LAW FOR NON-LAW STUDENTS

Third Edition

Cavendish
Publishing
Limited

London • Sydney

LAW FOR NON-LAW STUDENTS

Third Edition

Keith Owens, LLB, MA
Chair of the Law Subject Group
University College Northampton

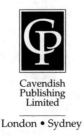

Cavendish
Publishing
Limited

London • Sydney

Third edition first published in Great Britain 2001 by Cavendish Publishing Limited, The Glass House, Wharton Street, London WC1X 9PX, United Kingdom

Telephone: +44 (0)20 7278 8000   Facsimile: +44 (0)20 7278 8080

Email: info@cavendishpublishing.com

Website: www.cavendishpublishing.com

British Library Cataloguing in Publication Data

Owens, Keith
Law for non-law students – 3rd ed
1 Business law – England 2 Business law – Wales
I Title
346.4'2'07

ISBN 1 85941 671 3

Printed and bound in Great Britain

PREFACE

When writing under such a broad remit as this, it is difficult to know exactly what to include and what to exclude. Previous editions have not contained any material on agency or negligence. I have decided to include these because so many business courses include them in the syllabus nowadays. I have also tried to put the law in its practical business context so that the reader knows why the law has developed as it has, rather than simply presenting the reader with a set of somewhat abstract rules.

It would be helpful if readers would give some feedback about the book. For example, what do you think could usefully be expanded and what do you think could be omitted without any loss? I would also be pleased to learn of areas which you find difficult to understand – I can then work on trying to simplify the text for any future edition.

If you would care to email me with your views at Keith.Owens@Northampton.ac.uk, I will try to reply within a reasonable time, though there are some times of the year where it might be weeks rather than days!

Keith Owens
Northampton
July 2001

CONTENTS

Contents

Contents

TABLE OF CASES

TABLE OF STATUTES

1

TABLE OF STATUTORY INSTRUMENTS

INTERNATIONAL INSTRUMENTS

Other Legislation

CHAPTER 1

THE LEGAL SYSTEM

INTRODUCTION

This book begins by looking at the legal system. It is not intended to give a comprehensive view: there are specialist texts which will do that. It is intended to tell you enough about the system so that you know how it works in relation to business matters.

It is difficult to undertake any activity in business which does not have a legal consequence. Any sale of goods or supply of services, for example, has potential legal complications. However, this does not mean that business people need to consult their solicitors before their every move. Disputes tend to be resolved by negotiation and compromise. Only in extreme cases is recourse taken to legal action. This is because legal action is not only expensive in relation to the costs that need to be paid to the justice system (not least to one's professional legal advisers), but it is also expensive in relation to the working time lost to the business enterprise because key personnel are needed to prepare statements, consult with legal advisers and, ultimately, to attend court for possibly several days to give evidence. Although the greater part of the costs paid to the justice system may be reclaimed from your opponent if you win, winning is never guaranteed; and even if you do win, the cost of tying-up your enterprise's personnel cannot be reclaimed.

It is common when concluding a contract to put a clause in it to the effect that any disputes shall be referred to arbitration. This means that the dispute will be solved by an arbitrator (a sort of referee – further reference will be made to arbitrators later on). In this case, the need to attend court is replaced by the need to give evidence to the arbitrator, who may be prepared to be more accommodating than the courts to the needs of your business: for example, evidence may be given by written statement or may be given outside normal business hours. Nevertheless, a significant amount of time will still be taken up.

In practice, wherever possible, business people avoid recourse to the legal system and rely on self-help. Why, then, is it necessary for a business person to learn the law at all? Can't all disputes be solved by common sense and compromise? The answer is that, to some extent, this is what happens. But common sense solutions usually involve negotiations. For example, your customer wishes to reject a freezer she has bought from you because, although it performs its function perfectly well, it had some cosmetic damage which, to put right, will cost between 15% and 25% of the purchase price. You offer a discount of 15%. She argues for 25%. In the end you agree on 20%.

Negotiations can be pursued much more effectively if you, as a negotiator, are aware of the legal principles that a court would follow if it were to decide your dispute. It enables you to quantify, in percentage terms, your chances of winning should the matter have to be resolved by a court or arbitrator. For example, has your customer the legal right to reject the freezer because of cosmetic rather than functional damage? Under s 14 of the Sale of Goods Act 1979, it is probable that, especially if she is a consumer, she does have that right. Her chances of winning the case, should she seek to reject the goods and you refuse to accept this rejection, are high, let us say in the region of 95%. You will, therefore, bear that in mind when conducting your negotiations and, having succeeded in persuading your customer to accept the goods for a reduction of 20% of the price, you will probably be quite satisfied with your efforts.

COMMON LAW AND CIVIL LAW

This section deals with the relationship between common law and civil law. Until relatively recently, this was largely of academic interest. However, since European Union law is based on civil law and since the English courts must now take account of Union law, where appropriate, in reaching their decisions, the relationship between the two has become of practical importance.

There are two important systems of law which have been developed in the Western world. These are:

(a) Roman law; and

(b) English law.

Many other states throughout the world have based their legal systems on one of these two systems. Countries which have based their system on Roman law, including the EU, are said to have a 'civil law' system. Countries which have based their system on English law are said to have a 'common law' system.

Common law systems

English law ('English' includes Welsh, but excludes Scottish and Northern Irish) is called common law. This means that the law is common to the whole country, in contrast to law which does not apply throughout the whole country but which varies according to local custom. Common law originally consisted mainly of principles established by judges in cases brought before them, which the judges then applied to similar cases arising in the future. Such law is called case law. However, nowadays, legislation enacted by

Parliament (also called statute law), which mainly takes the form of Acts of Parliament and statutory instruments, has become the most important source of domestic law, though, for example, most of the law of contract is still based on case law rather than statutory law. The term 'domestic law' is used to denote areas of law which are not affected by European Union law. Where an area of law is affected by European Union law, the legislation of the European Union is the supreme source of law.

Those countries which have a legal system based on English law and, therefore, have common law systems, include many former British colonies, for example, Australia, New Zealand, the USA (except Louisiana) and Canada (except Quebec). They also include Northern Ireland. The significance of this is that if there is no English authority on a particular point of law, the judge may seek guidance from the law of other common law countries.

Example

In *Ready Mixed Concrete v Ministry of Pensions* (1968), the court had to decide whether lorry drivers who delivered concrete for Ready Mixed Concrete Ltd were *employees* of the company, or whether they were *self-employed* contractors. The issue was complicated by the fact that, although the drivers were designated 'self-employed', there were a large number of factors (for example, they were compelled to wear the company's uniform and provide sick certificates when they were incapable of work through illness, among other things), which pointed towards the conclusion that they were, in law, employees. Because there had been no analogous English case, the court referred to a USA case and a Canadian case to help in establishing criteria which would act as a guide to whether, in such cases, the workers are truly self-employed or whether, in reality, they are employees.

Civil law systems

Most of the countries of Western Europe, their colonies and former colonies have a 'civil law' system. Scotland, through its ancient alliances with France and the Netherlands, has a civil law system. The Scots complain, with some justification, that their system has become adulterated by virtue of the many parliamentary enactments which apply indiscriminately throughout the UK. In addition, because certain principles of Scottish law are identical to those of English law, each country has borrowed quite liberally from the law of the other. For example, the seminal case in English law on establishing liability for negligence is a Scottish case. Nowadays, the principal differences relate to the law of contract and tort (civil wrongs, which in Scotland are called 'delict') and to criminal law. On the other hand, in respect of many areas of statutorily created modern law (employment law relating to unfair dismissal, equal pay, etc), Scottish law is identical to English law.

Differences between civil law and common law

European Union law is a civil law system. The civil law has a fundamentally different approach to both the creation and interpretation of statute law to that adopted by English law. This means that, if they are to apply European Union law (which now takes precedence over any conflicting domestic law in the UK), many UK courts are having to familiarise themselves with a system that is essentially alien to them.

Civil law creates statutory law (usually called 'codes') by laying down a series of broad principles, leaving the judges to interpret what they mean. In this they may seek assistance from previously decided cases involving similar issues and from the opinions of eminent textbook writers. In contrast, UK statutes are much more detailed, attempting to cover all foreseeable eventualities. Of course, not every eventuality is foreseen, so that judges in UK law also have an interpretive role, which involves reference to previous cases and other sources of help, including textbook writers. However, we should not make too much of this supposed distinction, since regulations and directives, some of which are very detailed, have been issued in order to amplify the Treaty of Rome and other primary legislation of the European Union.

In relation to *interpretation* of statutes, the English method is to look at the *literal* meaning of the words used and to give effect to them. It is immaterial if the literal meaning results in a different consequence to what was intended, providing the result is not manifestly absurd or meaningless. If that is the case, the literal meaning can be modified, but only in so far as it is necessary to make sense of the provision.

Example of the literal approach to statutory interpretation

Fisher v Bell (1961)

The Restriction of Offensive Weapons Act 1959 provided that it is an offence to 'offer for sale' a number of offensive weapons, including flick-knives. A shop-keeper displayed a number of flick-knives in his shop window, with price tags attached. Was he guilty of an offence? Although the purpose of the Act was clearly to penalise those who sought to supply dangerous weapons to the public, it was held that no offence had been committed because it is an established part of contract law that goods with prices attached are not being offered for sale. Therefore, applying the literal approach, there had not been an offer for sale.

The civil law method, on the other hand, is to look at the purpose of the provision and to interpret the words used in such a way as to give effect to that purpose. This is often called the 'purposive' approach. The tension between the literal approach (which is still used in purely domestic legislation) and the purposive approach (which should be used when interpreting a statute passed in pursuance of our obligations under the European Treaties) is causing some problems in the English courts.

Example of the difference in the interpretation of statutory law

The Transfer of Undertakings Regulations 1981 were passed in order to give effect to EEC Directive 77/187. This is aimed at protecting the employment of persons who are employed in a business which is transferred to another business. The Regulations provide that the contract of employment of those persons employed by the transferring business *immediately before* the transfer, shall transfer to the new owner. The question has arisen as to what *immediately before* means, since buyers who wish to avoid the burden of having the seller's employees transferred with the business have induced the seller to dismiss the employees shortly before the transfer is due to take place. The legal effectiveness of this was underpinned by a 1986 Court of Appeal decision in which the words *immediately before* were given their literal meaning, and it was held that employees dismissed three hours before the transfer took place were not employed *immediately before* the transfer. However, in the later case of *Litster v Forth Dry Dock and Engineering Co Ltd* (1989), the House of Lords adopted the purposive approach and held that the words *immediately before the transfer* must be interpreted in a manner which enables the regulations effectively to fulfil the purpose for which they were made, that is, that of giving effect to EEC Directive 77/187, which was issued with the aim of protecting employment.

Different meanings of 'civil law' and 'common law'

It is important to be aware that the expressions 'civil law' and 'common law' can mean radically different things according to the context in which they are being used.

'Civil law' may be used with one of three meanings:

(a) it may mean that part of a country's law which is not criminal law (in fact, that is the context in which most laymen will find it being used);

(b) it may mean, as we have used it above, a system of law based on Roman law; and

(c) to a person in the armed services it may mean any law which is applicable to civilians (that is, law which is not military law).

'Common law' may also be used with one of three meanings:

(a) it may mean the whole system of English law, both case law and statute law, which is the sense in which we used it above;

(b) it may mean law which was developed by the judges in the early common law courts, in contrast to the law which was developed by successive

Chancellors in their own court (called the Court of Chancery), in order to mitigate the rigour and inflexibility of the common law. Such law is called 'equity'. Where equity and common law conflict, equity prevails; and

(c) it may be used to mean that part of the law (both common law and equity), which remains case law rather than statute law.

It is important when you are reading about the law, to identify which of the possible meanings the author is giving to either of these two expressions.

The relationship between equity and common law

We have said that the term 'common law' may be used to distinguish the law which was applied in the old common law courts from the 'equity' applied in the Chancellor's court, the Court of Chancery. The common law courts and the Court of Chancery were incorporated into the new High Court of Justice, as Divisions of that court, as a result of the Judicature Acts 1873–75. The administration of the rules of common law and equity was fused at the same time. However, it is still important to know whether a right or remedy derives from common law or from equity. We will examine the reasons why after we have looked at the development of equity.

Equity came about because of the rigid and inflexible approach of the common law judges in a number of situations. For example, in medieval times, if Alan borrowed £50 from Bill, Alan might be required to sign a document called a 'bond' in which he agreed to repay the loan. Suppose he repaid the loan, but failed to have the bond cancelled. Bill then claims repayment of the loan, relying on the bond as evidence that the money was owed. The common law courts would refuse to look beyond the evidence of the bond and Alan would have to repay the loan a second time.

If the common law judges had been willing to adapt the law in situations where a rigid application of the common law led to injustice, there would have been no need for equity. However, the judges tended to be intransigent, with the result that, in the early days of the law, where a litigant failed to get justice from the courts of common law he might petition the King to do justice. The King would pass such petitions to his Chancellor, who was an ecclesiastic and was, in effect, the King's chief minister. The Chancellor, being a churchman, would decide the matter according to what he thought that a person of good conscience should do in the circumstances.

Petitions grew in number to the point where a special court, the Court of Chancery, had to be established in order to deal with them. A prime example can be found in the law relating to mortgages.

Example of equity in relation to mortgages

A mortgage consists of putting up property as security for a loan. Suppose Ann wished to borrow £10,000 from Ben against the security of land called Greenacre, worth £30,000. At common law, she would convey Greenacre to Ben (that is, make Ben the legal owner of Greenacre), subject to a contractual agreement that Ben would reconvey Greenacre to her if she repaid the loan of £10,000 on time. If she failed to do so, Ben remained the owner of Greenacre and, moreover, Ann still owed the £10,000. Against such a palpably unjust state of affairs, the Chancellor intervened. Equity would allow Ann an additional period of time in which to redeem the mortgage (that is, pay off the loan) and, failing that, the court would order that the property should be sold, that Ben should recoup his loan out of the proceed,s and that Ann should receive any balance left over. Such a balance is called the 'equity of redemption'.

The law relating to mortgages was not the only area of law in which equity intervened in order to apply ideas of fairness. The common law was defective in relation to remedies. The only remedy available to a claimant at common law consisted of a money payment called damages. However, there are numerous situations where damages are not an adequate remedy. For example, suppose that Carol continuously trespassed on David's land. For David to have to keep going to court to claim damages would be unduly burdensome. Equity, therefore, invented the remedy of the injunction: an order to Carol to desist from trespassing on David's land, which, if she disobeyed, amounted to contempt of court, for which she could be punished.

The classic example of the intervention of equity is in relation to the law of trusts. A trust occurs where one party, D (the donor) gives property to T (the trustee) to hold or administer on behalf of B (the beneficiary). A common modern example is where a husband with a wife and, say, two children, wishes his children to become the ultimate owners of his estate after his death, but, should his wife survive him, wishes his wife to enjoy the income from the estate during her lifetime. The husband does not wish to make his widow the owner of the estate in case she should remarry and take the property out of the family, thus depriving his children of the property. The solution is to create a trust by which the husband (the donor) transfers the legal ownership to trustees, to administer on behalf of his widow (the beneficiary) during her lifetime. After her death the trust may be wound-up and the trust property be divided between the husband's two children, who become the owners of the property. The problem with the trust, originally, was that if the trustees appropriated the trust property to their own use and the beneficiaries complained to a common law court, the common law judges would simply enquire as to who was the legal owner of the trust property. The answer was that the trustees were the legal owners. The common law judges regarded that as concluding the matter, thus depriving the beneficiary of the property.

However, if the beneficiaries petitioned the Chancellor, the Chancellor would order the trustees to act according to the dictates of good conscience and to account for the trust property to the beneficiaries.

In the early days of equity there was no conflict between the Chancellor and the common law judges. However, as equity became increasingly intrusive, litigants began playing off one against the other. Thus, the Chancellor would imprison a defendant for refusing to obey the Chancellor's order to act in accordance with good conscience, only for the Court of King's Bench to release him from prison, using the prerogative writ of habeas corpus, on the ground that his imprisonment was unlawful. (The writ of habeas corpus is still in use today and may be used by anyone claiming that he is being unlawfully detained.)

In the early 17th century, the question arose in the Earl of Oxford's case as to what the outcome should be where the rules of equity and common law conflicted. King James I decided the issue and came down in favour of equity prevailing over common law. This is the rule at the present day.

However, it is important to note in this respect that if, for some reason, equity refuses to exercise its discretion in favour of a person who is claiming an equitable right or remedy, the common law rule regarding the situation will then apply.

Until the late 19th century, an issue which involved questions of common law and questions of equity might have to go to two courts in order to be decided – a lengthy and expensive process.

Example

Wood v Scarth (1855 and 1858)

The plaintiff made a contract with the defendant which the defendant then refused to carry out. The only remedy which the common law will give for breach of contract is an award of damages. However, equity developed a number of other remedies, one of which is a decree of specific performance. This is an order by the court that the defendant will carry out the contract as agreed. The plaintiff therefore sued the defendant in the Court of Chancery, seeking an order of specific performance. However, the disadvantage with equitable remedies, from the plaintiff's point of view, is that they are given at the discretion of the court. This means that even though the claimant has a valid claim for breach of contract, the court will not necessarily order the defendant to perform it. In this case, the court refused to grant the decree because the defendant had entered into the contract by mistake. The mistake did not invalidate the contract, but the court thought that to grant a decree of specific performance would be unduly hard on the defendant.

The plaintiff then brought a case in a common law court, claiming damages. It was held that the defendant's mistake was no answer to the plaintiff's claim and damages were awarded accordingly.

The Judicature Acts of 1873 and 1875 completed the fusion of common law and equity as far as procedure is concerned. Nowadays, in similar circumstances, there would be need to bring only one case in which damages and specific performance could be claimed in the alternative.

It would be a mistake to think that, nowadays, equity will always intervene to correct what are seen as injustices in the common law. In the early days of equity it was criticised for its unpredictability: 'Equity varies with the length of the Chancellor's foot.' Following such criticisms, efforts were made to achieve greater consistency, in consequence of which equity became as hidebound with precedent as the common law.

Nevertheless, equity has been invoked a number of times during the relatively recent past in order to do justice in particular cases. In the law of contract, the doctrine of promissory estoppel (see Chapter 5) has been created. This has eroded the common law rule in *Pinnel*'s case. In relation to remedies, an area which has been a traditional concern of equity, the *Mareva* injunction and the *Anton Piller* order have emerged as new remedies.

The *Mareva* injunction freezes assets under the control of the defendant to prevent them being moved out of the jurisdiction of the English courts to a place where the claimant would not be able to get at them. The *Anton Piller* order permits the claimant to enter the defendant's premises in order to prevent the defendant from destroying, concealing or removing evidence in the form of documents or property (for example, pirated video cassettes). Both the *Mareva* injunction and the *Anton Piller* order are now regulated by statute and are now called a 'freezing order' and a 'search order' respectively.

Since the creation of the High Court of Justice by the Judicature Acts of 1873 and 1875, the administration of common law and equity have been 'fused' together. However, matters which were formerly dealt with in the Court of Chancery are still dealt with in the Chancery Division of the High Court and common law matters still dealt with in the Queen's Bench Division of the High Court, which corresponds to the old common law court of Queen's (or King's) Bench. If a claimant is claiming both damages (a common law remedy) and an injunction (an equitable remedy), for example, the case may be brought either in the Queen's Bench Division or the Chancery Division of the High Court.

Why distinguish between common law and equity?

There are two reasons why it is necessary to be able to distinguish between an equitable right or remedy and a common law right or remedy. The first reason is that equitable rights and remedies are given only *at the discretion of the court*, whereas any common law right or remedy is given *as of right*. Nowadays, the court's discretion is exercised according to settled principles; equity no longer 'varies with the Chancellor's foot'. There is a variety of circumstances in which the court will refuse to exercise its discretion in a party's favour. For example, you will recall that at the outset equity was used to prevent the defendant (or 'respondent') from acting against the precepts of good conscience. What, then, if the petitioner (that is, the person seeking equity's help) had himself failed to act in accordance with good conscience? In such a case, equity would adopt the maxim 'he who comes to equity must come with clean hands' or 'he who seeks equity must do equity' and would refuse to help the petitioner. A good example is to be found in the contract case of *D and C Builders v Rees* (1966), where Rees was being sued for the balance of a debt after D and C Builders had promised they would accept, in full settlement, the amount which had already been paid. Common law supported D and C's claim, but Rees argued that equity should not allow D and C to go back on their promise. The court held that, normally, equity would not allow D and C to go back on their promise. However, Mrs Rees had brought undue pressure to bear on D and C in order to obtain their promise. Equity would, therefore, not exercise its discretion in Rees' favour since Mrs Rees had not herself behaved equitably.

The second reason lies in the maxim 'equity acts *in personam*' (in relation to the person), whereas common law is said to act '*in rem*' (in relation to the thing or property). What this means is that a common law title (that is, right of ownership) to property is good against any other claimant, whereas an equitable title to property is a personal right which can always be defeated by a common law title, where the legal owner has no notice of the equitable right.

Example of common law title prevailing over equitable title

Stan has given property to Terry to be held on trust for Ursula. As we have already seen, Terry will have a legal (that is, common law) title to the property, whereas Ursula's right is equitable. Suppose that Terry sells the trust property to Vera, who buys it in good faith and without any knowledge of Ursula's claim to the property. In such a case, Vera would become the legal owner of the property, leaving Ursula with an action for damages for breach of trust against Terry.

If, however, Vera had notice of Ursula's interest in the property, Vera's claim would be defeated.

Since trusts are by no means the only situations where a person may obtain an equitable title to property (for example, an informal assignment of an insurance policy as security for a debt may give an equitable title to the assignee), students who go to work in a financial services environment may frequently encounter equitable titles to property.

THE SOURCES OF LAW

An academic study of the sources of law can involve extensive discussions as to classification of sources, and may involve enquiries not only as to where the law comes from, but also from where it derives its validity. We will confine our studies to a practical descriptive account of where to look for present-day law.

The main sources of modern United Kingdom law are:

(a) legislation of the European Union;

(b) cases decided by the European Court of Justice as to the interpretation of the European Union legislation;

(c) legislation by Parliament or powers delegated by Parliament; and

(d) case law from cases decided by judges in English, Scottish or Northern Irish courts, as appropriate.

Legislation of the European Union

The United Kingdom acceded to the European Union (formerly called the European Community) on 1 January 1973. The European Communities Act 1972, which came into effect on the same date, incorporated European Union law into our own domestic system without the requirement for any further legislation. Accession to the Union made a fundamental constitutional change in relation to the sources of law. Whereas previously, the UK Parliament had been the supreme law-maker, that role is now performed by the legislative organs of the European Union. Because many of the provisions of European law are derived from French or German law, the UK courts are increasingly looking at the French or German domestic law in order to interpret European law.

Example of supremacy of European Union law

Factortame v Secretary of State for Transport (No 2) (1991)

The Merchant Shipping Act 1988, enacted by the UK Parliament, provided that 75% of the directors and shareholders of companies operating fishing vessels in UK waters must be British nationals. This prevented ships *owned* by British companies but *controlled* by Spanish nationals from fishing in British waters. An action was brought to challenge the validity of the provisions in relation to the European Union's common fisheries policy. However, there was likely to be a substantial delay in obtaining a definitive ruling and, meanwhile, the Spanish controlled company was losing revenue. They, therefore, asked the courts to suspend the relevant provisions of the 1988 Act to allow them to fish until their rights had been finally decided. The House of

Lords ruled that there was no such power in domestic law, but referred the matter to the European Court of Justice to determine whether European law required the Act to be suspended. It was held that national courts are under a duty to give effect to community law where there is, or might be, a conflict between national law and community law. Accordingly, the House of Lords granted an injunction suspending the effect of the 1988 Act until the matter had been resolved by the European Court of Justice. The decision was historic in that it was the first time a UK court had ever prevented the operation of an Act of Parliament.

It is important to note that European law affects only a relatively small area of activity, mainly employment, competition between enterprises, agriculture and fishing. However, its scope is growing. Note that in relation to matters in respect of which there is no Union legislation, domestic law (that is, that of the relevant country) applies.

The idea behind European Union legislation is that each Member State shall incorporate into its own domestic law the principles laid down in the Union legislation. Should the Member State fail to do so, or should the domestic legislation prove defective, the European Commission may bring infringement proceedings in the European Court of Justice. If these are successful, the Member State concerned must then take steps to remedy domestic legislation.

Example of infringement proceedings

EEC v United Kingdom (1982)

Article 119 of the Treaty of Rome lays down a principle of equal pay for equal work as between men and women. The UK interpreted this as meaning that equal pay must be given for similar work. It enacted the Equal Pay Act 1970 to give effect to this principle. However, a directive was issued in 1975 which made it clear that the principle of equal pay was wider than the UK perception: it covered not just equal pay for similar work, but also equal pay for work of equal value. In 1982, the European Commission brought infringement proceedings against the UK in the European Court of Justice, alleging that the UK Equal Pay Act 1970 was defective in that it failed to cover work of equal value. The European Court of Justice found in the Commission's favour. As a result, the UK introduced Regulations in 1983 to amend the Equal Pay Act 1970 (as from 1 January 1984) so that it allowed a woman (or man, where appropriate) to claim that their work was of equal value.

The legislation of the European Union consists of primary legislation and secondary legislation.

Primary legislation

This consists of a number of treaties, protocols, council decisions, etc, the principal of which is the Treaty of Rome, which founded the EEC. This legislation can be directly enforced through the courts of Member States if the state's domestic legislation does not give the rights which the European legislation contains. The main criteria which such legislation must meet before it can have direct effect are that, first, it must be sufficiently clear and precise and, secondly, it must leave no room for discretion to be exercised by Member States. Legislation which may be enforced directly is said to be 'directly applicable'. Legislation which may be directly enforced against the State is said to have a 'vertical effect'. Legislation which may be directly enforced against individuals (here we include legal individuals such as limited liability companies) is said to have a 'horizontal effect'.

Case showing horizontal effect of direct applicability of the Treaty of Rome

MacCarthys v Smith (1978)

A man was employed as a stockroom manager and was paid £60 per week. He left the job, and four months later a woman was appointed at a wage of £50 per week. She brought a claim for equal pay. The Court of Appeal held that she could not succeed under the Equal Pay Act 1970, since the Act requires comparison with a man in the same employment, whereas Ms Smith was comparing herself with a man who had left the employment before she had begun. However, the court referred the matter to the European Court of Justice in order to determine whether she could succeed under Article 119 of the Treaty of Rome. It was held that she succeeded under Article 119, which repaired the deficiency in domestic legislation. The Court held that a woman should receive equal pay for the same work even though the person with whom she was comparing herself was a male predecessor.

Secondary legislation

The following secondary legislation may be made under the authority of Article 189 of the Treaty of Rome:

(a) regulations;

(b) directives; and

(c) decisions.

EC regulations

These are directly applicable, both vertically and horizontally. For example, Regulation 1612/68 provides regulations for the free movement of workers within the Union. Any person prevented from moving from one EC state to another for the purpose of working would be able to pursue the matter through the courts, relying on Regulation 1612/68.

EC directives

EC directives are said to be solely 'vertical' in effect, in that they are addressed to the Member States and the state must give legislative effect to them before they become law (though national courts are required to interpret the resultant national legislation in a manner which reflects the wording and purpose of the directive: *Marleasing SA v La Comercial Internacional de Alementacion Case* C-106/89 (1990). In respect of directives concerned with rights in employment, it has been held that the vertical effect means that because they are addressed to the State, directives are not directly applicable in relation to employees of private employers. However, it has been held that because they are addressed to the state, they can be directly applicable in respect of (that is, they can confer rights upon) state employees.

Case showing how a directive which generally has a vertical effect can have a horizontal effect in relation to state employees

Marshall v Southampton and South West Hampshire Area Health Authority (Teaching) (1986)

A Health Authority requirement that women should retire at an earlier age than men infringed 75/117/EEC (the Equal Treatment Directive). It was held that, because Ms Marshall was a state employee, the vertical nature of the directive meant that she could take advantage of it, although an employee in the private sector would not have been able to.

This would seem to give public sector employees an unfair advantage over their private sector counterparts. However, a subsequent case decided by the European Court of Justice shows how, while preserving the vertical effect for state employees only, it is possible, using indirect means, to give a directive horizontal effect for *all employees*. (Newcomers to law will find that circumventing an established principle, while at the same time paying lip service to it, is a favourite game of lawyers.)

Case illustrating how a directive can be given horizontal effect by indirect means

Francovich v Italian Republic (1992)

The Italian government failed to introduce legislation to protect employees in consequence of the insolvency of their employer. The Italian government should have done this in order to comply with Directive 80/987.

Francovich attempted to claim his loss from the Italian government, relying on the directive. The question arose as to whether the directive was directly applicable. The European Court of Justice confirmed that the directive could not have direct effect between an employee and a private employer. However, the court ruled that if the employee of a private employer is disadvantaged by the State's failure to implement a directive, the employee may claim damages from the *State* providing three conditions are met. These are:

(a) that the result required by the directive includes the conferring of rights for the benefit of individuals;

(b) that the content of these rights may be determined by reference to the provisions of the directive; and

(c) that a causal link exists between breach of the obligation of the state and the damage suffered by the persons affected.

In the event, it was held that condition (b) was not met: that is, the rights conferred by the directive were not sufficiently precise on which to base a claim. However, the European Court of Justice clearly envisages national courts adjudicating upon claims against the state founded upon the failure to implement appropriate directives and awarding damages where appropriate.

Decisions of the Commission

A decision may be addressed to a Member State, to a number of Member States, or to an individual. The decision is binding on those to whom it is addressed. A decision may be appealed against in the European Court of Justice.

Example

Re Pioneer Hi-Fi Equipment (1980)

In this decision, the Commission imposed fines of around seven million ecus (European Currency Units – an ecu was about 70 pence) for market-sharing practices contrary to Article 85 of the Treaty of Rome. Article 85 outlaws certain anti-competitive practices. Pioneer brought proceedings in the European Court of Justice in order to annul the decision. However, the decision was confirmed, although the fine was reduced owing to the Commission's miscalculation regarding the length of time for which the practices had been in operation.

Decisions of the European Court of Justice

Any national court or tribunal dealing with a case which raises issues of Union legislation may refer the matter to the European Court of Justice (ECJ), for a ruling regarding the interpretation of the legislation. If the issue is raised in a national court or tribunal from which there is no further appeal, the matter *must* be referred to the ECJ. This is the effect of Article 177 of the Treaty of Rome.

There have been numerous references to the ECJ under Article 177. An example of this is the case of *MacCarthys v Smith* (above, p 13) in which the ECJ ruled that a restriction in the Equal Pay Act 1970, to the effect that a woman could compare herself only to a man in the same employment for the purposes of claiming equal pay, infringed Article 119 of the Treaty of Rome. This ruling becomes part of the national law and overrides national legislation which is inconsistent with it. Note, however, that an individual may not make direct application to the ECJ.

The other main area of adjudication of the ECJ is in respect of appeals from the decisions of the Commission. An example can be seen in the case of *Re Pioneer Hi-Fi Equipment* (above), in which the ECJ confirmed the decision of the Commission but reduced the fine imposed.

The ECJ sits in Luxembourg. The Court consists of 13 judges, six advocates-general and a registrar. An advocate-general is allocated to each case. It is his job to analyse the case for the Court and to suggest what the Court's decision should be. The Court, which sits as a full court (that is, all 13 judges) and delivers one judgment, is not compelled to agree with the opinion of the advocate-general but does so in about 75% of cases. Unlike the case with English courts, no dissenting opinion is given by any judge who does not agree with the majority.

The Single European Act 1986 added a new Court of First Instance to be attached to the European Court of Justice. This new Court has limited jurisdiction (it does not deal with references under Article 177 or infringement proceedings brought against a Member State, for example) and appeal from its decisions is made to the European Court of Justice.

Note that the European Court of Justice should not be confused with the European Court of Human Rights, to which it is wholly unrelated. The European Court of Human Rights operates under the auspices of the council of Europe, of which most European countries, including those from the former Soviet bloc, are members. The Court and the European Commission of Human Rights were established under the 1950 European Convention on Human Rights, to which the UK is a signatory. The Convention establishes various basic rights and freedoms and it is through the Commission and the Court that these are enforced. References to the court should be a thing of the past following the incorporation of the Convention into domestic law under the Human Rights Act 1998. The Court sits in Strasbourg, which is the headquarters of the Council of Europe.

Legislation by the UK Parliament

Legislation consists of an express and formal laying down of rules of conduct. It is almost invariably created by *Act of Parliament* (sometimes called 'statute') or by the *delegated authority* of Parliament. Occasionally, however, law having statutory force may be created by exercise of the royal prerogative (effectively by the Cabinet of the day). Increasingly, legislation is being made under powers delegated by Parliament. In 2000, there were 45 Acts of Parliament but no less than 3,400 pieces of delegated legislation.

Uses of legislation

Legislation may be put to one of four uses. The obvious ones are to *create* new law or to *amend* existing law. For example, the Data Protection Act 1984 *created* new law with the purpose of, among other things, safeguarding the privacy of persons about whom personal details may be stored on a computer. The Race Relations (Remedies) Act 1994 *amended* the law on remedies for successful complainants under the Race Relations Act 1976, by removing the limit on the amount of compensation payable under the 1976 Act.

Two less obvious uses of legislation are:

(a) to *consolidate* existing statutory law when the statute law relating to a particular topic has become unwieldy. This involves the repeal (that is, cancellation) of the existing provision and its replacement with (usually) identical provisions in the consolidating Act. Nowadays, in order to avoid this type of problem, a new Act *amends* the old Act so that when the old Act is reprinted containing the new provisions, the whole of the old law and the new law is there in one Act. For example, the Sale and Supply of Goods Act 1994, the Sale of Goods (Amendment) Act 1994 and the Sale of Goods (Amendment) Act 1995 all amended the Sale of Goods Act 1979, so that there remains only one Act. If new sections are needed, they are usually numbered the same as an existing section but given a letter as a suffix, for example, s 20A; and

(b) to *codify* the law. This means that the case law on a particular topic is drawn together in an Act of Parliament. A famous codifying statute was the Sale of Goods Act 1893 (which was added to over the years and all the relevant provisions have now been consolidated in the Sale of Goods Act 1979). There have been proposals, from time to time, which have failed to make much progress, to codify the law of contract. On the other hand, much of the criminal law has been codified.

The above categories are not self-contained, and one statute may well perform more than one of the above functions.

Types of legislation

There are two types of legislation:

(a) Act of Parliament (this is also called 'statute'); and

(b) delegated legislation.

Act of Parliament

Parliament consists of two 'houses', the House of Commons and the House of Lords. Both are housed at the Palace of Westminster. The House of Commons consists of 651 Members of Parliament who are elected by voters from a particular geographical area, known as a 'constituency', to represent them. In practice, the Member will belong to a political party (except for the very rare independent member) and will vote on parliamentary issues in accordance with the instructions given by his political party, enforced by officials quaintly known as 'Whips'. The political party which can command the majority of the votes forms the government. The House of Lords has almost 700 members. It is not a democratically elected body. It consists mostly of life peers appointed by the government of the day. There are also almost 100 hereditary peers. In addition, the two Anglican Archbishops of Canterbury and York and some senior Anglican Bishops are members.

Types of Bill

An Act starts life as a Bill. The Bill may be a Government Bill or it may be a Private Member's Bill. Either of these is called a Public Bill. There is also a category of Bills called Private Bills. These usually have restricted aims, such as the compulsory purchase of land for a particular purpose, and are usually promoted by public authorities.

'Private Member's Bill' is the name given to a Bill which is sponsored by an individual Member of Parliament, rather than by the government. Because parliamentary time is limited, there is a ballot to decide which Members are allowed to put their Bills forward. Even where a Member wins time by virtue of the ballot, his Bill is unlikely to become law – procedures exist which make it fairly easy for objectors to block the progress of a Private Member's Bill. Yet, occasionally, the government will make time for a Private Member's Bill to go through the stages necessary for it to become law. This may happen where the government does not wish to be too closely associated with a controversial Bill which it would, nevertheless, like to see enacted as law. Examples are the Matrimonial Causes Act 1937, which introduced the modern concept of divorce into the law, and the Abortion Act of 1967, which legalised abortion in certain circumstances.

How a Bill becomes an Act

A Bill may be introduced in either House of Parliament. An exception is a 'money' Bill – one dealing with taxation or loans – which may only be introduced in the House of Commons by a Minister of the Crown. To become an Act, the Bill must go through the following stages in both Houses: a formal first reading, at which the title of the Bill is announced but no more; a second reading, at which the Bill may be debated but not amended (to save parliamentary time there is a procedure whereby the second reading may be done in Committee); a Committee stage, at which the Bill is discussed in detail and, where appropriate, amendments proposed; a Report stage, where the amendments may be debated and, where appropriate, referred back to the Committee; and a third reading. It must then receive the Royal Assent, which nowadays, by convention, is not refused – the last time the Royal Assent was refused was by Queen Anne, in relation to the Scottish Militia Bill 1707. Because the House of Lords is not an elected assembly, its power to reject a Bill put forward by the Commons has been removed and replaced by a delaying power: it may delay a Bill for a period of one year (except for a money Bill where the period is one month), after which the Bill may become law despite the opposition of the Lords.

A Bill usually has a number of *clauses*. Clauses may be added, deleted or amended during the parliamentary process which leads to a Bill becoming an Act. When the Bill becomes an Act, the clauses become *sections* of the Act.

Each Act has a short title (for example, Consumer Credit Act 1974) and an official reference. Since 1963 the official reference has consisted of the calendar year in which the Act was passed, together with a chapter number (this simply perpetuates the fiction that Parliament passes one piece of legislation during a parliamentary session and that that piece of legislation is divided into a number of chapters. In practice, one can determine the chronological order of the Acts passed in a parliamentary session by the chapter number). The official reference of the Consumer Credit Act 1974 is '1974 Chapter 39'. This means that it was the 39th Act to be passed in 1975.

The Act is arranged in sections, sub-sections and paragraphs. There may, on occasions, also be sub-paragraphs.

Example

Alice is claiming that she has been unfairly dismissed from her employment, having walked out of her employment. She did this because her employer, having promised payment if she worked overtime, is now refusing to pay. To succeed in her claim, she will first have to prove that she has been dismissed within the meaning of the Employment Rights Act 1996.

Section 95, sub-s (1), para (c) of the Act, which would normally be written s 95(1)(c), may well cover her case. Section 95(1) provides:

(1) an employee shall be treated as dismissed by his employer if, ... –

    (a) the contract under which he is employed by the employer is terminated by the employer (whether with or without notice),

    (b) he is employed under a contract for a fixed term and that term expires without being renewed under the same contract, or

    (c) the employee terminates the contract under which he is employed (with or without notice), in circumstances in which he is entitled to terminate it without notice by reason of the employer's conduct.

Other important features of Acts of Parliament

Somewhere in each Act, usually towards the end, will be an 'interpretation section', that is, a section which defines key words and phrases to be found in the statute. In the Consumer Credit Act 1974, for example, this is s 189.

At the end of the Act there will usually be a number of appendices, called 'Schedules'. In the Consumer Credit Act there are five.

Schedules often expand upon matters which are contained in the main body of the Act. For example, s 53 of the Sex Discrimination Act 1975 provides that there shall be an Equal Opportunities Commission, while Sched 3 to the Act makes detailed provision regarding the appointment, remuneration, tenure of office of Commissioners, appointment of staff, and other matters relating to the organisation and operation of the Commission.

Any Acts which are repealed by the new Act will usually be listed in a Schedule. This is done in Sched 1 of the Trade Union and Labour Relations (Consolidation) Act 1992. A consolidation Act, which you will remember, repeals several old Acts and incorporates the repealed provisions in one new Act, may contain a Destination Table which, very helpfully, shows where the provisions of the old repealed Acts are to be found in the new Act. Thus, there is a Destination Table at the end of the Trade Union and Labour Relations (Consolidation) Act 1992, which shows where to find in the new Act, the provisions of the old Acts which were repealed by Sched 1.

When does the Act come into force?

An Act may come into force in one of several ways. Whichever way is used, it comes into force at the first moment of the appropriate day. The day may be appointed by the statute itself for its commencement. It may be a day which is designated by a person, often a Secretary of State, to whom the Act expressly gives this power. It is increasingly common for different sections of an Act to be brought into force at different times by using this procedure. If neither of these applies, the Act comes into force on the day on which it receives the Royal Assent.

Status of a statute

Statute is the supreme source of law in the United Kingdom in the sense that, theoretically, Parliament may enact any law it wishes, no matter how arbitrary or unjust in effect it may be: there is no written Constitution under which a Supreme Court may declare a statute invalid. Judge-made law is subsidiary to statute law. However, as we have seen, UK law is now subsidiary to law made by the European Union so that, where UK law and EU law conflict, EU law will prevail.

You will note that the statute, somewhat chauvinistically, uses masculine pronouns. However, there is a general rule of interpretation contained in the

Interpretation Act 1978 that the male embraces the female, so that Alice, in our example above (p 19), is included within the ambit of the Act even though it talks in terms of 'he' and 'his'.

Delegated legislation

Due to the complexity of modern government, it is often necessary for Parliament to delegate some of its law-making powers to others. Such legislation is called delegated legislation. It has the force of an Act of Parliament, but, unlike an Act of Parliament, the validity of the delegated legislation may be challenged in the courts. This is done either on the ground that the person to whom the power was delegated has exceeded the power given to them by Parliament or, alternatively, that they have failed to follow the correct procedure for bringing the delegated legislation into force.

There are three types of delegated legislation:

(i) Regulations, orders or rules

Whether delegated legislation takes the form of regulations, orders or rules (or, indeed, is given some other name) is a somewhat arbitrary decision, since there seems to be no meaningful distinction between them. Nowadays, most delegated legislation takes the form of regulations. Each of the three, whatever it is called, is created by statutory instrument made under an enabling power which is contained in an Act of Parliament.

It is becoming increasingly common for an Act of Parliament to provide a statement of general principle (though not nearly as general as a 'code' in civil law), leaving the detail to be filled out later in the form of regulations. The procedure for doing this is set down in the Act concerned. It usually allows a Minister of the Crown to make regulations, often, but not always, following consultations with interested parties. Regulations made under statutory instrument are also a useful way of providing machinery for updating monetary amounts to keep pace with inflation, without the need to pass fresh Acts of Parliament.

Example

Sections 44 and 151 of the Consumer Credit Act 1974 give the Secretary of State the power to make regulations relating to certain aspects of advertising consumer credit facilities. Section 182 states how this power is to be exercised and s 189 defines certain terms used. The Consumer Credit (Advertisements) Regulations 1989 are, therefore, made under the powers given by ss 44, 151, 182 and 189 of the Consumer Credit Act 1974.

(ii) Bye-laws

Most bye-laws are made by local authorities, though certain public undertakings have power to make them. Power to make bye-laws must be given by statute. Almost invariably they require approval by the appropriate government minister.

(iii) Order in council

Certain powers are conferred by the constitution or by Parliament through a statute, upon the Queen, acting upon the advice of the Privy Council. In practice, these powers are exercised by the Cabinet (all of whom are Privy Councillors) or by a member of the Cabinet. When an order is issued under these powers, it takes the form of a statutory instrument.

Statutes on the web

The texts of all Acts of Parliament from 1988 and all statutory instruments from 1987 can be found on the Internet at http://www.hmso.gov.uk. There is a useful explanatory note attached.

Interpretation of statutes

Once a statute or a regulation has passed into law, it is often necessary for a court to decide what the statute means. For example, suppose a statute is passed which provides that it is an offence to *park* a *vehicle* so that it *obstructs* the *highway*. This appears to be perfectly straightforward but, in practice, problems of interpretation would soon arise. For example, is a vehicle *parked* if it is stationary but the driver is at the wheel with the engine running? Is a *vehicle* still a vehicle within the meaning of the statute if it is incapable of self-propulsion because it has broken down? Is there an *obstruction* if other vehicles can circumvent the parked vehicle? Does the word *highway* include pavements and grass verges to either side of the roadway?

Some assistance may be gained from the Interpretation Act 1978, which defines certain expressions commonly used in statutes. In addition, as we have seen, modern Acts usually contain an interpretation section, which stipulates the meaning to be given to words used in the Act. Where judges are uncertain as to the extent of the meaning of a word used in a statute, they may use the Oxford English Dictionary as an aid to interpretation. For example, in the *Attorney General's Reference (No 1 of 1988)* (1989), the question arose as to whether a person 'obtained' information if it were volunteered to him. The House of Lords consulted the Oxford Dictionary as to the meaning of 'obtain'.

There are a number of rules which guide the courts when they are interpreting statutes. However, there have been such rapid changes in the way that the interpretation of statutes has been approached over the past few years that it is strongly arguable that our traditional domestic rules of interpretation are no longer paramount.

First, the Human Rights Act 1998 must be applied when interpreting all legislation, both primary and secondary. This is potentially tremendously far-reaching (for more detail see below).

Secondly, the law of the European Union is encroaching more and more on domestic law. Since much of this law is derived from French or German domestic law, the UK courts are increasingly turning to French and German law in order to interpret what the law means. For example, in *King v Tunnock* (2000), an agent was claiming compensation under the Commercial Agents (Council Directive) Regulations 1993. Compensation in this context is a concept of French law. The court, therefore, made reference to French law in order to decide how compensation should be calculated.

Thirdly, what may be seen as a by-product of the UK joining the EU is that our domestic rules of interpretation have been expanded to incorporate a European rule of interpretation – the purposive rule. This looks at the purpose for which the statute has been passed and interprets its provisions in order to promote that purpose. This contrasts with the principal domestic rule of interpretation, the literal rule, which may often have the effect of frustrating the purpose of the statute.

Thus, the domestic rules, which are set out below, must be read subject to the comments made above.

Literal rule

The basic rule is the literal rule, which means that a word must be given its literal meaning even if this gives a result which does not accord with what Parliament intended. An example was given when we were talking about the basic differences between common law systems and civil law systems in their approach to statutory law (see p 4 above).

Surprisingly to those outside the law, the courts were not permitted, until recently, to refer to debates in Parliament which led to the passing of the Act in question. However, a recent House of Lords case, *Pepper v Hart* (1993), has held, contrary to the previous practice, that debates reported in *Hansard* can be referred to in order to assist the interpretation of statute, in the following circumstances:

(a) the legislation must be ambiguous, obscure or lead to an absurdity;

(b) the parliamentary materials relied upon must consist of one or more statements by a minister or other promoter of the Bill, together with such other parliamentary material as is necessary to understand such statement; and

(c) the statements relied upon must be clear.

Although this does not go as far as the purposive approach of the European Court, it is a move in that direction, and as law handed down by the European Union becomes increasingly pervasive, it is to be expected that English methods of statutory interpretation will become harmonised with those of the ECJ.

Golden rule

Sometimes the application of the literal rule would lead to a manifest absurdity or would result in the provision being meaningless. In this case, the golden rule allows the literal wording of the provision to be modified, but only so far as is necessary to remove the absurdity or to give the provision some meaning.

Example

R v Allen (1872)

The Offences Against the Person Act 1861 provided that whosoever, being married, should marry during the lifetime of their spouse, committed the offence of bigamy. Since it is not legally possible to marry during the lifetime of one's spouse (unless of course there has been a legal annulment or dissolution of the marriage), using the literal rule it was not possible to commit the crime of bigamy. Therefore, the courts modified the language of the provision to read 'whosoever being married goes through a ceremony of marriage', commits the crime of bigamy.

Mischief rule

There is an old rule, called the 'mischief rule', which has rarely been applied. This is to the effect that a court will, where possible, interpret a statute in such a fashion as to remedy the 'mischief' that the statute was passed to remedy. In practice, the literal rule tends to be applied even though it may have the effect of failing to remedy the mischief (see, for example, *Fisher v Bell*, p 4). The 'mischief' rule is, however, closely related to the purposive rule, dealt with below.

Purposive rule

In relation to provisions passed to give effect to the UK's obligations under EC legislation, there is a willingness to look at the purpose of a provision and take a purposive view of its meaning. See the example given in relation to the interpretation of the Transfer of Undertakings (Protection of Employment) Regulations 1981, above, p 5.

Statutory interpretation and the Human Rights Act 1998

The importance of this Act, in relation to the legal system, cannot be emphasised too greatly. It has the potential to affect every single area of activity which our law seeks to regulate – even, it seems, the rights of a finance company under the Consumer Credit Act. It came into force on October 2000, and it incorporates the European Convention on Human Rights into our domestic law. Previously, if a question of infringement of the Convention arose, there was a long-winded process whereby the matter was referred to the European Court of Human Rights (ECHR) at Strasbourg (not to be confused with the European Court in Luxembourg, which deals with European Union law). This procedure should be no longer necessary now that the Convention has become directly applicable in domestic law.

Statutory interpretation and compatibility with the Act

The Human Rights Act itself affects every other statute in the legal system, both those which were passed before the Act and those which have been passed since. The Act makes a sweeping provision that all legislation is to be interpreted in a way compatible with the European Convention. Thus, provisions in legislation or rules of common law which have not previously been challenged (perhaps because of the time and expense required to bring a case before the ECHR,) but which appear to infringe one of the human rights given by the Convention, are now open to challenge in a much more simple and straightforward manner than in the past. Courts must presume that legislation is intended to be compatible with the Convention. As the Government observed in the White Paper which preceded the Act:

> This goes far beyond the present rule which enables the courts to take the Convention into account in resolving any ambiguity in a legislative provision. The courts will be required to interpret legislation so as to uphold the Convention rights, unless the legislation itself is so clearly incompatible with the Convention that it is impossible to do so.

In addition, in respect of all new legislation, the minister in charge of it must make a declaration that it is compatible with the Convention. He may make a statement that it is not compatible, but that the Government nevertheless intends to proceed with it. Where existing legislation has been found by the ECHR to infringe the Convention, it may be amended. For example, the Insolvency Act 2000 has amended s 219 of the 1986 Act to prevent self-incriminatory answers, given under compulsion under the Companies Act 1985, being used in evidence against that person. This follows the case of *Saunders v UK* in the ECHR, where it was found that the use of such answers infringed the right of a person not to incriminate himself.

Declaration of incompatibility

If legislation cannot be interpreted so as to be compatible with the Convention, the court must make a 'declaration of incompatibility'. This does not give the courts the power to ignore the legislation; however, any order to be made under the legislation may be postponed in order to give the Government the right to respond. It is envisaged that the Government will respond quickly to such declarations, and there is provision for a 'fast track' procedure for amending the law in such cases. If not, the aggrieved party will have to use the old procedure of applying to the ECHR.

In *Wilson v First County Trust* (2001), a lender completed documentation which mis-stated the amount of credit given. Under the Consumer Credit Act, this meant that the agreement could not be enforced. Even though the customer may have lost nothing because of the mis-statement, the court was not permitted to order that the agreement should be enforced. The Court of Appeal held that this was incompatible with Article 6 (right to a fair trial) and Protocol 1, Article 1, which guarantees peaceful enjoyment of possessions (because as a result of the Act, the finance company lost its money). The court does not have the power to strike down the legislation in such a case. The court proposed to make a 'declaration of incompatibility' which would then put the onus on the Government to change the law. The case was, therefore, adjourned to allow the Crown to put its side of the argument, should it wish to oppose the making of the declaration (see Chapter 24 for more detail).

Public authorities

The Act places a duty on public authorities, including courts and tribunals, to conduct themselves in a way which is compatible with the Act. In the case of public activities which have been privatised, this provision will apply.

Absolute, derogable and qualified rights

Some rights are absolute, such as the right to life or the prohibition of torture. That right cannot be taken away. In relation to some rights, the Government may enter a derogation (that is, can claim an exemption). Many rights are 'qualified rights' in which it is necessary to balance the public interest against the rights of the individual. Thus, the right to freedom of expression is subject to the law relating to defamation (which protects a person's reputation) – though such law could be challenged on the ground that it is more restrictive than it need be in order to protect the individual's reputation.

Meaning of 'human rights'

To the layman, 'human rights' tends to have a restricted meaning. It tends to mean the right not to be arrested arbitrarily for no cause, the right not to be tortured by law enforcement agencies in order to extract a confession, and the right to be protected against similar wrongdoings by the state. However, the notion of human rights has long progressed beyond a few rudimentary propositions and now represents a sophisticated body of rights.

Main human rights

The European Convention on Human Rights sets down a list of human rights in the form of a number of Articles. These include basic ones, such as the right to life, the right not to be the subject of slavery or forced labour, and the prohibition of torture and inhuman treatment. They also include:

Article 6   The right to a fair trial

This is wide-reaching. It includes pre-trial proceedings as well as the trial itself, and so covers the whole judicial process. It has been held to apply where suspects on a criminal charge have been denied access to a solicitor; where a court refused to hear a negligence action on its merits, ruling that it was against public policy to allow the case to proceed; and where the Consumer Credit Act has provided that an agreement which was not entered into according to the provisions of the Act could not be enforced by the creditor, thus depriving the creditor of his money: the Court of Appeal held that the company should have been entitled to argue its case in court.

Article 8   The right to respect for private and family life, home and correspondence

Article 9   Freedom of thought, conscience and religion, including the right to manifest religion or belief in public or private worship, teaching, practice and observance

Article 10 Freedom of expression, including the right to receive and impart information and ideas without interference

Article 11 Freedom of assembly and association, including the right to form and join trade unions

Article 13 The prohibition of discrimination on any ground such as sex, race, colour, language, religion, political or other opinion, national or social origin, association with a national minority, property, birth, or other status

Thus, employment law protects the employee or would-be employee from discrimination on the grounds of sex, race or disability. It is foreseeable that claims will emerge (some already have) claiming protection from discrimination on the grounds of sexual orientation, religion, or even age (which could conceivably be brought under 'or other status').

There are a number of Protocols which include the right to peaceful enjoyment of possessions, the right to education, and the right to free elections.

Case law, governed by the doctrine of binding precedent

In most other legal systems, including civil law systems, decisions made in previous cases simply form part of the material (though necessarily an important part) which a court may take into account in reaching its decision. However, English law has a doctrine of *binding precedent*. Binding precedent means that a judge, in deciding the case before him or her, is *bound* to follow a ruling of law which was laid down by a higher court on a previous occasion. The binding ruling is called the *ratio decidendi*, meaning 'the reason for the decision'. The Court of Appeal (unlike the House of Lords) is also bound by its own previous decisions (though the previous court would probably have been made up of different personnel, of course).

Any ruling of law which is not necessary to the decision (and, given the verbosity of lawyers, including the present writer, there are plenty of those) is called *obiter dicta*, meaning 'things said by the way', and is regarded as being of persuasive authority for future courts. Other persuasive authorities include decisions of courts which are not binding on the present court, including those of courts in other common law countries and opinions of eminent textbook writers.

Previous decisions are collected together and published in volumes as law reports. The most important series of reports is called simply the *Law Reports*. They are published by the Incorporated Society of Law Reporting. There is often some time-lag between the case being heard and the report being published. The reports are comprehensive, containing the arguments of counsel (that is, the barristers who are instructed to argue the case in court on behalf of the litigants), as well as the judgment, which is revised by the judge before publication. Only a limited number of cases can be reported. The *Law Reports* tend, therefore, to report cases which establish an important new principle of law. If a case is reported in the *Law Reports*, it is the *Law Reports'* version which must be cited in court, not any other report which may have been made.

There are four sets of *Law Reports*. These are Appeal Cases (AC), Queen's Bench (QB), Chancery (Ch) and Family (Fam). The Family Division was not established until 1972. Before 1972, the third division of the High Court was Probate, Divorce and Admiralty (PDA).

Appeal Cases contain reports from the House of Lords and the Privy Council. Appeal Cases do not, as might have been thought, contain appeals from the Court of Appeal. These are reported in the volume of reports for the High Court Division in which the case started, or, where a case has proceeded to appeal from the county court, in the volume for the Division of the High

Court which it would have been started in had it been started in the High Court.

There are two sets of general law reports which publish reports weekly. The *All England Law Reports* (All ER) are published by a private publisher, Butterworths, and the *Weekly Law Reports* (WLR) are published by the Incorporated Council of Law Reporting. There are also a large number of specialist reports. Students of business studies might come across *Lloyds Reports* (Lloyds Rep), which report cases dealing with commercial law and the *Industrial Relations Law Reports* (IRLR), which report cases relating to employment (or industrial) law.

References to law reports in the Table of Cases are made as follows:

Chappell & Co Ltd v Nestlé Co Ltd [1960] AC 87; [1959] 2 All ER 701.

This means that a report of the case can be found in the Incorporated Council of Law Reporting's series of Appeal Cases for 1960 at p 87. Alternatively, it may be found in the second volume of the *All England Law Reports* series of reports for 1959, at p 701.

For those without access to a law library, the Incorporated Council of Law Reporting has an excellent updating service called Daily Law Notes on the web. It is to be found at http://www.lawreports.co.uk/indexdln.htm.

How precedent works

In practice, the doctrine of binding precedent is not nearly so rigid as the theory. There are two main reasons for this.

First, if a court which is deciding a case wishes to reach a different decision from that by which it is apparently bound, it is a relatively easy matter to 'distinguish' the present case from the previous one by ruling that the facts are different in principle and that, therefore, the rule of law to be applied is different. It is not uncommon, nowadays, to apply very tenuous distinctions in order to be freed from rules of law laid down in earlier times under different social, political or economic conditions.

Example of 'distinguishing'

In *Balfour v Balfour* (1919), a husband promised to pay his wife £30 per month maintenance during a period of enforced separation. He failed to pay and the wife sued him for breach of contract. It was held that her claim failed because agreements between spouses are not enforceable as contracts, since it is not envisaged that such agreements will have legal consequences.

In the later case of *Merritt v Merritt* (1970), a husband and wife were separating and the husband promised to pay his wife £40 per month out of which she had to pay the outstanding mortgage payments on the matrimonial home. He also made a written agreement to transfer the house to her when she had paid off the mortgage. He made the promised payments, but refused to keep his promise to transfer the house to her when she had paid off the mortgage. She sued for breach of contract. It was argued on the husband's behalf that she should fail because the agreement was between spouses and, following the case of *Balfour v Balfour*, there was, therefore, no intention that his promise should be legally enforceable. However, it was held that the agreement was enforceable as a contract. The earlier case of *Balfour v Balfour* could be *distinguished* on the ground that in that case the parties were living together in amity when the agreement was made, whereas in the present case the agreement was made after the parties had separated.

Questions of fact rather than law

Secondly, the great majority of cases involve issues of *fact* rather than law. The first task of any court or tribunal is to decide what the facts of the case are, in the event of a dispute, then to apply the law to the facts.

Most civil cases are tried by a judge alone or, in the case of certain tribunals, by a panel chaired by a legally qualified person. In such a case the judge or panel decides what the facts are. In the case of a trial by jury, the fact-finding process is done by the jury, having been told by the judge what the law is.

It is important to distinguish between a question of law and a question of fact for three main reasons.

First, a finding of fact can, as a general rule, be overturned by an appeal court only if the finding is wholly perverse in the sense that no *reasonable* court or tribunal could come to that finding on the evidence presented to it. *An appeal court will not overturn a finding of fact by a lower court or tribunal simply because the appeal court would have come to a different decision on the evidence presented.*

Secondly, certain appeal rights are limited to appeal on point of law only. For example, appeals to the House of Lords and to the Employment Appeal Tribunal (among others) may only be brought on point of law.

Thirdly, only a decision on a point of law constitutes a legal precedent.

So, how do you tell the difference between point of fact and point of law? The answer which the authors of an eminent textbook have given is that an issue of fact is one which, if the case were being heard with a jury (but don't forget that the vast majority of civil cases aren't), would be an appropriate issue to be decided by the jury. The difficulty with this is that one then has to progress to the question, what issues are appropriate to be decided by the jury? A suggested answer, which is admittedly broad and general but will cater for most cases, is that a question of *law* is a matter of general principle. A question of *fact* is how the general principle applies to the particular case.

Example

Kathryn is being sued for breach of contract. On Monday she offered to sell a quantity of building bricks to Len at a very favourable price, giving him until Friday to accept. On Tuesday she changed her mind and alleges that she telephoned Len to tell him of this. On Wednesday Len posted a letter accepting Kathryn's offer, which she received on Thursday. Len is now stating that Kathryn did not telephone him to withdraw her offer and that, even if she had, she could not withdraw the offer because she had initially told him that it was to remain open until Friday. There are two questions to be answered here:

(a) Did Kathryn telephone Len to withdraw the offer? and

(b) Can an offer be withdrawn before it has been accepted even if a time limit has been given for acceptance and the time limit has not been reached?

The first question is a point of fact, since it is a question concerned solely with the case of Kathryn and Len. The second question is a point of law, since it involves a general principle which may be applied to all similar cases. (The answer which the law has given to the second question is 'yes'.)

Advantages and disadvantages

The system of judicial precedent has advantages and disadvantages. As is often the case, the disadvantages may consist of the advantages considered from a different point of view!

The advantages (and disadvantages) include:

(a) It is practical rather than theoretical.

Case law develops the law through practical examples rather than trying to predict what will happen in the future and trying to legislate for it in advance.

The other side of the coin is that case law gets made only when there is an appropriate case to cover the facts. English courts will not answer hypothetical legal problems so, unless an appropriate case gets to court, an important legal point may remain uncertain for many years. The only way to settle undecided points, in the absence of case law, is for Parliament to find the parliamentary time to legislate. However, legislation regarding a significant body of law tends to take priority over legislation dealing with the isolated point, even though the isolated point may be very important.

In addition, since taking a case to the higher courts such as the Court of Appeal and the House of Lords is expensive, it may mean that an important point which arises is made the subject of a settlement out of court. Thus, for example, in *Bernstein v Pamson Motors* (1987), the High Court ruled that a car purchaser lost his right to reject a faulty car after having possessed it for only three weeks. The decision was subject to criticism and an appeal was lodged. Many commentators thought that the appeal would be successful and a more generous time allowance given to the purchaser. However, the defendant settled the matter out of court before the appeal. Thus the purchaser's rights remain uncertain (though for a more generous approach, but in a slightly different context, see *Truk v Tokmakidis* (2000)).

(b) Certainty through detail.

Because of the large number of cases decided, the law is rich in detail. This means that a large number of fact situations are the subject of a legal ruling, which, in turn, means that there is a large degree of certainty in the law. See, for example, Chapter 3 and the law relating to distinguishing offers from invitation to treat. Although only the most important cases are included in this text, they cover advertisements in newspapers, auction sales, catalogue lists, supermarket sales, public transport and ticket machines. This enables the lawyer to be able to predict the outcome of a case with some certainty in many areas, though precedent didn't help the Northampton auctioneer who refused to sell two machines to the lowest bidder in an auction 'without reserve'. This proved to be an expensive mistake which could perhaps have been avoided if the auctioneer had had an elementary knowledge of the case law relating to auctions (see *Barry v Heathcote Ball* (2000)).

The disadvantage which arises from the detail is that there is too much of it. There is a significant (and increasing) number of law reports which the well-stocked legal library needs to hold. Holding hard copies takes up a great deal of space and, whether copies are hard or electronic, they are very costly.

(c) Flexibility.

It is argued that the law can adapt to new fact situations through the application of established principle. It is not necessary to pass a new Act of Parliament in order to introduce new law. This is true to a certain extent. There has been a dramatic upsurge in negligence claims over the past few years owing to the willingness of the courts to apply the existing law to new situations. The law relating to promissory estoppel in contract, for example, circumvented an old but commercially inconvenient principle of law in order to be more appropriate for modern commercial conditions and practices.

The disadvantage in this is that case law is retrospective in effect. This point was made by the law reformer, Jeremy Bentham (1748–1832), who argued that all law should be codified (that is, put into legislation), so that people would know the law in advance. For example, in *Donoghue v Stevenson* (1932) (see Chapter 27), the manufacturer who was sued by the consumer appeared, under the existing law, to have a perfectly valid defence. It was only by a 3:2 vote in the House of Lords that it was established that he was liable. To Bentham, and some jurists following after him, establishing liability in this way is wrong. He called it 'dog's law' and compared it to the way a person makes rules for his dog: he waits until it does something wrong and then beats it! Those who support Bentham would argue that there should have been legislation in place which established that the manufacturer was liable, before the event. However, this argument to some extent overlooks the fact that legislators can never foresee every possible fact situation so that, although the main principles of liability may be set down in legislation, there will always be a role for judges to decide, after the event, what the legal effect of the parties' action was.

Further general disadvantages are:

(i) that an out-of-date or unjust principle of law may become established as law because no subsequent case is brought to court, which might give the courts the opportunity to overrule the earlier decision; and

(ii) that important principles of law which may affect the lives of a significant proportion of the population are decided by individuals who have not been democratically elected.

CLASSIFICATION OF LAW

There are various ways of classifying legal liability. By far the most useful classification for practical purposes is into (i) civil; or (ii) criminal. The basic difference is that an infringement of criminal law renders you liable to *prosecution* and, if you are convicted, you are liable to be *punished*; an infraction of the civil law means that the injured party may *sue* you and, if you are found liable, you are likely to have to pay a monetary compensation called *damages* or have some other remedy awarded against you.

One important reason for being able to distinguish between criminal and civil liability is that you can always compromise a claim in relation to the civil law, that is, you can bargain with the claimant (the person or company which is bringing the action against you) with a view to avoiding court action. However, in the case of a criminal offence, although there is a discretion in all cases whether or not to prosecute (and, indeed, some bargaining may take place: for example, a local council may withhold a prosecution in relation to an unlawful notice misleading consumers about their rights, if the person responsible undertakes to remove the notice and not to display a similar notice in future), whether to prosecute is the unilateral decision of the authorities responsible for enforcing the law.

Criminal law

A crime may be defined as 'a legal wrong for which the offender is liable to be *prosecuted* and if *convicted* punished by the state'.

Most lay-persons, if asked to define a crime, will do so in terms of the *conduct* prohibited. Thus, they will suggest that a crime is an act against public morality, or against the 'public good'. However, it is not possible to define a crime by reference to the wrongful activity which constitutes a crime. There are two main reasons for this. First, it would be extremely difficult to frame a definition which included all criminal activity but at the same time excluded all non-criminal acts. Secondly, since standards of morality and notions of 'public good' frequently change, one's definition would need continual updating.

It is, therefore, necessary to approach the problem from the point of view of the *consequences* of the conduct: the twin factors of liability to *prosecution* and liability to *punishment* if convicted. Thus, murder is a crime, but so too is negotiating consumer credit without a licence, contrary to the Consumer Credit Act 1974. Both offences contain the common elements highlighted above, though, of course, the respective punishments will vary greatly.

Civil law

Although most laymen's perception of law is confined to criminal acts, in fact by far the greater part of our law is civil law. Perhaps the only definition we can offer is that civil law is that part of the law which is not criminal law. However, if we describe civil law we will say that its distinguishing feature is that it is concerned with the rights and duties of individuals (including legal individuals such as limited liability companies) as between themselves.

Although the state provides the machinery by which civil disputes may be resolved and the judgment of the court enforced, it has no further involvement in the matter.

The main areas of civil law with which a business may be concerned are:

Law of contract

This is concerned with the enforcement of promises, usually in the form of agreements. Such agreements may be formal written agreements or informal oral agreements, or even agreements to be implied from conduct.

Law of tort

A tort is a civil wrong, other than a breach of contract or a breach of trust (both of which are civil wrongs but are not torts), which may be remedied by an action for damages. Unlike contract (with which, nevertheless, there is some overlap) the duty which is breached in committing a tort is fixed by the law, whereas the duty which is breached in committing a breach of contract is a duty undertaken voluntarily as a result of a promise to the other party. There are quite a number of individual torts. The most prominent ones include negligence, nuisance, trespass (to person, to goods, or to land), defamation, breach of statutory duty, and deceit. In practice a person in business is most likely to be concerned with negligence and breach of statutory duty.

Commercial law or mercantile law

These terms tend to be employed interchangeably. They comprise the special rules relating to specific types of contract such as sale of goods, supply of services, hire purchase, insurance, consumer credit, carriage of goods, etc.

Company law

Most companies are formed so as to have limited liability for their debts. This is regarded as a privilege conferred by the law, so that it is not surprising that this privilege is subject to fairly detailed regulations about raising money, the allotment of shares, company meetings, insider dealings, etc. This is the subject matter of company law.

Employment law (or labour law or industrial law)

This can be divided into two parts. First, there is the part which regulates individual employment rights, for example, the rules relating to unfair dismissal, the right to redundancy payment, equal pay, etc. Secondly, there is the part which relates to collective activity, for example, the law relating to industrial action, admission to and expulsion from trade unions, etc. Some employment law, particularly in the area of health and safety, is criminal law.

Land law

The main areas which concern businesses are the law relating to the relationship of landlord and tenant and planning law.

Terminology

Criminal and civil law each have their own particular terminology. In a criminal case there is a *prosecution*. The person bringing the case is called the prosecutor. The accused (or the defendant) is first charged and then prosecuted. The accused may plead 'guilty', in which case the defence lawyer may make a plea in mitigation (that is, the lawyer explains special circumstances surrounding the crime which tend to show that the accused is not as blameworthy as it might appear, in the hope that this might persuade the court to be lenient when handing down the sentence). The accused may, on the other hand, plead 'not guilty', in which case a trial will follow. If the accused is convicted (that is, found guilty) a plea in mitigation may be made. The accused will then be sentenced. If the accused is found 'not guilty', he will be acquitted.

In a civil case, the claimant brings an *action* against the defendant. (Alternatively, you can say that the claimant *sues* the defendant.) The defendant defends the case by denying liability. If his denial of liability is successful he will be found not liable (for tort, breach of contract or whatever). If his denial is unsuccessful he will be found liable. The court will then make an award to the claimant.

In an industrial tribunal, the complainant (or applicant) brings a case against the respondent.

In an appeal case, the appellant brings the appeal against the respondent.

Relationship between civil and criminal law

It is extremely important to understand that a particular course of conduct can give rise to consequences in both civil law and criminal law at the same time.

For example, the crime of murder (and most other criminal offences involving physical injury) will almost invariably involve the torts (that is, the civil wrongs) of assault and battery. The crime of causing criminal damage, for example, by throwing a missile at a car, will amount to the tort of trespass to goods. The crime of causing death by dangerous driving will amount to the tort of negligence; the crimes of dangerous driving or driving without due care and attention, assuming that they result in physical damage to another person or to his property, will amount to the tort of negligence.

Despite the fact that many crimes also amount to torts, it is, in practice, very rare for the victim of a crime to bring a civil action against the wrongdoer, unless the wrongdoer is covered by an appropriate insurance policy. The main reason for this is that it is a waste of time and money to sue a defendant who is unlikely to be able to afford to pay the amount of any award of damages which is made against him. Thus, to refer back to the examples of murder and criminal damage, neither the murderer nor the person who commits the criminal damage will be insured and, therefore, it is unlikely to be worth suing them. On the other hand, the motorist who drives without due care and attention must by law be insured against the risk of personal injury to third parties, including passengers, and the risk of damage to the property of third parties. Since, in such a case, the party who has suffered the damage is really suing the insurance company, a civil action will be worthwhile.

Proving your case

A further practical point is that (as we have already said) most civil cases are settled out of court. In this event, the defendant makes an offer to the claimant which is dependent upon the claimant withdrawing his case. In cases where there is a substantial amount of money at stake, there is often a protracted process of negotiation before a settlement is finally reached.

Where the defendant's conduct is a criminal offence in addition to being a civil wrong, it is useful to the claimant's civil case if the defendant has been the subject of a successful criminal prosecution before the civil case comes to court. The reason for this is that although, surprisingly, a conviction for a criminal offence is not *conclusive* evidence that the defendant committed the offence of which he was found guilty, a criminal conviction may be used in a civil case to raise the presumption that the defendant was guilty of the offence for which he was convicted. This means that it is up to the defendant to prove that he didn't do what he was alleged to have done, rather than, as would normally be the case, the claimant having to prove his case from scratch.

Example

Ted is convicted in a magistrates' court of driving without due care and attention when he hit Sarah's car from behind. Should Ted or his insurance company refuse to compensate Sarah in respect of the damage, with the result that Sarah had to bring a civil case for damages, she could use the conviction as evidence that Ted had been negligent. It would then be up to Ted to prove that he hadn't been negligent (though if he is successful it won't overturn the conviction!). In practice, Ted will find this extremely difficult to do.

Compensation in a criminal case

Strictly speaking, compensation is the job of the civil law. However, under the Powers of Criminal Courts (Sentencing) Act 2000, where a person is convicted of a criminal offence, the court which is sentencing him or her may, in addition to a sentence or instead of a sentence, make a compensation order. In practice, this power is not used as often as it might be. This is partly because the Court of Appeal has said that compensation orders should not be used where the criminal might be tempted to commit further crimes in order to meet his or her obligations, and partly because in cases where civil liability is not absolutely clear-cut, the criminal courts prefer to leave the matter to be dealt with by a civil court. The maximum compensation that can be awarded in the magistrates' court is £5,000. In the Crown Court it is unlimited. Note that the power to award compensation does not apply to road traffic offences, except in relation to damage to a vehicle which is the subject of an offence under the Theft Acts (for example, a car which has been stolen or has been taken away and driven without the owner's consent). Note, too, that a victim of violent crime may apply to the Criminal Injuries Compensation Authority for appropriate recompense. This will be done where, as is usual, the perpetrator of the crime is not worth suing for damages.

THE COURTS

There are two types of court structure in the English legal system. One structure deals with (mainly) criminal cases and one structure deals with civil cases. Nearly all criminal cases are dealt with by the magistrates' court, leaving only a few of the more serious to be dealt with by the Crown Court. Most civil cases are dealt with by the county court and by various administrative tribunals which have been superimposed upon the general court system (most notably the industrial tribunals), leaving only a small minority to be heard by the High Court.

Figure 1.1   The structure and operation of the civil courts

The civil courts deal with a wide number of matters, including claims in contract and tort. The court where a case is first heard is called a Court of First Instance. In relation to most business matters, two courts have first instance jurisdiction. These are:

(a) the county court; and

(b) the High Court, usually the Queen's Bench Division of the court, but sometimes the Chancery Division.

The whole system of civil justice has been radically overhauled following the reforms proposed by Lord Woolf. Following a comprehensive inquiry, he produced a Report, *Access to Justice* in two stages: an Interim Report in 1995 and a Final Report in 1996. He identified the key problems of the civil justice system as being 'cost, delay and complexity'. In consequence of the Report, the Civil Procedure Act 1997 and the Civil Procedure Rules 1998 were introduced and came into effect in April 1999.

The overall purpose of the reforms is to make the court system more user-friendly. Civil cases, even the vast majority which were settled out of court, were renowned for:

(1) delaying tactics: often used by defendants to wear down a claimant who was refusing to settle for the terms proposed by the defendant;

(2) vast amounts of unnecessary paperwork: justified on the ground that it ensured that every possible point was covered; and

(3) undue cost: in many small claims cases the legal costs were greater than the amount recovered in damages.

A new system of case management conducted by judges, modelled on American lines, was introduced with the objective of reducing the time taken for cases to be resolved and, in consequence, saving costs. Under the previous system, if one of the parties did not produce appropriate documentation to time, the onus was on the other party to bring the matter before the judge and to obtain an order to compel the defaulting party to comply. Under the case management system, it is the judge's responsibility to ensure that the procedures (for example, exchange of witness statements) are completed by the appropriate time. If they are not, a penalty is applied either by the Civil Procedure Rules or by the judge. However, the judge retains an overriding discretion and may give relief from a sanction imposed by the Rules. The exercise of this discretion has already been the cause of a number of appeals. It will be interesting to see whether the appeals reduce as the process settles down.

In addition, Alternative Dispute Resolution (of which arbitration is the most important example for businesses), which is aimed at keeping the case out of the court system, is encouraged. Central to the system of case management will be an efficient computerised system. It should be noted that not everyone agrees that the case management system saves time and costs.

Pre-action protocols (PAPs) are an innovation intended to encourage early but well-informed settlement. These have been introduced for claims of clinical negligence and personal injury. They were drafted after consultation with interested parties and are intended to do away with what tended to happen under the old system whereby the parties behaved like fighters in a boxing match, testing each other out by a long period of sparring before getting down to the actual fight. They require the claimant to send a letter detailing his claim including an explanation of why the defendant is thought to be at fault. The defendant has 21 days to acknowledge the letter, identifying an insurer where applicable, and a further three months in which to investigate the claim, at the end of which he should either admit liability or deny it, giving reasons. There are procedures whereby the claimant may obtain early access to medical records and whereby the parties may agree on expert evidence (preferably one report rather than the multiple reports commonly used in the past) to be used in the claim. The protocols encourage the use of Alternative Dispute Resolution. If a party fails to comply properly with a PAP, this may be taken into account, in effect to penalise the non-compliant party, particularly when the court is considering the question of costs.

Each case will be allocated to a 'track'. There are three tracks:

- Small claims track; this is for cases where the amount claimed is £5,000 (formerly £3,000) or less. The £5,000 limit applies to *personal injury cases* unless the amount of general damages claimed exceeds £1,000 (general damages represents damages quantified by the court, for example, pain and suffering, rather than a specific amount of loss, such as lost earnings; for *housing repair cases*, the cost of repairs must not exceed £1,000 and the value of any other claim for damages must not exceed £1,000).

These cases will normally be heard by a junior judge called a 'District Judge'. The hearings are intended to be relatively informal. If the parties consent, a paper adjudication may be given. Costs awarded to the winning party are restricted to: the summons issue fee; reasonable travelling expenses to and from court; up to £260 for legal advice and up to £200 for an expert's report. The parties need not attend the hearing. Parties may consent to the hearing of a claim using the small claims track even if the value of their claim is above the £5,000 limit. In such a case, the costs are not limited to the sums set out above.

- Fast track: this is for claims where the amount claimed is more than £5,000 but less than £15,000; the pre-trial procedures are standard and are designed to avoid complexity and to be relatively streamlined. The trial must be estimated by the judge managing the procedure to last a maximum of one day (five hours). If a trial requires expert evidence (for example, the cause of a brake failure which results in a car crash), it is intended that the parties will agree on a single expert witness (rather than each side tendering its own expert was the case under the old procedure) and that the expert will give his/her evidence in writing. The intention is that this will save costs by avoiding multiple experts and by avoiding the need for the witness to appear in court.

- Multi-track: these are cases where either the claim is for £15,000 or more or cases of a lesser amount which involve points of special importance or are of special complexity. This track offers a variety of procedures (for example, pre-trial reviews, case management conferences, standard directions by the court as to what is to be done), intended to be selected for their particular relevance to the case in question. Formality has been relaxed so that, for example, a case management conference may take place over the telephone.

A matter for complaint about the new civil justice system is that one of its aims is to make the courts self-financing through the fees charged to litigants. There is a strong argument that the state should treat justice as it treats health and ensure that no-one is denied justice because they lack the means to pay for it.

A relatively minor objective of the reforms was to simplify the language used in the civil legal process. To give three examples, the 'plaintiff' (the person bringing a case) is now the 'claimant'; 'pleadings', which consisted of a formal exchange of statements between the parties, intended to narrow down the issues in dispute, are now called 'statements of case'; an Anton Pillar Order (that is, an order to search premises in order to discover evidence) is now 'a search order'.

Appeals

The Bowman Report (1997) suggested wide-ranging reforms to the system of appeals. The main aims were to cut down the number of multiple appeals which are possible and to cut down the use of expensive judicial time by making more use of the possibility of appeal to a single judge or, where appropriate, two judges. The Access to Justice Act 1999 made provision for some of the recommendations. For example, the Court of Appeal is now properly constituted with only one judge (formerly two were required). The Act also made provision whereby the Lord Chancellor may, by Order, prescribe new appeal routes. There is a new power under the Act whereby the Master of the Rolls can order that an appeal being heard by a lower court may be transferred to the Court of Appeal in relation to issues which are causing difficulty.

The county court

There are about 240 of these in England and Wales. They were created by the County Courts Act 1846. Quite why they are called county courts no-one knows, since neither the individual courts nor the circuits into which they are organised have anything to do with counties.

They are staffed by circuit judges, who are the more senior, and by district judges. They have a wide jurisdiction including: actions in contract, tort, probate, bankruptcy, winding-up of companies, admiralty matters, equity matters, children and matrimonial property, undefended divorce, cases under the Consumers Credit Act 1974 and the Race Relations Act 1976.

Under the new system, the county court will hear small claims track, fast track and straightforward multi-track cases.

However, certain cases must be set down for hearing in the High Court. These are: professional negligence; fatal accidents; fraud or undue influence; defamation; malicious prosecution or false imprisonment; and claims against the police.

The High Court

The High Court consists of three divisions: Queen's Bench, Chancery, and Family. It is Queen's Bench that hears commercial cases, though Chancery has jurisdiction to hear matters relating to companies, partnerships, mortgages and equitable remedies such as injunctions.

The High Court will hear the more complex or important multi-track cases under the new system.

A High Court case will normally be heard by a High Court judge, though simpler cases can be released to be heard by a circuit judge. The High Court is based at the Royal Courts of Justice in the Strand. There are, in addition, 23 provincial centres at which High Court cases may be heard.

A High Court judge whose name is George Brown will be called Mr Justice Brown when he is being written about. This is normally abbreviated to Brown J. The situation is complicated by the fact that Brown J will be addressed in court as 'My Lord' and 'Your Lordship'. However, he is not a Lord unless he holds the title independently of his position in the legal profession. High Court judges are invariably knighted, so that Mr Justice Brown, who is called 'My Lord' in court, will be Sir George Brown in private life. Not surprisingly, lay-persons, even journalists experienced in writing about judicial proceedings, frequently become confused about what to call a High Court judge!

If George Brown had been a circuit judge before he became a High Court judge, he would have been called Judge Brown. He would have been called 'Your Honour' in court and would be written about as Judge Brown or, His Honour, Judge Brown.

Commercial actions may be tried in the Commercial Court, which is part of the Queen's Bench Division. Procedure is simplified and the case is heard by a specialist judge. The court has power to sit as arbitrator. In an effort to woo commercial litigants away from private arbitration, it has been proposed that the court should have a general power to sit in private (it has such a power where trade secrets, etc, are involved or where it acts as arbitrator). Such a proposal was included as part of the Administration of Justice Bill 1970, but was defeated in the Commons.

The court acts as a point of reference for arbitrators. Any party to an arbitration can require the arbitrator to 'state a special case' on an issue of law, to be considered by the Commercial Court. If the arbitration is in the Commercial Court itself, the reference is made to the Court of Appeal. There are probably more cases heard in the Commercial Court by way of reference from arbitration than are started in the court directly.

There are clear advantages in using the Commercial Court as arbitrator where there are likely to be substantial points of law involved. When sitting as arbitrator the court may sit at any place convenient to the parties – the hearing does not have to be in the law courts; and as a special case can be referred to the Court of Appeal during the hearing, one stage of the appeal process is dispensed with, with benefits in speed and cost.

Court of Appeal (Civil Division)

Appeals from the county court or the High Court are heard by the Court of Appeal. The appeal will normally be heard by three Lords Justices of Appeal (or the Master of the Rolls and two Lords Justices of Appeal). When George Brown becomes a Lord Justice of Appeal, he will be written about as Lord Justice Brown, which is abbreviated to Brown LJ. He is still called 'My Lord' or 'Your Lordship' in court and is still Sir George Brown. If George became the Master of the Rolls, who is the senior judge in the Court of Appeal (Civil Division), he would be called Sir George Brown, Master of the Rolls (usually abbreviated to MR).

Appeal may be made on point of fact (subject to certain limitations) or on point of law. In practice, unless the conclusion which the lower court has reached is entirely unsupported by the evidence, an appeal on point of fact will fail. The Court of Appeal may reverse or uphold the decision of the lower court or it may substitute a new judgment. Exceptionally, it has power to order a new trial, for example, where evidence has been improperly admitted or rejected.

House of Lords

This is the final domestic court of appeal. It hears appeals form the Court of Appeal and, in certain circumstances, from the High Court. It hears appeals on point of law only. Either the court below or the Appeal Committee of the House of Lords must certify that a point of law of general public importance is involved. There is provision for direct appeal from the High Court in civil cases, thus 'leap-frogging' the Court of Appeal. All parties must consent and the appeal must raise a point of law of general public importance relating wholly or mainly to a statute or statutory instrument.

A case in the House of Lords is usually heard by five Lords of Appeal in Ordinary (often referred to as 'Law Lords'). Law Lords are life peers, so that when they are addressed as 'My Lord' this reflects their civil status as well as their judicial status. Thus, when Brown LJ is elevated to the House of Lords, he will become Lord Brown.

Tribunals

Since the Second World War, there has been a great upsurge in the use of administrative tribunals, rather than courts, to do certain types of judicial work. Although most tribunals have a legally qualified chairman, most tribunals also have lay-persons involved in giving judgment. For example, an industrial tribunal, which deals with employment matters, has a legally qualified chairman plus two lay-persons: one representative from each side of industry. An important defect of tribunal justice, from the point of view of the public, is that legal aid (that is, state-funded professional assistance) is not available for a tribunal case so that the applicant must either represent him or herself, receive assistance from a body such as a trade union, or pay for professional assistance out of their own pocket. The latter can make a case not worthwhile pursuing since, unlike a court case, a tribunal rarely awards costs to a successful party.

Arbitration

It is common for commercial contracts to contain a provision that any dispute shall be referred to an arbitrator for decision. The arbitrator may be named; he may be designated by his office; he may be left to be chosen by a designated third party; or the contract may provide for the parties each to nominate an umpire who will then agree on an arbitrator. Doubtless there are variations on these methods.

The arbitrator need not be a lawyer. However, where an arbitration involves a difficult point of law, the arbitrator may refer it to the High Court and either party may request the arbitrator to submit a point of law for decision by the High Court. Arbitrations have the advantage that they are usually quicker than normal legal proceedings, they are heard in private, and they may be held in a place and at a time convenient to the parties. It is also said that arbitrations are cheaper, but this is not necessarily so.

Costs

One of the major drawbacks to litigation is the very high cost involved. The court has a discretion in the award of costs. The normal rule in England is that the winning party receives his costs from the other party. However, this is by no means inflexible, and where one party brings a case simply to vindicate his legal rights without securing any other advantage, the court may well make him pay his own costs. In a case where there are multiple issues and the claimant wins on some and loses on others, the claimant may be awarded a proportion of his costs. At the moment, an employment tribunal rarely awards costs, though there is power to do so if the applicant's claim is vexatious or frivolous. However, where following a pre-hearing review it is found that the applicant has no case, the applicant can be made to pay a deposit of £500 against costs if he insists in proceeding with the case.

Example of cost where the claim is compromised

Builders (B) claim that they are owed £2,000 by Customer (C) in respect of maintenance work done on C's premises. C claims that the work was defective and, since it will cost £1,000 to complete the work to the initial specification, C is prepared to offer £1,000 in full settlement. After some negotiation between C and B's solicitors, C offers £1,500 in full settlement, on the terms that each party will pay its own costs. The solicitor charges £70 per hour for the cost of his service and adds 50% profit costs and VAT. (The profit costs might be less if B is a large client, more if the matter is particularly complex.) If B accept this offer, they will receive £1,500 less solicitor's costs of (say) five hours' work = £80 + 50% = £120 x 5 = £600 plus (reclaimable) VAT at 17.5%.

Example of costs where claim is litigated (that is, taken to court)

If B refuses the offer and institutes legal proceedings to recover the debt, C is likely to pay £1,500 into court. 'Paying in' is a useful tactic because it means that if the court awards B less than the £1,500 paid in, B must pay all the costs which accrue after the date the money is paid in. (The normal rule about costs is that the party who wins the case is entitled to recover their costs from the losing party.) The judge is not informed about any amount paid in until after he has given judgment and is about to make an order in relation to costs.

Costs escalate when the matter is litigated. In the first place, there are certain pre-trial proceedings which are often lengthy and drawn out (and therefore costly!) and secondly, the trial itself is expensive. It is not possible to give an estimate of the costs of a full blown court trial, since there are so many variables, but if the matter is at all complex or involves a substantial amount of money, your solicitor may well instruct a barrister to appear on your behalf. If the hearing is in the High Court (rather than the county court) or goes to appeal, then generally a barrister must be instructed.

In employment tribunal cases, the norm is for each party to pay its own costs, although there is a little used power to award costs where one of the parties has acted frivolously, vexatiously or otherwise unreasonably. If the matter is one which, under the terms of a contract, is heard by an arbitrator rather than a court, the costs may be lower than for a court case, but often only marginally so. The rule with arbitrations is that, unless the parties have agreed otherwise, costs are awarded as they would be in relation to a court case.

Don't forget that in addition to the costs mentioned above, a legal case can also generate considerable indirect costs, for example, in relation to time lost from work by attending at the solicitor's office, preparation of relevant documents, time lost to attend the court hearing, etc. Because of the cost and complexity of legal action, the manager tends, for example, to remedy the minor breaches of contract which occur daily at many workplaces, both by customers and by employees, by informal negotiation rather than by legal action. Although the manager may feel threatened when a new piece of legislation which affects his undertaking and carries criminal penalties comes into force, he is relieved to find that enforcing authorities such as the Health and Safety Inspectorate, the Trading Standards Department or the Environmental Health Department, tend to work on a policy of advice and conciliation rather than prosecution, except in serious cases.

CRIMINAL COURTS

Figure 1.2   The structure and operation of the criminal courts

Although statute has created a wide range of criminal offences aimed at regulating the conduct of businesses, it is relatively rare that business people are brought before the courts for the commission of such offences.

The reason is twofold. First, some of the agencies entrusted with upholding the law prefer to work on the basis of conciliation. They give help and advice to the business community and only if that help and advice is blatantly ignored will a criminal prosecution ensue, as a general rule. Thus, if you provide consumer credit without having a licence, which is an offence under s 39 of the Consumer Credit Act 1974, unless you are recalcitrant, you are more likely to be counselled and warned about your future conduct than you are to be prosecuted. Secondly, some agencies such as the VAT branch of Customs and Excise, the Inland Revenue, etc, will often agree penalties as an alternative to prosecution.

Thus, despite the fact that the business community commits an abundance of criminal offences daily (albeit mostly inadvertently!), relatively few business people end up being prosecuted.

Types of criminal offence

For the purposes of determining which court is to try an offence, there are three types of criminal offence:

(a) summary offences. These are triable only by magistrates;

(b) offences triable only on indictment. These are very serious offences and may be tried only at the Crown Court by a judge and jury; and

(c) offences triable either way. There are a large number of such offences. What happens in such cases is that both the prosecution and the defence are permitted to make representations to the examining magistrates as to whether the trial should be a summary one in the magistrates' court or a trial on indictment in the Crown Court. If the magistrates decide that the trial should be on indictment, that is an end to the matter. If, however, they decide it should be a summary trial, the accused must be told that he has the right to trial by jury in the Crown Court should he so choose. In practice, many such defendants opt for summary trial in order to get the matter out of the way there and then.

Magistrates' court

The magistrates' court hears 98% of criminal cases. The trial is before a minimum of two and a maximum of seven magistrates (though there are several functions which one magistrate alone can perform), unless the magistrate is a paid magistrate called a 'stipendiary', in which case he can try a case sitting alone. The magistrate is called by his or her normal name and is addressed in court as 'Your worship' or, less formally, simply as 'Sir' or 'Madam'.

The magistrates are lay-persons, most of whom have only a rudimentary knowledge of the law. For this reason they are assisted by a clerk. The clerk for any Petty Sessional Division must have a five years magistrates court qualification (that is, they must have had a right of audience in relation to all magistrates courts proceedings for five years and so will be a barrister or solicitor), though the clerk who appears in court on any particular day may well be unqualified.

Appeals from the magistrates' court may be made by the defendant to the Crown Court. The appeal takes the form of an entire re-hearing of the case, with witnesses giving their evidence all over again. (This contrasts with the normal form of appeal which is simply conducted by examining the paperwork from the court below.) The appeal is heard by a judge together with not less than two and not more than four lay magistrates. There is no jury.

A further appeal may be made on point of law only to a Divisional Court of the Queen's Bench Division of the High Court. This may be brought by either the prosecution or the defence. It is heard by three judges. If a point of law is the only matter at issue between the defence and prosecution, the defence will often make their appeal direct to the Divisional Court, thus cutting out the Crown Court.

A final appeal may be brought to the House of Lords, providing the Divisional Court certifies that a point of law of general public importance is at issue and either the House of Lords or the Divisional Court gives permission to appeal.

Crown Court

A Crown Court trial is called a trial on indictment, and is conducted by a judge, before a jury.

Appeal from the Crown Court lies to the Court of Appeal (Criminal Division). Such an appeal is not a re-hearing of the case, though if the appearance of fresh evidence is thought to warrant it, the court has power to order a fresh trial before judge and jury if it wishes.

House of Lords

There is a final appeal on point of law to the House of Lords, providing the Court of Appeal certifies that a point of law of general public importance is involved and either the Court of Appeal or the House of Lords gives permission to appeal.

Legal advice and assistance

The extent to which legal advice and assistance should be available either free of charge or at a subsidised rate is a moot point. Ideally, everyone should have unrestricted access to legal services. However, this is simply not practicable. The existing scheme in 1998/99 cost the exchequer £1,622 million. The cost of civil legal aid and that of criminal legal aid were similar, at around £650 million each. The remainder was made up of legal aid for family matters. The scheme restricted legal aid in civil cases to the relatively poor. In criminal cases, in order to ensure that there could be no accusation of unfairness because the defendant was not properly represented, the scheme tended to give the defendant the benefit of any doubt. This meant that, in a number of high profile cases, defendants who were apparently wealthy both before and after their cases suffered from relative poverty at the time their means came to be assessed for the purposes of legal aid.

In order to try to reduce the rapidly rising amount spent on legal aid, new provisions have been enacted to try to promote value for money, on the one hand, while ensuring quality of service on the other. The provision of legal aid and advice has been overhauled by the Access to Justice Act 1999. It establishes a Legal Services Commission to run two new schemes. The

Commission will replace the Legal Aid Board. The new schemes will be called the Community Legal Service and the Criminal Defence Service. The Community Legal Service will provide legal aid in civil and family cases. A funding code will set out the criteria for funding individual cases. Community Legal Service Partnerships will be formed in each local authority area. The Legal Services Commission, the local authority and others will plan the provision of legal services in each area in order to ensure that the services provided are appropriate to local needs.

The purpose of the Criminal Defence Service is to secure the provision of advice, assistance and representation for persons facing criminal charges. Contracts for doing this will be entered into with lawyers in private practice or will be by salaried persons employed directly by the Legal Services Commission.

The conditional fee, introduced by the Courts and Legal Services Act 1990, has been reformed by the Access to Justice Act 1999. This is a 'no win no pay' arrangement. The client enters into an insurance in order to ensure payment of the other party's costs should he lose. If he wins, the solicitor is entitled to charge up to 100% in addition to his normal fee. The Law Society (the governing body for the solicitors' profession) has recommended that solicitors curtail their fee to 25% of the damages recovered if this is less than the 100% 'uplift'. The 1999 Act improves the position of the claimant in that it provides for the defendant to pay the 'uplift' charged by the claimant's solicitor and also the insurance premium paid by the claimant. It is hoped, by the Government, that these changes will make conditional fees more attractive to litigants seeking a non-monetary award. As things stood before the 1999 Act, the successful claimant had to pay the insurance fee and the 'uplift' out of the damages secured from the other party. Thus, anyone seeking a non-monetary award would be out of pocket whether he won or lost. The changes made by the 1999 Act mean that a person who is successful in seeking a non-monetary award should not be out of pocket in relation to costs.

The Legal Services Commission is given wide powers in relation to its provision of aid. It may, for example, make loans to enable people to purchase the appropriate aid.

Legal aid is not available to corporations.

Advocates in court

The legal profession is divided into two branches: solicitors and barristers.

A solicitor may be in partnership or may be a sole practitioner. Solicitors traditionally deal with out-of-court matters such as the conveyancing of property, drawing up of wills or trust documents, formation of companies, issuing the documents to begin a legal action, and dealing with all ancillary matters such as taking statements from witnesses.

A barrister is traditionally an advocate: that is, a person who appears in court on behalf of a litigant. A barrister is often referred to as 'counsel' and is regarded as a specialist. Thus, when a solicitor is not sure whether a client has a case which is winnable if it were taken to court (or defended), the solicitor will often seek 'counsel's opinion'. It is useful for a solicitor to do this in a case which is not straightforward, since if he acts on counsel's opinion, it will usually protect him from an action for negligence, should the client be dissatisfied with the way in which the case has been pursued.

Barristers are sole practitioners, though certain aspects of their professional undertakings resemble a partnership. Barristers work from a set of offices called 'chambers', which house several barristers. They employ administrative staff, cleaning staff, etc, in common. The chief of the administrative staff is the 'clerk', whose particular job is to negotiate fees with solicitors who bring work to the chambers. The fee for a 'brief' is customarily a set amount with daily 'refreshers'. Thus the fee for a brief which is marked £10,000 with a £1,000 per day refresher would be £12,000 if the case lasted two days. A senior barrister may apply to 'take silk'. This means that he or she is entitled to wear a silk gown rather than one made of an ordinary material called 'stuff'. A barrister who takes silk becomes a Queen's Counsel, normally abbreviated to 'QC'. A QC appears in court assisted by a 'junior' barrister.

Barristers used to have a monopoly of advocacy work in cases which were begun in the higher courts, that is, Crown Court, High Court, etc, but, under the Access to Justice Act 1999, it is now possible for a solicitor to act as an advocate in the higher courts, though, oddly enough, they are not yet permitted to wear the horsehair wig which is the trademark of the barrister. To do this, the solicitor must undertake a special advocacy qualification.

Many barristers and solicitors are employed by organisations such as the Crown Prosecution Service or by large corporations. Before the Access to Justice Act 1999, there were professional rules which restricted the right of audience (that is, the right of appearing in court as an advocate) and did not permit employed barristers or solicitors to appear in certain courts. These rules have now largely disappeared, allowing employed advocates rights of audience on equal terms with those in private practice.

Where to find the law

The most obvious source is a textbook. However, a textbook only tells you the writer's view of what the law is: although the law relating to many issues is settled beyond dispute, in other cases it is not, in which case a text writer can only give you his view of the law (though good writers will examine other possibilities) and it is by no means certain that a court or tribunal will decide a case in accordance with the writer's view, however eminent they may be.

If you wish to go to the source material, the primary sources of law are *statutes* and *decided cases* (that is, cases which have been decided by judges).

Where to find statutes

Copies of individual statutes can be purchased from Her Majesty's Stationery Office (HMSO), High Holborn, London W1. They can be ordered through most booksellers. They can also be found in most decent-sized public libraries. Library copies are usually found in bound volumes, each containing several Acts. Statutes published by HMSO are those which are cited in court. They are known as the Queen's Printer's copy and contain the words of the statute and nothing else. One needs to be careful when using a library copy in a bound volume, since statutes are sometimes amended by subsequent legislation and the bound volume fails to reflect this. In such a case, a copy of the individual statute must be acquired. The texts of statutes and statutory instruments may be found on the Internet at http://www.hmso.gov.uk. The service is free of charge, apart, of course, from the phone call and service provider's fees.

Where to find law reports

Large public libraries usually have at least one set of general law reports; some 'general sets', that is, reporting all types of cases which make an interesting point of law; and some specialist reports, that is, those dealing with a particular area of activity, for example, the Industrial Relations Law Reports, which deal, as the name suggests, only with employment cases. Most university libraries subscribe to one or more databases to be found on the Internet such as Lexis and Lawtel.

On the web

Below is a list of useful website addresses:

http://www.lawreports.co.uk/indexdln.htm (this gives summaries of recent cases)

http://www.hmso.gov.uk (this gives access to the full text of statutes or statutory instruments)

http://www.oft.gov.uk (this is the Office of Fair Trading website. The Annual Report gives useful information about a number of areas of law, particularly the law relating to consumer credit and that referring to unfair contract terms)

http://www.asa.org.uk (the website of the Advertising Standards Authority) http://www.hull.ac.uk/lib/fsheets/eucase.htm (this contains reports of the European Court of Justice)

http://www.companies-house.gov.uk (basic information about registered companies and the work and services of Companies House)

http://www.lawlinks/gateways.htm (links to a variety of useful legal websites)

http://www.legalwebsites.co.uk (gives a wide range of websites for all aspects of law)

http://webjcli.ncl.ac.uk (the web Journal of Current Legal Issues. Quality articles on a wide range of current issues and developments)

CHAPTER 2

CONTRACTS AND WHAT THEY ARE USED FOR

WHAT IS A CONTRACT?

A contract is a *promise* or *set of promises* which the law will enforce. It usually does this by awarding damages for non-performance or for defective performance, but sometimes the court will order the party in default to carry out the contract or not to breach it.

Bilateral contracts

Most major business contracts take the form of an *agreement* consisting of reciprocal promises. This is called a bilateral contract. If either party entirely fails to carry out their part of the agreement, or carries it out defectively, the other may sue for breach of contract.

Example

Amy is a tour operator. She contracts with Beth, an air broker, whereby Beth will provide an aeroplane to undertake specified flights to Spain during the summer from May to September, at a total cost of £250,000. This creates an obligation on both parties. If either party fails to fulfil her obligations, the other may sue for breach of contract. If the breach is sufficiently serious in effect, the innocent party may, in addition, repudiate the contract, bringing it to an end.

Unilateral contracts

It is possible to have a contract where only one party makes a promise, that is, there is no agreement as such. Such contracts are called unilateral contracts. The difference between a bilateral contract and a unilateral contract is that in a bilateral contract each party makes a promise or promises to the other. If any promises are broken each may sue the other.

In a unilateral contract (which are sometimes called 'if' contracts based on the idea that one party says to the other, 'if you will do such and such, then I will do so and so'), one party's promise is dependent upon the other party performing an act requested by the offer and doesn't become operative until that act has been performed.

Example

Charles guarantees David's overdraft with Eastern Bank (that is, Charles agrees to pay if David defaults). This is a unilateral contract whereby Charles is saying to the bank, 'If you will make a loan to David, I will guarantee its repayment'. This does not bind the bank to make the loan, and Charles cannot sue for breach of contract if the loan is not made. However, if the loan is made, the bank is entitled to look to Charles for repayment of it should David default.

Claims for restitution

It is possible to have an obligation to pay money to another party for work carried out without there being a binding contract. In such a case, the parties may have tried to formulate a contract but the contract has failed to come into existence, and the party claiming the money is said to have a claim for restitution.

Example

Edward is a builder and requires a quantity of windows and other glasswork to put in the houses of an estate he is building. He begins negotiations with Fiona, a glazier, to enter into a contract whereby Fiona will supply the glasswork. Negotiations proceed slowly because of failure to agree on certain essentials. Meanwhile, Edward asks Fiona to start work in anticipation of an agreement. After Fiona has done some work, negotiations break down irretrievably and Fiona stops work. There is no contract, so neither party can sue for breach of contract. However, Fiona may claim what is called a *quantum meruit* (meaning 'as much as it is worth') under the law relating to restitution, for the work she has done. The court will award her a reasonable sum for the work.

The theory of 'agreement'

Classical legal theory is based on the idea that rights and duties arising from a contract are fixed by *agreement* between the parties. However, the idea of a contract being governed by 'agreement' is not entirely realistic, and probably never was. There are a number of reasons for this.

In the first place, there are many contracts in which a stronger party dictates to the weaker party the terms on which the dominant party is willing to contract. It is immaterial that the weaker party wouldn't agree with the terms given a free choice; it is a case of take it or leave it. Once the weaker party has entered into the contract, he or she is regarded as having agreed to its terms.

Secondly, the law, particularly statute law, may give the parties no option in the matter. For example, if the parties to a sale of goods contract agree to exclude from the contract the implied term that the goods shall be of satisfactory quality, and if the sale is a consumer sale, the agreement to exclude the term will be void under s 6 of the Unfair Contract Terms Act 1977.

Thirdly, there are inevitably situations where the parties haven't given any thought to a particular matter which arises during the course of the contract. The approach of the law in such cases is twofold:

(a) Sometimes, the courts preserve the fiction that they are simply giving effect to the parties' agreement by deciding the dispute according to what the court deems to be the *intentions* of the parties. This is done by looking at what the parties have said, done and written, and then concluding what an objective third party would have deemed to be the parties' intentions in the matter. Where these 'intentions' consist of obligations to be carried out as part of the contract, they may be categorised as *implied terms* of the contract.

(b) An alternative approach of the law was to prescribe rules which are imposed on the parties. In early law, these prescribed rules applied only if there was no agreement to the contrary. In modern law, some of the prescribed rules will apply even if there is an agreement between the parties and will operate to override that agreement if it conflicts with the legal rule.

Scope of the law of contract

The law of contract is concerned with the enforcement of promises. Although in the minds of most lay-persons, a contract is a formal document full of legal verbiage, formality is needed for very few types of contract. The majority can be, and are, made verbally, or even by conduct. When you order a cup of coffee in a café, you are making a contract with the café, and although the transaction is straightforward, the café is impliedly promising you: (i) that the coffee complies with the description applied to it; (ii) that it is of satisfactory quality; (iii) that it is fit for its purpose; and (iv) that the café has the right to sell you the coffee. The café may, further, make express promises to you, such as, that the coffee contains cream and sugar. All these promises, both express and implied, are contractual, and if they are broken, for example, if the coffee turns out to be tea or if it is adulterated with poison, the café will be liable to you for breach of contract.

The remedies that are available to the injured party are:

(1) *Damages*

This is a money payment which aims at putting the innocent party in the position he would have been in if the contract had been carried out.

(2) *Rescission*

This is a cancellation of the contract which puts each of the parties back into the position they were in before the contract; for example, A enters into a contract with B whereby B will purchase a painting from A for £10,000. B rescinds (that is, cancels) the contract because of A's misrepresentation that the painting was by Renoir when, in fact it, wasn't. B is entitled to his £10,000 back and A is entitled to have the painting returned to him.

(3) *A decree of specific performance*

This is an order to the defaulting party to carry out the contract. Note that it is awarded in only three circumstances:

(i) where the subject matter of the contract is land;

(ii) where the subject matter of the contract is commercially unique goods; or

(iii) where the remedy of damages would not properly compensate the claimant.

A decree of specific performance will never be awarded in the case of a contract of employment.

(4) *Injunction*

Injunctions are of two types: mandatory, which is an order of the court to someone to carry out an obligation; and prohibitory, which is an order of the court to someone to refrain from doing something which is a breach of contract.

(5) *Declaration*

This simply declares the rights of the parties in the matter, without making any order. It is often used in conjunction with an injunction, that is, both remedies are sought together.

(6) *Rectification of documents*

This is an order of the court to rectify the wording of a document where it fails to represent accurately the verbal agreement of the parties.

THE PRACTICAL USE OF THE LAW OF CONTRACT

There is a tendency to think of the law of contract as a means of bringing defaulting parties to court. While it is true that in certain types of contract, for instance consumer credit contracts, there is a relatively high incidence of court action, actions for breach of contract in cases involving two commercial parties are a relative rarity. It is more normal for disputes to be settled by agreement or, where one of the parties proves intransigent, for the matter to be left unsettled. In the latter case, there is often a consequent termination of the commercial relationship between the two.

Even where actions are brought, businesses tend to prefer to use private arbitration rather than the ordinary court system. This may either be provided for in the contract itself, or agreed by the parties as a means of resolving the dispute after the dispute arises.

The main aim of commercial parties in making a contract is to lay down, with as much clarity as possible, what each party is expected to do under the contract. In addition, it should state what the parties' responsibilities are to be in the case where the contract doesn't go as planned, for example, if performance is interrupted by industrial action.

Where a contract is of high value, or is intended to last for some length of time, it is particularly important that some thought is given to planning the contract.

The law of contract is commonly used for the following purposes:

(a) to recover a debt on a contract;

Example

Anne sells a quantity of bricks to Builders Ltd for £1,000 on 30 days' trade credit. Builders Ltd fails to pay for the goods. Anne may sue Builders Ltd for the price agreed in the contract.

(b) to recover the value of goods or services paid for under a contract which have not, in fact, been supplied. Strictly speaking, this is a claim for restitution;

(c) to recover damages for breach of contract where the contract has not been carried out at all (note the special legal meaning of the word 'recover' in this context: the claimant is not really recovering anything since, in the ordinary use of the English language, one cannot 'recover' what one never had in the first place);

Example

Chris orders and pays £5,000 in advance for office carpeting to be supplied by Carpets Ltd. Carpets Ltd fails to supply the carpet. Chris has two claims here, though both may be consolidated in the same legal action. The first is a restitution action to claim his money back. The second is an action for damages for breach of contract, the amount of damages being the difference between the £5,000 which Chris had agreed to pay Carpets Ltd and the amount that Chris will have to pay a different contractor in order to get the job done. Thus, if Chris has to pay Flooring Ltd £6,000 to do the job, Chris will be entitled to £1,000 damages for breach of contract.

In examples (a) and (b), it is possible that the failure of Builders Ltd to pay for the bricks and of Carpets Ltd to supply the carpet is due to insolvency. In such a case, Anne and Chris will claim from the liquidators of Builders Ltd and Carpets Ltd. Such a claim will, at best, yield only a proportion of what Anne and Chris have actually lost, and in many cases, because of prior claims to the assets of the insolvent companies, Anne and Chris will receive nothing.

(d) to recover damages where one party has purported to carry out his part of the bargain but has done so defectively.

In practice, by far the greater part of breach-of-contract actions are concerned with defective performance rather than non-performance.

Example

Fiona has installed double glazing units in Gemma's factory at a cost of £20,000. Some of the work is faulty, and although Fiona is given the opportunity to rectify the faults, she says she can't fit the work into her work schedule. Gemma calls in Harriet to rectify the defects at a cost of £2,000. Gemma will be entitled to this amount as damages for breach of contract.

Standard form contracts

Nowadays the use of 'standard-form' contracts is widespread. A standard-form contract is a contract where some, if not all, of the terms are determined in advance by one party or the other and are printed in a standard form. Sometimes the terms are negotiable, but often it is a case of one party saying to the other, 'These are the only terms on which I am willing to do business – take it or leave it.'

A standard-form contract may have been specially drafted on its behalf by the enterprise's own lawyer, or it may have been drafted by a trade association for the use of its members. In some cases, where members of one trade association regularly contract with members of another, model terms are negotiated between the two. For example, the Plant Contractors' Association and the Federation of Civil Engineering Contractors have produced a set of model terms to be used in plant-hire contracts.

In drafting standard-form contracts, it is important to be aware of the Unfair Contract Terms Act 1977. This does not, as its title would imply, control *all* unfair contract terms, but only unfair terms which aim at *excluding* or *limiting* the liability of one party for breaches of contract, negligence, or breach of statutory duty. As a general rule, its effect is that any term which aims at excluding or limiting liability in the event of a breach of contract must, in a standard form contract made between commercial enterprises, satisfy the test of reasonableness; the exclusion of terms implied into contracts for the sale, supply, hire or hire-purchase of goods is void if the sale is a consumer sale; terms which attempt to exclude liability for death or personal injury are void. Only in very rare circumstances will a term which is aimed at excluding or limiting liability for breach of contract be unconditionally valid. The Unfair Terms in Consumer Contracts Regulations must also be borne in mind.

Formal and informal contracts

No written formality is needed for most types of contract. They can be, and are, made verbally, or even by conduct. A simple oral contract is as enforceable as the most complex written one.

Nevertheless, it is customary for important commercial contracts to be made in writing. This facilitates *proof* of what the agreement is in the event of a dispute. It is also convenient as a *source of reference*, since the rights and obligations of business contracts are often extensive and much too detailed to commit to memory; a building contract, for example, will usually need detailed plans and will contain exact specifications as to the materials which are to be used.

Some contracts *must* be made in writing. The most important of these are:

(a) a contract for the sale of land (or other disposition of land or any interest in land, for example, a lease): s 2 of the Law of Property (Miscellaneous Provisions) Act 1989. Note, here, that 'land' includes things permanently attached to the land, the most obvious example being buildings;

(b) a regulated consumer credit agreement, within the meaning of the Consumer Credit Act 1974, must be made in writing in the prescribed form in order to be 'properly executed': s 61 of the Consumer Credit Act. If it is not properly executed, it is enforceable only on order of the court: s 65 of the Consumer Credit Act.

IMPORTANCE OF THE LAW OF CONTRACT

The law of contract is of fundamental importance to any enterprise because it is at the base of all types of business agreement. There is a wide range of types of business agreement. Some examples are given below:

Type of contract	Example
Sale of goods	Purchase of vehicles, business stationery, etc
Supply of services	Contract cleaners engaged to clean premises
Hire purchase	Hire of a vehicle coupled with option to purchase
Hire of goods	Hire, lease, rental of office equipment
Employment	Engaging a worker to be employed by the business

| Lease | Lease of shop, offices, factory, etc |
| Agency | Northern Bank collects a cheque from Counties Bank on behalf of the business |

GENERAL PRINCIPLES AND SPECIFIC CONTRACTS

Each of the above types of agreement is regulated by the general law of contract. This means that there is a body of *general principles* of contract which apply to the contract, irrespective of what type of contract it is. The result is a common, consistent set of rules applied to all types of contract, so that, for example, all contracts are formed by a process whereby one party makes an 'offer' which the other 'accepts'.

However, there are limits to which you can treat dissimilar types of contract in the same way and still produce satisfactory outcomes in practice. Because of this, it is necessary to augment (or sometimes replace) the general rules of the law of contract with specially created rules for particular types of contract. Therefore, each of the above types of agreement also has its own special set of rules. Most of the general principles are to be found in *case law*, while most of the special rules are *statutory*.

Example of how the general rules and specific rules operate

Ben, a computer dealer, alleges that Alice has contracted to buy a computer from him but is now refusing to take delivery. She asserts that she never ordered the computer. The rules governing this matter are the general rules relating to the formation of a contract, to be found in case law.

If, on the other hand, Alice took delivery of the computer and is now alleging that the computer is defective, s 14 of the Sale of Goods Act 1979, will apply. This enactment applies, as one might deduce from its name, only to contracts for the sale of goods. Section 14 requires that the computer shall be of satisfactory quality and fit for its purpose. The court will have to decide whether it is or not.

CHAPTER 3

HAVE WE GOT A CONTRACT?

In relation to any legal action arising out of a contract, the first question which must be answered is, 'Have we got a contract?'

In contractual theory, a contract is formed by a process whereby one party makes an *offer* to the other. The other party then *accepts* the offer and there comes into being a binding contract. For example, an offer may be made by one party sending a quotation to the other and the acceptance made by the other party writing back to accept it.

If the offer is not accepted, it may come to an end in one of several ways. The most important ones are: it may be rejected; it may lapse, either because a time limit which has been put upon the offer has expired, or because there has been too long a delay between the offer being made and a purported acceptance of it; it may be 'accepted' subject to conditions, in which case the original offer is cancelled and replaced with a new offer, called a *counter-offer*, containing the new conditions. The termination of offers is dealt with in more detail later in the text.

HAS AN OFFER BEEN MADE?

The first thing to consider in deciding whether there is an agreement is whether an offer has been made. If an offer has been made, it can be *accepted* and can, therefore, turn into a contract, notwithstanding the fact that the person who has made the offer (the 'offeror') has since changed his mind and no longer wishes to contract, though we will see that if this change of mind is communicated to the person to whom the offer was made (the 'offeree') *before* the acceptance is made, this will have the effect of cancelling the offer.

Whether an offer has been made depends upon whether the person making the offer had a definite *intention* to make an offer. The question of whether a party has an intention to make an offer is *objective* rather than *subjective*. This means that if the matter goes to court, the court will determine the parties' intentions by asking what a reasonable third party would have deduced, looking at the parties' words and deeds. In such circumstances, it is no use a party saying, 'It may look as if I was making an offer but I didn't intend to.' If it looks, to an objective third party, as if there was an intention to make an offer, it will be held that an offer has been made.

Anything which is a step in negotiations, but which does not amount to an offer, is called an 'invitation to treat'. An *invitation to treat* cannot be accepted and, therefore, it cannot be turned into a contract.

Example

Step 1: Builder is asked by Client to quote for an extension to Client's factory. This is an invitation to treat and does not bind Client to accept Builder's quotation.

Step 2: Builder submits a quotation for £200,000. This will usually be an offer which Client may accept or reject.

Step 3: Client writes a letter accepting the offer. A binding contract comes into existence at this stage and if either party attempts to withdraw from it, the other will have an action for breach of contract.

This is, of course, a greatly simplified version of what happens in relation to a major commercial contract. Negotiations may take place over many months before all the terms of the contract are finally agreed by the parties and a contract is formed.

The courts have developed certain guidelines to determine whether there was an intention to make an offer or not. The interesting thing about this area of the law is that many of the cases involve not, as one would expect, a person attempting to enforce a contract which the other party denied existed, but the issue of whether an offer for sale has been made for the purposes of a prosecution being made under the criminal law.

Examples of invitations to treat

The following have been held to be invitations to treat:

(a) A display of goods on the shelves of a self-service store.

The customer makes an offer to buy when he or she presents the goods to the cashier at the check-out. The offer may there be accepted or rejected by the cashier.

Pharmaceutical Society of GB v Boots (1953)

The defendants adapted a branch in Edgware to self-service. As a result, it became necessary to determine at what stage a contract comes into existence in a self-service transaction in a shop. The reason is that s 18(1) of the Pharmacy and Poisons Act 1933 required that a registered pharmacist must be present when poisons listed in Part 1 of the Poisons List were sold. A registered pharmacist, who was empowered to prevent, if he thought fit, the customer purchasing any restricted drug, was stationed at the check-out. Thus, if the display of goods on the supermarket shelf was an offer which was accepted when the customer took the goods from the shelf and placed them in his basket, then Boots were committing a criminal offence by not having a pharmacist present when the goods were sold. If, however, either the customer placing the goods in his basket was an offer, or the customer presenting the goods at the check-out was an offer, then in either case the acceptance (and therefore the sale) would take place at check-out, and Boots would not be committing an offence. It was held that the offer was made when the customer presented the goods to the cashier at the check-out and the contract came into being when the cashier duly accepted the offer (presumably by ringing up the price of the goods on the till).

This result was similar to that in the US case of *Lasky v Economy Grocery Stores* (1946), in which the plaintiff picked up a bottle of tonic in a supermarket and was about to place it in the basket provided by the store when it exploded, causing her injury. She sued for breach of contract. Her claim failed since there was no contract in existence at the time the bottle exploded. However, a significant difference between the analysis in this case and that in the *Boots* case is that in *Lasky*, the display of goods on the shelves was an offer which was accepted when the customer reached the check-out. There appears to be no practical significance in this difference of analysis as far as the law of contract is concerned, since in either case, no contract would be formed until the assistant at the check-out accepted the customer's offer to buy. However, where a statute makes it a criminal offence to offer certain goods for sale, the offence would be committed by placing them on the shelves under the US analysis, but not under the English analysis.

Note: nowadays, if such circumstances arose in a case governed by English law, a person in the plaintiff's position might still have difficulty in gaining compensation for her injuries. A breach of contract action is the most attractive, since the plaintiff would simply have to show that the defective goods caused her injuries. She would not have to show who caused the defect in the goods, nor would she have to show that the defects had been caused by the defendant's negligence. In an action based on breach of contract, the store would be *strictly liable* (that is, the injured party would not have to prove that the store was in any way blameworthy) under s 14 of the Sale of Goods Act (see Chapter 18). However, as we have seen, it is unlikely that a court would hold that a contract had come into existence.

There are two other possibilities whereby the injured party might obtain damages. One is an action against the producer under the Consumer Protection Act 1987. The other is an action for the *tort of negligence* against anyone whose negligence might have caused the explosion. The difficulty in either of these cases is that the claimant would have to prove what caused the explosion. With an aerated product, such as tonic water, contained in a glass bottle, there are sundry possibilities: the producer (or manufacturer) of the bottle might have manufactured it defectively; the producer of the tonic might have chosen to use a bottle which turned out to be insufficiently robust to contain the drink; the air pressure in the bottle might have been too great; the carrier of the goods between the producer and the store may have damaged the bottle; the store may have damaged the bottle; the store may have stored the bottle at an incorrect temperature ... and so forth.

A further difficulty in respect of an action under the tort of negligence is that the claimant would have to prove not only that the defendant had been the cause of the explosion, but also that the explosion had been caused through the defendant's negligence (that is, by the defendant failing to take reasonable care in the circumstances of the case). The pitfalls in an action relating to injuries caused by unsafe products are examined in more detail in Chapter 25.

(b) A display of goods, with a price tag attached, in the window of a shop.

Fisher v Bell (1961)

A shop-keeper was prosecuted under the Restriction of Offensive Weapons Act 1959 for offering for sale a flick-knife, contrary to the provisions of the Act. He had displayed the knife in his shop window with a ticket which said, 'Ejector knife – 4s'. He was acquitted on the ground that the display of an article in a shop window with a price attached is an invitation to treat, not an offer.

This means that if, for example, a car in a showroom displays a price of £3,000 in error for £4,000, a potential buyer cannot accept this 'offer' so as to create a binding contract.

In practice, if goods are mis-priced to the customer's advantage, a retail outlet will often sell the goods for that price despite the fact that they are not legally bound to do so. The main reason for this, apart from preserving goodwill, is that it is a criminal offence under Part III of the Consumer Protection Act 1987 to mis-price goods. Although in most cases it is relatively easy to mount a successful defence to a criminal charge, it may be easier and more cost-effective to sell the goods slightly more cheaply than to argue the matter out with the Trading Standards Department (which conducts investigations in such cases and decides whether to prosecute).

(c) An advertisement in a newspaper, stating that goods were for sale and giving the price.

Partridge v Crittenden (1968)

An advertisement was placed in a periodical which said: 'Bramblefinch cocks, bramblefinch hens, 25s each.' An RSPCA inspector sent the money for a hen and was duly sent one. The defendant was then charged with offering for sale a wild bird, contrary to the provisions of the Protection of Birds Act 1954. The advertisement was relied upon as being the evidence of an offer having been made. *Held*: the advertisement was not an offer for sale, merely an invitation to treat. Although the words 'For sale' were not used in the advertisement, the outcome would probably have been the same if they had been.

On the other hand, an advertisement which offers a prize or reward in return for a particular act being performed by the offeree (that is, where acceptance of the offer creates a unilateral contract) will normally constitute an offer. See, for example, *Carlill v Carbolic Smoke Ball Co* (1893), in which the defendants manufactured a medicinal product called the carbolic smoke ball. If used in the prescribed manner, the smoke ball would, claimed the manufacturers, ward off a variety of ailments, including influenza. In order to promote the product, the defendants advertised that they would pay £100 to anyone who caught 'flu after using the product in the prescribed manner. As evidence of their sincerity in the matter, they had deposited £1,000 at the Alliance Bank in Regent Street. Ms Carlill used the product as prescribed but, nevertheless, caught 'flu. She claimed the £100 reward. The defendants came up with a variety of (sometimes ingenious!) defences to her claim, which are dealt with throughout this book as their relevance arises. One of the defences was that no offer had been made to Ms Carlill. However, the court held that an offer had been made to the world at large and that this offer was accepted and thus turned into a contract by anyone who came forward and fulfilled the terms of the offer.

(d) A mere statement of price, without any indication that the person making the statement was willing to sell.

Harvey v Facey (1893)

H sent a telegram to F: 'Will you sell Bumper Hall Pen? Telegraph lowest cash price.' The defendant replied: 'Lowest price for Bumper Hall Pen £900.' The plaintiffs then telegraphed: 'We agree to buy Bumper Hall Pen for £900 asked by you ...' The defendants refused to sell and were sued for breach of contract by the plaintiffs. *Held*: the defendant's telegram was not an offer to sell but was merely an indication of the lowest price they would accept if they did make an offer to sell.

Similarly, in *Clifton v Palumbo*, the owner of a large estate was negotiating to sell it and wrote: 'I am prepared to offer you or your nominee my Lytham estate for £600,000. I also agree that a reasonable and sufficient time shall be granted to you for the examination and consideration of all the data and details necessary for the preparation of the Schedule of Completion.' It was held that this was a mere statement of price, not an offer to sell.

However, where it seems that an offer was intended and was perceived by the other party as such, the courts may hold that a statement of price is an offer.

Bigg v Boyd Gibbins (1971)

The defendants wanted to purchase the plaintiff's house to make an access road for a new estate. The plaintiffs wrote to the defendants: 'For a quick sale I would accept £26,000.' The defendants wrote back: 'I accept your offer,' and asked the plaintiffs to contact the defendant's solicitors. The plaintiffs wrote back saying: 'I thank you for your letter accepting my price of £26,000. My wife and I are both pleased that you are purchasing the property.' The defendants subsequently refused to proceed with the sale and the plaintiffs sued. The defendants argued that, following *Harvey v Facey* and *Clifton v*

Palumbo, the plaintiffs' first letter was a mere statement of price, not an offer. *Held* by the Court of Appeal: each case depends upon its particular facts. In this case the plaintiffs' letter had been an offer which had been accepted by the defendants. Therefore, a contract had been formed which the court would enforce.

Price lists and catalogues with prices stated in them will usually be invitations to treat.

(e) An advertisement that an auction of specific goods was to take place.

Harris v Nickerson (1873)

An advertisement that specified goods would be sold by auction on a particular day was held not to be an offer to sell to the highest bidder. Indeed, it was held that there was no obligation to hold the auction at all. Therefore, when the auction was cancelled, the plaintiff was unable to reclaim his travelling and subsistence expenses in an action for breach of contract.

(f) An auctioneer who calls for bids at an auction.

The bidder makes the offer, which the auctioneer may accept by the fall of the hammer or by other indication (see s 57 of the Sale of Goods Act 1979), or may reject, for example, by accepting a higher bid or by withdrawing the goods from the sale.

British Car Auctions v Wright (1972)

Auctioneers were charged with offering for sale an unroadworthy vehicle. It was held that the invitation to bid for the car was an invitation to treat, not an offer for sale.

If the auction is advertised 'without reserve', there is an obligation to sell to the highest bidder ('without reserve' means that the seller does not stipulate a minimum price at which the goods must be sold. At many sales, the seller imposes a reserve price, and if the goods do not reach that price they are withdrawn from the sale).

In *Barry v Heathcote Ball* (2000), an auction was advertised as being 'without reserve'. Two new engine tuning machines, worth approximately £14,000 each, were among the lots. The claimant bid £200 each for the machines. The auctioneer withdrew them from sale and sold them a few days later as a result of an advertisement for £750. The claimant sued, arguing that as the auction was 'without reserve', the machines should have been sold to the highest bidder.

Held: the defendant was in breach of contract. Under s 57(3) of the Sale of Goods Act, the seller could have put a reserve price on the machines. The Act did not specifically deal with auctions without reserve, but s 57(4) provided that unless a sale was notified to be subject to a bid by or on behalf of the seller, it was not lawful for the seller to bid himself or employ any person to bid at the sale. The act of the auctioneer in withdrawing the machines was tantamount to the auctioneer bidding on behalf of the seller. In an auction 'without reserve' it was not possible to withdraw the lots simply because the bids were not high enough.

Examples of offers

The following have been held to be offers:

(a) The running of a bus service by a bus company.

The offer is accepted when the passenger 'puts himself either on the platform or inside the bus': *Wilkie v LPTB* (1947). Presumably if the bus goes past without stopping, the offer of carriage is revoked! The reasons for holding the operation of a bus service to be an offer are now no longer valid, although this case remains as an authority unless and until it is superseded. In any case, a significant number of bus tickets are now obtained in advance of the journey, in which case the offer and acceptance takes place at the time the ticket is bought.

(b) The existence of a ticket machine at a car-park.

The precise time at which the offer is made in a slot machine transaction may be of some practical importance, for example, in determining whether an exemption clause has been effectively incorporated into the contract (the clause is ineffective if not). In *Thornton v Shoe Lane Parking* (1971), the question arose as to when the offer and acceptance takes place in relation to a contract made by an automatic ticket machine. Lord Denning MR said: '... the offer is made when the proprietor of the machine holds it out as being ready to receive the money. The acceptance takes place when the customer puts his money into the slot.'

The other two judges were, however, unwilling to commit themselves as to when, precisely, the offer and acceptance took place.

In the case of a self-service petrol pump, it has been held that the pump is an offer which the customer accepts when he puts the petrol into his tank: *R v Greenberg* (1972).

In the case of the normal vending machine, the neatest analysis is that the intending customer makes the offer, which is then accepted if the machine supplies the goods, or rejected (if the machine is faulty, or has run out of supplies, for example) as the case may be.

TERMINATION OF AN OFFER

There are seven ways in which an offer may terminate. These are:

(a) it may be accepted and thus become part of a contract;

(b) it may be rejected;

(c) it may be revoked;

(d) it may lapse due to the passage of time;

(e) it may lapse due to the death of the offeror or the offeree;

(f) it may lapse because the subject matter has undergone a significant change which makes it impossible to carry out the terms of the offer: see Chapter 9; and

(g) it may be cancelled by a counter-offer.

We will deal with these in turn.

Acceptance

An acceptance is the manifestation of an unqualified agreement to all the terms of an offer. A qualified acceptance amounts to a counter-offer, the effect of which is to cancel the original offer (so that it can no longer be accepted) and to replace it with a fresh offer which the original offeror is free to accept or reject. (See below for more detail about counter-offers.)

The normal rule is that an acceptance takes place and, therefore, a contract is formed, when the acceptance is communicated to the other party (that is, when the other party hears it or reads it). The normal rule applies to telephone, telex, and (presumably) fax and any other form of instantaneous electronic written communication. However, it does *not* apply when the acceptance is by post. A special rule called the 'postal rule' applies.

The 'postal rule'

In circumstances where the post is a reasonable method of communicating the acceptance, the acceptance is complete (and therefore the contract is formed) as soon as the letter of acceptance is put into the post. This rule also applies to telegrams.

Adams v Lindsell (1818)

A were in business at Bromsgrove, Worcestershire. L were in business in St Ives, Hunts. On 2 September 1817, L wrote to A offering to sell them a quantity of wool. The letter asked for a reply in the course of the post (which appears to have meant by return of post). Unfortunately, L directed their letter to Bromsgrove, Leics, so that it didn't reach A until 7 pm on 5 September. The same evening, A wrote and posted an acceptance of the offer. The letter of acceptance reached L on 9 September. The defendants had expected a reply by 7 September, and not having received one, proceeded to sell the wool to a third party on 8 September. A sued L for breach of contract. *Held*: the contract was formed when A posted their letter of acceptance. Further, the offer had not lapsed when L didn't receive a reply in the expected course of the post, since the delay was due to L's fault. Thus the defendants were in breach of contract.

Note: in deciding the case as they did, the court were clearly anxious to avoid penalising the plaintiffs for the mistake of the defendants. It is unfortunate that they chose to do this by ruling that the contract was formed when the letter of acceptance was put in the post: the second reason they gave, that is, that because the offerees communicated the acceptance as soon as they were able, the offer had not lapsed (as it normally would when acceptance wasn't received by return of post) would have been sufficient by itself. The court could then have gone on to hold that the acceptance was effected on 9 September and thus gave rise to a valid contract. However, the reason they chose to hold that the contract was formed on the 7th, when the acceptance was posted, was because the law relating to termination of an offer by revocation had not been developed at the time *Adams v Lindsell* was decided. The court didn't refute the (erroneous) argument that an offer to sell goods is revoked if, before the offer is accepted, the goods have been sold to a third party. They chose to meet the problem by holding that the contract was formed before the goods were sold to the third party (that is, when the letter of acceptance was posted on the 7th). It was not until later in the century that it became the rule that an offer is not revoked until notice of the revocation is communicated to the offeree.

The 'postal rule' can cause difficulty because in all other contractual situations, a communication takes effect when it is *communicated* to the other party (which may mean when he receives it or when he reads it or even when he ought to have read it – but it certainly doesn't mean when it is posted). Thus the postal rule is out of step with the other rules relating to postal communications, and in a manner which could cause difficulties to the offeror through no fault of his own: for example, the rule applies even where the letter of acceptance is *delayed* or *fails to arrive at its destination*.

Household Fire Insurance v Grant (1879)

The defendant made a written application for shares in the company on the terms that he paid a deposit of one shilling per share and agreed to pay the other 19 shillings within one year of the shares being allotted to him. The company secretary posted a letter of allotment (that is, he accepted the defendant's offer) from Swansea. The defendant never received it. However, his name had been placed in the company's Register of Members and dividends of five shillings were credited to his account. The company went into liquidation and the liquidator sued Grant for the balance of the purchase price of his shares. *Held* by the Court of Appeal (Bramwell LJ dissenting since he disliked the idea of an unknown liability being imposed on the offeror): that the defendant was liable. It was suggested that the justification for the postal rule is that when the letter is posted the Post Office becomes the common agent of both parties. That suggestion has subsequently been widely disapproved and nowadays the argument would find few supporters.

Despite the practical difficulties it may cause, *Adams v Lindsell* was confirmed by the House of Lords in *Dunlop v Higgins* (1848) and by the end of the century it was firmly established law.

Recalling an acceptance once it has been posted

One problem which hasn't been resolved is whether an acceptance may be recalled before it reaches the offeror. For example, if A posts a letter accepting B's offer, may he phone, for example, before the letter acceptance is delivered and cancel the acceptance? In principle, the answer should be 'no', since otherwise the offeree would be enabled to have his cake and eat it, that is, he could accept by letter in the knowledge that, if he were to change his mind shortly afterwards, he could recall the acceptance. However, there is no English decision on the point.

Displacing the operation of the postal rule

It is possible for the offeror to displace the operation of the postal rule by stipulating, as a term of the offer, that an acceptance of the offer will not be deemed to be valid until it is received at the offeror's address (usually within a specified time). Alternatively, the operation of the rule may be displaced by *implication*.

Holwell Securities v Hughes (1974)

It was held that the words 'The said option shall be exercisable by notice in writing to the intending vendor', were sufficient to displace the operation of the postal rule. The use of the word 'notice' in the offer implied that the acceptance was not complete until actual notice reached the offeror. In fact, the letter of acceptance never reached the offeror (though a copy reached his solicitor several days before the offer was due to expire) and it was held that there had been no valid acceptance when the letter of acceptance was posted.

It seems that this decision is indicative of a trend in judicial thinking aimed at cutting down the scope of the anomalous postal rule.

The normal rule

An oral acceptance is not compete until it is heard by the offeror. This rule applies to acceptances by telephone and other electronic forms of instant communication, as well as to the situation where the parties are in each other's presence.

Entores v Miles Far Eastern Corp (1955)

E in London made an offer to M in Amsterdam by means of a telex. The offer was accepted, acceptance being typed out in Amsterdam and received on the plaintiff's telex in London. There was a breach of contract and the question arose as to where the contract had been made. The defendants argued that the postal rule applied to telex and that, therefore, the contract had been made in Amsterdam. *Held* by the Court of Appeal: where communication is instantaneous (for example, where the parties are face to face or talking on the telephone) or almost instantaneous (for example, telex), acceptance is complete only when it is received by the offeror.

Similarly, in *Brinkibon v Stahag Stahl und Stahlwarenhandelsgesellschaft MBH* (1983), there was a telexed acceptance from Vienna. The House of Lords held that the contract was made in Vienna. Lord Wilberforce refused to hold that a telex message *always* took effect when received on the machine at the other end. He said:

> The message may not reach or be intended to reach, the designated recipient immediately; messages may be sent out of office hours, or at night, with the intention, or on the assumption, that they will be read at a later time. There may be some error or fault at the recipient's end which prevents the receipt at the time contemplated and believed in by the sender. The message may have been sent and/or received through machines operated by third persons. And many other variations occur. No universal rule can cover all such cases: they must be resolved by reference to the intentions of the parties, by sound business practice and in some cases by a judgment where the risks should lie.

Acceptance by conduct

An acceptance may be made by conduct. In the case of a unilateral contract, acceptance by conduct is the norm. For example, in *Carlill v Carbolic Smoke Ball Co*, it was held that the fact that Ms Carlill used the smoke ball in the manner prescribed by the defendants was a sufficient act of acceptance of the defendants' offer. However, in a bilateral contract, with its insistence that an acceptance must be communicated and that mere mental assent is not enough, an acceptance by conduct will be exceptional, at least in as far as it relates to obligations to be performed at some time in the future. For a rare example, see:

Brogden v Metropolitan Railway Co (1876)

Brogden had supplied the railway company with coal for many years without a formal agreement. Eventually Brogden suggested, and the railway company agreed, that there ought to be one, and the railway company's agent drew up a draft agreement and sent it to Brogden for approval. Brogden filled in some spaces which had been left blank for the purpose, including the name of an arbitrator, and sent the draft back to the company's agent. The agent merely put the contract in a drawer and nothing more was done with it. Nevertheless, the parties acted on the terms of the draft for two years, at the end of which Brogden denied that the contract existed. *Held* by the House of Lords: although the draft was not a contract, since Brogden had inserted new terms which had not been agreed by the railway company, nevertheless, the parties had indicated by their conduct that they mutually approved the terms of the draft. A contract was formed either when the railway company ordered its first load of coal under the terms of the draft, or, at the latest, when Brogden supplied it. The contract was formed by conduct, its terms being contained in the draft.

Where the offeror prescribes a particular method of acceptance

If the offeror prescribes a particular method of acceptance it would seem that the offeree is free to use an alternative method of accepting, providing:

(a) that the acceptance reaches the offeror at least as soon as it would have done by the prescribed method; and

(b) that the chosen alternative offers no disadvantages to the offeror when contrasted with the prescribed method.

Yates v Pulleyn (1975)

The defendants owned certain building land which the plaintiffs wanted to buy. The defendants granted the plaintiffs options to acquire the land in portions. The options had to be exercised by notice in writing to the defendants, 'such notice to be sent by registered or recorded delivery post'. The plaintiffs purported to exercise the option by ordinary post. The defendants denied that the option was validly exercised. *Held* by the Court of Appeal:

(a) the person making the offer may stipulate the manner in which it is to be accepted;

(b) the question of whether such a stipulation is mandatory or merely directory is a matter of construction;

(c) if, on true construction of the words used by the offeror, the stipulation is mandatory, no other method of communication will do; and

(d) if the stipulation is merely directory, then communication of acceptance by a mode which is no less advantageous to the offeror than the directed mode, will be sufficient to constitute a valid acceptance.

The difficulty with such a case is to be able to tell when a stipulation is merely directory and when it is mandatory. Such fine distinctions tend to be lost on the lay-person who is apt to assume, quite naturally, that if an offeror stipulates that an acceptance is to be by registered post, he or she means registered post and that, therefore, whatever the reason for the stipulation, it ought to be mandatory.

Effect of offeree's silence

An offeror may not impose contractual liability on an offeree by stating that the offeree's silence will be taken for an acceptance.

Felthouse v Bindley (1862)

The plaintiff discussed with his nephew, John, the purchase by the plaintiff of a horse belonging to John. The plaintiff wrote to John saying: 'If I hear no more about him, I consider the horse mine at £30 15s.' John did not reply to this letter. Six weeks later, the defendant, an auctioneer who had been employed by John to sell his farming stock, sold the horse by mistake, having been told by John not to sell it because it was already sold (to the plaintiff). The plaintiff sued the auctioneer for the tort of conversion. To succeed he had to prove that he was the owner of the horse, which in turn involved proving that he had a valid contract for the purchase of the horse. *Held:* there was no contract for the sale of the horse because, among other things, the nephew had not communicated acceptance of his uncle's offer. Mere mental assent was insufficient to form the contract.

However, the offeror may dispense with the need to communicate acceptance: in other words, he may impose liability upon himself by dispensing with the need for the offeree to communicate acceptance. This will often be the case with a unilateral contract: see, for example, *Carlill v Carbolic Smoke Ball Co* (1893), where it was not necessary for Ms Carlill to write to the Smoke Ball Company in order to inform them that she intended to use their smoke ball in the prescribed manner and that if she then caught 'flu she would claim the £100 reward. It was sufficient that she performed the act stipulated by the offeror and then caught 'flu.

Inertia selling and the Unsolicited Goods and Services Act

Because of an increase in inertia selling in the 1960s, the Unsolicited Goods and Services Act 1971 was passed with a view to improving the position of the recipient of unsolicited goods (among other things). Inertia selling is where goods are sent to a recipient who has not requested them, with a statement to the effect that if he does not return them within a certain number of days, he will be deemed to have purchased them. The main effect of the civil provisions of the Act is that the recipient of unsolicited goods may treat them as an unconditional gift, providing that he has no reasonable cause to believe that they were sent to him for the purposes of trade or business and has neither agreed to acquire nor return them. A previous provision, requiring the recipient to give notice to the sender or to keep the goods for six months before they become his, has been removed by the Consumer Protection (Distance Selling) Regulations 2000. The present position contrasts with the position at common law, under which the recipient had to keep the goods for six years before he acquired ownership of them (although at least one enterprising recipient succeeded in claiming storage charges in respect of the goods!).

Tenders

It is quite common for organisations which require particular goods or services to invite suppliers to 'tender' for them. The practice is either to prepare a shortlist of suppliers (perhaps those with which the organisation has dealt in the past) and to invite those on the list to tender or, alternatively, to place an advertisement in an appropriate publication (newspaper, trade journal, etc) inviting any interested supplier to tender. Such an advertisement will almost invariably be an invitation to treat. The customer organisation will send out particulars of tender to the interested supplier. The supplier will then tender in accordance with the required specifications. For example, the customer may want tenders for the supply of certain office supplies. The supplies will be listed, for example, 50 reams of A4-size photocopying paper, 10 reams of A3-size photocopying paper, 5,000 A4-size plain brown envelopes, etc. The tender may be a one-off, per week, per month, etc. This will be specified. The tender may further specify an exact quality of the items required.

A specific tender (that is, one where all the terms as to quantities to be supplied are certain at the outset) is an offer which can be accepted in the normal way. The customer is under no obligation to accept the lowest tender, but it would seem that he is under a contractual obligation to consider all the offers. This is the effect of *Blackpool and Fylde Aero Club Ltd v Blackpool Borough Council* (1990), in which the plaintiffs had been invited to tender for the concession of operating pleasure flights from the council's airport. The council failed to consider the plaintiff's tender. The plaintiff sued for damages. *Held:* despite the fact that the defendants had not undertaken to accept any of the tenders, the defendants had nevertheless impliedly contracted to consider all the tenders. The defendants were therefore liable in damages.

Sometimes, the quantities required are not specified. In such a case the tender may be completely open-ended or the customer may specify an upper limit, for example, up to 5,000 envelopes 'per week'. Such a tender is called a 'general tender'. A general tender is a standing offer, which is accepted each time goods are ordered. A general tender may, therefore, be revoked at any time, leaving the supplier with legal liability only in respect of orders which have been accepted but have not yet been fulfilled (if any): see *Great Northern Railway v Witham* (1873). Further, the party accepting a general tender need order no goods under the tender: *Percival v LCC* (1918). However, should he promise to take all his needs of goods of a particular type from the tenderer, although the party accepting the tender need order no goods at all, if he does have need for goods of the type included in the tender, he must order them from the tenderer.

Cases in which there is no apparent offer and acceptance

It is not always easy to analyse the formation of a contract into terms of offer and acceptance. For example, it is quite common in certain types of contract such as building, engineering and civil engineering, for the work which is to be done under the contract to be started (and sometimes even finished!) before the terms of a contract are agreed.

Retrospective acceptance and contracts by conduct

As a general rule, if the work under the contract has commenced and afterwards the parties come to an agreement, the courts will hold that the agreement is retrospective. The contract is therefore governed by the terms of the agreement.

Trollope and Colls v Atomic Power Constructions and Others (1962)

The plaintiffs were subcontractors for the civil engineering aspects of building a new power station for the CEGB (one of the defendants). The plaintiffs had submitted a tender which stated that their price for their part of the work would be £9 million. The tender also contained a price adjustment clause which allowed the plaintiff to adjust the price for variations in the cost of labour and materials during the course of completing the work. The CEGB made numerous changes to the tender, including changes to the price adjustment clause. These changes were detrimental to the plaintiffs who, nevertheless, at a meeting between themselves and the CEGB on 11 April 1960, agreed the changes. By this time the plaintiffs had already done a considerable amount of the work which the tender covered. They later regretted having made the agreement of 11 April. They therefore tried to escape from it, arguing that there was no valid contract. Instead, they were entitled to payment for the work they had already done, on the basis of a *quantum meruit* (this means 'as much as it is worth' and is an amount assessed by the court in circumstances where the plaintiff has done work for which it has been intended that he will be paid, but no contract for payment exists). *Held*: the agreement of 11 April operated retrospectively, since both parties had throughout worked on the assumption that a binding agreement would be entered into at some stage. Therefore, the plaintiffs were bound to complete the work and were entitled to payment on the basis of the agreement of 11 April.

If the work has greatly progressed or has been finished, without agreement ever having been reached, then, providing there are no major sticking points between the parties, the courts will say that there is a *contract by conduct* (see *Brogden v Metropolitan Railway Co* (1877), the facts of which are given on p 71).

In the following more modern case, the court concluded that the parties had in stages, during the time the work was being carried out, come to an agreement regarding the important terms of the contract. The agreement therefore constituted a contract. However, the court said that even if it was wrong on that point, there was clearly a contract by conduct since the contract had been completed without any significant disagreement remaining unresolved between the parties.

Trentham Ltd v Archital Luxfer (1993)

This case involved a claim by Trentham against Archital in respect of defects in Archital's performance of a contract to design and install windows in an industrial estate. Archital defended the claim by asserting that there was no contract between them and Trentham, and that, therefore, they could not be in breach of contract.

Trentham (T) were engaged as main contractors in erecting industrial units. The work included the design, supply and fitting of aluminium windows. Archital (A), who were window suppliers, submitted a quotation for the work based on their own conditions of supply. T was not prepared to accept this but made a counter offer. This was the same as A's offer, but incorporated T's standard terms and was subject to a form of sub-contract being entered into and immediate return of the attached acknowledgment slip. Neither of these conditions was met. Nevertheless, A started work under the 'contract'. There was further correspondence and meetings between the parties, at the end of which it was clear that T's standard conditions were accepted by A. There remained three points about which it was argued that there had been no agreement: (i) payment procedure; (ii) whose responsibility was it to insure windows left on the site by A, which were yet to be incorporated into the building; (iii) disputes procedure.

The judge found that payment procedure had been agreed on the basis of the timetable contained in T's standard conditions. He found that A had accepted the risk to unfixed windows. It was argued in the Court of Appeal that there was no evidence to support that contention, but the Court dismissed this argument. T had clearly refused to accept the risk and A had said that they were seeking an insurance quotation from their brokers. They continued to deliver goods to the site, to perform work and to receive stage payments and must, therefore, have accepted the risk. The point about dispute resolution was not a matter essential to the contract. In any event, there was evidence to show that the parties had agreed on an adjudicator and stakeholder. The trial judge had concluded that there was an offer and acceptance even though certain matters were left to be resolved after the work had begun: see *Trollope and Colls v Atomic Power Construction* (1962). The Court of Appeal agreed with the judge but added that, even if he were wrong, in the case of a contract which has been fully carried out it would be implausible to find that there was no contract. There could be a contract by conduct, as in *Brogden v Metropolitan Railway Co* (1877), even though such a contract could not be analysed precisely in the terms of offer and acceptance and even if the contract came into existence after part of the work had been carried out and paid for.

However, in a contrasting case, where the parties *never reached agreement*, it was held that there was no contract.

British Steel v Cleveland Bridge and Engineering Co (1984)

The plaintiffs and defendants were negotiating a contract under which the defendant would buy four steel nodes from the plaintiff. The defendant issued a letter of intent stating their intention to buy the nodes and asked the defendant to start work on the nodes pending the issue of a contract. However, the defendant wanted the contract to be on terms which imposed unlimited liability on the plaintiff for consequential loss arising from late delivery. This proved a stumbling block in the negotiations and as a result no formal contract was ever entered into. Meanwhile, the plaintiff had manufactured and delivered all but one of the nodes: the final one was delayed by an industrial dispute at the plaintiff's plant. The defendant refused to pay for the three nodes which had been delivered, and argued that the plaintiff was in breach of contract in not delivering the fourth. *Held*: as the parties had failed to agree on a significant term of the proposed contract, there was no contract and, therefore, no breach of contract. Therefore, British Steel were able to claim, under the law of restitution, a reasonable sum for the work they had done.

The crucial point in the *British Steel* case is that the parties were very clearly not in agreement about an important term of the contract. In *Trentham Ltd v Archital Luxfer*, although the facts were similar, a different conclusion was reached because the work was concluded without any major disagreement between the parties.

Attempts to avoid having to find a strict offer and acceptance

The difficulty with the 'offer and acceptance' analysis is that, in practice, it may be difficult to pinpoint exactly when an offer has been made and exactly when it has been accepted. Of course, in many cases it doesn't matter exactly when the contract was made, since neither party is attempting to deny the existence of the contract or trying to deny that a particular term is part of the contract and thus the matter is not in issue. However, in a case where the formation of the contract must be pinpointed exactly (for example, if the question arises as to whether an exemption clause is incorporated into the contract or whether an offer has been revoked before it has been accepted), it is necessary to find an offer by one party and its acceptance by the other.

Attempts have been made to get away from this rather restricting analysis of the formation of a contract which, in certain cases, is rather strained and artificial. The chief proponent of change was Lord Denning MR, and in a case involving the sale of a council house, he argued that it is not necessary to find a strict offer and acceptance in order to find that a contract has been formed.

Gibson v Manchester City Council (1979)

In November 1970, the council sent G details of a scheme whereby council tenants could purchase their rented properties. G applied immediately in writing. The council replied on 10 February 1971, saying: 'The corporation may be prepared to sell the house to you at the purchase price of £2,725 less 20%, £2,180 (freehold).' The letter gave details about a mortgage and said: 'This letter should not be regarded as a firm offer of a mortgage. If you would like to make a formal application to buy your council house, please complete the enclosed application form and return it to me as soon as possible.'

G filled in the form and returned it, but left the space for the purchase price blank, saying in a covering letter, dated 5 March 1971, that the property was in need of some repair, and asking that the council either repair the property or reduce the purchase price. The council replied on 12 March declining either to reduce the price or to undertake the repairs. G replied on 18 March, asking the council to proceed with the purchase as per his original application.

Two months later, before formal contracts had been exchanged, control of the council passed from the Conservatives to Labour, and the policy of the new council was against the sale of council houses. No further sales were to take place *unless a legally binding contract to sell had already been entered into* under the previous council. The question arose, therefore, whether the correspondence amounted to a legally binding contract (note that in the case of a sale of land, the contract formerly had to be *evidenced* in writing in order to be binding: nowadays it must be made in writing).

G had the advantage that in a previous similar case, *Storer v Manchester City Council* (1974) (in which, however, the correspondence had gone a stage further), the Court of Appeal had ruled that a contract did exist. The Court of Appeal made a similar ruling in G's case, Lord Denning having this to say about the issue of whether there had been an offer which had been accepted:

> We have had much discussion as to whether Mr Gibson's letter of 18 March 1971 was a new offer or whether it was an acceptance of the previous offer which had been made. I do not like detailed analysis on such a point. To my mind it is a mistake to think that all contracts can be analysed into the form of offer and acceptance. I know that in some textbooks it has been the custom to do so; but, as I understand the law, there is no need to look for strict offer and acceptance. You should look at the correspondence as a whole and at the conduct of the parties and see therefrom whether the parties have come to an agreement on everything that was material. If by their correspondence and their conduct you can see an agreement on all material terms, which was intended thenceforth to be binding, then there is a binding contract in law even though all the formalities have not been gone through. For that proposition I would refer to *Brogden v Metropolitan Railway Co* (1877).

The Council appealed to the House of Lords. The appeal was successful. The House of Lords, though acknowledging that there may be exceptional cases which don't fit into the normal analysis of offer and acceptance, held that in this particular case, where the negotiations of the parties were fully documented, there was no reason for departing from the conventional analysis. The Lords distinguished *Storer*'s case from the present case, pointing out that S's case had reached a stage further than G's in that the council had written to S: 'I understand you wish to purchase your council house and enclose the Agreement for Sale. If you will sign the agreement and return it to me, I will send you the agreement signed on behalf of the Corporation in exchange.' The House of Lords considered that this difference was vital. It amounted to an offer, which S accepted when he signed the agreement. There was no such document in G's case. The council had said merely that they 'may be prepared' to sell the house. Thus the necessary offer and acceptance could not be found. The House of Lords held that as the exchanges between the parties were well-documented and as they did not show a clear offer and acceptance, there was no contract.

Offers made by, and accepted to, a central party

The problem has arisen as to what is the position if the offer is made and accepted via a central party. In *Clarke v Dunraven* (1897), entrants in a yacht race sent in their entries to the club secretary. It was, nevertheless, held that they were in a contractual relationship with one another. A similar principle applies in relation to persons who subscribe for shares in a company. They are deemed to be in a contractual relationship with one another and with the company, on the terms of the company's Articles of Association, that is, the rules governing the internal management of the company (see s 14 of the Companies Act (1985)).

Collateral contracts

Sometimes the concept of a *collateral* contract is employed where A has entered into a contract with B relying on representations made by C. In such a case there is not, apparently, a contractual relationship between A and C.

Shanklin Pier v Detel Products (1951)

The plaintiffs, who owned a pier, entered into a contract with a painting contractor to have the pier repainted. The plaintiffs had the right under the contract to specify the paint used. After discussion with the defendant paint manufacturers who promised that a particular paint manufactured by them would last seven to 10 years, the plaintiffs specified that the contractors should use that paint. The contractors did so, but the paint proved unsatisfactory and lasted only three months. Normally when a contractor uses unsuitable materials he can be sued for breach of contract. The difficulty here was that the contractor had used paint specified by the plaintiffs. The plaintiffs, therefore, sought recompense from the defendants. The difficulty in the way of this action was that, on the face of it, the plaintiffs had no contract with the defendants, as the paint had been bought by the contractors. The court surmounted this difficulty by holding that there was not one, but two, contracts involved in the transaction. Under the first contract, the plaintiffs hired the contractors to paint the pier. Under the second contract, which was collateral to the first, the plaintiffs had a contract with the defendants whereby the defendants promised that if the plaintiffs specified the use of the defendants' paint for the painting of the pier, the defendants would promise that it would last seven to 10 years.

Rejection

A rejection is a refusal of the offer. It takes effect when it is communicated to the offeror.

Revocation

If an offer is revoked it means that it is cancelled. Revocation is a withdrawal of the offer by the offeror and must not be confused with rejection.

An offer may be revoked at any time before it has been accepted. This is the case even if the offeror has agreed to keep the offer open for a specified period of time. The reason is that the law will not enforce a promise unless consideration has been given for the promise (see Chapter 5).

Routledge v Grant (1828)

G offered to take a lease of R's premises, an answer to be given within six weeks. Three weeks later G withdrew his offer. Later, but before the six weeks had expired, R purported to accept G's offer. *Held*: the offer had been effectively revoked by G before R had accepted it. There was therefore no contract.

There are two exceptions to the rule that an offer can be revoked at any time before it has been accepted.

Options

If the offeree has paid a sum of money, called an option, to the offeror in consideration of which the offeror has agreed to keep the offer open for a specified length of time, the offeror must leave the offer open for that length of time and may not revoke it. For example, A Ltd may grant B an option, for the price of, say, £50, to buy 1,000 shares at £1 each, exercisable six months from the date of the option. If, at the end of six months, the value of the shares has risen, B will exercise the option, that is, buy the shares. If, on the other hand, the value of the shares has fallen, B will not purchase the shares and will simply have lost the money which he paid for the option.

Mountford v Scott (1975)

S granted an option for the sum of £1, under which M could purchase S's house for the sum of £10,000 if he exercised the option within six months. Before the option was exercised, S purported to withdraw the offer. *Held*: because S had granted M an option for a valuable consideration, S was not free to withdraw the offer.

Note: the Law Commission, in its Working Paper No 60 (1975), has made the following proposals relating to firm offers for which no consideration has been given by the offeree:

(a) an offeror who has promised that he will not revoke his offer for a definite time should be bound by the terms of that promise for a period not exceeding six years, provided the promise has been made in the course of a business;

(b) such a promise need not be evidenced in writing;

(c) it should be capable of applying to land or interests in land;

(d) a firm offer to which (a) applies should be capable of acceptance by the offeree during the time that the offeror is bound by his promise, notwithstanding his purported revocation of it; and

(e) an offeror who breaks a promise by which he is bound under (a) should be liable in damages to the offeree.

No action has been taken on these proposals to date.

Unilateral contracts

It would seem that unilateral contracts are an exception to the rule that an offer may be revoked at any time before it has been accepted. Note in this respect that the offer in a unilateral contract is not accepted until the offeree has *completed* the task stipulated by the offeror. Thus, if the general rule were to be applied to unilateral contracts, the offeror could wait until an offeree had substantially completed the stipulated task and could then revoke his offer. For example, suppose A offered a prize of £10,000 for the winner of a walking race from Northampton to London. Although 100 people, say, set out, only one accepts the offer and that is the winner of the race, so that if, when the leader has reached Luton, A revokes the offer, application of the general rule would give the answer that the offer has been validly revoked. A modification of the general rule is therefore needed in order to do justice.

Errington v Errington (1952)

A father bought a house for his son and daughter-in-law to live in. The father put down £250 in cash and borrowed the remaining £500 of the purchase price from a building society, repayable at 15s per week. He told the daughter-in-law that the £250 was a present to them. He handed her the building society book and told her not to part with it and that the house would be theirs when they had paid off the mortgage. He further said that when he retired he would transfer the house into their names. The couple paid the building society instalments regularly and had paid off a good deal of the money when the father died. His executors sought possession of the property on the grounds that it was part of the father's estate. The couple argued that they were entitled to remain in possession until they had paid off the mortgage, at which time the house would become theirs. *Held* by the Court of Appeal: the father's promise had created a unilateral contract under the terms of which, if the couple paid off the mortgage, the house became theirs. The offer could not be revoked while they were still trying to accept the offer by paying off the instalments. Once the offeree, to the knowledge of the offeror, has begun to perform the task required for the acceptance of the offer, the offeror cannot revoke the offer without giving the offeree a reasonable chance of completing the act of acceptance.

Communication of the revocation

In order to be effective, the revocation must be communicated to the offeree.

Byrne v Van Tienhoven (1880)

Events took place as follows: 1 October, VT in Cardiff posted an offer to B in New York, offering to sell them 1,000 boxes of tinplates; 8 October, VT posted a letter purporting to revoke their offer; 11 October, B received offer and telegraphed acceptance; 20 October, B received VT's letter of revocation. The question arose as to whether the posting of the letter of revocation was a sufficient communication of it. *Held*: although the acceptance was complete as soon as the telegram had been handed in at the Post Office, the letter of revocation didn't take effect until it reached the plaintiffs on 20 October. Since, by then, the plaintiff had already accepted the defendant's offer, there was a valid contract for the sale of the tinplate.

Difficulty might arise where, for example, the offeror posts a revocation to the address to which the offer was posted, only to find that the offeree is not at that address at the time, and that the offeree subsequently accepts the offer in ignorance of the letter of revocation. Another example might be where the letter of revocation is delivered to the offeree's premises at 9 am, opened at 9.30 am by a secretary and not read until 11 am. Suppose a letter of acceptance is posted at 10 am. Is there a contract? The answer is that if the court takes the strict view of 'communication' it will hold that communication does not take place until the revocation actually comes to the notice of the offeree. However, it may be that the court will take the view that communication is deemed to take place when the revocation ought reasonably to have come to the notice of the offeree.

On the face of it, communication of revocation should be made by the offeror to the offeree. However, it has been held that revocation was effective if the offeree got to know, by whatever means, that the offeror no longer wished the offer to remain open.

Dickinson v Dodds (1876)

On Wednesday, Do handed Di a written offer to sell certain houses: 'This offer to be left over (that is, remain open) until Friday 9 am.' On Thursday afternoon Di was informed by B that Do had been offering or agreeing to sell the property to A. At 7.30 on Thursday evening, Di left a formal letter of acceptance at the house where Do was staying. On Friday morning B (who was acting on Di's behalf) handed a duplicate of the letter of acceptance to Do and told him verbally what the letter contained. The day before Do had signed the contract to sell to A. The court made an order that he should specifically perform his contract with Di. Do appealed and the question for determination was whether the offer to Di had been effectively revoked. The Court of Appeal held that it had, James LJ saying:

> The plaintiff clearly knew that Dodds was no longer minded to sell the property to him as plainly and as clearly as if Dodds had told him in so many words, 'I withdraw the offer'.

Note that the headnote to the case, which says that it seems that the sale of property to a third party would of itself amount to a withdrawal of the offer, seems to be based upon an example given by Mellish LJ. However, at the beginning of his speech, he makes it clear that, if property on offer to A is subsequently sold to B, the offer to A is revoked only if A has notice of the sale.

Where the offer of a unilateral contract is made to the world at large or a class of persons (rather than to a particular person), it would seem that the offer may be effectively revoked if the offeror gives notice of revocation through the same channel that the original offer was published.

Lapse of time

Where a time limit is placed upon an offer, it must be accepted within the time limit; otherwise it lapses. Where no time limit is placed upon the offer, it must be accepted within a reasonable time. What is a reasonable time will depend on the particular circumstances of the offer.

Lapse due to death

The rule here depends upon whether the death is that of the offeror or that of the offeree.

Death of the offeror

Where the offeror has died after making the offer, it appears that an acceptance after his death will be valid, providing:

(a) that the contract can be performed from the deceased's estate (thus acceptance of an offer to provide a personal service will lapse); and

(b) that the offeree was unaware of the offeror's death at the time he accepted the offer.

Bradbury v Morgan (1862)

The deceased had written to B asking them to give credit to T and offering to guarantee the debt up to a maximum of £100. (A guarantee of credit or an overdraft is a standing offer which is 'accepted' each time money is advanced on the credit or overdraft.) The credit was continued after the deceased's death, since B were unaware of the death. B brought an action on the guarantee against the deceased's executors. *Held*: the defendants were liable for money advanced by B after the deceased's death before B had notification of it.

Death of the offeree

It is widely believed that the death of the offeree will always cause the offer to lapse, although there is no direct English reference on this point.

Counter-offer

Where, in response to an offer, the offeree introduces new terms or proposes to alter existing terms, he is making a counter-offer, the effect of which is to extinguish the original offer and replace it with the offeree's proposed alternative. It is then up to the original offeror whether or not he accepts the alternative terms proposed by the offeree. If he does not, the offeree is not then permitted to accept the original offer, because it has been extinguished by his counter-offer.

Hyde v Wrench (1840)

On 6 June, the defendants wrote to the plaintiff offering to sell his farm for £1,000. The plaintiff's agent immediately called on W and made an offer of £950, which W wished to have a few days to consider. On 27 June, W wrote to say that he couldn't accept the offer. H then wrote to W purporting to accept

W's offer to sell for £1,000. It was held that there was no contract. W's offer to sell had not been accepted. Instead, H had made a counter-offer to buy for £950. The effect of this was that it destroyed the original offer and replaced it with a new one. The new offer had been rejected and, therefore, there was no contract.

Battle of the forms

One difficulty regularly encountered by sales managers is the problem of 'the battle of the forms'. This is the term given to the quite common situation where two contracting parties each send standard forms to the other in an attempt to ensure that their own preferred terms of business prevail over the other party's. A supplier makes an offer on his or her standard form which contains the supplier's terms of supply. The customer makes an 'acceptance' on his or her standard form which contains the customer's terms of purchase. In the event of a conflict between the two sets of terms, whose terms will prevail?

Butler Machine Tool Co v Ex-Cello (1979)

On 23 May, B offered to sell E a machine for £75,535, delivery to be in 10 months' time. The offer included a condition that all orders were accepted only on B's terms, which were to prevail over any terms in E's order. One of B's terms was that any increase in the cost of manufacture after the order was placed but before delivery was made, should be added to the price payable. On 27 May, E submitted a purchase order on which was printed their own terms of purchase. These did not, of course, include a price-variation clause. At the bottom of the order was a tear-off slip which read, 'We accept your order on the terms and conditions stated thereon'. On 5 June, B returned the tear-off slip. They also wrote a covering letter which stated that, 'your official order is being entered in accordance with our revised quotation of 23 May'.

B demanded an additional £2,892 from E under the price-variation clause and E refused to pay. *Held* by the Court of Appeal: E's order of 27 May was a counter-offer which B had accepted when they returned the tear-off slip on 5 June. (B's letter referring to their quotation of 23 May was held, on rather doubtful grounds, to be intended to identify the machine and the price and not to incorporate B's terms and conditions printed on the back of the document.) If the tear-off slip had not been returned, there would have been no contract, because of lack of acceptance, at least until the machine had been delivered and accepted by the buyer (in which case there would have been an acceptance by conduct).

This case has far-reaching implications for business. Before this case was decided it was thought that if X's terms of sale included a term to the effect that X's terms were to prevail over any terms subsequently tendered by Y, this was sufficient to give X's terms priority. It is clear from the *Butler* case, however, that, in a battle of the forms, the terms which are the last to be tendered will prevail.

It was also thought that a simple price variation clause in a contract would fall foul of the rule requiring 'certainty' in contracts and would, therefore, not be effective unless it contained a precise formula indicating how the revised price was arrived at. Hence, motivated by the raging inflation of the 1970s, a number of trade associations prepared price-variation formulae for incorporation into members' contracts, though many companies selling relatively low priced goods continued to rely on a clause permitting them to raise their prices by an unspecific amount. However, in the *Butler* case this point was not really argued, because the main issue was whether the clause was incorporated into the contract. If Butler had managed to clear that hurdle they may well have been defeated by the 'uncertainty of terms' argument, although there are a number of cases where an agreement which allows one party to vary it unilaterally, without reference to any precise formula, has not been held to be void on the ground of uncertainty. (However, in the Unfair Terms in Consumer Contracts Regulations 1994, among the list of terms which a court may regard as being unfair is included terms 'providing for the price of the goods to be determined at the time of delivery or allowing the seller of goods or the supplier of services to increase their price without in both cases giving the consumer the corresponding right to cancel the contract if the final price is too high in relation to the price agreed when the contract was concluded.)

So what should a company in Butler's position do in future in order to ensure that their terms and conditions prevailed over those of a prospective purchaser?

The best way for a supplier of goods or services to make sure that the contract is made on his or her terms of supply, is to make all offers on a standard form bearing the supplier's terms and conditions. This is sent to the purchaser in duplicate. The purchaser is required to accept the offer by returning one of the copies of the form, duly signed on behalf of the purchaser.

An alternative method is for the parties to agree on a particular set of terms which appear to be fair to both parties, such as those supplied by a trade association.

If a business normally concludes by telephone contracts supplying goods or services, a copy of the supplier's terms and conditions should be sent to the customer at the outset, preferably before any order is made or accepted. It should contain a space for the customer's signature, and wording which indicates that the customer accepts that all transactions are to take place on the supplier's terms. This will not prevent the customer's terms and conditions becoming applicable if the supplier accepts an order on those terms. It might, however, deter the customer from subsequently tendering the customer's own terms and conditions.

An enterprise which deals with telephone customers in relation to low-value transactions is in a difficult position regarding the incorporation of its terms into the contract, particularly where the customers are irregular or one-off. It will often be impracticable to notify terms to the customer in advance of the transaction and to obtain the customer's signed agreement to this. In such cases, the supplier should state over the telephone that the sale or supply is to be on the supplier's terms and should then send the customer a copy. A difficulty with this is that in the event of a dispute, a court or arbitrator might say that the supplier's terms are not incorporated in the contract because the precise terms were not made known to the other party at the time the contract was made. On the other hand, because the supplier made known that the sale or supply was subject to terms, and subsequently made the precise terms known to the other party, the court or arbitrator may rule in the supplier's favour.

It should not be assumed that all communications from the offeree to the offeror, which apparently propose new terms, amount to a counter-offer. It may be that the offeree is simply asking for clarification of the terms of the offer or requesting further information about it.

Put in simple terms, this distinction is easy to make. If A offers to sell B a holiday at a particular resort, in a particular hotel, travel to be by air, A may legitimately ask B to confirm that the price includes a meal in flight and a midday meal at the hotel, without this amounting to a counter-offer. It is clearly a request for further information about the offer. However, in the leading case of *Stevenson v McLean* (1880), in which the distinction between a request for further information and a counter-offer was first made, it may appear to the objective observer that although the court held the offeree's communication to the offeror to be a request for further information, it in fact looks very much like a counter-offer.

Stevenson v McLean (1880)

McL wrote to S on Saturday offering to sell S some iron at 40s net cash per ton, open till Monday. On Monday S telegraphed McL saying: 'Please wire whether you would accept forty for delivery over two months, or if not, longest limit you would give.' (Net cash means immediate payment is required, so that the meaning of S's telegram is 'Will you give us credit?'.) McL received S's telegram at 10.01 on Monday and immediately sold the iron to a third party. At 1.25 pm, McL telegraphed S telling him that the iron had been sold. At 1.34 pm, the S telegraphed accepting McL's offer to sell at 40s cash. At 1.46 pm, McL's telegram was delivered to S. S sued McL for breach of contract. McL argued that S's telegram which they received at 10.01 am was a counter-offer which destroyed their original offer to sell and that as they had not accepted the counter-offer, there was no contract for the sale of the iron. It was held by Lush J that the plaintiff's telegram of 10.01 was simply a request for further information about the offer. It did not amount to a counter-offer.

Since the offer had been accepted by the plaintiff's telegram of 1.34 pm, the purported revocation of the offer by the defendant's telegram of 1.25 pm, which was not delivered until 1.34, was ineffective.

Cancellable agreements

At common law, once an offer has been made which has been accepted, a contract comes into existence which binds both parties. Thus, if one party changes his mind and does not wish to proceed with the contract, he will be in breach of contract. However, because of the incidence in modern times of high pressure selling, and because transactions are becoming increasingly complicated so that an instant decision is not necessarily a considered decision, various statutory provisions allow a cooling-off period. Most of these cooling-off rights are in favour of consumers.

The Consumer Protection (Cancellation of Contracts Concluded Away from Business Premises) Regulations 1987 give a 7 day cooling-off period to a customer who enters a contract to buy goods or services during an unsolicited visit by the trader to the customer's home, or place of work, or someone else's home. The visit is unsolicited if the customer agrees to it as a result of an unsolicited contact during which the trader indicates he is willing to make a call. The Regulations provide that the trader must give the customer a written notice of his right to cancel and a detachable form must be provided on which the customer may exercise this right. The customer has 7 days from the date of the making of the contract in which to cancel. He must do this in writing, which takes effect when it is posted, but it need not be on the detachable form provided.

There are a number of exceptions to the Regulations. These include: where the contract is for a cash price of £35 or less (including VAT); contracts to buy, sell, dispose of, lease or mortgage land, to finance or provide bridging finance for the purchase of land, for the construction or extension of a building or other erection on land; contracts for the supply of food, drink or other goods intended for current consumption by use in the household and supplied by regular roundsmen; contracts which provide credit of £35 or less; and contracts which are covered by certain other legislation, such as the Insurance Companies Act 1982, the Financial Services Act 1986 and the Banking Act 1987.

The Consumer Protection (Distance Selling) Regulations 2000 also provide for a cooling-off period of 7 working days after goods are delivered or, in the case of the contract for a service, 7 working days after the contract is made.

The Timeshare Act 1992 gives a 14 day cooling-off period for contracts made in the UK or where one of the parties is located in the UK.

The Insurance Companies Act 1982 gives the proposer (that is, the customer), under a long-term insurance contract, a 10 day cooling-off period.

If the proposer exercises his right, his offer is revoked (if the insurance company has not yet accepted it) or the contract is rescinded. The proposer is entitled to the return of any premiums paid if he exercises his right of cancellation.

The Consumer Credit Act 1974 gives a cooling-off period of 5 days (longer in certain circumstances) if the contract is concluded away from the business premises of the creditor or supplier and if oral representations were made to the debtor during the antecedent negotiations. This cooling-off period applies whether or not the creditor or supplier visited the debtor's home. If there was a visit to the debtor's home, the fact that the debtor requested it does not affect his rights – unlike with the Consumer Protection (Cancellation of Contracts Concluded Away from Business Premises) Regulations 1987, which require the visit to be unsolicited.

The Consumer Protection (Distance Selling) Regulations 2000

The upsurge in home shopping has prompted the government to introduce a comprehensive protection scheme for the consumer by way of the Distance Selling Regulations. These require, among other things, certain information to be given to the consumer and a right of cancellation for the consumer (that is, a cooling-off period).

The Regulations apply to distance contracts. 'Distance contract' means any contract concerning goods or services concluded between a supplier and a consumer under an organised distance sales or service provision scheme. It is run by the supplier who, for the purpose of the contract, makes exclusive use of one or more means of distance communication.

Thus, Internet sales and mail order sales will be the main form of distance contract.

Writing or other durable medium

The provisions requiring information to be given to the consumer usually require it to be given in writing or in another durable medium available to the consumer. The 'durable medium' probably includes fax and email. They are certainly acceptable for communicating the right to cancel. Whether it would include giving it over the Internet, which could be printed off like an email, is a moot point. In any case, many distance selling companies appear to be playing safe for the moment and giving the information in writing.

Exceptions

There are a number of exceptions, including certain contracts for the disposition of an interest in land (except for a rental agreement), financial services contracts, automated sales, public pay phones and auctions.

Some of the Regulations, including those relating to the provision of information and the right to cancel, do not apply to:

(a) contracts for food, drinks and other goods delivered to the consumer's residence or workplace by regular roundsmen;

(b) contracts for the provision of accommodation, transport, catering or other leisure services where the supplier undertakes to provide the services on a specific date or within a specific period; and

(c) timeshare contracts, since they are largely controlled under different legislation.

Information to be supplied

The following information must be supplied prior to the contract:

(a) the identity of the supplier and, where the contract requires payment in advance, the supplier's address;

(b) a description of the main characteristics of the goods or service;

(c) the price of the goods or services including all taxes;

(d) the delivery costs, where appropriate;

(e) the arrangements for payment, delivery or performance;

(f) the existence of a right to cancel;

(g) the cost of using the means of distance communication except where it is calculated other than at the basic rate;

(h) the period for which the offer or the price remains valid; and

(i) where appropriate, the minimum duration of the contract, in the case of contracts for the supply of goods or services to be performed permanently or recurrently.

These are listed in reg 8.

Substitute goods or services

The supplier must also inform the consumer:

(a) whether he proposes, in the event of the goods ordered by the consumer being unavailable, to substitute goods or services of equivalent quality and price; and

(b) that the cost of returning any such goods in the event of cancellation by the consumer would be borne by the supplier.

Right to cancel

The supplier must also give the consumer information about his right to cancel and about arrangements for the return of the goods, should the consumer decide to cancel. It may be given by writing, fax or email.

Regulation 10 makes provision about the right to cancel. If this is complied with by the supplier, the cancellation period ends on the expiry of 7 *working days* beginning with the day after the day on which the consumer receives the goods or, if the contract is for the supply of a service, the day on which the contract was concluded.

Where the supplier has not initially complied with reg 8, but does so within three months, the right to cancel the cancellation period is 7 working days after the consumer receives the information.

If no information about the right to cancel is given, the right to cancel ends at the expiry of 3 months and 7 working days, beginning with the day after the day on which the consumer receives the goods or, in the case of services, concluded the contract.

The right may be exercised by:

(a) leaving it at the address last known to the consumer band addressed to the supplier, in which case it takes effect on the day on which it was left;

(b) sending it by post to the last known address of the supplier, in which case it takes effect when posted;

(c) sending it by fax to the last known fax number; and

(d) sending it by email.

In the case of both fax and email, the notice is given on the day it is sent. Although the Regulations make reference to the address, etc, 'last known' to the consumer, in the majority of cases the address will be the one from which the supplier still operates.

Any related fixed-sum credit agreement is also cancelled, so that if, for example, goods are bought on credit, two contracts are cancelled: the contract of sale and the contract for credit.

Exceptions to the right to cancel

(a) Where a contract for the supply of services has, with the customer's agreement, begun before the end of the cancellation period, providing Regulation 8 regarding the provision of information has been complied with.

(b) Where the price of goods or services to be supplied is dependent upon the fluctuations of the financial services market, which cannot be controlled by the supplier.

(c) For the supply of goods of a personalised nature or which by reason of their nature cannot be returned or which are liable to deteriorate or expire rapidly.

(d) For the supply of audio or video recordings or computer software if they are unsealed by the consumer.

(e) For betting, gaming or lottery services.

Recovery of sums paid

On cancellation, the supplier must reimburse any sum paid by or on behalf of the consumer. This includes any sum which was paid to someone other than the supplier (usually to a finance company) under a credit agreement.

The reimbursement must be done as soon as possible and in any case within a period not exceeding 30 days, beginning with the day on which the notice of cancellation is given.

If a term of the contract provides for the consumer to return the goods after cancellation, the supplier may make a charge to the consumer, not exceeding the direct costs of recovery, if the consumer does not comply or if the consumer returns the goods at the supplier's expense.

Care of the goods

During the cancellation period, the consumer must retain possession of the goods and must take reasonable care of them.

Performance of the contract

Unless otherwise agreed, the supplier must perform the contract within 30 days, beginning with the day after the day the consumer sent his order to the supplier.

Making the contract by electronic means

We have seen that legislation has been introduced with a view to regulate distance selling. Increasingly this is via the Internet, or, less frequently, by email. In addition, the Government (which has set a target for 90% of its routine procurement of goods to be done electronically by 2001) has passed the Electronic Communications Act 2000, among other things, to facilitate secure on-line transactions. The Act provides for a register to be set up listing persons who are approved for the purposes of providing cryptography services, for example, in relation to the recognition of electronic signatures. However, it is not compulsory for providers to register – but those who do so will have the advantage that it is known that their service meets certain standards. It also provides for the recognition of electronic signatures in legal proceedings, in order to facilitate legal transactions taking place over the Internet. (It is now possible, for example, to register a limited liability company using the Internet.) There is also provision for removing obstacles contained in other legislation: in relation to the use of electronic means of storage of records, for example.

Contracting by email

In contracting by email, it would seem that the rule relating to acceptance of offers should be on the same basis as the 'instantaneous communication' rule relating to telex. We have already examined the case of *Brinkibon v Stahag Stahl* (1982) and seen that acceptance by telex took place when received. However, the court refused to rule that a telexed acceptance *always* takes effect when received. It may be, therefore, that where there are special circumstances, the court may apply a different rule. For example, Amy makes an offer by email to sell goods to Barry. Barry despatches an acceptance at 3 pm, aware that Amy will have left the office by that time and so will not read the acceptance until the morning. At 4 pm, Barry receives an offer from Carl to sell similar goods to those Amy was offering, but at a cheaper price. He accepts the offer and sends an urgent email to Amy, which will appear written in red at the top of her screen, informing her that he wishes to reject her offer. It may well be, in such circumstances, that Barry's rejection would be valid, even though the acceptance arrived first.

Contracting over the Internet

A contract over the Internet is perhaps not quite so straightforward. In particular, if an international dimension is present, as is the case with many consumer transactions nowadays, the situation may be quite complex. It is beyond the current scope of this text to discuss international transactions.

In relation to transactions in England and Wales, many websites which sell goods are set up rather like a supermarket. The shopper acquires a basket, tours the store and clicks on the items he wishes to buy. It seems clear that the list of items is an invitation to treat. When he reaches the check-out he is asked to provide details of his credit or debit card. He is then asked to click on an icon, in order to confirm the transaction. The screen usually has a display of what the customer is agreeing to buy. He then receives an email from the seller confirming the transaction from their point of view. The neatest analysis of this situation is that the request to click on the icon is an offer to sell, which the customer accepts when he clicks as requested. The email is simply confirmation from the supplier that the electronic acceptance has got through.

However, this does not seem to be the case. The EC Directive on Electronic Commerce provides:

Where a recipient, in accepting a service provider's offer, is required to give his consent through technological means, such as clicking on an icon, the contract is concluded when the recipient of the service has received from the service provider, electronically, an acknowledgement of receipt of the recipient's acceptance.

Thus, the customer's click on the 'proceed' icon is the offer and the supplier's email is the acceptance. Therefore, if the supplier wishes to change his mind having received the offer from the customer, he is free to do so by failing to send the confirmatory email.

CHAPTER 4

CERTAINTY OF TERMS AND SUBJECT MATTER

If an offer or any important terms of an offer are not certain, any purported acceptance is ineffective and there will be no contract. The uncertainty may arise in one of two ways:

(a) where the parties have left one or more of the important terms of the contract unresolved; or

(b) where the parties are at cross-purposes.

Where the parties have left one or more of the important terms of the contract unresolved

In such a case, the action is usually brought by a party who finds the contract inconvenient and is seeking a way to escape from it. Sometimes the terms are so uncertain that the courts cannot give contractual effect to the agreement. An example is to be found below in the case of *Scammell v Ouston* (1941). On other occasions, the court is able to find a way to resolve the uncertainty and, therefore, give effect to the contract.

Scammell v Ouston (1941)

O wished to acquire a new pantechnicon for use in his furniture-removing business. Following discussions with S in which it was assumed that hire-purchase terms would be available and in which a trade-in price was fixed for O's old vehicle, O sent in a written order saying: 'This order is given on the understanding that the balance of the purchase price can be had on hire-purchase terms over a period of two years.' S completed the new van and arrangements were made with a finance company to give hire-purchase, though the terms were not agreed. Then it seems that S changed their mind about taking O's old van in part-exchange, as they were not satisfied with its condition, and they asked him to sell it privately. O sued for breach of contract. *Held* by the House of Lords: S's defence, to the effect that there was no contract until the HP terms had been agreed, succeeded. There was evidence that HP terms varied widely and no evidence to show which, if any, the parties favoured.

Similarly, where an offer is expressed as being 'subject to contract', there is no valid offer because the offer is regarded as being uncertain in its terms, (though a better reason for denying the existence of a contract might be that there is no intention to make an offer and that, therefore, there is no firm offer which can be accepted).

Getting rid of the uncertainty

The courts have made it clear that, where it is evident that the parties had contractual intention, they will make every effort to give effect to that intention. This has been done in the following types of case:

(a) Where there had been a previous course of dealing between the parties, which could be referred to in order to clarify the uncertain terms

Hillas and Co v Arcos (1932)

H had agreed to buy from A, '22,000 standards of softwood goods of fair specification over the season 1930'. The agreement contained an option to buy 100,000 standards in 1931. No difficulties arose regarding the 1930 contract, but when H tried to exercise their option for 1931, A argued that the contract was too vague since the contract contained no details as to the kind or size of timber or the manner of shipment. However, the House of Lords held that as there had been no serious difficulties in carrying out the contract for 1930, there was no reason why it could not be carried out for 1931.

(b) Where the contract itself provided the means of resolving the uncertainty via an arbitration clause

Foley v Classique Coaches (1934)

F, who owned a service station, agreed to sell certain land to the coach company on condition that the company would buy its petrol from him. The contract for the sale of land was made subject to the defendants entering into another agreement to purchase from the plaintiff all the petrol required for their coach business. Both contracts were entered into, the petrol contract being described as supplemental to the land contract. The petrol sale contract provided that the coach company would buy its petrol from F, 'at a price to be agreed by the parties in writing from time to time'. Another clause in the agreement provided for disputes arising out of the agreement to be submitted to arbitration. After three years, the coach company felt that it could get its petrol at a better price elsewhere and wrote to F repudiating the petrol contract. It was argued that there was no binding contract on the ground that, because the price of the petrol had not been agreed, the contract lacked certainty. *Held*: that although the parties had failed to agree a price for the petrol, the contract provided a means by which any dispute as to price could be settled, that is, by referring the matter to arbitration. Thus the contract itself provided the means of rendering an apparently uncertain term certain. The court was concerned to distinguish the decision in *May and Butcher v R* (1934) below, and it is clear that in deciding that there was a contract in *Foley*'s case, they were influenced by the fact: (a) that the parties had managed to act on the agreement for three years (see *Hillas v Arcos* above); and (b) that the contract for the sale of the land had been conditional upon the petrol contract being entered into, that is, if there had been no petrol contract the plaintiffs would not have been willing to sell their land.

It seems that where the contract is executory (that is, has not been carried out), a contract in which the price has not been fixed will be void for uncertainty. It follows that a contract which provides for arbitration will be ineffective, since the parties cannot use the terms of a void contract in order to make it valid. It seems, too, that the provisions of s 8 of the Sale of Goods Act 1979, which provide for a reasonable price to be paid where the price of the goods has not been fixed by the contract (a similar provision is made in respect of the supply of services by the Supply of Goods and Services Act 1982), do not apply where the contract is executory. This rule has been established by case law and does not seem to accord with the wording of s 8 of the Act, which makes no distinction between executory and executed obligations.

May and Butcher v R (1934)

M and B claimed to have a contract for the purchase of certain tentage. The terms of the alleged contract were as follows:

(3) The price or prices to be paid, and the date or dates on which payment is to be made by the purchasers to the Commission for such old tentage shall be agreed upon from time to time between the Commission and the purchasers as the quantities of the said old tentage become available for disposal and are offered to the purchasers by the Commission.

(10) It is understood that all disputes with reference to or arising out of this agreement will be submitted to arbitration in accordance with the provisions of the Arbitration Act 1889.

The House of Lords held that there was no contract. The arbitration clause was to deal with matters arising out of the agreement, but, in the opinion of the House of Lords, until the price was fixed there was no agreement and, therefore, nothing to which the arbitration clause could relate.

The question also arose as to whether s 8 or s 9 of the Sale of Goods Act 1893 (now re-enacted in the Sale of Goods Act 1979) operated so as to make certain the uncertain term as to price. Briefly s 8 provides that in a sale of goods the price: (i) may be fixed by the contract; (ii) may be left to be fixed in a manner agreed in the contract; or (iii) may be determined by a course of dealing between the parties. Where none of these has been done, the buyer must pay a reasonable price. Section 9 provides that if the agreement provides for a price to be fixed by a third party and the third party fails to fix a price, the contract is void. Lord Buckmaster thought that the provision for the parties to agree in the future was analogous to allowing a third party to fix a price. As the parties could not agree a price, therefore, the contract was void. Viscount Dunedin said that the 'reasonable price' provision of s 8 of the Sale of Goods Act applies only if the parties are silent as to price in their agreement. He went on to say that the parties were not silent as to price, in that they had agreed that the two parties were to agree the price in the future. The result of that was that the 'reasonable price' provisions did not apply and there was no contract. Lord Warrington of Clyff repeated this argument.

(c) Where a term may be implied by statute in order to resolve the uncertainty

Thus, for example, s 8 of the Sale of Goods Act 1979 may be used to resolve an uncertainty in a contract for the sale of goods, regarding the price to be paid by the buyer.

(d) Where a term may be implied by the courts or by common law in order to resolve the uncertainty

Certain contractual terms have become well-established at common law because they have been consistently implied into certain types of contract: for example, it is an implied term in a contract of employment that the employee will perform his duties with due skill and care. Occasionally, the court may be persuaded to imply a particular term into a particular contract. However, it will only do this if the missing term is something which the parties would have inserted themselves had they thought about it. Thus in implying the term, the court is purporting to give effect to the intentions of the parties. The court will only imply a term into a particular contract if the suggested term is something which is necessary in order to give the contract business efficacy, that is, it is something which should go without saying. It is not sufficient simply to show that such a term would be a reasonable one to imply.

The Moorcock (1889)

The defendants owned a wharf and had agreed to allow the plaintiff shipowner to discharge his ship at their jetty, which extended into the River Thames. Both parties realised that the vessel would rest on the river bed at low tide. The boat was damaged when it rested on a ridge of hard ground at low tide. The plaintiffs sued in respect of the damage. The defendants argued that they had not contracted that the mooring would be safe. *Held*: there was an implied term in the contract to the effect that the mooring would be safe. Such an implied term was needed in order to give business efficacy to the transaction.

The topic of implied terms will be dealt with in more detail under the heading 'terms of the contract'.

(e) Where a term may be implied by local custom or by trade custom

Most local and trade customs have now been absorbed into the common law, so that, in practice, custom is an unlikely source of an implied term. For a case where a term was implied by trade custom, see *Smith v Wilson* (below, Chapter 7, p 158).

Where the parties are at cross-purposes

In a case where one party intends to contract on a particular set of terms and the other party accepts, thinking he is accepting a different set, the contract will be void for uncertainty only if, taking an objective view, it is not possible to say what the terms of the contract were.

Raffles v Wichelhaus (1864)

R sold W 125 bales of cotton to arrive *ex peerless* from Bombay. The cotton was shipped on a vessel called the *Peerless* which sailed in December. W thought that the ship which was meant by R was a ship called *The Peerless* which sailed from Bombay in October. Consequently, when the cotton arrived W refused to take delivery. R sued for breach of contract. *Held*: because of the latent ambiguity, W was not liable.

Scriven Bros v Hindley (1913)

S employed N, an auctioneer, to sell hemp and tow. Hemp is of greater value than tow. Two separate lots were mentioned in the catalogue: one of 47 bales and the other of 176 bales. However, the catalogue failed to state that one lot was hemp and the other lot tow. The goods had arrived on the same ship and bore the same shipping mark. It was highly unusual for two different commodities to bear the same shipping mark. H's manager examined the hemp but not the tow because he was not interested in bidding for tow. H's buyer made a bid for tow believing it was hemp: the bid was high for tow. The auctioneer realised that the bid was high but thought that the bidder was making a mistake as to value of tow. *Held*: there was no contract since H thought they were buying hemp when S was selling tow.

On the other hand, a party cannot be allowed to escape the consequences of his contract simply by alleging that he has made a mistake. If the mistake of the mistaken party is not induced by a misrepresentation or latent ambiguity, the contract will stand: that is, if, on an objective view of what the parties said or wrote, there appears to be a contract, the court will give damages for its breach, or may make an order for specific performance of the contract.

Tamplin v James (1880)

An inn and adjoining shop were put up for sale by auction. Behind the premises were two pieces of garden which had been used by the inn and the shop but were not owned by the sellers. The particulars of sale did not mention the gardens nor did the plans of the property being auctioned. The lot was not sold at the auction but the defendant bought it immediately afterwards by private treaty. He then refused to complete the sale. He argued that he thought the gardens were included in the sale since he knew that they were used by the shop and the pub. *Held*: in the absence of any misrepresentation by the plaintiff, the court would order specific performance of the contract. To do otherwise would make it too easy for a person to escape the consequences of their bargain by asserting they had made a mistake.

However, looking at the matter objectively, there may be a contract, for the breach of which the law will give damages, but equity will refuse to exercise its discretion to give the equitable remedy of specific performance. This happened in *Wood v Scarth* (1855), where the defendant agreed to grant the lease of some premises to the plaintiff. Negotiations were conducted through the defendant's agent, who, in addition to the rent payable, was supposed to have agreed a premium of £500 to be paid by the plaintiff to the defendant. The agent concluded the contract without mention of the premium. When the defendant discovered this, he refused to execute the lease. The plaintiff claimed specific performance of the contract. *Held*: it would cause undue hardship to the defendant if specific performance of the contract were granted. Nevertheless, in a separate action, the plaintiff was granted damages for breach of contract.

CHAPTER 5

CONSIDERATION

A person wishing to enforce a contractual promise must show that he or she has provided *consideration* for it.

Consideration consists of a *promise* to confer a *benefit* on the other party or a promise to do something which is *detrimental* to one's self. An *act* which has the effect of conferring a benefit or which amounts to a detriment may also be a consideration. In a bilateral contract, the consideration will have the dual effect of being beneficial to the other party and detrimental to one's self. For example, if Amrat promises to sell Barry a computer for £1,000, Amrat will confer the benefit of the computer on Barry and will undergo the detriment of losing the ownership of the computer. Conversely, Barry will confer the benefit of £1,000 on Amrat and will undergo the detriment of losing the £1,000.

If this element of benefit or detriment is not present, the promise will be unenforceable. For example, Clara has promised to give David £500 on his 21st birthday: David cannot sue for the money if Clara refuses to pay. The reason is that David has given no consideration for Clara's promise. David has not conferred, or promised to confer, a benefit on Clara or undergone, or promised to undergo, a detriment to himself.

PURPOSE OF CONSIDERATION

Consideration originally acted as a filter mechanism to decide whether or not a promise should be enforced: promises which were given for a consideration were enforceable, those which were not given for a consideration were not enforceable. As such, under classical contract law, consideration was regarded as a fundamental ingredient of a contract and it meant that gratuitous promises could not be enforced unless they were made by 'deed'.

Promises contained in a formal document called a 'deed' are an exception to the rule that promises made without consideration will not be enforced. At common law, a deed had to be signed, sealed and delivered in order to be effective. It also had to be witnessed. The Law of Property Act 1989 has removed the requirement for a deed to be sealed, where it is made by an individual and also where it is made by a company incorporated under the Companies Acts, providing it is signed by a director and the company secretary or by two directors, and the document makes it clear that it is intended to be a deed of the company. The other common law requirements still apply, though you should note that 'delivered' in this context does not mean that possession has been transferred, as it does in the context of a sale of goods, for example. It simply means that the person intending to be bound by it has conducted himself to that effect. In addition to not requiring consideration, a deed has the further distinguishing characteristic that the limitation period (that is, the period within which a legal action must be brought to enforce the deed) is 12 years in contrast to the six years which applies to a contract not made by deed.

Nowadays, as we shall see, the law has developed to the extent where virtually any promise made in a commercial context, except for one which is clearly gratuitous, is treated as having been made for a consideration and is, therefore, enforceable.

Incidentally, it is a common misconception that a contract cannot be enforced unless one party has actually carried out at least part of his or her promised consideration, for example, has given a deposit to the other party as part of the agreed purchase price. This is not correct. Provided there has been an exchange of promises whereby each party will provide something of value, each promise is enforceable in the sense that if one party refuses to perform his or her part of the bargain the other may sue for damages.

DEFINITION OF CONSIDERATION

The two most commonly quoted definitions of consideration are:

(a) a valuable consideration ... may consist either in some right, interest, profit or benefit accruing to one party, or some forbearance, detriment, loss or responsibility given, suffered or undertaken by the other;

Currie v Misa (1875)

The main criticism of this definition is that it fails to make it clear that the promisee (that is, the person to whom the promise has been made and who is trying to enforce it) does not need to have actually given the benefit, etc, or suffered the detriment, etc, for him to have given consideration. It is sufficient if the promisee has *promised* to give benefit or suffer detriment.

(b) an act or forbearance of one party or the promise thereof, is the price for which the promise of the other is bought, and the promise thus given for value is enforceable. (*Dunlop v Selfridge* (1915), Lord Dunedin (quoting Pollock, *Principles of Contract*, 8th edn, p 175).)

This definition emphasises the importance of the promise in that it indicates clearly that on one side of the equation there is always a promise, whether the contract is bilateral (or multilateral) or whether it is unilateral.

In a bilateral contract, the equation is:

promise = promise.

In a unilateral contract, the equation is:

act or forbearance = promise.

It must be pointed out that while this is the theory, there may be some difficulty in fitting the theory to situations that arise in practice.

SUFFICIENCY OF CONSIDERATION

To amount to a valid consideration, the consideration must be 'sufficient' (sometimes expressed as 'valuable', sometimes as 'real').

What this means is that the consideration must be something of value in the eyes of the law. It has been argued that a valid consideration should have an economic value. However, there are a number of cases where the act or promise that was found by the court to be the consideration was of doubtful economic value.

An early case on the sufficiency of consideration held that it was no consideration to promise to refrain from doing what one had no right to do. Nowadays, the case might well be decided on the basis that it was a family arrangement in which there was no intention to create a legal relationship.

White v Bluett (1853)

A father lent his son a sum of money in respect of which the son executed a promissory note (that is, a written promise to repay the money) in favour of his father. Later, the father died and the father's executors sued the son on the promissory note. The son's defence was that his father had told him he would regard the promissory note as having been discharged if the son would refrain from complaining about the father's (admitted) unfair treatment of the son in relation to the distribution of the father's property among his children. The son did cease to complain and argued that, because of this, the promissory note should be discharged. *Held*: a promise to refrain from doing something which one had no right to do was not a sufficient consideration.

In a relatively modern case, it was held that wrappers from bars of chocolate amounted to consideration.

Chappell v Nestlé Co (1960)

C owned the copyright to a piece of music called 'Rockin' Shoes'. Section 8 of the Copyright Act 1956 permitted a person to make a record of a musical work for the purpose of selling it retail, providing that the copyright owner was given notice that this was being done and was paid a royalty of $6^{1/4}\%$ of the normal retail selling price. N approached H, who were record manufacturers, and asked them to produce a record of 'Rockin' Shoes' which was to be sold to persons who, having bought three bars of Nestlé's chocolate, sent in the wrappers, together with 1s 6d. H gave notice of their intention to use the song and to pay C a royalty of 6.25% of 1s 6d. C refused to accept this, since 1s 6d was substantially below the price at which normal commercially produced records were sold. They sued for breach of copyright, arguing that the three wrappers were part of the consideration for the record. *Held*, by the House of Lords: the wrappers were part of the consideration, even though they were of no direct value to Nestlé and were thrown away when received. Lord Somervell stated:

> A contracting party can stipulate for what he chooses. A peppercorn does not cease to be good consideration if it is established that the promisee does not like pepper and will throw away the corn.

CONSIDERATION MUST BE SUFFICIENT BUT NEED NOT BE ADEQUATE

On first sight this rule appears to represent a contradiction in terms. To most laypeople 'sufficient' means the same as 'adequate'. However, what the rule means is that although consideration must be sufficient to support a contract (that is, it must have some value in the eyes of the law), it need not be adequate in the sense that it matches in value the consideration of the other party.

Thomas v Thomas (1842)

The plaintiff was the widow and the defendant the executor of J Thomas, deceased. The defendant had entered into an agreement with the plaintiff, whereby the defendant would convey to the plaintiff a life interest in the former matrimonial home for as long as she should remain a widow and unmarried, on the payment of £1 per annum towards the ground rent and on promising to keep the premises in good and tenantable repair. The reason the defendant entered into this agreement was because the late J Thomas had wished it. The plaintiff now complained that the defendant had not kept his part of the bargain. The defendant argued that there was no consideration for his promise. *Held*: although the wishes of the deceased could not amount to consideration, the promise by the widow to pay £1 per annum and to keep the premises in good repair was a sufficient consideration.

Thus, an essentially gratuitous promise (that is, one which is tantamount to a gift) can be enforced providing the promisee has given a nominal consideration which the court is prepared to regard as sufficient. For example, a kindly farmer may allow the local football team to use one of his meadows as a football field, for a nominal consideration of, say, 5p per annum. (Why not let them have it free of charge? The answer is that it is possible for a non-owner of land to become its owner by a rule of law called 'adverse possession'. This is not possible if the owner asserts his ownership by charging a rent, however nominal.) A peppercorn (see the quote from Lord Somervell, above) has been traditionally used as a nominal consideration. Note, however, that in insolvency proceedings any contract to sell assets at an inordinately low price is liable to be set aside.

THE COMPROMISE OF A LEGAL CLAIM

Most legal cases are compromised before they reach a court hearing. The compromise often takes the form of one party offering a sum of money in settlement of the claim and the other party accepting the settlement and agreeing to discontinue his action. Suppose Helen, driving her car carelessly, runs into Ivy and then, under the threat of legal action, Helen promises to pay Ivy an agreed sum in damages. This agreement creates a contract. Thus, if Helen fails to pay the money, Ivy may rely on the contract as evidence of her entitlement to it. She does not need to prove the original act of negligence which gave rise to the compromise agreement: the law regards Ivy as having given consideration for Helen's promise, by virtue of the fact that she agreed to give up her right of action against Helen for negligence.

However, what is the position if the legal right which was given up was non-existent, so that, in effect, the claimant has given nothing for the defendant's promise to pay? Is the giving up of a worthless claim a sufficient consideration for the defendant's promise to pay?

Example

Fred verbally agrees to sell Graham a house. Fred changes his mind and Graham threatens to sue for breach of contract. If Graham's claim went to court, the court would almost certainly hold that Fred's promise was not actionable as a breach of contract since it was not made in writing, as required by s 2 of the Law of Property (Miscellaneous Provisions) Act 1989. However, neither of the parties is aware of this, and, in consequence, Fred agrees to pay Graham an agreed sum in damages if he will refrain from taking the matter to court. On discovering the legal position, Fred refuses to pay the agreed sum.

It would seem that, despite the probable invalidity of Graham's claim, the law will enforce Fred's promise to pay as a contract. A practical reason was given by Bowen LJ in *Miles v New Zealand Alford Estate Co* (1886), where he said that the reality of a claim that was compromised must be judged, not by the state of the law as it is ultimately discovered to be, but by the state of the knowledge of the person who concedes the claim. If the law were otherwise, then every claim would have to be tried in court to determine whether it was valid or not, before it could be compromised!

Where the mistake of the parties is one of *fact* rather than *law*, it may be that there is an equitable jurisdiction which will set the contract aside.

Magee v Pennine Insurance Co (1969)

It was stated on an insurance proposal form, filled in by a third party and signed by M, that M held a provisional licence. It named his two sons as drivers. Their licence details were entered correctly. Several years and several renewals later, the car was being driven by the younger son (for whom, in fact, it had been bought) when it was involved in a crash. The insurance company agreed to pay M £385 in settlement of his claim against them. Before the money had been paid, the insurers found out that the statement that M had held a provisional licence was untrue – in fact he had never held a licence. The insurers refused to pay on the grounds that they were entitled to avoid the contract because of M's mis-statement. M sued to enforce the compromise contract. The court found as a fact that M had not been dishonest in making his statement. However, the Court of Appeal found that as the contract of compromise had been made under a fundamental mistake as to the true facts, the contract could, in equity, be set aside.

PAST CONSIDERATION IS NO CONSIDERATION

There are two situations in which the law regards a promised consideration as being past and therefore the person to whom it has been promised cannot sue to enforce it.

The first example of past consideration is where one party to a contract makes an additional promise to the other party which is not part of the promises which form the offer and acceptance.

Roscorla v Thomas (1842)

The plaintiff paid the defendant £30 for a horse. After the contract was made, the defendant promised that the horse was sound and free from vice. The plaintiff sued on this promise. *Held:* because the promise came after the sale, the consideration for the promise was past.

However, the mere fact that a promise is to be performed at a future date does not make it past consideration. It is quite customary to make promises which are to be carried out in the future and, providing the promise forms part of the offer and acceptance, it is regarded as having been given for a valid consideration.

Similarly, if *both* parties were to make a further promise, each promise would be regarded as consideration for the other and therefore the parties would have validly varied their original contract.

The second situation in which past consideration arises is where one party does an act voluntarily and subsequently the person who has benefited from the act promises to pay for it.

Re McArdle (1951)

A person voluntarily carried out improvements to a house. After she had done the improvements, the owners signed a paper promising to reimburse her for the work. When she sued on the promise she failed because the consideration on which she relied was past.

Exceptions to the rule

There are three exceptions to the rule that past consideration is no consideration. These are:

(a) *Where an act or service is performed, and a subsequent promise to pay for it or confer some other benefit on the promisee is made, the subsequent promise is enforceable if:*

   (i) the act or service was performed at the request of the other party;

   (ii) it was assumed from the outset by both parties that the act or service was to be paid for; and

   (iii) the promise would have been legally enforceable if it had been promised in advance.

The first of these conditions was laid down in the old case of *Lampleigh v Braithwaite* (1615).

Lampleigh v Braithwaite (1615)

B, having killed a man, asked L to try to obtain a pardon for him. L did so, riding to Royston to see the King. In consideration of this, B agreed to pay L £100. L sued for the money and B pleaded past consideration. *Held*: a 'mere voluntary courtesy' (for example, if L had volunteered to ride to see the King) would not amount to a consideration, but consideration was present here because the act in question was performed at the request of the defendant.

The second condition was emphasised in *Re Casey's Patents*.

Re Casey's Patents (1892)

Patents were granted to Stewart and Charlton in respect of an invention. Casey agreed with S that he would 'push' the invention. Later, Stewart wrote to Casey saying: '... in consideration of your services as the practical manager in working ... our patents ... we hereby agree to give you one third share of the patents ...'

The patents were later transferred to Casey and, after the death of Stewart, S's executors wrote asking for the return of the patent. C refused to return it, claiming that he was entitled to a one-third share. One of the questions which arose in the Court of Appeal was whether C had given consideration for the assignment of the one third share, or whether his alleged consideration was past. *Held*: the rendering of the service by C raised the implication that it would be paid for. Normally, the court would fix a reasonable amount of remuneration for the service (a *quantum meruit*). However, as the parties had themselves fixed an amount, that is, a one third share of the patent, the court would accept that as being a reasonable remuneration.

Pao On v Lau Yiu Long is a more complex example.

Pao On v Lau Yiu Long (1980)

PO owned shares in a company called Shing On. The main asset of the company was a building which was under construction. LYL were shareholders in a company called Fu Chip, which wished to acquire the building. In February 1973, PO agreed to sell to Fu Chip their shares in Shing On. (This would make Fu Chip the owner of the building Fu Chip wished to acquire.) The price of the shares was to be the issue to PO of shares in Fu Chip. By selling these shares, PO would get the required price for the building. The value of each share was, at the time, $2.50. PO agreed to retain 60% of the shares allotted to them until after 30 April 1974. (Presumably if they had been allowed to sell all the shares at once, the market in the shares would have become depressed to the detriment of the remaining shareholders in Fu Chip.)

However, a difficulty with this agreement from PO's point of view was that the value of the shares might fall between the date of the contract and 30 April 1974, with the result that PO would not get as much as they had expected from the deal. To guard against this, PO and LYL entered into a subsidiary agreement whereby LYL agreed to buy 60% of the allotted shares from PO on or before 30 April at $2.50 per share. Thus, PO was guaranteed a price of $2.50.

In April 1973, after the agreements had been made but before the main agreement had been carried out, PO realised that the subsidiary agreement did not give them the opportunity of any profit, should the shares *rise* in price before 30 April 1974. Therefore, PO refused to complete the main agreement with Fu Chip unless LYL agreed to cancel the subsidiary agreement and replace it with a different agreement which would not require LYL to buy the shares but would require LYL to *indemnify* PO should the value of the shares fall below $2.50. The sale of the building under the main agreement then took place. PO retained 60% of the shares in Fu Chip as agreed, until 30 April 1974, at which date the share value was below $2.50. LYL refused to indemnify PO, arguing, among other things, that the consideration for their promise was past. *Held* by the Privy Council: PO's promise not to sell the shares until 30 April 1974 was a sufficient consideration for LYL's subsequent promise since: (i) the promise not to sell was at the request of LYL; and (ii) the parties understood at the time the main agreement was made that the restriction on selling the shares must be compensated for by the benefit of a guarantee against a drop in price; and (iii) such a guarantee was legally enforceable.

The rule regarding past consideration means, for example, that if after having negotiated a contract, one party promises an increase in price (unless, of course, the contract itself contains an appropriate price variation clause), the promise to pay the additional amount is unenforceable, since it has been given without a matching consideration. However, although the courts have upheld this principle in theory, in practice, in the interests of commercial expediency, they have proved willing to circumvent this rule and hold that the promise to pay the additional amount is enforceable (see, for example, *Williams v Roffey Bros* below).

(b) *Section 25 of the Limitation Act 1980*

This provides that no action may be brought on a simple contract beyond six years from the date when the cause of action arose. The action is said to be 'statute-barred'. However, s 29 of the Act provides for an extension of the ordinary time limit where the cause of action is a debt on a contract. In such a case, if the debtor acknowledges the debt in writing (or if he part-pays the debt), the six years' limitation begins to run again from the date of the acknowledgment (or part-payment). The debtor cannot argue that the consideration for his written acknowledgment is past (note that neither a written acknowledgment nor a part-payment can revive a debt once it has become statute-barred).

(c) *Section 27 of the Bills of Exchange Act 1882*

In relation to the payment of debts by way of a bill of exchange (of which a cheque is the most common example), s 27 of the Bills of Exchange Act 1882 provides that:

... valuable consideration for a bill may be constituted by:

(i) any consideration sufficient to support a simple contract;

(ii) any antecedent debt or liability.

It is often said that (ii) means that consideration for a bill of exchange may be past consideration. With respect, this view is difficult to support since any antecedent debt or liability created by a past consideration is not a debt or liability. The true effect of the provision seems to be that if a cheque is given in settlement of a statute-barred debt, the antecedent debt is sufficient consideration to allow the payee to sue on the cheque.

Price-variation clauses

Where the parties are entering into a contract which is going to be performed at a date significantly into the future, it is a wise precaution for the supplier to build a price-variation clause into the contract. A properly drafted clause can operate to increase the contract price in the event of inflation, or an unexpected increase in the price of labour or materials, or (in the case of an international contract) a devaluation of the currency in which the contract price is to be paid. If such a clause is not inserted, and one of the events we have mentioned above materialises, the seller may be faced with the dilemma of either completing the contract at a reduced profit (or even at a loss) or refusing to continue with the contract and be confronted with a claim for damages for breach of contract.

Existing obligations as consideration

Sometimes a party will rely on an existing legal or contractual duty as his consideration for the promise of the other party. This is the case where one party asks for an increase in price from the other party because he has underpriced the contract. If a price variation clause has been inserted in the original contract, there will be no difficulty in raising the price in accordance with the terms of the clause. If there is no price variation clause, the problem of consideration arises.

For example, Rex agrees to build an extension to Sarah's hotel for a price of £200,000. Because of an increase in the price of materials, Rex requires a further payment of £20,000 if he is to make a reasonable profit on the deal. In such a case, Sarah is legally entitled to refuse to make any additional payment. However, if Rex's response to Sarah's refusal is to say that he will do no further work on the extension, this may place Sarah in difficulties. On the one hand, she would succeed in an action against Rex for breach of contract. On the other hand, bringing the action would be costly, stressful and time-consuming and there is no guarantee that, at the conclusion of the case, Rex would have the financial ability to pay any award of damages. There is the further problem that Sarah would have to hire a different contractor to finish the job. This would inevitably lead to delay and additional cost. Although in theory this would be borne by Rex, in practice the plaintiff never recovers entirely what the breach of contract has cost him, even assuming the defendant can afford to pay.

The most practical way out will normally be for Sarah to accede to Rex's request for the additional £20,000. However, in such a case the classical law of contract would regard Rex as having provided no consideration. Because he is already contractually bound to do what he is promising to do as his consideration (that is, build the extension), he is really providing nothing in return for Sarah's promise to pay the additional £20,000. He therefore would not be able to enforce Sarah's promise to pay the additional £20,000.

Although the attitude of the classical law is logical, it does not, as we have seen, accord with commercial realities. However, as we shall see, the attitude of the law towards this strict view of consideration appears to be changing.

The reason for the attitude of the classical law seems to be partly related to public policy: that is, it is contrary to public policy to allow an existing legal duty or an existing contractual duty to be used as a base for further bargaining between the parties, since it might lead to one party imposing undue pressure on the other. Denning LJ argued that in cases where no issues of public policy arise, agreement to perform an existing duty should be valid consideration because it confers a benefit on the promisee: see *Williams v Williams* (1957). The subsequent Court of Appeal decision in *Williams v Roffey Bros* (1990) (see below) appears to have gone a substantial way towards adopting the view of Denning LJ. The case has far-reaching implications. It appears to decide that where an additional promise is exacted from one party subsequent to the original contract, as an additional price for the carrying out of the original obligation, this may constitute a consideration sufficient to allow the promisee to sue on the promise.

It remains to be seen what effect the decision in *Williams v Roffey Bros* will have in the longer term and it is, therefore, necessary to place the case in the context of the pre-existing law.

Duties laid down by law and duties laid down by contract

An existing obligation may take the form of a duty laid down by law or a duty laid down by contract.

Duty laid down by law

If the plaintiff has promised to do a duty which he is bound by law to do, he is not regarded as having provided consideration.

Collins v Godfroy (1831)

G promised C that he would reimburse him for his loss of time while acting as a witness at a trial involving G. G subpoenaed C as a witness. C attended for six days but wasn't called. He sued G upon his promise to pay. *Held:* C had given no consideration for G's promise to pay since he was bound by law to act as a witness when he was subpoenaed to do so. (Note that nowadays, a subpoenaed witness is entitled to payment.)

Duty under a contract

Where the promisee is already bound by contract to the promisor to carry out his promise, the law doesn't regard him as having given good consideration for the promise.

Stilk v Myrick (1809)

The plaintiff, a seaman, had agreed to sail with a ship to the Baltic and back at a wage of £5 per month. During the course of the voyage, two of the seamen had deserted. The captain, having vainly tried to fill the jobs of the two deserters at Cronstadt, agreed with the remainder of his crew that they should split the wages of the two deserters between them should they be unable to fill the vacancies at Gothenberg. The vacancies remained unfilled and the ship sailed home short-handed. The plaintiff sued for his share of the deserters' wages. *Held:* there was no consideration for the captain's promise (in that the seamen were only agreeing to do what they were already bound to do).

Exceptions to the above rules

(a) *If the promisee promises to do* more *than the duty imposed upon him by* law, *or by* contract, *he will have supplied sufficient consideration for the other party's promise.*

Glasbrook Bros v Glamorgan CC (1925)

Glasbrook owned a colliery near Swansea. The mine's employees were on strike and, following a hostile demonstration by 500 to 600 of the workers, the colliery manager was informed that the strikers were going to get the safety men out on strike. Unless the safety men went into work, the mine would quickly be flooded. The colliery manager then asked the local police to billet 100 men on colliery premises in order to protect the safety men. Otherwise, the safety men wouldn't come in to work as they were frightened. The police superintendent was of the opinion that it would be sufficient to keep a mobile force at the ready. They would be able to respond quickly enough if the apprehended danger to the safety men materialised. However, if police were to be billeted at the colliery, a force of 70 would be sufficient. The colliery manager agreed to have 70 men billeted at the colliery and to pay the police authority specified rates per day for the services of the men, plus travelling expenses. The colliery also agreed to feed them and to provide sleeping accommodation. The total bill came to around £2,000. Glasbrook refused to pay on the ground that the police were bound by law to provide protection. The police authority sued for the money. Glasbrook counterclaimed for around £1,300, this being the cost of feeding and housing the policemen who guarded the colliery. *Held,* by the House of Lords: although the police were under a duty to provide protection, they had a discretion as to what form the protection should take. In this case they thought that a mobile force would be sufficient. Since the respondents had insisted on a resident garrison, the police, in agreeing to provide it, had given consideration sufficient to support Glasbrook's promise to pay.

In relation to contractual duties, the case of *Hartley v Ponsonby* (1857) is illustrative of a promise to perform more than the original contract required and, therefore, to provide consideration.

Hartley v Ponsonby (1857)

A ship had left England with a crew of 36, but on arrival in Port Phillip a number of the crew deserted, leaving only 19, of whom only four or five were able seamen. The captain tried to recruit fresh crewmen but failed. He therefore promised the plaintiff, an able seaman, and the rest of the able seamen, a remuneration of £40 if they would assist in sailing the ship from Port Phillip to Bombay with a crew of 19 hands. The ship reached Bombay safely, the plaintiff having carried out his duty. On arrival in Liverpool, he was paid his normal remuneration but was refused the extra £40. *Held:* because the ship was unseaworthy being sailed by only 19 men, the plaintiff would have been within his rights to refuse to sail from Port Phillip to Bombay. He was, therefore, able to make that voyage the subject of a fresh contract between himself and the ship's captain.

Modern willingness to find consideration

In modern cases, the willingness to find a consideration moving from the promisee in circumstances where a consideration consisted of an existing legal or contractual duty began to become quite pronounced, particularly in a Court of Appeal influenced by Lord Denning MR (as he became).

Ward v Byham (1956)

W was the mother of an illegitimate child and B was the father. B and W co-habited until B threw W out of the house. B then paid a neighbour £1 per week to look after the child. When W secured a position as a housekeeper, she asked for the child to come and live with her and asked for the £1 per week to maintain the child. The father replied that he was willing to let her have the child and pay the £1 per week allowance, providing that W could prove that the child would be well looked after and happy and providing that the child was allowed to decide for herself whether or not she wished to live with W. The child opted to live with her mother and B paid the £1 per week until W married her employer. B then stopped the payments and W sued. B's defence was that under s 42 of the National Assistance Act 1948, the mother of an illegitimate child had a duty to maintain it. Therefore, W was only promising to do what she was already under a legal duty to do and had therefore not provided consideration for B's promise to pay. The Court of Appeal held that B was bound by his agreement. Morris and Parker LJJ were of the opinion that W had provided consideration in that she had promised to do more than the duty imposed upon her by statute in that she had promised to look after the child well and see that it was happy and let it decide for itself who it wished to live with. Denning LJ, on the other hand, thought that the performance of an existing duty ought to be good consideration since it confers a benefit on the promisee.

In *Williams v Roffey Bros* (1990), the Court of Appeal built on the propositions put forward by Denning LJ in *Ward v Byham* (1956) and gave a judgment which affirms that a promise to perform an existing contractual obligation can amount to consideration, providing its effect is to confer a benefit on the promisee.

Williams v Roffey Bros (1990)

R contracted with the Shepherd's Bush Housing Association to refurbish 27 flats in a block called Twynholm Mansions. On 21 January 1986, R subcontracted the carpentry work to W for an agreed price of £20,000. By the end of March, W was in financial difficulties because the agreed price was too low for him to operate at a profit. The main contract contained a time penalty clause (that is, a stipulation that the main contractor would pay certain sums to the Housing Association if the contract were not completed on time). On 9 April, at which time W had completed the work on the roof and nine flats and partially completed the other 18 flats, R agreed to pay W an extra £10,300. This represented £575 for each further flat completed and was promised because of R's fear that they would incur a penalty if W did not complete the carpentry on time. The issue of consideration (there was also the issue of partial performance which it is unnecessary to consider here) was whether the promise to complete an existing obligation was sufficient to support the promise to pay the extra money. Classical theorists would say no, basing their answer on *Stilk v Myrick* (1809). However, we have seen that in the modern era there has been some dissatisfaction with the classical law. In the present case, it was held that the defendants secured a benefit by their promise to pay the additional amounts and that, therefore, the plaintiffs had provided a consideration. Glidewell LJ summarised the law as follows:

(a) if A has entered into a contract with B to do work for, or supply goods or services to B in return for payment by B; and

(b) at some stage before A has completely performed his obligations under the contract B has reason to doubt whether A will, or will be able to, complete his side of the bargain; and

(c) B thereupon promises A an additional payment in return for A's promise to perform his contractual obligations on time; and

(d) as a result of giving his promise, B obtains in practice a benefit, or obviates a disbenefit; and

(e) B's promise is not given as a result of economic duress or fraud on the part of A; then

(f) the benefit to B is capable of being consideration for B's promise, so that the promise will be legally binding.

All three judges affirmed the correctness of the decision in *Stilk v Myrick*, but in the view of Glidewell LJ:

> It is not ... surprising that a principle enunciated in relation to the rigours of
> seafaring life during the Napoleonic wars should be subjected during the
> succeeding 180 years to a process of refinement and limitation in its application
> in the present day.

One important circumstance in which the courts will be unwilling to find a
benefit in the performance of an existing contractual obligation, was laid
down in *Re Selectmove* (1995). In that case it was held that the ruling in
Williams v Roffey Bros could not apply in circumstances where the existing
obligation was to pay a sum of money rather than to provide goods or
services. Thus, if a creditor agrees to accept the payment of a lump-sum debt
by instalments, this cannot amount to a contractual agreement (though, as we
shall see when we come to examine promissory estoppel, the agreement may
not be entirely devoid of legal effect).

Relevance of economic duress

A further factor to be taken into account where a contract is renegotiated, is
that if a party threatens that he will not perform his obligations unless the
other party makes an additional promise (usually to pay an additional sum of
money), such a threat may amount to economic duress. Let us return to our
example of Rex and Sarah, given earlier in the chapter. Suppose that Rex
knows that Sarah is desperate to have the extension to her hotel completed on
time, since she has taken substantial bookings for it and will suffer
considerable loss if the extension is not completed on time. Rex refuses to
continue work unless Sarah promises him the extra £20,000 he is demanding.
A court may decide that this amounts to economic duress. If this is the case,
the promise to pay the extra money is voidable (that is, can become void) at
Sarah's option.

North Ocean Shipping v Hyundai Construction Co (1979)

Here, H agreed to build a ship for N at a fixed price of US $30,950,000. N
agreed to pay the price in five instalments as the work progressed. H agreed
to open a letter of credit to provide security for the repayment of the
instalments should H default in performance of the contract. N paid the first
instalment on April 28 1972. On 12 February 1973, the US dollar was
devalued. H therefore claimed an increase of 10% on the four remaining
instalments. N didn't agree that any increase was due and offered to submit
the disagreement to arbitration. H declined the offer and told N that if N
didn't agree to the extra 10%, H would terminate the contract and refund the
first instalment. If they had done this, N would have had a clear action for
breach of contract. However, N had entered into a very advantageous
agreement with Shell whereby the new vessel would be chartered to Shell for
a period of three years, and they would have lost this contract if H had carried
out their threat. (Note: damages to compensate for the loss of this specially

lucrative contract would probably not have been recoverable if H had carried out their threat to repudiate the contract and N had sued for breach of contract in consequence: see *Victoria Laundry v Newman* (1949).) N, therefore, told H that although N were under no obligation to make additional payments to H, they were prepared to make the additional payments without prejudice to their rights. They added that no doubt H would increase their letter of credit correspondingly. H replied promising to increase the letter of credit. The increases in the instalments and in the letter of credit were duly effected and the tanker was delivered on 27 November 1974.

On 30 July 1975, N claimed the return of the excess 10%. They explained that they had refrained from reclaiming the money until then because H had another ship under construction for N, and N were afraid that if they sued before the other tanker had been delivered, H might have refused to deliver it. It was held by Mocatta J that the promise to increase the letter of credit was consideration for N's promise to increase the instalments. Thus, the exception in *Hartley v Ponsonby* (above) applied.

His Lordship then had to consider whether N could recover the additional 10% because it had been paid under coercion. It was held that the extra 10% had been paid under economic duress, and this made the contract to pay the 10% voidable. However, since the power to set aside a contract on the ground of economic duress is an equitable one, the maxim of equity which states that 'delay defeats equities' is applicable. N had delayed in making their claim. Because of this, they must be taken to have affirmed the contract and thus were not entitled to the repayment of the 10%.

Note:

(a) that the distinction between hard bargaining to protect one's own interests, which is legitimate, and economic pressure sufficient to amount to duress, which is not legitimate, may be a fine one. For example, in the *Pao On* case (above), the facts of which did not, in principle, differ greatly from the *North Ocean Shipping* case, it was held that there had been no duress, simply hard bargaining;

(b) a contractual obligation to one party can be made the subject of a fresh contract with a third party. This is so even though no additional promise is made.

Scotson v Pegg (1861)

S had contracted with a third party, T, that they would deliver a cargo of coal to T or to the order of T. T sold this cargo to P and T directed S to deliver the coal to P. P subsequently made an agreement with S whereby 'in consideration that S, at the request of P, would deliver to the defendant' the cargo of coal, P promised to unload it at a stated rate. S sued P because P failed to honour the agreement. P pleaded that S had given no consideration for his promise, since he was already under a contractual duty to T to deliver the coal. *Held*: S succeeded. Wilde B thought that S might have found it advantageous not to comply with his contract with T, so that S's contract with P was a detriment to him. Further, S agreed to part with the cargo to P which was a benefit to P.

In *New Zealand Shipping Company v Satterthwaite* (1975), Lord Wilberforce, delivering the majority opinion of the Privy Council, said:

> An obligation to do an act which the promisor is already under an existing obligation to do, may quite well amount to valid consideration and does so in the present case: the promisee obtains the benefit of a direct obligation, which he can enforce. This proposition is supported and illustrated by *Scotson v Pegg* which their Lordships consider to be good law.

Before *Williams v Roffey Bros* tidied up the law, there existed the anomalous situation where if A was under a contractual obligation to B, he could make the existing obligation the subject of a fresh contract with C. He could not, however, make it subject to a fresh contract with B without agreeing to do something additional in order to form the 'consideration' element.

PART-PAYMENT OF DEBT

Where the promisee is under an existing contractual duty to pay a debt, but the creditor has agreed to accept part-payment of it in full settlement of the debt, the question which arises is the reverse of that which arose in *Stilk v Myrick* (above). In that case, the question was whether the promisee had given consideration for the promisor's promise to pay something additional to the contracted wages. In the case where the part-payment of a debt is accepted in full satisfaction for the debt, the question arises as to whether the promisee has given consideration for the promisor's promise to forgo the remainder of the debt.

At common law, the rule is that part-payment of a debt is no satisfaction for the whole debt. This rule is known as the rule in *Pinnel*'s case, although the rule had been part of the law of England for more than a century before *Pinnel*'s case was heard.

Pinnel's case (1602)

Pinnel sued Cole on a debt of £8 10s due on 11 November 1600. Cole's defence was that he had paid Pinnel £5 2s 6d on 1 October and that Pinnel had accepted this as full satisfaction for the debt. The court affirmed that payment of a lesser sum on the due day in satisfaction of a greater sum cannot be any satisfaction for the whole debt.

The rule was the subject of some criticism since critics, although accepting the need for consideration at the creation of the contract, could see no logic in requiring consideration to be provided in a situation concerned with the discharge of a contract. (However, if one thinks in terms of enforcement of promises, which appears to be the approach of the common law, it is immaterial *when* the promise is made: the simple rule is that a promise for which no consideration has been given will not be enforced.)

That this is the case was confirmed by the House of Lords in an 1884 judgement underpinning the rule in *Pinnel's* case.

Foakes v Beer (1884)

B had obtained judgment against F for £2,090 19s for debt and costs. F agreed to settle the judgment by paying £500 down and £150 per half-year until the whole debt was paid, and B agreed not to take any further action should the sum of £2,090 19s be duly paid. F paid the £2,090 19s. However, judgment debts bear interest, and interest of £360 had accrued on the debt. F refused to pay the interest, arguing that he had kept to his part of the agreement and that B had agreed to take no further action on the judgment if he did so. B sued for the interest. *Held*: she was entitled to the money. Her promise to take no further action was not supported by any consideration moving from F.

Exceptions to the rule in *Pinnel's* case

Three exceptions to the rule in *Pinnel's* case were confirmed in the case itself. The exceptions laid down in the case were:

   (a) payment of a smaller sum at the creditor's request before the due day is good consideration for the creditor's promise to forgo the balance, since it is to the creditor's benefit to be paid early and early payment is a detriment to the debtor;

   (b) payment of part of the debt at a different place to the place it is due is sufficient satisfaction because again the creditor receives a benefit and the debtor suffers a detriment; and

   (c) payment of the debt in kind rather than in cash is a sufficient satisfaction, since it is up to the creditor what value he places on a non-monetary consideration:

     ... the gift of a horse, hawk or robe, etc, in satisfaction is good. For it shall be intended that a horse, hawk, or robe, etc, might be more beneficial to the plaintiff than the money in respect of some circumstance, or otherwise the plaintiff would not have accepted it in satisfaction ...

Two further exceptions emerged later (there were, in fact, three, but since the third is no longer an exception we will not consider it here).

Compositions with creditors

Sometimes an insolvent debtor will make a composition with his creditors whereby he agrees to pay each of them a proportion of the debt which is owing to them. This is generally advantageous to both parties, since the creditors tend to get more than they would if the debtor was made bankrupt and the debtor avoids certain of the disadvantages of being made bankrupt.

The difficulty arises if, despite the agreement, one creditor seeks to enforce his right to the remainder of the debt owing to him. What is the consideration for his promise to forgo the balance of his debt? As between the creditors themselves, no doubt the mutual promises to forgo the balance of their debt would be sufficient consideration. However, the debtor cannot rely on this consideration.

A pragmatic solution to the problem is to say that an individual debtor may not sue in defiance of the agreement he has made with the remainder, since such an action would be a fraud on the remainder. This solution was adopted in *Woods v Robarts* (1818) and *Cook v Lister* (1863). It is a solution of convenience rather than principle.

Where a third party part-pays the debt of another

A similar problem arises where a third party part-pays the debt of another, having extracted a promise from the creditor that the part-payment will be treated as full satisfaction for the debt. It would seem that, following the rule in *Pinnel's* case, the debtor has given no consideration for the creditor's promise not to proceed against him on the debt.

Welby v Drake (1825)

D owed W £18. D's father had paid W £9, which W had promised to accept in full satisfaction for the debt. Held: the payment of £9 by D's father operated to discharge the debt. Lord Tenterden CJ said:

> If the father did pay the smaller sum in satisfaction of this debt, it is a bar to the plaintiff's now recovering against the son; because by suing the son, he commits a fraud on the father, whom he induced to advance his money on the faith of such advance being a discharge of his son from further liability.

Thus, again, the problem was solved in a pragmatic way by holding that to sue the son would be committing a fraud against the father.

PROMISSORY ESTOPPEL

Although the exceptions given above are well established exceptions to the rule in *Pinnel's* case, they apply in only very few cases, so that even despite them, the overall application of the rule remained largely untouched. What was required was for an exception to the rule which would apply in the majority of cases. In other words, a new rule was required to which the rule in *Pinnel's* case would become the exception!

The seeds of an appropriate rule were to be found in the *equitable doctrine of waiver*, which had existed for a long time and was a well-established exception to the requirement that to be enforceable, a promise must be supported by consideration.

Hughes v Metropolitan Railway Co (1877)

H had given his tenant MR Co, on 2 October 1874, six months' notice to effect certain repairs in accordance with the terms of the lease. If the repairs were not completed by 22 April 1875 (that is, within six months), MR Co were liable to forfeit the lease. However, in November 1874, MR Co wrote to H offering to sell back the lease (a lease of well-situated business premises can be a valuable asset and is often the subject of a sale) and saying that they would do no work under the repair notice until they heard from H. On 1 December, H replied saying he would consider the matter on hearing the price required. On 30 December, MR Co quoted a price of £3,000. On 31 December, H replied saying that the price asked for 'is out of all reason' and asking for a modified proposal. No other communication was made until 19 April 1875 (three days before the repair notice was due to expire) when MR Co stated that as the negotiations had not resulted in a sale and the weather was now favourable, repairs would commence. H replied that there had been ample time to complete the repairs since the negotiations had broken off at the end of December and on 28 April, H issued a writ to recover the lease from MR Co from the premises on the ground that they had failed to complete the repairs in accordance with the repair notice.

Held by the House of Lords: negotiations for the sale of the lease had had the effect, in equity, of suspending the repair notice. The suspension came to an end on 31 December 1874 and the MR Co were entitled to six months from that date in which to effect the repairs.

Note: it was clear that if the tenants were going to sell the lease, they were not going to embark on the required repairs; in fact, they had said as much to H. H, in undertaking negotiations to buy back the lease, had impliedly promised the MR Co that he would waive his strict legal rights and not enforce the repair notice. When negotiations broke down, the waiver came to an end and H was entitled to resume his strict legal rights.

The principle produced by *Hughes v Metropolitan Railway Co* is called 'waiver'. A waiver is produced where:

(a) one party makes a promise (which may be either express or implied) to the other, that he will not insist upon his strict legal rights under the contract, intending the other party to act on the promise; and

(b) the other relies on the promise by acting on it.

If these conditions are met, the promisor cannot resume his strict legal rights unless it is equitable for him to do so. One situation in which it will normally be equitable to allow a promisor to resume his strict legal rights will be where he gives reasonable notice of his intention to do so to the other party, so that the landlord in *Hughes v Metropolitan Railway Co* was able to resume his strict legal rights to get the repairs done, but only after giving reasonable notice of his intentions.

Waiver is often used where one party to a contract is unable to meet the date agreed for performance. For example, let's suppose that the date agreed for the delivery of goods by A to B is 1 November. A is unable to meet this date and, therefore, B agrees that delivery by 1 December will suffice. B is not then permitted to go back on the waiver he has granted and to resume his strict legal rights by suing A for breach of contract when the goods don't arrive on 1 November.

Sometimes, a waiver is granted without a new time limit being substituted for the old one, in which case the obligation must be completed within a reasonable time.

Charles Rickards v Oppenheim (1950)

R sold Rolls Royce chassis to O. O required a body to be built on the chassis and R agreed to have it built, subcontracting the work. The work was to take six months or, at the most, seven months, and should therefore have been ready by the end of March. The work wasn't completed by the end of March but O continued to press for delivery. Eventually, he wrote to R and said that if the car wasn't ready by 25 July, he would buy another car instead. The car wasn't ready so O bought a replacement. R completed the car in October and then sued O when he refused to take delivery, arguing that he had waived the original time limit and that, therefore, R's obligation was to complete the car within a reasonable time. The Court of Appeal held that O had waived the original delivery date but that he was permitted to resume his right to a delivery date by giving reasonable notice. This he had done.

It was this principle of waiver which was adapted by Denning J (as he was then) to apply to a part-payment of debt. The principle, as it has been applied to cases of part-payment of debt, is called 'promissory estoppel' (estoppel is a rule of evidence which, broadly speaking, 'estops', that is, prevents, a person who makes a statement from later denying the truth of the statement).

Central London Property Trust v High Trees House (known as 'the *High Trees* case') (1947)

Under a lease dated 24 September 1937, HTH leased a block of flats from CLPT for 99 years at an annual rent of £2,500 per annum. HTH then relet the flats to individual tenants. Because of the onset of the war, the flats couldn't be fully let and it became clear to the parties that HTH couldn't pay the rent it owed to CLPT out of the rents received from tenants. It was therefore agreed that the rent should be reduced to £1,250 per annum. HTH paid the reduced rent from 1941 onward. By the beginning of 1945, all the flats in the block were let. On 21 September 1945, CLPT wrote to HTH stating that henceforth the full rent must be paid and stating the amount of arrears back to 1941. CLPT then sued HTH for the full amount of the rent for the quarters ending 29 September and 25 December. The defendants argued:

(a) that there was an agreement that the rent should be £1,250 only and that agreement should last till the end of the lease; alternatively

(b) that the plaintiffs were estopped from alleging that the rent exceeded £1,250 per annum; alternatively

(c) that by failing to demand rent in excess of £1,250 before their letter of 21 September 1945 (received by the defendants on 24 September 1945), CLPT had waived their rights in respect of any rent in excess of £1,250 up to 24 September 1945.

Held by Denning J: a number of cases, including *Hughes v Metropolitan Railway Co* (1877), had established an equitable principle, similar to that of estoppel, to the effect that a party making the kind of promise made by CLPT was not allowed to act inconsistently with it. There was no consideration to support the defendant's contention that the agreement of the plaintiffs to accept half rent constituted a permanent variation of the contract. However, even though the plaintiff's promise was not a contractual promise, it was effective in equity to prevent the plaintiffs from going back on their promise to accept half rent because of the unusual situation brought about by the war. Once war-time conditions were at an end, the plaintiffs were entitled to resume their legal right to the full rent. The plaintiffs were therefore entitled to the full rent they were claiming for the quarters ending 29 September and 25 December 1945. They were, however, 'estopped', by their promise to accept half rent, from trying to reclaim unpaid rent from the earlier period.

The principle established by the *High Trees* case became known as 'promissory estoppel'. The principle of promissory estoppel is as follows:

> If one party, by his conduct, leads another to believe that the strict rights arising under the contract will not be insisted on, intending that the other should act on that belief, and he does act on it, then the first party will not afterwards be allowed to insist on the strict legal rights when it would be inequitable for him to do so ... He may on occasion be able to revert to his strict legal rights for the future by giving reasonable notice in that behalf or otherwise making it plain by his conduct that he will thereafter insist on them. (Lord Denning MR in *WJ Alan & Co v El Nasr Export and Import Co* (1972).)

The similarity between the principle of promissory estoppel, and that of waiver, to which we referred earlier, may be illustrated by the following case.

Brikom Investments v Carr and Others (1979)

In this case, a lease was being negotiated which required tenants to keep the roofs of the building in good repair. The tenants objected that the roofs were in need of substantial repair at that time, which meant that as soon as they signed the lease they would become responsible for repairing a seriously defective roof. The landlord therefore agreed to put the roof into a reasonable state of repair at his own expense. This promise was made in writing to some tenants, and orally to others. Relying on this, the tenants signed the leases which included the repair clause. Subsequently, the plaintiffs repaired the roof but then sought a contribution from the defendants, who included some original tenants and some assignees from the original tenants. In the case of the tenants, it was held that they were not liable since they had the benefit of a collateral contract to the effect that the landlord would carry out the initial repairs. In the case of the assignees, Lord Denning MR thought that promissory estoppel prevented the landlord from claiming against them. Roskill and Cumming-Bruce LJJ thought that the landlord was prevented from enforcing his rights because he had waived them.

Conflict between common law and equity

One difficulty with Denning J's attempt to circumvent the rule in *Pinnel's* case is that the rule had been confirmed by the House of Lords in *Foakes v Beer* (see above), and that no conflicting equitable principle had been mentioned in *Foakes v Beer*. However, Denning J pointed out that at the time *Foakes v Beer* was decided, the principles of equity and common law had only recently been fused, and added that at the present day, when law and equity had been joined together for over 70 years, principles must be reconsidered in the light of their combined effect. This explanation is not entirely convincing, but in view of the fact that, in practice, the principle of promissory estoppel has gained a wide judicial acceptance, it is perhaps rather late to try to argue that it conflicts with *Foakes v Beer* and, therefore, does not exist.

The principle of promissory estoppel, as it is currently applied

Denning J's novel application of the principle that the House of Lords laid down in *Hughes v Metropolitan Railway Co* created some controversy and misunderstanding at first. It was said that he was trying to abolish the doctrine of consideration.

'A shield not a sword'

Denning J soon had an opportunity to restate the doctrine of equitable estoppel in the case of *Coombe v Coombe*. In this case, Denning LJ (as he had now become), emphasised the point he had made in the *High Trees* case to the effect that equitable estoppel cannot be used to justify the *enforcement* of a promise for which no consideration has been given: it can only be used as a *defence* to an action. His colleague, Birkett LJ employed a striking metaphor when he said that the principle must be used 'as a shield not a sword'.

Coombe v Coombe (1951)

Mrs C started divorce proceedings and obtained a decree nisi (this amounts to a provisional decree of divorce). Mr C promised to pay her maintenance of £100 per annum free of tax. He failed to pay and Mrs C sued on the promise. It was found as a fact that there was no consideration for the husband's promise. Nevertheless, Byrne J held that she was entitled to succeed following the equitable principle laid down in the *High Trees* case. The Court of Appeal allowed the husband's appeal on the ground that the equitable principle could be used only as a defence, not as a cause of action.

Note: in *Crabb v Arun District Council* (1976), the plaintiff was permitted to sue on a promise for which he had given no consideration. The principle which permitted this was estoppel, but a *proprietary* estoppel rather than a *promissory* estoppel. Even after the *Crabb* case, it would still appear to be correct law that a promissory estoppel must be used as a defence rather than a cause of action.

Suspensory or extinctive of strict legal rights?

An important question, which has yet to be finally answered in respect of promissory estoppel, is whether the doctrine operates merely to suspend strict legal rights or whether it extinguishes them altogether. In other words, if A promises B that he will accept £50 in full satisfaction for a debt of £100, does this *extinguish* A's right to the balance of £50? On the other hand, does it merely *suspend* A's right so that A can subsequently change his mind and go back on his promise? We have seen that its close relative, waiver, operates to *suspend* strict legal rights and that those rights can be revived on giving reasonable notice. It has been argued that promissory estoppel produces the same effect and that it is, therefore, suspensory in effect.

The judgment of the Privy Council in *Ajayi v Briscoe* (1964) may give some help in answering the question. The Privy Council stated that the doctrine of promissory estoppel operates subject to the following conditions:

(a) that the promisee must have altered his position (presumably in reliance on the promise);

(b) that the promisor can resile from his promise on giving reasonable notice, which need not be formal notice, giving the promisee reasonable opportunity of resuming his position; and

(c) the promise only becomes final and irrevocable if the promisee cannot resume his position.

Lord Denning consistently stated that the doctrine may be extinctive as well as suspensory, and also denied the need for the promisee to act upon the promise other than by observing the new agreement as it stands after the promise. He tended to concentrate his attention on whether or not it was equitable to allow the promisor to go back on his promise. If it was, as it was in the case of *D and C Builders v Rees* (1966) (see below), then the common law rule in *Pinnel's* case will apply. If it is not equitable to allow the promisor to go back on his promise, then the principle of promissory estoppel, as laid down in the *High Trees* case, will apply.

It would seem to be preferable to apply this relatively simple question, that is, whether it is equitable to allow the promisor to go back on his promise in the circumstances, rather than to complicate the issue by requiring the promisee to have altered his position and by indulging in non-productive debates as to whether the doctrine is suspensory or extinctive.

One thing that is clear in relation to contracts of continuing obligation where one of the obligations is suspended, is that if no express or implied time limit for the operation of the waiver had been given, strict legal rights can be resumed on giving reasonable notice.

Tool Metal Manufacturing Co v Tungsten Electric Co (1955)

TM agreed to the suspension of certain contractual terms which required TE to make certain payments to TM. The suspension was pending a new contract being entered into. No payments were made from 1939 onwards. In 1944, negotiations for the new contract broke down. In 1945, TE sued TM for breach of contract and TM counter-claimed for the payments due to them under the contract, not from 1939, but from 1 June 1945. TE's claim failed. The question of TM's counter-claim was then pursued. The Court of Appeal held that TM could demand a resumption of the contractual payments only on giving reasonable notice, and that as they had given no such notice their claim failed. TM then started a second action claiming a resumption of the payments from 1 January 1947 and the question became whether TM's counter-claim in the first action amounted to notice that they intended to resume their legal rights. The House of Lords held that the counter-claim did amount to such notice and, therefore, TM's claim succeeded.

The equitable nature of promissory estoppel

A final point which needs to be made is that promissory estoppel, being of equitable origin, is available only at the discretion of the court (unlike the common law remedy of damages which *must* be given if the claimant makes out his case).

There are a variety of circumstances where the court will refuse to exercise its discretion in favour of a particular claimant. One of particular relevance to promissory estoppel is where the promisee has extorted the promise by applying undue pressure. *'He who seeks equity must do equity'* is one of the principles of equity which means that the person claiming an equitable relief must have behaved equitably himself.

D and C Builders v Rees (1966)

In that case, R had some building work done for him by D and C Builders (Donaldson and Casey). After taking into account a payment made on account, there remained £482 to be paid. The plaintiffs pressed for payment unsuccessfully over a period of several months. Finally, Mrs Rees phoned them and stated that they could have £300 in full settlement and that that was all they would get. Donaldson and Casey talked it over. Their financial position was poor to such an extent that if they didn't get some money urgently, their company would become insolvent. D telephone Mrs Rees, who knew the desperate position that D and C were in, and told her that they would accept the £300 in part-payment and give her a year in which to pay the rest. She refused this, saying that she would never have enough money to pay the balance. She then gave them a choice of £300 or nothing. D accepted the £300, telling her he had 'no choice'. She gave them a choice of receiving a cheque on Saturday or cash on Monday. D opted for the cheque on Saturday and when he went to collect it, took with him a pre-prepared receipt for £300. Mrs R insisted that the words 'in completion of the account' be added to the receipt. D and C then claimed the balance of the account from R. R argued:

(a) that part-payment by cheque, being payment which was different in kind from that in which the debt was due (all debts are due in cash unless the contract states otherwise) amounted to an accord and satisfaction for the whole debt. R relied on the authority of *Goddard v O'Brien* (1882) in support of this proposition.

The Court of Appeal held that part-payment by cheque was, in this case, no different from part-payment in cash, so that R's argument on this point failed;

(b) that D and C were estopped from claiming the balance of the debt since they had promised to accept £300 in full settlement.

Lord Denning MR and Danckwerts LJ held that R had secured D and C's promise by putting undue pressure on the creditor. The benefit of promissory estoppel was, therefore, not available to her.

In a case where the debtor makes promises in order to defer the payment of a debt, it will not be inequitable for the creditor to go back on his promise to defer payment if the debtor fails to meet the agreed deferred payments as they become due.

Re Selectmove (1995)

The company owed the Inland Revenue substantial amounts of tax and national insurance contributions. In July 1991, in order to avoid the Revenue presenting a petition to wind up the company, the managing director offered to pay future liability as and when it became due, commencing in August 1991, and to repay arrears at £1,000 per month commencing in February 1992. In October 1991, at which time the company had paid only one month's tax and insurance as it became due, the Revenue demanded the arrears in full.

After that date, payments which were made pursuant to the managing director's offer were paid late. The Revenue served a winding up petition in September 1992. The company contended that the Revenue had accepted the proposal made by the company's managing director for the payment of the outstanding debts. It was held that: (a) the Revenue never signified acceptance of these proposals and that the silence of the Revenue could not be taken as signifying acceptance; (b) even if there was an agreement there was no consideration for it. The ruling in *Williams and Roffey Brothers* (1991), to the effect that the performance of an existing contractual or legal obligation can amount to consideration because it confers a benefit on the other party, cannot apply where the obligation is to pay a sum of money rather than to provide goods or services; (c) the doctrine of promissory estoppel could not apply even if there had been an agreement, since the company had not kept its part of the alleged agreement (which, in any case, the local collector had not the authority to make). It was not, therefore, inequitable to allow the Revenue to go back on the agreement.

PROPRIETARY ESTOPPEL

Where a person, relying on the promise of an owner of land that he will acquire some rights in relation to the land, does an act in reliance on the promise, the court may enforce the promise even though no consideration has moved from the promisee. The principle is very similar to that of promissory estoppel, with the vital difference (though Salmon LJ in *Crabb v Arun DC* doubted whether the distinction between promissory and proprietary estoppel was useful) that the promisee may use the estoppel as a cause of action.

In many of the cases, the promisee has spent money on the land in reliance on the promise, but the principle applies even though the reliance took a different form.

Crabb v Arun District Council (1976)

C owned a piece of land to which access was via a right of way over land owned by the council. There was only one point of access over the entire piece of land. C wished to divide the land into two parts and sell it. The difficulty with this was that there would be access to only one of the pieces of land. He therefore agreed with the council that he would be given a right of way which would permit access to the second piece of land. The council attempted to go back on the promise. C sued. *Held*: the council's promise added to the fact that they had put gates at the two points of access created an estoppel in favour of C. The council was not permitted to go back on its promise.

CONSIDERATION MUST MOVE FROM THE PROMISEE

In a bilateral contract, each party is both a promisor and a promisee. For example, suppose Alice agrees to sell a book to Bertha for £10: Alice is the promisor of the books and the promisee of £10. Conversely, B is the promisor of the £10 and the promisee of the books. Therefore, either Alice or Bertha may sue on the contract, but no one else. In a unilateral contract, there is only one promisee. That person must show that consideration, in the form of an act or forbearance, has moved from him to the defendant.

This rule, in effect, provides that a person who has given no consideration may not sue on a contract. This rule is very similar, if not identical, to the rule that a third party may not sue on a contract. It is arguable that a person may be a party to an agreement yet not give consideration for it, and thus is defeated from suing by the rule 'consideration must move from the promisee'. However, the counter-argument is that a person cannot be a party to a contract unless he has given consideration. The rule has a number of practical effects in relation to business transactions. These are dealt with fully in the Chapter 11.

CHAPTER 6

INTENTION TO CREATE LEGAL RELATIONS

Even though a person has made a promise which is supported by consideration, this doesn't necessarily mean that the promise is contractual. The law requires that the promise should have been made, looking at the matter objectively, with the intention that the promisor should be legally bound.

It follows, as we shall see, that if one party expressly states, when he makes his promise, that he doesn't intend to be legally bound, it is difficult to infer an intention to create legal relations. However, in most cases, the matter of intention isn't dealt with in the agreement. It is, therefore, left to the court to infer the intentions of the parties. For the purpose of analysis, contracts are divided into two broad classes. These are: (a) domestic promises; (b) commercial promises. We will deal with them in turn.

DOMESTIC PROMISES

These are promises made between friends and relatives. The presumption here is that there is no intention to create legal relations. However, this presumption is rebuttable (that is, it can be displaced) by evidence which shows that, looking at the matter objectively, there *was* an intention to create a legal relationship.

Where husband and wife are living together on friendly terms, the presumption that they do not intend any agreement to create a legal relationship will be difficult to displace. Thus, an agreement by the husband to pay his wife a monthly allowance will be unlikely to be contractual.

Balfour v Balfour (1919)

D was a civil servant working in Ceylon (now Sri Lanka). D and his wife, P, came home to England when D was given some leave. P, following medical advice, remained in England. Before leaving to resume his duties, D promised to allow her £30 per month during their enforced separation. Later, D wrote saying that it would be better if they remained apart. P, in consequence, obtained a decree of divorce *nisi*. She sued D for breach of his promise to pay her the £30 per month. Sargant J gave judgment for the wife, holding that the husband was under an obligation to maintain his wife and that the parties had contracted the extent of the maintenance. *Held*, by the Court of Appeal: allowing the husband's appeal, that the husband's promise, having been made when the parties were living together in amity (in other words, not having been made in consideration of a separation), was unenforceable since it was not intended that the promise was to be legally binding. In giving their reasons, the judges resorted to the now familiar 'floodgates' argument, that is, if this agreement were held to have legal consequences, wives would be suing husbands on the strength of trivial promises to such an extent that a whole lot of new courts would be needed to cope with the actions. (Note: two of the judges were of the opinion that the wife had given no consideration – another reason why the husband's promise was unenforceable.)

However, where spouses make a separation agreement, the presumption that no legal relations are intended will normally be rebutted. The agreement will, therefore, be regarded as a contract.

Merritt v Merritt (1970)

The husband (H) left the wife (W) for another woman. H and W had a meeting at which H agreed to pay W £40 per month maintenance and also agreed in writing to the effect that if W paid all the charges in relation to the matrimonial home (which was in their joint names), until the mortgage payments to the building society were completed, H would transfer the property into her sole ownership. W paid off the mortgage. H refused to transfer the property to her. She sued for a declaration that she was the sole beneficial owner and for an order to compel H to transfer the property into her sole name. H defended the case by arguing that the agreement was a domestic arrangement, not intended to give rise to a legal obligation, and also that W had given no consideration for his promise. *Held* by the Court of Appeal: the agreement was enforceable since it had been made when the parties were not living together in amity. Further, W had given consideration for H's promise since the payment of the balance of the mortgage was a detriment to W and a benefit to H in that he was relieved of his obligation to the building society.

Note that in *Pettit v Pettit* (1970), Lord Diplock stated that *Balfour v Balfour* (above) should not be taken as authority for the proposition that an agreement between a husband and wife which is made while they are living together in amity can *never* have legal consequences. He stated that, while the law would refuse to enforce the promise on the ground that no legally binding agreement was intended, if the parties had carried out the promise, the carrying out of the promise could affect proprietary rights. In such a case, the husband or wife might acquire rights, not through the law of contract, but by applying the law of property. However, the subsequent case of *Merritt v Merritt* (above), in which the nature and extent of this proprietary right could usefully have been explored, was decided solely on contract principles relating to the intention to create legal relations.

The above cases all relate to agreements between husband and wife, but the presumption that no legal relationship is intended extends to contracts between other relatives and between friends. An example of its application is to be found in *Jones v Padavatton*.

Jones v Padavatton (1969)

Mrs P was Mrs J's daughter. She had been married but was now divorced, with a young child. P had a job in the Indian Embassy in Washington in the United States. J wished her to go to England and there to qualify as a barrister. J promised that if P would do as she wished, she would make her a monthly maintenance allowance of £42. P reluctantly gave up her job and, in 1962, came to England, bringing her child with her. She began to read for the bar, her fees and maintenance being paid for by J. In 1964, because P was experiencing difficulties living in one room in Acton, J bought a large house, to be occupied partly by P and partly by tenants. P was to take her maintenance money from the money received from the tenants, though no arrangement was made as to what was to happen to the surplus, if any. In 1967, J and P quarrelled and J claimed possession of the house from P. P counter-claimed for £1,655 which she had paid out in connection with running the house. At the date of the hearing J had passed only a part of the Part 1 exams and still had Part 2 to pass.

Two agreements were in question. The first was the agreement whereby the daughter gave up her job and came to live in England to read for the bar, relying on the mother's promise to maintain her. The second was J's promise to allow P to occupy the house and take the rent in lieu of maintenance. At the county court hearing, the mother's claim for the possession of the house was dismissed. Her appeal was unanimously upheld by the Court of Appeal. Danckwerts and Fenton Atkinson LJJ held that there was no intention to create legal relations in either of the two agreements. Salmon LJ found that the first agreement created a contract by which the mother agreed to maintain P. However, it was implied that the agreement should last only for a sufficient time to allow the daughter a reasonable opportunity to pass the bar exams. Five years was a reasonable period for this, and since five years had elapsed since the agreement was formed, the contract had come to an end. Salmon LJ found that the terms of the second agreement were uncertain and could, therefore, not be given contractual effect.

A good contrasting case is *Parker v Clark*.

Parker v Clark (1960)

The plaintiffs were Commander and Mrs P and the defendants were Mr and Mrs C. The Ps were in their late fifties and owned a cottage in Sussex. Mrs P was the niece of the Cs, who were both in their late seventies. Mrs C wrote to Mrs P suggesting that the Ps should sell their house and go to live in Torquay with the Cs. A detailed schedule for the sharing of household expenses was set out. To get over the difficulties caused by the Ps selling their house in Sussex, the Cs would leave their house in Torquay and its contents to Mrs P, her daughter and her sister, when they passed away. The Ps agreed to this proposal and sold their house, lending some of the proceeds to their daughter so that she could acquire a flat. The parties had, in effect, entered into two agreements: the first an agreement that if the Ps sold their house in Sussex, the Cs would leave their house to Mrs P jointly with her sister and daughter; the second that if they would share household expenses, the Ps could live rent free with the Cs. Unfortunately, after a year or so, there was some unpleasantness between the parties and the Ps, having been asked to leave, left as an alternative to being evicted. The Ps sued for breach of contract. The Cs defended the case by arguing, among other things, that the arrangements were family arrangements, not intended to have legal consequences. *Held*: the agreements were legally binding. The Ps were awarded £1,200 damages for breach of the contract whereby they lived with the Cs rent free. Mrs P was awarded £3,400 for the loss of her promised inheritance.

See, also, *Simpkins v Pays* (1955). Three people living in the same house jointly entered a newspaper competition. The entries were made in the defendant's name and there was no regular rule about who should pay the entry fee and postage. One week the entry won. The plaintiff claimed his share. *Held*: the parties intended to create a legal relationship.

In *Peck v Lateu* (1973), it was held that an agreement between two women to share whatever prizes either of them might win at bingo, was legally binding.

In *Snelling v John G Snelling Ltd* (1972), three brothers were co-directors of a family company, JGS Ltd. Each had made loans to JGS Ltd. The company, needing further finance, borrowed money from a finance company. Each brother agreed with the finance company not to reduce the balance of his loan to JGS Ltd until the finance company had been repaid. The purpose of this agreement was to prevent the brothers using the loan from the finance company to repay themselves rather than use the money for the needs of the business. The brothers further agreed with one another that if any of them resigned before the loan to the finance company was repaid, he would forfeit the loan made by him to JGS Ltd. One brother resigned and claimed the repayment of the loan he had made to the company. Among other issues, the question arose as to whether his agreement with his brothers was intended to be legally binding. *Held*: this was not a family arrangement like that in *Balfour v Balfour* (above). The family relationship had already been destroyed by disagreements and nothing but the biological tie remained between them. The agreement was, therefore, enforceable.

COMMERCIAL PROMISES

The presumption with commercial promises is that they are intended to be legally binding. However, again, the presumption is a rebuttable one.

There are three situations to consider. These are:

(a) advertising puffs;

(b) honour clauses and similar clauses intended to deny the existence of an intention to be bound; and

(c) cases in which an intention to create legal relations is denied, as a matter of policy, by the courts or by statute.

We will deal with these in turn.

Advertising puffs

Advertisers often describe their goods or services in an optimistic manner designed to attract customers. Such promises are often vague in content and, therefore, any attempt to enforce them would probably fall foul of the general rule that a contract must be certain in its terms.

However, the advertiser will not always escape liability on the grounds that his statement was a 'puff'. In *Carlill v Carbolic Smoke Ball Co* (1893), the defendants claimed that their offer to pay a reward of £100 to anyone who caught 'flu after using their smoke ball in the prescribed manner, was merely an advertising puff. It was held that the Company's promise was intended to be legally binding, particularly in view of their claim to have deposited £1,000 with their bankers 'to show our sincerity in the matter'.

The Advertising Standards Authority is responsible for monitoring advertising. If an advertisement is thought to infringe the Control of Misleading Advertising Regulations 1988 and 2000, reference may be made to the Office of Fair Trading, who may secure an undertaking that the offender will cease producing the advertisement or, if no undertaking is forthcoming or an existing undertaking is breached, may seek an injunction from the courts to restrain publication of the advertisement. In 2000, Clockwork Orange Ltd gave a written undertaking to stop producing misleading advertisements for its Fuel Cat product.

Honour clauses

The parties can negative their presumed intention to create legal relations by inserting an 'honour clause', or similar clause announcing their intention not to be bound, into their contract. This is seldom done in commercial agreements generally, though there is evidence that many commercial parties who enter into contractual relations have, in practice, no intention of enforcing the agreement by legal action, should things go wrong.

The leading case on honour clauses in relation to normal commercial contracts is *Rose & Frank v Crompton*.

Rose & Frank v Crompton (1925)

The plaintiffs were a New York firm which was given sole selling rights in the USA and Canada by the defendants, who were an English firm which manufactured paper tissues. The contract conferring the rights contained the following clause:

> ... this arrangement is not entered into, nor is this memorandum written, as a formal or legal agreement, and shall not be subject to legal jurisdiction in the law courts either of the United States or England, but it is only a definite expression and record of the purpose and intention of the three parties concerned to which they each honourably pledge themselves with the fullest confidence, based on past business with each other, that it will be carried through by each of the three parties with mutual loyalty and friendly co-operation.

The contract was for three years from 1913, with an option to extend. It was in fact extended to March 1920, but the defendants terminated it without notice in 1919. Before the termination, the defendants had received and accepted several orders from the plaintiffs. The plaintiffs sued, claiming breach of contract. *Held* by the House of Lords: the defendants were not in breach of the 1913 agreement, since it expressly stated that it was binding in honour only. However, each individual order placed under the agreement and accepted by the defendants created a separate contract. Thus the defendants were in breach of the contracts to supply the orders they had accepted before repudiating the 1913 agreement.

Honour clauses are also used by football pools' promoters to avoid legal liability should a competitor claim that he has submitted a winning entry but that the pools company has lost it (or some similar denial of liability).

Jones v Vernons Pools (1938)

The plaintiff claimed that he had sent the defendants a winning football pool coupon. The defendants denied having received the coupon and, in denying liability, relied on a clause which was printed on every coupon, to the effect that the transaction should not give rise to any legal relationship or be legally enforceable but binding in honour only. The court held that this effectively negatived any intention to create a legal relationship.

See, also, *Appleson v Littlewood Ltd* (1939), in which the Court of Appeal followed the *Jones* case.

It has been held, however, that if the parties to a commercial contract wish to rebut the presumption that a legal relationship is intended, they must do so in clear terms.

Edwards v Skyways (1964)

The defendants were an airline. They wished to make a number of pilots redundant. Under his contract with the company, E was entitled, on termination of his contract of employment, to choose one of two options in relation to his contributions to the defendant's pension scheme. He could: (a) withdraw his own contributions to the fund; or (b) take the right to a paid-up pension at the age of 50. His union negotiated with the defendants and as a result of the negotiations it was agreed that if E would take option (a) the defendants would make him an *'ex gratia'* payment approximating to the amount of his own contributions: in other words, he would receive back double the money he had paid in. The plaintiff chose this option, but the defendants refused to make the *ex gratia* payment. When the plaintiff sued, the defendants argued, among other things, that the words *'ex gratia'* meant that there was no intention to create legal relations. *Held*: the onus was on the party seeking to escape liability to prove that there was no intention to create legal relations. Here they had not done so. The words *'ex gratia'* simply meant that there was no pre-existing liability on the company's part. It did not mean that their offer, once accepted, would not be binding in law.

Cases in which the existence of an intention to create legal relations is denied by the courts or by statute

There are certain cases in which, as a matter of policy, the courts or statute have denied the existence of an intention to create a legal relationship.

Willmore v South Eastern Electricity Board (1957)

The plaintiffs wished to install infra-red ray electric lamps for the purpose of rearing chicks. A steady heat was necessary for this purpose. The plaintiffs, therefore, consulted the defendant's engineer who told them that the electric current supplied by the defendants would be suitable. The plaintiffs completed an application form for the supply of current. The plaintiffs bought lamps from the defendants who approved their installation. On a number of occasions the voltage failed (that is, there were electricity cuts) and, as a result, the plaintiff's chicks died. They sued for breach of contract. *Held*: the defendants supplied electricity pursuant to a statutory duty and there was, therefore, no intention to create legal relations.

Triefus v Post Office (1957)

The Post Office lost two registered packets belonging to the plaintiffs. Compensation for their loss was restricted to £2 18s. The plaintiff sued for breach of contract. *Held*: there was no contract since there was no intention to create legal relations. (For statutory provisions to the effect that the Post Office shall not be liable in tort for the loss or delay of a postal packet see s 29 of the Post Office Act 1969. For statutory provisions which limit the liability of the Post Office in tort for the loss of a registered packet see s 30 of the same Act.)

In *Pfizer v Minister of Health* (1965), it was held that there was no contract between a chemist and his patient, even if the patient pays a prescription fee, in respect of a prescription filled under the NHS. The reason given was that the chemist is under a statutory duty to fill the prescription and since a contract is consensual (that is, entered into by consent), this negatived the existence of a contract.

Note, however, that the real reason why there is no contract in such cases is one of policy. It is unrealistic, in view of the restrictions increasingly placed upon contracting parties by statute, to regard a contract as being based wholly on agreement. Furthermore, there are cases in which the law does, when it suits the law's purpose, impose an essentially contractual obligation on an unwilling party. An example is the doctrine of 'agency of necessity', where, if A acts on behalf of B in an emergency, A is entitled to recover his costs from B, despite the fact that agency is normally a consensual relationship.

A statutory provision, which may also be explained on the ground of policy, relates to collective agreements. Collective agreements are agreements between one or more unions and one or more employers intended to regulate the terms and conditions of employment of employees covered by the agreement. Section 179 of the Trade Union and Labour Relations (Consolidation) Act 1992 provides that such an agreement shall be conclusively presumed *not to have been intended to be legally binding* unless:

(a) it is in writing; and

(b) it contains a provision that the parties intend the agreement to be a legally enforceable contract.

Letters of comfort

Sometimes one party sends another a 'letter of comfort' or 'letter of intent'. Whether the writer intends to be legally bound will depend upon the circumstances, particularly the wording of the letter and what reliance the recipient reasonably placed upon it. Viewed objectively, the letter may be intended merely as reassurance and, in such circumstances, will not give rise to contractual liability.

Kleinwort Benson v Malaysian Mining Corp (1989)

M sent out a letter of comfort in respect of a loan which was being made, by K, to one of M's subsidiaries (legally a separate company for the default of which M would not be legally liable unless they expressly undertook legal liability, for example, by guaranteeing repayment of the loan). The letter of comfort stated that it was M's policy that the subsidiary 'is at all times in a position to meet its liabilities in respect of the loan'. The subsidiary was not able to meets its liabilities in respect of the loan and, therefore, K sued M, arguing that M's written assurance created a legal liability whereby M should be liable for the repayment of the loan. It was held that the letter was simply a statement of the company's present policy. It did not amount to a contractual undertaking.

CHAPTER 7

THE TERMS OF THE CONTRACT

A normal business contract, whether written, verbal or made by conduct, consists of a promise or set of promises. These promises are called 'terms' and may be *express* or *implied*.

An express term is what the parties said or wrote or included by their conduct.

An implied term is a term which the parties did not expressly agree but which is necessary in order to make the contract work in a business sense.

Implied terms mainly come from statute (for example, Sale of Goods Act 1979 implies a number of terms into contracts for the sale of goods) or from the common law (for example, the terms implied into a contract of employment). Occasionally, however, the court may be prepared to imply a term into a particular contract because the court thinks that the parties intended that such a term should be included.

It is misleading to think that implied terms are the only way in which the law may intervene to lay down rules which may govern a contract. For example, the Sale of Goods Act 1979 lays down rules as to the time when ownership of goods passes from buyer to seller; the Employment Rights Act 1996 lays down minimum periods of notice which an employer or employee must give in order to terminate a contract of employment.

Some of these rules apply only if the parties have not reached a contrary agreement. For example, the rules which govern the transfer of ownership from a seller to a buyer of goods come into this category. Other rules apply irrespective of agreement between the parties. For example, the rule which gives the employee a right to a minimum period of notice to terminate her contract of employment cannot be overridden by agreement between the parties.

In respect of matters about which the parties are free to agree their own terms, there are a number of ways of doing this. Some are willing to agree on a set of terms which have been prepared by a trade association and appear to be fair to both parties; some are willing to contract only on their own terms or the terms of their own trade association; occasionally the parties agree a compromise where they adopt certain terms from one standard contract and certain terms from the other. In the latter case, this is sometimes done by making a one-off contract specially for the purpose, but is more commonly done by using one party's standard terms as the basic contract and adding a memorandum or letter which states in what way the terms are to be amended.

If the latter course is adopted, it is important to make clear reference to the standard form which is the basis of the contract and to make it clear that the amending letter or memorandum is just that. If this is not done properly, there is the danger that the letter or memorandum which is aimed at amending the terms will be treated as setting down the only terms of the contract.

CONTENTS OF THE CONTRACT

There are two important questions we need to answer about promises or statements which are made while negotiating a contract:

(a) which promises are part of the contract and which (if any) are not; and

(b) what is the importance of each promise relative to other promises (unless we intend to treat all the promises as equally important which, as we shall see, is not really practicable)?

To save repeating explanations of terminology, it is more convenient to deal with the questions in reverse order.

Relative importance of contractual terms

Once we have established which promises are part of the contract, we must then decide what the consequence is to be if the promise is broken. The main question here is whether a particular breach entitles the innocent party to *repudiate* the contract, in addition to claiming damages, or whether the innocent party is entitled *only to damages*. Of course, it is possible for the parties to provide in the contract that in the event of one party failing to fulfil a particular obligation, the innocent party shall have the right to repudiate the contract. Unfortunately, things can and do happen during the course of the performance of a contract which, though clearly a possibility in retrospect, did not occur to the parties at the time the contract was entered into. It is necessary, therefore, for the law to provide a mechanism whereby it can determine the consequences of a particular breach of contract.

One possibility would be to frame the law so that the consequences of breaking any of the promises in a contract are the same: (a) always repudiation plus damages; or (b) always only damages. However, (b) could force an innocent party to continue putting up with fundamentally flawed performance of a contract and being able only to claim damages; on the other hand, (a) could lead to innocent parties, for whom the contract had become inconvenient, claiming repudiation as a result of a breach of no real consequence.

Therefore, we really need an analysis which will allow repudiation where this seems appropriate and will entitle the innocent party to claim only damages in other situations.

Example

Alfred books a skiing holiday in Austria with Flybynight Tours. His flight is to depart at 11 pm on Friday 14 December and he is to stay for two weeks. Suppose two alternative situations (ignoring, for this purpose, the usual exemption clauses contained in such a contract):

(a) Flybynight write to Alfred a few weeks before he is due to depart, informing him that two flights have been consolidated and, as a result, his flight is to depart at 2 am on the 15th. He is disappointed at losing three hours of his holiday.

(b) Flybynight write to Alfred a few weeks before departure saying that they can't now take him to Austria because of overbooking on that holiday but will, instead, take him to the French Pyrenees. He is dissatisfied with this because he particularly likes Austria and the skiing is not so good in the Pyrenees.

In example (a), Alfred will probably seek a refund of part of the holiday price by way of damages. He is unlikely, however, to want to cancel the holiday and, moreover, it is arguably unjust to allow him to do that in respect of a relatively minor breach. In example (b), however, the breach is a serious one and Alfred is likely to want to cancel the holiday and, in addition, claim damages for the extra cost (if any) of booking an alternative holiday in Austria.

We can solve the problems thrown up in Alfred's case in one of two ways. First, we can look at the promises made by the tour company (that is, the terms of the contract) and place them into two categories of importance. We can then go on to say that breach of the more important promises will give rise to the remedies of *repudiation and damages*, whereas breach of the less important promises will give rise *only to an action for damages*. Thus, the term as to time of departure will be a minor promise, breach of which can be remedied by damages; the location of the holiday will be a major term of the contract, breach of which may be remedied by repudiation of the contract plus damages.

The difficulty with this approach is that a particular promise can be breached in a variety of ways. Thus, although we have said that the promise as to time of departure is a minor one, let us say that the departure was put back for 72 hours so that Alfred was going to lose three days of his holiday. In such a case, categorising the terms of the contract is not particularly helpful, since treating the term regarding time of departure as a less important promise gives Alfred a right to damages only, no matter how seriously it is breached. However, the *consequence* of the breach is clearly much more serious if it leads to a 72-hour delay than it is if the delay is only three hours.

This brings us to the second possible approach to the problem. Instead of categorising the promises or terms, we can wait and see the consequence of the *breach* of a particular term. If the breach is very serious, repudiation may be allowed in addition to damages; if not, the only remedy allowed is damages.

The traditional common law approach to the problem was to categorise the *promises* made by the parties. It called the important promises *'conditions'* and the less important promises *'warranties'*. Breach of condition entitled the innocent party to *repudiate*: breach of warranty entitled the innocent party only to *damages*.

However, the limitations of the conditions/warranties approach led, in the early 1960s, to the idea of approaching the problem from the other end. Instead of categorising *promises*, this approach categorises *breaches*. The terms of the contract are not given names but are called *'innominate'*, meaning 'no name'. (Sometimes they are called 'intermediate'.) Breaches are divided into *repudiatory* and *non-repudiatory*. Serious breaches are repudiatory and give the innocent party the right to repudiate the contract. Less serious breaches are non-repudiatory and give the innocent party the right to damages only.

It would be helpful if the 'innominate terms' approach had entirely superseded the conditions and warranties approach and that the standard method of deciding the consequences of a breach is to look at the seriousness of the breach rather than the type of term that has been breached. Unfortunately, it is not so simple. The 'conditions and warranties' dichotomy of the common law has become the unhappy bedfellow of the more modern 'innominate terms' approach, with the result that sometimes contracts are analysed on a conditions/warranty basis, sometimes on the innominate terms basis, and sometimes (see, for example, *The Hansa Nord*, below) on a mixture of the two.

(Note: it has been argued that in reality the early common law did, in fact, look at the consequences of breach when deciding whether a contract could be repudiated for failure to perform. In *Poussard v Spiers* (1876), an opera singer was not available to begin the start of the 'run' of an opera for which she had been engaged. A substitute had to be promised a four week engagement to replace P. When P became fit again, about a week into the run, she offered to sing but the defendants refused her offer. In *Bettini v Gye* (1876), B was engaged on a 15-week contract to sing in theatres, halls, etc. He was not available for four out of six days of rehearsal because he was ill. In both cases, the court was faced with the question of whether the unavailability of the plaintiff 'went to the root of the matter'. In the *Poussard* case, it was decided that P's unavailability went to the root of the contract and that, therefore, the defendant was not at fault in repudiating the contract. In the *Bettini* case, it was held that B's unavailability did not go to the root of the contract and that, therefore, G had wrongfully repudiated the contract. This appears to be the same test as was proposed in the 1962 case of *Hong Kong Fir Shipping v Kawasaki Kisen Kaisha* (1962), which marked the beginning of the modern 'innominate term' approach.)

We will now examine the two approaches in more detail.

CONDITIONS AND WARRANTIES

Until recently, unless the situation were governed by a statute (such as the Sale of Goods Act), the law approached the problem by looking at the contract and asking which of the terms (that is, promises) the parties intended to be of fundamental importance and which were intended to be of relatively minor importance. It categorised the more important promises, breach of which give the innocent party the right to repudiate the contract, as *conditions* and the less important, which give a right only to damages, as *warranties* (though be careful when using this terminology because both words are sometimes used, confusingly, with different meanings).

The term 'condition' is not defined in any statute. However, it means a term which is of fundamental importance to the contract. Breach of a condition will entitle the innocent party to:

(a) repudiate the contract; and

(b) claim damages for breach of contract.

Alternatively, the innocent party may, if they wish, *affirm* the contract and claim damages only.

The term 'warranty' is defined in the Sale of Goods Act 1979 (though note that this definition will hold good for any type of contract, not just in relation to a sale of goods) as an agreement which is collateral to the main purpose of the contract. Its breach entitles the innocent party to damages but does not entitle him to repudiate the contract.

Certain implied terms in the Sale of Goods Act (and in other statutes relating to the supply of goods) are categorised as either conditions or warranties by the statute concerned.

In situations where there is no statutory guidance, the court asks 'What was the intention of the parties at the time the contract was made?' This approach, like most instances of situations where the court purports to determine the initial intentions of the parties after an event has taken place, is somewhat artificial. However, conventions grew up which had the advantage of certainty. Thus, in charterparties (these are contracts for the hire of a ship, usually either for a particular time period or to undertake a particular voyage), stipulations as to the time a vessel would be available to load or stipulations as to its route on voyage, were usually regarded as conditions, so that the charterer knew that if the vessel wasn't ready on time, or if it deviated from its stated route, he could repudiate the contract.

A typical case is *Behn v Burness* (1863). In this case, a ship was chartered to carry coal from Newport to Hong Kong. A statement was made in a charter-party to the effect that the ship concerned was now lying in the port of Amsterdam. In fact, the ship was in Niewdiep, about 62 miles from Amsterdam, and was late arriving at Newport. It was held that the statement about the whereabouts of the ship was a *condition* of the contract, since it enabled the charterer to calculate at what time the ship would arrive at the port of loading. Breach of that condition entitled the charterers to repudiate the contract.

A more modern example is to be found in *The Mihalis Angelos* (1971). In this case, a vessel was chartered under a charter-party dated 25 May 1965 for a voyage from Haiphong in North Vietnam to Hamburg. The charter stated that she was 'expected ready to load under this charter about 1 July 1965'. At the time of the charter the vessel was in the Pacific on her way to Hong Kong. She arrived in Hong Kong on 23 June, but did not complete the discharge of her cargo until 23 July. Furthermore, in order to maintain her class on Lloyds shipping register she would have to undergo an examination which would take two days. Then it would take a further two days to reach Haiphong. The charterers repudiated the charter-party on 17 July on the ground that when they made the statement about the vessel being ready to load on 1 July, the owners had no reasonable expectation that this would be so. *Held* by the Court of Appeal: the clause in the charter relating to readiness to load was a *condition* of the charter. Because the condition had been broken, the charterers were entitled to repudiate the contract.

INNOMINATE TERMS

The categorisation of terms into conditions and warranties was thought by many to be capable of producing unsatisfactory results in practice. In particular, there have been cases where an innocent party has taken advantage of a breach of condition to escape from an inconvenient contract, even though the damage caused by the breach of condition was little or nothing.

For example, in *Arcos v Ronaasen* (1933), sellers agreed to supply a quantity of wooden staves half an inch thick. When they arrived in London, about 85% of them were found to be between half an inch and nine-sixteenths of an inch thick and 9% were found to be between nine-sixteenths of an inch and five-eighths of an inch thick. The staves were required for making cement barrels and the slight differences in thickness did not impair their use for that purpose. Nevertheless, it was held that the width of the staves was part of their description and since the Sale of Goods Act (s 13) says that it is an implied *condition* that goods shall correspond with the description, the buyer was entitled to *repudiate* the contract because the condition had been breached.

Similarly, in *Re Moore and Co and Landauer and Co* (1921), sellers agreed to sell a quantity of tinned fruit to be packed in cases each containing 30 tins. When the fruit was delivered, it was found that although there was the correct quantity of tins, only about half the cases contained 30 tins, the rest contained 24. The arbitrator found that 24 tins to the case was as commercially valuable as 30 to the case. Nevertheless, the Court of Appeal held that the buyers were entitled to repudiate the contract since the goods did not comply with the description applied to them. (But note that since the House of Lords decisions in *Ashington Piggeries v Christopher Hill* (1971) and *Reardon Smith Line v Hansen-Tangen* (1976), it might well be held that the packaging of the goods was not part of the description. Note, too, that under the Sale and Supply of Goods Act 1994, in non-consumer cases, the condition implied by s 13 can be treated by the courts as a warranty – that is, there is no right of rejection – where the breach is trivial.)

In an attempt to make the law more flexible, the Court of Appeal in *Hong Kong Fir Shipping Co Ltd v Kawasaki Kisen Kaisha Ltd* (1962) ruled that not all contractual terms could be labelled a 'condition' or a 'warranty', since many contractual terms could be breached in a serious way or in a minor way. The correct way to view the breach of such terms was to see whether the breach had sufficiently serious consequences to justify the innocent party repudiating the contract or whether the innocent party's interests would be sufficiently taken care of by an award of damages. Thus, the 'innominate' term was introduced into English law.

There are certain difficulties in adopting the innominate term idea. First, the Sale of Goods Act 1979, the Supply of Goods (Implied Terms) Act 1973, and the Supply of Goods and Services Act 1982 all categorise certain terms implied into contracts for the supply of goods as conditions or warranties, and it is not open to the courts to overrule something which Parliament had laid down in a statute. Thus, the implied terms must remain as conditions and warranties.

Secondly, although the innominate term is more flexible than the conditions/warranties dichotomy, it is less certain. It is difficult to predict in advance whether the innocent party may or may not repudiate the contract. A look at the leading case will perhaps demonstrate this.

In *Hong Kong Fir Shipping Co v Kawasaki Kisen Kaisha Ltd* (1962), the plaintiffs chartered a vessel to the defendants for a period of 24 months from February 1957, 'she being fitted in every way for ordinary cargo service'. The vessel was delivered at Liverpool and immediately sailed for Newport in the USA to load a cargo for Osaka. The engine-room staff on the ship were incompetent and unable to cope with the ship's antiquated machinery, with the result that the ship was delayed for five weeks with engine trouble on the way to Osaka. At Osaka, 15 more weeks were lost because the engines had become further dilapidated through the inability of the staff to maintain them properly. It was not until September that the ship was made seaworthy. In June, the defendants had repudiated the charter. The plaintiffs sued for breach of contract. *Held* by the Court of Appeal: although the ship was unseaworthy until September, this breach did not entitle the charterers to repudiate the contract. Not all terms of a contract could be designated 'conditions' or 'warranties', the consequences of the breach of which are known in advance. Many were intermediate terms and in such a case it is the consequences of the breach which determine whether the innocent party is entitled to repudiate the contract or is entitled only to damages. In the present case, the delay which had already occurred when the charterers repudiated the contract on 6 June, and was likely to occur in the future, taken together with the steps that the shipowners had taken to remedy the defects, were not sufficient as to deprive the charterers of substantially the whole benefit that it was intended they should gain from the charter.

The innominate term was again used by the Court of Appeal in *The Hansa Nord* (1976). In this case, sellers agreed to sell to buyers a quantity of US citrus pulp pellets to be used in making cattle food, for delivery in Rotterdam. The contract was on the standard terms of the London Cattle Food Association, clause 7 of which provided 'Shipment to be made in good condition ... each shipment shall be considered a separate contract'. The sellers shipped 3,400 tons, the price of which was about £100,000. When the pellets arrived in Rotterdam, part of the contents of one hold (which in total held about 1,200 tons) was found to be damaged by overheating. The buyers rejected the whole shipment and claimed repayment of the purchase price. By this time the market price of the goods had fallen so that, even in perfect condition, they were worth only £86,000. The sellers refuted the buyers' claim. The goods were being stored in barges in Rotterdam with both the buyers and the sellers disclaiming ownership. The owners of the barges therefore applied to Rotterdam county court for an order that the goods be sold. Such an order was made and the pellets were bought by a Mr Baas for £32,720. The expenses of the sale were deducted, leaving about £30,000 which was paid into a Dutch bank to the order of 'to whom it may concern'. On the same day, Mr Baas sold the goods to the original buyers on the same terms as he himself had bought them. Having bought the goods, the buyers continued to ship them to their plant and use them in the normal way, except that with the damaged portion of the cargo they used smaller percentages in their compound feeds than would be normal with sound goods. There was no evidence that this difference in manufacture caused the plaintiffs any loss.

The dispute was referred to arbitration in accordance with a provision in the contract and the umpire held that the buyers were not entitled to reject the shipment. (It seems that the umpire was not satisfied that the goods had not been shipped in good condition. He blamed faults in the ship for the damage to the pellets.) On appeal to the Board of Appeal of the Grain and Feed Trade Association, it was held that the sellers had been in breach of the express condition in clause 7 that the pellets were to be shipped in good condition; the board made no finding that the pellets were unfit for their purpose and found that the goods were merchantable on arrival in Rotterdam in a commercial sense, though at a lower price than would be paid for sound goods, but they were not of merchantable quality within the meaning of the phrase as used in s 14 of the Sale of Goods Act. The Board, therefore, held that the buyers were entitled to reject the shipment for breach of the express condition contained in clause 7 and breach of the implied condition found in s 14 of the Sale of Goods Act. The sellers appealed to the High Court and the judge upheld the award of the Board. The sellers appealed to the Court of Appeal. *Held* by the Court of Appeal: the appeal would be allowed on the following grounds:

(a) The Sale of Goods Act does not require a rigid division of *all* the terms of a sale of goods contract into 'conditions' and 'warranties'. It was the duty of the court to see whether a stipulation was a condition of the contract, breach of which would entitle the innocent party to repudiate the contract. If it was not, then the court should look at the consequences of the breach. If the breach went to the root of the contract (that is, if it was sufficiently serious) the innocent party was entitled to repudiate the contract. Otherwise he was not. In this case, the stipulation in clause 7 that the goods were to be shipped in good condition was not a condition in the strict sense and the sellers' breach of it did not go to the root of the contract. Accordingly, the buyers were not entitled to reject the whole cargo because of the breach of clause 7 but were entitled only to damages. (Note: those terms which the Sale of Goods Act designates as 'conditions' or 'warranties' must remain conditions and warranties. What the Court of Appeal is saying here is that express terms of the contract and any implied terms which are not designated conditions or warranties by the Act, do not have to be divided into conditions and warranties. The court is free in such cases to use the innominate term approach.)

(b) The Board's conclusion that the pellets were not of merchantable quality could not be supported: the words were used in s 14(2) in their commercial sense, that is, saleable for the ordinary purpose for which goods of that description would be bought and sold. The fact that the pellets could only be resold at a reduced price was not conclusive evidence that they were not of merchantable quality. Accordingly, the buyers were not entitled to reject the cargo on the grounds that there had been breach of the implied condition that the pellets should be of merchantable quality, since there had been no breach of that condition.

CONCLUSION

The present state of the law seems to be as follows:

(a) The parties may, in their contract, state that the performance of a particular term is to be a 'condition' of the contract. However, even if they do this, there is no guarantee that the courts will treat it as such, as in the *Schuler AG v Wickman Machine Tool Sales* (1974).

Schuler agreed to give the plaintiffs, Wickman, for a period of four years, the sole selling right of certain machinery manufactured by Schuler. Clause 7(b) of the agreement provided that, 'It shall be a condition of this agreement that (i) 'Wickman shall send its representative to visit' six specified UK motor manufacturers, 'at least once in every week' in order to solicit orders. There were terms contained in 20 other clauses but none of them was described as a condition. Wickman's representative failed on a few occasions to visit the manufacturers as specified. Schuler sought to terminate the contract on the grounds that Wickman had broken a condition of the contract. The House of Lords held, Lord Wilberforce dissenting, that the parties cannot have intended to use the word 'condition' as a term of art, since it was manifestly unreasonable to construe the contract in such a way as to allow Schuler to repudiate the contract for a single breach. The term requiring weekly visits was, therefore, construed as an innominate term and the House decided that the consequences of its breach did not entitle Schuler to repudiate the contract.

In earlier editions of this book, I have suggested that if a contracting party wishes to be able to repudiate the contract in the event of a breach by the other party, he should specify that not only is the term a 'condition' of the contract, but should also provide that its breach will be regarded as a repudiatory breach. He might also add, for good measure, that even a minor breach will be regarded as justifying repudiation of the contract. This approach is rendered necessary because it seems that the courts are determined, in this type of case, to impose their own 'common sense' solutions wherever possible, rather than observe the agreement that has been made between the parties.

In the *Wickman* case, the House of Lords decided that the parties could not possibly mean what they had said, since what they had said was manifestly unreasonable. The Court of Appeal adopted a similar approach in *Rice v Great Yarmouth Borough Council* (2000). In this case, the claimant contractor contracted with the council to provide certain services over a four year period. The council terminated the agreement after seven months for breach of contract. In doing so, it relied on a clause in the contract which provided:

> If the contractor ... commits a breach of any of its obligations under the contract the council may terminate the contract ... the council may ... terminate the contractor's employment ... having immediate effect.

In interpreting this provision, the Court of Appeal used a 'common sense' approach. The contract did not designate any term as a 'condition' or indicate which terms were considered so important that any breach would justify termination. Therefore, it was only where there was a repudiatory breach or an accumulation of breaches that the right to terminate the contract would arise. A second point was to decide what would amount to a repudiatory breach. The court said that the correct approach was to look at the contractor's performance over a year and ask whether the council had been substantially deprived of the benefit of the contract from the breach or breaches. It might be that some breaches were so important that a single breach would have that effect. If it appeared from the contractor's performance over that one year that the council had been deprived of a substantial total of the standard of performance for which it had contracted, this might justify the inference that the contractor would continue to perform in a sub-standard manner over the remainder of the four-year contract and thus justify the repudiation of the contract.

(b) If a statute provides that a particular implied term is a condition or a warranty, the courts must treat it as such. Examples are to be found in the Sale of Goods Act 1979, the Supply of Goods and Services Act 1982, the Supply of Goods (Implied Terms) Act 1973, etc.

(c) If the contract is silent as to how a particular term is to be treated and the term is not governed by a statutory provision, it is open to the courts to decide whether the parties intended a term to be treated as a condition or whether the term is an innominate term. In *Barber v NWS Bank* (1995), the court treated an important term of a contract as a condition, since it was not susceptible to breach in a number of ways but could be breached in one way only. (For the facts, see Chapter 20, p 433.) Sometimes the court will treat a stipulation as a condition, even though there may be breaches of it which may not be serious, because such a term has been generally accepted by the courts as being a condition in the past. See, for example, the *Mihalis Angelos* (above) and *Bunge Corporation v Tradax Export SA* (1981).

In the *Bunge* case, a contract for the sale of soya-bean flour required the buyers to give at least 15 days notice of probable readiness of vessels and of the approximate quantity to be loaded. A port of loading was then to be nominated by the seller. The final date for shipment was 30 June, which meant that the buyers should have given notice by the 15th. They didn't do so until the 17th and on the 20th the sellers repudiated the contract on the ground of the buyer's failure to give 15 days' notice and also claimed $317,500 damages for breach of contract, the market price of the goods having fallen considerably. The umpire held that the seller was entitled to repudiate and awarded the damages claimed. The award was confirmed by the Trade Association. However, the case went on to the High Court where Parker J held that the term as to 15 days notice was an innominate term, the breach of which did not go to the root of the contract. The Court of Appeal ruled in favour of the seller, holding that the term in question was a condition of the contract. The court did this mainly on the ground that stipulations as to the time when something must be done in commercial contracts have always been regarded as being 'of the essence' and failure to observe time stipulations has always entitled the innocent party to repudiate.

WHICH STATEMENTS ARE PART OF THE CONTRACT?

We have seen that in order to indicate the importance of the terms of a contract they may be (though they are not always) divided into 'conditions' and 'warranties'. A further way of categorising a term of a contract is by the method by which it becomes incorporated into the contract. Thus terms may be *expressly* incorporated and be called 'express terms', or they may be *impliedly* incorporated and be called 'implied terms'.

However, it may be that a statement made to induce a contract is not incorporated into the contract at all. If such a statement proves to be false, the remedy will be for *misrepresentation* not for breach of contract.

Express terms

An express term is what the parties actually said or wrote. Where a contract is made wholly by word of mouth, what the parties said is a matter of fact to be found by the court.

On the face of it, few difficulties should arise where the terms of a contract are reduced to writing, but in practice this is where the legal difficulties lie.

Where a contract is made on the standard terms of one of the parties and it purports to incorporate the terms of another document, problems may arise as to whether the other party has sufficient notice of the terms of the other document. This problem often arises in connection with exemption clauses, and we will study it further in that context.

The 'Parole Evidence' rule

There is a general rule to the effect that evidence cannot be admitted to add to, vary or contradict the terms of a written document. Lawrence J expressed it as follows in *Jacobs v Batavia and General Plantations Trust* (1924):

> It is firmly established as a rule of law that parole evidence cannot be admitted to add to, vary or contradict a deed or other written instrument.

The rule has been eroded by a number of exceptions to such an extent that the Law Commission proposed in 1976 that what was left of the rule should be abolished. In 1986 in its Working Paper 154, the Law Commission stated that legislation was no longer necessary to abolish the rule since it no longer existed. However, since it has not been abolished by statute and has been circumvented rather than abolished by case law, it is necessary to look at the exceptions.

Implied terms

An implied term may be incorporated into a contract by statute, by common law, or by trade custom or usage (or by the court, but in such a case the term isn't pre-existing). In each case, parole evidence is admitted to prove the existence of the implied term.

Evidence to show that there is no agreement

Extrinsic evidence may be brought to show that although there is, apparently, a valid agreement, that agreement is not operative.

In *Pym v Campbell* (1856), a contract was entered into which was not to be performed unless it was approved by a third party. The third party didn't approve. The plaintiff alleged breach of contract, arguing that the parole evidence rule did not permit the defendant to adduce evidence to add to, vary or contradict the written contract. *Held*: the defendant was not seeking to vary the terms of the agreement; he was seeking to show that there was no agreement at all (since the condition as to the third party's approval hadn't been met). Evidence to show that there was no agreement was admissible.

Evidence to prove a mistake or a misrepresentation

A party who has been misled by an oral statement may give evidence of that statement in order to support an argument that the contract is void or voidable or that the document should be rectified or that he is entitled to damages.

Evidence to show that the written document was not intended by the parties to be the complete contract

There is a presumption that a document which appears to be a complete contract is, in fact, the complete contract.

However, sometimes a plaintiff will be able to persuade the court that, although a written document appears to be the whole contract, it was intended by the parties to be only part of the contract – the other part being oral:

Although when the parties arrive at a definite written contract the implication or presumption is very strong that such contract is intended to contain all the terms of the bargain, it is a presumption only, and it is open to either of the parties to allege that there was, in addition, an express stipulation not intended to be excluded but intended to continue in force with the express written agreement. (Lord Russell in *Gillespie Bros & Co v Cheney, Eggar & Co* (1896).)

The problem most frequently arises in connection with the discussion of whether something that was said by one party to the other was a contractual term or a mere representation. A mere representation which turns out to be false is called a misrepresentation and, until the mid-1960s, with advent the House of Lords' decision in *Hedley Byrne v Heller* and the Misrepresentation Act 1967, the remedies for breach of contract were, generally speaking, substantially more favourable to the plaintiff than the remedies for misrepresentation. Even nowadays, there are situations where a breach of contract claim will give a remedy where a misrepresentation claim will not or, if it does, will give an inferior remedy. Thus, there are a number of cases in which the plaintiff has argued that a written contract was only part of the contract and was intended to be read in conjunction with the oral statements of the parties. We will deal with this in detail when we consider the difference between the mere representation and the contractual term.

MERE REPRESENTATIONS AND ADVERTISING PUFFS

One difficulty which arises in English law is that things said or written by the parties to a contract, in connection with the contract, are not necessarily regarded as being part of the contract. They may, instead, be an advertising puff (or commendation), or a mere representation.

Advertising puffs

We have seen in our study of 'intention to create legal relations' that it is common for advertisers to make exaggerated claims for their goods or services. Providing these claims are made in general terms and are substantially a matter of opinion, the maker of the claim will incur no legal liability should the claim prove to be unfounded. The reason for this is that English law has always given advertisers some licence in the formulation of commendatory claims.

This probably causes no great difficulty in relation to most contracts. No one really believes that 'Sudso Washes Whiter' or that drinking a particular type of lager endows the drinker with superhuman powers. However, if more specific claims are made (as in *Carlill v Carbolic Smoke Ball Co*, for example), the claims of the advert may be treated as contractual promises or representations.

Mere representations

It often happens that one party to a contract makes a statement, either orally or in writing, in order to induce the other party to enter into the contract. In such a case, providing the statement is not an advertising puff, it might be assumed that the statement becomes a term of the contract. However, this is not necessarily so. The statement may be a *mere representation*. A *mere representation* which turns out to be false is called a misrepresentation.

It is often difficult to decide whether a statement is a *contractual term* or whether it is a *mere representation*. However, it is necessary to do so because the principles on which the remedy for breach of contract is determined are different from the principles on which the remedy for a misrepresentation is determined. The remedy for breach of contract depends either on the seriousness of the breach or the importance of the term which is breached and liability is strict (that is, exists irrespective of any fault on the part of the party who is alleged to be in breach). On the other hand, the remedy for misrepresentation depends upon the state of mind of the representor at the time he made the misrepresentation. While, nowadays, these different approaches may give substantially the same results, this is not always so. (See, for example, *Oscar Chess v Williams* (1957), where W made a false statement about the age of a car which she sold to the plaintiff. If W's statement about the age of the car had been held to be a contractual term, the plaintiff would have been entitled to damages, but as it was held to be a mere representation, the plaintiff got no remedy at all. Note that although the law on misrepresentation has changed since this case, the outcome of the case would probably be the same if it were heard today. Note, too, that damages for misrepresentation, being awarded on a tort of deceit or tort of negligence basis, are awarded on different principles to the award of damages for breach of contract.)

Furthermore, while a statement of future intention may amount to a contractual term, it cannot be a misrepresentation should the representor change his mind subsequent to making the statement. In such a case, again, it will be to the representee's advantage if the statement is held to be a contractual term.

Distinguishing between mere representations and contractual terms

The distinction between the two depends upon what the court, looking at the matter objectively, presumes to have been the intention of the parties. The court must decide whether the party who made the statement intended to make a contractual promise or not: *Heilbut Symons v Buckleton* (1913). In this case, the appellants, who were rubber merchants in London, underwrote a large number of shares in a company called Filisola Rubber and Produce

Estates. They instructed J, who was the manager of their Liverpool office, to obtain applications for the shares in Liverpool. J mentioned the company to W. B later telephoned J from W's office, saying: 'I understand that you are bringing out a rubber company.' J replied: 'We are.' B then asked J if he had any prospectuses. J said he hadn't. B then asked if it was all right. J replied: 'We are bringing it out.' B replied: 'That is good enough for me.' B then took a large number of shares in the company.

For a short time the shares traded at a premium, but when it was discovered that there was a large deficiency in the number of rubber trees that the prospectus had said were on the Filisola estate, the shares dropped in value. B sued for fraudulent misrepresentation and breach of contract, arguing that it was a contractual term that the company was a rubber company and that, in fact, it wasn't a rubber company at all. The case was tried with a jury, which held that there was no fraudulent misrepresentation. However, they found that the company could not properly be described as a rubber company and that the appellants or J, or both, had made a contractual promise to the effect that it was a rubber company. Thus the trial judge awarded B damages for breach of contract. The House of Lords held that the statement that the company was a rubber company was not intended to be a contractual promise. B's main interest was in whether the company was 'all right', not in whether it was a rubber company. B's claim for damages therefore failed.

There are certain factors which the courts use in order to assist them in ascertaining the intentions of the parties:

(a) It will be presumed that a document which looks like a complete contract is, in fact, the whole contract.

This derives from the parole evidence rule. Evidence will, therefore, not usually be admitted to add to, vary or contradict the document. Oral statements which are not incorporated into the document will, therefore, tend to be regarded as representations rather than contractual terms.

For example, in *Whittington v Seale Hayne* (1900), breeders of prize poultry were induced to take a lease of land by an oral representation that the land was in a sanitary condition. In fact, the drainage required extensive work. The plaintiff claimed damages for breach of contract and rescission of the contract for misrepresentation. *Held*: the oral statements were not part of the contract. Since the lease made no mention of the drainage, the plaintiff was entitled to rescission for misrepresentation but not to damages for breach of contract.

In *Routledge v McKay* (1954), a motor-cycle was first registered on 17 October 1930. One owner performed extensive alteration to the machine so that, in many respects, it looked like a later model, and managed to get a registration book which gave the date of registration as 9 September 1941. The present seller bought the machine after that had taken place and was not responsible for the wrong entry in the log book. On 23 October 1949, the seller, in answer to a question by a prospective buyer (the plaintiff), said that it was late 1941 or 1942. On 30 October, the seller and the plaintiff entered into a contract of sale and signed a memorandum of agreement which didn't mention the date of registration. The buyer discovered the true date of registration and sued the seller for breach of contract. *Held*: the statement as to the date of registration was a mere representation not a contractual term. Since (in those days) there was no remedy in damages for a misrepresentation which wasn't made fraudulently, the plaintiff lost his case.

The courts have, however, been willing to circumvent this rule in order to do justice in certain cases. They have done this in one of two ways:

(i) The court has held that the written document does not represent the whole contract, that is, the contract consists of both the written document and the oral representations.

An example of this approach is to be found in *Quickmaid Rental Services v Reece* (1970). In this case, Mr Reece was persuaded by a salesman employed by Quickmaid to sign a rental agreement for a drinks dispensing machine to be installed on the forecourt of Mr Reece's garage, which was on the same main road as a number of other garages. To allay Mr Reece's fears about competition from machines installed at other garages, the salesman promised Mr Reece that no other machine would be installed in the same road. Mr Reece was upset when he discovered that, within three months of this promise, a machine had been installed at a different garage in the same road, and, moreover, the second machine was in a better position for getting custom. Because of this, and because he had had some trouble with the machine, Mr Reece stopped paying the rental. The company sued Mr Reece, arguing that their promise about not installing another machine was not a term of the contract. (It was not a misrepresentation either, since, by a much-criticised quirk of the law, a statement of future intention cannot be a misrepresentation unless it can be shown that, at the time the statement was made, the representor had no such intention.) *Held* by the Court of Appeal: the statement regarding the installation of no other machine in the same road, was a term of the contract even though it was not incorporated into the written rental agreement. Moreover, the term was a condition of the contract and the breach of that condition entitled Mr Reece to repudiate the contract.

In *Walker Property Investments v Walker* (1947), the defendant took the lease of a flat from the plaintiffs. During the negotiations, he stipulated that if he took the lease he was to have the use of two basement rooms and also the garden. This was agreed verbally, but the lease made no mention of it. *Held* by the Court of Appeal: the lease and the oral agreement should be read together to form the complete contract.

(ii) The court may hold that the oral agreement forms a separate *collateral* contract (that is, a contract which stands by the side of the written one). This is an alternative method of achieving the same effect as the approach under (i) above, and, moreover, one which does less violation to established rules of contract law.

In *De Lassalle v Guildford* (1901), the plaintiff leased a house from the defendant. During the course of negotiations the plaintiff said that he would not execute the lease until he received an assurance from the defendant that the drains were in good order. The defendant gave this assurance, whereupon the plaintiff executed the lease. The lease made no reference to the drains which were, in fact, not in good order. The plaintiff sued for breach of contract. *Held*: the oral statement about the drain was a separate collateral contract, whereby the defendant was saying to the plaintiff: 'I promise to put the drains in order in return for you signing the lease.' The plaintiff was entitled to damages for the defendant's breach of the collateral contract.

Sometimes, a court may hold that a statement is contractual for both reasons, using them as alternatives. In *Couchman v Hill* (1947), a heifer belonging to the defendant was put up for auction. The catalogue described the animal as 'unserved'. The plaintiff asked both the auctioneers and the owner to confirm that the heifer was unserved and when they did, he bought it. The heifer was not unserved and died shortly afterwards as a result of carrying a calf at too young an age. *Held* by the Court of Appeal: either there was a collateral contract to the effect that the heifer was unserved; or the documents formed only part of the contract and the oral statements could be added to the documents in order to form the complete contract.

(b) If the statement materially precedes the contract in time, it will tend to be treated as a representation rather than as a contractual term.

In *Hopkins v Tanqeray* (1864), a statement made before the day of an auction was held to be a mere representation rather than a contractual term. Moreover, the court felt that holding the statement to be a contractual term would have given the plaintiff an advantage over the other bidders at the auction. In both *Couchman v Hill* and *Harling v Eddy* (1951), the relevant statement was made shortly before the contract was made. *Harling v Eddy* was another auction case in which the appearance of a sickly-looking heifer in the auction ring failed to excite any interest. No-one bid for her. The owner thereupon said that there was nothing wrong with her and that he would guarantee her in every respect. The plaintiff bought her and three months later she died of tuberculosis. The plaintiff sued for breach of contract. A problem for the plaintiff was condition 12 of the printed conditions of sale which said that no animal was sold with a 'warranty' unless this appeared on the purchaser's account. Nevertheless, the Court of Appeal held that the statement made in the auction ring was a contractual term.

In *Routledge v McKay* (above), a further reason why the defendant's statement as to the year of manufacture of the motor-cycle was held to be a mere representation was that it was made a week before the contract was entered into. However in the Irish case of *Schawel v Reade* (1913) (decided by the House of Lords), the gap between the statement and the contract was three weeks, yet the statement was treated as part of the contract.

(c) If the statement was made by someone *without* special knowledge to someone *with* special knowledge, the statement will tend to be treated as a mere representation.

In *Oscar Chess v Williams* (1957), the defendant tendered a second-hand Morris in part-exchange for a new Hillman Minx. The registration book of the Morris showed the year of manufacture as 1948 and the defendant confirmed this. The plaintiffs therefore gave her £290 in part-exchange. Eight months later the plaintiffs found that the date of the manufacture of the Morris was not 1948 but 1939 (the specification of the model had not changed in the intervening years because of the war). The registration book had been fraudulently altered, presumably by a previous owner. The appropriate trade-in price was only £175. The plaintiffs sued for £115 damages, being the difference between the price they had allowed Mrs W and the true value of the Morris. The statement as to the year of the Morris had been made at the same time as the agreement for the new Hillman. There was nothing in writing. So, on the face of it, the indicators were in the plaintiffs' favour. This is how the county court judge decided the case. However, his judgment was overturned by the Court of Appeal, who regarded the crucial factor as being that the statement was made by a layperson with no special knowledge of cars, to someone who was a car specialist. Thus, the statement was a mere representation and the plaintiffs were not entitled to damages for breach of contract.

(d) If, on the other hand, the statement is made by someone with special knowledge to someone without special knowledge, the statement will tend to be a contractual term.

In *Dick Bentley Productions v Harold Smith* (1965), Bentley asked Smith to find him a well-vetted Bentley car. Smith said that he had such a car and that it had done only 20,000 miles since it had been fitted with a replacement engine and gear-box. Bentley went for a short run in it and then bought it. In fact, it had done nearly 100,000 miles since it had been fitted with the replacement engine and gear-box, and the car proved unsatisfactory. Bentley sought damages for breach of contract. *Held:* the defendant's statement was a term of the contract. *Per* Denning LJ:

> Here we have a dealer, Mr Smith, who was in a position to know, or at least to find out, the history of the car. He could get it by writing to the makers.

Salmon LJ seemed to base his decision on the concept of the collateral contract. However, it seems clear that the superior knowledge of the defendant was the crucial factor which led to his statement about the engine and gear-box being treated as contractual.

IMPLIED TERMS

It could be argued that anything the parties fail to agree expressly should not be part of the contract. That, certainly, was the attitude of the early common law, which was concerned mostly with contracts concerning land and contracts for the sale of goods. In respect of sales of land, the contracts tended to be elaborate and in writing (they *must* be made in writing now), with the consequence that it was fair to conclude that if the parties hadn't put a particular term in the contract, they didn't intend that term to be there. In the case of the sale of goods, most persons bought goods from people they knew and it was usually relatively simple to spot defects in the proffered goods before the sale. (An exception then, as now, was with transport. Many of the earlier cases involved defective horses – nowadays it's cars!)

However, with the coming of the industrial revolution, contracts of sale in which the buyer hadn't seen the goods prior to delivery began to become relatively common. Either the courts had to insist that if the buyer wanted protection he had to enter into a formal contract, including all the terms on which the parties wished to rely (such formality is often found in primitive systems but is usually abandoned as both the legal system and the economy begin to develop) or, if the informality of sales of goods was to be preserved without potential injustice to the buyer, implied terms had to be developed. The formal contract solution would have been a clearly retrograde step. Therefore, from the early 19th century, the courts began to imply terms into contracts of sale. The process of implication of terms continued, until most types of contract nowadays have certain terms implied into them.

An implied term can come from one of four sources:

(a) the court;

(b) common law;

(c) custom; or

(d) statute.

The first source implies a term as a matter of fact, that is, it must be shown that, viewed objectively, the parties *did* in fact intend to imply such a term in their contract. The other three sources imply terms as a matter of law, that is, on the basis that the parties *must have* intended to include such a term in their agreement.

The court

An implied term will start life as a term implied into a particular contract by the court. If the issue never comes up for discussion again, it will remain a one-off.

However, a court will not imply a term simply because it would be reasonable to imply such a term. In order for a term to be implied it must be shown that, viewed objectively, the parties *must* have intended such a term to be implied.

One way in which a litigant might establish such an intention is to show that the contract would lack business efficacy (that is, the contract would be ineffective in a business sense) without the implication of the term. For example, in *The Moorcock* (1889), the owner of a vessel called *The Moorcock* agreed to hire a mooring alongside a jetty in the Thames. When the tide ebbed, the vessel rested on the bottom of the river and, because of the presence of a ridge of rock, suffered damage. The owners of the vessel sued in respect of the damage. The owners of the jetty argued that they hadn't promised that the bottom of the river would be safe for the ship. *Held*: as both parties envisaged that the ship would rest on the river bed at low tide, there was an implied term in the contract that the bed would be reasonably safe for this purpose.

Another test, which was suggested by McKinnon LJ in *Shirlaw v Southern Foundries* (1939), is that of the 'officious bystander'. He said:

> *Prima facie* that which in any contract is left to be implied and need not be expressed is something so obvious that it goes without saying; so that, if while the parties were making their bargain, an officious bystander were to suggest some express provision for it in the agreement, they would testily suppress him with a common 'Oh, of course'.

Common law

A term is implied by the common law when, as a result of a series of consistent decisions, the courts apply a similar term into all contracts of the same type. The terms implied by the Sale of Goods Act and the Supply of Goods and Services Act began as terms implied by the common law. Nowadays, notable areas of law where terms are still implied by common law rather than statute include employment law, the law of agency, and contracts between banker and customer.

Custom

A term may be implied into a contract by trade custom or local custom. It is very rare for a term to be implied by either, since the conditions to be met, especially in the case of a local custom, are very restrictive. In the case of a trade custom, it must be proved:

(a) that the custom is very well known throughout the trade;

(b) that the custom is reasonable; and

(c) that the custom is certain.

In *Smith v Wilson* (1832), it was held that a trade custom to the effect that an order for 1,000 rabbits meant that 1,200 should be supplied, was valid.

The rules for the implication of a custom which is restricted to a particular locality are similar but with the addition that the custom must have existed since 'time immemorial', that is, since 1189, though in practice evidence of long usage will suffice as long as there is no evidence that the custom didn't exist as far back as 1189.

Custom is not an important source of implied terms nowadays.

Statute

An important source of implied terms nowadays is statute. The codification of implied terms by statute began with the Sale of Goods Act 1893 (now re-enacted as the Sale of Goods Act 1979). The process continued with the Marine Insurance Act 1906. Then came the Hire Purchase Act 1938, which governed contracts of hire-purchase up to a certain value. (The implied terms are now contained in ss 8, 9, 10 and 11 of the Supply of Goods (Implied Terms) Act 1973, and apply irrespective of the value of the transaction or the credit given.) The most recent Act to imply terms is the Supply of Goods and Services Act 1982, which deals with three areas: (i) a supply of goods which is not sale within the legal definition; (ii) contracts of hire; (iii) contracts for services.

Relationship between express terms and implied terms

As a general rule, an express term will take precedence over an alleged implied term which conflicts with it. For example, in *Les Affreteurs Reunis SA v Walford* (1919), W, a broker, had negotiated a charter-party between the owners of a ship called the SS Flore and a company called Lubricating and Fuel Oils Co Ltd. A clause in the charter-party provided that the owners, on signing the charter, would pay Walford a commission of 3% on the estimated gross amount of the hire. The commission was not paid and Walford brought a legal action against the owners. The owners pleaded in their defence that there was a term implied by custom that commission on charter-parties was not paid until the hire charges had actually been earned. *Held*: the alleged custom was in conflict with the plain words of the agreement. In such a case, effect must be given to the agreement of the parties.

Note, however, that statute has occasionally created 'non-excludable' implied terms. Examples are to be found in the Sale of Goods Act 1979, so that, to give a precise example, s 13(1) provides that where there is a contract for the sale of goods by description, there is an implied condition that the goods will correspond with the description. Section 6(2)(a) of the Unfair Contract Terms Act 1977 provides that, as against a person dealing as a consumer, this term cannot be excluded or restricted by reference to any contract term. Thus, if Electro Ltd sell a television to Bloggs, a consumer, and a clause in the agreement provides that the condition implied by s 13 of the Sale of Goods Act is excluded, the clause will have no effect and the implied term will still be applicable.

CHAPTER 8

UNFAIR CONTRACTS

The courts have sometimes been faced with contracts which are manifestly unfair to one of the parties and have been asked to set them aside for that reason. However, there is no general power in English law to set aside contracts simply because they are unfair. Instead, English law has tackled various potential sources of unfairness, some more positively than others, with the result that the law has developed in a fragmentary manner. Sometimes it will be possible to find a reason to set aside an unfair contractual term, sometimes not.

The main areas of law dealing with unfairness are:

(a) the law relating to duress and undue influence. This area of law has significant potential for development into an area which would give a general protection to weaker parties in a contract. However, despite the attempts of Lord Denning in *Lloyds Bank v Bundy* (1975) to establish a set of general principles uniting the cases in which the courts have refused to enforce a contract because of the inequality of bargaining power between the parties, this seems unlikely to develop into settled principles without statutory intervention;

(b) statutory provisions contained in the Consumer Credit Act 1974, the Insurance Companies Act 1982 and the Financial Services Act 1986 allow cancellation of agreements in certain circumstances;

(c) ss 137–40 of the Consumer Credit Act 1974 provide for the courts to reopen extortionate credit bargains;

(d) other provisions, for example, the restraint of trade doctrine, which have been used by the courts to set aside unfair contracts;

(e) the Unfair Contract Terms Act (UCTA) 1977 (together with other statutory and common law rules), which control unfair exemption clauses. It is important to note that the Act does not, as its title would imply, control unfair contract terms generally; and

(f) as from 1 July 1995, the Unfair Terms in Consumer Contracts Regulations, which deal with unfair terms generally (for the first time in English law) but only in relation to consumer contracts. This purports to put into effect EEC Directive 93/13/EEC, aimed at controlling unfair terms in consumer contracts. This development is perhaps the most significant control over unfair terms in contracts and it remains to be seen whether the principles contained in the regulations will be expanded in the future to apply to business contracts. The Regulations were re-drawn in 1999.

UNCONSCIONABLE CONTRACTS IN THE USA

The United States Uniform Commercial Code provides a model which shows how the use of unfair terms generally might be the subject of control. It gives the court wide powers that it may use to combat 'unconscionable' contracts. 'Unconscionable' means 'contrary to good conscience'.

The US Uniform Commercial Code 2–302 provides:

(1) If the court as a matter of law finds the contract or any clause of the contract to have been unconscionable at the time it was made, the court may refuse to enforce the contract, or it may enforce the remainder of the contract without the unconscionable clause, or it may so limit the application of any unconscionable clause as to avoid any unconscionable result.

The Commercial Code has been given wide application. It has been used to adjust the price in a contract where a sale of goods was made for approximately two and a half times their reasonable retail value: *Toker v Westerman* (1970). In that case, an 'unconscionable contract' was defined as:

... one such as no man in his senses and not under a delusion would make on the one hand, and as no honest and fair man would accept on the other ... It has been said that there must be an inequality so strong, gross and manifest that it must be impossible to state it to a man of common sense without producing an exclamation at the inequality of it.

The code has been applied, as in the *Toker* case above, where there is an inadequacy of consideration. In English law inadequacy of consideration has never been a reason, in the absence of some vitiating factor such as misrepresentation or duress or undue influence, for intervening in the parties' contract. If a person makes a poor bargain that is his misfortune.

The 'unconscionable contract' doctrine has also been applied in a situation where a person 'of poor education' who was the lessee of a filling station, signed a contract containing an onerous indemnity clause prepared by an oil company's lawyers. It was held that he wasn't bound by his signature: *Weaver v American Oil Co*. English law would say that he was bound by his signature unless the document were misrepresented to him. (There is a provision in s 4 of the Unfair Contract Terms Act (UCTA) 1977 which provides that indemnity clauses must satisfy the test of reasonableness but this only applies if the party disadvantaged by the clause is dealing as a consumer.) Thus, in English law, Weaver would have been bound by the contract he signed. (See, for example, *L'Estrange v Graucob*, below.)

DURESS AND UNDUE INFLUENCE

If a contract (or a gift) is obtained by undue pressure, the court may set it aside. There are two concepts under which it does this: duress and undue influence.

Duress

Duress is a common law concept which originally meant actual violence or threats of violence. Originally, such pressure probably made a contract void. The concept of duress has since been extended to cover threats to property or business, in addition to violence or threats of violence to the person. Nowadays, the weight of opinion seems to be that duress makes the contract voidable: see, for example, *Pao On v Lau Yiu Long* (1980).

The difference between 'void' and 'voidable' is crucial: if a contract is void it is treated as never having been made, so that all property transferred or money paid under the contract can be reclaimed; if a contract is voidable it is valid until such time as it is repudiated. This means that if a third party acquires rights in the subject matter while the contract is valid, the original owner becomes unable to reclaim the subject matter. In addition, if the innocent party delays his repudiation of the contract beyond a reasonable time, the contract cannot be rescinded ('rescission' means the process by which each party is returned to the position he was in before the contract was made). For an explanation as to the ways in which a claim for rescission may be defeated, see Chapter 10, p 247.

In *Universe Tankships Inc of Monrovia v International Transport Workers' Federation* (1982), Lord Scarman identified two elements of duress:

(1) pressure amounting to compulsion of the will of the victim; and

(2) the illegitimacy of the pressure exerted.

In *Pao On v Lau Yiu Long* (1980), it was held that in order to amount to duress there must be a coercion of will so that there was no true consent. Determining whether there has been no true consent involves examination of the following factors:

(a) whether the person alleged to have been coerced did or did not protest;

(b) whether, at the time he was allegedly coerced, he did or did not have an alternative course of action open to him, such as an adequate legal remedy;

(c) whether he was independently advised; and

(d) whether, after entering the contract, he took steps to avoid it.

Violence or threats of violence

Violence or threats of violence amount to duress. There is a modern example in contract in the case of *Barton v Armstrong* (1975). In this case, B, the managing director of a company, resented the interference of A, the chairman. A was removed as chairman and B was informed that the company's principal lender would not advance any more money. B believed that if the money owed to A was settled, further finance would be forthcoming. A threatened to kill B and had made several threatening phone calls. B therefore made an agreement whereby the company would pay A $140,000 and purchase A's shares in the company. The lender still refused to lend and the company was soon in financial difficulties. *Held*: the agreements were voidable. Duress need not be the sole reason for entering into them. Once unlawful pressure had been proved, it was up to the other party to show that the threats had had no effect on the decision to contract.

Duress to goods and economic duress

Originally, duress to goods was not sufficient to make a contract voidable. In *Skeate v Beale* (1841), B owed S some rent. S seized goods in order to sell them to satisfy the rent arrears. B contracted with S to pay the arrears in return for which S would return B's goods. S returned B's goods. B paid part of the arrears but refused to pay any more, since he argued that he had paid all that was due. S sued on the contract. B argued that it should be set aside as it had been obtained by duress. The court held that the contract could not be set aside because of duress even if the seizure was wrongful, because it covered more rent than was due. The correct course of action, said the court, was not to enter into a contract and then bring an action to have it set aside but, instead, to bring an action in respect of the unlawful seizure. The court also gave the opinion that if the full amount of money demanded by the defendant had been paid, the excess over the amount of rent due could not have been recovered in an action for money had and received (such an action is nowadays called 'restitution').

In *Universe Tankships Inc of Monrovia v International Transport Workers' Federation* (1982), a ship called the 'Universe Sentinel', having unloaded its cargo at Milford Haven, was 'blacked' by ITF (a trade union) as part of its campaign against ships flying 'flags of convenience', that is, they are registered in countries which don't require them to observe internationally agreed standards in relation, among other things, to the terms and conditions of employment of their crews. The blacking meant that the ship was unable to leave port. The union would release the ship only if a contribution of $6,480 was made to its funds. The sum was paid. After their ship had successfully left port, the owners sued for the return of their money on the ground of economic duress. The House of Lords held that the claim succeeded, since the pressure put on the owners was illegitimate. (If the action of the union had come within the ambit of a 'trade dispute', as then defined by s 29 of the TULRA 1974, the pressure would have been legitimate and the money irrecoverable.)

Any other type of undue pressure is generally categorised as economic duress. In the past 15 years or so, this type of duress has become recognised as sufficient to render a contract voidable. However, it can be difficult to draw the line between hard bargaining and duress. In the *North Ocean Shipping* case and in *Atlas v Kafco*, it was held that the later 'agreements' were voidable for duress. However, in the *Pao On* case, which seems little different in principle, it was held that the pressure was simply hard bargaining.

In *North Ocean Shipping Co v Hyundai* (1979), H agreed to build a ship for N at a certain price in dollars. The dollar was devalued by 10%. H therefore threatened to abandon a contract to build a ship for N unless N agreed to increase the contract price to compensate for the devaluation. N agreed under protest because they had arranged a lucrative charter of the ship on its completion. The ship was completed and delivered. N did not try to reclaim the additional 10% until nine months later because they had a second ship under construction by H and feared that if they commenced legal action before the second ship was delivered, delivery would be withheld by H. *Held*: N's agreement to pay the additional 10% was voidable because of duress. However, N's delay in reclaiming the money meant that they had affirmed the contract and that money was, therefore, no longer recoverable.

In *Atlas v Kafco* (1989), A operated a delivery service and K were importers of basketware into the UK. K had won a contract to supply Woolworths with their goods and approached A to carry the goods from Wisbech to various Woolworth stores. A contract was arranged between A and K after an employee of A had visited K's warehouse and seen a sample of the goods that were to be carried. A rate was agreed of £1.10 per carton. However, it seems that A's employee made only a visual inspection of the cartons – he took no measurements – and was later surprised when he saw how many large cartons there were in a load. The trailers would hold only 200 cartons, whereas he had calculated the average load as being 400 to 600 cartons. At a meeting between A and K, A therefore refused to transport any more of the cartons unless K paid a minimum rate of £440 per trailer load. The success of K was highly dependent upon their contract with Woolworths and it would have been difficult, if not impossible, for K to find alternative carriers to meet their delivery dates. Some time after the meeting, one of A's drivers arrived at K's premises with a document specifying a new rate of £440 minimum per trailer. K reluctantly signed the new agreement because if they had not done so A would not have delivered their goods. K later refused to pay the new rate, arguing that there was no consideration for the agreement to pay the new rate and that the agreement for the new rate had been extracted by duress.

Held: the agreement to pay the new rate had been made under duress and, furthermore, there was no consideration for it.

In *Pao On v Lau Yiu Long* (1980), on the other hand (for facts, see Chapter 5), it was held that a threat to break a contract to sell shares was no more than the unfair use of superior bargaining power, against which the law offered no protection. It did not amount to duress.

Undue influence

Equity developed the idea of undue influence in order to relieve the weaker party of the burden of a contract induced by undue pressure. Nowadays, (although, as we have seen, it was not always the case), any contract brought about by a threat to do something unlawful is likely to be held voidable because of duress. On the other hand, undue influence can be pleaded where there has been undue pressure (or where the law presumes there has been undue pressure), without there having been any threats at all.

In some cases, the undue pressure is brought to bear by the other contracting party, but in an increasing number of cases we are faced with a familiar problem: which of two innocent parties should suffer for the wrongdoing of a third?

For example, suppose Husband wishes to borrow money from Northern Bank. The bank requires a security for the loan and Husband suggests the matrimonial home owned jointly by himself and Wife. Husband persuades Wife to sign the appropriate papers by putting undue pressure on her or by misrepresenting the circumstances of the loan. Husband is then unable to repay the loan, with the result that the bank wishes to take possession of the house in order to sell it to recover the money it has loaned. The question arises as to whether the bank may take possession of the home or whether Wife may have the transaction between herself and the bank set aside on the ground of her husband's undue influence or misrepresentation (as appropriate).

A similar question would arise if the matrimonial home were owned by the wife and the husband offered the home, with the wife's agreement, as security for a loan made to the husband.

The answer to this question will depend upon the wife being able to prove one of two things: either (a) the husband was the agent of the bank for the purpose of procuring the wife's signature to the appropriate documentation; or (b) that the bank had notice of the undue influence or misrepresentation. Such notice may be actual notice, where the bank is actually aware of the irregular circumstances. This will be very rare. Much more common is constructive notice. This means that the circumstances of the loan (or the guarantee of the loan, where this is the case) are such that a reasonably prudent banker should recognise the warning signs and should make further enquiry into the circumstances of the loan or guarantee.

Holding the husband (or other dominant party in the transaction) to be the agent of the bank (or other third party) has not found much favour with the courts. One case in which this analysis was accepted was *Avon Finance v Bridger* (1985). In this case, an elderly couple had left the financial arrangements for buying their retirement home entirely in the hands of their son. He had borrowed money on the security of the home. He needed to obtain his parents' signatures in relation to this transaction, but did this by telling them that the document they were signing was in connection with the building society mortgage he was obtaining on their behalf. The son failed to keep up the payments on his loan and the plaintiffs sought possession of the parents' property in order to enforce their security. It was held that the son was the agent of the finance company for the purpose of obtaining the parents' signatures. Because of this agency, the finance company was responsible for the son's fraud and undue influence. It was, therefore, as if they had committed these wrongdoings themselves, and the transaction by which the parents had offered their home as security was therefore set aside.

The agency analysis has not found much favour elsewhere. For example, in *CIBC Mortgages v Pitt* (1993), it was held that, where a husband procured his wife's signature to documents offering the matrimonial home as security for a loan, the husband was not the agent of the bank. Similarly, in *Barclay's Bank v O'Brien* (1993), the agency analysis was rejected by the House of Lords as 'artificial and misleading'.

In relation to *constructive notice*, the circumstances must be such as to put a prudent banker on enquiry, that is, to alert him that something may be wrong. It may be the case that, where the loan is ostensibly made to both parties, there are no suspicious circumstances which should put the bank on enquiry.

In *CIBC Mortgages v Pitt* (1993), the husband and wife jointly owned the matrimonial home. The husband wished to borrow money on the security of the home in order to speculate in shares. The wife was unhappy about this but, following what the court held to constitute actual undue influence on the part of the husband, she agreed. Since banks are understandably reluctant to loan money for the purpose required by the husband, the bank was told that the money was to be used to buy a holiday home. The wife signed the appropriate documentation without reading it. The husband was, at first, successful in his dealings, which involved using the shares he bought as security to borrow money in order to finance further dealings. However, while such a method may work well while the market is rising, it encounters difficulties in a falling market and, as a result of the stock exchange crash of 1987, the husband was no longer able to service the loan of £150,000. The plaintiff bank sought to possess the matrimonial home in order to realise its security. The wife defended the claim on two grounds: she had been induced to enter into the transaction: (a) as a result of her husband's misrepresentations as to the purpose of the loan; and (b) because of the undue influence of her husband. It was held by the trial judge that there had been no misrepresentation by the husband to the wife; and that Mr Pitt had not acted as the agent for the bank. (In which case, as we have seen, the bank would have been responsible for the undue influence of the husband and would not be entitled to enforce the security against Mrs Pitt.) It was also held, by the House of Lords, that there were no circumstances which ought to have put the bank on enquiry in respect of the transaction. As far as the bank was concerned, it was a straightforward transaction to enable the joint owners of the matrimonial home to acquire a holiday home.

However, in *Barclay's Bank v O'Brien* (1993), also heard by the House of Lords, the facts were different and resulted in a different outcome. In this case the husband and wife jointly owned the matrimonial home, subject to a mortgage of £25,000. The husband wished to increase the overdraft of a company of which he was a shareholder. It was agreed that the overdraft would be increased to £135,000 (reducing to £120,000 after three weeks), with the matrimonial home being used as security. The bank manager instructed that the husband and wife were to be given an explanation of the nature of the transaction and that, if there appeared to be any doubts surrounding the transaction, the bank staff should suggest that independent legal advice should be obtained. This was not done and the wife signed the appropriate documents, having been told by her husband that the amount being secured was £60,000 and for three weeks only. She signed without having been given any advice as to the nature and possible consequences of the transaction. The company defaulted on the loan and the bank sought to enforce the security. It was held that there was no undue influence. However, the bank was fixed with constructive notice of the husband's misrepresentation regarding the loan. A significant difference between this case and *Pitt* was that in *Pitt*, the loan was apparently for the benefit of both parties offering the security whereas, in the present case, it was for the advantage of only one of the parties. The House of Lords summarised the position as follows:

> Where one cohabitee has entered into an obligation to stand surety for the debts of the other cohabitee and the creditor is aware that they are cohabitees:
>
> (a) the suretyship will be valid and enforceable by the creditor unless the suretyship was procured by undue influence, misrepresentation or other legal wrong of the principal debtor;
>
> (b) if there has been misrepresentation, undue influence, or other legal wrong by the principal debtor, unless the creditor has taken reasonable steps to satisfy himself that the surety entered into the obligation freely and in knowledge of the true facts, *the creditor will be unable to enforce the surety obligation* because he will be fixed with constructive notice of the surety's right to set aside the transaction; and
>
> (c) unless there are special circumstances, a creditor will have taken reasonable steps to avoid being fixed with constructive notice if the creditor warns the surety (at a meeting not attended by the principal debtor) of the amount of her potential liability and of the risks involved, and advises the surety to take independent legal advice.

Not all cases involve cohabitees, though it is clear that where the circumstances indicate the possibility of irregularity (as they often will, particularly where one party, who is not a cohabitee, acts as surety for the debt of another), the lender has the duties which were set out in the *O'Brien* case.

Banco Exterior Internacional SA v Thomas (1997)

Mrs Dempsey, a widow, guaranteed an overdraft of up to £75,000 given by the bank to Mr Mulchay, who was her close friend. She charged her residence as security for the loan. In return, M was to pay Mrs D a weekly income of £125. Mrs D was not a customer of the bank and before the bank would accept her guarantee it referred her to an independent solicitor who advised her as to the nature and legal effect of the guarantee. The court found that there was no reason to doubt that she understood the advice given. He did not advise her as to the wisdom of the arrangement. However, the title deeds to the property were lodged with Mr Frere-Smith, a solicitor who had acted for Mr and Mrs D in the past. Mrs D visited Mr Frere-Smith, who advised her in the strongest terms that her arrangement with M was ill-advised. She nevertheless proceeded to sign the guarantee and the charge on 12 February 1985. When M's overdraft exceeded the amount of the guarantee, the bank sought to enforce their security. Before the action came to trial, Mrs Dempsey died and her executors were defending the claim. Their defence was as follows: (i) Mrs D was induced by M's undue influence to provide security for M's overdraft; (ii) the bank was on notice of the undue influence; (iii) the bank was not entitled to enforce its security. The trial judge found that although the bank did not have actual or constructive notice of undue influence, it was put on notice by a telephone call made by Mr Frere-Smith to the bank on 5–6 March informing them of the circumstances under which Mrs D had signed the guarantee and the legal charge. A letter had followed on 11 April limiting the charge to £30,000. M's overdraft already exceeded £30,000 before the events of March had put the bank on notice. The bank was, therefore, entitled to £30,000 and no more.

Held by the Court of Appeal: the trial judge was wrong to hold that the guarantee and charge were affected by undue influence. Even if there were a presumption of undue influence, it had been rebutted by the fact that Mrs D had had independent legal advice from two solicitors but nevertheless decided to proceed with the transaction.

Classification of undue influence

In *Barclays' Bank v O'Brien* (1993), the House of Lords adopted the classification of undue influence suggested by the Court of Appeal in *Bank of Credit and Commerce International v Aboody* (1992). There are two basic situations, which are as follows.

Class 1   Actual undue influence

In this situation, there is no special relationship between the parties and the person asserting that undue influence had been applied must affirmatively prove it. It must be proved by the weaker party that the contract was entered into as a result of the undue influence of the stronger party.

In *Williams v Bayley* (1866), the son gave the bank several promissory notes upon which he had forged the endorsements of his father. At a meeting between the three parties, the banker made it clear that unless the father undertook responsibility the son would be prosecuted. The father agreed to make a mortgage to the bank in return for the promissory notes. *Held*: the agreement was void on the ground of undue pressure.

It would seem that once undue pressure has been proved, the contract may still be held to be valid if the stronger party can show that the weaker party nevertheless exercised free and independent judgment: *Barton v Armstrong* (1975).

Class 2   Presumed undue influence

In this situation, there is a relationship of trust and confidence between the parties of such a nature that it is fair to presume that the dominant party abused that relationship in procuring the weaker party to enter into the transaction. In such a case, undue influence is *presumed* to have been exerted without the need for the weaker party to prove that it has. If the dominant party wishes to enforce the transaction, the burden of proof falls on the dominant party to show that the weaker party entered into the transaction in consequence of having exercised independent judgment.

As we have seen, many of these cases involve wives guaranteeing their husband's borrowings by agreeing to put up the matrimonial home as security. The wife can raise a presumption of undue influence in such cases by showing that the transaction was to her manifest disadvantage. (If she cannot do this, she will need to demonstrate actual undue influence.) If the wife succeeds in raising the presumption of undue influence, the bank is fixed with constructive notice (that is, the bank is deemed to know) that the wife has a right to have the transaction set aside as against her husband and, in consequence, as against the bank.

The bank can avoid this result by showing that the wife entered into the transaction of her own free will, with full realisation of the possible consequences. The case law shows that the best way for the bank to do this is to insist that the documentation be completed in the presence of a qualified legal practitioner. (It has recently been held that a qualified legal executive is appropriate for the task – it does not have to be a solicitor.) The wife must then submit the documentation, together with a certificate from the legal practitioner, to the effect: (a) that she has received independent legal advice (that is, independent from the bank); and (b) that she understood the transaction; and (c) she was entering into it of her own free will.

Note: although we have been speaking in terms of wives claiming undue influence, similar principles will apply to any case of presumed undue influence.

In a recent case involving no less than eight appeals by wives, the Court of Appeal laid down useful guidance as to what level of legal advice is necessary in such cases. (Note that these principles will also apply to sureties other than wives.) The ideal is for the bank to ensure that the wife has had independent legal advice, with the husband not being present. This does not ensure that the wife will not go ahead in defiance of legal advice, but it does mean that the bank's security will almost certainly be protected. It has been made clear (see *Inche Noriah v Bin Omar* (1929)) that legal advice is not an absolute pre-requisite for a bank to be able to enforce its security, but cases where it will be able to do so in the absence of legal advice must be very rare.

In *Royal Bank of Scotland v Etridge (No 2)* (1998), eight appeals by wives claiming to have been induced to charge the matrimonial home, either by the husband's undue influence or his misrepresentation, were considered. The Court of Appeal laid down the following guidelines:

(a) if a wife deals with a bank through a solicitor, whether it is her own solicitor or a solicitor who is acting for both herself and her husband, the bank was entitled to assume that the solicitor had given proper professional advice and had considered and advised upon any potential conflicts of interest;

(b) if the wife did not approach the bank through a solicitor, it would be sufficient to protect the bank if the bank urges her to obtain independent legal advice. This is especially so if the solicitor confirms that he has explained the transaction and the wife appeared to understand it;

(c) there is not always a conflict of interest between husband and wife. It is therefore not necessarily wrong for the same solicitor to advise them both. The fact that the solicitor was prepared to advise the wife indicates that he considered himself to be independent;

(d) the bank is not required to enquire as to what advice the solicitor has given to the wife. Nor is it obliged to enquire whether the advice was adequate;

(e) if the bank introduces the solicitor to the wife, the solicitor is acting as the wife's solicitor and owes a duty to the wife. The bank is not regarded as having notice of what the solicitor advises the wife. (So that, if she disregards advice not to proceed with the loan or guarantee, the bank is not fixed with notice of what the solicitor advised her to do. Therefore, the bank could enforce the agreement); and

(f) if the solicitor advises the wife negligently, she will still be bound by her agreement with the bank, but she will have an action against the solicitor in respect of any loss she suffers.

In *Barclay's Bank v Coleman* (2000), the meanings of 'manifest disadvantage' and 'independent legal advice' were considered by the Court of Appeal. The case was yet another where a wife had signed documents granting a second charge over the matrimonial home in favour of a bank in order to secure her husband's borrowings in respect of a property he was purchasing in New York. The crucial point was that the certificate of independent legal advice was signed by a legal executive employed in a solicitor's practice. The trial judge held that although the bank was not entitled to rely on the certificate in order to show that the wife had had independent legal advice, nevertheless a presumption of undue influence could not arise because the wife had not shown that the transaction was to her manifest disadvantage: the transaction was to the future benefit of the family. The trial judge's findings were overturned by the Court of Appeal. The court held:

(a) that the manifest disadvantage should not be looked at in a narrow way. The charge upon the matrimonial home covered all moneys owed to the bank for the time being, so that although the wife had charged the home for the purpose of buying a property in New York, the charge did not simply cover debts in respect of that property. On balance, this was a manifest disadvantage; and

(b) the fact that the certificate of independent legal advice was signed by a legal executive did not invalidate it. The certificate confirmed that the full effect of the contents of the legal charge had been explained to the wife, that it was understood by her and that she had signed the charge of her own free will. It had been given by the legal executive acting within the authority given to him by his principal. Thus, although there was presumed undue influence because of the manifest disadvantage of the transaction to the wife, the bank had taken reasonable steps, in relying on the legal executive's certificate, to avoid being fixed with notice of the wife's right to set the transaction aside.

One element of *presumed* undue influence which does not apply in the case of *actual* undue influence is that the party seeking to set the contract (or gift) aside must show that the transaction is to his *manifest disadvantage*.

Presumed undue influence is of two types:

Class 2A

Certain relationships give rise to a presumption of undue influence as a matter of law. Established categories of special relationship include solicitor and client, doctor and patient, parent and child. Note that the child is regarded as being 'emancipated' only when the child may be taken to have broken free of the parent's influence, so that, in one case, it was held that the presumption of undue influence existed in the case of a married woman who was, nevertheless, still greatly influenced by her mother: *Lancashire Loans v Black* (1934).

Husband and wife is not among this category, but it is not difficult, in an appropriate case, to bring a case of husband and wife within class 2B, or within class 1.

Class 2B

This category does not automatically give rise to a presumption of undue influence. It requires the party who is seeking to avoid the agreement (the surety) to demonstrate, as a matter of fact, that there exists a special relationship between the surety and the person for whom the surety is being given (the beneficiary), whereby the surety relies on the beneficiary for advice. If the surety is able to demonstrate that this special relationship exists (as it may often do between husband and wife), this raises a presumption of undue influence in favour of the surety.

In *Lloyds Bank v Bundy* (1975), D, an elderly farmer, and his son had been customers of the bank for many years. D had put a charge of £7,500 on the farmhouse to secure his son's company's overdraft. He had been advised by his solicitor that this was the most he could afford. Son and assistant bank manager visited the defendant and told him that the bank would allow the company's overdraft to increase only if D increased the charge to £11,000. The defendant signed. The evidence showed that the assistant manager knew that D relied upon the bank for advice and that the farmhouse was the defendant's only assets. *Held*: the contract would be set aside for undue influence. The bank had a conflict of interest and the defendant had not received independent advice.

Similarly, in *Credit Lyonnais Bank Nederland NV v Burch* (1997), the surety agreement was set aside even though the bank's solicitors had written to the surety and had advised her that, since the guarantee she was signing was unlimited, she should take independent legal advice. She replied to the bank's solicitors informing them that she understood the full implications of the transaction. In this case, an employee guaranteed her employer's bank borrowings, putting up her own home (valued at £100,000) as security. When the employer's business failed, the bank wished to enforce the agreement. The employee pleaded 'undue influence'. It was held by the Court of Appeal that the guarantee could not be enforced. The agreement was clearly so disadvantageous to the employee that the bank should not have allowed her to go ahead without explaining: (a) the full extent of the employer's borrowing; (b) the full implications to the employee in the event of the bank seeking to enforce the guarantee; and (c) the bank should have ensured that the employee had received independent legal advice.

Contrast *National Westminster Bank v Morgan* (1985). Husband and Wife were joint owners of their home. H was unsuccessful in business and unable to meet the mortgage payments. H negotiated a refinancing arrangement with the bank. It was secured by a charge on the matrimonial home. The bank manager visited the house so that W could execute the charge. During the visit W made it clear that she had little faith in H's business ability and wanted the charge only to cover the mortgage, and not to finance her husband's business. The bank manager assured her that the charge covered only the mortgage liabilities. This was said in good faith, but was incorrect: the charge was unlimited in extent and covered all H's liabilities to the bank, though in fact no such liability was incurred. W obtained no independent legal advice. H fell into arrears with repayments and the bank brought an order for possession. W contended that the charge should be set aside. *Held*: although the relationship between the bank manager and W was confidential, it did not cross the line so as to give rise to dominance by the bank manager and, therefore, there was no presumption of undue influence. In addition, the transaction was to W's advantage.

Rescission

Duress or undue influence makes a contract (or gift) voidable. This means that equity will rescind it. Rescission means restoring the parties to their pre-contract position. However, this does not need to be precisely possible, providing that the court is able to do justice between the parties.

In *O'Sullivan v Management Agency and Music* (1985), the plaintiff was a composer and performer of popular music. He had made a number of agreements with the defendants relating to management, ownership of copyright, etc, while he was unknown. They proved to be disadvantageous to him when he became famous. He sought to rescind the contracts on the ground of undue influence. The defendants argued that rescission was not possible. The parties could not be restored to their pre-contract positions because the defendants had, meanwhile, undertaken considerable work on the plaintiff's behalf. *Held*: rescission could be ordered where a precise restoration to the pre-contract position was not possible, providing the court was able to do justice between the parties. In this case, the contracts, which were procured by undue influence, would be set aside, subject to the defendants being paid a reasonable remuneration for the work they had undertaken.

In *Dunbar Bank v Nadeem* (1997), it was held that where a party is seeking to set aside a contract of surety on the ground of undue influence, that party must account to the lender for any benefit the surety had received from the loan.

Because the remedy of rescission is equitable, the usual bars to rescission apply (dealt with fully in Chapter 10). Thus, lapse of time will defeat a claim.

In *Allcard v Skinner* (1887), P donated, without being permitted access to legal advice, £7,000 to a religious institution known as the 'Sisters of the Poor'. She had become a sister in 1871 and remained one for eight years. When she left, there remained only £1,671 of the money she had donated. Six years later, she sued for its return. *Held:* she was entitled to set aside the agreement in principle but six years' delay, during which she had access to legal advice, was too long.

In *North Ocean Shipping v Hyundai* (1979), a claim for rescission made nine months after the duress had ceased was held to be too late.

Contrast *Morley v Loughnan* (1893): £140,000 was extorted from an epileptic by a Plymouth Brother. Six months after the donor's death, an action was brought to recover the money. The action was successful.

ALLOWING THE CONSUMER SECOND THOUGHTS

A number of statutes have introduced controls aimed at allowing the consumer to have second thoughts after entering into particular types of agreement. Prominent examples include long-term insurance contracts, consumer credit contracts, timeshare contracts, distance selling and contracts concluded away from trade premises.

The Insurance Companies Act 1982 provides that the insurer, under a long-term insurance contract, must provide the insured with a statutory notice informing the insured of his right to cancel the agreement. The proposer of the insurance (that is, the customer) has 10 days after receiving the notice or up to the end of the earliest day on which he knows the contract has been entered into and that the first or only premium has been paid, whichever is the later. If the proposer cancels, it either revokes his offer or rescinds the contract. If a premium has been paid this must be refunded.

Section 67 of the Consumer Credit Act 1974 provides that a consumer credit agreement which is made following oral representations to the debtor, which is signed away from trade premises and which is not secured on land, is cancellable. This provision was made following a spate of complaints about high-pressure doorstep salesmen pressurising people who were at home alone, into entering credit agreements for goods they didn't really need (encyclopaedia salesmen were particularly active). They regretted making the agreement after the salesman had left, but as the law used to stand, they were unable to do anything about the matter once their signature was on the contract. The cancellation must take place within five days of the debtor receiving his statutory copy of the unexecuted agreement. This period of grace is often called a 'cooling-off' period.

The Consumer Protection (Cancellation of Contracts Concluded Away from Business Premises) Regulations 1987 give a seven day cooling-off period to a customer who enters a contract to buy goods or services during an unsolicited visit by the trader to the customer's home, or place of work, or someone else's home. For more detail regarding these Regulations, see Chapter 3.

The Consumer Protection (Distance Selling) Regulations 2000 also provide for a cooling-off period of seven working days after goods are delivered or, in the case of the contract for a service, seven working days after the contract is made.

The Timeshare Act 1992 gives a 14 day cooling-off period for contracts made in the UK or where one of the parties is located in the UK.

RE-OPENING OF EXTORTIONATE CREDIT BARGAINS

Sections 137–40 of the Consumer Credit Act 1974 allow the court to reopen an extortionate credit bargain. Under s 138, a bargain is extortionate if it requires the debtor or a relative of his to make payments which are grossly exorbitant, or it otherwise grossly contravenes ordinary principles of fair dealing. In determining whether a credit bargain is extortionate, regard shall be had to evidence concerning interest rates prevailing at the time the agreement was made; factors such as the debtor's age, experience, business capacity and state of health; and the degree to which the debtor was under financial pressure. The court may also take regard of any other relevant considerations.

RESTRAINT OF TRADE

The doctrine of restraint of trade, while not primarily aimed at unconscionable contracts, has been used in an *ad hoc* manner in order to negative the effects of contracts which the courts think have been unfair.

In *Schroeder v Macaulay* (1974), Macaulay, a promising but unknown song writer, entered into a contract with S whereby he gave S his exclusive services for five years. Under the contract, M assigned to S the copyrights in all his compositions during the contract period. However, S was not bound to publish any of M's compositions, which meant that if good material remained unpublished, M could not recover the copyright and sell the material to a different publisher. If M's royalties under the contract exceeded £5,000 in the first five years, the contract was automatically extended by another five years. S could terminate the contract with a month's notice but M had no right of termination. It was argued that the agreement was voidable because it was an unreasonable restraint of trade. The court accepted this argument. Lord Wilberforce pointed out:

Any contract by which a person engages to give his exclusive services to another for a period, necessarily involves extensive restriction during that period, of the common law right to exercise any lawful activity he chooses in such manner as he thinks best. Normally the doctrine of restraint of trade has no application to such restrictions: they require no justification. But if contractual restrictions appear to be unnecessary or to be reasonably capable of enforcement in an oppressive manner, then they must be justified before they can be enforced.

UCTA 1977 AND OTHER STATUTORY AND COMMON LAW CONTROLS OVER THE USE OF EXEMPTION CLAUSES

An exemption clause is a clause in a contract by which one of the parties seeks to exclude or limit his liability.

Such clauses may be used for one of two main purposes:

(a) to determine in advance which party is to bear the risk of certain eventualities materialising (and, presumably, to insure against such eventualities); and

(b) to exploit (and often abuse) the superior economic power of the supplier of goods or services over the consumer of goods or services.

The first purpose is a legitimate, and indeed necessary, method of risk allocation in contracts between businessmen. However, the use of exemption clauses for the second purpose, particularly against consumers (members of the motor trade were particularly enthusiastic users), brought the whole concept of exemption clauses into disrepute, with the result that the use of exemption clauses in order to attain morally dubious ends, tended to obscure their legitimate use. This led, inevitably, to legislative control over their use.

The most significant legislative control is exercised by the Unfair Contract Terms Act 1977, though the Unfair Terms in Consumer Contracts Regulations 1994, which are dealt with later, arguably provide a more comprehensive protection against the use of unfair terms, providing the complainant is a consumer. Under the terms of UCTA 1977, certain exemption clauses are void. This means that they cannot be validly incorporated into a contract. Thus, where it is clear that the clause is void, it is unnecessary to consider whether or not it is incorporated into the contract. However, most exemption clauses in dealings between businesses are not void but must satisfy the requirement of reasonableness. In such a case (and in the few cases of business exemptions which are not regulated by the Act), the first requirement of the clause is that it must be incorporated into the contract in question. If the clause in question is not in the contract, it becomes irrelevant whether it is reasonable or not – it is not binding!

(Note: in a number of the cases at which we shall be looking in connection with the question of whether the exemption clause has been incorporated into the contract, the case on its facts would have a different outcome today. However, the cases are still valid authority on the principles of incorporation.)

In our study of exemption clauses, we shall look at two questions:

(a) when is an exemption clause incorporated into a contract?; and

(b) how can a seemingly valid exemption clause be defeated?

Incorporation into the contract

In order to be valid, an exemption clause must be incorporated into the contract in question.

There are two methods of incorporating an exemption clause into a contract:

(a) by signature; and

(b) by notice.

Signature

A person who signs a contractual document is bound by its terms whether he reads them or not or whether, having read them, he understands them or not. In *L'Estrange v Graucob* (1934), L signed a sales agreement for the purchase of an automatic cigarette-vending machine. It was printed on brown paper and some of the clauses were in very small print. One of these was 'Any express or implied condition, statement or warranty, statutory or otherwise not stated herein is hereby excluded'. The machine became jammed and unworkable after a few days. L claimed the repayment of the instalment of the purchase price which she had paid. She claimed that she wasn't bound by the exemption clause since she hadn't read it. *Held*: the fact that she had signed the document meant that she was bound by its terms.

(Note: if this case were heard today, the exemption clause would have to satisfy the requirement of reasonableness, under the Unfair Contract Terms Act. One of the criteria to which the court must have regard in deciding whether the exempting term was reasonable is 'whether the customer knew or ought reasonably to have known of the existence and extent of the term'. The term in question would probably have failed the test of reasonableness on this criterion alone.)

Sometimes a person will be induced by fraud or misrepresentation to sign a contract which contains exemptions. In such a case, the misrepresentation will override the exemption clause. In *Curtis v Chemical Cleaning* (1951), the plaintiff took a white satin wedding dress to the defendant's dry-cleaning shop for cleaning. She was asked by a shop assistant to sign a paper headed 'receipt'. It contained the following clause: 'The company is not liable for damage howsoever arising.' She asked what the effect of the document was and was told that it exempted the company from certain types of damage, particularly, in her case, the risk of damage to the beads and sequins on the dress. The plaintiff signed the document without reading it. The dress was returned with a stain on it. The plaintiff sued for damages. The defendants couldn't explain how the stain came to be there but relied on their exempting condition. *Held*: the shop assistant, albeit innocently, had misrepresented the effect of the exemption clause. The company could not, therefore, rely on the clause to exempt them from liability.

Notice

Often, the exemption clause is printed on a document which is simply handed by one person to the other, or it is posted up, for example, on a wall or a door where the contract is made. In neither case has the party adversely affected by the clause signed any document. If the clause is actually brought to the other party's notice, there tends to be no difficulty. It is in cases where the clause has not been brought to the other party's notice where the difficulties arise. In such a case, the clause will be incorporated into the contract only if the court finds that reasonable notice of its existence has been given to the party adversely affected. Such notice is called 'constructive notice'.

In deciding whether reasonable notice has been given, the courts tend to be influenced by one or more of the following factors:

(a) The steps taken to bring the notice to the other party's attention

An exemption clause is effective only if reasonable steps were taken to bring the existence of the clause to the other party's attention. This is illustrated by *Interfoto Picture Library v Stiletto Visual Programmes* (1988). It illustrates that the claimant who relies on an onerous clause, whether or not it is an exemption clause, must take reasonable steps to bring it to the attention of the other party. In this case, the plaintiffs ran a photographic library. They sent a selection of transparencies to the defendant with a delivery note stating that if the transparencies were not returned within 14 days they would be charged at the rate of £5 per day each. The defendants did not read the clause and did not return the transparencies for a month. They received a bill for nearly £4,000. *Held*: the clause could not be enforced. The more onerous or unusual the clause, the greater the steps which needed to be taken to draw it to the attention of the other party.

Where it is asserted that the clause is part of a contract, the notice in which it is contained must be part of the contract. If the notice is contained in a document, the question arises whether the document is part of the contract. If, looking at the document objectively, it can be said that the document was intended to be part of the contract, it will be treated as such. Difficulties have arisen, mainly with the so called 'ticket cases', but the problem is of potentially wider application than that: for example, in *Davis Contractors v Fareham UDC* (1956), the question arose as to whether certain conditions (which, in essence, amounted to exemption clauses) in a letter attached to a tender were part of the contract that was eventually concluded without mention of the conditions. The court said 'no', the letter was not part of the contract.

In relation to exemptions contained in tickets, Lord Hodson, speaking in *McCutcheon v MacBrayne* (1964) approved the following three questions, put in *Parker v South Eastern Railway Co* (1877), as establishing the correct test as to whether a ticket was a contractual document. The three questions are:

(a) did the passenger know that there was writing on the ticket?;

(b) did he know that the ticket contained, or referred to, conditions?; and

(c) did the railway company do what was reasonable in the way of notifying prospective passengers of the existence of the conditions and where their terms might be considered (that is, where the terms can be found if they're not on the ticket)?

A leading case is *Chapleton v Barry UDC* (1940). The plaintiff wished to hire two deck-chairs. He approached a pile of chairs owned by the defendants behind which was a notice saying, 'Hire of Chairs 2d per session of three hours'. The notice requested intending hirers to obtain a ticket from the deck-chair attendant and retain it for inspection. On the back of the tickets was printed, 'The council will not be liable for any accident or damage arising from the hire of the chairs'. The plaintiff took two chairs and was given two tickets which he put in his pocket without reading. When he sat on one of the chairs, it collapsed and he was injured. He claimed damages. In its defence, the council sought to rely on the exemption clause on the ticket given to the plaintiff. *Held*: the exemption clause was not binding on the plaintiff. There was nothing in the defendants' notice to indicate that their liability was restricted in any way, and it was unreasonable to communicate such conditions by means of a document which appeared to be simply a receipt.

However, there is no rule of law to the effect that tickets are always simply receipts and not contractual documents, and in modern trading conditions, where it is well-known that tickets often contain conditions, it may well be that even an unread ticket is treated as a contractual document. In *Mendelssohn v Normand* (1970), the plaintiff had frequently left his car in the defendants' garage. He had always received a ticket which said that the company 'will not accept responsibility for any loss or damage sustained by the vehicle, its accessories or contents, howsoever caused'. The Court of Appeal held that the ticket was a contractual document and as the plaintiff had accepted it without objection, the plaintiff must be taken to have agreed to its terms. (The exemption clause was, however, invalidated on other grounds.)

In *Thornton v Shoe Lane Parking* (1971), the plaintiff drove to the entrance to the defendant's multi-storey car-park. He had not been there before. Outside the entrance was a notice which said 'All cars parked at owners' risk'. The notice also contained details of the parking charges. As the plaintiff drove into the park, a light turned from red to green and a ticket was issued from an automatic machine. The ticket recorded the time at which the plaintiff went into the park and it also stated that the ticket was issued subject to conditions which were displayed inside the premises. These were posted up at intervals around the interior of the park. One of the conditions purported to exempt the defendants from liability for personal injury to customers, howsoever caused. The plaintiff saw the time printed; he also saw that there were other words on the ticket, but he didn't read them. The plaintiff was injured, partly through his own negligence, but partly through the negligence of the defendants. He claimed damages. The defendants sought to rely on the exemption clause. *Held* by the Court of Appeal: *per* Megaw LJ and Sir Gordon Willmer, that the defendants had not done what was reasonable to bring the exemption to the notice of the plaintiff at or before the time when the contract was made. (Lord Denning MR held that the ticket came too late in the transaction to be viewed as part of the contract; the other two gave no opinion on that point.)

A contrasting case is *Thompson v LMS* (1930). In this case, the plaintiff was illiterate. She gave her niece, Miss Aldcroft, (who was held by the court to be her agent for the purpose of purchasing the ticket) the money to buy her an excursion ticket from Manchester to Darwen. On the front of the ticket was printed 'Excursion. For conditions see back'. On the back were the words: 'Issued subject to the conditions and regulations in the company's timetables and notices and excursion and other bills.' The excursion bills referred to the conditions in the railway company's timetables. The conditions in the timetable provided that excursion ticket holders should have no right of action against the railway company in respect of any injury howsoever caused. In getting off the train at Darwen, the plaintiff slipped and injured herself when the train drew up at the place where the platform ramp begins. She claimed damages. The railway company relied on the exemption clause. *Held*: the plaintiff had had reasonable notice of the exemption clause. Lord Hanworth MR said that the fact that the plaintiff couldn't read didn't help her (taking into account the state of education in this country and the legal authorities on the matter). The time of the train was ascertained by Miss Aldcroft's father (who seems also to have been regarded as the plaintiff's agent), who specifically asked at what time and under what circumstances there was an excursion available for intending travellers.

In *Richardson Steamship Co v Rowntree* (1894), an exemption clause was printed in small type and was rendered less obvious by a red ink stamp on the ticket. It was held that Rowntree was not bound by the clause: she did not know of its existence and the company had failed to give reasonable notice of it.

(b) Was notice given in time?

An exemption clause is incorporated into a contract only if notice of it is given before or at the time of the contract. If notice is given after the contract is concluded, the clause will be ineffective (unless the consistent course of dealing exception applies – see below). The leading case is *Olley v Marlborough Court Hotel* (1949). Mr and Mrs O arrived at a hotel as guests. They paid for a room in advance and went up to their room. Posted on one of the walls was the following notice: 'The proprietors will not hold themselves responsible for articles lost or stolen unless handed to the manageress for safe custody.' Mrs O closed the self-locking door of the bedroom and handed in the key at the reception desk. While she was out, a third party took the key and stole certain of the wife's furs. The wife sued the hotel in respect of her loss. The hotel argued that they were protected by the exemption notice. *Held:* the notice came too late in the transaction and was not, therefore, part of the contract.

Course of dealing

A controversial aspect of 'constructive notice' is that it may be created as a result of a consistent course of dealing between the parties. In *Spurling v Bradshaw* (1956), the plaintiffs were warehousemen with whom the defendant had dealt for many years. The defendant delivered to the plaintiff eight barrels of orange juice for storage. He later received a written document (which the plaintiffs called a 'landing account'), acknowledging receipt of the barrels. The document referred the recipient to 'contract clauses' printed on the back. One of these exempted the plaintiffs from any 'loss or damage occasioned by the negligence, wrongful act or default' of themselves or their servants. When the defendants came to collect the barrels, some were empty, some were leaking badly and some contained dirty water. The defendant refused to pay the storage charges and the plaintiff sued. The defendants counter-claimed for damages for breach of an implied term in the contract to the effect that the plaintiffs would use reasonable care in carrying out the contract or alternatively for negligence. The plaintiffs pleaded that the exemption clause excused them from liability. The defendants argued that the exemption clause came too late in the transaction. However, the defendant admitted that he had received many similar 'landing accounts' over the years in respect of other goods but that he had never bothered to read them. *Held* by the Court of Appeal: the defendant was bound by the exemption clause because his long course of dealing with the plaintiff was sufficient to amount to reasonable notice of the exemption clauses contained on the back of the 'landing account'.

Despite criticisms of the rule and despite attempts to restrict its scope (notably the judgment of Lord Devlin in *McCutcheon v MacBrayne* (1964), in which his Lordship suggested that it was necessary for the party seeking to rely on the exemption clause to show actual rather than constructive knowledge in relation to previous dealings), it is clear that constructive knowledge based on a previous course of dealing is firmly established.

In *British Crane Hire Corp v Ipswich Plant Hire Ltd* (1975), the Court of Appeal went further and incorporated a clause on the basis that both parties were in the same line of business. In this case, both the plaintiffs and the defendants were companies who hired out earth-moving equipment. The defendants found themselves in urgent need of a crane. They agreed over the telephone to hire one from the plaintiffs. The hire cost was agreed but no mention was made of the plaintiffs' conditions of hire. It was the plaintiffs' practice to impose conditions and they therefore sent the defendants a printed form containing the conditions and asked the defendants to sign it. One of the conditions provided that the defendants would be liable for all expenses arising out of the crane's use. Before the defendants signed the form, the crane sank in soft ground but without any fault on the part of the defendants. The plaintiffs sued the defendants for an indemnity for the cost of recovering the crane. The defendants argued that the indemnity clause was not part of the contract. *Held* by the Court of Appeal: since the defendants used a similar clause themselves (as did all companies in this type of business), they must be taken to have contracted on the plaintiff's terms of business.

(Note: one of the reasons that the Court of Appeal gave for holding that the indemnity clause was incorporated into the contract was that the parties were of equal bargaining power. This might, since the Unfair Contract Terms Act 1977, be a reason why the clause was reasonable, but is irrelevant to the question of whether the clause was incorporated. The crucial factor which led to the clause being incorporated appears to be not so much the equality of bargaining power but the fact that the parties were in the same business, so that the defendants could reasonably be expected to know that such clauses were standard when hiring heavy cranes like the one in question.)

In contracts involving consumers, the courts have been less willing to hold that an adverse exemption clause was incorporated by a course of dealing. In *Hollier v Rambler Motors* (1972), H telephoned R and asked them whether they would repair his car. R agreed. Whilst the car was in R's garage, it was damaged by a fire caused by the negligence of R. H claimed damages in respect of his loss. He had dealt with the company three or four times in the previous five years and on each occasion had signed a form which stated: 'The company is not responsible for damage caused by fires to customers' cars on the premises.' R therefore argued that H was bound by this exemption clause even though he had not been asked to sign a form incorporating the clause on the present occasion. *Held* by the Court of Appeal: the number of transactions involved was not sufficient to amount to a course of dealing and that, in any case, the wording of the clause was not sufficiently clear to exclude liability for negligence.

In *McCutcheon v MacBrayne* (1964), McCutcheon's brother-in-law, McSporran, shipped McCutcheon's car on MacBrayne's ship. The ship was negligently rammed into a rock and sank. McCutcheon sued in respect of the loss of his car. MacBrayne argued that condition 19 of their conditions of carriage, which purported to exempt them from liability in respect of any loss caused by their negligence, applied to the contract of carriage. McSporran had regularly shipped his brother-in-law's car and sometimes he was asked to sign a 'risk note' incorporating condition 19 and sometimes not. This time he hadn't been asked to sign. Nevertheless, argued MacBrayne, condition 19 was incorporated into the present contract because of a consistent course of dealing between the parties. *Held* by the House of Lords: condition 19 was not incorporated into the present oral contract and, therefore, MacBrayne's were liable. Three of their Lordships were of the opinion that the present contract, being oral, was different from previous written contracts and that it could not be assumed that the exemption clause was incorporated into it. Two of their Lordships were of the opinion that, since McSporran was sometimes asked to sign a risk note and sometimes not, the course of dealing between the parties was not consistent.

Defeating an exemption clause

An exemption clause may be defeated for one of the following reasons:

(a) it is rendered invalid as a result of statutory provision;

(b) because the *contra proferentem* rule applies;

(c) because the party seeking to rely on the clause is not a party to the contract; or

(d) because it has been subsequently overridden.

Exemption clauses, especially those aimed at depriving a consumer of his rights, were frowned upon by the courts, which developed a number of weapons which were used effectively against exemption clauses. The war against exemption clauses was waged particularly strongly by the Court of Appeal under the influence of Lord Denning MR. The Court developed a doctrine of 'fundamental breach', the effect of which was to prevent, as a matter of law, a party using an exemption clause to excuse his breach of contract if the breach was so fundamental that, in effect, the party seeking to rely on the clause was not carrying out his contractual obligations at all. However, in 1966, in the *Suisse Atlantique* case, the House of Lords held that whether an exemption clause covered a particular breach of contract was a matter of construction. If it did, there was no rule of law which prevented it from operating to excuse the breach. Following this decision, which virtually restored *carte blanche* to unscrupulous users of exemption clauses, legislation aimed at controlling the use of exemption clauses became inevitable. An interim measure in relation to the supply of goods was passed in 1973, to be repealed and re-enacted along with much wider measures in 1977 by the Unfair Contract Terms Act. A comprehensive measure aimed at protecting consumers was passed in 1994 in the shape of the Unfair Terms in Consumer Contracts Regulations.

We shall deal in turn with the reasons why an exemption clause may be defeated.

Statutory provision

An exemption clause may be defeated because it is prohibited by statute or because, where a statute has allowed the clause subject to the test of reasonableness, the clause has been found to be unreasonable. We shall look at this area under two headings:

(a) the Unfair Contract Terms Act; and

(b) other statutory controls over exemption clauses.

Unfair Contract Terms Act 1977

The title of the Act is somewhat misleading since:

(a) it implies that all unfair terms are within the ambit of the Act, whereas only unfair exemption clauses and ancillary clauses are caught by the Act; and

(b) it deals with unfair exemptions from tort liability in addition to unfair contract exemptions.

The Act applies only to business contracts (including consumer contracts), so that a contract between two private persons is not caught by the Act.

Unconditionally valid clauses

Under the Act, virtually all exemption clauses are either 'void' or must be subjected to the test of reasonableness. The only circumstances in which an exemption clause can be unconditionally valid are if:

(a) the clause does not seek to exempt the terms implied in a supply of goods; and

(b) neither of the parties is dealing as a consumer; and

(c) the contract is not on the standard form of the party seeking to rely on the exemption clause.

This combination of circumstances will be rarely encountered in practice.

Whether a clause is unconditionally valid, void, or must satisfy the test of reasonableness depends upon:

(a) the legal context in which the clause is being used; and

(b) the type of person against whom it is used.

It is probably most convenient to structure a study of the Act by looking at it from the point of view of the context in which the exemption clause is used. We will, therefore, use the following headings (including 'Misrepresentation', the provisions in respect of which are contained in the Misrepresentation Act 1967 but are closely related to those of the 1977 Act, by which they were amended):

(a) contracts for the sale, supply, hire or hire-purchase of goods;

(b) negligence;

(c) contractual obligations generally;

(d) indemnity;

(e) guarantees;

(f) misrepresentation.

We shall deal with each type of obligation in turn.

Contracts for the sale, supply, hire or hire-purchase of goods

In order to understand fully the effect of the Unfair Contract Terms Act, it is necessary to know, at least in outline, the nature of the terms which the Sale of Goods Act 1979 implies into a sale of goods (see Chapter 18). A knowledge of the Sale of Goods Act is probably sufficient, since the terms implied by the Act are the model on which terms are implied into other contracts for the supply of goods.

Sections 6 and 7 of the 1977 Act control the use of exemption clauses in contracts for the sale, supply, hire or hire-purchase of goods. An exemption clause used in such a contract will either be void or, alternatively, it must meet the requirement of reasonableness. In no such contract may an exemption clause be unconditionally valid.

Clauses which seek to exempt s 12 of the Sale of Goods Act or its equivalent

Any clause which purports to exclude or limit the operation of s 12 of the Sale of Goods Act (that is, the implied term dealing with the seller's right to sell the goods), or its equivalent in relation to goods transactions other than sale, is *void*. In the case of the other implied terms, the exemption may be valid if used in a contract where both parties are dealing in the course of business and the exemption satisfies the test of *reasonableness*. However, in the case of s 12 or its equivalent, it is immaterial against whom the clause is used: it is void in all events.

Clauses which seek to exempt s 13, 14 or 15 or their equivalents

Such clauses are void if they are used against a person dealing as a consumer.

If a clause which seeks to exempt s 13, 14 or 15 or their equivalents is used in a contract between two businesses, the clause must satisfy the test of reasonableness.

For example, Alan sells a computer to Beth. A term in the contract states that 'All conditions and warranties, express or implied, by statute or otherwise, are hereby excluded'. If Alan and Beth are both private persons, the exemption clause will not be invalidated by the Unfair Contract Terms Act, since the Act applies only to business contracts. If Beth is dealing as a consumer, the exemption clause will be void. If both Alan and Beth are dealing as business people, the clause will be subject to the test of reasonableness.

Negligence

Under s 2, certain attempts to exempt oneself from the consequences of negligence will be void. Others must be reasonable. In no case will an exemption clause which attempts to exempt from negligence be unconditionally valid without at least the need to satisfy the test of reasonableness.

'Negligence' is a tort (which, in essence, places liability upon a person who breaches his duty to act with reasonable care). However, by s 1 of UCTA, it is given an extended definition to cover, in particular: the breach of a contractual duty to exercise reasonable care or skill in the performance of the contract; any common law duty to exercise reasonable care or skill; the common duty of care which arises under the Occupiers' Liability Act 1957, that is, the duty to make premises reasonably safe for the purposes for which a visitor is invited to use them.

Section 2 of the Act provides:

(i) a person cannot by reference to any contract term or to a notice given to persons generally or to particular persons, exclude or restrict his liability for death or personal injury resulting from his negligence;

(ii) in the case of other loss or damage, a person cannot so exclude his liability for negligence except in so far as the term or notice satisfies the requirement of reasonableness.

In either case, a person's agreement to or awareness of the exemption clause is not of itself to be taken as indicating his voluntary acceptance of the risk.

Contractual obligations generally

This is a very broad heading which encompasses all types of contractual obligation. The effect of s 3 of UCTA is that a clause seeking to exempt contractual obligations generally will be either unconditionally valid or must be reasonable.

Typical circumstances where s 3 will apply include: exemption clauses in holiday contracts which exclude or limit liability for late departure or for the need of the tour operator to allocate the customer different accommodation from that which was booked; an exemption clause which seeks to excuse the seller from liability in the event of late delivery in a sale of goods contract.

There is an overlap between s 3 and other sections of the Act, notably s 2 and ss 6 and 7, and where those sections apply it may be more advantageous to rely on them rather than on s 3 as a means of invalidating the exemption clause. For example, Drew sells a hand-built car to Lucy, a consumer, in the course of a business. He purports to exempt himself from liability for death or personal injury caused by negligence and from liability for breach of ss 12, 13, 14, or 15 of the Sale of Goods Act. Drew has constructed the car brakes negligently and the defects in them result in Lucy suffering an injury. If Lucy were to rely on s 3 of UCTA in order to challenge the validity of the exemption clause, the clause would be subjected to the test of reasonableness. If, however, she uses s 7 to challenge the exemption clause in respect of the attempt to exclude the implied terms (s 2 could be used in respect of the personal injury caused by negligence but would not be necessary since the injury arises from the goods not being of satisfactory quality nor fit for their purpose), the reasonableness or otherwise of the clause does not arise, since the clause is void. (Similarly, s 2 renders void the attempt to exclude liability for personal injury caused by negligence.)

On the other hand, there are other circumstances in which the provisions of s 3 overlap with those of s 2, where it appears to be immaterial which provision the victim of the exemption clause relies upon, since the effect of both sections is that, in the circumstances, the exemption clause must satisfy the test of reasonableness (though note that, in theory, the test of reasonableness is different in each case!). Examples include exemption clauses in contracts for the developing and printing of photographic film, which typically limit the liability of the film processor to supplying an unexposed replacement film should the processing be faulty.

Section 3 of the Act provides that in a case where either:

(a) one of the parties is a consumer; or

(b) one of the parties is dealing on the other's standard terms of business,

the non-consumer or the party on whose standard terms the parties are contracting cannot:

(i) when himself in breach of contract, exclude or restrict any liability in respect of the breach; or

(ii) claim to be entitled either (i) to render contractual performance substantially different from that which was reasonably expected of him; or (ii) in respect of the whole or part of his contractual obligation, to render no performance at all,

except insofar as the contract term satisfies the requirement of reasonableness.

It follows from this that an exemption clause which is included in a contract which does not involve a person dealing as a consumer and does not contain standard terms can be unconditionally valid.

Indemnity

The effect of s 4 of the Act is that indemnity clauses used in consumer contracts must be reasonable. An indemnity is a promise to assume liability on behalf of another. For example, a compulsory motor insurance requires the insurer to indemnify the policy holder in respect of third party liabilities, so that if Cliff, while driving his car, negligently injures Joanne, Cliff's insurance company will indemnify him in respect of the damages he must pay to Joanne.

Sometimes, indemnity clauses can be used unfairly. For example, several years ago, I came across a clause (one of 30 closely typed) in a contract for the removal of household furniture which required the customer to indemnify the removal firm in respect of any legal liability incurred during the course of the move. This meant that if, for example, the firm's pantechnicon ran into a pedestrian and injured him, the customer would be liable to indemnify the removal firm (or the removal firm's insurers) against the damages it would have to pay. Since the customer's attention was not specifically drawn to this clause, and since there was no offer of suitable insurance, the indemnity clause was probably unfair and it is extremely unlikely that it would have passed the test of reasonableness should it ever have become an issue in court.

Guarantees

The word 'guarantee' is used here in the sense of a consumer guarantee, whereby the person offering the guarantee (usually the manufacturer) promises to repair or replace goods which become faulty, usually within a limited period of time. (The normal legal sense of 'guarantee' is a promise to be liable for the debt or default of another person if that person is unable to pay.)

Section 5(1) of the Act provides:

In the case of goods of a type ordinarily supplied for private use or consumption, where loss or damage:

(a) arises from the goods proving defective while in consumer use; and

(b) results from the negligence of a person concerned in the manufacture or distribution of the goods;

liability for the loss or damage cannot be excluded or restricted by reference to any contract term or notice contained in, or operating by reference to, a guarantee of the goods.

Misrepresentation

Section 3 of the Misrepresentation Act 1967 provides that any contract term which excludes or restricts liability for misrepresentation or any remedy available to another party by reason of a misrepresentation, must satisfy the test of reasonableness, as contained in the UCTA 1977.

Section 13 clauses

Sections 2–7 of the Act apply to clauses which seek to exclude or restrict liability. However, there are clauses which can achieve similar effects without exempting liability. Strictly speaking, therefore, they are not exemption clauses.

Section 13 of the Act deals with such clauses. It provides that clauses which do the following are void, or must be reasonable according to what an actual exemption clause would be in the same circumstances:

(a) make liability or its enforcement subject to restrictive or onerous conditions.

Examples

> *'Any claims of defective workmanship must be submitted within three days of the completion of the contract.'*

> *'All defective goods must be returned carriage paid to the manufacturer before any claim may be entertained.'*

(b) exclude or restrict any right or remedy in respect of the liability, or subject a person to any prejudice in consequence of his pursuing any such right or remedy.

Examples

> *'In the event of a breach of contract by the seller, the purchaser shall not be entitled to reject the goods.'*

> *'All claims will be subject to a deposit of £1,000, to be forfeited should the claim fail.'*

(c) exclude or restrict rules of evidence or procedure.

Example

> *'The signing of the delivery note by the purchaser shall be conclusive evidence that the goods were of satisfactory quality, fit for their purpose and in accordance with the contract.'*

To avoid arbitration clauses being brought into question, s 13(2) provides that an agreement in writing to submit present or future disputes to arbitration is not a clause excluding or restricting liability. It will, therefore, be valid. A liquidated damages clause is probably also outside the ambit of s 13(1).

Dealing as 'consumer'

In some cases, notably with contracts for the sale, etc, of goods, the status of an exemption clause depends upon whether the person against whom the clause is being used is 'dealing as consumer'. Section 12(1) of UCTA provides that a party 'deals as consumer' if:

(a) he neither makes the contract in the course of a business nor holds himself out as doing so; and

(b) the other party does make the contract in the course of a business; and

(c) in the case of a contract governed by the law of sale of goods or hire-purchase, or by s 7 of this Act, the goods passing under or in pursuance of the contract are of a type ordinarily supplied for private use or consumption.

Note that (c) applies only to contracts for the sale, etc, of goods.

In *R & B Customs Brokers v UDT* (1988), it was held that a Colt Shogun vehicle bought by a company partly for business use and partly for private use by one of its directors was not purchased in the course of a business. In reaching this decision, the court applied the test in *Davies v Sumner*, as to whether there was any regularity of dealing in cars. As the answer was 'no' the vehicle was not purchased 'in the course of a business' and, in consequence, was a consumer sale. However, in *Stevenson v Rogers* (1999), a case decided in relation to provisions in the Sale of Goods Act, it was held that a seller sells in the course of a business if he sells goods in the course of his business activity, even though the sale is ancilliary to his main business and even though he does not deal in such goods. Thus, it may well be that if Steve buys a computer from a solicitors' practice, Steve will be dealing as a consumer.

Section 12(2) provides that in an auction sale, in no circumstances is the buyer to be treated as dealing as consumer. Under s 12(3), a party who asserts that another does not deal as consumer bears the burden of proof.

Reasonableness

We have seen that in many cases an exemption clause must satisfy the test of 'reasonableness'. Under s 11(5), the burden of proving that a clause is reasonable is upon the party who claims that it is.

Oddly, the Act contains no less than *three* different tests of reasonableness, depending upon the legal context in which the exemption clause in question is used or depending upon its source. In addition, if the exemption clause is a *limitation* clause, which seeks to limit liability to a specified sum of money rather than to exclude it entirely, the provisions of s 11(4) will apply. This provides that:

> Where by reference to a contract term or notice a person seeks to restrict liability to a specified sum of money, and the question arises ... whether the term or notice satisfies the requirement of reasonableness, regard shall be had in particular ... to:
>
> (a) the resources which he could expect to be available to him for the purpose of meeting the liability should it arise; and
>
> (b) how far it was open to him to cover himself by insurance.

In *St Albans City and District Council v ICL* (1996), the plaintiff council suffered loss because of an error in a computer program supplied by the defendants, a large company trading worldwide. The loss amounted to £650,000. The defendants sought to rely on a limitation clause in the contract, which purported to limit their liability to £100,000. *Held*: the limitation clause was unreasonable since a large corporation like ICL was well able to insure against potential liability, which would otherwise have to be borne by the community charge payers of St Albans.

The three reasonableness tests

The first test, contained in s 11(1), relates to *contract terms* and to *misrepresentation*; the second relates to ss 6 and 7 of the Act (*contracts for the sale, supply, hire and hire-purchase of goods*). This has as its base s 11(1) but, in addition, incorporates a set of criteria set out in Sched 2 of the Act; the third is contained in s 11(3) and relates to *exemptions contained in a notice not having contractual effect*.

Contract terms and misrepresentation

The test of reasonableness set out in s 11(1), which applies to exemptions or limitations contained in *contract terms* or *liability for misrepresentation or attempts to exclude or restrict any remedy for misrepresentation*, is that:

> ... the terms shall have been a fair and reasonable one to be included having regard to the circumstances which were, or ought reasonably to have been, known to or in the contemplation of the parties when the contract was made.

However, in *Woodman v Photo Trade Processing* (unreported), the judge was prepared to apply the criteria set out in Sched 2 (see below), although, according to the strict wording of the Act, those criteria apply only to contracts for the sale of goods, not for the supply of services, as was the case in *Woodman*. He rationalised its application to a contract for services on the ground that similar factors needed to be taken into account as with a disposition of goods. In this case, W took photos of a friend's wedding. He took them to Dixons to be processed. Dixons were agents of the defendants. A notice on the wall of Dixons' shop read:

> All photographic materials are accepted on the basis that their value does not exceed the cost of the material itself. Responsibility is limited to the replacement of films. No liability will be accepted, consequential or otherwise, howsoever caused.

W received back only 13 negatives and prints from a roll of 36. He claimed damages. PTP relied on their exemption clause, arguing that the clause was reasonable on the ground that it enabled them to give a low-cost service to the public: accepting liability in such circumstances as W's would mean that they would have to charge more for their services. However, the court was clearly influenced by the fact that W was given no choice in the matter – he was forced to accept the terms offered. The judge applied the criterion, set out in Schedule 2, whether there were alternative means by which the customer's need could have been met. There were not. The court, therefore, suggested that a two-tier service would be reasonable: those who wanted low-cost allied with risk could opt for that and those who wanted special care taken could opt for an alternative which would give compensation if things went wrong. W was therefore awarded £75 damages to reflect the fact that the lost photos were irreplaceable.

In *Walker v Boyle* (1982), clause 17 of the National Conditions of Sale, which are habitually used by solicitors as a standard-form contract in house sales, provided that: 'No misdescription shall annul a sale.' (Normally, a misrepresentation will allow the purchaser to rescind the contract, which would mean that the purchaser would refuse to complete the sale.) The question arose as to whether this clause satisfied the test of reasonableness imposed by s 3 of the Misrepresentation Act 1967. It was held that the defendant had not discharged the burden of showing that the clause was reasonable and that the purchaser (to whom a misdescription had been made) was entitled to refuse to complete the sale.

Sale, supply, hire and hire-purchase of goods

The terms of s 11(1) also apply to these types of contracts but, in addition, the criteria set out in Sched 2 of the Act apply.

Schedule 2 provides that regard shall be had to any of the following which appear relevant:

(a) the strength of the bargaining positions of the parties relative to each other, taking into account (among other things) alternative means by which the customer's requirements could have been met;

(b) whether the customer received an inducement to agree to the term, or in accepting it had an opportunity of entering into a similar contract with other persons, but without having to accept a similar term;

(c) whether the customer knew or ought reasonably to have known of the existence and extent of the term (having regard, among other things, to any custom of the trade and any previous course of dealing between the parties);

(d) where the term excludes or restricts any relevant liability if some condition is not complied with, whether it was reasonable at the time of the contract to expect that compliance with that condition would be practicable; and

(e) whether goods were manufactured, processed or adapted to the special order of the customer.

In *RW Green v Cade Bros Farm* (1978), the plaintiffs were seed-potato merchants. They had had regular dealings with the defendants, who were farmers. These dealings had taken place on the standard conditions of the National Association of Seed Potato Merchants. The conditions provided that:

(a) notification of rejection, claim or complaint must be made to the seller within three days after the arrival of the seed at its destination; and

(b) any claim for compensation would be limited to the amount of the contract price of the potatoes.

One deal was for 20 tons of King Edward potatoes. In fact, the potatoes were infected with a virus which could not be detected by inspection at the time of delivery. As a result, the seed was planted and it was not until it came up some eight months later that it was found to be useless. The plaintiffs sued for the price of the potatoes and the defendants counter-claimed for damages for loss of profits. *Held*:

(a) The defendants' counter-claim for damages for breach of s 14 of the Sale of Goods Act was successful: the clause which required the claim or complaint to be made within three days was unreasonable. The plaintiffs had argued that such a clause was necessary because potato seed was a perishable commodity. The judge accepted that the clause might be reasonable in respect of defects which were discoverable upon reasonable examination, but where, as here, the defects were latent, the clause was not reasonable.

(b) However, the clause in their contract with the plaintiff limiting the amount of compensation payable was reasonable, and because of this, damages were limited to the amount of the contract price. The factors which influenced the judge were:

(i) the defendants had dealt with the plaintiffs for many years on terms which included the limitation clause;

(ii) the terms had been the subject of discussion between the National Association of Seed Potato Merchants and the National Farmers' Union; and

(iii) although it would have been difficult for the defendants to have obtained seed potatoes from a merchant other than on the conditions in the contract with the plaintiffs, it was possible to obtain seed stock certified by the Ministry of Agriculture as being virus free, but at a much higher price.

This meant that criteria (a), (b) and (c) of Sched 2 were met.

A contrasting case, in which the House of Lords considered the requirement of reasonableness, is *George Mitchell v Finney Lock Seeds Ltd* (1983). Finney Lock were a firm of seed merchants. They contracted to sell to Mitchell 30 lbs of Dutch winter cabbage seed for £201.60. M planted 63 acres with the seeds. The resultant crop was worthless, partly because the seed which had been delivered was autumn seed, not winter seed, and partly because, in any case, the seed was of low quality. M sued for damages of £61,000 for loss of profit. F relied on a standard clause in their conditions of sale which limited their liability to replacing the defective seeds or refunding payment. *Held*: F's limitation clause was unreasonable and, therefore, F were liable to compensate M for loss of profits. The main factor which swayed the House of Lords was that F gave evidence that they attempted to negotiate settlements above the price of the seeds in cases where they considered the customer's complaint to be 'genuine' and 'justified' – a tacit admission that their limitation clause was unreasonable. Two further factors were in favour of M: (a) F had been negligent in that, irrespective of its quality, the variety of seed supplied to M could not be grown commercially in the area where M's farm was situated; (b) farmers could not be expected to insure against losses of this kind, but F could insure against happenings such as occurred in this case without needing to increase their prices significantly.

Exemption clauses imposed by notice

The reasonableness test for exemption clauses imposed by notice is contained in s 11(3) and is that:

> ... it should be fair and reasonable to allow reliance on it, having regard to all the circumstances obtaining when the liability arose or (but for the notice) would have arisen.

Criteria to be taken into account in deciding whether the notice is fair and reasonable were set down by the House of Lords in *Smith v Eric S Bush* (1989). In that case, a prospective purchaser of a house applied to a building society for a mortgage. The building society instructed a surveyor to survey and value the property. The survey reported that there were no major defects in the house. It was, however, done negligently. When the purchaser sued for negligence (there was no contractual relationship between the buyer and the surveyor, but the surveyor knew that the buyer would rely on his report and, therefore, a duty of care in negligence arose), the surveyor relied on an exemption clause disclaiming liability for negligence, contained in a form which the plaintiff had had to sign before the valuation could be undertaken. The report itself contained a similar clause. The issue of whether it was reasonable arose and the House of Lords, *per* Lord Griffiths, held that the following criteria were to be applied (the comments which Lord Griffiths added are included in abbreviated form):

(a) Were the parties of equal bargaining power?

If the court is dealing with a one-off situation between parties of equal bargaining power, the requirement of reasonableness would be more easily discharged than in a case such as the present where the disclaimer is imposed on the purchaser who has no effective power to object.

(b) In the case of advice, would it have been reasonably practicable to obtain the advice from an alternative source, taking into account considerations of costs and time?

The surveyor argued that it would have been easy for the plaintiff to have obtained his own report. The plaintiff argued that this would have meant paying twice for the same thing and that people at the bottom end of the market have enough financial pressure without paying twice for the same advice.

(c) How difficult is the task for which liability is being excluded?

In the case of a dangerous or difficult task there might be a high risk of failure which would be a pointer towards the reasonableness of excluding liability. A valuation, however, should entail no difficulty: it is work at the lower end of the surveyor's field of expertise.

(d) What are the practical consequences of the decision on the question of reasonableness?

This must involve the sums of money potentially at stake and the ability of the parties to bear the loss involved, which, in turn, raises the question of insurance. We are dealing in this case with a loss which will be limited to the value of a modest house and against which it can be expected that the surveyor will be insured. Bearing the loss will be unlikely to cause significant hardship if it has to be borne by the surveyor but it is, on the other hand, quite possible that it will be a financial catastrophe for the purchaser, who may be left with a valueless house and no money to buy another. The result of denying the surveyor the right to exclude liability will result in distributing the risk of his negligence among all house purchasers through an increase in his fees to cover insurance, rather than allowing the whole of the risk to fall on the one unfortunate purchaser.

Held: it would not be fair and reasonable to allow the surveyor to exclude liability in the circumstances of this case, though no ruling was made as to the position of purchasers of industrial property, blocks of flats or expensive dwelling houses, as it may be that the expectation of the behaviour of the purchaser is different.

In an unreported case (1996), it has been held that where the parties were of equal bargaining power, and it was clear that the valuation was made solely for the purpose of the defendant's client and was not intended to be shown to or relied on by any third party, then a third party who relied on the valuation (which had been made negligently) was unable to recover his losses from the valuer.

Contracts excluded from the provisions of the Act

Schedule 1 to the Act provides that the provisions of ss 2–4 do not apply to the following contracts:

(a) contracts of insurance;

(b) any contract so far as it relates to the creation or transfer of an interest in land or to the termination of such an interest;

(c) any contract so far as it relates to the creation or transfer of a right or interest in any patent, trade mark, copyright, registered design, technical or commercial information, or other intellectual property, or relates to the termination of any such right or interest;

(d) any contract so far as it relates to the formation or dissolution of a company or to its constitution or the rights or obligations of its corporators or members; and

(e) any contract so far as it relates to the creation or transfer of securities or of any right or interest in securities.

Furthermore, other legislation may override the provisions of the Act. Section 29 provides that nothing in the Act removes or restricts the effect of, or prevents reliance on, any contractual provision which is authorised or required by the express terms or necessary implication of an enactment or, being made with a view to compliance with an international agreement to which the UK is a party, does not operate more restrictively than is contemplated by the agreement. Thus, for example, the Merchant Shipping Acts 1894 to 1983 place various limitations on the liability of a shipowner in the event of death or personal injury to a passenger, loss of or damage to goods, etc, where there is no fault on the part of the shipowner (under the law of contract, the shipowner would be strictly liable for all damage caused in breach of contract). This legislation will override the 1977 Act.

Other statutory restrictions on exemption clauses

Section 151 of the Road Traffic Act 1960 provides that a clause in a contract for the conveyance of a passenger in a public service vehicle which purports to negative or restrict the liability of the carrier in respect of death or bodily injury to the passenger while being carried in, entering or alighting from the vehicle, shall be void.

Note: this situation will now also be covered by s 2 of UCTA, which is broader in effect, because it would also cover persons who are not travelling under a contract of carriage. In *Gore v Van Der Lann* (1967), the RTA provisions were held to protect a passenger travelling on a free pass, on the rather improbable ground that she had a contract with the bus company, whereas in *Wilkie v London PTB* (1947), they didn't protect an employee travelling on a free pass.

Section 43 of the Transport Act 1962 contains similar provisions to protect passengers travelling on British Rail. Again, the UCTA provisions are wider because they also protect those who are not travelling under a contract.

The Road Traffic Act 1988 provides that all drivers must be insured in respect of liability for the death or bodily injury of their passengers (which can arise only if the driver concerned has been negligent) and that any agreement or notice which seeks to limit or exclude liability in the event of death or bodily injury to the passenger is void. It is also compulsory to insure in respect of liability for the death or bodily injury to other road users and against liability for damage to the property of third parties. In these cases, too, negligence is the basis of liability. There are further provisions which seek to prevent the insurance company repudiating their obligations under the contract of insurance, should the insured person cause damage in respect of which compulsory insurance applies, in circumstances which would ordinarily render the policy voidable at the option of the insurance company.

Note: the UCTA 1977 imposes a narrower restriction than the RTA 1988, in that the former covers only passengers who are being transported in the course of a business, whereas the RTA 1988 covers all passengers.

The contra proferentem *rule*

Contra proferentem is a rule of evidence whereby any doubt or ambiguity in an exemption clause must be resolved *against* the person seeking to rely on the clause.

In *Wallis v Pratt* (1910), the plaintiff purchased from the defendant certain seed described as 'common English sanfoin'. The seed was, in fact, a different, lower quality seed called 'giant sanfoin'. The contract excluded liability in respect of 'all *warranties*'. The plaintiff claimed damages and the defendant argued that he was protected by the exemption clause. *Held* by the House of Lords: (i) the defendant had broken a *condition* of the contract; (ii) the breach was not covered by a clause which referred only to 'warranties'; (iii) although the buyer was compelled by the Sale of Goods Act to treat the breach of condition as a breach of warranty (because he had 'accepted' the goods instead of exercising his right to reject them), this did not turn the breach of condition into a breach of warranty. The defendants were, therefore, not protected by their exemption clause and were liable to pay damages to the plaintiff.

Similarly, in *Andrews v Singer* (1934), the plaintiffs entered into a written contract with the defendants for the purchase of several 'new Singer cars'. One of the clauses in the contract protected the seller from liability in respect of breach of 'all conditions, warranties and liabilities implied by statute, common law or otherwise'. One of the cars which was delivered under the contract was second-hand, having been run for some 500 miles. The plaintiff claimed damages for breach of contract. The defendant relied on the exemption clause in the contract. *Held*: the description of the cars as 'new' was an *express* term not an *implied* one and it was, therefore, not covered by the exemption clause.

Third parties and exemption clauses

Only the parties to a contract are bound by the contract. Thus, an exemption clause may be defeated because the person seeking to rely on it is not a party to the contract. Perhaps the most common attempt to circumvent this rule is where an employer provides in his conditions: 'Neither the company *nor its servants* will be liable ...' This is called a 'Himalayas' clause after the name of the ship in the case of *Adler v Dickson* (1955), where the effectiveness of such a clause was considered. It would appear that the clause would not protect employees (servants) of the company, since they are not parties to the contract.

For a further exploration of third parties and exemption clauses, see Chapter 11.

The subsequent overriding of an exemption clause

An exemption clause may fail because it has been subsequently overridden by an oral undertaking given at the time of the contract. In *Mendelssohn v Normand* (1970), the plaintiff left his car in the defendants' garage. He received a ticket which said that the company 'will not accept responsibility for any loss or damage sustained by the vehicle, its accessories or contents, howsoever caused ... no variation of these conditions will bind the (proprietors) unless made in writing signed by their duly authorised manager'. The plaintiff was about to lock the car, as he usually did, when the attendant told him he couldn't do so as the attendant would need to move it. The plaintiff explained that there was a suitcase containing jewellery on the back seat. The attendant, therefore, agreed to lock the car once he had moved it. When the plaintiff returned, he found the car unlocked with the key in the ignition. The case containing the jewellery had gone. The plaintiff claimed damages and the defendant pleaded that he was protected by the exemption clause. *Held*: the attendant's undertaking to lock the car, and thus ensure that its contents were safe, overrode the condition printed on the ticket.

The Unfair Terms in Consumer Contracts Regulations 1999

These regulations came into effect on 1 October 1999, amending earlier Regulations. They are based on EC Directive 93/13. They are wider than the Unfair Contract Terms Act in the sense that they apply to any and all unfair terms, not simply unfair exemption clauses. They differ from UCTA in at least three respects:

(a) they apply only to consumer transactions, whereas UCTA applies to all business transactions;

(b) UCTA makes certain exemptions void whether they are, in substance, unfair or not. The regulations require that, in order to render a term 'not binding', the term must contravene the requirement of 'good faith'; and

(c) the regulations apply only where the term in question has not been individually negotiated (that is, to standard terms), whereas many of the provisions in UCTA are capable of applying to terms which have been individually negotiated (that is, to non-standard terms).

The main provisions of the regulations are as follows.

Terms to which the regulations apply

The regulations apply to any term in a contract between a seller or a supplier and a consumer, where the term in question has not been individually negotiated. A term is not to be regarded as having been individually negotiated if it has been drafted in advance and the consumer has not been able to influence it. Where a specific term or aspects of it have been individually negotiated, the regulations apply to the rest of the contract if an overall assessment of it indicates that it is a pre-formulated standard contract. If a seller or supplier claims that a term was individually negotiated, it is up to him to prove that it was.

Regulation 6 provides that, in so far as it is in plain and intelligible language, no assessment shall be made of the fairness of any term which: (a) defines the main subject matter of the contract; or (b) concerns the adequacy of the price or remuneration.

Note: in the United States, agreements in which the price was unconscionable have been re-opened by the courts. However, the wording of Article 4 of the directive excludes terms as to price, where these are in plain and intelligible language.

Consequences of using an unfair term

Regulation 8 provides that an unfair term in a contract concluded with a consumer by a seller or supplier shall not be binding on the consumer. However, the contract shall continue to bind the parties if it is capable of continuing in existence without the unfair term.

Meaning of 'unfair term'

Regulation 5 provides that 'unfair term' means any term which, *contrary to the requirement of good faith*, causes a significant imbalance in the parties' rights and obligations under the contract, to the detriment of the consumer.

In assessing whether or not the term is unfair, the court must take into account the nature of the goods or services for which the contract was made and all the other circumstances regarding the making of the contract, and all the other terms of the contract or any other contract on which it is dependent. The test does not seem significantly different from the test of 'reasonableness' under UCTA.

Schedule 2 of the regulations provides a non-exhaustive list of terms, amounting to 17 paragraphs, which may be regarded as being unfair.

An example of a contract with unfair terms which breached the requirement of good faith is *Falco Finance v Gough* (1999). A loan was taken out at a concessionary rate of interest which, however, was lost if the debtor defaulted even in a minor way. The full rate would then be payable, calculated on a flat rate, without any credit being given for payments already made, which added £125 per month to the debtor's payments. Furthermore, the basis of the calculation which was performed when the borrower wished to redeem the loan was based on a formula which was disadvantageous to the borrower and, taken with other redemption conditions, was unfair. The court found that it was so easy to default on the terms of the mortgage that it was virtually impossible to maintain the right to the concessionary rate. It was held that the terms in question were unfair terms within the meaning of the Unfair Terms in Consumer Contracts Regulations 1994.

Regulation 10 makes it the duty of the Director General of Fair Trading (DG) to consider complaints. He may seek an injunction to prevent the continued use of the term or of a term having a similar effect. A new provision in these Regulations is that a qualifying body may also apply for an injunction to prevent the continued use of an unfair term. These include the Consumers' Association, statutory regulators, such as the Data Protection Registrar, the Financial Services Authority, the Rail Regulator, the Director General of Telecommunications and trading standards departments of local authorities. The DG or a qualifying body may take an undertaking from the user of the term. Although the Regulations do not specify this, the undertaking will be to the effect that its use will be discontinued or it will be modified.

A qualifying body (except the Consumers' Association) is under a duty to consider a complaint if it has told the DG it will do so. (This presupposes that the DG will inform a qualifying body that he has a complaint which comes within their jurisdiction and that, if they do not wish to investigate, he will do so.)

Regulation 13 provides for the DG and qualifying bodies to require traders to produce copies of their standard form contracts and to give information about their use. Should the information not be given, the DG may apply to court for an order that the default should be rectified.

The DG must be notified about undertakings given to qualifying bodies and the outcome of any application for an injunction. He has a duty to publicise details of court orders and undertakings given.

The Court of Appeal has recently heard a case relating to an application for an injunction by the DG, in which an appeal to the House of Lords is pending. In *Director General of Fair Trading v First National Bank plc* (2000), the question arose as to whether the terms of a regulated agreement were unfair under the Unfair Terms in Consumer Contracts Regulations 1994 (now 1999). In this case, a contractual term provided for interest to be payable at the contractual rate on any judgment made against a defaulter. Thus, interest would be paid on interest. The DG was concerned that borrowers who consented to judgment and to pay by instalments would find themselves faced with a surprise bill for interest, when they thought they had paid off the judgment. The bill for interest arising from this provision would sometimes be larger than the judgment debts itself. The DG argued that the contractual terms regarding interest was unfair within the meaning of the regulations in that, contrary to the requirements of good faith, it caused a significant imbalance in the parties' rights and obligations, to the detriment of the consumer. The Bank's argument was that the interest provision was a 'core term' in the agreement and was, therefore, exempt from the control of the Regulations. Regulation 3 provides that, as long as the term is in plain, intelligible language, no assessment shall be made of any term which: (a) defines the main subject matter of the contract; and (b) concerns the adequacy or the price or remuneration as against goods or services sold. The Court of Appeal held that the term did not fall within (a) or (b), since it did not concern the main subject matter, nor did it concern the adequacy of the remuneration, since it only applied where the borrower was in default and then simply provided for the continuation of the contractual rate after judgment. The provision caused an unfair surprise and, therefore, did not satisfy the requirement of good faith. It also caused a significant imbalance in the rights and obligations of the parties.

The Office of Fair Trading (OFT) has a specialist Unfair Contract Terms Unit. In 2000, the International Air Transport Association (IATA) agreed to make changes to its recommended consumer contract following intervention by the OFT which challenged no less than 30 terms as being potentially unfair and unenforceable.

Action by the OFT is ongoing in relation to package holiday contracts which purport to take away consumer rights under the Package Travel, Package Holiday and Package Tour Regulations 1992.

CHAPTER 9

IMPOSSIBILITY

It sometimes happens that the parties make a contract which is impossible to carry out. Sometimes the obligation created by the contract is impossible to carry out at the time the contract is made. The reason for this is usually the incidence of an event which occurred, unknown to the parties, before the contract was made. More commonly, the impossibility is caused by a supervening event, that is, something which happens after the contract is made.

In principle, there is no reason why a party should not contract to do something which is impossible and to be liable damages for breach of contract should he or she fail to carry out the promised impossible obligation. Indeed, the early law adopted a theory of 'absolute' liability in relation to contractual obligations. This meant that a party was absolutely bound to carry out what he or she had promised even though an unforeseen event made that impossible.

In *Paradine v Jane* (1647), a tenant was unable to occupy premises which had been leased to him. The reason for this was that an armed force, hostile to the King, had expelled him. The tenant refused to pay the rent and was sued for it. *Held*: the tenant was bound to pay the rent. If non-performance of the contract was to be excused in particular circumstances, this should be provided for in the contract.

The 'absolute contract' rule was never fully applied in contracts which required personal service, and since *Paradine v Jane* it has been modified in a number of other situations.

In a case where a supervening event affects the performance of the contract, the contract itself may provide a solution. For example, because the law is still relatively strict in relation to the circumstances in which it will allow a party to be excused performance of a contract on the grounds of impossibility, it is common for a contract to contain a *force majeure* clause which exempts performance in certain circumstances. A typical *force majeure* clause will exempt liability in the case of strike or other industrial action, storm, flood, adverse weather (this appears mainly in building and civil engineering contracts) and governmental action.

THE CIRCUMSTANCES IN WHICH IMPOSSIBILITY MIGHT AFFECT THE CONTRACT

Impossibility does not mean that it is necessarily physically impossible to carry out the contract. What it means is that the contract as carried out will be radically different from the contract that was envisaged when it was made.

Impossibility may affect a contract in one of three situations:

(a) the impossibility may arise before the contract is entered into;

(b) it may arise after the offer is made but before it has been accepted; or

(c) it may arise after the contract has been made.

Some, but not all, textbook writers analyse the first situation as 'common mistake', that is, each party mistakenly believes that it is possible for the contract to be carried out. The second situation is highly unusual and has happened only once in a reported case. It therefore tends to be ignored when legal writers are dealing with the issue of impossibility: it is treated as a problem of offer and acceptance. The third situation is universally dealt with under the heading 'frustration'.

The relationship between common mistake and frustration has been acknowledged by text writers and by some judges as being simply two different sides of the same coin. That being so, there appears to be no reason why the principles relating to the two concepts could not be harmonised. The difficulty with harmonising these concepts at this stage of the law's development is that each concept has developed separately. There is, for example, statutory provision regarding the financial consequences which follow when a contract is frustrated, but there is no such provision in the case of common mistake. Instead, in what is, nevertheless, a parallel type of development, equity has ruled that a contract affected by common mistake may be set aside (that is, cancelled) on whatever terms the court thinks fit, if any. The analogy between the equitable treatment of common mistake and the treatment of the financial consequences of frustration by the Law Reform (Frustrated Contracts) Act 1943 cannot be pushed too far, since the equity in common mistake allows the court to impose terms beyond those related to the financial obligations of the parties, whereas the 1943 Act only allows the court to adjust the financial outcome. So, for example, in the case of *Grist v Bailey*, which was a case of common mistake, the court set aside a contract to sell a house, the price of which was affected by a common mistake, but on terms that the buyer should have the option of entering into a fresh contract for the purchase of the house at an appropriate price. Such terms cannot be imposed where a contract is frustrated.

We will now deal with the three 'impossibility' situations in turn.

IMPOSSIBILITY ARISING BEFORE THE CONTRACT IS MADE

A contract may be impossible to carry out at the time it is made. For example, A may contract to sell his car to B on the shared assumption that the car is in existence. Unknown to either party, the car was stolen and destroyed earlier in the day so that, at the time the contract is made, the car no longer exists. This situation is sometimes called 'common mistake', meaning a mistake common to both parties; other writers call it 'initial impossibility'.

Where both parties believe that the subject matter of the contract is in existence at the time the contract was made, but, in fact, the subject matter has ceased to exist, the contract will be void. The leading case is *Couturier v Hastie* (1856). Corn being shipped from Salonika to London became overheated and started to ferment. It was sold at Tunis and, therefore, ceased to exist as a commercial entity. In ignorance of this, S sold corn to B. S brought an action for the price of the goods. The action failed on the grounds that at the time the contract was made, there was nothing to contract about.

The principle which was thought to have been laid down in *Couturier v Hastie* was embodied in s 6 of the Sale of Goods Act 1893 (now 1979) as follows:

> Where there is a contract for the sale of specific goods and the goods, without the knowledge of the seller have perished at the time when the contract is made, the contract is void.

This provision has been criticised on the ground that it does not necessarily follow that because an action for the price of the goods failed in *Couturier v Hastie*, the contract was void. The court did not say that the contract was void (they did not use the term 'mistake' either) and it is possible that if the action had been one for damages for non-delivery, it might have succeeded.

However, since s 6 of the Sale of Goods Act 1979 now provides in express terms that such a contract will be void, this does not seem to leave a disappointed buyer much room for manoeuvre, unless, as in *McRae v Commonwealth Disposals Commission*, he can argue that the seller promised that the goods were in existence and is, therefore, liable for breach of that promise (see below).

In *Strickland v Turner* (1852), an annuity was bought on the life of someone who, unknown to either party, was already dead. It was held that the buyer had received nothing for his money and that his payment must be returned. In *Scott v Coulson* (1903), a life insurance policy was sold, both parties assuming that the insured was alive. In fact, he was dead and this rendered the policy more valuable. *Held*: the contract for the sale of the policy was void. In *Galloway v Galloway* (1914), P and D entered into a separation agreement on the mistaken assumption that they were married to one another. In fact, they weren't. *Held*: the agreement was void.

A common factor running through the above cases is that both parties mistakenly thought that the subject matter of the contract was in existence at the time the contract was made.

Contrast *McRae v Commonwealth Disposals Commission* (1951), in which D, carelessly but not fraudulently, sold a non-existent tanker to P. Nowadays, P would almost certainly be able to sustain an action for negligent misrepresentation against D, but such an action wasn't possible at the time. P sued for breach of contract. *Held*: D had warranted (that is, contractually promised) that the tanker existed and was, therefore, in breach of contract. The High Court of Australia pointed out that the circumstances which led to the mistake were entirely the fault of the Commission, and the court clearly felt that it was unjust to allow the Commission to rely upon their own mistake in order to avoid the contract. (This reasoning is very similar to the rule that a party cannot argue that a contract is frustrated when his own conduct has brought about the frustration. The frustration is said to be 'self-induced': see below.) In addition, the court pointed out that s 11 of the Victoria Sale of Goods Act, which corresponds to s 6 of the English Sale of Goods Act, makes the contract void where the goods have perished at the time the contract is made. In this case the goods had not perished – they had never existed.

An alternative analysis

Atiyah, in his *Introduction to the Law of Contract*, argues that where the impossibility consists of the non-existence of the subject matter there are three possible situations:

(a) the *seller* took the risk of the subject matter not existing at the time the contract is due to be performed and is therefore in breach of contract if the contract is not carried out;

(b) the *buyer* took the risk of the subject matter being non-existent and is therefore liable to pay the price even though he has not got the goods; or

(c) neither the buyer nor the seller took the risk and that therefore the contract is void at common law.

In other words, he is saying that it is a matter of interpretation of the contract. This view is not widely accepted, because the express terms of s 6 of the Sale of Goods Act provide that where the subject matter of a contract for the sale of specific goods has perished unknown to either party, the contract is void. However, in *McRae v Commonwealth Disposals Commission*, as we have seen, the court decided that the seller had warranted the existence of *non-existent* goods. Also, it is possible that Atiyah's analysis could apply to *perished* subject matter which does not consist of goods, and is, therefore, not governed by the Sale of Goods Act.

Note: where one party is aware of the mistake of the other he cannot take advantage of it: the contract will be void. See, for example, *Hartog v Colin and Shields* (1939), in which the price of goods was quoted wrongly by mistake of the seller in circumstances in which the buyer cannot have reasonably supposed that the offer contained the seller's real intention.

Mistakes as to quality

In order for a common mistake to be operative in the sense that it makes the contract void at common law, the mistake must make the subject matter of the contract different in substance from what the parties believed they were contracting for. If the mistake is merely as to one of the *qualities* possessed by the subject matter, without rendering it substantially different, then the contract will not be void. (Note that most mistakes as to quality are brought about by representations made by one of the parties. If those representations are false, the law relating to misrepresentation will, nowadays, normally give the innocent party a remedy.)

In the difficult case of *Bell v Lever Bros* (1932), Bell and Snelling, directors of a subsidiary of Lever Bros, received £30,000 and £20,000 compensation respectively, when their company was taken over and their services were no longer required. However, they had breached their contracts with L in that they had been engaged in business on their own account which conflicted with their duty to L. If L had known this, they could have terminated the contracts of B and S without the need to pay compensation. L claimed that the compensation contract was voidable for fraudulent misrepresentation. It was held that there was no fraudulent misrepresentation since B and S had forgotten about the breaches of duty when they made the compensation contract and had, therefore, not been fraudulent. L also tried to raise the issue of common mistake (confusingly for students it was called mutual mistake by their Lordships), that is, L was arguing that the contract was void because it was impossible to carry out. *Held*: a contract is void at common law only if the parties entered into it in consequence of a fundamental mistake which related to an essential and integral element of the subject matter of the contract. In this case, there was no such mistake. The mistake which existed was not as to *what* was being bought but was as to the *quality* of what was being bought.

Per Lord Atkin:

> ... I have come to the conclusion that it would be wrong to decide that an agreement to terminate a definite specified contract is void if it turns out that the agreement had already been broken and could have been terminated otherwise. The contract released is the identical contract in either case and the party paying for the release gets exactly what he bargains for. It seems immaterial that he could have got the same result in another way or that if he had known the true facts he would not have entered into the bargain.

Note that this decision was only by a three to two majority. A factor which affected at least one of the majority, Lord Thankerton, was that Lever Bros were extremely anxious to terminate the contracts of B and S and he was not convinced that L would have refused to enter into the contract to terminate the contracts of employment even if they had known the full facts. The two dissenting judges, while appearing to agree with the statements of law made by the majority, thought that the erroneous assumption made by both parties (that is, that they were dealing with a contract which could only be terminated by what amounts to a damages payment) was fundamental to the contract between the parties.

Equitable relief

Because of the strictness of the common law, equity has been invoked in order to try to do justice between parties to a contract affected by a common mistake. The authority for this stems from the House of Lords case *Cooper v Phibbs* (1867), in which the purported owner of a fishery leased it to the actual owner. When the true ownership was discovered, the owner applied for the lease to be set aside. It was held by the House of Lords that the lease was voidable but that equity permitted the court to impose terms (that is, conditions) upon the parties. The court imposed a term in this case that the owner should compensate the purported owner for the money that had been expended upon improving the fishery. Despite the fact that in *Bell v Lever Bros* Lord Atkin had criticised *Cooper v Phibbs* on the grounds that the correct view was that such a contract was void not voidable, two of three judges in the Court of Appeal held in *Solle v Butcher* that equity may set aside, on terms, a contract where the parties were under a common misapprehension either as to facts or as to their relative and respective rights, provided:

(a) that the misapprehension was fundamental; and

(b) that the party seeking to set it aside was not himself at fault.

This is broader than the common law power to rule the contract void in the case of a common mistake. The equitable rule applies whether or not the mistake renders the contract void. In *Solle v Butcher* (1950), a tenant agreed to rent a flat at £240 per annum, both parties thinking that fundamental alterations to the flat had brought it outside the ambit of rent control. In fact the alterations had not done that and, therefore, the maximum rent which could be charged was £140 per annum. However, if the landlord had realised that the Rent Acts still applied, he could have served a notice on the tenant *before the lease was entered into* which would have enabled him to raise the rent to £250. However, he could not do that once the lease was in existence. The plaintiff claimed repayment of the overpaid rent. The defendant counter claimed that the lease was void or voidable for mistake, arguing that the subject matter had, by reason of the alteration, undergone a fundamental change. *Held* by the Court of Appeal: confirming that the contract was not void because the alterations had not altered the identity of the flat, that the mistake nevertheless made the contract voidable in equity. According to Lord Denning:

> A contract is … liable in equity to be set aside if the parties were under a common misapprehension either as to facts or as to their relative and respective rights, provided that the misapprehension was fundamental and that the party seeking to set it aside was not himself at fault.

The judgment of Lord Denning stated that the party seeking to take advantage of the mistake should not be at fault, and it was found as a fact that the landlord in this case was not at fault. The court therefore set the contract aside on terms that the defendant allowed the plaintiff to remain in possession while the defendant served the statutory notice which would allow him to increase the rent. Having done that, the defendant must grant the plaintiff a new lease at the permitted amount, not exceeding £250 per annum.

In *Grist v Bailey* (1967), B entered into a contract to sell a house to G for £850, 'subject to the existing tenancy'. Both parties thought that the house was occupied by a sitting tenant (that is, a tenant whose right to occupy was protected by law). In fact, the sitting tenant had died and though his son became entitled to claim the benefit of the protected tenancy, he did not do so. That meant that the house could be sold with vacant possession, which made it worth more than £2,000. B refused to complete the contract so G sued for specific performance. B counter claimed for rescission of the contract on the ground that the contract was void or voidable for mistake. *Held*: there was a common mistake. This was a mistake as to a quality of the subject matter and as such could not render the contract void at common law. However, the mistake was fundamental in the sense that the seller would never have agreed to sell if she had realised the correct facts. Goff J also added that he did not consider the defendant to be sufficiently at fault to disentitle her from being relieved of her bargain, though a number of commentators have remarked that, as owner of the property, she was in the best position to know the status of her tenants and the judgment had the effect of relieving her from a bad bargain made through her own carelessness. The contract was set aside on terms that B must give G the opportunity to enter into a new contract for the sale of the house at a proper vacant possession price.

IMPOSSIBILITY ARISING AFTER THE OFFER HAS BEEN MADE BUT BEFORE IT HAS BEEN ACCEPTED

Where, after the offer is made but before it has been accepted, the subject matter of the offer undergoes a significant change (for example, a car which is the subject matter of the offer is destroyed by fire), the offer will lapse and the purported acceptance will be ineffective. There will be no contract. This is because the basis of the offer has changed so fundamentally that it is no longer possible to carry out the contract which was envisaged when the offer was made. Alternatively, it may be said that the offer is made subject to the condition that the subject matter will remain in substantially the same state between the offer being made and the acceptance of it.

In *Financings v Stimson* (1962), S signed a form at the premises of a car dealer, on 16 March, by which he offered to take a car on hire-purchase terms from F. The form said that the agreement was only to become binding on signature on behalf of F. On 18 March, S paid a deposit of £70 and took the car away. He was dissatisfied with it and on 20 March returned it to the dealer and said that he didn't want it but would forfeit his deposit. On 24 March, the car was stolen from the dealer's premises and badly damaged. On 25 March, F, not knowing that S had returned the car nor that it had been damaged, signed the HP agreement. S refused to pay the instalments due under the agreement and was sued. *Held* by the Court of Appeal: the offer was conditional upon the car remaining in substantially the same condition until the moment of acceptance. Because that condition was not fulfilled, the acceptance was invalid and no contract was formed.

IMPOSSIBILITY WHICH ARISES AFTER THE CONTRACT IS MADE

This situation is usually called 'frustration': it is said that the contract has been frustrated. It sometimes happens that, after the contract has been made, events occur which make it difficult, if not impossible, for A to perform his contract with B. If the supervening events make it impossible for the contract to be carried out, or at least render the type of performance which is possible fundamentally different from what was envisaged, the contract will become terminated by operation of law under the doctrine of frustration.

However, it is by no means easy to escape from one's contractual obligations by pleading frustration. Consider the following examples:

(a) A has contracted to manufacture goods for B. A's work-force has gone on strike so that he is unable to deliver goods on time.

(b) A has contracted to supply goods to B and is relying on components to be supplied by C in order to complete the contract. C's work-force has gone on strike, with the result that, although A has a ready and willing work-force, he is unable to manufacture the contracted goods.

(c) A has contracted to hire out one of a fleet of coaches to B. The night before the contract is due to be performed, the coach which A intended to supply in satisfaction of his contract with B is destroyed by fire.

In each of these cases, the layman might sympathise with A and be of the opinion that A ought not to be liable for a breach of contract which is not his fault. However, the law will usually take the attitude that his inability to perform the contract is A's misfortune and that if he wished to escape the consequences of non-performance in the circumstances specified, he should have stipulated this in the contract.

In each case, the law probably would not regard performance as being impossible. In example (a), A could have hired an alternative work-force. In example (b), he could have obtained components from an alternative supplier. In example (c), he could have supplied an alternative coach. Admittedly, if in example (b), the contract specified that components from that supplier should be used and if, in example (c), the contract specified the use of the coach that was burnt, A might be excused for non-performance, as we shall see later. To put it in legal terms, he might succeed in claiming that the contract was frustrated. However, as a general rule, in respect of the circumstances set out in the examples, each contract is said to be 'absolute' in the sense that non-performance is not excused and B will, therefore, have an action for breach of contract.

As we have seen from the examples above, the law does not lightly excuse a person from performing his contractual undertakings. It is worth bearing in mind that in order to excuse one's self from performance of a contractual obligation, it is not sufficient to show simply that the event responsible for the non-performance is beyond one's control. It is necessary to go further and to show that the event has made the performance of the contract impossible in relation to the commercial venture originally envisaged.

Where the party adversely affected by the event is able to prove this, he will be excused performance and will not be liable for breach of contract. In such a case, the contract is said to be discharged because of frustration. The effect of frustration is that the contract is treated as having been discharged by operation of law. This means that neither party can sue the other for damages for breach of contract. However, this does not mean that the contract is void. The financial consequences of frustration are now governed by the Law Reform (Frustrated Contracts) Act 1943, which provides a basic rule that money paid in advance in pursuance of the contract can be recovered by the payer, but modifies this by giving the other party the right to claim for expenses that have been incurred in pursuance of the contract. We shall look at the financial consequences of frustration in more detail in due course.

The circumstances in which a contract is frustrated

The overriding situation in which a contract is frustrated is where the venture has become impossible to carry out, either in the sense that it is physically or legally impossible or that the obligation has become radically different, because of supervening events. In practice such impossibility arises in one of three circumstances. These are:

(a) supervening illegality;

(b) physical impossibility;

(c) where the contract as carried out would be radically different from what was originally envisaged by the parties.

Supervening illegality

'Supervening' means 'coming after', so that we are talking about a contract which becomes illegal after it has been made. There are two circumstances, in practice, where the contract will be discharged under this heading because of frustration. These are:

(a) Where legislation is passed which makes the contract, or further performance of it, illegal.

In *Re Shipton Anderson & Co and Harrison Bros Arbitration* (1915), a contract was made for the sale of some wheat which was being stored in a warehouse in Liverpool. Before the title to the wheat had passed to the buyer, the government requisitioned the wheat under wartime emergency powers legislation. *Held*: the seller was discharged from the need to perform the contract because performance was rendered impossible by the government's lawful requisition of the goods.

In *Marshall v Glanville* (1917), Marshall was appointed as the defendants' sales representative for the Midlands, North of England and Scotland. He was appointed on terms which entitled him to a commission on all sales in those areas, whether or not the sales were effected by him personally. On 12 July 1916, he joined the Royal Air Corps. He would have been compelled to join the forces four days later by virtue of the Military Service Acts. He claimed commission on sales effected after he joined the forces. *Held*: his contract determined (that is, came to an end) because further performance had become unlawful and thus Marshall was not entitled to commission on sales made after he had joined the forces.

(b) Where the contract is due to be performed in a country which, as a result of the outbreak of war, becomes enemy territory.

In *Fibrosa Spolka Akcyjna v Fairburn Lawson Combe Barbour Ltd* (1943) (usually known as 'the *Fibrosa* case'), an English company agreed to manufacture some machinery for a Polish company, delivery to made at a place called Gdynia, in Poland. After the contract was made, but before delivery of the machinery was due, war broke out between Britain and Germany and German troops occupied Gdynia. In consequence of this, the contract became frustrated.

Supervening physical impossibility

Where it becomes physically impossible to perform a contract due to supervening events, the contract will be frustrated. Physical impossibility may arise in one of a number of ways:

(a) Where the subject matter of the contract is destroyed.

Where the subject matter of the contract is destroyed after the contract is made, the contract is frustrated. In *Taylor v Caldwell* (1863), the parties entered into a contract whereby the defendants agreed to let the plaintiffs have the use of the Surrey Gardens and Music Hall on four future days, 17 June, 15 July, 5 August and 19 August, for the purpose of giving four grand concerts and day and night fêtes. The plaintiffs agreed to pay £100 per day for the hire of the gardens and hall. After the agreement was made, but before the first of the four booked dates, the hall was destroyed by fire, without the fault of either party. The concerts could not be given as intended. *Held*: as neither party was at fault in respect of the destruction of the hall, the contract was discharged, neither party being liable to the other.

(b) Where one of the parties, or something essential to the performance of the contract, becomes unavailable.

A contract may become discharged because of frustration where someone or something which is essential for its performance becomes unavailable and the contract, as it could be performed, would be substantially different from what was envisaged at the outset.

In order for the contract to be frustrated because of unavailability, it is essential that the contract stipulated the use of the particular person for its performance. It is not sufficient that one of the parties simply intended to use a particular person or a particular thing to perform the contract.

For example, Painters Ltd is a small painting and decorating company. Albert contracts with the company whereby they will paint his house during June. The company intends to use Bill, one of its employees, to execute the contract. Unfortunately, Bill falls ill and the remainder of the company's small workforce is so committed elsewhere that Albert's contract cannot be completed until December at the earliest. The contract would not be frustrated unless it stipulated the use of Bill and, even then, because a viable alternative (that is, taking on another painter) is available, the court may well decide against ruling that the contract had been frustrated. Albert would therefore be entitled to damages for breach of contract.

A decided case which illustrates this point is *Tsakiroglou v Noblee Thorl* (1962). In this case, there was a contract for the sale of Sudanese groundnuts to be shipped cif (this means 'cost, insurance and freight', which means that the seller's price includes the cost of the goods, the cost of transport from door to door, and the insurance costs) to Hamburg during November/December

1956. It was assumed that the goods would be shipped via the Suez canal. On 7 October, the sellers booked cargo space in a vessel due to call at Port Sudan during the months of October and November. On 2 November, the Suez canal was closed to shipping. The seller failed to ship the goods. The buyer sued for damages for breach of contract. The seller claimed that the contract had been frustrated by the closure of the Suez canal. *Held* by the House of Lords: since no particular shipping route had been agreed in the contract, the sellers were bound to choose a route which was practicable in the circumstances. *Further, even if the contract had stipulated that the goods were to be shipped by the Suez canal, the House thought that the contract would not have been frustrated by the closure of the canal*, since shipping via the Cape of Good Hope, though costing more in freight and perhaps insurance, was not an obligation radically different from shipment via Suez.

Contracts requiring personal service

Where, in a contract requiring personal service, the person by whom the service is to be given has died or is incapacitated for the period of the contract, the contract may be frustrated. In *Robinson v Davison* (1871), the plaintiff contracted with the defendant that she would play the piano at a concert on 14 January 1871. She was ill on that date. The plaintiff sued for breach of contract. *Held*: the contract was not absolute but dependant on the defendant being well enough to perform. She was therefore not liable for breach of contract.

Similarly, where the contract in question is intended to last for a particular period of time, any period of unavailability within that time (other than a temporary unavailability), will frustrate the contract, providing that the interruption renders the performance of the contract to be substantially different from that which was originally undertaken. Thus, in *Morgan v Manser* (1948), Manser was a comedian who worked under the name of Charlie Chester. In February 1938, he contracted with the plaintiff whereby for a period of 10 years from that date, Morgan would act as his manager. The contract provided, among other things, for the comedian to accept no work except through the agency of Morgan. Manser was called up into the forces in June 1940. He was discharged in February 1946. He had allegedly breached his contract with Morgan in October 1945 by accepting work which had not been secured for him by Morgan and since February 1946, he had failed to observe the terms of the contract altogether. The question arose as to whether Manser was in breach of contract or whether the contract was frustrated. *Held*: the interruption was sufficient for the contract to have become frustrated.

Similarly, in *Unger v Preston Corporation* (1942), the plaintiff was a refugee from Nazi Germany. He was engaged by the Corporation as a full-time school medical officer. He was interned as an enemy alien in June 1940 and released in May 1941. He claimed his salary for the time during which he was interned. *Held*: any interruption of the contract other than a purely temporary interruption frustrated the contract, and in this case the interruption was sufficient to frustrate the contract. (Contrast *Nordman v Rayner and Sturgess* (1916), in which a long-term agency contract was not frustrated when the agent was interned as an enemy alien. Since the agent was an Alsatian who was anti-German, the court decided that the internment was not likely to last long, and, in fact, it lasted only one month.)

In *Hare v Murphy Bros* (1974), a sentence of imprisonment of one year was held to frustrate a contract of employment. In *FC Shepherd v Jerrom* (1985), J was an apprentice plumber. He was 21 months into his four year contract when he was sent to Borstal for six months to two years for his participation in a motor-cycle gang fight. He was released after six months. His employer refused to take him back. He claimed unfair dismissal under the provisions of the Employment Protection (Consolidation) Act 1978. *Held* by the Court of Appeal: the contract was frustrated. The contract was therefore discharged by the frustration rather than by a dismissal by the employer.

Note: most contracts of employment are nowadays terminable by notice. In such a case, the court is reluctant to conclude that the contract has been frustrated, particularly where the reason for the frustration is that the employee was a long-term invalid (or likely to become one). The reason for this is that statute has given employees rights to compensation for dismissal where the reason is redundancy or where the dismissal is 'unfair'. Where an employee's contract is found to be frustrated, then he is not regarded as having been dismissed for the purposes of a redundancy payment or compensation for unfair dismissal (the contract has come to an end by operation of law). Therefore, the preference is to rule that the employee has been dismissed and for the court or tribunal to decide whether, on its merits, the dismissal was fair (or the employee has been made redundant, as the case may be).

Contracts which require the availability of some particular thing to enable them to be performed

The rules as to unavailability apply not only to a person necessary for the performance of the contract, but to any particular thing which is necessary for performance. Again, it would appear that the contract is not frustrated if an alternative method of performance is readily available and the contract as performed would not be substantially different to the performance which was originally envisaged.

In *Jackson v Union Marine Insurance* (1874), the plaintiff was the owner of a ship which had been charted to go from Liverpool to Newport to load a cargo for San Francisco. This was to be done with all possible dispatch. The ship sailed from Liverpool on 2 January and, on 3 January, ran aground in Caernarvon Bay whilst on its way to Newport. It was not refloated until 18 February and could not be completely repaired until the end of August. On 15 February, the charterers repudiated the charter and chartered another ship.

The plaintiff, who had insured himself against the possibility that he would be unable to carry out the charter, claimed on his insurance. The insurance company argued that they were not liable since the charterers could be sued for breach of contract. The question the court had to decide was whether the plaintiff could have sued the charterers for breach of contract or whether his contract with the charterers was frustrated. (If it was, he was entitled to the insurance money.) *Held*: the time needed for refloating and repairing the ship put an end to the charter in a commercial sense. Hence, the contract was frustrated.

Where the contract as performed would be radically different from what was envisaged

Sometimes, although the performance of the contract doesn't become impossible, a supervening event occurs which makes the performance of the contract fundamentally different from what the parties envisaged when they made the contract. Such was the case when, due to the King's illness, the coronation of Edward VII was postponed. Many people had rented rooms along the route of the coronation procession in order to watch the coronation. The contracts could, of course, still be carried out. The rooms were still there to be used, and those which had been rented with the benefit of the catering could still have the caviar, champagne, etc, which they had contracted to have, but there was no procession to watch. The Court of Appeal held that such a contract was frustrated: see *Krell v Henry* (1903). In this case, it was said that the contract was frustrated because the coronation and the procession were the foundation of the contract. Vaughan Williams LJ contrasted the present case with the case of a person who had contracted to take a cab at an enhanced price to take him to Epsom on Derby Day. For some reason the race was called off. The judge asserted that in such a case the contract would not be frustrated because the seeing of the Derby was not the foundation of the contract. He went on to say that each case must be judged on its own circumstances and that three questions must be asked:

Firstly, what, having regard to all the circumstances, was the foundation of the contract?

Secondly, was performance of the contract prevented?

Thirdly, was the event which prevented the performance of the contract of such a character that it cannot reasonably be said to have been in contemplation of the parties at the date of the contract?

A contrasting case to *Krell v Henry*, and one which some commentators have had difficulty in distinguishing from that case, is *Herne Bay Steamboat Co v Hutton* (1903). As we have previously emphasised, the law does not lightly relieve a person of his contractual obligation. In *Herne Bay Steamboat Co v Hutton*, the defendant chartered a steamboat, 'Cynthia', for two days, 28 and 29 June 1902, to take out a party (that is, paying passengers) for the purpose of 'viewing the naval review and also for a day's cruise round the fleet'. The Naval Review in question was to have been conducted by Edward VII. However, it was cancelled because of his illness. Notice of cancellation was published four days before the review was due to take place. The owner of the boat thereupon wired to the charterer: 'What about Cynthia? She ready to start six tomorrow,' but received no answer. The owners employed Cynthia on other work and then claimed for the agreed cost of the charter, less the money they had earned employing the boat elsewhere during the two days in question. The defendants argued that the contract had been frustrated. (They also argued that the consideration of the plaintiffs had totally failed, because before the Law Reform (Frustrated Contracts) Act 1943, if money was payable before the contract was due to be performed, it remained payable even though the contract had been frustrated.) *Held* by the Court of Appeal: the contract had not been frustrated. Vaughan Williams LJ, returning to a theme that he had pursued in *Krell v Henry* (above), said:

> I see nothing that makes this contract differ from a case where, for instance, a person engaged a brake to take himself and a party to Epsom to see the races there, but for some reason or other, such as the spread of infectious disease, the races are postponed. In such a case it could not be said that he could be relieved of his bargain.

Another case in which it was held that there was no commercial impossibility was *Davis Contractors v Fareham UDC* (1956). In this case, in July 1946, contractors entered into a contract to build 78 houses for a sum of £92,425, within a period of eight months. They had submitted a tender in March 1946, saying in an attached letter that the tender was subject to adequate supplies of labour and building materials. No such provision was made in the written contract, however, and due to the shortage of skilled labour and building materials, the work took 22 months to complete and the contractors had to meet additional expenses of £17,651. They argued that they should be entitled to recover this additional expense either (a) because their letter attached to the tender should be incorporated into the contract, or (b) because the original contract had been frustrated by the unforeseen shortages of labour and materials and replaced by a new contract under which, as no price had been agreed, they were entitled to a *quantum meruit*. *Held:* (a) the letter attached to the tender was not incorporated into the contract; and (b) the contract was not frustrated. Lord Radcliffe said:

> ... it is not hardship or inconvenience or material loss itself which calls the principle of frustration into play. There must be as well such a change in the significance of the obligation that the thing undertaken would, if performed, be a different thing from that contracted for.

His Lordship went on to say that the appellants' case seemed to him to be a long way from a case of frustration. Two factors prevented the application of the doctrine of frustration: first the delay was caused by known risks (and could, therefore reasonably have been provided for in the contract) and secondly, the council had made known the penalties for delay and the contractors should take into account the risks of delay in calculating the price at which they would complete the work.

Note: the attitude of the court, though seemingly harsh, is probably justified in that all sorts of circumstances may arise during the currency of the contract which have the effect of making it less advantageous to one party than that party anticipated. Raging inflation is one example. The wise tenderer builds in a price-increase clause to allow for it. The unwise one takes the risk. If that risk proves to be unjustified, he cannot then seek to escape the consequences of his bad bargain.

EXCEPTIONS TO THE DOCTRINE OF FRUSTRATION

There are a number of possible exceptions to the doctrine of frustration. These are:

(a) self-induced frustration;

(b) where the parties expressly provide for the frustrating event; and

(c) sales and leases of land.

Self-induced frustration

Where a party has brought about the frustrating event by his own conduct, he cannot claim that the contract is discharged by frustration.

The leading case is *Maritime National Fish v Ocean Trawlers* (1935). In this case, the appellants renewed their charter of the respondents' trawler, the St Cuthbert, for 12 months from 25 October. It was agreed that the trawler should be used for fishing only. At the time the charter was renewed, both parties were aware of a Canadian statute which made it an offence to fish with an otter trawl without a licence from the minister. The St Cuthbert could only operate with an otter trawl. The appellants, who were operating five trawlers in all, applied for five licences. The minister granted only three licences but left it to the appellants to name the trawlers to which the licences were to apply. The appellants didn't include the St Cuthbert in their list and claimed that the charter of the St Cuthbert was frustrated. The respondents brought an action for the price. At first instance, it was held that the charter had been frustrated. On appeal, it was held that the contract was not frustrated, because: (a) despite the fact that they knew of the statute the appellants had inserted no protective clause in the charter. They must, therefore, be deemed to have taken the risk that a licence would not be granted; and (b) if there was frustration of the venture, it resulted from the deliberate act of the appellants and they could not rely on their own act to substantiate a plea of frustration. On appeal, the Privy Council held that the contract was not frustrated because the doctrine of frustration assumes that frustration arises without fault on either side. In this case, the frustration was self-induced and, therefore, the appellants were unable to rely on it.

A further example is to be found in *Ocean Tramp Tankers v VO Sovfracht* (1964). In this case, the *Eugenia* was chartered for a trip out to India via the Black Sea from the time the vessel was delivered at Genoa. When the charter was being negotiated both parties realised that the Suez canal might be closed, but were unable to agree what should be done if this happened. However, a 'war clause' in the charter forbade the charterers from bringing the vessel into a dangerous zone without the consent of the owners. The vessel sailed from Genoa and arrived at Port Said at the time when it was a dangerous zone. The vessel became trapped in the canal. The charterers argued that, as a result, the charter had become frustrated. (The possibility of self-induced frustration was realised, but the charterers argued that if they had never entered the canal they would have had to go round the Cape, which would have meant that the contract would have been fundamentally different from that which had been agreed.) *Held* by the Court of Appeal: the charterers could not rely on the fact that the ship was trapped in the canal as frustrating the contract, since the frustration was self-induced. On the further point that even if the ship hadn't been trapped in the canal the contract would have been frustrated, the court held that this was not so, since the difference in the two voyages (that is, via the Cape of Good Hope as opposed to via Suez) was not so radical as to produce frustration.

However, if one party alleges that the other is at fault in relation to the alleged frustrating event, that party has to prove the allegation. If, therefore, the cause of the frustrating event is unexplained, it will not be presumed that the frustration is self-induced. In *Joseph Constantine Steamship Line v Imperial Smelting Corp* (1942), the respondents chartered the appellants' steamship Kingswood to proceed to Port Pirie, Australia, to load a cargo. While she was anchored in the roads off Port Pirie, a violent explosion occurred which resulted in such a delay that it was agreed that the commercial venture was frustrated. The contract was, therefore, *prima facie* frustrated. The question arose as to whether the explosion amounted to self-induced frustration. The Court of Appeal held that it is up to the party who is *prima facie* guilty of failing to perform his contractual obligations to prove that the frustration occurred without fault on his part. However, the Privy Council reversed this judgment, ruling that once a *prima facie* case of frustration has been established it is up to the party alleging that the frustration was self-induced to prove it.

Where the parties expressly provide for the frustrating event

Generally speaking, if there is an express clause in the contract which covers the occurrence of a certain event, frustration cannot be pleaded when that event happens. However, it may be that the event is more extreme in form than was envisaged by the contract. In such a case, the contract may be frustrated despite an express term in the contract to the contrary.

In *Pacific Phosphate Co v Empire Transport* (1920), a contract was made in 1913 by which ship-owners undertook to provide charterers with certain vessels in each of the years 1914 to 1918. It was a clause of the contract that if war broke out, the contract could be suspended at the option of either party, to continue after the end of the war. However, after the start of the First World War, it was held that the contract was frustrated, not simply suspended, because the war suspension clause did not envisage such a large-scale war with so many dislocating effects.

Sales and leases of land

There is considerable authority for the proposition that there is a rule of law that leases of land and sales of land could not be frustrated. The reason is that both of these are more than contractual arrangements: they give the lessee (or purchaser) an estate in the land. Thus, leased property is still there even though the lessee may, for example, be unable to live in it. Similarly, if a house is contracted to be sold and before completion it is destroyed, the contract will not be frustrated. This rule will normally cause inconvenience rather than hardship, since it is recognised that the risk of such destruction falls on the prospective purchaser once contracts have been exchanged and he will, therefore, usually insure against the risks of fire, etc.

An illustrative case is *Northern Estates v Schlesinger* (1916). In this case, a person who became an enemy alien had taken a lease of a flat. He became unable to reside in it because wartime legislation forbade him to. *Held*: the lease was not frustrated simply because the tenant was unable personally to reside in the flat.

Although it will be difficult to show that a sale or a lease has been frustrated, there is no rule of law to the effect that they cannot be. The matter was discussed by the House of Lords in *Cricklewood Property and Investment Trust v Leighton's Investment Trust* (1945). In this case, a building lease of 99 years' duration was entered into in May 1936, by which L leased land to C, and C promised to build shops upon it. Before any building had taken place, the Second World War broke out and restrictions were placed on the supply of building materials so that the shops which the lessees had promised to erect could not be erected. L sued for the rent due under the lease and C pleaded that the lease had been frustrated. *Held* by the House of Lords: the lease was not frustrated because the period of interruption, that is, from 1939 to 1945, was not sufficient in duration, when compared with the overall length of the lease, to frustrate the contract. However, conflicting views were expressed *obiter* on the question of whether a lease could ever be frustrated. Two of their Lordships thought that a lease could be frustrated if, for example, some vast convulsion of nature swallowed up the property altogether or buried it in the depths of the sea, or, in the case of a building lease, if legislation were subsequently passed which designated the building area as a permanent open space. However, two of their Lordships denied that a lease could ever be frustrated and the fifth expressed no opinion.

It remains true to say, however, that whatever the correct rule is, there is no example in English law of a lease or a contract for the sale of land having been held to be frustrated. It may be that this is because there has been no occurrence in relation to either a lease or a sale of land which the court has felt to be sufficiently drastic to justify frustration. Certainly in *Hillingdon Estates v Stonefield Estates* (1952), a compulsory purchase order which was placed on a property after the contract of sale but before the conveyance, was held not to frustrate the contract. In *Amalgamated Investment v John Walker* (1976), developers contracted to buy land and buildings with the object of knocking down the buildings and redeveloping the site. They particularly asked the vendors whether the existing buildings were listed by the Department of Environment as being of special architectural or historic interest, since there is a duty to maintain such buildings in their existing state and in good repair and, of course, it is extremely difficult to secure consent for the demolition of such buildings. The vendors replied that the building wasn't listed, but, unknown to them, the Department intended listing the building and did so the day after the parties had exchanged contracts on the building. The purchase price was £1,710,000; however, the value of the land with the listed building upon it was only £210,000. The purchasers pleaded: (a) that the contract was void for mistake; and (b) that the contract was frustrated. *Held* by the Court of Appeal: (a) the contract was not void for mistake since at the time the contract was made the building wasn't listed; and (b) although the court was prepared to assume that a contract for the sale of land can be frustrated, the contract wasn't frustrated in this case since, although the listing reduced the value of the property, it could not be said that the commercial foundation of the contract had been removed. It was still possible for the purchasers to obtain planning permission to carry out their original intentions in respect of the land: the listing simply made it much more difficult.

FINANCIAL CONSEQUENCES OF FRUSTRATION

The common law position

At common law, the financial consequence of frustration was, in effect, that the contract was 'frozen'. Any money which had been paid to the other party before the frustrating event was not recoverable, and any money which was payable but hadn't been paid had to be paid. Thus, in *Chandler v Webster* (1904), the facts of which were similar to *Krell v Henry* (above), the contract for the use of the room for viewing the coronation stipulated that the price of the room, £141 15s, was payable immediately. The plaintiff had paid £100 on account, and sued to recover this sum. The defendant counter-claimed for £41 15s. *Held*: The plaintiff failed and the defendant's counter-claim succeeded. (*Krell v Henry* was different, since the rent for the room didn't become due until after the procession.)

This treatment of frustrated contracts attracted widespread criticism. In particular, it was thought that where the consideration given by one party had totally failed, the other party ought to be entitled to recover the money he had paid, or property he had transferred. In the *Fibrosa* case (above), the House of Lords ruled that money paid in pursuance of a contract where the consideration had totally failed was recoverable by the party who had paid it. However, this solution gave rise to as much dissatisfaction as the earlier one in *Chandler v Webster* (above). There was thus a need for legislation in order to attempt to reach a just result as between the parties.

THE LAW REFORM (FRUSTRATED CONTRACTS) ACT 1943

This altered the law so that first, a party who has incurred expenses in pursuance of the contract can, under certain conditions, be awarded the whole or part of such expenses, and secondly, a party who has conferred a valuable benefit on the other party in pursuance of the contract can be awarded the whole or part of the value of the benefit.

Money paid or payable before the frustrating event

Section 1(2) of the Act provided that money paid or payable before the frustrating event was recoverable, or ceased to be due, as the case may be.

Entitlement to expenses

However, s 1(2) went on to say that a party to whom money was paid or payable before the frustrating event, and who had incurred expenses in pursuance of the contract, might recover the whole or part of his expenses. In order that a sum in respect of expenses may be awarded, the following conditions must be met:

(a) the claimant must have received an advance payment or contract must provide for one to be payable;

(b) the payment must have been made, or if not made, must have become due, before the frustrating event;

(c) the party claiming expenses must have incurred the expenses in pursuance of the contract before the frustrating event;

(d) the court must deem it just in the circumstances to award the claimant a sum of money in respect of expenses; and

(e) the sum awarded must not exceed the amount of the sum paid or payable before the frustrating event.

Thus, if the *Fibrosa* case (above) had been heard after the Act, the first three conditions would certainly have been met in considering the English company's claim for expenses. They had received £1,000 advance payment before the frustrating event, and they had incurred expenses in preparing to fulfil their contractual obligations. Thus, the court could allow them to retain up to the amount of £1,000 in order to assist in defraying their expenses, if the court thought it just to do so in the circumstances. (Of course, if the expenses had been less than £1,000, they would have been allowed only the amount of their expenses.)

Compensation for conferring a benefit on the other party

At common law, a person who partially performs a contract is entitled to no reward for his partial performance unless:

(a) the partial performance amounts to a substantial performance of the contract; or

(b) the party who has only partially performed his obligation has been prevented from complete performance because of the fault of the other party; or

(c) the contract is divisible rather than entire, that is, there is a term, express or implied, that payment will become due for less than complete performance.

It is rare that any of these conditions are met in a frustrated contract, with the result that, at common law, the person who had conferred a benefit on the other party, without completing performance, would be entitled to no payment. A classic example of this is to be found in *Cutter v Powell* (1795). In that case, Cutter, a seaman, signed on to crew a ship from Jamaica to Liverpool at a wage of £31 10s. After almost two months as a member of the crew, and 19 days before the ship reached Liverpool, Cutter died. His widow claimed a proportion of his wages as a *quantum meruit*. *Held*: the contract was entire and, as Cutter had only partially performed his obligation, he was entitled to nothing.

In the case of seamen, this rule was modified by provisions which are now contained in the Merchant Shipping Act 1970.

In the case of rent, annuities (including salaries and pensions), dividends and other period payments in the nature of income, the Apportionment Act 1870 provided that they should be considered as accruing from day to day and apportioned accordingly.

However, these two provisions related to relatively narrow areas and in respect of contracts not involving seamen's wages or the matters covered by the Apportionment Act, the common law rule remained. A good example is to be found in *Appleby v Myers* (1867), where the plaintiffs agreed to install machinery in the defendant's factory. When the installation was almost complete, the factory burnt down, destroying all the contents including the machinery. *Held*: the plaintiffs were entitled to no payment.

Because of the injustice caused by the common law rule, s 1(3) of the 1943 Act provided that where, for the purpose of the performance of the contract, one party has, before frustration, obtained a valuable benefit from the other, the court may make such an award of compensation as it feels just in the circumstances. The award must not exceed the amount of the valuable benefit conferred. Moreover, the concept of 'valuable benefit' does not include the payment of a sum of money (this is dealt with by s 1(2)).

Section 1(3) was considered in the complex case of *BP Exploration Co (Libya) Ltd v Hunt* (1982), in which BP carried out extensive exploration work in order to discover a large oil field on a concession held by Hunt. It was held, among other things, that the valuable benefit conferred did not consist of the exploration, but of the enhanced value of the field after oil was struck. It would seem, therefore, that a valuable benefit must be something tangible. Thus, it may be that the outcome of *Appleby v Myers* would be the same even following the 1943 Act.

EXCEPTIONS TO THE 1943 ACT

The Act does not apply to the following contracts:

(a) a contract for the carriage of goods by sea;

(b) a charterparty;

(c) a contract of insurance; and

(d) a contract to which s 7 of the Sale of Goods Act 1979 applies, or any other contract for the sale, or for the sale and delivery, of specific goods, where the contract is frustrated by reason of the fact that the goods have perished.

There are two possible situations here:

(a) A has agreed to sell specific goods to B. Without any fault on the part of A or B, the goods have perished before the risk has passed to B. The agreement is void under s 7 of the Sale of Goods Act 1979. This means that B cannot sue A for breach of contract. However, the risk of the loss of the goods falls on A and he will be the loser unless he carries suitable insurance.

(b) A has sold specific goods to B but has remained in possession of them, or has agreed to sell specific goods to B on terms that B was the risk-bearer at the time of the frustrating event. The goods are destroyed without the fault of either party. The contract is frustrated. However, the loss is with the party who bore the risk. (Note: in the type of sale outlined in this example, the ownership of the goods, and therefore the risk, will usually, but not always, have passed to B.)

CHAPTER 10

MISREPRESENTATION

Sometimes a person is induced to contract by a statement which is not part of the contract. Such a statement is called a 'representation' and, if it turns out to be false, it is called a misrepresentation.

We have seen (see Chapter 7) that, in cases where the court thinks there is justification on practical grounds, a statement which would normally be classed as a representation (or, indeed, would be given no legal status at all – for example, a statement of future intention), is given the status of a contractual term. The relative ease with which the courts manage to justify this, conceptually, leads one to the conclusion that the law of misrepresentation is anachronistic and now that the law of contract has reached a developed state, could be dispensed with. It seems that the perpetuation of the concept has little positive value when weighed against the difficulties with which this area of law abounds.

Before the Misrepresentation Act 1967, the position of the victim of an innocent (that is, non-fraudulent) misrepresentation, when contrasted with the position of the victim of a breach of contract, was generally (though not always) inferior. The 1967 Act greatly improved the position of the victim of an innocent misrepresentation, but even now the remedies available for misrepresentation have not been entirely assimilated to the remedies for breach of contract. There are two reasons for this:

(a) The 1967 Act gives damages as if misrepresentations were fraudulent, that is, on the basis of the tort of deceit, which compensates *all* damage directly flowing from the tort. Damages for breach of contract, on the other hand, compensate only loss which flows naturally from the breach (that is, was a likely consequence of the breach). One effect of this is that in a case where there is a substantial amount of unlikely loss, a victim of misrepresentation may be better off; where there is a substantial expectation loss (see Chapter 16, p 325), the victim of a breach of contract is likely to be better off. This is explained more fully later.

(b) The damages available under the 1967 Act in respect of a wholly innocent misrepresentation (that is, a mis-statement which the representor had reasonable grounds to believe was true) are restricted to damages *in lieu of rescission*. Such damages will compensate for the fact that the claimant is not being granted a rescission of the contract, but they will not compensate the claimant for his entire loss (see example on p 251). If, on the other hand, such a mis-statement is contractual, the representor in effect warrants the truth of his representation so that, when it turns out to be untrue, he is liable for all damage which was likely to flow from his breach of contract.

Furthermore, a statement of intention which is made in a contract will give rise to a breach of contract if it is not carried out. A statement of intention which is not part of a contract is only actionable as a misrepresentation if the representor had no such intention at the time he made the statement.

DEFINITION OF MISREPRESENTATION

A misrepresentation is an *untrue statement* of *fact* which *induces* another to make a contract.

We will examine the meaning of the emphasised words in turn.

Untrue

'Untrue' includes a statement which, though literally true, is intended to and does have the effect of misleading.

In *R v Kylsant* (1932), a company advertised in its prospectus that even through years of depression it had paid dividend, thus implying that it was financially sound. The company had, in fact, paid dividend through depression, but had failed to add that the dividend had been paid out of financial reserves accumulated before depression. *Held*: that this half-truth was intended to mislead and was thus a misrepresentation.

Statement

This is usually spoken or written, but it may be by conduct.

In a very old case, a man dressed himself in an undergraduate cap and gown in order to take advantage of a discount that an Oxford trader offered to students. He didn't say he was a student but was, nevertheless, guilty of a misrepresentation.

In *Aprilia v Spice Girls* (2000), Aprilia is a company based in Italy which manufactures, among other things, scooters. It sells them in Europe and the United States. The Spice Girls Limited was a company formed to promote a singing group called the Spice Girls. At the beginning of 1998, the Spice Girls consisted of five singers called Geri Halliwell, Emma Bunton, Victoria Adams, Melanie Brown and Melanie Chisholm. They each took a professional name which portrayed their individual character. Geri Halliwell left the band on 29 May 1998. Aprilia had signed a contract whereby they could use the Spice Girls to promote the sale of their scooters on 6th May 1998, which was to last until March 1999. Aprilia claimed that Spice Girls Ltd, by their conduct in signing an agreement involving all five of the girls, when they were aware that one would be shortly leaving, was a misrepresentation by conduct. The promotional material involved all five Spice Girls. There was one particular photo-shoot in which considerable expense was incurred. If Aprilia had known that one girl was leaving the group, they would not have signed the contract. It was held that Spice Girls Ltd, by their conduct in appearing at the photo-shoot, had made a representation that, to the best of their knowledge, none of the girls would be leaving the band before March 1999.

Can silence be a statement?

The general rule is that a person has no duty voluntarily to disclose material facts which are within his knowledge. This principle is known as *'caveat emptor'*: it means 'let the buyer beware'.

For example, in *Keates v Cadogen* (1851), a landlord rented a house without telling the tenant that it was in a ruinous and dangerous condition. It was held that the landlord had no duty of disclosure. (It would have been different if the tenant had asked the landlord questions about the house's condition and the landlord had answered them untruthfully.)

There are three important exceptions to the rule of *caveat emptor* and, in these circumstances, there is a duty of disclosure whether or not questions are asked. The three are as follows.

(a) Representations made untrue by later events

If one person makes a statement to another in order to induce him to contract, and after the representation is made but before the contract is entered into, the representation becomes untrue, the representor owes a duty to the representee to correct the original statement. If the representor remains silent and the statement is not corrected, this amounts to a misrepresentation.

In *With v O'Flanagan* (1936), O was a doctor who wished to sell his practice. W was interested, and in January O represented that the income from the practice was £2,000. O fell ill and by May, when the contract was signed, receipts had fallen to about £5 per week. This was not, however, mentioned before the contract was signed. W claimed rescission of the contract on the ground of misrepresentation. *Held*: in these circumstances, failure to correct the previous statement was a misrepresentation.

(b) Contracts of the utmost good faith

In certain types of contract where one party alone has full knowledge of the material facts, that party is required to show the utmost good faith. (You will sometimes see this concept expressed in Latin as *'uberrima fides'* or *'contracts uberrimae fidei'*.) This means that the normal rule of *caveat emptor* does not apply and that the party in possession of the facts must make full disclosure of them.

There are five types of contract where full disclosure is required. These are as follows.

(1) Contracts of insurance

Every contract of insurance requires full disclosure of all material facts.

This means that although, in practice, the insurance company will ask you questions about anything they regard as material, you must, nevertheless, disclose anything that is material to the risk they are insuring whether or not they ask you about it expressly. The reason for this rule is to enable the insurer to fix a premium appropriate to the risk he is taking. A fact is material if it would affect the mind of a prudent insurer, even though the insured doesn't appreciate that it is material. For example, in *Locker and Woolf Ltd v Western Australian Ass Co* (1936), in making a proposal for fire insurance, the proposer stated that no insurance proposal by him had previously been declined by another company. In fact, another company had previously refused to issue a policy of motor insurance. *Held*: the policy of fire insurance was voidable for non-disclosure.

The duty of disclosure is confined to facts which the assured knows or ought reasonably to know. If, in proposing a life insurance, the proposer states that his health is sound, fully believing this to be so, the contract cannot be rescinded if it turns out that the proposer was, in fact, suffering from a terminal disease (though, in practice, insurance companies make the proposer warrant the truth of his answers, so that if an answer turns out to be untrue, the proposer is strictly liable for breach of contract).

(2) Contracts to take shares in a company

Such contracts are often made in reliance on a prospectus issued by the promoters of the company. The Companies Act 1985 sets out a long list of details which a company must disclose in its prospectus. Failure to disclose the facts in relation to any of these items will be a misrepresentation.

(3) Family arrangements

This term covers a wide range of agreements between relatives designed to preserve harmony within the family, preserve family property, etc. In such an arrangement, there must be full disclosure of all material facts known to each party, even though no enquiry has been made about them. Examples of family arrangements include: an agreement to abide by the terms of a will which hasn't been properly executed; an agreement to vary the terms of a valid will, etc.

(4) Sales of land

A person selling real property is under a duty to disclose all matters within his knowledge relating to the title to the land, for example, the existence of restrictive covenants, etc. Note: There is no duty to disclose defects in the property itself.

(5) Partnerships

During the existence of a partnership each partner owes to the other a duty to disclose all matters within his knowledge which affect the partnership business. This rule applies only after the partnership has come into existence. It does not apply to an agreement to create a partnership.

(c) Where there is a fiduciary relationship between the parties

A fiduciary relationship may arise in one of several circumstances. The first is where the relationship between the parties is such that any contract between them is presumed to have been induced by undue influence. Such relationships include: parent and child; doctor and patient; solicitor and client, etc. In such a case, the duty of the dominant party includes full disclosure but goes beyond that (see Chapter 8). In other cases, such as principal and agent and business partners, full disclosure is the full extent of the duty owed by one to the other.

Fact

In order to amount to a misrepresentation should it be found to be untrue, a representation must be one of fact. The following do not amount to representations of fact: statements of law, future intention and opinion.

Statements of law

If an untrue representation is a statement of law, the person misled does not have a remedy for misrepresentation.

For example, A is negotiating the sale of his car to B. He correctly tells B that the car was first registered in 1983. When B asks about the MOT test certificate, A tells him that only cars more than five years old need a certificate (when in fact all cars more than three years old need a certificate). B believes him, only finding out some time later that he has been misled. B has no remedy for misrepresentation since A's statement was a statement of law.

Statements of future intention

A representation as to what the representor will do in the future will generally not amount to a misrepresentation if the representor subsequently changes his mind.

However, a statement of future intention will amount to a misrepresentation if at the time the representation was made, the representor had no intention of carrying out his stated intention.

In *Edgington v Fitzmaurice* (1885), E was induced to lend money to a company following representations by its directors that the money would be used to expand the business. In fact, the directors intended to use the money to pay off the company's debts. E sued the directors for misrepresentation. They defended the action by arguing that their statement was one of future intention and, as such, could not be a misrepresentation. *Held*: the defendants were liable for misrepresentation. *Per* Bowen LJ:

> There must be a mis-statement of existing fact; but the state of a man's mind is as much a fact as the state of his digestion. It is true that it is very difficult to prove what the state of a man's mind at a particular time is, but if it can be ascertained, it is as much a fact as anything else. A misrepresentation as to the state of a man's mind is, therefore, a mis-statement of fact.

Of course, a statement of future intention may amount to a contractual promise (see *Quickmaid Rental Services v Reece*, Chapter 7, p 153 above), in which case, although there will be no remedy for misrepresentation, there will be a remedy for breach of contract.

Statement of opinion

A statement of opinion is, as a general rule, not a statement of fact.

In *Bisset v Wilkinson* (1927), the seller of a piece of land told the buyer that, in his opinion, the land would carry 2,000 sheep. However, the seller was not a sheep farmer and had no knowledge (nor did he claim to have) of the requirements of sheep. In fact, the land would carry nowhere near the stated figure. *Held*: the statement was one of opinion and, though it proved to be incorrect, it was not a misrepresentation.

There are two exceptions to the rule that a statement of opinion is not a representation:

(1) Where one party has some special knowledge on which to base his opinion

In *Smith v Land and House Property Corp* (1884), S put a hotel up for sale, saying that the hotel was let to a 'most desirable tenant' at a rent of £400 per annum. In fact, the tenant had not paid the rent for the previous quarter and, although he had paid the quarter before, had only done so after threat of legal action. Between the time when the defendants contracted to purchase the hotel and the time when the sale was completed, the tenant went bankrupt. The defendant refused to complete the sale. *Held*: the statement by S was a misrepresentation because he was in a position to know that the tenant was undesirable. The defendants would not, therefore, be ordered to complete the sale.

See also *Esso v Mardon* (p 243 below) where an expert opinion as to the potential number of gallons which a petrol station would sell, was held to be a representation.

(2) *Where the party who has stated the opinion does not, in fact, hold that opinion*

For example, Alice sells Matthew a painting which she says was painted, in her opinion, by Picasso. In fact, she holds no such opinion. Alice's statement is not a statement of opinion but is a misrepresentation.

Induces

A false statement does not, in itself, render its maker liable for misrepresentation. For misrepresentation to be established, it must be shown that the representation was intended to induce, and did in fact induce, the representee to make the contract.

A false statement of fact will, therefore, not amount to a misrepresentation in law where:

(1) *The statement did not affect the representee's judgment*

In such a case, it cannot be said that the false statement induced the contract. In *Smith v Chadwick* (1882), S brought an action against the promoters of a steel company for misrepresentation. They had stated in the company prospectus that a Mr JJ Grieves MP was a director of the company. In fact, he had withdrawn his consent to act on the day before the prospectus was issued. However, the evidence showed that S had never heard of JJ Grieves at the time he read the prospectus, so that the statement, though untrue, could not be said to have affected S's judgment.

(2) *The statement was not known to the intended representee*

In *Horsfall v Thomas* (1862), H made a gun for T. T paid for it by means of two bills of exchange. H sued T on one of the bills and T's defence was that after he had fired six rounds from the gun, it burst. T claimed that the breech of the gun had been defective and that a plug of metal had been driven into the breech to conceal the defect. However, it appeared that, at the time of accepting the bills of exchange, T had never seen the gun or, if he had, he had never examined the gun. Thus, any attempt to conceal the defect could not have had a misleading effect on his mind.

(3) *The representee knows at the time the contract is made that the representation is false*

(4) *The representee relies on his own judgment rather than on the representation of the other party*

In such a case, the representee cannot claim to have been misled by the misrepresentation. However, it is not sufficient that the representee should have been given the opportunity to discover the truth – his knowledge must be full and complete. In *Redgrave v Hurd* (1881), R, a solicitor, inserted an advertisement in the *Law Times* for a partner, 'an efficient lawyer and advocate, about 40, who would not object to purchase advertiser's suburban residence ...'. H replied to the advert and R told him that the practice was worth £300–£400 per annum. Papers were produced by R which showed an income of less than £200, but when H queried this, R produced further papers which, he said, made up the balance. Relying on that statement, H agreed to purchase the house and a share in the practice. After the contract but before the conveyance, H found out that the gross takings of the practice were less than £200 per annum. He refused to complete the sale. *Held*: H had relied on R's statements, not on his own judgment. It was immaterial that H could have discovered the untruth of R's statements, he was entitled to rely on them being true.

REMEDIES FOR MISREPRESENTATION

The remedies for misrepresentation are:

(a) damages; and/or

(b) rescission of the contract.

Since the Misrepresentation Act 1967, there have effectively been four types of misrepresentation, with slightly differing remedies for each. These are: fraudulent, statutory, negligent and wholly innocent.

(Note that before the Act (or at least before *Hedley Byrne v Heller*) there was no distinction between negligent and wholly innocent misrepresentation, both types being classified as *innocent* misrepresentation (as distinct from fraudulent misrepresentation): this is a point which must be borne in mind when reading pre-Act cases.)

DAMAGES

Damages may be awarded either:

(a) for the tort of deceit (in respect of a fraudulent misrepresentation); or

(b) for the tort of negligence; or

(c) under s 2(1) of the Misrepresentation Act 1967 (statutory misrepresentation).

(Note: damages in lieu of rescission may be awarded in respect of a non-fraudulent misrepresentation under s 2(2) of the 1967 Act. We will deal with this when we deal with rescission.)

Damages for the tort of deceit

Damages for the tort of deceit may be awarded where the false statement has been made fraudulently. A fraudulent statement is one that:

(a) is known by the representor to be false; or

(b) is made without belief in its truth; or

(c) is made recklessly without any regard as to whether it was true or false.

The leading case on the definition of fraud is *Derry v Peek* (1889), in which a tramway company had power under a special Act of Parliament to run trams by animal power and, if they secured the consent of the Board of Trade, by mechanical or steam power. Derry and others were directors of the company. They had issued a prospectus inviting the public to subscribe for shares in the company. In the prospectus they said that they had the power to run trams powered by steam and that this would result in considerable economies to the company. The directors, when making this statement, had assumed that Board of Trade permission was a formality. However, in the event it wasn't granted, the company was wound up and disappointed investors sued the directors for fraud. *Held*: the statement was not made fraudulently since the directors honestly believed that the statement they made was true.

(Note that the law was quickly changed by the Director's Liability Act 1889 (now part of the Companies Act 1985), so that directors were liable to pay damages for negligent mis-statements made in prospectuses. However, this made no inroad into the general position, that there was no liability to pay damages for a misrepresentation made other than fraudulently.)

Differences between damages for deceit and damages for breach of contract

The general rule for an award of damages in tort is that they are intended to put the innocent party in the position he would have been in had the tort not taken place, as far as money can achieve this. Contract damages, on the other hand, are intended to put the innocent party in the position he would have been in if the contract had been carried out. This means that where the innocent party has made a potentially profitable bargain, he might be better off if the misrepresentation were treated as a breach of contract and damages awarded on a contract basis.

On the other hand, the rules relating to remoteness of damage (that is, the rules which limit the extent of the damage for which compensation may be awarded) are more generous in the tort of deceit, where all *direct* damage, even though it may not have been likely, is compensable. In breach of contract, the damage either has to flow naturally from the breach (that is, it must be a likely result of the breach) or must be within the contemplation of both parties as a possible consequence of the breach. Thus, where, for example, there is consequential damage which would be too remote as far as contract is concerned (for example, the suffering of sleepless nights, the need to take out an overdraft to compensate for losses caused by the misrepresentation, etc), the innocent party may be better off if his damages are assessed on a tort of deceit basis. For example, in *Doyle v Olby Ironmongers* (1969), the plaintiff needed to take out an overdraft as a result of a *fraudulent misrepresentation* which was made to him. It was held that he could recover the expenses of the overdraft. However, in *Pilkington v Wood* (1953), where the plaintiff needed an overdraft in consequence of a *breach of contract*, it was held that the expenses of the overdraft were not recoverable as they were too remote.

(The rule as to remoteness of damage in relation to the tort of deceit is also different from the rule as to remoteness of damage in the tort of negligence. In negligence, the general requirement is that damage of the type that was *foreseeable* is recoverable.)

An example of the difference between the rules relating to remoteness in contract, and those relating to the tort of deceit, is to be found in *Doyle v Olby Ironmongers* (1969). P purchased the business for £4,500 and paid £5,000 for the stock. When P went into occupation of the business, he found that a number of false statements had been made to him. In particular, he had been told that the trade was two-thirds retail and one-third wholesale and that all of the trade was 'over the counter' (which should have meant that there was no need to employ a travelling salesman). However, he discovered that about half the trade was wholesale and that to maintain that trade he would have to employ a travelling salesman. D couldn't afford to employ a travelling salesman since he had used all his available cash to buy the business, and he had had to borrow in addition. Therefore, all of the wholesale trade was lost. In 1964, P brought an action for damages for fraud and conspiracy against Olby (Ironmongers) Ltd and several members of the Olby family.

The trial judge treated the statement that all the trade was over the counter as being a term of the contract. He decided that the measure of damages should be the difference between what D had paid for the business and what the business was actually worth. Having decided that the price paid for the goodwill was £4,000, the judge held that the loss of the wholesale trade reduced the value of the business by about 35–40% which, as a round figure, gave £2,500. Thus, damages were assessed at £1,500. However, the Court of Appeal *held* that the basis of assessment for fraud was different to that for breach of contract. In addition to damages for the reduced worth of the business (which the Court of Appeal put at £2,500), D was entitled to compensation for the strain and worry which the defendant's misrepresentations had caused him and, also, the cost of servicing his bank overdraft which had been made necessary by the defendant's misrepresentations. This figure was put at £3,000, giving a total of £5,500.

The leading case on damages for fraudulent misrepresentation is now *Smith New Court Securities v Scrimgeour Vickers* (1996). The defendants owned 28,141,424 shares in Ferranti which they wished to sell. They offered the shares to the plaintiffs. In a deal of this magnitude, the plaintiffs would normally have expected to have bought the shares at the lower end of the market price (which the evidence placed at between 78p and 82p per share) and to have resold them immediately to institutional clients. The evidence was that such clients would not have been prepared to buy at more than 80p unless Smith gave a special recommendation, which they were not prepared to do. However, following fraudulent misrepresentations by R, an employee of the defendants, that two other buyers had made bids for the shares – one of them at 81p per share – the plaintiffs agreed to buy them, not with a view to short-term gain, but with a view to re-selling them in the market over a longer period. They agreed to pay 82 and a quarter pence per share, making a total price of £23,141,424. Unfortunately, unknown to either party, a further fraud (which was nothing to do with either of the parties to this case) had been perpetrated on Ferranti. This meant that the shares were worth a great deal less at the date of the transaction between Smith and Scrimgeour: the share value was around 44p per share.

Two main issues arose: firstly, should the defendants be responsible for the effect of the fraud of a third party? The trial judge and the House of Lords thought 'yes' while the Court of Appeal said 'no'.

The answer to the first question directly affected the answer to the second question, which was, on what basis should damages be awarded? Should they be awarded on the difference between the price that Smith paid (that is, 82p) and the price Smith would have been prepared to pay without R's fraudulent misrepresentation (that is, 78p), which was what the Court of Appeal thought? Or should it be the difference between what Smith paid and what the shares were actually worth at the date of the purchase, which is what the trial judge awarded? The House of Lords held that neither was the true measure of damages. The true measure was the difference between what Smith had paid for the shares and what they eventually were able to sell them for. In fact, this turned out to be slightly more than the trial judge's assessment and a great deal more than the Court of Appeal's.

Lord Browne-Wilkinson laid down seven points governing liability for fraudulent misrepresentation:

(a) the defendant is bound to make reparation for all damage *directly* flowing from the transaction;

(b) although such damage need not have been foreseeable it must have been directly caused by the transaction;

(c) in assessing such damage, the plaintiff is entitled to recover, by way of damages, the full price paid by him;

(d) as a general rule, the benefits received by him include the market value of the property acquired as at the date of the acquisition; but such general rule is not to be inflexibly applied where to do so would prevent him obtaining full compensation for the wrong suffered;

(e) although the circumstances in which the general rule should not apply cannot be comprehensively stated, it will not normally apply where either: (i) the misrepresentation has continued to operate after the date of the acquisition of the asset; or (ii) the circumstances of the case are such that the plaintiff is, by reason of the fraud, locked into the property;

(f) in addition, the plaintiff is entitled to recover consequential losses caused by the transaction; and

(g) the plaintiff must take all reasonable steps to mitigate his loss once he has discovered the fraud.

Tort of negligence

In 1963, the case of *Hedley Byrne v Heller* (1964) established the possibility of a common law action for damages in tort for negligent misrepresentation.

Before *Donoghue v Stevenson* (1932), a person could not be liable in tort arising out of a transaction in respect of which that person had a contractual liability. This was because it was thought that to impose a tort liability was to undermine the doctrine of privity of contract. For example, if Linda was liable to Malcolm for breach of contract in respect of defective goods, she could not also be liable in negligence to Norah, who had been injured by the goods, since she had no contract with Norah. *Donoghue v Stevenson* altered the position by holding that a manufacturer owed a duty of care, under the tort of negligence, to a consumer of his product despite the fact that he also owed a contractual duty to the purchaser (that is, the retailer).

However, this duty was restricted to a duty not to cause physical injury or damage to property. There was no duty to avoid causing *pure economic loss*. This view was affirmed in *Candler v Crane Christmas and Co* (1951), where a potential investor relied on accounts prepared by an accountant on behalf of the company in order to invest in the company. The accounts had been prepared carelessly and failed to show the true financial position of the company. In consequence, the plaintiff lost his investment. He sued the accountants for negligence. *Held*: there was no liability in negligence for pure economic loss.

Until 1963, an award of damages for misrepresentation was possible only if the misrepresentation had been made fraudulently. In such a case, an action was brought for the tort of deceit (see above). In 1963, the case of *Hedley Byrne v Heller* overruled *Candler v Crane Christmas and Co* and established the possibility of a common law action for damages in tort for negligent mis-statement resulting in pure economic loss.

In the *Hedley Byrne* case, P were advertising agents. They had been asked by a company called Easipower to insert some adverts in the press and on television on Easipower's behalf. This would involve giving Easipower credit of up to £100,000 and, as advertising agents are *del credere* agents (this means that, contrary to the normal agency rule, the agents are liable to pay the principal), P wanted to be sure that Easipower were financially sound. They therefore sought a reference from D, who were Easipower's bankers. D replied, 'without responsibility on the part of the bank or its officials', that Easipower was 'a respectably constituted company considered good for its ordinary business engagements. Your figures are larger than we are accustomed to see'.

To those who are used to dealing with bank references, this reference was a warning, and D intended it as such because Easipower had an overdraft with the bank and the bank knew that they were about to call in this overdraft. This meant that Easipower would almost certainly have difficulty in paying P. However, P went ahead and placed the advertising. When Easipower went into liquidation, unable to pay their advertising bill of £17,000, P sued D for negligently giving a favourable reference. P lost the case because it was held that D's exemption clause, whereby they accepted no responsibility for the accuracy of the reference, was effective to exempt them from liability. However, the importance of the case lies in the fact that the House of Lords stated that the maker of a negligent mis-statement may be liable in tort to the representee.

It is difficult to say in exactly what circumstances the representor becomes liable. The House held that for A to owe B a duty of care in respect of any statement made to him, A and B must be in a special relationship. Lord Pearce, in dealing with the question 'in what circumstances does the special relationship exist which gives rise to a duty of care?' said:

> ... the answer to that question depends upon the circumstances of the transaction. If, for instance, they disclosed a casual social approach to the inquiry no such special relationship or duty of care would be assumed ... To import such a duty to a representation must normally, I think, concern a

business or professional transaction whose nature makes clear the gravity of the inquiry and the importance and influence attached to the answer.

Despite an attempt by the Privy Council (in *Mutual Life and Citizens' Assurance Co v Evatt* (1971)) to restrict the duty of care to cases where advice is given by a professional person (and possibly only where it is the professional person's business to give advice), it seems possible that the English courts do not accept any such restriction. For example, in *Anderson v Rhodes* (1967), D were held liable for P's loss following a negligent misrepresentation that a financially unsound company was creditworthy, though this was decided before the Evatt case.

The case of *Caparo v Dickman* (1990) laid down four conditions to be met if a duty of care was to exist in the case of pure economic loss. In this case, D were auditors for Fidelity. They had prepared annual accounts on the strength of which C (the plaintiff) bought shares in Fidelity and mounted a successful takeover bid. C alleged that the accounts were inaccurate and showed a profit of £1.3 m when they should have shown a loss of £400,000. Had C known the true state of affairs, they would never have bid for F. They sued in negligence to recover their loss. *Held*: D owed no duty of care in respect of the accuracy of the accounts, either to members of the public who relied on the accounts to invest in the company or to any individual existing shareholder who relied on the accounts to increase his shareholding. Auditors prepare accounts not to promote the interests of potential investors but to assist shareholders collectively to exercise their right to control the company.

Four conditions must be met for a duty of care to exist in respect of pure economic loss:

(a) the defendant must be fully aware of the nature of the transaction which the claimant had in contemplation;

(b) he must either have communicated that information directly or must well know that it will be communicated to him or a restricted class of persons of which D is a member;

(c) he must specifically anticipate that the claimant will properly and reasonably rely on that information when deciding whether or not to engage in the transaction; and

(d) the purpose for which P does rely on that information must be a purpose connected with interests which it is reasonable to demand that the defendants protect.

The court thought that if a duty were owed to all potential investors, this would result in unlimited liability on the part of the auditors.

A different result was reached in *Morgan Crucible v Hill Samuel* (1991). In this case, the plaintiffs mounted a takeover bid for First Castle Electronics. The target company mounted a defence in which they compared Morgan Crucible's profit record with First Castle's, concluding that MC compared unfavourably with FC and urging shareholders not to accept the plaintiff's bid. In making the statements about profit records, reliance was made on accounts recently prepared by the auditors and endorsed by Hill Samuel. MC therefore increased their bid. FC's directors recommended that the shareholders should accept the bid. MC later alleged that the accounts were prepared negligently and were misleading. *Held*: it was not sufficient that it was foreseeable that MC would lose as a result of the financial statements; there had to be a sufficient proximity between the plaintiff and the defendants. In addition, it had to be just and reasonable to impose liability on the defendant. In this case, some of the representations were made after the bid was made and because the bid had been made. Therefore, this case could be distinguished from *Caparo* since, in that case, the accounts had not been prepared for the purpose for which the plaintiff had relied on them. Thus, the defendants were liable.

In *Esso v Mardon* (1976), M was negotiating to take the lease of a petrol station owned by E. During the negotiations, M was told by one of E's senior sales representatives that the potential throughput of the station in the third year was in the region of 200,000 gallons. M had suggested that 100,000 might be a more realistic figure. However, he relied on the superior expertise of E's employee. In fact, the throughput was substantially less than 100,000 gallons. This made the station uneconomic and, therefore, in July 1964, M gave up the tenancy. He was granted a new tenancy at a lower rent. Nevertheless, the throughput remained insufficient to make the station economic. By August 1966, M was unable to pay for petrol supplied. E therefore claimed possession of the site and also claimed arrears of rent. M counter-claimed for: (i) breach of warranty; or (ii) damages for negligence. *Held*: E's statement was not a contractual term in the sense that they warranted that the throughput would be 200,000 gallons. However, it was a contractual term that the forecast should have been made with reasonable care and skill. As this was not the case, E were in breach of contract. The statement was also a negligent mis-statement within the meaning of the *Hedley Byrne* case. It was not a statement of opinion on the lines of *Bisset v Wilkinson* (1927), because the representor in this case had specialised knowledge which the representee did not have. (The facts occurred before the Misrepresentation Act 1967 came into force, so that the Act could not be used by the defendant. However, its application would have provided a similar result.)

Note, however, that the representee recovered damages on a tort of negligence basis, that is, he was put into the position he would have been in had he not taken the lease. He did not receive his expectation loss, which is the basis on which damages would be awarded for breach of contract, which would be the amount of profit he would have made if the throughput had been 200,000 gallons.

Nowadays, a person who has been induced to contract by a misrepresentation of the other contracting party will normally seek to rely on s 2(1) of the Misrepresentation Act 1967, though he will include a *Hedley Byrne* claim and a breach of contract claim so as to cover all possibilities.

Statutory misrepresentation

Until the case of *Hedley Byrne v Heller* (1963), the only remedy for a misrepresentation which was made innocently (that is, non-fraudulently) was rescission. This was the case even where the misrepresentation was made negligently and had the consequence that, where a non-fraudulent misrepresentation resulted in substantial financial loss, the innocent party was unable to reclaim his loss by way of damages. This was unsatisfactory, since allegations of fraud are not easy to prove (see, for example, *Derry v Peek* above) and, furthermore, allegations of fraud entitle the defendant to call for a jury, which increases the liability for costs should the plaintiff lose the case.

The case of *Hedley Byrne v Heller* mitigated the earlier law in that the House of Lords ruled that where a misrepresentation is made negligently, the innocent party can sue for the tort of negligence. However, the 1967 Misrepresentation Act went a stage further in that it provided for a party who makes a misrepresentation to be liable to pay damages:

> ... notwithstanding that the misrepresentation was not made fraudulently unless he proves that he had reasonable grounds to believe ... that the facts represented were true.

Both statutory misrepresentations and negligent mis-statements are statements which, though made honestly, are made without the sufficient care which should have been given in the circumstances, so that a statutory misrepresentation overlaps to some extent with the common law of negligent mis-statement established by the *Hedley Byrne* case. An important difference between statutory misrepresentation and negligent mis-statements is that the rule in *Hedley Byrne* can apply to situations in which the representor and representee have no contractual relationship, whereas s 2(1) applies only 'where a person has entered into a contract after a misrepresentation has been made to him by another party thereto'.

The statutory remedy for misrepresentation offered by s 2(1) of the Misrepresentation Act is generally thought to offer a superior remedy to that offered by the tort of negligence, in that:

(a) the representee does not have to prove that the representor owed him a duty of care (though it is difficult to imagine circumstances in which one contracting party would not owe the other a duty of care);

(b) the claimant who uses *Hedley Byrne* has to prove negligence in the normal way, whereas with s 2(1) there is a *presumption* of negligence and it is up to the defendant to prove that he had reasonable grounds for believing his statement to be true; and

(c) the rules as to remoteness of damage differ: under s 2(1) the damages are assessed as if the misrepresentation had been made fraudulently, which means that *all direct damage* is recoverable (see *Smith New Court Securities v Scrimgeour Vickers* (1996), above); under *Hedley Byrne* the damages are assessed on a negligence basis, which means that only damage of the type that is *foreseeable* is compensable.

The second defendant (D2) was a car dealer; the first defendant (D1) was his customer. D1 wished to take on hire-purchase a car owned by D2. However, D1 had insufficient cash to pay a deposit which the claimants (R), a finance company, required before they would finance the agreement. The two defendants therefore submitted incorrect figures to R, which made it appear that D1 had paid a greater deposit than was actually the case. D2 then sold the car to R, who let it on hire-purchase to D1. As a consequence of the fraud perpetrated by D1 and D2, R lent more money than they would otherwise have done. D1 fraudulently sold it to an innocent third party, who obtained a good title under s 27 of the Hire-Purchase Act 1964. R therefore sought to recover their loss from D1 and D2, relying on s 2(1) of the Misrepresentation Act 1967. There were three possibilities:

(a) that R had lost nothing since, under the transaction between R and D2, R had obtained ownership of a car which was worth at least the sum which they had lent to D1 under the hire-purchase agreement; or

(b) that R had lost the outstanding instalments which were owed to them by D1 and the additional money which R had loaned because of the fraudulent statements made to them by D1 and 2 (this solution would still have left R out of pocket on the deal); or

(c) that R had lost the difference between what R had loaned and the instalments which D1 had repaid. This solution would repay to R the full amount of their loss.

The issue to be resolved was whether R were entitled only to their foreseeable loss (which they would be awarded if their damages were to be assessed according to the rules of negligence) or whether they were entitled to the full amount of their direct loss, to which they would be entitled if the damages were awarded on the basis of the tort of deceit.

Held: the measure of damages under s 2(1), according to the clear words of the statute, is 'as if the representation had been made fraudulently', that is, on the basis of the tort of deceit, rather than the tort of negligence. The court gave judgment in favour of the finance company against the dealer for £3,625.24.

The earlier case of *Howard Marine v Ogden* (1978), indicates the sometimes complex relationship between the statutory action under s 2(1) of the Misrepresentation Act, an action for the tort of negligence at common law, and an action for breach of contract.

O were excavating specialists. They won a contract which involved transporting excavated earth out to sea in order to dispose of it. To do this, they hired two barges from HM. When asked how much, in tonnes, the barges would transport, HM had, from memory, unintentionally given an incorrect carrying capacity, which was greater than the barges would actually hold – though it would have been relatively easy to have looked up the figure in the barges' documents. Owing to the fact that the barges would not carry as much as had been expected, the job proceeded more slowly than it should have done, resulting in extra costs for O. O therefore refused to pay the hire cost. HM sued. O counter-claimed for their losses caused by the fact that the barges' carrying capacity was lower then HM had claimed, as follows;

(a) breach of contract; or,

(b) the tort of negligence; or,

(c) statutory misrepresentation within the meaning of s 2(1) of the Misrepresentation Act 1967.

The three judges in the Court of Appeal were unanimous in deciding that H had not intended their statement as to the carrying capacity of the barges to be a contractual term. One judge thought that HM should be liable for common law negligence; one thought that HM were not liable for negligence and the third expressed no opinion. However, O won their case because two of the three judges decided that HM were liable for misrepresentation under s 2(1) of the 1967 Act. They thought the representation as to the load carrying capacity of the barge was an important matter and, in finding HM liable, they were influenced by the fact that HM's representative could easily have looked up the carrying capacity and thus given the correct answer when O had asked about the matter.

Wholly innocent misrepresentation

This is where the maker of an untrue statement had reasonable grounds for believing that his statement was true. For example, the owner of a house informs a prospective purchaser that the house is free from damp. She does this relying on a recent surveyor's report. The information is incorrect. This would be a wholly innocent misrepresentation for which the purchaser's remedy would be rescission or damages *in lieu*. (Of course, the owner of the house or the purchaser might bring an action against the surveyor for negligence.) The remedy for a wholly innocent misrepresentation, as stated, is rescission or damages in lieu of rescission under s 2(2) of the 1967 Act.

RESCISSION

'Rescission' means that the parties are substantially restored to their pre-contract position.

This idea is sometimes expressed by the Latin term *'restitutio in integrum'*. Each party must give back what he has gained under the contract. For example, if A sells B a chair for £500, having misrepresented that it is an antique, the contract is rescinded by B giving back the chair to A and A giving back the £500 to B.

Rescission is an equitable remedy, given at the discretion of the court. However, this discretion is not absolute: it is exercised according to established rules and the courts have laid down four circumstances in which they will refuse to exercise their discretion in favour of the claimant. These are:

(a) where the claimant has delayed in asserting his claim to rescission

Delay in equity is often called *'laches'*. In the case of fraudulent misrepresentation or breach of fiduciary duty, delay is calculated from the time the plaintiff discovered the fraud entitling him to rescind. However, in the case of non-fraudulent misrepresentation, delay is probably calculated from the time when, with reasonable diligence, the representee should have discovered the misrepresentation. (The difference is explained by the fact that, in fraudulent misrepresentation, there has been a deliberate attempt to conceal the truth and it is therefore felt to be unjust to penalise the representee in these circumstances.)

There is no set time limit within which a claim for rescission has to be made to avoid being guilty of *laches*. In *Oscar Chess v Williams* (1957), where eight months elapsed between the contract and the claim for rescission, it was held that the delay was too long, even though the claim was made immediately the truth was discovered.

In *Leaf v International Galleries* (1950), the plaintiff was sold a drawing of Salisbury Cathedral which was represented as being by the famous artist, Constable. The representation was not fraudulent. It was not until five years later, when L wished to sell the painting, that he discovered that the drawing was not by Constable. He claimed rescission of the contract (in 1950, damages were not available for misrepresentation unless it were fraudulent). It was held that five years was too long a delay, despite the fact that L made his claim immediately on discovering the truth.

(b) where the claimant has affirmed the contract

Even where the representee discovers the untruth of the representations fairly soon after the contract was made, he must opt unequivocally to rescind the contract. If he does not, the court may conclude that he has affirmed it (that is, indicated an intention to go on with the contract despite the misrepresentation).

In *Long v Lloyd* (1958), the defendant was a haulage contractor who advertised a lorry for sale for £850. His advert said that the lorry was 'in exceptional condition'. The plaintiff, who was also a haulage contractor, saw the lorry at the defendant's premises in London and, two days later, took it for a trial run. He found that the speedometer was not working, a spring was missing from the accelerator pad and that it was difficult to engage top gear. The defendant asserted that there was nothing wrong with the lorry other than what the defendant had found and also asserted at this stage that the lorry would do 11 miles to the gallon.

The plaintiff bought the lorry for £750. He then drove it from London to his place of business in Sevenoaks. Two days later he drove it to Rochester, on a round journey of 40 miles, to pick up a load. During the journey the dynamo ceased to function, there was a crack in one of the wheels, an oil seal was leaking badly and it did only five miles to the gallon. The same day the plaintiff told the defendant of these defects. The defendant offered to pay half the cost of a reconstructed dynamo but denied knowledge of the other defects. The plaintiff accepted the offer.

The next day the plaintiff's brother drove the lorry to Middlesborough. It broke down the following night. The plaintiff thereupon asked for his money back but the defendant refused to give it to him. The lorry was subsequently examined by an expert who pronounced it to be unroadworthy. The plaintiff claimed rescission of the contact. *Held* by the Court of Appeal: the remedy was not available to the plaintiff since, although his journey to Rochester could be regarded as a testing of the vehicle in a working capacity, the acceptance of the defendant's offer to pay half the cost of a reconstructed dynamo and the subsequent journey to Middlesborough amounted to an affirmation of the contract.

Note that since the Misrepresentation Act 1967, the plaintiff in a similar case would almost certainly succeed in an action for damages for statutory misrepresentation under s 2(1) of the Act.

(c) Where it is not possible to restore the status quo

In some cases it is not possible to restore the status quo. This will be the case where the subject matter of the contract has been wholly or partly consumed or, for example, where the subject matter of a contract is a mine, where the mine has been substantially worked or worked out.

In *Clarke v Dickson* (1858), the plaintiff invested money in a partnership to work lead mines in Wales. Four years later the partnership capital was converted into shares in a limited company. Shortly afterwards the company commenced winding up proceedings, at which time the plaintiff discovered that certain statements which had been made to him were false. He claimed rescission of the partnership contract. *Held*: rescission could not be granted since the partnership was no longer in existence, having been replaced by the limited company. It was therefore not possible to restore the parties to their original positions.

Note that it is not necessary that the parties are restored precisely to their pre-contract position. In *O'Sullivan v Management Agency and Music* (1985), it was held to be sufficient if the court was able to do justice between the parties (see above, Chapter 8, p 174).

(d) Because third parties have acquired rights in the subject matter

Misrepresentation renders a contract voidable. This means that, until the innocent party rescinds the contract (for example, by telling the other party that they wish to end the contract), the contract is valid. Thus, while the contract is valid, the guilty party may dispose of the subject matter to a third party, and, providing that the third party takes the subject matter in good faith and for value and without notice of the misrepresentation, the third party acquires a good title to the subject matter. If the claim for rescission is made after third parties have acquired rights in the subject matter, rescission will not be granted. Thus, the time at which the innocent party effectively rescinds the contract is of paramount importance where a third party is claiming that he has acquired rights under the contract.

There has been some litigation on the question of 'what does the original owner have to do in order to indicate that he is rescinding the contract'? The original answer was 'tell the misrepresentor' (that is, the other party to the contract). This is all very well if the other party remains available to be told. But what about the situation where A sells his car to B and takes a cheque in payment? The cheque is dishonoured. This is a misrepresentation, since a person who proffers a cheque in payment impliedly represents that it will be honoured. However, a fraudulent person will often abscond in circumstances where it will not be possible for the innocent party to inform him that he is rescinding the contract. In such a case, will informing the police of the fraud and asking them to recover the subject matter of the contract be sufficient to rescind the contract with the rogue?

In *Car and Universal Finance v Caldwell* (1963), C sold his car to a firm called Dunn's Transport on 12 January. He was paid by a cheque signed by W Foster and F Norris on behalf of the firm. He presented it to the bank for payment the following day and it was dishonoured. (Presumably he presented the cheque to the bank on which it was drawn, or got special clearance, because it normally takes at least three working days and often more before a cheque is cleared.) He immediately told the police and asked them to recover his car. On 15 January, a firm of car dealers called Motobella bought the car from Norris with notice that he had not come by it honestly. On the same day Motobella sold it to G & C Finance, who bought it in good faith. Tied in with the sale was a fictitious HP proposal, put forward by Motobella, that the car would be taken on HP by a fictitious person called Knowles. On 20 January, the police found the car in the possession of Motobella. On 29 January, C's solicitor wrote to Motobella informing them that C claimed the car. On 3 August, G & C sold the car to Car and Universal who took it in good faith.

It was held by the Court of Appeal (unanimously) that C retained title to the car (that is, he still owned it), because he had avoided the contract with Dunn's Transport at the time he asked the police to recover the car. As this was on 13 January, two days before Motobella sold it to G & C Finance, G & C Finance had acquired no rights in the car.

Note: The Law Reform Committee (Cmnd 2958) recommended that the seller should not be able to avoid a sale which was rendered voidable by the buyer's misrepresentation, until he had informed the buyer of his decision. This proposal has not, to date, been given statutory effect.

CIRCUMSTANCES IN WHICH ENTITLEMENT TO RESCISSION MAY ENTITLE THE INNOCENT PARTY TO A PAYMENT OF MONEY

Entitlement to rescission does not necessarily entitle the innocent party to damages. However, there are two circumstances in which entitlement to rescission may entitle the innocent party to a payment of money. The first is where he is entitled to an indemnity. The second is where, in the case of an innocent (that is, non-fraudulent) misrepresentation, he is granted damages in lieu of rescission.

Indemnity

Where the innocent party is entitled to rescission, he is also entitled to an indemnity. An indemnity is not the same as damages and does not consist of compensation for the total damage that the innocent party has suffered. It consists only of money which the innocent party was *bound to expend under the terms of the contract*.

A good example of the distinction between an indemnity and damages is to be found in *Whittington v Seale Hayne* (1900), in which the plaintiffs were breeders of poultry. They leased certain property for use as a chicken farm, having enquired as to whether the premises were in a sanitary condition and having been assured that they were. In fact, the premises turned out to have poor drainage. The water supply was poisoned and, in consequence, the farm manager became ill and the poultry died. The local authority declared the house and land unfit for habitation and required the plaintiffs to renew the drains, as required by a term of their lease. The plaintiffs claimed rescission of the contract for misrepresentation and (since damages were available only for fraudulent misrepresentation at that time), for an indemnity against the following losses: loss of stock £750; loss of profit on sales £100; loss of breeding season £500; removal of stores and rent £75; medical expenses £100. *Held*: the plaintiffs were entitled to an indemnity only in respect of money necessarily laid out in consequence of the obligations contained in the lease. Thus they had to pay the rent, the rates and the repairs ordered by the local authority and only in respect of these items could an indemnity be granted.

Damages *in lieu* of rescission

In cases of contracts induced by an innocent (that is, negligent or wholly innocent) misrepresentation, the court may declare that the contract is to remain in existence and may give the plaintiff damages in lieu of an award of rescission.

This was an innovation of the Misrepresentation Act 1967. It gives the court a discretion and is done by s 2(2) of the Act which states:

> Where a person has entered into a contract after a misrepresentation has been made to him otherwise than fraudulently, and he would be entitled by reason of the misrepresentation to rescind the contract, then, if it is claimed in any proceedings arising out of the contract that the contract ought to be or has been rescinded, the court or arbitrator may declare the contract subsisting and award damages in lieu of rescission, if of the opinion that it would be equitable to do so, having regard to the nature of the misrepresentation and the loss that would be caused by it if the contract were upheld, as well as to the loss that rescission would cause to the other party.

The circumstances in which the court has the power to award damages *in lieu* of rescission are not certain and await authoritative decision. In *Thomas Witter Ltd v TBP Industries Ltd* (1996), it was held that damages *in lieu* of rescission could be granted either: (i) if the right to rescind had ever existed; or, at least, (ii) if the right existed at the time the plaintiff sought to rescind. Of course, these two options could give different results according to the circumstances. If, for example, the plaintiff delayed in making his claim, he could nevertheless be awarded damages *in lieu* of rescission if option (i) were regarded as being the correct interpretation of s 2(2). If option (ii) were regarded as being the correct interpretation, the plaintiff could not be granted damages *in lieu*.

Note, too, that damages under s 2(2) are only *in lieu of rescission*. This does not mean that the innocent party is entitled to compensation for the full extent of his losses. The following example should illustrate what this means:

Suppose A purchases a market garden from B. The price is £150,000, made up of £30,000 goodwill and business, £25,000 stock and £95,000 freehold premises. A tells B that he is principally interested in developing the flower sales of the business and, in particular, in growing and selling exotic flowers. B negligently represents that the land and greenhouses are entirely suitable for this without the need for adaptation. This is untrue, with the result that B is now claiming:

(a) rescission of the contract; and

(b) damages for misrepresentation, including £2,000 loss of stock, £10,000 loss of profits and £5,000 other expenses caused by the misrepresentation.

As the misrepresentation is negligent, A will be entitled to the damages set out in (b), relying on s 2(1) of the 1967 Act. However, let us suppose that, although the court holds that A is entitled to rescission, it emerges during the course of the hearing that A has discovered how to adapt the premises for growing exotic flowers and that he would not be unwilling to keep the business. The court may decide, in view of the difficulty of undoing a sale of real property (and particularly as B may have invested the proceeds of his sale to A in other real property), to hold that the contract subsists (that is, remains in existence) and to give A damages *in lieu* of rescission. They will thus have to value the business as it was, against the price that A paid (or alternatively to assess the amount of money that A would have to expend to give the property the attributes which B negligently represented that it had) and to award A the difference as damages *in lieu* of rescission. So that, supposing that A had to spend £5,000 in adapting the premises so that they would grow exotic flowers, the £5,000 will be given as damages *in lieu*.

Recognising that there may be an overlap between damages awarded under s 2(1) and damages *in lieu* of rescission awarded under s 2(2), in order to avoid the same damage 'being awarded twice over', s 2(3) provides that damages awarded under s 2(2) shall be taken into account when assessing damages under s 2(1).

REMEDIES FOR MISREPRESENTATION

Type	Damages	Rescission
Fraudulent (common law)	For tort of deceit. All direct damage flowing from the deceit is recoverable	Claim within a reasonable time from the discovery of the fraud
Negligent (common law)	For tort of negligence. Only damage of the *type* that is *foreseeable* is recoverable	Claim within a reasonable time within which the misrepresentation ought, with reasonable diligence, to have been discovered BUT under s 2(2) Misrep Act 1967, the court may declare the contract subsisting (ie still in existence) and award damages *in lieu* of rescission
Negligent (statutory)	On tort of deceit basis, (which means that all direct damage is recoverable), under s 2(1) Misrep Act. Can only be used where the parties have a contractual relationship	As above
Wholly innocent (ie neither fraudulent nor negligent)	No damages as such	As above

Notes on the above:

(a) That the statutory action under s 2(1) offers two advantages to the representee over the action available at common law:

   (1) the representor has to prove that he had reasonable grounds for believing that his representation was true: at common law it is up to the representee to prove that the representor had no reasonable grounds for believing that his representation was true. This reversal of the burden of proof is an important advantage to the representee;

(2) damages are awarded on the basis of the tort of deceit, which may be more advantageous than the tort of negligence.

(b) If there is no contractual relationship between representor and representee (as there wasn't in the *Hedley Byrne* case), the claimant must use the common law action: the statutory one is not available to him.

(c) In all cases where the representation has been made non-fraudulently it is open to the court to declare the contract subsisting and to award damages in lieu of rescission. However, note that this is not an award of damages as such, it simply compensates the representee for the fact that rescission has not been awarded.

(d) That a money payment called an indemnity can be awarded with rescission but it does not amount to an award of damages: it covers only what the representee was *compelled* to pay out under the contract.

(e) That the term 'innocent misrepresentation' is used in the cases, particularly pre-Misrepresentation Act cases, to mean a misrepresentation made without fraud. It could, however, be negligent. The term 'wholly innocent misrepresentation' is a term invented by text writers to indicate a misrepresentation that is made without fraud or negligence.

CHAPTER 11

PRIVITY OF CONTRACT

At common law, a contract cannot, as a general rule:

(a) confer benefits; or

(b) impose obligations,

on any persons except the parties to the contract.

Although the reason for the second aspect of the rule is quite clear, (that is, no one should have contractual obligations imposed upon them without their consent), the reason for the first aspect was not quite so clear-cut. There seemed to be no reason at all if A wished to make a contract with B for the benefit of C, why he should not be allowed to do so, subject to certain safeguards and exceptions. Indeed, the first aspect of the rule has, for a long time, created problems in many normal commercial transactions. The courts were, therefore, constrained to acknowledge a significant number of exceptional situations in which the rule did not apply. However, the basic rule remained. Although the courts were willing, by dint of some nifty legal footwork, to get round the rule in some cases in order to do justice (see, for example, *Beswick v Beswick*, below), in other cases they were not willing to do so, with the result that justice was not done (see, for example, *Scruttons v Midland Silicones*, below). It could be fairly said that by the end of the 19th century, the rule which prevented the parties from contracting in order to confer a benefit on a third party was creating far more problems in commercial situations, despite the exceptions, than would be created if the rule were to be abolished.

The Contracts (Rights of Third Parties) Act 1999 has now created a very broad exception to the rule. We can say that the rule has almost been abolished, but not quite. Not every contract which confers a benefit on a third party will qualify as an exceptional case. We will, therefore, consider the 1999 Act and, at the same time, the exceptions which were created before the Act, because if a contractual term is not enforceable under the term of the 1999 Act, it may still be enforceable because of one of the pre-existing exceptions.

CONFERRING BENEFITS ON THIRD PARTIES

An early example of how the doctrine of privity operated to prevent a third party suing on a contract can be found in the case of *Price v Easton* (1833). E promised P that if X did certain work for E, E would discharge a debt owed by X to P. X did the work, but E failed to pay P. P sued on E's promise. It was held that P's claim failed. Lord Denman said that he failed because he could show no consideration moving from him to the defendant. Littledale J said that P failed since he was not a party to the contract between X and E.

In a case like this, which is, in effect, a three-sided transaction to which each side has brought consideration, the effect of the doctrine may be formal only. P could (presumably) have sued the third party on the debt owed to P, and the third party could have sued E in respect of the work done for E. What the law didn't permit was P to sue E directly.

However, in cases where the third party has provided no consideration the doctrine may have a substantive effect, in that it will defeat the third party's claim or defence. A good example is to be found in *Beswick v Beswick* (1968). Peter Beswick, who was old and in ill-health, was assisted in his business as a coal merchant by his nephew, who was the defendant. In March 1962, PB assigned the business to his nephew in consideration of which the nephew agreed to employ him as a consultant at a fee of £6.50 per week for the remainder of his life and, after his death, to pay an annuity to his wife (that is, the defendant's aunt and the plaintiff in the case) of £5 per week. After his uncle died, the defendant paid his aunt the first weekly payment of £5 but paid nothing thereafter. She sued for breach of contract, first in her own capacity, and second on behalf of her late husband as his administratrix. She claimed a declaration and specific performance of the agreement. The Vice-Chancellor in the Chancery Court of the County Palatine of Lancaster dismissed the action. The Court of Appeal unanimously granted Mrs B a decree of specific performance in her capacity of administratrix of her late husband's estate. The defendant appealed to the House of Lords, which held unanimously that Mrs B was entitled to enforce the agreement in the name of her late husband and, moreover, she was entitled to a decree of specific performance to enable her to do this. She was not, however, entitled to enforce the agreement in her own name, since she was not a party to the contract between her husband and her nephew.

In this case, justice was done by the fact that, in addition to suing in her own right, the wife also sued on behalf of her husband's estate, since she was the administratrix of her husband's estate. The House of Lords was, therefore, able to give judgment in favour of the husband. However, a difficulty presents itself in relation to what damages should be awarded. The basic question is: 'What has the husband's estate lost by virtue of the nephew's breach of contract?' It is arguable that the answer is little or nothing, in which case the court should award only nominal damages. A further problem is that any award of damages would go to the husband's estate and would benefit the person entitled to the residue of the estate, which would not necessarily be the person whom it was intended to benefit (in this case, the widow). The House of Lords circumvented this problem by awarding the equitable remedy of specific performance, which is an order to the defendant to carry out the terms of the contract, that is, pay the pension to the widow. This circumvention could not be universally relied upon, however. For example, what would have been the case if the husband had left a will and had appointed his nephew as its executor? In addition, since equitable remedies are discretionary, there may be circumstances, for example, an undue delay in claiming the remedy, in which the court would not be prepared to grant a decree of specific performance.

THE CONTRACTS (RIGHTS OF THIRD PARTIES) ACT 1999

The Contracts (Rights of Third Parties) Act 1999 significantly alters the law of privity of contract in favour of a third party who wishes to rely on a provision in a contract which has been made for his benefit.

Promisor and promisee

Before we go any further, we need to remind ourselves what is meant by the terms 'promisor' and 'promisee', since these terms must be understood in order to make sense of what follows. In a bilateral contract, both parties are both promisee and promisor. The promisor is the person who makes the promise and the promisee is the person to whom the promise is made. If we use the case of *Beswick v Beswick* (above) as an example, uncle Beswick was the promisor of the coal business. He was, on the other hand, the promisee of the £6.50 consultancy fee and the promise to pay Mrs Beswick £5 per week after his death. Nephew Beswick was the promisor of the £6.50 and the £5 per week, on the one hand, and the promisee of the coal business on the other. The claimant in a contract action is always the promisee, that is, he is suing on the promise which was made *to him* by the promisor and which the promisor has broken – hence the action.

Basic right of third party to sue

Section 1(1) provides that a person who is not a party to a contract may enforce a contract term *in his own right* if the contract expressly provides he may. He may also enforce a term if that term purports to confer a benefit on him. Section 1(6) provides that the third party may also enforce any exclusion or limitation clause which is for his benefit. However, sub-s (2) provides that he may not enforce such a term if it appears that the actual parties did not intend him to be able to enforce it. Section 4 provides that the above provisions do not affect the right of the promisee (that is, the contracting party) to enforce the contract. If the promisee has obtained an award of damages under the contract in respect of the third party's loss, the court must take that into account in any award it makes to the third party.

Types of third party who can sue

Sub-section (3) states that the third party must be expressly identified in the contract by name, as a member of a class, or as answering to a particular description. This seems designed to overcome problems such as those encountered in *Southern Water Authority v Carey* (1985), where it was not possible to name the third parties in whose favour the main contractor intended to contract, because they hadn't yet been appointed. (For a full explanation of the problems which preceded the 1999 Act, and which may still exist if the contract is not brought within the terms of the 1999 Act, see the section below on 'Privity of Contract and Exemption Clauses', p 271).

Sub-section (3) also provides that the third party need not be in existence at the time the contract is made on his behalf. Again, this provision seems to be aimed at the rule in agency where, if the principal does not exist when the agent makes the contract on his behalf, the principal cannot ratify the contract. A typical situation is where an 'agent' makes a contract on behalf of a limited company which has not yet been formed. Under pre-existing law, it could not be enforced by the company, but this provision seems designed to ensure that it can be. Of course, the provision is capable of much wider application than simply unformed companies. A contract to benefit an unborn child would seem to come within the provision.

Sub-section (5) gives the third party the right to use any remedy in enforcing the contract that would have been available to him if he had been a party to the contract, and the rules relating to damages, specific performance, injunctions, etc, shall apply accordingly.

Rights of the parties to rescind or vary the contract

In the past, opponents of proposals to reform the law in order to give rights to a the third party have often relied strongly on the objection that such rights would interfere with the right of the parties themselves to rescind (that is, cancel) or vary (that is, amend) the contract. Section 2 deals with this situation by restricting the rights of the parties to rescind or vary the contract but, where the contracting parties provide for something different, provides that the wishes of the parties override the provisions of the Act.

Section 2(1) provides that where a third party has a right to enforce a term of a contract, the parties may not, by agreement, vary the contract in such a way as to extinguish or alter his entitlement, without his consent, unless:

(a) the third party has communicated his assent to the term to the promisor (that is, the person against whom the term is being enforced); or

(b) the promisor is aware that the third party has relied on the term; or

(c) the promisor can reasonably be expected to have foreseen that the third party would rely on the term and the third party has in fact relied on it.

Communication may be by words or conduct and takes place when received by the offeror.

However, an important exception to these provisions is contained in s 2(3). Where, in the contract, the parties have provided that the contract can be rescinded or varied without the consent of the third party, or have provided that the consent of the third party is required in circumstances specified in the contract, such a term displaces the requirements of s 2(1), that is, the contract term is applied rather than the terms of the Act.

Dispensing with consent

Section 2 also deals with problems arising out of obtaining the third party's consent. Section 2(4) and (5) provide that consent may be dispensed with by a court or tribunal if:

(a) the consent cannot be obtained because the whereabouts of the third party cannot reasonably be ascertained; or,

(b) where the third party is mentally incapable of giving his consent; or

(c) where it cannot reasonably be ascertained whether the third party has relied on the term which benefits him or not.

If the court orders that the consent of the third party may be dispensed with, it may impose such conditions as it thinks fit, including an award of compensation to the third party.

Promisor's (that is, defendant's) right to set-off, defence and counter-claim

Section 3 gives the promisor the right to claim a set-off or put forward a defence if the set-off or counter-claim arises from the contract and is relevant to the term, and the defence or set-off could have been used if the proceedings had been brought by the promisee (that is, the party to the contract who has extracted the promise in favour of the third party). It also gives a right to set-off or defence if the right is provided for expressly by the contract and would have been available if the proceedings had been brought by the promisee. The promisor is also given any right to set-off or defence that would have been available to him if the third party had been a party to the contract, and a right to counter-claim in respect of any matter not arising from the contract that would have been available had the third party been a party to the contract.

It also provides that where a third party seeks to enforce a term for his benefit (including in particular a term purporting to limit or exclude liability) he may not do so if he could not have enforced the contract if he had been a party to it. Note: this provision appears to be saying, among other things, that if an exemption clause does not satisfy the test of reasonableness (which would prevent the promisee from relying on it), it cannot be relied on by the third party.

Exceptions

No rights of enforcement are conferred on a third party in respect of:

(a) a contract on a bill of exchange, promissory note or other negotiable instrument (negotiable instruments have their own special rules relating to third party rights);

(b) a contract binding on the members of a company under s 14 of the Companies Acts (that is, the provision to the effect that the Memorandum and Articles of Association of a company constitute a contract between the company and its members and also as between the members themselves);

(c) a contract of employment against an employee (a contract of employment is a personal matter between the parties in which it would be inappropriate to allow a third party to intervene);

(d) any term of a worker's contract against a worker;

(e) a term of a relevant contract against an agency worker;

(f) a contract of carriage of goods by sea (thus, in the case of *Scruttons v Midland Silicones* (below), if this provision had been in place, it would have allowed Scruttons to rely on the exemption clause in the shipping contract made between the shipping line and Midland Silicones); and

(g) contract of carriage of goods by rail, road or air, which is subject to the rules of an international transport convention, except that a third party may rely on an exemption clause in such a contract.

EXCEPTIONS TO THE RULE

The rule which prevents the contract from conferring benefits on third parties has been found to be commercially inconvenient in a number of circumstances and to operate against public policy in others.

Therefore, a number of exceptions to the rule have been created. These are:

Assignment

Section 56 of the Law of Property Act 1925

Agency – the undisclosed principal

Certain insurance contracts

Trusts

Collateral contracts

Negotiable instruments

Bankers' commercial credits

Bills of lading

Section 14 of the Companies Act 1985

Assignment

A party to a contract may assign the benefit of contractual rights to a third party. The formalities for doing this are kept to a minimum. There are two types of assignment: (a) statutory (or legal) assignment; and (b) equitable assignment.

Statutory assignment

The statutory provisions relating to the method and effect of a statutory assignment of debts and other *choses in action* are to be found in s 136 of the Law of Property Act 1925. A *chose in action* is used to describe personal property rights which can be asserted only by legal action, not by taking possession. Examples include debts, shares in a company, insurance policies, and negotiable instruments such as cheques, copyrights, etc.

The rules are:

(a) the assignment must be in writing;

(b) written notice must be given to the debtor; and

(c) the assignment must be unconditional: it must be of the whole *chose*, not part of the *chose*, and must not be subject to any conditions.

Equitable assignment

If the conditions set out in s 136 are not complied with, the assignee may be left with an equitable assignment; the assignment will not give the legal title to the *chose*, but it may be effective in equity to give an equitable title. One consequence of this is that the assignee cannot sue in his own name: he must join the assignor as plaintiff in the action. Notice to the person liable on the *chose* does not have to be given, but if it is not, one of two consequences may ensue.

First, if the person liable makes payments to the assignor in ignorance of the assignment, the assignee is bound by them. For example, suppose A owes B £1,000 and B assigns the debt to C without giving notice to A. If A pays £200 to B in part-payment of the debt, C cannot then pursue A for that amount. He may only sue A for the balance of £800.

Secondly, under the rule in *Dearle v Hall* (1828), if the *chose* is assigned to a subsequent assignee who has no notice of a prior assignment, the subsequent assignee will gain priority over the earlier assignee. For example, suppose A owes B £1,000. B assigns the debt to D having already assigned it to C. D gives notice but C does not. D's assignment will take priority, even though C's was first in time.

Subject to equities

Any assignment, statutory or equitable, is subject to equities. In *Roxburghe v Cox* (1881), K assigned monies due to him as a result of a sale amounting to £3,000 to R. The debt was paid into K's account with C on 6 December. R gave notice of the assignment to C on 19 December. K's account was overdrawn by £647 on 6 December. It was held that C was entitled to set off the £647 owed to them against the money assigned.

The debtor may set off any debt which arises out of the same contract, or is closely connected with the same contract, as that which gives rise to the assigned debt, even though it hadn't accrued at the time of the assignment.

If the debt has neither accrued at the time that notice of the assignment is given, nor arises out of the same or a related transaction, a set-off cannot be claimed.

Section 56 of the Law of Property Act 1925

Sub-section (1) states that:

> A person may take an immediate or other interest in land or other property, or the benefit of any condition, right of entry, covenant or agreement over or respecting land or other property, although he may not be named as a party to the conveyance or other instrument.

The question arose in the case of *Beswick v Beswick* (1968) as to whether the words 'or other property' allowed the plaintiff, who was the widow of the contracting party and was the person for whose benefit the contract was made, to sue on the contract in her own right.

The full facts are given above but, essentially, a husband made a contract to benefit his wife and the question arose as to whether she could enforce the contract in her own name. Lord Denning MR and Danckwerts LJ held that she was entitled to succeed in her personal capacity under s 56(1) of the Law of Property Act 1925. The defendant appealed to the House of Lords, which held that she was not entitled to enforce the agreement in her own name, using s 56 of the Law of Property Act. It was held that s 56 of the Act applies only to real property (that is, land and things affixed to the land such as buildings). A difficulty with this conclusion is that s 205 of the Law of Property Act 1925 (on which the Court of Appeal had relied in coming to their conclusion that the widow could sue in her own name), states that:

(1) In this Act, unless the context otherwise requires, the following expressions have the meanings hereby assigned to them respectively, that is to say:

(i) 'Property' includes any thing in action, and any interest in real or personal property.

If s 205 is taken literally (and it is arguable that it ought to be), it would seem fairly clear that the words 'or other property' in s 56 include *personal* property as well as *real* property. However, the House of Lords resisted this interpretation, pointing out that the Act was a consolidating Act and that Parliament could not have intended that an enactment which referred mainly to real property could be used to dispense with the doctrine of privity of contract. The House was, therefore, of the opinion that the word 'property' as used in s 56 excluded personal property.

Agency

An agent (A) is a person who is appointed by a principal (P) in order to make a contract with a third party (T) on the principal's behalf. (Note that occasionally there are agency situations where the agent is employed merely to effect an introduction and not to conclude a contract: most agency contracts with estate agents are of that type.) Typical of commercial agents are insurance agents, travel agents, auctioneers, stock-brokers, etc.

It is clear that where P appoints an agent to make a contract with T, the law treats the contract as if it had been made directly by P with T. Questions of privity of contract do not, therefore, arise. For an example, see *Dunlop v New Garage* (1915), in which the facts were similar to those in *Dunlop v Selfridge* (below), except that in the agreement between the middleman and New Garage, the middleman was clearly designated as Dunlop's agent for the purpose of the contract of sale. It was held that the contract of sale was between Dunlop and New Garage, and that the interposition of an agent did not affect the privity of contract between those parties.

The undisclosed principal

A difficulty arises in cases where A fails to tell T that he is contracting on behalf of P. In such cases, P is called an undisclosed principal. If the reality of the situation is that A is really contracting on behalf of P, the law will give effect to the contract even though the principal is undisclosed. If, however, the law of agency is simply being used as a method of by-passing the doctrine of privity, a claim that A is contracting on behalf of an undisclosed principal will not succeed.

In *Dunlop v Selfridge* (1915), Dunlop were manufacturers of tyres and Selfridge was a retail store. Dunlop entered into a written agreement with Dew & Co, who were suppliers of motor accessories, whereby Dew bought certain of Dunlop's products for resale to the retail trade. Dew promised that they would not sell tyres below Dunlop's list price, and, acting as Dunlop's agents, would obtain a similar undertaking from persons to whom Dew sold the tyres. In return for this undertaking, Dew obtained special discounts from Dunlop and were allowed to pass up to 10% of the discount on to their own customers. Selfridge accepted an order from two of their customers for Dunlop's tyres, at cut prices. They ordered these tyres from Dew, who, in turn, ordered them from Dunlop. On 2 January, the day the tyres were delivered, Selfridge gave Dew an undertaking that they would not resell them below Dunlop's list price. (In fact, the undertaking was signed several days later, but was dated 2 January.) One of the orders was delivered. Selfridge subsequently told the other customer that he could have the tyre only at list price. Nevertheless, Dunlop sued Selfridge for breach of contract, asking for damages in respect of the breach and an injunction to prevent further sales below list price. *Held*, by the House of Lords: even though Dunlop may have been undisclosed principals in respect of the undertaking not to cut prices, the only parties to the contract of sale were Dew and Selfridge. Therefore, Dunlop failed because they were not parties to the contract of sale and had provided no consideration to the sale agreement between Dew and Selfridge, which had been entered into before ever Dunlop became involved.

Certain insurance contracts

As a general rule, the doctrine of privity applies to insurance contracts. However, the doctrine can easily be avoided by assigning the policy to the person one wishes to benefit.

In certain cases, however, a strict application of the rule of privity could cause commercial inconvenience and even injustice. These cases have been tackled on an *ad hoc* basis, whereby statute has provided for circumstances where a third party can sue on an insurance made for his benefit. Thus, a policy of insurance taken out by a husband or wife for the benefit of the other spouse, or of a child of the family, is enforceable by the beneficiary; in road traffic cases, a compulsory third party insurance is enforceable against the insurance company by any person whom it purports to cover. However, despite these and other exceptions, the basic doctrine of privity has remained applicable to insurance contracts.

Trusts

It is an established principle of equity that if D (the donor) gives property to T (the trustee) in order that T may apply the property for the benefit of B (the beneficiary), this creates a trust. Equity will ensure that T carries out his obligations under the trust and that he doesn't use the trust property for his own benefit. Provided the trust is constituted with the proper formalities, the property given by D is treated as a gift and B can enforce the trust against T.

However, suppose that D promises T that he will, in future, confer a benefit on B in return for consideration from T. Does this create a binding obligation sufficient to enable B to sue D on the promise? In other words, can there be a trust of a promise?

In *Tomlinson v Gill* (1756), G promised a widow that he would pay her late husband's debts. One of the creditors (T) sued on the promise. It was held that a trust had been created with G as the donor, the widow as the trustee and T as the beneficiary.

The difficulty with this case is that in 1756 the doctrine of consideration wasn't nearly so established as it is today, and, clearly, the widow had given no consideration for G's promise. Almost certainly, therefore, T's claim would fail nowadays, on the ground that the widow had given no consideration to G.

However, in *Gregory and Parker v Williams* (1817), consideration was present in the agreement. P owed money to both G and W. P agreed with W that he would sign the whole of his property over to him, if W would pay P's debts to G. P assigned the property as agreed, but W failed to pay P's debts to G. G and P sued to compel W to perform his promise. *Held*: P must be regarded as a trustee for G and therefore the claim against W must succeed.

In *Les Affreteurs Reunis v Walford* (1919), W negotiated a charterparty between Les Affreteurs, who were the owners of the SS Flore, and an oil company. LA promised the oil company that they would pay a commission to W of a sum estimated to be 3% of the gross amount of the hire. W didn't originally join the charters as plaintiffs, but when W applied to do so, LA made no objection and the case proceeded as if they had been joined. *Held*, by the House of Lords: the charterers were trustees of LA's promise to pay the commission to W.

However, in *Vandepitte v Preferred Accident Insurance* (1933), Lord Wright said that:

> ... the intention to constitute a trust must be affirmatively proved; the intention cannot necessarily be inferred from the mere general words of the (insurance) policy.

In *Re Schebsman* (1944), Lord Greene MR said:

> ... it is not legitimate to import into the contract the idea of a trust when the parties have given no indication that such was their intention. To interpret this contract as creating a trust would, in my judgment, be to disregard the dividing line between the case of a trust and the case of a simple contract made between two persons for the benefit of a third.

In *Beswick v Beswick* (1968), it was argued in the Court of Appeal that the agreement between uncle and nephew in favour of the uncle's widow created a trust in favour of the widow. The court held that it did not, and the point was not pursued in the House of Lords. Thus, the doctrine of the trust is clearly of limited value in attempting to circumvent the doctrine of privity at the present day.

Collateral contracts

A collateral contract is one which stands by the side of the main contract. It is usually a highly artificial device but it has proved useful and flexible in the doing of justice, not least in cases where the plaintiff would otherwise be defeated because of lack of privity of contract.

In *Shanklin Pier v Detel Products* (1951), the plaintiffs, who owned a pier, entered into a contract with contractors to paint the pier. Under the contract, the plaintiffs had the right to specify the paint to be used. A director of Detel travelled to Shanklin in order to try to get the contract to supply the paint. He told the plaintiffs that a particular paint manufactured by Detel would last seven to 10 years. The plaintiffs consequently specified that the contractors should use that particular paint. The paint proved unsatisfactory and lasted only three months. The plaintiffs therefore sought to sue the manufacturers for breach of contract. The obvious objection to such an action was that there was no privity of contract between the plaintiffs and the defendant. Detel's contract for the supply of the paint had been with the contractors. Had the contractors chosen the paint themselves, Shanklin would have had no difficulty since they would have sued the contractors for breach of the implied term that the paint would be of merchantable quality and the contractors, in turn, would have made a similar claim against Detel. However, the contractors were not in breach of contract with Shanklin, since they had used the paint specified by Shanklin. Therefore, unless Shanklin were able to sue Detel, they had no redress. *Held*: Detel's promise to Shanklin that the paint would last seven to 10 years was a collateral contract, in which Detel promised that if Shanklin would specify the use of their paint, Detel promised that it would last seven to 10 years.

Negotiable instruments

A negotiable instrument is a *chose* in action which can be freely transferred, either by delivery or endorsement, from one person to another. Negotiable instruments were created because of commercial need. Originally, they were validated by commercial custom, then by judicial recognition and finally by legislation.

The most common example of a negotiable instrument is a bank note. In practice these give rise to few legal problems. However, cheques, bills of exchange and promissory notes (among other documents) are also negotiable instruments, and these quite often give rise to problems. (Note that since the Cheques Act 1992 provided that crossing a cheque with the words 'account payee only' renders the cheque non-negotiable, the vast majority of cheques issued will not be negotiable instruments, since it is the general practice nowadays to issue cheques bearing such a crossing.)

Although most cheques are not, in fact, negotiated, in order to avoid undue complication, we will take the cheque as our example of how a negotiable instrument is an exception to the doctrine of privity. Suppose Andrew sells goods to Bertha and Bertha gives Andrew a cheque for their value. Andrew then endorses the cheque in favour of Clarence, who has supplied goods to Andrew. The cheque is dishonoured. Clarence may sue Bertha for the value of the cheque even though Clarence was not a party to the contract between Bertha and Andrew.

Negotiability is similar to assignment but has the following differences:

(a) the holder of a negotiable instrument can sue in his own name. A statutory assignee can do this but an equitable assignee cannot;

(b) a negotiable instrument is not transferred subject to equities. An assignment is always subject to equities;

(c) no notice of the transfer of a negotiable instrument need be given to the person who is liable on the instrument. In a statutory assignment notice is essential and in an equitable assignment it is desirable in order to establish the priority of one's claim as against a competing assignee; and

(d) an assignee can acquire no better title to the assignment than his assignor, which means that if A assigns to B, the assignment is stolen by C and assigned to D who takes it in good faith and for value, without any notice of the defect in C's title, D will have no rights against A. However, if A draws a cheque in favour of B, the cheque is stolen by C and negotiated to D who takes it in good faith and for value, without any notice of the defect in C's title, D will be entitled to the amount of the cheque.

Bankers' commercial credits

Commercial credits are much used in international trade. Suppose B in Britain wishes to buy goods from S in Japan. B doesn't wish to pay for the goods in advance of shipment, since something may go wrong whereby S fails to ship the goods. On the other hand, S doesn't want to ship the goods without being sure of securing payment. A solution which will satisfy both sides is the banker's commercial credit. What happens is that the seller puts a clause in the contract of sale requiring B to open a credit in S's favour at B's bank. The credit is to be payable to S when S presents the shipping documents to the bank. S will usually require the credit to remain irrevocable for a particular period of time. B agrees with his bank to do this. The bank notifies S that it has opened an irrevocable credit in his favour which he can draw upon as soon as he presents the shipping documents to the bank. In this way, S is assured of his money.

The question has arisen as to what happens if the bank refuses to honour its promise to pay S. The problem is often regarded as one of privity of contract, in that S is seeking to enforce an agreement made between B and B's bank, to which S is not a party. However, the present author of *Cheshire, Fifoot and Furmston's Law of Contract* (1996) regards the problem as one of consideration. He argues that S is, in reality, seeking to enforce a promise by the bank to himself, such promise being in the nature of a unilateral contract.

Despite the fact that there has been much litigation on the subject of commercial credits, no bank has yet taken the point that they are not contractually bound by the agreement. If the unilateral contract analysis is accepted, there would appear to be little difficulty in finding consideration for the bank's promise: S has acted to his detriment in shipping the goods which, without the bank's promise, he would not otherwise have done.

If the problem is regarded as one of privity of contract, then bankers' commercial credits must be regarded as being a practical exception to the rule of privity.

Bills of lading

Where goods are carried by sea, the seller generally arranges the contract to ship the goods with a carrier. The contract is evidenced by a document called a 'bill of lading'. When the goods are shipped to the buyer, the seller endorses the bill of lading and sends it to the buyer. This gives the buyer the title to the goods which the bill of lading represents. A problem, at common law, was that if the goods failed to arrive or were delivered in a damaged state, the buyer had no contractual remedy against the carrier because there was no privity of contract between them. To remedy this, the Bills of Lading Act 1855 provides for a transfer of the consignor's rights and liabilities, in relation to the carrier, to a named consignee or endorsee to whom property in the goods passes upon or by reason of the consignment or endorsement. This allows the person to whom the goods were consigned, to sue the defaulting carrier.

Section 14 of the Companies Act 1985

This provides that the registered memorandum and articles of the company bind the company and its members as if they had been signed and sealed by each member. The memorandum of the company is a document which regulates the relationship of the company with the outside world. The articles of a company are its internal rules of government specifying such things as how many directors there shall be, how they shall be appointed, when they shall retire, what types of shareholding there shall be, what are the rights of the respective shareholders, etc.

PRIVITY OF CONTRACT AND THE TORT OF NEGLIGENCE

One method which has been used in an attempt to circumvent the rule of privity is to sue for negligence instead. Negligence is a tort and requires the plaintiff to prove that, among other things, the defendant owed him a duty to take care in relation to the activity claimed of. Generally, whether a duty of care is owed depends upon whether it is foreseeable that the defendant's actions will cause damage to the plaintiff, and, if so, whether there is a sufficiently proximate relationship between the two. Sometimes, in special cases, factors of policy are taken into account.

The early law would not allow the doctrine of privity to be circumvented by using the law of tort. Thus, if A had potential contractual liability to B, he could not have a concurrent liability to C in respect of the same transaction. However, in the landmark case of *Donoghue v Stevenson* (1932), it was held that a manufacturer of goods could be liable to a consumer of goods for damage caused by a defect in the manufacturer's product. This was extended by analogy to situations such as defective repairs. However, the damage had to involve physical damage caused by the defect, to either the defendant or his property: it could not be pure economic loss. Thus the plaintiff could not claim, in an action for negligence, in respect of defects in the product itself, since such a claim is regarded as pure economic loss. Such a claim must be brought by the party who bought the product and the claim will be for breach of contract.

This distinction between physical damage and pure economic loss has caused difficulties in practice. In *Junior Books v Veitchi* (1983), C contracted with Junior Books (J) to build a factory for them. J were entitled to nominate sub-contractors, though it is more usual for the contractors to select their own sub-contractors. J nominated the defendants as sub-contractors to lay the floor. The sub-contractors did so negligently with the result that cracks appeared in the floor, which then had to be relaid at considerable cost. The normal procedure in such a case would have been for J to have brought an action for breach of contract against C, and for C to have sought an indemnity from Veitchi (V). However, an exemption clause in the contract between J and C persuaded J that a better course of action would be to sue V. V's defence was that the loss suffered by J was pure economic loss and, as such, could be remedied only by an action for breach of contract. It was held by the House of Lords that J succeeded. The decision appears to turn largely upon the fact that J actually selected V to lay the floor and because of this there was a relationship of special proximity between the two, akin to a contractual relationship, which enabled J to succeed.

The *Junior Books* case has not received much judicial support since it was decided, although subsequent efforts have been made to recover pure economic loss by relying on a tort action rather than on contract. In *Simaan General Contracting v Pilkington Glass (No 2)* (1988), S were main contractors for building a building for a Sheikh in Abu Dabi. The Sheikh required the glass in the building to be of a particular green colour and this was specified in the main contract. S contracted with sub-contractors to fit the glass and the sub-contractors bought the glass from P, who are glass manufacturers. There was no contract between S and P though the successive sub-contracts contained the specifications regarding the colour of the glass. The glass provided by P was unsatisfactory, since it was not the colour specified and, in any case, was not of a uniform colour. The Sheikh refused to pay S for the building until the glass was replaced. This caused S significant economic loss which they sued to recover. *Held*: the plaintiff's loss was pure economic loss and, as such, was not recoverable by the plaintiff against the defendant. (Under English law, S would have been able to recover against their sub-contractor for breach of contract. The sub-contractor could, in turn have sued P for an indemnity. In practice such actions are usually combined.)

It seems that the *Junior Books* case must now be confined to its own facts and that, generally, an action in tort will not be allowed where its effect is to circumvent the doctrine of privity and to recover pure economic loss.

The law of tort has been used, controversially, in other circumstances to recover pure economic loss in the absence of a contractual relationship between plaintiff and defendant. In *Ross v Caunters* (1980), a solicitor failed to ensure that a will was properly executed with the result that a beneficiary under the will was disappointed. She sued the solicitor. It was held that she could recover her loss. The decision has been widely criticised on the grounds that liability in contract usually depends upon an undertaking made by the plaintiff to a defendant or upon the defendant relying upon a representation made by the plaintiff. Thus, in the *Junior Books* case, as has been pointed out, it was this special reliance by the plaintiff on the defendant which gave rise to a liability, in tort, analogous to a contractual liability. But in the *Ross* case, this factor was not present. The Law Commission Paper 121 states that the decision is defensible on the grounds that the person who suffered the loss would have no valid claim, whereas the person who had the valid claim would have suffered no loss (that is, the testator's estate would succeed in an action for breach of contract, but since there had been no loss to the husband's estate, the damages awarded would have been nominal). The House of Lords has recently confirmed the correctness of the principle in *Ross v Caunters* in *White v Jones* (1995). In this case, a father became reconciled to estranged daughters. He therefore instructed his solicitor to make a will in their favour. The solicitor unduly delayed in drafting the will and before it was executed, the father died. It was held that the daughters were entitled to damages from the solicitor in relation to their loss of expectation.

PRIVITY OF CONTRACT AND EXEMPTION CLAUSES

It is expected that, in cases like the ones cited in this section, the contracts will now be framed so that they will be covered by the 1999 Act. However, if the contracts are not framed in that way, these situations will be governed by the pre-existing law.

Parties to a contract often try to allocate risks relating to damage which may be caused during the performance of the contract. Thus, a building contractor who is employed to carry out work on a building may seek to exempt himself from liability for any damage he causes by using an appropriate exemption clause. What this means, in effect, is that it is the owner's responsibility to insure the building against the appropriate risks.

Carriers of goods also frequently use clauses which either exclude liability or limit liability. Again, the intention of the parties is that the owner of the goods shall effect suitable insurance against the loss of, or damage to, the goods.

One difficulty with trying to allocate the risk of loss or damage arising during the performance of a contract may occur when a main contractor contracts with the employer not only to exempt or limit his or her own liability for breach of contract, but also the liability of the *sub-contractors* who are working under the main contractor. The appointment of sub-contractors is extremely common in the building trade. For example, C contracts with O to carry out substantial alterations and extensions to O's building. The contract provides that neither C, nor his sub-contractors, shall be liable for any damage caused to the building while the contract is being carried out. E, an electrical sub-contractor, causes the building to be damaged by fire. O will normally sue E using the tort of negligence. O will need to prove that E had a duty of care to avoid causing the damage (a requirement that would normally cause little difficulty), that E breached that duty and that the damage resulted from this breach.

The problem that arises when E tries to take the benefit of the exemption clause which is in the contract negotiated by O and C, is that there is no privity of contract between O and E and therefore, on the face of it, it appears that E cannot take advantage of the clause. (For those whose reaction is that E ought to be liable since the fire was his fault, I would emphasise that the real question in these cases is, 'Who should provide the insurance cover?'. The answer is, 'The party who has undertaken to bear the risk'. Hence it is generally no hardship for O to be liable, since the liability will be met by his insurers.)

One way of getting round the rule of privity is, as we have seen, for the party who inserts a term in a contract intending to benefit a third party, to contract as the agent for the third party. For example, if O is contracting with C and inserts a term which is intended to benefit E, C may do so as the *agent* of E, in which case the term will be binding on O. If, however, C fails to mention E, or fails to mention that C is acting as E's agent, there will be no agency and the term intended to benefit E will not be binding. This problem might still arise even after the 1999 Act.

In *Scruttons v Midland Silicones* (1962), Midland Silicones shipped a drum of chemicals from America to London. The carrier of the goods was a shipping company called the United States Lines. MS made a contract with the USL which limited the latter's liability for damage to $500. Scruttons were stevedores in London. They had a contract with USL whereby they discharged the USL's vessels in London and acted as agents in the delivery of the goods to their final destination. This contract limited Scruttons' liability for damage to $500. Scruttons negligently dropped MS's drum causing damage to the value of £593.

MS sued Scruttons for the tort of negligence, claiming £593. Scruttons argued, among other things, that the USL were their agents for the purpose of extracting the promise from MS that their liability would be restricted to $500, that is, that USL had made the contract limiting their liability to $500 on Scruttons' behalf.

Held: there is a general rule that a stranger to a contract (in this case Scruttons), cannot take advantage of the provisions of the contract, even where it is clear from the contract that some provision in it was intended to benefit him. The agency argument, put forward on behalf of Scruttons, could only succeed if:

(a) the contract made it clear that Scruttons were intended to be protected by its provisions;

(b) the contract made it clear that USL, in addition to contracting on their own behalf, were contracting as *agents* for Scruttons;

(c) USL had authority from Scruttons to do that; and

(d) that any difficulties about consideration from Scruttons to MS were overcome. (In modern times, the law of consideration has developed to the extent that this is unlikely to cause a problem: the consideration would be that Scruttons were conferring a benefit on MS by unloading their chemicals.)

Judgment was therefore given in favour of Midland Silicones – reluctantly by Lord Reid, who presumably was unhappy about the fact that because Scruttons had a contract with USL which limited Scruttons' liability to $500, Midland Silicones were effectively obtaining the additional damages from USL, with whom they had contracted a limitation of liability to $500. Thus, MS were obtaining from the USL a sum of money which they had promised to forgo.

The requirement that the principal should be known to the agent when contracting with the third party on the principal's behalf causes particular difficulty in the case where a main contractor undertakes work, intending to appoint several sub-contractors. In such a case, the main contractor often cannot contract as the *agent* of the sub-contractors because, at the time the main contract is entered into, the names of the sub-contractors are not known and, as we saw in the *Midland Silicones* case, the persons for whose benefit the term is inserted must give their consent to the main contractor acting as their agent. In recent cases, the courts have found a way round this problem in order to prevent one of the parties to the contract from suing a third party, after having agreed in a contract that they wouldn't sue.

In *Southern Water Authority v Carey* (1985), the water authority had entered into a contract with main contractors for the building of sewage works. The contract was made on the standard form of the Institute of Mechanical Engineers/Institute of Electrical Engineers, clause 30(iv) of which limited the contractor's liability to defects which appeared within 12 months of the completion of the work. The clause also purported to apply the same limitation to the liability of sub-contractors, servants and agents. The water authority sued two sub-contractors for negligence after the 12 month limit had expired. The sub-contractors argued that they were protected by clause 30(iv).

Held: the sub-contractors could not claim the benefit of clause 30(iv) since they were not parties to the contract. The main contractor could not have contracted with Southern Water Authority as their agent since there was no evidence that the sub-contractors had authorised the main contractors to do this. (Indeed, it would have been difficult since their names were not known at the time the main contract was entered into!) However, liability for the tort of negligence is dependent upon a duty by the defendant to take care not to injure the plaintiff. The court held that although the limitation of liability clause in the contract could not directly benefit the defendant, it nevertheless had the effect of negativing the duty which the defendant would otherwise have owed to the plaintiff, to take care not to injure the plaintiff. Therefore, the defendant was not liable for his negligence. (The practical effect of this judgment is that the Water Authority's insurance company had to foot the bill for the damage rather than the defendant or his insurance company – presuming he was insured.)

In *Norwich City Council v Harvey* (1989), the facts were similar but, unlike the previous case, the contract did not purport to exempt the sub-contractor but simply allocated the risk of fire to the employer. It was held that the allocation of risk clause meant that the sub-contractor owed no duty of care to the employer.

Both these cases are clearly influenced by the fact that the clauses used were well-known risk-allocation devices in the building trade. Even so, it is doubtful whether the principle contained in the cases could be applied in a case like *Scruttons,* simply because Midland Silicones were never made aware that United States Lines intended Scruttons to take the benefit of the exemption clause.

DAMAGES TO BE AWARDED TO THE THIRD PARTY

We have seen that there are problems in making an appropriate award to a third party in respect of the third party's losses. In *Beswick v Beswick*, an award of damages would not have sufficed, therefore the court awarded a decree of specific performance. In *Jackson v Horizon Holidays* (1975), J booked a holiday with H. The holiday was not in accordance with the contract. J was awarded damages for the unsatisfactory holiday and the disappointment suffered in consequence, on behalf of himself, his wife and his children. However, in the later case of *Woodar Investment Development v Wimpey* (1980), the *dictum* of Lord Denning to the effect that the father had made the contract for the benefit of his wife and children and could therefore recover damages for their loss, was expressly disapproved, as a general principle, by the House of Lords. The House suggested that the damages were in respect of his own loss or that the case came within a special category of cases such as one person ordering a meal for a party in a restaurant, or hiring a taxi for a group, which called for special treatment. In the *Woodar* case itself, Woodar extracted a promise from Wimpey to pay £150,000 to Transworld Trade Ltd (a third party) on the completion of a contract. The money was not paid. The question arose as to whether Woodar's damages could include the amount of Transworld's loss. It was held that unless Woodar could prove that the failure to pay the money to Transworld had resulted in a loss to themselves, Woodar would be entitled only to nominal damages in respect of this breach of contract.

We are thus left with the odd situation where, if the contracting party brings an action to enforce a contract in which a third party is accorded a benefit, damages will be nominal unless the plaintiff can prove damage to himself. On the other hand, if a decree of specific performance is appropriate, the third party may effectively be given full benefit by the making of such a decree. However, if the third party is able to bring an action in tort because the contract has been carried out negligently, the third party will be entitled to claim his loss. Furthermore, there are special circumstances, such as holidays, restaurant meals and group transport bookings, in which the party who made the booking may be entitled to claim damages on behalf of all the participants.

An exception to the rule in the *Woodar* case (above) has been established in building contracts where a constructor has constructed a building that is defective, but at the time the defect is discovered, the building is owned by a third party. In *Linden Gardens Trust v Linesta Trust Disposals* (1993), a property developer contracted with a construction company whereby the construction company would construct buildings for the property developer. The property developer then assigned his rights in the property to a third party. However, when defects developed, the third party was unable to sue the construction company because there was no privity of contract. Therefore, the property developer sued. The objection to this was that the property developer had suffered no loss. However, in order to avoid creating a 'legal black hole' the property developer was allowed to recover damages on behalf of the third party.

However, where the construction company and the third party create a legal relationship, under which the third party is enabled to sue the construction company, the developer will be unable to claim damages: he will have suffered no loss. In *Panatown v McAlpine* (2000), the defendant had entered into a contract with P whereby Mc would construct a building on land owned by Unex. Unex and Panatown were part of the same group, and the contract was structured in this way for VAT advantages. Thus the benefit of the building was to go to U, but P was the employer of the constructor. The building was allegedly defective and P sued Mc. However, this case was different to the *Linden Gardens* case because U had entered into a duty of care deed (DCD) with Mc which was expressly intended to overcome the privity of contract problem. Thus, there were two contracts: a contract between P and Mc for the construction of the building and a contract between U and Mc (made by deed, so the absence of consideration between them is immaterial), whereby U was given the right to sue Mc. *Held* by the House of Lords: where a contractor was in breach of a contract with the employer to construct a building for a third party, the employer could not recover substantial damages if it had been intended (as in this case) that the third party should have the right to bring an action.

Note: the *Panatown* case was decided before the Contract (Rights of Third Parties) Act 1999, discussed above, came into effect. The Act would appear to do away with the need to perform legal gymnastics such as entering into DCDs or alternatively for the courts to circumvent the doctrine of privity by allowing substantial damages to be claimed by a contracting party on behalf of a third party.

IMPOSING LIABILITIES ON THIRD PARTIES

It is a general rule that parties to a contract cannot impose liabilities on third parties. Apart from the law of agency, where a principal is liable on a contract made on his behalf by an agent, there are two main exceptions to this rule. These are:

(a) obligations running with real property; and

(b) novation.

We will deal with them in turn.

Obligations running with real property

It has long been a principle of land law that obligations in respect of leased property may 'run with the land'. This means that the obligations bind successive purchasers, lessees, etc, of the land. For example, suppose Allan, a landlord, has leased property to Barbara. Allan then sells the leased property to Carol. Carol may sue Barbara for the breach of any of the tenant's obligations set out in the lease, even though she is not a party to the contract between Allan and Barbara. Similarly, Barbara could sue Carol for any breach of the landlord's obligations under the lease.

During the 19th century, the above principle was extended to include certain promises (called 'restrictive covenants') made when freehold property is sold.

In *Tulk v Moxhay* (1848), Tulk was the owner of several plots of land in Leicester Square. In 1808, he sold one of these plots to a person named Elms. Elms agreed for himself, his heirs and assigns, to 'keep the Square open as a pleasure ground and uncovered with buildings'. After several conveyances, the land was conveyed to Moxhay, who intended to build on it. T sought an injunction to prevent M building on the land. M admitted having bought the land with notice of the covenant, but argued that as he himself hadn't entered into the covenant, he wasn't bound by it. *Held*: equity had a jurisdiction to prevent, by way of injunction, any act inconsistent with a restrictive covenant on land, providing the land was acquired with notice of the covenant. Thus, M was bound by the covenant even though he hadn't made it himself.

The principle that a seller of real property can create duties which bind successive purchasers providing they have notice of the duties, has become an established principle of land law. Since the Land Charges Act 1925, restrictive covenants can be registered at the Land Registry. If a restrictive covenant is registered, it counts as notice to a prospective purchaser (such notice is called 'constructive notice') and he will be bound by the covenant whether he has actual knowledge of it or not, providing:

(a) the original seller or his successors in title retain a proprietary interest in other land in the neighbourhood, which will benefit from the covenant; and

(b) the covenant is negative in form, that is, a promise not to do something, for example, a promise not to use a private residence to carry on a business.

If the covenant is not registered at the Land Registry, actual notice of the covenant must be given before it can become binding. Attempts have been made to extend the principle in *Tulk v Moxhay* (above) to contracts concerning goods: that is, to have a restrictive covenant running with goods.

In *Lord Strathcona SS Co v Dominion Coal Co* (1926), a ship called the Lord Strathcona had been chartered by her owner A to B for a number of years for use by B during the summer season on the river St Lawrence. The terms of the charter required B to return the vessel to A in November each year. While the charterparty (that is, the contract of charter) was still in force, A sold the vessel to C, who resold it to D. D, who had notice of the charterparty between A and B, refused to deliver the vessel to B for use during the summer season. B obtained an injunction against D restraining D from using the vessel in any way that was inconsistent with the charterparty. D's appeal to the Privy Council was dismissed.

However, the English courts have consistently refused to accept the principle contained in the judgment as part of English law: see, for example, *Port Line v Ben Line Steamers* (1958).

Novation

Though the benefits of a contract may easily be transferred to a third party by assignment, it is not possible to dispose of the obligations under a contract in this way, except with the consent of the other party to the contract. This can cause problems when a complete business is sold, since the seller will usually have uncompleted contracts on his hands. The only possible way for the seller of the business to transfer the obligations under the contracts to the purchaser is by a process called novation. This really amounts to a cancellation of the obligation of the seller and its replacement by a fresh obligation undertaken by the purchaser. It works as follows.

Suppose Albert has contracted with Bill to make some machinery for Bill. Albert wishes to sell his business to Clara before he has completed his contract with Bill. Albert cannot make Clara legally liable to Bill unless Bill consents.

The solution is for the parties to make a three-sided agreement whereby Albert assigns to Clara the benefit of his contract with Bill, Clara agrees with Albert to take over his obligations under the contract, and Bill agrees with Clara that he will accept her as his contracting party in place of Albert.

CHAPTER 12

MISTAKEN IDENTITY AND MISTAKES WITH DOCUMENTS

A recurrent problem in the law of contract concerns the situation where a rogue induces a contract by fraud, under which he receives property, and then sells the property on to an innocent third party.

Where a rogue induces a contract by fraud, the rule is that the contract between the rogue and the original seller is *voidable* owing to the rogue's deceit. 'Voidable' means that the contract is *valid* until it is *repudiated* by the innocent party. The original owner of the goods then has an action for damages for fraudulent misrepresentation (that is, for the tort of deceit) and, providing that nothing has been done to prevent him rescinding the contract, he will be entitled to claim rescission against the fraudulent party.

Once the innocent seller has discovered the fraud, he will usually take steps to avoid the contract. This he can do by informing the rogue of his intentions. However, if, as is often the case, the rogue has absconded, it will be sufficient to take all practicable steps to rescind, which will usually consist of informing the police of the fraud and asking them to recover the property which has been transferred under the contract (see *Car and Universal Finance v Caldwell* (1965), of which a condensed account appears in Chapter 10). The innocent seller will then be entitled to resume possession of the goods.

WHERE A THIRD PARTY HAS ACQUIRED RIGHTS

However, as we saw in our study of misrepresentation, one of the reasons that rescission may be refused by the court is because a third party has acquired rights in the subject matter of the contract.

Example

Alice advertises her Volvo car for sale. Jones offers to buy it for £5,000.

Alice accepts the offer and accepts Jones's cheque for £5,000.

Jones sells the car to Rex, a used car dealer, for £3,000.

Jones's cheque is dishonoured.

Who owns the Volvo?

The normal rule where someone sells goods to which he has a defective title, is *'nemo dat quod non habet'*, which means that 'no one can give what he hasn't got'. A transferor of property is unable to pass on a better title to it than he himself has. A thief, who has no title, cannot pass on a title, and stolen goods must always (except in the very rare case where the owner might be estopped from asserting his title) be returned to their original owner even if they are found in the possession of someone who has purchased the goods from the thief in good faith.

There are a number of exceptions to the *nemo dat* rule, and one of them is where a person obtains a *voidable* title to property. 'Voidable', you will recall, means that the contract is *valid* until the innocent party *repudiates* it. The effect of this, where, for example, the subject of the voidable contract is goods, is that providing the rogue sells to an innocent third party *while the contract is still valid*, the third party gets a good title. (If the contract is a sale of goods, good title is given by s 23 of the Sale of Goods Act; however, in other cases, the common law will operate to pass a good title.) In such a case, the innocent party will be left only with an action for damages against the rogue, an action which, bearing in mind that only a minority of such criminals are apprehended by the police and bearing in mind that when they are apprehended they will usually have no funds available to satisfy judgment against them, will usually be valueless. Thus, the *innocent seller* is the one who suffers for the fraud perpetrated by the rogue.

So, in our example above, provided Rex buys the car in good faith and without notice of Jones's fraud, Rex will get a good title to the car. Alice will therefore lose £5,000. Note that if Rex 'bought' the car *after* Alice had taken appropriate steps to rescind the contract, Rex would *not* get a good title, since the contract would have been effectively avoided by Alice thus preventing the subsequent acquisition of any rights by Rex (unless s 25 of the Sale of Goods Act 1979 applies – see Chapter 20, p 427).

MISREPRESENTATION OF IDENTITY

Does it make any difference to the legal consequences in a case where Jones calls himself, not Jones, but by a different name?

Example

Alice advertises her Volvo car for sale. Jones, calling himself 'Smith', offers to buy it for £5,000. Alice accepts the offer and accepts 'Smith's' cheque for £5,000.

Jones sells the car to Rex, a used car dealer, for £3,000.

Jones's cheque is dishonoured.

In principle, this will make no difference. As a general rule, the use of a false name (for example, where a rogue called 'Jones' uses the pseudonym 'Smith' because it happens to be on the cheque he has stolen) will simply render the resultant contract voidable for misrepresentation. As we have seen, this will usually mean that the third party will obtain a good title to the property.

However, there is a rule, dating from relatively early in the development of the law of contract, to the effect that an offer can only be accepted by the person to whom it is made. In *Boulton v Jones* (1857), J had often dealt with Brocklehurst. J sent Brocklehurst a written order for 50 feet of leather hose on the day on which (unknown to J) Brocklehurst had transferred his business to his foreman, Boulton. Boulton filled the order and J used the goods, believing that they had been supplied by Brocklehurst. When Boulton asked for payment, J refused to pay because he had a set-off against Brocklehurst which he had intended to use in payment for the goods. *Held*: J was not liable to pay the price of the goods to Boulton, since he had intended to contract with Brocklehurst and not with Boulton.

As the law has developed, the rule has become that if an offer is accepted by any person other than the person to whom it was made, the resultant contract is *void*. In this context, 'void' means that the contract between the innocent seller and the rogue is treated as though it had never taken place: therefore the rogue is unable to claim even a voidable title to the goods and the owner is thus entitled to reclaim his goods from any subsequent innocent purchaser.

So, if Jones calls himself 'Smith', can Alice argue that the car still belongs to her because the contract she has entered into is void on the ground that she intended to enter into a contract with the person whom Jones said he was, rather than with Jones? The answer is that if the rogue has misrepresented his identity in such a way that the innocent party can claim that he intended to contract, not with the rogue, but with the person whom the rogue represented himself to be, the contract may be void. In such a case, the law may regard the identity of the buyer of being a matter of fundamental importance to the contract and may take the view that (to use our 'Smith' and 'Jones' example above) Alice intended to contract not with Jones but with Smith, and no one else but Smith. In such a case, she would recover her car.

THE DEVELOPMENT OF THE LAW
RELATING TO 'MISTAKEN IDENTITY'

The law in these so called 'mistaken identity' cases was developed in the latter half of the 19th century. The approach of the courts to the matter was relatively unsophisticated. The question was treated as being one of offer and acceptance and the analysis was that if the offer was accepted by a person other than the person to whom it had been made, the purported acceptance was invalid and the resultant contract void (though it would perhaps be more accurate, analytically, to say that the contract never came into being).

Some textbook writers, following the *Cheshire, Fifoot and Furmston* analysis, categorise mistaken identity cases under the heading of a 'unilateral mistake' by one party as to the identity of the other. While this is no doubt a useful analytical tool, it must not be lost sight of that the courts generally use the 'offer and acceptance' analysis and it is this approach which we will take in our studies.

When is the contract void?

The courts have distinguished between two situations:

(a) where, despite a misapprehension as to the identity of the other party, the person under the misapprehension had nevertheless intended to contract with the person with whom he had, in fact, contracted (in such a case the contract is simply voidable for misrepresentation); and

(b) where the party under the misapprehension had intended to contract only with the party whom he had been told that he was contracting with. In such a case the contract is void for mistaken identity.

The test here is 'objective', that is, would a reasonable third party have concluded that the mistaken party had intended to contract with the person who had misrepresented his identity or had intended to contract *only* with the person whom the rogue misrepresented himself to be.

In making this distinction, the courts have tended to emphasise one factor, and one factor only, as a criterion for making the decision, they ask: 'Was the identity of the other contracting party of fundamental importance to the person misled?' If it was, the contract is void. If not, the contract is only voidable.

Not surprisingly, the principles to be invoked in answering this rather broad question have given rise to much judicial *dicta* and have had textbook writers suggesting tests of their own (some of which bear little relation to the way in which the courts, in practice, tackle the question). We can, however, venture the following propositions:

(a) A contract cannot be void for mistaken identity unless there is confusion between two distinct entities.

In *King's Norton Metal Co v Edridge, Merret & Co* (1897), the plaintiffs were metal manufacturers in Worcestershire. They received a letter from Hallam and Co in Sheffield. It was on headed paper on which was an illustration of a large factory and which stated that the company had depots in Belfast, Ghent and Lille. The letter requested a quotation for the supply of a quantity of brass rivet wire. The quotation was sent and subsequently an order was received and dispatched. The goods were never paid for. It later transpired that the goods had been sold to the defendants by a person called Wallis, who had set up in business as Hallam and Co. The defendants had taken the goods in good faith. The plaintiffs sued for the return of the goods, alleging that their contract with Wallis was void on the grounds that they had intended to contract with Hallam and Co and not with Wallis. *Held*: there was a contract for the sale of goods between the plaintiffs and Wallis, trading as Hallam and Co. There was only one entity and, therefore, the plaintiff must have intended to contract with that person, that is, the person who wrote the letters. The contract was, therefore, not void but was voidable for fraud. This means that the innocent third party obtained a good title to the goods.

Contrast *Sowler v Potter* (1940). The defendant, then known as Ann Robinson, was convicted of permitting disorderly conduct at a café. Shortly afterwards she applied for a lease from the plaintiff under the name of Ann Potter. The estate agent who had acted on behalf of Mrs Sowler in negotiating the lease stated that he remembered the conviction of Ann Robinson and would not have dealt with Ann Potter if he had realised that she was really Ann Robinson. The contract was held to be void for mistake, though the decision has been criticised on the ground that there was only *one entity* who at one time called herself Ann Robinson and at another Ann Potter.

Note that when, as here, there are only two parties involved, it is unusual for the plaintiff to claim that the contract is void. That is because the plaintiff usually requires rescission of the contract which can be gained by relying on misrepresentation alone. However, it will be remembered that misrepresentation renders the contract voidable, that is, it is valid until it is repudiated. In *Sowler v Potter*, the plaintiff was seeking damages for trespass from the time the contract was made. She could only succeed in her claim if the contract was void from the outset. If the contract was only voidable Potter would have had the right to occupy the premises until the contract was rescinded, which means that she wouldn't have become a trespasser until after that time.

(b) The contract will be void if, looking at the matter objectively, the court concludes that the person under the misapprehension intended to contract with a third person and only with that third person.

The leading case is *Cundy v Lindsay* (1878). In that case, a rogue called Blenkarn used premises in Wood St, Cheapside. Based in the same street was a reputable concern called Blenkiron and Co. Signing his name in such a manner that it looked like Blenkiron and Co, B sent an order to L in Belfast for a large number of handkerchiefs. He sold the handkerchiefs to C and absconded with the proceeds. L brought an action against C for the tort of conversion, asserting that their contract with Blenkarn was void and that therefore the handkerchiefs still belonged to them. *Held* by the House of Lords: L intended to contract with Blenkiron and Co. As Blenkiron knew nothing of the contract it was a nullity and therefore the effect was as if B had stolen the goods, that is, that the goods still belonged to L.

Two older cases illustrate the point: *Boulton v Jones* (1857), a condensed account of which is given above, and *Hardman v Booth* (1863). In this case, one of the plaintiffs went to the offices of Thomas Gandell & Co. There they took an order for goods from Edward Gandell, who was the son of the proprietor of the firm. Edward Gandell had led the plaintiff to believe that he was ordering goods on behalf of the firm of Thomas Gandell and gave the plaintiff one of the firm's cards. The plaintiff sent the goods to the premises of Thomas Gandell & Co (they were invoiced to 'Edward Gandell & Co'), where they were intercepted by Edward Gandell and pawned to the defendant in consideration of advances made by the defendant to a business which Edward Gandell conducted with a person called Todd. The plaintiffs now sued the defendants for the conversion of their goods. *Held*: there was no contract between the plaintiffs and Edward Gandell since the plaintiffs intended to contract with no one but Thomas Gandell & Sons.

(c) Where the parties are in each other's presence, there is a *prima facie* presumption that the person who has been misled intended to contract with the person who is, in fact, in front of him and not with an absent third party. This presumption may, however, be displaced by evidence that the misled party intended to contract only with the absent third party.

This gloss on the law does not appear to have been present in the 19th century cases. It emerged in the 1919 case *Phillips v Brooks* and it was probably the result of judicial policy-making in that it was felt that if one of two innocent people had to suffer for the fraud of a third, then the person to suffer should be the one who had facilitated the fraud by handing over his goods to a third party without a sufficient check on that third party's creditworthiness.

In *Phillips v Brooks* (1919), a rogue called North entered the plaintiff jeweller's shop and selected some pearls and a ring to the value of £3,000. He produced a cheque book and wrote out a cheque for £3,000 saying: 'You see who I am, I am Sir George Bullough,' and he gave an address in St James's Square. The plaintiff went into the back of his shop where he checked the name and address in a directory. He then asked 'Sir George' whether he would like to take the goods with him. The reply was: 'You had better have the cheque cleared first but I should like to take the ring as it is my wife's birthday tomorrow.' The following day, North pawned the ring to the defendant. The cheque given to the plaintiff by the rogue was then dishonoured. The plaintiff sought to recover the ring from the defendant. *Held* by Horridge J in the High Court: although the plaintiff asserted that he had no intention of making a contract with any other than Sir George Bullough, it was inferred by the court that the seller intended to contract with the person who was present 'and there was no error as to the person with whom he contracted ...'.

This case was not consistent with the earlier authorities we have looked at. However, when, in a similar case, the Court of Appeal had the opportunity to overrule it, they did not do so. They did, however, distinguish the case from that with which they were dealing, which was a case called *Ingram v Little* (1961).

In this case, the three plaintiffs were joint owners of a Renault Dauphine car who had advertised it for sale. A person who called himself 'Hutchinson' offered to buy it. A price of £717 was agreed. Hutchinson brought out his cheque book but was told that payment by cheque was not acceptable. He then said that he was PGM Hutchinson of Stanstead House, Stanstead Road, Caterham. One of the plaintiffs went to the nearby Post Office and checked in the telephone directory that PGM Hutchinson was listed as living at that address. The plaintiffs then allowed 'Hutchinson' to take the car in exchange for a cheque. 'Hutchinson' sold the car to the defendant and then disappeared and remained untraced. Hutchinson's cheque was dishonoured. The question before the court was whether the plaintiffs intended to sell to the person who was present (that is, the rogue) or whether they intended only to sell to PGM Hutchinson. In the course of his judgment Pearce LJ said:

> An apparent contract made orally *inter praesentes* (that is, between people in each other's presence) raises particular difficulties. The offer is apparently addressed to the physical person present. *Prima facie*, he, by whatever name he is called, is the person to whom the offer is made. His physical presence, identified by sight and hearing, preponderates over vagaries of nomenclature. Yet clearly, though difficult, it is not impossible to rebut the *prima facie* presumption that the offer can be accepted by the person to whom it is physically addressed.

He then went on to hold that the refusal of the plaintiff to accept the cheque demonstrated quite clearly that she was not prepared to sell on credit to the physical person in her drawing-room, though he had presented himself as a man of substance. She was prepared to sell only to PGM Hutchinson. 'Only when she had ascertained (through her sister's short excursion to the local Post Office and investigation in the telephone directory) that there was a PGM Hutchinson of Stanstead House in the telephone directory did she agree to sell on credit.' It seems that in order to show that the offer was not made to the person physically present, the offeror will have to show that the identity of the offeree was of particular importance.

In *Ingram v Little*, Pearce LJ attempted to explain the matter as follows:

> To take two extreme instances. If a man orally commissions a portrait from some unknown artist who had deliberately passed himself off, whether by disguise or merely verbal cosmetics, as a famous painter, the impostor could not accept the offer. For though the offer is made to him physically, it is obviously, as he knows, addressed to the famous painter. The mistake in identity on such facts is clear and the nature of the contract makes it obvious that identity was of vital importance to the offeror. At the other end of the scale, if a shopkeeper sells goods in a normal cash transaction to a man who misrepresents himself as being some well-known figure, the transaction will

normally be valid. For the shop-keeper was ready to sell the goods for cash to the world at large and the particular identity of the purchaser in such a contract was not of sufficient importance to override the physical presence identified by sight and hearing.

The actual judgment in *Ingram v Little* has been widely criticised. If the court had held that *Phillips v Brooks* was out of line with earlier authorities and had overruled the case, the judgment would have been unexceptionable. However, the Court of Appeal acknowledged the correctness of the principle in *Phillips v Brooks* but then went on to hold that the present case did not fall within it: a difficult decision to defend on the facts.

The correctness of the principle in *Phillips v Brooks* has been confirmed by the Court of Appeal in *Lewis v Averay* (1972). In this case, L advertised a Mini-Cooper S motor car for sale. A man arranged to see the car. He tested it and said he liked it. L and the man went to the flat of L's fiancee where the man told them that he was Richard Greene, the actor who had played Robin Hood in the television series. A price of £450 was agreed for the car and the man wrote a cheque for the amount which he signed 'RA Green'. L was reluctant to part with the car for a cheque and said he would retain the car to do some small jobs on it, which would allow 'Greene' to obtain the cash amount of the sale. 'Greene' persisted that he wished to take the car and produced an admission pass to Pinewood Studios, bearing an official stamp, a photograph and the name 'RA Green'. L allowed the man to take the car. The car was then sold by 'Greene' (passing himself off as Lewis, because Lewis's name was in the registration document) to Averay. Greene's cheque was dishonoured and Lewis sued Averay for conversion. *Held* by the Court of Appeal: L intended to sell the car to the man in his presence. The contract was therefore voidable for fraud and as A had obtained title to the car before L had avoided the contract, the car belonged to A.

Conclusions

In *Ingram v Little*, Devlin LJ (who delivered a dissenting judgment) pointed out that the fundamental question was: 'which of two innocent parties shall suffer for the fraud of a third?' He suggested that the loss should be apportioned between the innocent parties, either equally, if the loss was pure misfortune, or, if there was some fault by an innocent party, the loss should be apportioned according to fault.

The Law Revision Committee, in their Twelfth Report (1966), concluded that although the power of apportionment was attractive at first sight, there were overriding objections to it. These included:

(a) that such a power would give judges a wide and *virtually unrestrained discretion*, which would introduce significant uncertainty and increase litigation, an area where reasonable certainty is important;

(b) that the *practical and procedural difficulties* which would ensue if there were a chain of purchasers involved, would make a system of apportionment unworkable;

(c) that the owner of goods who has been *in no way at fault* should not have to contribute to the loss; and

(d) that even if, as had been further suggested, the power of apportionment should be restricted to involve only the final 'purchaser' in the chain and the owner, it would leave out any intermediate purchaser who may have been negligent. The Committee pointed out that the *good faith of the first purchaser* from the rogue is *often in doubt*, though it is difficult to prove anything against him.

The Committee went on to recommend that in all cases where goods are sold under a mistake as to the buyer's identity, the contract should, as far as third parties are concerned, be voidable and not void. As we have seen, this probably represents the law now (except for exceptional cases) where the parties are in each other's presence. However, it would appear, illogically, that *Cundy v Lindsay* prevails in cases where the parties are not in each other's presence.

Section 25 of the Sale of Goods Act 1979

The student may have encountered the provisions of s 25 of the Sale of Goods Act 1979 (s 9 of the Factors Act 1889 is to much the same effect) and wonder why, in cases of mistaken identity such as *Ingram v Little*, the third party does not acquire a good title under the terms of the section. The short answer is that the section requires the buyer (that is, the rogue) to be in possession of the goods with the consent of the seller. If the contract is void for mistaken identity, the rogue's possession is not with the consent of the seller, it is akin to theft by the rogue.

Estoppel

Estoppel is a rule of evidence whereby if A makes a representation of existing fact to B, aware that B intends to act upon it, then if B does act upon it to his detriment, A is estopped from denying that his representation was true. See, for example, *Henderson v Williams* (1895), which is explained in Chapter 20, p 417.

Estoppel was the second ground for the decision in *Citibank NA v Brown Shipping and Co* (1991). In this case, a rogue managed to dupe Citibank and Midland Bank into drawing banker's drafts, for substantial amounts of money, against the accounts of a client (who had an account at both banks), in favour of Brown Shipping. A person purporting to be the client's messenger (presumably the rogue) collected the drafts and presented them for payment, in cash, by Brown Shipping and absconded with the proceeds. On both occasions, before paying the 'messenger', Brown Shipping checked with the banks that the drafts were in order and on both occasions was assured that they were. The two banks were not able to debit the client's account with the amounts of the drafts, because the client had not given them a mandate to do so. Therefore, in an attempt to recover their loss, they sued Brown Shipping for the return of the cash. They argued that they were entitled to the return of the cash because they had made a mistake as to the identity of the person with whom they were dealing. The judge held that if there was a mistake, it related to the identity of the messenger who delivered the draft to Brown Shipping. In order for the delivery to be void, Citibank and Midland would have to show that the identity of the messenger was of vital importance. This they had failed to do. In addition, even if there were a mistake of identity, Citibank and Midland would be estopped from relying on it because in relation to the transactions in question, they had both assured Brown Shipping that the drafts were not forgeries and that they had been issued in the ordinary course of business. It was in reliance on these assurances that Brown Shipping paid the money.

Offeree knows offer is not meant for him

There is a similar category of cases which do not, however, involve mistaken identity: simply the purported acceptance of an offer which the offeree knew that the other party did not intend to make. See, for example, *Hartog v Colin and Shields* (1939). Initial negotiations for the sale of hare skins were conducted at a price per piece. When a formal offer was made this was at a price which was stated to be per pound (there are several pieces to the pound), though it was appropriate to the price which had been mentioned per piece. Not surprisingly, the offer was accepted with alacrity. The offeror, realising his mistake, contended that the contract should be set aside. The judge agreed on the grounds that, to the knowledge of the offeree, the offeror had made a mistake. However, it is clear that the judge was using the term 'mistake' in the lay-person's sense and that the reason there was no contract was that the offeree 'accepted' an offer which he knew the offeror never intended to make.

Rectification of documents

Parties often enter into a verbal agreement intending to enter into a later formal written agreement on the same terms. Sometimes the written agreement fails to reflect accurately the prior verbal agreement. In such a case, equity may rectify the written document so that it expresses correctly the terms agreed by the parties. In *Joselyne v Nissen* (1970), the plaintiff suggested to his daughter that she should take over his car-hire business. If she accepted, she would pay all the household expenses of the house which they both shared. A formal contract was entered into by virtue of which the defendant took over the business. After honouring the informal verbal agreement to pay the household expenses for a time, she eventually refused to continue payment. The plaintiff brought an action for rectification of the written agreement to include the daughter's obligation to pay the household bills. The defendant argued that there had been no antecedent contract in which such liability had been agreed. The court rejected her argument and ordered rectification of the contract relating to the acquisition of the car-hire business.

However, equity will not rectify a document if it represents the agreement correctly even though the agreement was based on the incorrect assumption of both parties. In *Rose v Pim* (1953), R had received an order from one of their customers for 'Moroccan horsebeans described as feveroles'. R did not know what feveroles were and asked their own supplier what they were and whether they could supply them. P told R that feveroles were simply horsebeans and that they could supply them. An oral contract for horsebeans was entered into and when the contract was reduced to writing, again the goods contracted for were described as 'horsebeans'. In fact, there were three types of Moroccan horsebean of which feveroles was one. P supplied feves in satisfaction of the contract. R sought rectification of the written agreement so that it read, 'feveroles'. *Held*: rectification would not be granted since the written agreement accurately recorded the verbal one.

Documents mistakenly signed

Where a party mistakenly signs a contractual document, he may plead *non est factum* (it is not my deed), thus escaping from the consequences of the contract providing:

(a) the document which is signed is radically different from that which he intended to sign; and

(b) he was not careless in signing the document.

In these cases, we are faced with the familiar problem of which of two innocent parties should suffer for the wrongdoing of a third. The typical scenario is that a rogue obtains the signature of an innocent party, by fraud, to a document which allows him to obtain money from a third party on the strength of the document. The rogue disappears with the money. The question is whether the signatory, or the person who relied on the signatory's signature, is bound by it. An example would be where the rogue secured the signature of the innocent party to a cheque; the cheque is paid by the bank to the rogue, without any negligence on the bank's part. Does the bank or the innocent account holder suffer the loss?

The general rule of English law is that if you sign a document you are bound by its terms whether you read it or understand it or not. A relatively modern illustration is to be found in *L'Estrange v Graucob* (1934), in which the plaintiff attempted to escape from the consequences of a document she had signed on the ground that, although it was legible, it was in small print and she had not read it. *Held*: she was bound by the document.

An exception was established in the 16th century in *Thoroughgood's* case (1584), where it was held that if an illiterate person had had a deed read over to him incorrectly and he subsequently signed it, he was not bound by his signature. Thoroughgood had been told that the effect of the deed was to relieve the tenant of land owned by Thoroughgood from arrears of rent. In fact, it gave the tenant rights in the land which enabled him to sell it to an innocent third party. Thoroughgood sued to recover the land, pleading *'non est factum'* – it is not my deed. *Held*: the plea was successful and Thoroughgood was entitled to recover his land.

The exception has subsequently been extended to benefit persons who can read, but have nevertheless been duped into signing a document which they did not intend to sign. However, the law does not allow a person to escape from the consequences of his signature very easily and it will be only in rare cases that the plea of *'non est factum'* succeeds.

The leading case is *Saunders v Anglia Building Society* (1971). Here, Mrs Gallie, a widow aged 78, agreed to make a deed of gift of her house to her nephew, to whom she had left the house in her will, so that he could raise money on the security of the house. A condition of the gift was that she was to remain in occupation until she died. A deed was drafted by her nephew's friend, Lee, who was heavily in debt. In the nephew's presence, Lee asked her to sign the document. She did as she was asked without reading the document, as she had broken her glasses. The deed was not a deed of gift but an assignment of her leasehold interest in the house to Lee. Lee borrowed money from the building society on the strength of the document and then defaulted on the repayments. The building society sought to realise its security by repossession of the house. Mrs Gallie pleaded that the assignment was void since it was not her deed. *Held*: she could not escape from the consequences of her signature. To do so, she would have had to have shown:

(a) the document which she signed was radically different from that which she intended to sign; and

(b) she was not careless in signing the document.

The deed of gift which Mrs Gallie intended to sign was not radically different in nature from the assignment which she in fact signed. In addition she had been careless in signing the document, since, although the document was full of legal intricacies, she could have ensured that the person named in the document was the person she intended to benefit.

CHAPTER 13

CAPACITY

A sober adult of sound mind has full contractual capacity. However, a number of persons have a restricted capacity to contract. The main categories are minors, persons of unsound mind, drunks and corporations. This chapter is restricted to a consideration of the capacity of minors. The capacity of corporations is dealt with in Chapter 29, p 672.

A minor is a person under the age of 18. The present age of majority was fixed by the Family Law Reform Act 1969. Until the Act came into effect on 1 January 1970, the age of majority was 21 and minors tended to be called 'infants' – points to bear in mind when reading the cases, almost all of which were decided before the 1969 Act came into force.

As a general rule, although a minor may become liable on a contract, a minor is not bound by any contract to the same extent as an adult would be. The minor is protected by the law from his own lack of experience. The extent and nature of the liability of a minor depends upon the type of contract under discussion. There are four categories of minors' contracts:

(a) contracts for necessaries;

(b) beneficial contracts of service;

(c) voidable contracts;

(d) any contract not falling within the first three categories.

We will deal with them in turn.

NECESSARIES

The word 'necessaries' means goods or services necessary to reasonably maintain the minor in his station in life at the time of the delivery of the goods or the supply of the services. In respect of goods, 'necessaries' is defined by s 3 of the Sale of Goods Act 1979 as 'goods suitable to the condition in life of the minor ... and to his actual requirements at the time of sale and delivery'. Note that 'necessaries' are not confined to necessities such as food, drink, clothing and lodging. In *Chapple v Cooper* (1844), Parke B described necessaries as including 'the proper cultivation of the mind', so that education is a necessary; 'the assistance and attendance of others may be necessary', thus servants may be a necessary to an appropriate class of person. He added:

> But in all these cases it must first be made out that the class itself is one in
> which the things furnished are essential to the existence and reasonable

advantage and comfort of the infant contractor. Thus, articles of mere luxury are always excluded, though luxurious articles of utility are sometimes allowed.

In *Ryder v Wombwell* (1868), a minor with an income of £500 per annum, the son of a baronet, bought jewelled cuff-links for £12 10s each and an antique goblet to give to a friend. The jury found that the articles were necessaries but the court set aside the verdict as there was no evidence on which it could be based.

In *Chapple v Cooper*, an infant widow was liable to pay for the funeral of her late husband.

In *Peters v Fleming* (1840), the court refused to disturb a verdict by the jury that a gold watch chain and other items of jewellery were necessaries to a minor undergraduate.

If the minor is already suitably supplied with a particular item, then even though the supplier does not know this, the item does not qualify as a necessary. In *Nash v Inman* (1908), a Savile Row tailor sought to recover £122 in respect of items of clothing including 11 fancy waistcoats. *Held*: the minor was already supplied with suitable clothing and, therefore, the clothing was not 'necessaries'.

Where the necessaries take the form of goods, the minor's obligation is limited to paying a reasonable price for the goods, provided they have been delivered to him. Thus a minor's liability to pay for necessaries differs in two respects from the liability of an adult in similar circumstances: first, the minor need only pay a reasonable price, not the contractual one, so that, should a minor have agreed to pay £5,000 for a car which is reasonably worth only £3,000, the minor will have to pay only £3,000, not £5,000 as would an adult in similar circumstances; secondly, the minor is not liable on an executory contract to supply him with necessary goods. Thus, there would be no question of a minor being liable for damages as a result of his refusal to take delivery of goods he had contracted for – again, unlike the liability of an adult in similar circumstances. It is argued, therefore, that minors' liability is quasi-contractual (that is, based on restoring the value of a benefit received and thus preventing the unjust enrichment of the minor), rather than contractual.

It seems that where the necessaries are goods, the quasi-contractual argument is to be preferred. Where the necessaries are not goods, the question of the basis of liability has been rendered somewhat more difficult by the case of *Roberts v Gray* (1913). In this case, a minor was held to be liable on an executory contract for education – though it is at least arguable that this was, in reality, a beneficial contract of service in respect of which an executory contract is binding. Gray wanted to become a professional billiards player and made a contract with Roberts whereby R and G would accompany each other on a world tour and play matches together. R expended much time and trouble on the preparations and incurred some liabilities. G failed to carry out the agreements. *Held*: R was entitled to damages for breach of contract.

If a contract for necessaries contains onerous terms, it is void: *Fawcett v Smethurst* (1914), in which a minor hired a car under terms that he should be absolutely liable for any damage to the car, whether it was caused by his negligence or not. *Held*: the contract was not binding since it contained onerous terms.

BENEFICIAL CONTRACTS OF SERVICE

A beneficial contract of service (that is, employment) is binding upon a minor. The concept of 'contract of service' includes contracts analogous thereto by which a minor is enabled to earn his living: *Chaplin v Leslie Frewin* (1966) in which a minor, the son of the famous actor Charlie Chaplin, contracted to give publishers the sole right to publish his memoirs, which were entitled *I could not smoke the grass on my father's lawn,* and gave an account of disreputable conduct, including drug-taking. He sought to restrain the publication of his memoirs, first on the grounds that the contract wasn't of a type that could be binding and secondly, on the ground that, in any case, the contract was not beneficial. *Held*: the contract was of the type that could be binding on the minor since it enabled him to earn a living and that the contract was beneficial, despite the fact that, as carried out, it brought the minor into disrepute: '... the mud may cling but the profits will be secured.'

Note that a trading contract will not bind the minor: see *Cowern v Nield* (1921), where a minor who was a hay and straw dealer was paid in advance for a consignment of hay which he failed to deliver. *Held*: he was not liable to repay the price.

A contract is binding if it is beneficial overall, even though some aspects are not beneficial: *Clements v London and North Western Railway* (1894), in which a minor joined an employer's industrial injury scheme which was more beneficial than the statutory one, since it covered a wider range of accidents. However, the measure of compensation was lower. *Held*: the contract was beneficial.

In *Doyle v White City Stadium* (1935), a minor boxed under a contract which provided that if he was disqualified he lost. He sued for his £3,000 purse. *Held*: the contract was beneficial since the contract provided him with a means to earn his living and clean fighting was in the interest of everyone.

A contract that is not beneficial will not bind the minor. In *De Francesco v Barnum* (1890), a girl of 14 bound herself by apprenticeship deed for seven years to the plaintiff to be taught stage dancing. She agreed that she would not marry during the apprenticeship, and would not accept professional engagements without the plaintiff's permission. The plaintiff did not bind himself to find her engagements or to maintain her while she was unemployed. Her pay was 9d per night and 6d for matinées during the first three years and 1s per night and 6d for matinées after that period. The plaintiff could terminate the contract if D was found unfit for dancing. *Held*: the contract was not beneficial.

VOIDABLE CONTRACTS

Certain minors' contracts which involve subject matter in which the minor obtains a continuing interest are voidable in the sense that they bind both parties, but the minor can avoid the contract by repudiating it before majority or within a reasonable time thereafter. The principal examples of such contracts are contracts concerning land, partnership contracts, contracts to take shares in companies and marriage settlements.

In *Corpe v Overton* (1873), an infant agreed to enter into a partnership with the defendant in three month's time and to pay him £1,000 when the partnership deed was executed. He also made an immediate payment of £100 as security for the promise. He rescinded the contract as soon as he became of age and sued for the return of his £100. *Held*: the money was recoverable, since there had been a total failure of consideration.

In *Edwards v Carter* (1893), a marriage settlement was executed by which the father of the intended husband agreed to pay £1,500 a year to trustees who were to pay it to the husband for life and then to the wife and the children of the marriage. The intended husband, an infant at the time of the settlement, executed a deed binding him to vest in the trustees all the property he might acquire under the will of his father. A month later he came of age and three and a half years later he became entitled to an interest under his father's will. More than a year after his father's death, that is, about four and a half years after he came of age, he repudiated the agreement. *Held*: his repudiation was too late and was, therefore, ineffective.

The effect of repudiation is to relieve the minor of future liabilities: *Steinberg v Scala (Leeds)* (1923), in which P, an infant, applied for shares in a company and paid the amounts due on allotment and first call. She neither received dividends nor attended any meetings of the company and the shares appear always to have stood at a discount. Eighteen months after the allotment, while still an infant, she repudiated the contract and claimed to recover what she had paid. *Held*: her claim failed. By allotting the shares, the company had done all it had bargained to do by way of consideration.

There is some doubt at to whether the minor remains liable for accrued liabilities, though the better opinion is that he does not: in *North Western Railway Co v McMichael* (1850), a minor subscribed for shares and an action was brought to recover money in respect of a call on the shares. D pleaded that he had not ratified the purchase and had received no benefit under it.

However, if he had pleaded and substantiated repudiation, he would have had no liability to pay the call even though it had become due.

The minor can recover money paid or property transferred only if there has been a total failure of consideration: contrast *Corpe v Overton* (above) with *Holmes v Blogg* (1818), in which an infant paid a sum of money to a lessor as part of the consideration for the lease of premises in which he and his partner proposed to carry on their trade. He occupied the premises for 12 weeks but the day after he became of age he dissolved the partnership, repudiated the lease and left the premises. He failed in his attempt to recover what he had paid. There was no total failure of consideration since he had received the thing he had bargained for.

Restitution of property acquired under the contract can be ordered against the minor who repudiates: s 3(1) of the Minors' Contracts Act 1987.

OTHER TYPES OF CONTRACT

Contracts which don't fall within the first three categories are sometimes called 'voidable', but this is misleading since their effect is:

(a) they do not bind the minor, unless ratified by the minor after the age of majority: *Williams v Moor* (1843);

(b) they bind the other party: *Bruce v Warwick* (1815);

(c) however, the minor cannot claim specific performance of the contract (that is, he is restricted to claiming damages): *Flight v Bolland* (1828).

USE OF THE LAW OF TORT

The law of tort cannot be used to defeat the effect of the law of contract: in *Jennings v Rundall* (1799), an infant hired a mare for riding but injured it by excessive and improper riding. He was not liable in tort, since to allow him to be sued for negligence rather than for breach of contract would simply have been an indirect way of enforcing the contract. If the minor acts outside the parameters of the contract tort can be used against him: *Burnard v Haggis* (1863), in which, contrary to the express instructions of the owner, a horse hired for riding was used for jumping. *Held*: the minor was liable in tort because the action he had done was outside what was contemplated by the contract. See, also, *Ballet v Mingay* (1943), where an action for detinue to return borrowed articles which the borrower had unauthorisedly lent to a friend succeeded on similar grounds.

RESTITUTION

In any case where a minor acquires property under a contract which is unenforceable against him or which he repudiates, he may be required to perform restitution of the property: s 3(1) of the Minor's Contracts Act 1987. This provides where:

(a) a person ('the plaintiff') has, after the commencement of this Act, entered into a contract with another ('the defendant'); and

(b) the contract is unenforceable against the defendant (or he repudiates it) because he was a minor when the contract was made, the court may, if it is just and equitable to do so, require the defendant to transfer to the plaintiff any property acquired by the defendant under the contract, or any property representing it.

For the principles of restitution, see *Leslie v Shiell* (1914). In this case, it was held that a minor could not be compelled to restore a loan of £400 which he had obtained by fraud unless the exact notes and coins could be identified because to compel this would be to enforce the contract of loan, not apply the doctrine of restitution.

Contrast *Stocks v Wilson* (1913), in which a minor obtained goods on credit by misrepresenting his age and sold them. *Held*: although he could not be sued in tort for the value of the goods, he was accountable in restitution for the proceeds of the sale.

It would seem that *Leslie v Shiell* can be reconciled with *Stocks v Wilson* on the basis that, in *Leslie v Shiell*, to have forced the minor to repay the loan out of his general assets would inevitably have been to enforce the contract. However, in *Stocks v Wilson*, the minor was not made to pay the contract price for the furniture which he bought, but merely to account for the proceeds of the re-sale.

CHAPTER 14

ILLEGALITY

Certain contracts are said to be illegal. 'Illegal' in this sense does not mean that the contracts themselves are unlawful under the criminal law or even that they necessarily involve the commission of a criminal offence, though some contracts in this category will, no doubt, amount to criminal conspiracies. It simply means that the law regards the purpose of the contract to be unworthy and will, therefore, not lend itself to the enforcement of the contract.

If a contract is illegal, there is a general rule that no legal action will be permitted in order to enforce it (for those who like Latin, this is expressed as *ex turpi causa non oritur actio* – from an unworthy cause no right of action arises). Similarly, if the contract is illegal, not only may it not be enforced, in the sense that no action for damages will be entertained but, in addition, no action will be permitted in order to recover property transferred or money paid under the contract. This is expressed by another Latin maxim: *in pari delicto potior est conditio defendentis* – where the parties are equally to blame, the position of the defendant is the better.

Illegal contracts can be divided into three categories: contracts which involve a breach of the criminal or civil law; contracts contrary to public policy; contracts in restraint of trade (strictly speaking these are not a separate category – some breach the criminal law and some are contrary to public policy). In addition, certain contracts, such as wagering contracts, are void by statute. We will not examine wagering contracts since they are of interest to only a very small proportion of the business world.

There is a large list of illegal contracts, particularly in the 'contrary to public policy' category. The following are examples which are of most relevance to business.

CONTRACTS TO COMMIT A CRIME OR A BREACH OF THE CIVIL LAW

A contract which breaches criminal or civil law is illegal. Legal actions which seek to enforce the worst types of crime, such as contract killing, never come before the courts to be enforced, for fairly obvious reasons. If, however, someone who had been convicted of such a killing tried to enforce his right to the price for the killing, he would fail on the grounds that the contract was illegal.

The case of *Bigos v Bousted* (1951) illustrates the principle. D sent his daughter to Italy. Exchange control regulations, enacted by the Exchange Control Act 1947, were in force which made it a criminal offence to buy more than a small amount of foreign currency or to export more than a small amount of sterling for the purposes of tourism. To get round the restrictions imposed by the Act, D contracted with P that if P made £150 of Italian money available to his daughter in Italy, he would give P £150 when she came to England. D gave P some share certificates as security for the advance. The transaction went wrong and the money was not made available to D's daughter. D sought to recover share certificates. *Held*: the parties were equally to blame and therefore the court would not intervene to help D.

Contracts which result in a crime being committed because they are performed illegally

Such contracts are illegal if the purpose of the law is to prohibit such contracts. If, however, the illegality is incidental to the contract, the court will enforce it.

In *Anderson v Daniel* (1924), P sold D some agricultural fertiliser. P failed to give D an invoice showing the percentages of certain chemicals contained in the fertiliser. This was required by statute, which was passed for the protection of a class of the public, including the purchaser. *Held*: P could not recover the price since he had not performed the statute in the only manner permitted by the statute.

However, in *St John's Shipping v Joseph Rank* (1957), P contracted to carry goods for D. In doing so, P overloaded his ship, which was a criminal offence. D withheld a proportion of the cost of the freight, equivalent to that represented by the overload. P sued. D's defence was that P had, in overloading his ship, carried out the contract illegally. *Held*: although P's conduct was an offence, the overloading was incidental to the performance of the contract and did not affect P's right to claim the freight, particularly as the default was punishable by a fine, which would have resulted in P being punished for the same default twice over (though, in fact, the law provides abundant instances of just that!).

In *Hughes v Asset Management* (1995), H gave AM £3 million for the purpose of buying shares. A month later, following a fall in the market, H sold the shares for just under £1 million. H brought proceedings to recover the loss on the ground that although AM had been licensed to deal in securities under s 1 of the Prevention of Fraud (Investments) Act 1958, the individual who had made and signed the deal on behalf of AM was not licensed. It was argued that the agreement was, therefore, a nullity and void since the Act prohibited unlicensed persons from dealing in securities. *Held:* the purpose of the Act was to protect the investing public by imposing criminal sanctions on those who dealt in securities without a licence. The public interest was fully met by sanctions imposed by the statute and neither the words of the Act, nor the type of prohibitions imposed (which were directed against the persons making the deals, not the deals themselves or the contracting parties) showed any parliamentary intention that deals should be struck down or rendered ineffective.

Contracts where the subject matter is to be used for an illegal purpose

In *Langton v Hughes* (1813), L sold H some material which, to the knowledge of L, H intended to use in order to adulterate beer. The contract was illegal because it offended against a statutory provision which provided that only malt and hops may be used as flavouring in beer.

CONTRACTS WHICH ARE CONTRARY TO PUBLIC POLICY

There is some overlap between this category and the preceding one. For example, contracts to defraud the Revenue will amount to a criminal offence, in addition to being contrary to public policy.

Contracts where the subject matter is to be used for an immoral purpose

In *Pearce v Brooks* (1866), P agreed to supply B with a carriage on hire-purchase terms. B was a prostitute and intended to use the carriage for the purposes of prostitution. The carriage was an unusual one and the jury found that the plaintiffs knew of the purpose for which it was intended. *Held*: P was not entitled to recover payment for the carriage.

Contracts interfering with personal liberty

In *Horwood v Millar's Timber and Trading* (1917), a contract of loan provided that the borrower would not leave his job, borrow money, move house or dispose of his property without the consent of the lender. It was held that the contract was illegal as being an infringement of the borrower's personal liberty.

If, however, the court can be convinced that the restriction on freedom is to the ultimate benefit of the person whose freedom is curtailed, it may be that the contract will be enforced. In *Denny v Denny* (1919), a father promised to pay the debts of his profligate son and to make him an allowance if he did not go within 80 miles of Piccadilly Circus, gave up his disreputable associates, did not bet or borrow money or have any personal relations with bookmakers or moneylenders, etc. It was held that the contract was not illegal since the restrictions were imposed for the son's benefit.

Contracts which are prejudicial to friendly foreign relations

In *Foster v Driscoll* (1929), an agreement to export whisky to Canada, where it was to be re-exported to the United States and consumed there in contravention of that country's prohibition laws, was held to be illegal, since its object was to contravene the laws of a friendly foreign power.

Contracts to defraud the Inland Revenue

It is not uncommon for employers to enter into contracts with their employees whereby they are entitled to receive expenses, which are paid free of income tax, despite the fact that neither party expects the expenses to be incurred. Such contracts are illegal. The employee is not, therefore, able to claim any salary outstanding under the contract: *Napier v National Business Agency* (1951), nor is the employee entitled to the benefit of employment protection legislation which is given to those who are employed under a contract of employment. Thus, the employee will not be entitled to claim a redundancy payment or unfair dismissal, for example, in the event of his dismissal: *Corby v Morrison* (1980).

Contracts liable to corrupt public life

In *Parkinson v College of Ambulance* (1925), P paid money to secure a knighthood. The knighthood was not forthcoming and P sued to recover the money. *Held*: the contract was illegal and the money, therefore, was not repayable.

Contracts to oust the jurisdiction of the courts

A contract which prohibits any dispute being taken to court will be illegal. However, arbitration agreements are not illegal.

CONTRACTS IN RESTRAINT OF TRADE

At common law, any contract which restrained a party, either wholly or partially, from carrying on, or being employed in, a lawful trade or business, was void and unenforceable. However, the law was gradually relaxed until certain restraints were permitted, providing they were reasonable.

Restrictive covenants in contracts of employment and contracts for the sale of a business

An employer will sometimes wish to restrain his employee from using information gained in his employment on leaving that employment. This usually relates to the employer's customer base but may, occasionally, relate to the employer's trade secrets.

The best way to approach the matter is by placing an express restraint clause in the employee's contract of employment. This is because the terms implied into an employment contract by common law are restricted in scope and will often fail to give the employer the post-contract protection he requires. Similarly, when the owner of a business sells it, the buyer will often want some legal protection so that the seller cannot immediately set up in competition with him.

Restrictive covenants by which a party promises not to work in a particular business, in a particular geographical area and for a specified period of time, are *prima facie* void at common law because they act in restraint of trade. However, the law will give effect to a restraint clause providing three conditions are met:

(1) The employer must have an interest to protect which the law regards as meriting its protection. Typically, in a contract of employment, that interest will either be:

(a) the protection of the employer's trade secrets; or,

(b) protection of the employer's customer connections.

To be valid, therefore, a restraint clause must aim at protecting one or other of these interests – a restraint which is merely aimed at preventing the employee from subsequently competing with the employer will be invalid. In *Bull v Pitney Bowes* (1966), B had been required to join a non-contributory pension scheme. He had left the defendant's employment at the age of 45 after 26 years' service, and was entitled to a pension on reaching normal retirement age. One of the rules of the pension scheme was that, if on leaving the defendant's employment, the employee engaged in any activity which was in competition with or detrimental to the interests of the defendant, he would lose his pension rights if he failed to discontinue that activity when required by the defendant to do so. B entered into employment with a competitor of the defendant. He was asked to discontinue that employment and was told that he would forfeit his pension if he failed to do so. B asked for a declaration that the defendant's action was unlawful because it was in restraint of trade. *Held*: the rule permitting the forfeiture of the pension was void and unenforceable, since it was aimed merely at prohibiting competition with the employer. See, also, *Cantor Fitzgerald v Wallace* (1992), where it was held that an employer had no right or interest meriting protection where the main attribute of the job was individual skill and personality.

(2) The restraint must be reasonable as to:

(a) the time period of the restraint;

It is normal nowadays to use a period of between six months and two years. It has, however, been held that a lifetime's restraint was reasonable in the circumstances. In *Fitch v Dewes* (1921), a solicitor's clerk was restrained for life from practising within seven miles of Tamworth town hall. On the other hand, in *Eastes v Russ* (1914), where it was held that a lifetime's restraint imposed upon a pathologist's assistant was unreasonable.

(b) the geographical area of the restraint;

In *Nordenfeld v Maxim Nordenfeld* (1894), a worldwide restraint for 25 years was upheld against the seller of an arms-manufacturing business. However, this was justified because of the nature of the business being sold: there was only a very limited number of customers worldwide.

In employment contracts, although Eastern Hemisphere-wide and United Kingdom-wide restraints have been upheld, it will only be in a very rare case that such a restraint is justified. So, for example, a restraint on the manager of a butcher's shop in Cambridge not to carry on a similar business within five miles from the shop at which he was employed was held to be too wide and therefore invalid: *Empire Meat v Patrick* (1939). In *Lansing Linde v Kerr* (1991), a worldwide restraint was held to be too wide for the Managing Director of a fork-lift truck manufacturer, though a restraint extending to the UK would probably have been upheld.

(c) the activity which is being restrained. This must be no wider than is necessary to protect the employer's interest.

Thus, in *Attwood v Lamont* (1920), an attempt to restrain the manager of a menswear department in a department store from becoming employed in other activities undertaken by the store, failed as the restraint was too wide.

(3) The restraint must not be against the public interest.

It has never been made clear exactly what this means. It has been suggested that restraints upon employees who have an important skill (for example, doctors, engineers, etc) might offend against this requirement. However, in *Lyne-Pirkis v Jones* (1969), the Court of Appeal seems to have been prepared to uphold a restraint against a doctor, if they had found it to be reasonable.

It seems that a contract which indirectly seeks to impose an unlawful restraint will be void as being contrary to the public interest.

In *Kores v Kolak* (1959), two companies which manufactured similar products agreed that neither would employ any person who had been employed by the other during the last five years. The defendants broke this promise and were sued. It was held by the Court of Appeal that the contract was unreasonable as it provided a protection far in excess of what was required to protect the trading interests of each. However, Lords Reid and Hodson have since said that it would have been more correct to have found the contract void as being against the public interest.

Restraints by outside bodies, such as Trade Associations

In some cases, a restraint upon the employment of an individual or class of individuals is imposed not by a single employer but by a Trade Association or similar. In such a case, if the restraint is unreasonable, the courts will declare the restraint to be invalid as being contrary to public policy.

For example, the Jockey Club, which is the governing body of racing, used to have a rule that women would not be granted licences to train racehorses. A horse which was trained by an unlicensed trainer was not accepted to run in any races organised under the auspices of the Jockey Club, so that a woman who wished to become a racehorse trainer either had to train under a licence granted to a male (for example, her husband or a male employee, etc) or was restricted to training hacks for minor, non-Jockey Club races. Nowadays such a restraint would be contrary to the Sex Discrimination Act 1975. However, in 1966 an action was brought by an aspiring woman trainer, arguing that the rule barring women trainers was void as it was in restraint of trade. The Court of Appeal agreed and the restriction was declared void: see *Nagle v Fielden* (1966).

Similarly, in 1963, the existing 'retain and transfer' system operated by the Football League was declared to be in restraint of trade and, therefore, unlawful. Under this system, a player whose contract had expired could be retained by his club without wages until either a transfer to another club could be negotiated, on terms acceptable to his old club, or he signed a fresh contract: *Eastham v Newcastle United FC* (1964).

SOLUS AGREEMENTS

A solus agreement is one where a business agrees to take all of its supplies of a particular commodity or commodities from one source. The most common type of solus agreement is in relation to petrol stations agreeing to become 'tied' to one petrol company. Another example is 'tied' houses in the brewery trade.

The reason why the petrol service operator or the pub landlord agrees to restrict his freedom of purchase in this way is usually one of two: either the petrol company has an interest in the station and the operator is leasing it from them or has borrowed money from them by way of mortgage; or the petrol company has offered special discounts on the purchase price. The latter can be a compelling reason for a garage owner to enter into such an agreement: it enables him to be more competitive. The disadvantage of such an agreement is that the terms are largely dictated by the petrol company or brewery. Oddly enough, it seems that agreements by which a landlord who leases a pub from a brewery takes all his supplies from that brewery will be held to be valid simply because such agreements have been recognised for a very long time. Since the petrol business is of much more recent origin, the agreement is void unless it can be shown to be reasonable.

In *Esso v Harper's Garage* (1968), there were two solus agreements, one for about four years five months and the other for 21 years. It was held that the restraint of trade doctrine applied to such agreements and that the shorter one was valid, since it was reasonable in the interests of the petrol company being able to maintain a stable system of distribution. However, the 21 year restraint was too long. The Monopolies Commission suggested a maximum of five years duration for such agreements.

The issue arose in the *Esso* case as to how solus agreements, in which one party accepts a restriction on his ability to trade, differ in principle from restrictive covenants on the sale of property, where one party agrees to use premises for a particular purpose and no other. It is well-established law that the latter are valid. The House of Lords suggested that the difference lies in the fact that, in a solus agreement the party who accepts the restriction is giving up his right to trade freely, whereas a person who is purchasing or leasing property and accepts a restraint is doing so in order to acquire the property. He did not previously have any trading rights in relation to the property so that he is not giving up any right which he previously enjoyed. In other words, if a contract restricts an existing freedom it can be said to restrain trade: if it opens up a new economic opportunity, subject to restraint, it is not a restraint of trade.

The petrol companies reacted to the *Esso* case by looking for ways round it. One way was for the garage owner to lease his garage to the petrol company and for the petrol company to lease it back to a *company* controlled by the owner. The company, being in law a different person from the persons who control it, could then enter into a solus agreement of more than five years. The restraint of trade doctrine would not apply since the company had no previous right in the property and entered into the solus agreement in order to gain possession of the property. This was done in *Alec Lobb v Total* (1985), where Total bought and leased-back a petrol station. The lease-back included a solus agreement whereby the garage would take its fuel oil from Total for a period of 21 years. However, this was not a straightforward sale and lease-back, since it was clear that Total did not particularly want to do the deal: it was done at the request of the garage in order to give the garage some capital to enable it to continue trading. In addition, there was a 'break' clause in the lease which would have enabled Alec Lobb to escape from the clause after seven or 14 years. It was held that, in the circumstances, the restraint was legal and enforceable.

EFFECTS OF ILLEGALITY

As we have seen, the attitude of the courts to an illegal contract is that the courts will not enforce it, nor will they order the return of money paid or property transferred under the contract. However, the courts will enforce the plaintiff's rights in a case where the plaintiff is able to assert a claim irrespective of the illegality.

In *Bowmakers v Barnet Instruments* (1945), the plaintiffs let some machine tools to the defendants under three hire-purchase agreements. These were assumed to contravene an order made under the Defence of the Realm Regulations. The defendants sold two of the machines and refused to re-deliver the third to the plaintiffs, having made no payments under the agreement. In response to the plaintiffs' action for the tort of conversion (wrongfully dealing with the plaintiffs' goods as if they were the owners'), the defendants argued that they were not liable because the contract between themselves and the plaintiffs was illegal. *Held*: the plaintiffs were founding their claim, not on the illegal contract, but on their ownership of the goods. This was independent of the contract and the plaintiffs, therefore, succeeded.

In *Mohamed v Alaga & Co* (1999), the claimant made an agreement with the defendant firm of solicitors that he would introduce Somali asylum seekers to the defendants with a view to the defendant representing them in their application for asylum. He agreed to give help in completing the applications and, in return, was to be paid 50% of the legal aid fees as a commission. This was contrary to r 7 of the Solicitors' Practice Rules 1990, made under s 3 of the Solicitors Act 1974. It was held that the contract was illegal and, therefore, the claimant could not sue on the contract. However, the claimant would be allowed to sue for the value of work done, on a *quantum meruit* (as much as it is worth) basis. This would not require him to rely on the illegal contract.

Exceptionally, the court will order the return of money paid or property transferred under the illegal contract. The exceptions are:

(a) where the parties are not equally to blame (that is, *in pari delicto*) in respect of the illegality;

In *Hughes v Liverpool Victoria Friendly Society* (1916), Mrs Hughes was induced, by the fraud of the defendant's agent, to take over the payments of premiums in respect of an insurance policy in respect of which she had no insurable interest. The contract was therefore illegal. She sued for the return of the premiums she had paid. *Held*: since she entered into the agreement believing it to be a valid one, she was not in *pari delicto* with the insurance company and could therefore recover her premiums.

(b) where a party to a contract which has not been fully carried out, repents of the illegal contract in time.

In *Taylor v Bowers* (1876), Taylor, fearing that certain goods would be seized by his creditors, made a fictitious assignment of them to X. Without the knowledge of Taylor, X mortgaged the goods to Bowers, who knew of the fictitious assignment. Taylor sued Bowers for the recovery of the goods. *Held*: Taylor was entitled to succeed since the illegal purpose of interfering with the administration of justice had not been carried out.

In the similar but contrasting case of *Kearley v Thompson* (1890), K was a friend of a person who was subject to bankruptcy proceedings. K paid T, a firm of solicitors representing one of the creditors in the proceedings, a sum of money on condition that they did not appear at the public examination of the bankrupt nor oppose his discharge from bankruptcy. They did not appear at the public examination. K then decided not to proceed any further with the matter and sued for the return of the money. *Held*: he was not entitled to it, since the defendants had partially performed the contract and therefore K's repentance came too late.

There was a similar result in *Bigos v Bousted* (above, p 300) where the repentance came about because the deal had fallen through, not because the party reclaiming his property had thought the better of it.

SEVERANCE

Sometimes the illegal part of a contract can be severed from the lawful part, leaving the lawful part to be enforced. The test as to whether this can be done depends upon whether it is a question of a term of the contract being illegal or whether it is simply part of a term which is illegal.

Severance of terms

Whether an illegal term can be cut out of a contract in order to leave a valid contract depends upon whether or not the offending term is the main part of the consideration given by the person making the promise or whether it is ancillary to the main purpose. If the illegal promise is only ancillary, it can be severed so as to leave a valid contract. In *Goodinson v Goodinson* (1954), a wife contracted with her husband whereby, in return for the payment to her by the husband of a weekly sum by way of maintenance, she would indemnify him against all debts she incurred, would not pledge his credit and would not take any court proceedings for maintenance. The last promise was illegal since it ousted the jurisdiction of the court. *Held*: the promise not to take legal proceedings could be severed from the remainder of the agreement in order to leave a valid contract, since the promise not to sue was not the main consideration given by the wife.

Severance of part of a term

Where only part of a promise is illegal, the court will sever that part of the promise if it can do so without rewriting the offending term and without altering the sense of the term. This type of severance has arisen mainly in connection with contracts in restraint of trade.

In *Nordenfeld v Maxim Nordenfeld* (1893), N sold his arms business to a company and agreed that he would not engage in any business as a supplier of certain types of arms, nor would he engage in any business which would compete with the company in any way. The restraint against competing with the company in any way was clearly too wide, since it was a mere restraint against competition which, as we have seen, is not an interest which the law views as meriting its protection. The enforcement of such a clause would mean that if, for example, N set up in business as a tractor manufacturer and then, at a later date, the company set up as tractor manufacturers, N would have to cease his business since it competed with the company. However, the court held that the portion of the promise which related to not competing with the company could be severed from the remainder so as to leave a valid restraint.

In *Attwood v Lamont* (1920), A carried on business as a general outfitter in Kidderminster. His store had several departments and L was manager of the tailoring department. He signed a restraint clause which sought to prevent him from working as a tailor, dressmaker, general draper, milliner, hatter, haberdasher, gentlemen's, ladies' or children's outfitter within 10 miles of Kidderminster. It was admitted that the restraint was too wide in relation to the activity restrained, but A argued that the prohibitions against L working as anything other than a tailor could be *severed* leaving a valid restraint against L working as a tailor. It was held that the restraint against working as tailor could not be severed from the restraint against carrying on the other trades, since the restraint was, in the view of the court, one single restraint, which was too wide, and not a series of restraints which could be severed from one another.

CHAPTER 15

DISCHARGE OF CONTRACTS

Discharge of a contract means that a contract has come to an end: neither party has any further obligation under it. Discharge may be in one of four ways: by performance; by express agreement; by frustration; by acceptance by the innocent party of the guilty party's repudiatory breach, often called 'discharge by breach'. Discharge by frustration has been dealt with under the heading of 'Impossibility' in Chapter 9.

DISCHARGE BY PERFORMANCE

The rule at common law is that a party must perform exactly what he has promised to do, otherwise he cannot claim payment or performance from the other party. In this respect, the law draws a distinction between a contract which is 'entire', that is, that requires complete performance of the whole of the obligation, and a 'divisible' contract, under which the obligation can be sub-divided into two or more contracts. An example of the latter is stage payments in relation to the construction of a building. The contract may provide for payment to be made by the owner to the contractor in stages. The first payment may be due when the site is excavated and the foundations dug out, the second payment when the foundations are laid, and so forth. At each stage the contractor completes he will be entitled to payment: he does not need to complete the whole building before entitlement arises. The rule relating to entire contracts is illustrated by the old case of *Cutter v Powell* (1795). In that case, Cutter, a seaman, signed on to crew a ship from Jamaica to Liverpool at a wage of £31 10s. After almost two months as a member of the crew and 19 days before the ship reached Liverpool, Cutter died. His widow claimed a proportion of his wages as a *quantum meruit*. *Held*: the contract was entire and as Cutter had only partially performed his obligation, he was entitled to nothing. In the case of seamen, this rule was modified by provisions which are now contained in the Merchant Shipping Act 1970.

In the case of rent, annuities (including salaries and pensions), dividends and other periodic payments in the nature of income, the Apportionment Act 1870 provided that they should be considered as accruing from day to day and apportioned accordingly. The Law Reform (Frustrated Contracts) Act 1943 may apply in a case where, as in *Cutter*'s case, failure to perform was because the contract became frustrated.

However, in cases not specifically provided for by statute or which are not covered by the exceptions established at common law (see below), the rule relating to entire contracts remains. In *Bolton v Mahadeva* (1972), B agreed to install a central-heating system in M's home for £560. The system was defective and would cost £179 to put right. It was held that the contract was an entire contract and, since B had not performed it fully, he was entitled to no payment. (The doctrine of substantial performance did not apply because the defects were too great to say that the contract had been substantially performed.)

EXCEPTION TO THE ENTIRE CONTRACTS RULE

There are three exceptions to the rule. These are:

(a) where the contract has been substantially performed;

(b) where one party has accepted partial performance; and

(c) where performance is prevented by the wrongful act of the other party.

The doctrine of substantial performance

Where an entire contract has been substantially performed, the plaintiff may claim the agreed price for the work, less an amount which represents the incomplete or defective part. In *Hoenig v Isaacs* (1952), I employed H, who was an interior decorator, to decorate and to provide furniture for I's flat. The contract price was £750. The terms were 'Net cash as the work proceeds and the balance on completion'. The defendant made two payments of £150 as the work progressed but on being asked for the balance of £450 on completion of the work, paid only £100 as he alleged that the work had not been performed or that it had been done in an unskilful and unworkmanlike manner. The work was assessed and it was found that there were defects to a wardrobe and a bookcase which would require about £55 to put right. It was held that the contract had been substantially performed and H was therefore awarded the balance of the price, less the amount needed to put the defects right.

In *Dakin v Lee* (1916), the principle of substantial performance was justified as follows:

> Take a contract for a lump sum to decorate a house; the contract provides that there shall be three coats of oil paint, but in one of the rooms only two coats have been put on. Can anyone seriously say that under these circumstances the building owner could go and occupy the house and take the benefit of all the decorations which had been done in the other rooms without paying a penny for all the work done by the builder, just because two coats of paint had been put in one room where there ought to have been three?

It seems that in a case where one party makes it clear in advance that only entire performance will be accepted, the other will be entitled to no payment if he fails to perform his entire obligations, even if performance is substantial. In *Wiluszynski v Tower Hamlets LBC* (1989), W refused to perform an extremely small part of his contractual obligations under a contract of employment, since he was engaged in industrial action. His employer made it clear that if he did not perform his obligations in accordance with his contract, he would not be paid at all. When W sued for his salary, it was held that the doctrine of substantial performance did not apply, since his employers had made it clear that they were not willing to pay for anything less than complete performance of his obligations. (Note that what normally happens in such cases is that the employer makes a deduction in respect of the work which is not done; it is unusual for an employer to take the extreme action taken by Tower Hamlets LBC.)

Acceptance of partial performance

If one party indicates that he is willing to accept partial performance, the other party has an action for the appropriate proportion of the contract price. An example of this is contained in s 39 of the Sale of Goods Act, which provides that a buyer is not obliged to accept less goods than he contracted for, but if he does he must pay for them at the contract rate.

If, however, the innocent party is given no choice but to accept partial performance, this will not be regarded as a true acceptance. In *Sumpter v Hedges* (1898), S agreed to do some building work on H's land for a lump sum of £565. Before the work was finished (and after H had paid some of the price) S told H that he had run out of funds and could not, therefore, complete the work. H completed the work using materials which S had left on the site. S now sued for payment in respect of the work he had done and the materials which he had supplied. *Held*: S was not entitled to payment for the work he had done, because H had not accepted partial performance: since the building was on his land he had had no choice in the matter. However, S was entitled to payment for the materials which he had supplied.

Prevention of performance by the other party

Tender of performance (that is, offer of performance) is the equivalent of performance itself. In *Startup v Macdonald* (1843), S had a contract to sell oil to M within a certain time. He tendered the oil at 8.30 pm on the last possible day. M refused to accept it because of the lateness of the hour. It was held that S was entitled to damages for non-acceptance of the goods. (Note, however, that a delivery at a late hour will not always produce this result. Section 29(5) of the Sale of Goods Act 1979 provides that tender of delivery may be treated as ineffectual unless made at a reasonable hour. What is a reasonable hour is a question of fact.)

Where performance is prevented by the wrongful act of the other party, the innocent party is entitled to payment for what he has done under the contract, even though he has not completed his contractual obligations. In *Planché v Colburn* (1831), P agreed with C to write a book, to be part of a series, for £100. P began work on the book but C decided not to go ahead with the series. C refused to pay P for the work he had done, arguing that P was not entitled to payment as he had not completed the work. It was held that P was entitled to £50 in damages, since it was the default of the defendant which had caused P to abandon the work.

TIME OF PERFORMANCE

Where a time has been stipulated for performance, time is 'of the essence' if such is the intention of the parties. In such a case if performance is tendered otherwise than at the due time, the innocent party is under no obligation to accept and can bring an end to the contract.

In *Union Eagle v Golden Achievement* (1997), the appellant entered into a written contract to buy a flat from the respondent. The contract provided that completion was to take place before 5 pm on 30 September 1991, that time was of the essence of the contract, and that if the purchaser failed to comply with any of the terms and conditions of the contract, the deposit was to be forfeited. The purchaser was 10 minutes late tendering the balance of the purchase price and the completion documents. The vendor therefore informed the purchaser that the contract was rescinded and returned the cheques and documents to the purchaser. The purchaser claimed that equity should relieve him from the consequences of his lateness and claimed specific performance of the agreement.

Held: in cases of rescission of an ordinary contract of sale of land for failure to comply with an essential condition as to time, equity will not intervene unless there was conduct by the vendor amounting to waiver or an estoppel. A rule which gave the law certainty was required to enable the vendor to know he was free to resell the property. The vendor was, therefore, entitled to rescind the contract.

In mercantile contracts, the general rule is that time of performance is of the essence. For example in *Bowes v Shand* (1877), where goods were sold under a contract which required them to be shipped in March and April, the substantial majority were shipped in February. *Held*: the buyers were not bound to take delivery of the goods.

In equity, which was concerned mainly with time stipulations in contracts for the sale of interests in land, time was not regarded as being of the essence. Thus, failure to complete a contract for the sale of land in accordance with the time laid down in the contract did not entitle the innocent party to repudiate the contract unless, as in *Union Eagle v Golden Achievement* (above), time has been made of the essence. However, although the innocent party cannot refuse to accept late performance of a contract in which time is not of the essence, the offending party will be liable to pay damages: see *Raineri v Miles* (1981).

Where time was not originally of the essence, one party can make time of the essence by giving the other party reasonable notice of the requirement of performance by a particular time. In *Charles Rickards v Oppenheim* (1950), R sold a Rolls Royce chassis to O. O required a body to be built on the chassis and R agreed to have it built, subcontracting the work. The work was to take six months or, at the most, seven months and should, therefore, have been ready by the end of March. The work was not completed by the end of March but O continued to press for delivery. Eventually he wrote to R and said that if the car wasn't ready by 25 July, he would buy another car instead. The car wasn't ready so O bought a replacement. R completed the car in October and then sued O when he refused to take delivery, arguing that he had waived the original time limit and that, therefore, R's obligation was to complete the car within a reasonable time. The Court of Appeal held that O had waived the original delivery date but that he was permitted to resume his right to a delivery date by giving reasonable notice. This he had done.

DISCHARGE BY EXPRESS AGREEMENT

The problems with discharge by express agreement tend to centre upon the consideration for the discharge. Where Keith agrees to sell Brendan a car for £5,000, and both parties agree to cancel the deal, there is no problem. Both are relieved from their contractual obligations under the contract and the relief of one is consideration for the relief of the other.

Where the original obligation is replaced by another, the problem of consideration is overcome: the arrangement is called an 'accord and satisfaction'. For example, if Mick sells goods to Tim for £500 and Tim pays the £500, the contract is discharged by performance. If, on the other hand, Tim does not have £500 but offers to pave Mick's driveway in satisfaction of the debt, there is an accord and satisfaction, whereby Mick's entitlement to the £500 becomes the consideration for Mick entering into a fresh contract with Tim whereby Tim paves his drive.

Where the more difficult problem arises is in the case where one party agrees to discharge the other party from liability by releasing the other party from some or all of the other's contractual obligations, but without receiving anything in return. For example, suppose, in the example above, Mick had agreed to waive the debt of £500 so that Tim paid nothing for the goods supplied. This problem has been dealt with when the equitable doctrines of promissory estoppel and waiver were dealt with in Chapter 5.

DISCHARGE BY BREACH

Sometimes a party breaches a condition of the contract or, in the case of an innominate term, breaches the term in a way that amounts to a repudiation of the contract. In either case, the innocent party may affirm the contract and sue for damages or may accept the other party's repudiation and may regard himself as discharged from any further obligation under the contract (see Chapter 7).

In *Vitol SA v Norelf Ltd, The Santa Clara* (1996), the House of Lords had to decide whether formal notification of acceptance needs to be given by the innocent party to the defaulting party, or whether the innocent party, by failing to make further performance of the contract, accepts the defaulting party's repudiation. In this case, buyers of a cargo of propane gas at $400 per tonne wrongfully repudiated the contract by telex, which came to the sellers' notice on 11 March. The sellers failed to accept this repudiation expressly, but did not attempt to carry out the contract by attempting to deliver the goods. Instead, they sold the cargo elsewhere for $170 per tonne on 15 March. The buyers heard nothing further until they received a letter from the sellers' solicitor on 9 August claiming US $950,000 damages. The question arose as to whether the sellers had accepted the buyers' repudiation or not. If they had, they could claim damages from the buyers: if not, they were not entitled to damages. The House of Lords accepted the sellers' argument that their failure to perform the contract could amount to acceptance. An act of acceptance of repudiation does not have to be in a particular form; it is sufficient that the communication or conduct clearly and unequivocally conveys to the defaulting party that the innocent party is treating the contract as being at an end.

In *Federal Commerce and Navigation v Molena Alpha* (1979), the charterers of three ships were entitled under identical charterparties, that is, the contracts under which the ships were chartered, to make deductions from the hire charge in the event of certain occurrences, one of which was 'slow steaming'. A dispute arose over deductions made for slow steaming and in retaliation the owners of the vessel instructed the captains of the vessels to issue bills of lading endorsed 'subject to lien for freight', rather than indicating that freight had been pre-paid. (A bill of lading is a detailed receipt issued by the captain of a vessel when goods are loaded on to his vessel. The bill acts as a document of title so that goods are often sold while they are at sea. A lien on goods is the right to retain them pending payment of charges. Thus, what the owners of the vessels did in this case meant that the transported goods were unsaleable.) The charterers repudiated the contract. It was held that the action of the owners was a breach which went to the root of the contract. The charterers were therefore justified in their repudiation of the contract.

If one party announces his intention not to proceed with the contract, or does some act that prevents him from proceeding with the contract, before the contract is due to be performed, this is called an anticipatory breach. The consequence of an anticipatory breach is that the innocent party may accept the other party's repudiation and bring an action for breach of contract immediately: he does not need to wait until the time for performance arrives in order to see whether the other party changes his mind and decides to perform the contract. In *Hochster v De La Tour* (1853), H entered into a contract with D on 12 April whereby H would act as a tour guide for D beginning on 1 June. On 11 May, D informed H that he had changed his mind and did not wish to go on with the contract. On 22 May, H issued a writ claiming damages for breach of contract.

However, if one party acts in good faith, relying on what he genuinely believes to be his rights under the contract, the other party is not entitled to regard this as a repudiation of the contract. In *Woodar Investment Development v Wimpey* (1980), Woodar contracted to sell Wimpey a piece of land. The contract provided that Wimpey was entitled to rescind the contract if, *prior to completion* (that is, between the contracts being exchanged and the land being conveyed to Wimpey), a statutory authority shall have commenced to purchase the land. In fact, steps had been taken to effect a compulsory purchase *before* contracts were exchanged. Wimpey wished to escape from the contract because land prices had fallen and they therefore suggested a re-negotiation, stating that unless this were done they would exercise their right to rescind the contract relying on the compulsory purchase clause. It was held that Wimpey had not repudiated the contract since they thought that their action was within the terms of the contract, therefore they were not liable in damages for wrongful repudiation. (Woodar, in a bid to mitigate their loss, had sold the land to a third party after Wimpey had purported to rescind. Thus, Woodar rather than Wimpey were in breach of contract, though Wimpey made no claim against them.)

One danger in failing to accept an anticipatory breach of contract is that if the breach is not accepted as bringing the contract to an end and a frustrating event takes place before performance becomes due, the contract will be frustrated. In *Avery v Bowden* (1855), A chartered a ship to B. B agreed to load the ship with cargo at Odessa within 45 days. At Odessa, B told A's captain that he had no cargo for the ship and advised the ship to depart. The ship nevertheless remained. Before the 45 days had expired, the Crimean War broke out, frustrating the contract. *Held*: B's words of advice were not strong enough to amount to a repudiation of the contract. But even if they had been, the fact that A's captain insisted upon awaiting a cargo would have meant that he had not accepted the repudiation. The contract would have terminated through frustration. (In such circumstances, A would not, of course, be entitled to bring an action for damages.)

In some cases, the innocent party might be able to continue with the contract despite the guilty party's wrongful repudiation. For example, if Lucy contracts to decorate the interior of my house and I change my mind and repudiate the contract, there is nothing she can do to continue with the contract, since I will not allow her to enter my house. However, if I ask my local newspaper to place an advertisement stating that my car is for sale and, before the advert appears, I sell my car and request that the advertisement be withdrawn, the newspaper will be able to continue with the contract without my co-operation and may refuse to accept my repudiation of the contract.

In a case where the innocent party opts to continue with the contract rather than accept the repudiation, he does not owe a duty to mitigate his loss. He may continue with performance despite the other party's wishes. In *White and Carter (Councils) v McGregor* (1962), the House of Lords held that there is no duty to mitigate where the innocent party refuses to accept the guilty party's anticipatory breach as repudiating the contract. This is because, said the Lords, the duty to mitigate arises only where a contract is brought to an end by the breach. In this case, the plaintiffs were in the business of supplying litter bins to local authorities. The bins were paid for by persons who advertised their businesses on the bins. The defendant's manager (who had authority to make contracts on behalf of the business) contracted with the plaintiffs whereby they would advertise the defendants' garage business on litter bins for three years. Later the same day, the defendants wrote repudiating the agreement. At the time they received the letter, the plaintiffs had done nothing towards carrying out the agreement. Nevertheless, they refused to accept the repudiation. They prepared the advertisement plates and exhibited them, as agreed, for the next three years. They made no attempt to minimise their loss by finding other advertisers to take the defendants' place. They sued for the full contract price. *Held* by the House of Lords: the plaintiffs didn't owe a duty to mitigate their loss, since that duty arises only when the contract comes to an end. The contract hadn't come to an end by the defendants' repudiation since the plaintiffs had refused to accept the repudiation.

However, if the plaintiff has no legitimate interest in continuing the contract, it may be that a duty to mitigate arises: see *Clea Shipping Corp v Bulk Oil International (No 2)* (1984).

Where a contract is to be performed in stages, for example, a sale by installments, whether a repudiatory breach has taken place depends upon the ratio of the instalment missed to the contract as a whole and the degree of probability that the breach will be repeated.

In *Maple Flock Co Ltd v Universal Furniture Products* (1934), M contracted to sell U 100 tons of flock to be delivered at the rate of three loads per week as required. After delivery of 18 loads, U wrote to M stating that they would accept no further deliveries. The ground for doing this was that the 16th load had been analysed and had been found to contain a chlorine content of over eight times the government standard. *Held*: the buyers were not entitled to refuse to accept further deliveries under the contract. Whether U were entitled to refuse to continue with the contract on the basis of one defective load depended upon the application of two tests. The first test is the ratio, quantitatively, which the breach bears to the contract as a whole. The second test is the degree of probability or improbability that the breach will be repeated. Applying their first test, the court clearly did not regard a defective one-and-a-half tons out of a contract for 100 tons to be a very high ratio. On the second test, the court pointed out that there had been 20 satisfactory deliveries both before and after the delivery objected to and that there was no indication that there was anything wrong with any of the other deliveries. The court was of the opinion that the breach was an isolated instance and unlikely to be repeated.

CHAPTER 16

REMEDIES FOR BREACH OF CONTRACT

There are three principal remedies for breach of contract. These are:

(a) damages;

(b) a decree of specific performance; and

(c) injunction.

DAMAGES

Damages is the common law remedy for breach of contract. It consists of a payment of money. The purpose of damages in the law of contract is to put the injured party in the position he would have been in if the contract had been carried out. In *Sunley v Cunard White Star* (1940), D agreed to carry a machine belonging to P to Guernsey. However, the machine was delivered a week late. P were not able to show that they had an immediate use for the machine and were, therefore, not able to show that they had lost any profit. *Held:* P were entitled to £20, representing one week's depreciation of the machine, and the sum of £10 as interest on the capital cost.

Nominal damages

Liability for breach of contract does not depend (as some torts do) on the fact that the plaintiff has suffered damage. However, if the plaintiff has suffered no damage as a result of the breach, he will be awarded only nominal damages (that is, a conventional sum, say £2). In *Staniforth v Lyall* (1830), the charterer of a ship failed to load it. Employment was found for the ship elsewhere at no loss. *Held:* P was entitled to nominal damages only.

In addition to being awarded only nominal damages, the plaintiff may well be ordered to pay all or part of his own costs, though the normal rule is that costs are awarded against the losing party.

Punitive damages

As the name suggests, these damages have a punitive element. In English law, such damages are not awarded for breach of contract.

General damage

This consists of items which are not precisely quantifiable and must be left to the court to assess. Thus, pain and suffering, loss of amenities, disappointment, injured feelings or inconvenience are general damages. Loss of future earnings (that is, after the court case), loss of future profits, etc, are also general damages.

Until *Jarvis v Swans Tours* (1973), it was thought that, although damages for injured feelings are commonplace in tort, they had no application to breach of contract. This was because in *Addis v Gramophone Co* (1909), the House of Lords had refused to give any compensation for injured feelings to a manager who had been dismissed from his job in humiliating circumstances. He was entitled to damages for loss of salary and commission but that was all.

In *Jarvis v Swan's Tours* (1973), D advertised a house-party skiing holiday at the Hotel Krone in Morlialp, Switzerland, promising participants 'a great time'. They stated that the hotel's proprietor spoke English; that the hotel bar would be open several evenings in the week; that there would be a yodeller evening; that there would be the service of a representative; that there would be skis, sticks and boots for hire, among other things. In fact, the proprietor spoke no English; the hotel bar was an unoccupied annex which was open on only one evening; the yodeller evening consisted of one man from the locality who came in in his working clothes and sang four or five songs quickly; the representative was there during the first week but not the second; there were no appropriate skis for hire during the first week. Further, the house party consisted of 13 people during the first week, but only P during the second, and the skiing proved to be some distance from the hotel. P had paid £63.45 for the holiday. The county court judge assessed the defects at 50% but didn't take into account P's disappointment at having his fortnight's holiday ruined. On appeal, the Court of Appeal increased damages to £125, to take account of P's disappointment. *Jarvis* was followed in *Jackson v Horizon Holidays* (1975).

In *Heywood v Wellers* (1976), H employed a solicitor to obtain an injunction to prevent a third party molesting her. The solicitors failed to do this and H was molested. She suffered mental distress in consequence. *Held*: she was entitled to damages for mental distress.

However, the circumstances in which the court may award damages for mental distress are limited to contracts in which there is a 'mental element'.

In *Bliss v South East Thames Area Health Authority* (1985), a specialist was dismissed in breach of contract following his refusal to co-operate in psychiatric tests. He claimed damages for mental distress. It was held that damages for mental distress can be given only where a contract has a mental element, for example, where, as in a holiday contract, the plaintiff is promised enjoyment in addition to travel and accommodation (presumably you're not expected to enjoy yourself at work!).

Special damage

This consists of a specific item of loss which P must detail in his statement of claim. Thus, loss of profits, loss of earnings, etc, up to the date of the trial, will be special damage. (Loss of earnings or profit after the trial will be general damage.) The difference between the price paid for, for example, a holiday, a business, goods, etc, and the value of the defective holiday, business, or goods, etc, will be special damage.

AMOUNT OF DAMAGES

The general principle is that P must be put in the position he would have been in if the contract had been carried out. This means that, in theory, the law of contract compensates for loss of expectation. For example, if B buys a painting for £50,000, which is said to be by Picasso and, in breach of contract, it turns out to be by an unknown painter and is worth only £1,000, B is entitled as damages to the difference between what it is worth and *what it would have been worth* if it had been genuine. Thus, if the painting would have been worth £1 m, B will be entitled to £999,000 in damages. However, problems of proving the value of what one has contracted for mean that, in practice, the plaintiff will often be awarded only the loss he has suffered by relying on the other party's contractual promises.

Under influences from the USA, English academics are now accepting the categorisation of losses into:

Expectation loss and reliance loss

(a) Expectation loss

This is where P claims the value of what he had expected to get but hasn't got: he is to be put into the position he would have been in if the contract had been carried out.

(b) Reliance loss

This is where P has incurred expenditure as a result of the contract, which is lost because of D's breach of contract; P is to be put into the position he would have been in if the contract had never been made.

In addition, P may be entitled to the equitable remedy of restitution, whereby D has to repay any monies paid under the contract to P. As a general rule, restitution is only granted where there has been a total failure of consideration. Thus, in *McRae v Commonwealth Disposals Commission* (1951), where the plaintiff was sold and paid for a non-existent tanker, he was entitled to his money back.

Usually, P will be entitled to either expectation loss or reliance loss but not both. This is because, in order to arrive at an expectation loss, any reliance loss must be taken into account, since the reliance expenditure would have had to have been incurred in order to achieve the expectation. However, this is not always the case.

Suppose, for example, that A contracts to hire a concert hall from B for one night for £1,000. The tickets are printed and publicity issued at a cost of £1,000. B then wrongfully repudiates the contract with the result that A must pay £1,500 to hire similar hall from C. A will be entitled to expectation loss of £500 (the difference between what he expected to pay and what he had to pay for the hall) and reliance loss of £1,000 in respect of the wasted expenditure on the tickets.

If, on the other hand, the concert had to be cancelled altogether because there was no suitable substitute hall, A's claim might be as follows:

Expected total receipts:			£10,000
Less	printing and publicity	£1,000	
	hire of hall	£1,000	£ 2,000
			£ 8,000

Here the reliance loss was taken into account in quantifying the expectation loss.

To take a further example, suppose A sells an industrial machine to B on terms that B is to be responsible for dismantling the machine on A's premises and transporting it to his own. The cost of the machine is £5,000. The cost of dismantling and transporting is a further £5,000. Owing to a latent defect which was not apparent when B examined the machine on A's premises, the machine fails to function. If it had functioned properly, it would have been worth £30,000. As it is, it is worth nothing. Further, B would have made £1,000 profit from the machine from the date it was installed, to the date on which he could reasonably acquire a replacement. The claim for damages would be as follows:

(a) Expectation loss:	expected value of the machine	£30,000	
Plus	loss of profits	£1,000	
			£31,000
Less	restitution of price	£5,000	
	cost of removal, etc	£5,000	£10,000
			£21,000

(b) Reliance loss:	cost of removal, etc	£5,000	
Plus	restitution of price	£5,000	
			£10,000

Expectation loss is a superior claim to reliance loss in this example. However, this will not always be the case. Sometimes the claimant makes a bad bargain, in which case reliance loss may well be superior. Sometimes the expectation loss is so speculative that the court will not allow it. In *McRae v Commonwealth Disposals Commission* (1951), the defendants sold the plaintiffs a tanker for £285. In fact, the tanker did not exist. However, before they discovered this, the plaintiffs had spent around £3,000 in mounting a salvage expedition. In claiming expectation loss, they alleged that the tanker and its contents would have been worth £300,000. They based their claim on the average size of a tanker. The claim was dismissed as being too speculative and the plaintiffs were awarded their reliance loss instead (£3,000), plus restitution of the price of the tanker.

Expectation loss

We will examine two converse situations. The first is where the seller of goods or services is in default. The second is where the buyer is in default.

Seller in default

Expectation loss may occur where A has promised to sell goods to B but, on the date agreed for delivery, refuses to deliver. In that case, s 51 of the Sale of Goods Act 1979 provides that the buyer is entitled to damages equal to the difference between the contract price and the market price which prevails at the delivery date. In other words, the buyer is entitled to be compensated for the loss of his bargain.

Example: A agrees to sell 100 cwt of potatoes to B at £5 per cwt. A refuses to deliver. On the agreed delivery date, the market price of potatoes is £7 per cwt. B is entitled to £2 per cwt damages.

If no market exists, then the court must put a value on the goods. This may well be the amount that B has had to spend in purchasing the contracted goods. Thus, if, in the example above, there were no market in potatoes but B could show that he had had to pay £8 per cwt to purchase the contracted goods elsewhere, he would be entitled to £3 per cwt damages.

A good example of expectation loss is to be found in *Barry v Heathcote Ball* (2000). In this case, an auctioneer advertised an auction as being 'without reserve'. In the auction were two new engine tuning machines. They were being sold by Customs and Excise because the manufacturers had run into VAT payment problems. The auctioneer valued these at £14,000 each. If bought new from the manufacturers, they would have cost £14,521 each. The claimant bid £200 each. There were no other bidders and, although there was no reserve price, the auctioneer withdrew the machines from the sale and sold them privately for £1,500 some time later. The claimant argued, and the court accepted, that failure to sell the machines to him was a breach of contract. He argued that he was entitled in damages to the difference between the amount he had bid (£400) and the current value of the machines (£28,000). The court agreed with this analysis. It had been argued, on behalf of the defendant, that the machines were worth what they had been eventually sold for or that they were worth the maximum amount which the claimant had said he would have bid for them, that is, £1,000. However, the claimant had wanted to use the machines in his business, not to trade them. There was no evidence that he could have secured the machines for less than £14,000 each. Therefore, the measure of damages was the difference between what the claimant had agreed to pay for the machines and what it would cost him to buy replacement machines.

This principle, suitably amended, is of general application, and can be applied to subject matter other than goods.

For example: A agrees to hire a coach from B for a journey to Italy. The cost is to be £2,000. B withdraws from the deal. A has to pay C £3,000 to secure a suitable coach. A is entitled to £1,000 damages.

If the seller's default is that he has carried out the contract defectively, the measure of damages is the cost of curing the defect or the difference in value between what was tendered and what was due under the contract. Where the defect is relatively slight and the cost of cure is disproportionate, it may be that the court will value the breach on the basis of the amenity lost by the plaintiff, which is effectively a 'difference in value' award.

In *Ruxley Electronics and Construction v Forsyth* (1995), the question arose regarding the proper measure of damages for defective building works. F contracted with the plaintiffs to build a swimming pool in his garden. The contract expressly stated that the maximum depth of the pool should be 7 ft 6 in. F required it to be that depth for diving. In fact, the maximum depth of the pool was 6 ft 9 in and the maximum depth at the point where people would dive in was 6 ft. The question arose as to the measure of damages to which F was entitled. The trial judge made the following findings: (a) the pool as constructed was perfectly safe to dive into; (b) F had no intention or desire to fit a diving board and would be unlikely to form such a desire in the future; (c) there was no evidence that the shortfall in depth had decreased the value of the pool; (d) the only practicable method of achieving a pool of the required depth would be to demolish the existing pool and reconstruct a new one at a cost of £21,560; (e) he was not satisfied that F intended to build a new pool at such a cost (although F later gave the Court of Appeal an undertaking that he would build a new pool were he to be awarded the cost of reconstruction); (f) in addition such cost would be wholly disproportionate to the disadvantage of having a pool of only 6 ft as opposed to 7 ft 6 in and it would, therefore, be unreasonable to carry out the works; and (g) that the respondent was entitled to damages for loss of amenity in the sum of £2,500. The House of

Lords confirmed this award of damages, reversing the judgment of the Court of Appeal which had awarded F the cost of rebuilding the pool to the proper depth. While accepting that giving damages on the basis of the decrease in value (which was nothing, and therefore only nominal damages would have been given) was unfair, to rectify the unfairness by going to the other extreme and allowing the cost of reconstruction was unreasonable, since the pool could be used for the purpose for which it was required: evidence showed that a depth of 5 ft was adequate for safe diving without a diving board.

Section 53 of the Sale of Goods Act 1979 states that in the event of a breach of warranty of quality, the measure of damages is the estimated loss directly and naturally resulting and is, *prima facie*, the difference between the value of the goods at the time of delivery to the buyer and the value they would have had if they had been of the appropriate quality. However, the damage flowing naturally from the breach may, on occasion, be the cost of cure.

In *Bence Graphics International v Fasson UK* (1997), the defendants manufactured vinyl film, which they sold to the plaintiffs. The price of the film was £564,328. The plaintiffs used it to manufacture decals, printing words and symbols on the vinyl and cutting it to size. These decals were then sold to manufacturers of containers which were leased to shipping lines and were thus used all over the world. The decals were important in ensuring that the companies using the containers were able to identify them. The decals were warranted by the defendants for five years. However, the vinyl used to manufacture the decals degraded prematurely. The plaintiffs returned unused film to the value of £22,000. The defendants were clearly liable for breach of contract but the question arose as to what the measure of damages should be. Section 53(2) of the Sale of Goods Act 1979, enacting the first limb of the rule in *Hadley v Baxendale* (1854), provides: 'The measure of damages for breach of warranty is the estimated loss directly and naturally resulting, in the ordinary course of events, from the breach of warranty.' Section 53(3) goes on to say: 'In the case of breach of warranty of quality such loss is, *prima facie*, the difference between the value of the goods at the time of delivery to the buyer and the value they would have had if they had fulfilled the warranty.'

The trial judge held that the value of the decals at the time of delivery was nothing. The measure of damages was the difference between the value they would have had (£564,328) and the value at the time of delivery (nothing). The judge therefore awarded damages of £564,328. The defendants appealed, arguing that, since the defendants knew that the vinyl was to be made into decals, the damage flowing naturally from the breach was the amount of damages that the plaintiffs would have to pay in relation to claims made against them by their customers.

Held: the appeal would be allowed. Judgment for the plaintiffs was therefore amended to £22,000, representing the value of the vinyl which had been returned, plus damages to be assessed on the basis contended for by the defendants, that is, the damages that the plaintiffs would have to pay in relation to claims made against them by customers.

A disappointed buyer who made a good bargain is, in principle, entitled to claim the profit he would have made on the deal, providing this is not too remote (see, below, on 'remoteness'). However, such damage must be strictly proved and, in a case where the profit is at all speculative, the plaintiff may be restricted to his 'reliance loss'.

Buyer in default

In the converse case, where the buyer refuses to accept delivery of the goods, the measure of damages is, *prima facie*, the difference between the contract price and the market price on delivery day. However, again, where there is no market, the court may well accept evidence of the price at which the goods have been resold as being their market price. Again, too, the principle is of general application and applies, suitably amended, to subject matter other than goods.

In certain cases, the disappointed seller may be entitled to claim the loss of the profit he expected to make as a result of the contract. In *Thompson v Robinson* (1955), the defendants agreed in writing to purchase a Standard Vanguard motor-car from the plaintiffs. The defendants then wrongfully repudiated the contract. The plaintiffs consequently returned the car to their suppliers, who didn't ask for any compensation. The plaintiffs sued the defendants for breach of contract, claiming a loss of profit of £61. *Held*: the plaintiffs were entitled to claim their loss of profit from the defendants on the basis that, as the supply of Standard Vanguards exceeded the demand, the plaintiffs had, in effect, lost a sale because of the defendant's conduct.

It would seem, however, that where demand exceeds supply, the plaintiff will not be awarded a sum for loss of profit, since his ability to profit is limited by the number of cars he can get. In *Charter v Sullivan* (1957), the plaintiffs, who were motor dealers, agreed to sell a Hillman Minx car to the defendant. The defendant wrongfully repudiated the contract and the plaintiff resold the vehicle to another customer a few days later at the price which was to have been paid by the defendant. The plaintiff sued for breach of contract and claimed £97 15s damages. However, the plaintiff's sales manager gave evidence to the effect that they could sell all the Hillman Minx cars they could get. Thus, the claim that they had lost a profit because of the defendant's refusal to take the car was fallacious. If the plaintiffs could sell every Hillman Minx they could get, it followed that they would have sold the same number of cars and made the same number of fixed profits as they would if the defendant had carried out his promise. Therefore, the plaintiffs were awarded a nominal sum of £2 as damages.

In a case where a contract to sell *specific* goods is broken, and then the goods are resold elsewhere at a price equal to or greater than the original contract price, the seller will not be entitled to claim loss of profit. In *Lazenby Garages v Wright* (1976), L bought a second-hand BMW for £1,325. W agreed in writing to buy it from L for £1,670 but before taking delivery he changed his mind and refused to complete the purchase. Six weeks later L sold the car to someone else for £1,770. They then sued W for breach of contract, claiming £345 as loss of profit. *Held* by the Court of Appeal: L had suffered no loss since they got a higher price for the car than they had originally contracted for. The court refused to accept the argument that if W had bought the BMW as agreed, L could have sold a different car to the second purchaser.

Reliance loss

This is the loss which has been incurred in relying on the other party's promise.

As we have seen, the calculation of expectation loss will often include the reliance loss. Where this is the case, since a party cannot claim the same loss twice over, he must elect whether to ask for expectation loss or for reliance loss. In *Anglia Television v Reed* (1972), an actor was engaged to make a television film. The film had to be abandoned because of R's breach of contract. The plaintiff claimed the amount of expenditure which had been wasted because of the defendant's breach. Doubtless they opted for this rather than for a loss of profits claim because such a claim would have been speculative.

Note: the *Anglia Television* case laid down the controversial principle that, in appropriate cases, the plaintiff may be allowed to recover wasted expenditure which was incurred before the contract was entered into. Although it could not be said that the television company incurred the expenditure in reliance on the contract (since it did not exist at the time), they could argue that the contract was the cause of the wasted expenditure since, if Reed hadn't contracted to take part in the film, the company would have had time to engage another actor before production was due to take place.

A further example of a case where expectation loss was too speculative is *CCC Films v Impact Quadrant Films* (1985). The plaintiff had an agreement with the defendant whereby they would distribute the defendant's films in Europe. In pursuance of this agreement, the defendant formally delivered three films to the plaintiff in London. The plaintiff then handed them back and asked, in accordance with the contract, for them to be sent by registered post, insured, to Munich. The defendants sent the films by ordinary post and they were lost. The plaintiff claimed reliance loss only. Presumably a loss of profits claim would have been too speculative.

Note, however, that simply because the quantification of damages involves some element of speculation, this does not mean that damages may not be awarded. In *Chaplin v Hicks* (1911), a theatre manager agreed with the plaintiff that, if she would attend for interview with 49 others, he would select 12 out of the 50 and offer them a job. He failed to invite the plaintiff to interview. She claimed damages. He objected that even if she had attended she'd only have had a one in four chance of being selected. Nevertheless, damages of £100 were awarded.

Restitutionary damages

In an appropriate case, although the basis of damages in contract is normally to compensate for loss, restitutionary damages might be awarded. This was decided by the House of Lords in *Attorney General v Blake* (2000). George Blake was a spy who had written his memoirs. The Attorney General brought this case to try to prevent Blake receiving approximately £90,000 in royalties. Various legal principles by which this might be achieved were argued through the courts. However, the significant finding by the House of Lords was that damages for breach of contract are not confined to compensation for the loss which the innocent party has suffered but may, in appropriate cases, be awarded on a restitutionary basis (that is, to prevent the guilty party making a profit from his breach). Blake was in breach of his contract of employment with the Crown, under which Blake agreed not to divulge confidential information. The Attorney General was therefore entitled, on behalf of the Crown, to the profits which Blake had made from his breach.

REMOTENESS OF DAMAGE

Far-reaching damage may result from a breach of contract. The law, as a matter of policy, restricts the extent of the damage for which the defendant may be held liable.

The leading case on the question of remoteness of damage is *Hadley v Baxendale* (1854). The shaft in the plaintiff's mill was consigned to Greenwich using the services of the defendant, who was a carrier. The shaft was to act as a pattern for a new shaft. The defendants breached their contract in such a way that the shaft was not delivered at Greenwich at the time agreed and, because of the delay this caused in making the new shaft, the plaintiffs lost several days' production. They sued the defendants in respect of this loss. The appeal court divided recoverable damage into two types:

(a) that which flows naturally from the breach; and

(b) that which may reasonably be supposed to have been, in the contemplation of both parties at the time they made the contract, as the probable result of the breach of it.

It was held that the stoppage at the mill was not a natural result of the breach since, to give one alternative, the miller might have had a spare shaft. Nor was it in the contemplation of both parties at the time the contract was made, since there was nothing in the circumstances of the transaction to alert the carrier to the fact that a delay on his part might result in the mill being inactive. (Presumably if the miller had told the carrier that he had only one mill shaft and that, therefore, the return of the repaired shaft on time was imperative, the carrier would have been liable for the loss caused in consequence of the delay.)

The second limb of the rule has given rise to much academic discussion. In *Koufos v Czarnikow The Heron (No 2)* (1969), the House of Lords considered the meaning of the second limb of the rule in *Hadley v Baxendale*: that is, what is meant by the phrase 'reasonable contemplation'? In *Koufos v Czarnikow The Heron (No 2)*, the plaintiffs chartered a ship from the defendants in order to transport sugar which was to be sold at the sugar market in Basrah. The defendants knew that the plaintiffs were sugar merchants. They also knew that there was a sugar market at Basrah. They did not actually know that the sugar was to be sold immediately upon arrival but, according to Lord Reid, they knew that it was not unlikely that the sugar would be sold on arrival. The ship carrying the sugar deviated from the agreed route and, in consequence, was nine days late in reaching Basrah. The price of sugar had fallen between 22 November, when the ship should have arrived, and 2 December, when it actually arrived. The plaintiff claimed the difference between the price the sugar fetched and the price it would have fetched had it arrived on time. It was argued that the damage was too remote. Lord Reid applied the test of whether the damage was 'not unlikely' to result. He used the words as 'denoting a degree of probability considerably less than an even chance but, nevertheless, not very unusual and easily foreseeable'. He pointed out that the foreseeability test in tort imposes a much wider liability. The reason for this is because, in contract, if one of the parties wishes to protect himself against an unusual risk, he can direct the other party's attention to it before the contract is made. In tort, however, there is no such opportunity. In consequence, Lord Reid thought that the tortfeasor could not reasonably complain if he has to pay for some very unusual, but nevertheless foreseeable, damage which results from his wrongdoing. It was held that the damage was not too remote in this case as it was 'not unlikely' to have resulted from the breach.

One difficulty with distinguishing between remoteness of damage in tort and contract and in applying a different test in each case is that a contract can be breached in such a way that it gives rise to alternative claims in contract and tort. Lord Reid's view of the difference between the two has, therefore, attracted critical comment.

In *H Parsons v Uttley Ingham & Co* (1978), the Court of Appeal thought that it was absurd that the test for remoteness of damage should depend on the legal classification of the cause of action. (This is particularly so in areas where there is a substantial overlap between contract and tort, for example, in relation to the supply of services.) In this case, P owned an intensive pig farm on which they had a top grade herd. They entered into a contract with D whereby D would supply and erect a bulk-storage hopper for the purpose of storing pig food. D knew for what purpose the hopper was required. It was a term of the contract that the hopper should be fitted with a ventilated top. However, D sealed the ventilator for the purposes of transit and forgot to unseal it when it was installed. As the ventilator was 28 feet above the ground, P could not detect that it had been left closed. The result of this was that some of the pig food went mouldy through lack of adequate ventilation. P was not aware of this and continued to feed the food to the pigs. In consequence, the pigs developed a rare intestinal disease and 254 of them died. P sued for the loss of their livestock, valued at £10,000, and lost sales and turnover amounting to a further £10–20,000. D argued that they were liable only for the cost of the feed which replaced that from the hopper while the matter was being investigated: £18.02.

The Court of Appeal allowed the claim for loss of the pigs but not the claim for loss of profits. This conclusion was reached by two different routes. Lord Denning drew a distinction between claims relating to economic loss (that is, in this case, the loss of profits claim), where he said that such loss had to be in the contemplation of the parties at the time the contract was made, and those relating to physical loss, holding that, in the latter case, the test of remoteness is similar to that in tort, that is, it has to be a foreseeable consequence of the breach, though it may be more severe in extent than was foreseeable. (However, he cited no authority for this proposition and his ruling has been criticised on the ground that the distinction between economic loss and physical loss is not always easy to make.) Salmon and Orr LJJ found that the illness to the pigs was within the contemplation of the parties as being a serious possibility should the hopper be unventilated. They then went on to adapt the tort rule relating to extent of damage, and said that, providing the type of damage was within the contemplation of the parties, it is immaterial that the damage is more serious in extent than was contemplated. Thus, since it was within the contemplation of the parties that the pigs would suffer some illness, it was immaterial that the illness took the form of a rare virus which killed the pigs: the defendants were still liable for the loss of the pigs. However, the loss of sales and profit could not be said to have been within the contemplation of the parties at the time the contract was made and, therefore, these losses were too remote. The exact line of the reasoning of Salmon LJ is not entirely clear, but he seems to have been saying that since it was foreseeable that the pigs would suffer some illness, the fact that the illness took an extreme form resulting in death did not make the loss of the pigs too remote. However, since only illness was foreseeable, it was not in the contemplation of the parties that the pigs would die, resulting in loss of sales and profit and therefore that damage was too remote. The court was unanimous in their condemnation of the idea that the test for remoteness of damage should differ according to the cause of action pursued by the plaintiff.

Note: that the test of remoteness in cases where negligence is alleged is foreseeability of the loss. In *South Australia Asset Management v York Montague* (1996), financiers advanced money against the security of property which had been negligently valued. This caused loss when the properties were sold to realise the security. The loss was exacerbated by a general fall in the prices of property. The lenders argued that the valuers should be liable for *all* the losses which they had incurred because, had they known the true value of the property against the security of which they were lending, they would not have lent at all. *Held* by the House of Lords: the valuers were liable only for the foreseeable loss caused by their negligence. They were not liable for losses caused by the fall in the property market.

A claim for loss of exceptionally good profits will not be allowed unless the plaintiffs made known, expressly or impliedly, that exceptional profits were at risk unless the contract were carried out in accordance with its terms. If this is not the case, the plaintiff's claim will be limited to the normal amount of profit he would have made if the contract had been carried out correctly. In *Victoria Laundry v Newman Industries* (1949), P agreed to buy a boiler from D for the purpose of expanding their existing cleaning and dying business. D knew that the boiler was required immediately. However, the boiler was damaged while it was being dismantled by third parties on behalf of D. Delivery was delayed for five months. P claimed damages as follows: £16 per week loss of profit in respect of the large number of extra customers that could have been taken on; £262 per week which they could have made by virtue of an extremely lucrative dyeing contract which they had with the Ministry of Defence. *Held*: since D knew that P wanted the boiler for immediate use, they were liable for the ordinary profits which P had lost by reason of the delay in delivery. However, since they did not know of the extremely lucrative dyeing contract, they were not liable for the loss of profits related to the MOD contract.

An illustration of loss not being in the contemplation of the parties is provided by *Pilkington v Wood* (1953), P bought a house in Hampshire for £6,000. His solicitor negligently failed to notice that the title to the house was defective. Almost two years later, P went to work in Lancashire and wished to sell the Hampshire house in order to buy one in Lancashire. A purchaser for the Hampshire house was found (at £7,500, to include certain additional land since acquired by the plaintiff) but when P was unable to make a good title, the purchaser was not willing to pay the price. P claimed as damages:

(a) the difference between the market value of the house at the time it was purchased and the actual value with its defective title;

(b) expenses resulting from having to travel to Lancashire and to live in a hotel and phone his wife nightly, because of his inability to sell the Hampshire house; and

(c) the interest on the bank overdraft which he had taken in order to buy the Hampshire house.

It was held that only the first of these items was recoverable. The others were too remote as not being within the contemplation of the parties at the time the contract was made.

MITIGATION OF LOSS

Every party who suffers loss as a result of a breach of contract owes a duty to take reasonable steps to mitigate his loss. There is a parallel duty in the law of tort and, therefore, tort cases would seem to have equal applicability to contract. In *Brace v Calder* (1895), an employee of a partnership was dismissed when the partnership was dissolved and reconstituted. He was offered employment by the new partnership, to begin when his employment with the old one came to an end. He refused the new employment and sued for breach of contract (he had not been given the appropriate notice of termination). *Held*: the plaintiff owed a duty to mitigate his loss.

A tort case illustrates the principle of mitigation well. In *Luker v Chapman* (1970), the plaintiff lost his right leg below the knee in a traffic accident caused by the negligence of the defendant. In consequence, he was forced to give up his employment as a telephone engineer. He refused a clerical job and chose to do teacher training instead. It was held that he had a duty to mitigate his loss by accepting the clerical job. Thus, damages for loss of earnings would be based on the difference between his earnings as a telephone engineer and what he could have earned in the clerical job during the period of teacher training.

A difficult point arises in the case where the defendant is guilty of an anticipatory breach of contract (that is, he wrongfully repudiates the contract before the time appointed for performance). In such a case, the innocent party may accept the other party's repudiation and sue for breach of contract. On the other hand, he may treat the contract as still in being. If he does this, does he owe a duty to mitigate his loss? In other words, despite the fact that he knows his performance of the contract will be wasted since the other party no longer requires it, may he still go ahead and complete his part of the bargain (assuming, of course, that he is able to do so without the other's complicity)? In a controversial decision, the House of Lords answered 'yes': see *White and Carter (Councils) v McGregor* (1962). By a three to two majority, the House held that there is no duty to mitigate in such circumstances, because the duty to mitigate arises only where a contract is brought to an end by the breach. In this case, the plaintiffs refused to accept the defendants' purported repudiation of the contract. Since this meant that the contract was still in existence, the plaintiffs owed no duty to mitigate their loss (for full facts of this case, see Chapter 15, p 318).

However, it was suggested in the *White and Carter* case, by Lord Reid, that if the plaintiff had no legitimate interest, financial or otherwise, in continuing to perform the contract, a duty to mitigate might arise. This occurred in *Clea Shipping Corp v Bulk Oil International (No 2)* (1984). The defendants chartered a ship from the plaintiffs. The defendants wrongfully repudiated the charter. Despite the repudiation, the shipowners kept the ship fully crewed and ready to sail until the end of the charter period. It was held that the shipowners had no legitimate interest in doing this and should have mitigated their loss. They were therefore entitled only to damages rather than the hire charge for the ship.

LIQUIDATED DAMAGES AND PENALTY

The parties to a contract may agree beforehand what sum shall be payable as damages in the event of a breach by one or other of the parties. For example, a builder may agree with his customer that he shall pay damages of £100 per day for every day that the building he is constructing remains uncompleted after the date set for completion. The law may categorise the promised damages as *liquidated damages* or as *a penalty*.

Liquidated damages

Providing that the stated sum is a genuine attempt to pre-estimate the loss that the innocent party will suffer, the court will give effect to it. It is then immaterial whether the actual damage suffered is more or less than the amount provided for in the contract: the innocent party must accept the amount which the contract gives. In *Cellulose Acetate Silk Co v Widnes Foundry* (1933), the defendants entered into a contract to erect a plant for the plaintiff by a certain date. They also agreed to pay £20 per week damages for every week that they took beyond the stipulated date. They were 30 weeks late. The plaintiffs claimed their actual loss which was £5,850. *Held*: the defendants were bound to pay only £600 (that is, £20 x 30 weeks).

Penalty

On the other hand, the 'damages clause' may, in reality, be in the nature of a threat held over the other party to ensure his performance. In such a case, the sum specified as being payable is called a penalty. Since the penalty is intended to ensure performance, equity has ruled that the innocent party is sufficiently compensated by being given the actual amount of his loss.

Where, however, the stipulated penalty is insufficient to compensate the claimant, he has a choice:

(a) he may sue on the penalty clause, in which case he cannot recover more than the stipulated sum; or

(b) he may sue for breach of contract and recover damages in full.

It is sometimes difficult to determine whether a sum payable under a contract is liquidated damages or a penalty. Guidelines have been developed by the courts to assist in distinguishing between the two. These were summarised as follows in *Dunlop v New Garage* (1915):

(a) the fact that the parties may have used the expression 'penalty' or 'liquidated damages' is not conclusive. The court must decide whether the stipulated sum is a genuine pre-estimate of the probable loss (in which case it is liquidated damages) or not (in which case it is a penalty);

(b) the sum will be a penalty if it is extravagant and greater than the greatest possible loss which could follow from the breach;

(c) if the obligation of the promisor under the contract is to pay a sum of money by a certain date, and it is agreed that if he fails to do so he shall pay a larger sum, the larger sum will be a penalty. In *Betts v Burch* (1859), a contract for the sale of the stock-in-trade and furnishings of a pub provided that, in the case of default in performing the contract, either party would pay the other £50. It was held that this was a penalty, since if the buyer defaulted even to the extent of failing to pay £1, he would have to pay £50; and

(d) subject to the preceding rules, if there is only one event upon which a sum is payable, it is liquidated damages.

Interest on the late payment of commercial debts

The late payment of commercial debts is said to cost small firms millions of pounds in interest payments because they have to borrow money to fill a gap in their cash resources caused by the money which is owed to them. Some companies have attempted to rectify the situation by imposing in their conditions of sale a condition that interest should be paid on debts which are not settled within the given credit period (usually 28/30 days). However, if the customer ignores this and simply pays the net amount of the invoice, few creditors will take any further action, particularly where the creditor is a small company dealing with a larger one. In the first place, it is hardly worth the time pursuing the customer for a relatively small amount of interest (it is the cumulative effect spread over a period of time and a number of debtors which is at the root of the problem). Secondly, there is the possibility that customer relations will not survive such conduct and that the customer will be lost. Thus, unless the default of the customer amounts to a worthwhile amount in interest, the matter is rarely pursued.

One other method by which a large company is able to postpone the payment of a debt due to a small company, in this case, legitimately, is to stipulate for a longer period of credit. The author has encountered extreme cases where an internationally known company imposed a contractual term on its small company suppliers which gave it six months' credit in relation to payment for goods and services supplied under the contract. (Under the new Act (see below), if the debtor tries to extend the credit period after the contract was made, the new term must satisfy the requirement of reasonableness. However, it does not prevent an unreasonable credit period being 'agreed' as part of the initial contract.)

It must be questioned, therefore, for the reasons set out above, whether the Act which is now being brought into force to provide for interest on late payment of debts, will be of any great benefit to a small company whose larger customers habitually pay late. As you will see, the provisions of the Act are by no means straightforward. In particular, there are complex provisions which allow the parties to displace the Act and to make their own contractual agreement on interest. There are also provisions which give a wide discretion to the courts in implementing the right to interest. Despite these significant shortcomings, it may be that, although the Act in itself will have little effect, it will act as a signal to late payers that the government intends to alleviate the problem and that this may only be the first step. Such considerations may encourage late payers to behave more considerately. The Act may be taken as a signal that if the problem persists, the government may take stronger measures: perhaps making late payment subject to intervention by the Office of Fair Trading, perhaps even making it a criminal offence, and perhaps controlling at the outset the terms of contracts by which large companies insist upon extended credit from smaller ones.

Late Payment of Commercial Debts (Interest) Act 1998

Section 1 provides that it is an implied term in a contract to which this Act applies that any qualifying debt created by the contract carries simple interest. Most business debts will be qualifying debts. The Act applies to contracts for the supply of goods and services, apart from excepted contracts. Excepted contracts are consumer credit contracts, certain contracts such as mortgages intended to operate by way of security, and any contract designated by the Secretary of State as excepted.

The supplier and purchaser must each be acting in the course of a business. This provision may cause a difficulty, since in *Stevenson v Rogers*, for the purpose of s 14 of the Sale of Goods Act, it was held that any sale in the course of a business was sufficient to bring the sale within the scope of s 14. However, in *Davies v Sumner* it was held that for the purpose of the Trade Descriptions Act 1968, the sale needed to be integral to the purpose of the business. Thus, if a solicitors' practice sells a car belonging to the practice, would interest be payable if the buyer was a business buyer who paid late? The answer would be 'yes' if the *Stevenson v Rogers* test is applied, but 'no' if the *Davies v Sumner* test is applied. It is suggested that it would be unrealistic to apply the *Davies v Sumner* test in such a situation and that any sale by the business should qualify.

Statutory interest begins to run on the day after the relevant day for the debt. The provisions regarding the 'relevant day' become quite complex in respect of partially performed obligations, but for the most part the relevant day will be:

(a) the day agreed by the contract for payment unless the contract stipulates for payment in advance;

(b) if the contract stipulates for payment in advance, s 11 contains detailed provisions as to the relevant day but, broadly, these have the effect of the relevant day being the day on which the supplier performs his obligation. Thus, for example, Lisa enters into a contract with Mandy for the supply of a new computer. Mandy requires payment in two weeks in advance of the delivery date. Lisa fails to make this payment. Mandy may repudiate the contract and refuse to deliver the computer (remember that time is 'of the essence' for performance of obligations in a commercial contract). However, if despite lack of advance payment, Mandy supplies the computer, the relevant day will be the day of the supply and interest will begin to accrue from the following day;

(c) if the contract is one of hire, the last day of the hire period; or

(d) if none of the above applies, it will be the last day of the period of 30 days beginning with either (i) the day on which the obligation of the supplier was performed, or (ii) the day on which the purchaser has notice of the amount of the debt.

The Act allows the parties to contract out of it but subject only to strict safeguards. Section 8 provides that any contract terms which exclude the right to statutory interest are void unless the contract contains a substantial remedy for late payment.

Section 5 gives the court a wide discretion to disallow a claim, reduce the scope of a claim or to reduce the rate of interest. It allows the court to remit the statutory interest, either in whole or in part, where by reason of any conduct of the supplier the interests of justice require it. It also allows the court to reduce the statutory rate of interest. For example, Geri has received a bill from Victoria, payable in 30 days. However, Geri is arguing that previous goods supplied by Victoria, for which Geri has paid in full, have proved faulty. Geri is therefore claiming a set-off against the latest bill and has paid only part of it. Victoria is disputing this, and is claiming the unpaid portion of the bill. In addition, she is claiming interest under the Act. The court may take into account the reason why the bill was not paid and, even if it finds that Geri was wrong to have withheld payment, the fact that she had an arguable case may mean that the court will exercise its discretion and may remit the interest, in whole or in part, or may reduce the rate of interest for the whole or part of the period in question.

The rate of interest prescribed by regulations made under the Act is 8% over the prevailing Bank of England base rate.

At the moment, the Act is not fully in force and only small businesses may take advantage of its provisions. However, it is excepted to be fully in force by 2002.

SPECIFIC PERFORMANCE

The common law remedy for breach of contract was an award of damages. Thus, the only circumstances in which the performance of a contract was ordered at common law was if the contract required the payment of a sum of money. However, in certain cases, equity was prepared to order the defendant to perform what he had agreed to perform. It did this by making a decree of specific performance.

A decree of specific performance is exceptional. It will be made only where an award of damages is not an adequate remedy. Damages is not regarded as an adequate remedy in three circumstances:

(a) where the contract is for the sale of, or disposition of, an interest in real property (for example, land, houses, etc);

(b) where the contract is for commercially unique goods;

Section 52 of the Sale of Goods Act allows the court to make a decree of specific performance in a contract to sell specific or ascertained goods. The provisions of the Act do not fetter the court's discretion but, in practice, it seems that the courts will follow the rule from the old Court of Chancery that only where goods are not ordinary articles of commerce will a decree be made.

As a general rule, the court will regard damages as an adequate remedy if the plaintiff is able to purchase substitute goods. In *Cohen v Roche* (1927), a set of eight Hepplewhite chairs were regarded as ordinary articles of commerce and no order for specific performance was made. However, views may have changed by now!

In *Société des Industries Metallurgiques SA v The Bronx Engineering Co* (1975), B allegedly repudiated a contract to buy a machine from S and, in consequence, S told B that the machine would be sold to a Canadian buyer instead. B did not agree that he had repudiated the contract and obtained an injunction to prevent the machine being sold to Canada, pending the hearing of his action for specific performance of the contract. It was held that although the machine was not an 'ordinary article of commerce', S was not the only manufacturer of such machines. Therefore, specific performance would not be granted.

Where an alternative supplier of the goods is not available, specific performance may be granted. In *Sky Petroleum v VIP Petroleum* (1974), Sky operated petrol filling stations and had entered into a solus agreement with VIP whereby they would buy all their fuel supplies from VIP at fixed prices for a period of 10 years. Some three years into the agreement, at a time when there was a crisis in the Middle East and petrol was in short supply, the defendants purported to terminate the agreement on the ground of the plaintiff's alleged breach of contract. The plaintiff denied breach and, because the goods were not specific or ascertained and, therefore, a decree of specific performance would not be granted, the plaintiff sought an injunction to restrain the defendant from breaching the contract. Since the injunction had a similar effect to what a decree of specific performance would have had, the judge applied the test appropriate to specific performance in deciding whether or not to grant an injunction. He held that specific performance would have been available if the goods had been specific, because the goods were the only means of keeping the plaintiff's business going and they were not available elsewhere. Therefore damages would not have been an adequate remedy.

(c) where, exceptionally in other circumstances, damages would not be an adequate remedy.

A classic example of this is *Beswick v Beswick* (1968). We have already looked at this case in connection with privity of contract. You will recall that Mrs B's nephew purchased a coal business from Mr B on terms which included the payment of a pension to Mrs B after Mr B's death. The nephew refused to pay and Mrs B brought an action on behalf of her late husband to enforce the agreement. The difficulty with an award of damages was twofold: first, the House of Lords were of the opinion that Mr B's estate has suffered no loss attributable to the failure of the nephew to pay Mrs B her pension. Therefore nominal damages only would have been awarded. Secondly, even if the House had agreed that Mr B's estate was entitled to claim a realistic estimate of Mrs B's loss, the damages produced would have gone into the residue of Mr B's estate. Mrs B would not necessarily have been entitled to this. Therefore, in the circumstances, damages was not an adequate remedy and, in consequence, a decree of specific performance was granted.

In *Wolverhampton Corporation v Emmons* (1901), the plaintiffs contracted with the defendants whereby the defendants would demolish houses on a site and erect new ones. Although the defendants demolished the existing houses, they did not erect the new ones. The plaintiffs sued for specific performance. Normally damages would be an adequate remedy in a case such as this because the plaintiffs could contract with alternative builders to build the houses. However, it was not possible to do that in this case as the defendants were in possession of the site. Meanwhile, the plaintiffs were losing the income in rent they would have had from the new houses. *Held*: a decree of specific performance would be granted since damages did not provide an adequate remedy.

Specific performance is discretionary

The award of a decree of specific performance, because it is an equitable remedy, is discretionary. The exercise of discretion is not arbitrary, it is exercised according to established rules, such as 'he who seeks equity must do equity', 'he who comes to equity must come with clean hands', etc. However, where the court refuses a decree of specific performance, the plaintiff will usually be entitled to damages instead.

The court has refused a decree in the following circumstances:

Where the defendant is seeking to behave inequitably

The plaintiff sought to take advantage of a mistake by the defendant in pricing a property for sale: the defendant had already refused an offer of £2,000 but then wrote offering the land to the plaintiff for £1,250, intending to ask £2,250. The plaintiff accepted the offer by return of post and then, when the defendant refused to complete the contract, sued for a decree of specific performance. It was held that specific performance would not be granted: *Webster v Cecil* (1861).

Where compliance with a decree of specific performance would cause hardship to the defendant

In *Denne v Light* (1857), the defendant bought land which was surrounded by other land. On discovery that he had no right of way over the other land and could, therefore, not reach the land he had contracted to buy, he refused to complete the contract. A decree of specific performance was refused on the ground that it would cause hardship to the defendant.

Even if the hardship arises after the contract was made, the decree may be refused. In *Patel v Ali* (1984), the defendant contracted to sell her house. After the contract but before the conveyance she became disabled and heavily dependent upon her existing neighbours for help. It was held that specific performance of the contract would not be granted since this would cause hardship to the defendant.

Where the contract would require the constant supervision of the court

In *Ryan v Mutual Tontine* (1893), the defendants leased a flat to the plaintiffs, contracting that a porter would be in attendance to perform certain duties such as the delivery of letters, cleaning, etc. The porter had another job as a chef at a neighbouring establishment, and was frequently missing when he was required at the flats. The plaintiff sought specific performance of the contract. *Held*: specific performance would not be granted as this would require the constant supervision of the court.

However, in *Posner v Scott-Lewis* (1987), where the facts were similar, it was held that a decree would be granted. The court said that in deciding whether or not to grant a decree, the following considerations should be taken into account:

(a) is there a sufficient definition of what has to be done in order to comply with the order of the court?;

(b) will enforcing compliance involve superintendance by the court to an unacceptable degree?;

(c) what are the respective prejudices or hardships that will be suffered by the parties if the order is made or not made?

The court concluded that, in this case, the defendants could be ordered to appoint a porter within a defined time; such an order would not involve the constant supervision of the court, since if it was not complied with, the plaintiff could take steps to enforce compliance; compliance with the order would not be a hardship to the defendants.

Where the court would be unable to grant specific performance against the plaintiff: 'equality is equity'

In *Flight v Bolland* (1828), the court refused to grant a decree of specific performance to a minor on the ground that, owing to his minority, the contract could not have been specifically enforced against him.

A decree of specific performance is not available in a number of other circumstances. The principal example is a contract of personal service: it is seen as infringing a person's personal liberty if he were to be ordered to work for another. However, there is a growing trend nowadays to grant injunctions preventing someone from breaching a contract of personal service. It has been argued that this simply encourages the defendant not to breach his contract; it does not compel him to work under the contract (see *Warner Bros v Nelson*, below).

INJUNCTIONS

An injunction is an equitable remedy and, as such, is subject to the exercise of the court's discretion in a similar way to other equitable reliefs.

An injunction is an order by the court either to do something or not to do something. Breach of an injunction is contempt of court and is a serious matter.

An injunction may be prohibitory or mandatory. A mandatory injunction instructs the defendant to take positive steps to remedy a breach of contract which he has committed in the past.

A mandatory injunction is subject to the 'balance of convenience' test, that is, will the disadvantage to the defendant outweigh the advantage that the plaintiff will receive if an injunction is granted? Thus, the demolition of a building erected in breach of contract would not be ordered if the plaintiff will receive only a slight advantage from it, but in a case where a building was erected in breach of a restrictive covenant and the building blocked the plaintiff's sea view, the plaintiff was granted an injunction whereby the defendant was ordered to demolish the building.

A prohibitory injunction is granted to restrain the defendant from committing future breaches of contract. In *Lumley v Wagner* (1852), W agreed to sing at L's theatre for a period of three months. She contracted that during that time she would not sing elsewhere without L's written consent. An injunction was granted to prevent her singing elsewhere in breach of contract.

It was argued in *Warner Bros v Nelson* (1937) that to grant an injunction was tantamount to ordering specific performance of a contract of personal service and that, therefore, the injunction should not be granted. In this case, the famous film actress Bette Davis (whose real name was Nelson) was under exclusive contract to Warner Brothers. She proposed to go to work for a rival, in breach of her contract with Warner Brothers. *Held*: an injunction restraining her from doing so would be granted. Although it would have the effect of encouraging her not to breach her contract with Warner Brothers, it would not have the effect of forcing her to perform it, since she could, if she wished, take alternative employment in another field, as she was a woman of considerable ability.

This case can be contrasted with *Page One Records v Britton* (1967), in which the defendants, a pop group called 'The Troggs', contracted with the plaintiff whereby they would employ him as their manager for a period of five years. The contract further provided that they would employ no one else as their manager during that time. The parties had a serious disagreement, following which the defendants appointed another manager. The plaintiff sought an injunction restraining them from doing so. *Held*: the injunction would not be granted. In this case, the grant of an injunction would compel specific performance of the contract between the defendants and the plaintiffs, since the only alternative to appointing a new manager would be for the Troggs to manage themselves. This they did not have the ability to do. A prohibitory injunction was granted.

CHAPTER 17

SUPPLY OF GOODS AND SERVICES

We have seen that there is a body of general rules which apply to all contracts of whatever type. In addition, each type of contract has a number of rules which supplement (or, occasionally, replace) the general principles of contract law. We have no space to consider each type of specific contract which may be applicable to a business. We will, therefore, restrict the scope of this chapter to dealing with contracts by which the business gives or obtains the use of goods or services.

DISTINCTION BETWEEN VARIOUS TYPES OF GOODS AND SERVICES CONTRACTS

It is worth distinguishing at the outset between the various types of goods and service contracts which a business may enter into. This is because the different types of contract, although having similar consequences in many respects, may have different consequences in other respects. For example, if the sale of timber to be severed from land is regarded as a sale of goods (as it was in *Kursell v Timber Operators and Contractors* (1927)), then the contract does not have to be in writing (as it would have to be if the sale were regarded as the disposition of an interest in land); the timber would have to comply with the terms implied by ss 12–15 of the Sale of Goods Act: there are no real equivalents in relation to the disposition of an interest in land; property in the timber (that is, ownership of the timber) may pass from the seller to the buyer at a different time because the rules governing the passing of the property in a sale of goods are different to those governing passing of property in a disposition of an interest in land.

The most common contracts entered into by a business are as follows:

(a) sale of goods;

(b) hire-purchase;

(c) work and materials (including repairs);

(d) hire of goods (sometimes called 'lease of goods', sometimes called 'contract hire');

(e) contract for services; and

(f) contract of employment (sometimes called 'contract of service').

Contracts of employment differ so greatly from the others that we will not consider them here.

CONTRACTS FOR THE SUPPLY OF GOODS

A sale of goods is the archetypal contract by which a party secures possession and use of goods. A sale of goods is governed by the Sale of Goods Act (originally 1893, now 1979). This deals with matters such as the price of the goods, the right to reject the goods, the terms to be implied into the contract of sale, the time at which property (that is, ownership) of the goods passes from the buyer to the seller; the circumstances in which a non-owner of the goods can nevertheless pass on a good title to the goods; the remedies of the buyer, for example, if an incorrect quantity of goods is delivered; the rights of an unpaid seller, etc.

A contract which gives the right to possess and use goods may be one of three defined types, or it may be a residual contract under which goods are supplied. The three defined types are: contracts of sale of goods; of hire; of hire-purchase. The fourth, residual type may be any type of contract, not meeting the definition of a sale of goods, under which property in goods passes. A contract for the sale of work and materials is an example of the latter. This is a contract the substance of which is the skill of the worker rather than the transfer of goods: a contract to paint a portrait is an example.

What these four categories of contract have in common is that the terms implied by the law into the contract are similar in each case. Although the terms implied into a contract for the supply of goods are contained in three different Acts of Parliament, the terms implied into a sale of goods by ss 12–15 of the Sale of Goods Act 1979 are the basic implied terms, so that if you learn these, this will normally be sufficient for most purposes. The source of the terms implied into the other contracts is the Supply of Goods (Implied Terms) Act 1973 for contracts of hire-purchase; the Supply of Goods and Services Act 1982 for contracts of hire and residual goods contracts, under which property in goods is transferred but which do not come within the definition of a sale of goods. Because these contracts have the implied terms in common, the distinction between them is not always of great importance, but there are factors which they do not have in common which may still make it necessary to distinguish between them.

DEFINITION OF A SALE OF GOODS

Section 2 of the Sale of Goods Act 1979 defines a contract for the sale of goods as: '... a contract by which the seller transfers or agrees to transfer the property in goods to the buyer for a money consideration called the price ...'

A contract under which the right is given to possess and use goods may fail to meet the definition of a sale of goods for one of two main reasons:

(1) There is no sale or agreement to sell as required by s 2. The contract may be one of hire, hire-purchase or barter.

Hire

It is relatively easy to distinguish a contract of hire from a sale of goods, since it is never envisaged by the parties that property in the goods (that is, ownership) shall be transferred from the owner to the hirer.

A contract of hire is one under which one person bails (that is, gives entitlement to possession without ownership) goods to another in return for a payment. The payment may be a one-off, as in many cases of car hire, or it may be periodic, as where a householder hires a television. Hire contracts may be called 'rental agreements', 'leasing agreements', 'contract hire', etc, but legally they are all the same. Terms are implied into contracts of hire on similar lines to those implied into a sale or transfer of goods, by ss 7–10 of the Supply of Goods and Services Act 1982. If a hire contract comes within the definition of a 'consumer hire agreement', it will, in addition, be governed by the Consumer Credit Act 1974.

Hire-purchase

The distinction between a credit sale, a conditional sale and a hire-purchase contract is rather more subtle. A credit sale is a sale where the property in the goods passes to the buyer at the time of the sale, but the payment of the price is deferred by agreement. This is a sale of goods because the goods are sold not hired.

A conditional sale is a sale on credit terms under which the seller reserves title to the goods (that is, remains the owner) until a condition, usually the payment of the price, is met by the buyer. This, too, is a sale of goods because there is an agreement to sell.

A hire-purchase contract is a contract by which goods are delivered to a person who agrees to make periodic payments by way of hire, with an option to purchase the goods, which must be exercised at the latest at the completion of the hire period.

Hire-purchase contracts are governed principally by the Consumer Credit Act 1974, though the important *implied* terms are contained in ss 8–11 of the Supply of Goods (Implied Terms) Act 1973. Common law rules and other statutory rules will also be relevant.

When the hirer exercises his option to purchase, he enters into a contract for the sale of goods. Until that time, he is simply the hirer of the goods. This has important consequences in relation to transfer of title, that is, ownership, which will be dealt with in due course.

Because similar terms are implied into contracts of hire and hire-purchase as are implied into sale of goods, the distinction between a credit sale and conditional sale, on the one hand, and a contract of hire-purchase, appears to be significant only in respect of third party rights to goods which are wrongfully sold by the debtor (see Chapter 24, p 508) and even then the distinction between conditional sale and hire-purchase disappears in cases where the transaction is regulated by the Consumer Credit Act 1974 (that is, if the credit given is under £25,000 and the debtor is not a corporation). This, in fact, happened in *Forthright Finance Ltd v Carlyle Finance Ltd* (1997), where the pitfalls to a finance company of trying to dress up a conditional sale contract as a hire-purchase contract were clearly illustrated. F provided a car to S under what was described as a hire-purchase contract. The contract reserved title to the goods to F, but instead of the 'hirer' being required to exercise an option to purchase at the end of the 'hire' period, S was deemed to exercise the option when the last payment was made. Unfortunately for F, before the last payment was made, S wrongfully sold the car to C. F claimed the car back on the ground that it was only hired to S. *Held*: the contract, though described as 'hire-purchase', was really a conditional sale and therefore s 25 of the Sales of Goods Act operated to give C a good title to the car. (The agreement was not regulated by the Consumer Credit Act.)

Barter

A contract of barter is not a sale. Barter is where either: (a) goods are exchanged for goods; or (b) goods are exchanged for goods and some other consideration, such as money.

In the latter case, because there is money involved it may be difficult to determine whether the contract is one of barter or sale. However, it would seem that if the parties have put a money value on the goods involved in the transaction, the transaction will be a sale of goods. In *Dawson v Dutfield* (1936), the plaintiffs sold two second-hand lorries to the defendant. The price was £475, of which £250 was to be paid in cash and the balance by giving two other lorries in part-exchange. It was held that the transaction was a sale of goods. In a contrasting Irish case, a car was sold for £250 plus the trade-in of the customer's existing car. Since no monetary value had been placed on either the new car or the customer's trade-in, the contract was one of barter.

It is likely that little significance will attach to the difference nowadays, since the terms implied into a contract of barter and those implied into a sale of goods are substantially the same.

(2) The other main reason why a sale may fail to meet the definition of a sale of goods is because the property sold does not fall within the definition of 'goods'. In such a case, the sale may be one of land or a disposition of an interest in land; it may be a contract for work and materials or it may be a contract for the disposition of a chose in action (or, indeed, some other kind of contract).

Meaning of 'goods'

Section 61(1) provides that 'goods' includes all personal chattels other than things in action and money and, in particular, industrial growing crops and things attached to or forming part of the land which are agreed to be severed before the sale or under the contract of sale.

The expression 'personal chattels' includes tangible property, such as a briefcase or a pen, but would not include a leasehold interest in land. It does not include choses (that is, things) in action. Choses in action are rights which cannot be enforced by taking possession of the chose but can only be enforced by taking legal action. Examples include a cheque, shares in a company, debts, trademarks, copyrights, patents, insurance contracts, etc. Thus a cheque is, in itself, of no intrinsic value. If the cheque is not met, it is necessary to bring a court action to assert the right to the money which the cheque represents. Money is not goods, though money sold for curio value, such as currency which is no longer in circulation or money which is of value because of its metal content, such as a *kruggerand,* may be goods.

'Goods' does not include land or an interest in land. It may be significant whether a sale is of goods or of land because under the Law of Property (Miscellaneous Provisions) Act 1989, a contract for the sale or other disposition of an interest in land must be in writing, otherwise the contract cannot be enforced. There may be cases where, in the case of things fixed to the land, it is uncertain whether their sale is one of goods or one of land.

Industrial growing crops are goods. However, in *Saunders v Pilcher* (1949), a contract was made for the sale of a cherry orchard which was to include 'this year's fruit crop'. It was held that the sale was a sale of land.

'Goods' also includes 'things attached to or forming part of the land which are agree to be severed before the sale or under the contract of sale'. However, in *Morgan v Russell & Sons* (1909), the contract was for the sale of a slag heap which had been on the land for some time and had become overgrown. The buyer was to remove the slag heap from the land. It was held by the Court of Appeal that, because the slag heap had become merged with the land, the sale was one of land.

DISTINCTION BETWEEN A SALE OF GOODS AND A CONTRACT FOR WORK AND MATERIALS

It used to be important to distinguish between a sale of goods and a sale of work and materials. However, this was not, usually, because the substance of the law treated the two types of transaction differently. It was often for taxation reasons or reasons of form. It used to be the case, until 1954, that a contract for the sale of goods of more than £10 in value had to be evidenced in writing, otherwise it was unenforceable; for example, a disappointed buyer could not sustain an action against a seller who failed to deliver.

A contract for work and materials is one in which the substance of the contract is the skill of the worker rather than the materials which he provides incidentally to fulfil the contract. Contracts for work and materials are governed by the ordinary law of contract, and terms are implied into such contracts by the Supply of Goods and Services Act 1982. The 'materials' element, which is a supply of goods, is covered by ss 2 to 5 and the 'work' element, which is a supply of services, is covered by ss 13 to 15.

An example is *Robinson v Graves* (1935), in which an artist was commissioned to paint a portrait. The court had to decide whether the contract was for a sale of goods. The court asked, what was the substance of the contract: was it to supply goods, or was it for the skill of the seller? In this case the court decided that the contract was substantially for the skill of the seller and decided that the contract was one for work and materials. However, the outcome of such cases does not tend to be predictable. In *Lockett v Charles* (1938), a meal in a restaurant was deemed to be a sale of goods; in *Lee v Griffin* (1946), a contract to make a set of false teeth was a sale of goods. On the other hand, in *Dodd v Wilson* (1946), a contract between a farmer and a vet, whereby the vet would inoculate the farmer's cattle with a vaccine which the vet purchased for the purpose, was held to be a contract for work and materials.

Although the distinction does not usually affect the rights of the parties, there may be cases where it does. An example was found in *Hyundai Heavy Industries v Papadopoulos* (1980). In this case, the House of Lords had to decide whether a contract for the building and sale of a ship was a contract for the sale of goods or a contract for the sale of work and materials. Payment for the ship was to be made by installments. The buyers missed one installment and the seller therefore repudiated the contract. The issue was whether the installment that had been missed remained payable. If the contract was one for work and materials, the installment remained payable, since the payment related to on-going costs relating to designing and building the vessel. If the contract was one of sale of goods, the installment was not payable, since the buyer was not going to get what he had paid for (but, of course, the seller would be entitled to damages for breach of contract). The House of Lords held that the contract was a sort of hybrid. It was for work and materials while the ship was being built: it would have become a contract of sale once the ship was completed. The seller was therefore entitled to the missing instalment.

SUPPLY OF SERVICES (INCLUDING FINANCIAL SERVICES)

All the contracts we have already looked at involve the supply of goods in one form or another. However, many business contracts are for the supply of services: travel, cleaning, removals, exhibitions, banking, loans, insurance, etc. The basic framework of such a contract is contained in the common law. However, the Supply of Goods and Services Act 1982 implies some important terms into such contracts. If the contract involves credit or loan facilities, it may also be governed by the Consumer Credit Act 1974. (This Act does not simply apply to the normal 'consumer'; it can apply to a trader or a partnership but not a company.) The credit granted must not exceed £25,000, otherwise the common law, not the Act, applies. There are also some special rules which apply to the other types of contract, particularly contracts of insurance.

It may be that a contract will include elements of supply of goods and elements of service. While this has sometimes caused problems in the past, it would seem that nowadays it is a straightforward matter to imply the supply of goods implied terms into the 'goods' element of the contract and to imply the supply of services implied terms into the 'services' element. For example, a contract to service a car contains an element of labour (service) but also material, so that, if your complaint is that the new plugs don't function properly because they are defective, you will bring your claim under the implied term as to fitness for purpose or satisfactory quality of goods. If your complaint is that the new plugs don't function properly because they have been wrongly fitted, your complaint will be that the contract of service wasn't carried out with due care and skill (s 13 of the Supply of Goods and Services Act).

APPLICATION OF THE COMMON LAW
TO 'GOODS' CONTRACTS

Section 62(2) of the Sale of Goods Act 1979 states that 'the rules of common law ... except so far as they are inconsistent with the provisions of this Act ... apply to contracts for the sale of goods'.

Though there is no statutory provision to this effect, the same applies to the remainder of the 'goods' contracts and also to a contract for the supply of services: the common law applies unless there are conflicting statutory provisions. This means that the rules of the law of contract which relate to the formation of the contract, consideration, intention to create legal relations, capacity to contract, privity of contract, etc, all apply to the contracts with which we will be dealing.

Where there are conflicting statutory rules, these override the common law. Furthermore, there are occasionally special common law rules, applicable only to a certain type or types of contract, which conflict with the general common law rule. In this case, the special rule prevails. For example, there is a common law rule that if A sells goods to B under a conditional sale agreement and B then, in breach of the agreement, sells the goods to C, C obtains a good title to the goods. However, if A hires goods to B under a hire-purchase agreement and B wrongfully sells to C, A nevertheless retains his title to the goods. However, in a contract governed by the Consumer Credit Act 1974, A would retain his title to the goods in either case.

Formation of the contract

The formation of a contract for the sale of goods (other than a credit sale or conditional sale), a contract of barter, a contract for work and materials, a contract of service and a contract for services is governed by the rules of common law, that is, the contract may be made orally, in writing, or by conduct. However, a consumer credit contract (which includes a contract of hire-purchase, a contract of hire, a conditional sale and a credit sale) must be made in writing in the form laid down by the Consumer Credit Act 1974.

CHAPTER 18

SALE OF GOODS TERMS IMPLIED IN FAVOUR OF THE BUYER

Background to the implied terms

This chapter deals with certain terms implied into sale of goods contracts, by the Sale of Goods Act, for the benefit of the buyer. You often see these terms described as the buyer's 'statutory rights'.

These implied terms are contained in ss 12 to 15 of the Sale of Goods Act 1979 and provide that:

(a) the seller shall have the right to sell the goods (s 12 of the Act), so that if, for example, the seller sells goods which are stolen, the buyer has a right of redress;

(b) the goods shall correspond with the description which the seller has applied to them (s 13), so again a remedy is provided if the seller sells goods which have been mis-described;

(c) the goods shall be of satisfactory quality (s 14(2)), so the buyer has a legal complaint if the goods which he buys are faulty;

(d) if the seller has made known a particular purpose for which he requires the goods, the goods shall be fit for that purpose (s 14(3));

(e) if the goods are sold by sample, that the bulk of the goods will correspond with the sample, that the buyer will have a reasonable opportunity of comparing the bulk with the sample and that the goods will be free from any latent defect rendering them unsatisfactory (s 15).

These terms were designed to deal with different types of breach of contract by the seller and were intended to have comparatively little overlap. However, the term as to satisfactory quality (originally merchantable quality) and the term as to fitness for purpose each had odd pitfalls built into them. For example, the merchantability term applied only if the sale was by description. This led to two parallel developments. First, in order to avoid the buyer being defeated by a finding that goods did not need to be of merchantable quality on account of the fact that the sale was not a sale by description, the courts became progressively more liberal in relation to what they regarded as a sale by description. This, in turn, had a knock-on effect in relation to the interpretation of s 13. Secondly, the courts developed the implied term relating to fitness for purpose, so that instead of simply applying the term when a particular purpose was made known to the seller, the courts began to hold that if the buyer bought goods which were normally used for only one purpose (such as milk for drinking, a hot water bottle as a receptacle for hot water), the buyer had, by implication, made known a particular purpose for which he required the goods. The outcome of this was that it started to become normal for the buyer who had bought faulty goods to claim that the goods were not fit for their purpose, rather than that they were not of merchantable quality. There were other developments which led to the terms relating to description and quality being interpreted in unexpected ways, often overriding basic principle, to enable the courts to reach what they thought to be a desirable result in a particular case. In addition, there has been a number of amending statutes which, rather than tackling the fundamental structure of the implied terms, have tinkered with the law which was already in place. In 1987, the Law Commission Report on the Sale and Supply of Goods, in recommending various amendments to the Act, concluded that:

> ... it is doubtful how far a process of 'patching' the Sale of Goods Act can continue. If further alterations to our law of sale of goods are required, it might prove necessary to start from the proposition that it would be better to have a new Act or Acts ...

Having said that, it may be that despite the untidy development of the implied terms, the present situation is reasonably satisfactory in that it offers a substantial amount of protection to a disappointed buyer. It is clear that there is now a significant amount of overlap between s 14(2) (satisfactory quality) and s 14(3) (fitness for purpose), so that a buyer who buys defective goods can rely on either. He may also, in certain cases, be able to rely on s 13. And in some cases the buyer may, having no clear claim under the more obvious subsection, manage to succeed under the other. For example, in *R & B Customs Brokers v UDT* (1988), the buyer, having examined the goods and found the defect of which he was complaining, might well have failed under s 14(2) if the court had had to decide on the matter. However, the court did not need to decide, since they held that the buyer nevertheless succeeded under s 14(3). However, the courts do not always acknowledge that failure in one claim may nevertheless still allow success under a different provision. For example, in the case of *Harlingdon and Leinster Enterprises v Christopher Hull*, Slade LJ said: 'If the plaintiffs fail to establish a breach of contract through the front door of s 13(1), they cannot succeed through the back door of s 14.'

Caveat emptor

These implied terms were originally developed during the 19th century. It may seem obvious to us at the beginning of the 21st century that if we buy an object described as a 'coat', we expect that it will function as such. We do not expect to be provided with an item which comes apart at the seams the first time it is worn, and if it did, we would expect our money back. However, this proposition would not have been obvious to a lawyer of the 18th century.

The approach of the early common law was *caveat emptor*, meaning 'let the buyer beware'. This meant that it was the buyer's responsibility to satisfy himself as to the nature and quality of what he was buying. Thus, the early law gave the buyer of defective goods (including defects in title) a remedy in only two circumstances:

(a) Where the seller of goods had made a statement about the goods, which the seller *knew* to be false, the buyer could sue for the tort of deceit. The problem with the tort of deceit has always been the difficulty of proving that the seller *knew* that what he was saying about the goods was false: the seller might say, for example, that he was merely repeating what he had been told by a person who had sold the goods to him. If true, this may be negligence but it is not deceit. If not true, the difficulty is proving it. Because of this difficulty, this remedy for untrue statements has been added to in modern law, by equity, by the Misrepresentation Act 1967 and by the common law relating to negligence. These are dealt with in Chapter 10.

(b) Where the seller had given the buyer an express warranty (used here simply to mean an undertaking), which originally required a special form of wording. If the warranty turned out to be incorrect, the seller was liable, irrespective of his knowledge of the defect. Originally, he was liable for the tort of deceit in that the buyer had been deceived by his false warranty. Later he was liable for breach of contract because, by giving a warranty, he had assumed responsibility for the truth of what he said.

Any other statement was a mere representation, for the incorrectness of which the early law gave no remedy. The early law was, perhaps, not as unreasonable as it might appear when one takes into account that in the majority of sales the buyer was able to inspect the goods at the point of sale. In addition, goods did not tend to have the complex features which goods may possess nowadays, so the possibility of goods containing latent defects was significantly less.

At the end of the century the implied terms were codified in the Sale of Goods Act 1893. However, under notions of freedom of contract which prevailed at that time, s 55 of the Act allowed the benefits to the buyer to be limited, or even completely excluded, by 'agreement' between the parties. In practice, this allowed an economically stronger seller to get an economically weaker buyer to 'agree' to a term or terms which effectively excluded the seller's liability to comply with the terms implied for the benefit of the buyer. (This is called an 'exemption clause'. For a detailed discussion of exemption clauses, see Chapter 8, p 177 *et seq*.) Initially, perhaps because most of the contracts governed by the 1893 Act were commercial contracts where the parties might be expected to have more or less equality of bargaining power, this doesn't appear to have caused significant problems. However, with the rise of consumerism, the use of exemption clauses in sales of goods had become an absolute scandal by the 1960s. Therefore, in 1973, following a report by the Law Commission, the Sale and Supply of Goods (Implied Terms) Act radically changed the law in order to protect both consumer buyers and, perhaps a little controversially, though the protection takes a different form, commercial buyers. In consumer sales, the protection took the form of an absolute prohibition of the implied terms being excluded or limited. In sales to commercial buyers, there is no absolute prohibition on exclusions or limitations of liability (except the implied term relating to the right to sell – which cannot be excluded in any type of sale), but the Act imposed a requirement of 'reasonableness' if the terms were to be effectively excluded in a business sale.

The 1973 Act also took the opportunity to revise the substance of the implied terms themselves, partly to reflect developments brought about by judicial law-making during the period since 1893, and partly to try to clarify the standard which the seller had to meet in relation to the quality of the goods sold. These alterations now meant that in order to find the statutory law relating to the sale of goods it was necessary to refer to both the 1893 Act and the 1973 Act. In order to avoid this, the provisions of the two Acts were consolidated in the Sale of Goods Act 1979. The implied terms again underwent some modification as a result of another Law Commission report which led to the Sale and Supply of Goods Act 1994. This time, the Act took effect by making alterations to the Sale of Goods Act 1979. This type of approach often strikes students as a little odd – how can changes made in 1994 be included in an Act which was passed in 1979? However, simply altering the 1979 Act (though the alterations are not back-dated) means that the relevant law is still contained in one Act. Otherwise, we would be faced with the situation which led to the 1979 Act and would now be contemplating a Sale of Goods Act 2000 (or whenever), which would have been needed in order to consolidate the 1979 Act and the 1994 Act!

Victims of misrepresentation were given additional rights by the Misrepresentation Act 1967 (though the 1963 case of *Hedley Byrne v Heller* began the process of improvement in the position of victims of non-fraudulent misrepresentation).

Caveat emptor is a principle which, even with the rise of consumerism, has not been wholly discredited. It is the principle which the law still pursues in relation to the sale of land and indeed, subject to the exceptions contained in ss 14 and 15 of the Sale of Goods Act 1979, and analogous provisions relating to contracts of hire, hire-purchase and supplies of goods, still pursues in relation to the sale of goods. So, for example, the buyer of goods in a sale by a *private* seller is not protected by the provisions of s 14 in relation to goods being of satisfactory quality or fit for their purpose. If goods that he buys turn out to be defective, he has no right of complaint unless the seller has breached an express term of the contract, or unless the goods fail to correspond to the description which the seller has applied to them, or unless there has been a misrepresentation of the goods.

THE IMPLIED TERMS

The terms which the modern law implies in favour of the buyer come under four main headings. There is an implied condition that the seller has the right to sell the goods; an implied condition that goods will correspond with their description; an implied condition that the goods will be of satisfactory quality and fit for their purpose; and an implied condition that, in a sale by sample, the bulk of the goods will (among other things) correspond with the sample.

THE IMPLIED CONDITION THAT THE SELLER HAS THE RIGHT TO SELL

Section 12(1) implies a condition on the part of a seller that (except where s 12(3) applies) in the case of a sale he has a right to sell the goods and that, in the case of an agreement to sell, he will have a right at the time the property is to pass. Note that although this implied term is almost invariably referred to in the texts as an implied term as to title, in fact it goes further than that and implies a right to sell. The distinction is clearly illustrated by *Niblett v Confectioners' Materials Co* (1921), where, although the seller owned the goods and, therefore, had a good title to them, he still had no right to sell them because they infringed the trademark of a third party.

In this case, N bought 3,000 cases of condensed milk from C. It was agreed that the milk should be one of three brands, including the 'Nissly' brand. Two thousand cases of the other brands were delivered without a problem. However, when 1,000 cases of Nissly brand were delivered, it came to the attention of the Nestle company that this milk was being imported and they alleged that the Nissly brand infringed their registered trade mark. N did their best to sell, exchange or export the goods but found that the only way they could deal with the goods was to strip the labels off and sell them without marks or labels. The Court of Appeal held that, even though the sellers owned the goods, they did not have the right to sell the goods.

Perhaps the most common example of a seller without a title is where goods have been stolen. Example: O has his car stolen by T, who sells it to P1, who buys it in good faith. P1 sells it to P2. The police find the car in the possession of P2 and return it to its owner, which by now is probably O's insurance company. The company, having paid O in respect of his insured loss, would, in consequence assume the rights of ownership over the car. P2 has a right of action against P1 under s 12(1) of the Sale of Goods Act 1979. He may claim the full amount of the purchase price paid to P1, despite the fact that he may have had the use of the car for some time (see *Rowland v Divall* (1923)). P1 has a right of action against T, also under s 12(1) of the Sale of

Goods Act 1979. However, it will rarely be worthwhile pursuing the claim, so that P1 will normally end up as a substantial loser.

In *Rowland v Divall* (1923), D bought a car from T in April. T was a thief who had no title to the car. In May, D sold the car to R, a dealer, for £334. R did some work on the car before selling it, in July, to C for £400. The police traced the car to C and recovered it on behalf of the true owner. R refunded the £400 purchase price to C. D refused to refund R's purchase price but paid a lesser sum into court, representing the purchase price paid by R to D less a discount for the use of the car. As we have seen, the remedy for a breach of condition is that the buyer may repudiate the contract, return the goods and obtain his money back from the seller. However, under s 11(4) of the 1979 Act, if the buyer has 'accepted' the goods, the condition must be treated as a warranty, which means that the buyer is entitled only to damages. On the face of it, therefore, the seller's argument was correct: because the buyer had accepted the goods he was entitled to damages only, not to repudiate the contract and have his purchase price returned. However, the buyer's argument was that the breach by the seller, in failing to transfer the title to the goods, amounted to more than simply a breach of condition; it was a total failure of consideration. It was held that R was entitled to a refund of his full purchase price since he had paid for the *ownership* of the car, not its *use*. There had therefore been a total failure of consideration.

A further action which is rarely pursued is the owner's right of action against any or all of T, P1 and P2, for the tort of conversion (that is, wrongful interference with the owner's right to possess his goods). This is probably because the owner will often have been compensated by insurance for the loss of his goods. This means that the owner's rights in the goods are transferred to his insurers, who will usually sell the goods once they have been recovered, but will not pursue (because of the potential costs involved) their right of action for damages against the parties who have been in wrongful possession of the goods. Thus, the loss is spread across the community generally through the insurance premiums paid by those insuring their goods. This right of action is often ignored by those who put forward proposals for reform, arguing that P2 should be able to recover the purchase price only subject to a discount for the use that P2 has had out of the goods. If this were to be the case and, in addition, the owner pursued his right of action against P2, P2 would be paying for his use of the goods twice over, but without getting the ownership he had bargained for!

In some cases, there may be a doubt as to who is the true owner of stolen goods recovered by the police. In such cases the police will normally refuse to hand them to either party, pending a court decision as to title. If this happens, the original owner may sue the police, the party in whose possession the police found the goods or both, for the tort of conversion.

Providing that the buyer repudiates the contract for lack of title before any property has passed, the buyer may recover the price he has paid, even though the seller has meanwhile acquired a good title, capable of being passed to the buyer: *Butterworth v Kingsway Motors* (1954). B bought a car from KM. It turned out that it was owned by a hire-purchase company and had been wrongfully sold by the hirer, passing through a number of hands before it reached KM. The hire-purchase company reclaimed the car from B (though nowadays B would become the owner under the provisions of Part III of the Hire Purchase Act 1964). B therefore sued KM for the return of his purchase price. Meanwhile, the hirer paid off the balance of the hire-purchase price and became the owner. It was held that when the hirer became the owner, this 'fed' the titles of the intermediate purchasers. However, because B had repudiated the contract with KM *before* the hirer gained his title, B was entitled to a refund of his full purchase price.

Where the buyer has improved goods in the mistaken, but honest, belief that he had a good title to them, an allowance shall be made for the increase in value attributable to the improvement; a similar allowance shall be made in favour of a purchaser from the improver, or subsequent purchaser, where he is being sued by the true owner rather than the improver: s 6 of the Torts (Interference with Goods) Act 1977. For example, Bill buys goods from Claire, to which Claire had a defective title. Bill improves the goods. Donna buys the goods from Bill (for a price which reflects Bill's improvements). Although Donna will have to hand the goods back to their legal owner, she will be entitled to claim the cost of Bill's improvements.

Implied warranty of quiet possession

Section 12(2) implies a warranty that (except where s 12(3) applies):

(a) the goods are free from any charge or encumbrance not disclosed or known to the buyer before the contract is made; and

(b) the buyer will enjoy quiet possession of the goods except so far as it may be disturbed by the owner or other person entitled to the benefit of any charge or encumbrance so disclosed or known.

It is thought that in most cases where s 12(2) applies, the claimant will also have a claim under s 12(1). For example, in *Mason v Burningham* (1949), in which the plaintiff's claim related to a typewriter which she had bought and which turned out to have been stolen and had to be returned to its owner, her action was brought under s 12(2)(b), but the defendant would seem to have been liable had s 12(1) been relied upon.

However, for a case where s 12(2) but not s 12(1) was applicable, see *Microbeads AG v Vinhurst Road Markings* (1975). The defendants bought road-marking machines from the plaintiff in January and April 1970. The defendants refused to pay the balance of the purchase price and, when they were sued, defended the claim on the grounds that the plaintiffs were in breach of s 12 of the Sale of Goods Act 1979. A patent in the machines had been granted to a third party, Prismo, in 1972, at which time Prismo became entitled to restrain the buyer from using the machines. It was held that the plaintiffs were not in breach of s 12(1) since, at the time of the sale, they had a right to sell, the specifications in relation to the patent not having been filed until November 1970, after the machines were sold. They were, however, in breach of s 12(2)(b), since the warranty that the buyer will enjoy quiet possession of the goods is a continuing one.

Sub-sections (3), (4), and (5) of s 12 apply to the situation where it appears from the contract, or is to be inferred from its circumstances, that the seller intends to transfer a limited title, that is, only such title as he or a third party may have. The sub-sections provide:

(3) this sub-section applies to a contract of sale in the case of which there appears from the contract, or is to be inferred from its circumstances, an intention that the seller should transfer only such title as he or a third person may have;

(4) in a contract to which sub-s (3) above applies, there is an implied warranty that all charges or encumbrances known to the seller and not known to the buyer have been disclosed to the buyer before the contract is made;

(5) in a contract to which sub-s (3) above applies there is also an implied warranty that none of the following will disturb the buyer's quiet possession of the goods, namely:

(a) the seller;

(b) in a case where the parties to a contract intend that the seller should transfer only such title as a third party may have, that person;

(c) anyone claiming through or under the seller or that person otherwise than under a charge or encumbrance disclosed or known to the buyer before the contract is made.

Thus, a seller who has no knowledge of the history of the goods he is selling (for example, a pawnbroker selling an unredeemed pledge) will probably be taken to intend to transfer only such title as he actually has, which, of course, will depend upon the title that the person who pawned the goods had. In such a case, there is no implied condition that he has the right to sell the goods and the implied warranty of quiet possession is modified. The implied warranty that all charges and encumbrances known to the seller have been disclosed to the buyer remains.

Apart from this, the implied terms contained in s 12 cannot be excluded in any contract of sale of goods.

IMPLIED TERM AS TO CORRESPONDENCE WITH DESCRIPTION

Section 13(1) of the Sale of Goods Act 1979 implies a condition that where there is a contract for the sale of goods by description, the goods will correspond with the description.

For example, in *Raynham Farm v Symbol Motor Corp* (1987), a new Range Rover which had been seriously damaged by fire was restored to its 'new' condition. It was sold by the defendant as a new Range Rover. The plaintiff sought to reject it on discovering the truth. *Held*: the vehicle could not properly be described as 'new' since there would always be a lingering doubt about its soundness.

Section 13(2) goes on to provide that if the sale is by sample as well as by description, it is not sufficient that the bulk of the goods correspond with the sample if the goods do not also correspond with the description. Section 13(3) provides that a sale of goods is not prevented from being a sale by description by reason only that, being exposed for sale or hire, they are selected by the buyer.

Why is the implied term necessary?

Why, when the description applied to goods will be an express term of the contract (providing it is not a puff or a mere representation) is it necessary to have an implied term that the goods will correspond with the description?

Part of the answer is historical, but the implied term is of modern-day importance because of the following:

(a) The implied term is a condition (the breach of which entitles the innocent party to repudiate the contract), whereas an express term might be held to be a warranty, or, possibly, might be treated as an innominate term, the effect of the breach of which would not be clear until the consequences of its breach were seen. (This no longer applies in non-consumer sales where goods may no longer be rejected for a breach of s 13, where the breach is so slight that rejection would be unreasonable.)

(b) Under s 6 of the Unfair Contract Terms Act 1977, the duty to supply goods which correspond with the description cannot be excluded or restricted as against any person dealing as a consumer and further, can only be excluded or restricted as against a person dealing otherwise than as a consumer, if the exclusion or restriction fulfils the test of reasonableness.

The rules relating to the exclusion or restriction of an express term are not quite so strict. Any exclusion or restriction in a consumer sale, or where the parties have contracted on the other's written standard terms of business, must satisfy the test of reasonableness. Thus, the absolute prohibition which applies to the exclusion or restriction of the term implied by s 13 in a consumer sale, is replaced as regards the exclusion or restriction of an express term by allowing the exclusion or restrictions subject to the test of reasonableness. In relation to non-consumer sales, the reasonableness requirement which applies when seeking to exclude or restrict the operation of s 13 applies only where the parties are contracting on the other's written standard terms of business if the exclusion or restriction relates to an express term.

(c) Where it is an express term which is breached, the court may apply the doctrine of substantial performance, unless the parties have agreed otherwise or the circumstances of the contract indicate otherwise.

For example, in *Hoenig v Isaacs* (1952), a contract to decorate and furnish the defendant's flat was performed defectively. The contract price was £750. The defects would cost £50 to rectify. *Held:* the plaintiff was entitled to the contract price less the amount required to put the defects right. However, in relation to the condition implied by s 13, the courts have held that even a minor deviation between the goods described and those tendered under the contract is sufficient to entitle the buyer to reject the goods. In *Bowes v Shand* (1877), a quantity of rice which was contracted to be shipped during March and/or April, was shipped during February. It was held that the buyer was entitled to reject the goods. In *Arcos v Ronaasen* (1933), the contract was for wooden staves half an inch thick. Many of the staves were marginally larger or smaller, though this made no difference to their suitability for their intended use. *Held:* nevertheless, the goods did not correspond with their description and therefore the buyer was entitled to reject the goods. In *Re Moore and Landauer* (1921), the contract was for cases of Australian canned fruit to be packed 30 cans to the case. Although the correct quantity was tendered by the seller, some of the fruit was packed in cases of 24 cans. It was held that the buyer had a right to reject the goods as they did not correspond with their description.

It is arguable that this reason has lost much of its force since the Sale and Supply of Goods Act 1994. This inserts a new s 15A into the Sale of Goods Act 1979 and provides, in effect, that a breach of an implied term which results in damage so slight that it would be unreasonable for the buyer to reject the goods, may be treated as a breach of warranty (that is, the innocent party loses his right to rescind the contract), rather than a breach of condition. In other words, in the case of a breach in which the damage is trivial, the court may apply the doctrine of substantial performance. This provision applies only to sales which are not consumer sales. In consumer sales the right to reject for breach of condition, however slight, remains.

Relationship between s 13 and s 14

In many (but by no means all) cases where a breach of s 13 is involved, s 14(2) and/or s 14(3) will also be breached. In fact, many of the cases which discuss the meaning of a sale by description concern breaches of s 14(2) because, before the Supply of Goods Implied Terms Act 1973 altered the law, it was necessary, in order to succeed under s 14(2), to show that the sale was a sale by description. Thus, for example, if S sells a quantity of olive oil to B and the oil is actually only 50% olive oil and 50% corn oil, B would have an action under s 13 because the goods do not correspond with the description applied to them. B would also have an action under s 14(2) because the goods are not of satisfactory quality, in relation to the description applied to them. However, in considering the relative effects of the terms implied by ss 13, 14(2) and 14(3), one very important factor must not be overlooked: s 13 applies to *all* sales (unless validly excluded), whereas s 14(2) and s 14(3) apply only where the sale is *in the course of a business*. This means that a person who buys from a private seller can rely on the term implied by s 13 but that he cannot make use of the terms implied by s 14.

Scope of s 13

There are two principal questions to be answered in dealing with sales by description. These are, first, what amounts to a sale by description? and, secondly, which of the words used when describing goods to a purchaser are part of the description for the purposes of s 13?

What is a sale by description?

It is thought that the original intention of the draftsman of the Sale of Goods Act 1893 was that specific goods (that is, goods identified and agreed upon at the time of the contract) could not be the subject of a sale by description. The idea behind this was that if a buyer is buying something specific, he has the opportunity to examine it or have an expert examine it for him. If the goods do not then correspond with their description, for example, if a horse described as a 'thoroughbred racehorse' turns out to be a cart-horse, s 13 would not be breached because the buyer would be regarded as having bought the specific horse in front of him, not a horse corresponding to a description (although the buyer might have a remedy for breach of an express term of the contract or for misrepresentation). This harks back to the idea of *caveat emptor*. If, however, the buyer agrees to buy 500 cotton shirts, not yet in existence, the description is the only point of reference the buyer has in relation to the goods. If, therefore, the shirts offered in satisfaction of the contract turn out to be nylon, the buyer can reject them as not corresponding with the description applied to them.

The case law which preceded the 1893 Act had held that the sale of a specific article or articles could not be classified as a sale by description. This was a manifestation of the idea of *caveat emptor*. It was based upon the assumption that the buyer always sees a specific article before he buys it and thus has the opportunity to inspect it and to ascertain whether or not it conforms with any descriptive words which the seller may have applied to it.

On the other hand, if the goods which the buyer agrees to purchase are not specific, he will have only the seller's description, or, alternatively a sample, to rely on in order to know what it is that he is buying.

For example, let us imagine Deborah wishes to buy a new leather sofa. There are a number of possibilities:

(a) Deborah may see a sofa in a furniture showroom and agree to buy that specific sofa; or

(b) Deborah may order a sofa from a range which is described and illustrated in a catalogue; or

(c) Deborah may see a sofa in the showroom, which is for display purposes only, and she may ask the dealer to order a similar one for her.

Let us say that in each case the sofa is described as being manufactured from leather, but in each case, the sofa is made from a plastic imitation.

The original attitude of the law was that, because the sale in the first example is the sale of a specific sofa it could not be a sale by description.

Examples (b) and (c) are sales of unascertained goods because at the time Deborah has agreed to buy it, there is no specific sofa identifiable as the sofa which Deborah has agreed to buy: Deborah's sofa may be any one of many at the manufacturer's factory or, indeed, it may not even be manufactured yet!

As a general rule, a buyer will often see and have the opportunity to inspect specific goods before he agrees to buy them. On the other hand, he will often buy unascertained goods relying on the description given by the seller, for example, the sofa in the example given in the previous paragraph. Unfortunately, the law developed by regarding these assumptions as being invariably the case. Thus the rule developed that a sale of specific goods was not a sale by description: in a sale of specific goods, the buyer is agreeing to buy whatever the article in front of him happens to be, regardless of any descriptive words applied to it.

However, the need to distinguish between specific goods and unascertained goods (that is, goods not identified at the time of the contract), has never been wholly convincing. The application of such a rule would have meant that a person who bought specific goods which he had not seen, would have had no remedy against the seller of the goods should the goods have been misdescribed. It was, therefore, not long before the courts held that a sale of specific goods which the buyer had not seen, could be a sale by description. In *Varley v Whipp* (1900), the buyer bought a specific reaping machine which he had not seen but which was described to him by the seller as 'nearly new and used to cut only 50 or 60 acres'. This description was not correct. It was held that the sale was by description. Channell J said: 'The term "sale of goods by description" must apply to all cases where the purchaser has not seen the goods, but is relying on the description alone, as here where the buyer has bought by the description.'

Nowadays, the law has developed further so that a sale of specific goods which have been seen by the buyer may be a sale by description 'so long as [the item] is sold not merely as a specific thing but as a thing corresponding to a description': *Grant v Australian Knitting Mills* (1936). In *Godley v Perry* (1960), it was held that when a child asks for a catapult and is handed one over the counter, this is a sale by description. In *Beale v Taylor* (1967), a car was advertised in a newspaper as a '1961 Triumph Herald'. It had a disk on the back which said '1200', such a disk being displayed on the first model of the car which came out in 1961. The plaintiff went to see the car and bought it. The car turned out to be the halves of two different cars welded together. It was a private sale so the plaintiff was not able to rely on s 14. Instead, he argued that the car did not correspond with the description applied to it. The contrary argument was that the plaintiff had bought the specific car shown to him and that it was not, therefore, a sale by description. It was held that the sale was by description. The disk on the back of the car appeared to indicate that it was a 1961 model.

The sale will not be a sale by description if it is clear that the buyer relies upon his own judgment and not that of the seller. This is illustrated by the case of *Harlingdon and Leinster Enterprises Ltd v Christopher Hull Fine Art Ltd* (1991), in which the defendants were art dealers. They were asked to sell two paintings attributed to a German expressionist painter called Gabriele Munter. They contacted the plaintiffs who were art dealers who specialised in that field. The plaintiffs sent one of their employees, Mr Runkel, to look at the picture. Mr Hull made it clear that he was not an expert in relation to Munters, though he had a 1980 auction catalogue which attributed the paintings to Munter. Mr Runkel agreed to buy one of the paintings for £6,000. It turned out to be a forgery worth only £50 to £100. The plaintiffs claimed breach of s 13. It was held by the Court of Appeal that the sale was not a sale by description since Mr Hull had made it very clear that he knew nothing about the German expressionist school and Mr Runkel had therefore bought the paintings relying on his own judgment.

Which words are part of the description?

Words which describe goods may amount to express terms, terms implied under s 13, mere representations and advertising puffs. For example, a car is advertised as follows: 'Vauxhall Cavalier 1.6L 1994, red, five good tyres, engine reconditioned 2,000 miles ago, radio cassette, nice family car.'

It may be argued that all these words are part of the car's description, so that if it turns out that the spare tyre is bald or that the engine was reconditioned 30,000 miles ago, the car does not correspond with the description applied to it. However, it has been held that only words needed to *identify* the subject matter are part of the description. Other words fall into one of the other categories. (For an explanation of the law relating to the status of words used in statements, see Chapter 7.)

In *Ashington Piggeries v Christopher Hill* (1972), a clause headed 'quality and description', spoke of 'Norwegian Herring Meal of fair average quality' and set out minimum percentages of various ingredients which the meal was to contain. The House of Lords held that the description was 'Norwegian Herring Meal' and did not include the reference to 'fair average quality' nor the specification as to the ingredients. The House said that description equals identification and that, therefore, only so much is part of the description as is required to identify the goods. Therefore, although the herring meal contained an ingredient which generated a toxin which made it unsuitable for mink food, the House held that it was still properly described as herring meal because it was still identifiable as such.

It will be a matter of fact whether or not adulterated goods retain sufficient of the qualities required to be correctly identified by the description applied to them. In *Munro v Meyer* (1930), there was a contract to supply 1,500 tons of meat and bone meal. It was discovered that the meal had been adulterated with cocoa husks. *Held*: the goods did not conform with the description applied to them. Similarly in *Pinnock v Peat* (1923), the contract was for the sale of copra cake. The goods delivered were a mixture of copra cake and castor beans. *Held*: the goods did not correspond with their description.

According to Lord Wilberforce in *Reardon Smith Line v Hansen Tangen* (1976), 'identification' can be used in two senses. It can be used simply to indicate the whereabouts of the goods so that it was known which goods were meant. On the other hand, it can be used to identify an essential part of the description of the goods. If it is used in the first sense, the court may interpret the descriptive words more liberally than if they are used in the second sense. To show in simple terms what Lord Wilberforce seems to have meant by this, suppose a vessel is described as the oil tanker *Lucy* lying at Hull. The description 'oil tanker' is an essential part of the description of the goods so that if *Lucy* turned out to be a trawler, s 13 would have been breached. If, on the other hand, the oil tanker *Lucy* turned out to be lying at Immingham, then, if it was clear that this was the vessel referred to by the contract, the court may be prepared to hold that there had been no misdescription within the terms of s 13.

In the *Reardon Smith Line* case, the appellants had agreed to charter a vessel 'to be built by Osaka Shipbuilding Co and known as Hull 354 until named'. The yard at Osaka was not large enough to take the ship and, therefore, Osaka arranged for it to be built at the yard of an associated company called Oshima. Oshima gave it the number 004. When it was completed it complied with the specification for the vessel and was fit for the charter. However, by the time the vessel was ready, the demand for tankers had substantially diminished and the appellants refused to accept delivery of the vessel on the ground that vessel did not correspond with the description applied to it. *Held* by the House of Lords: that the vessel always was Osaka Hull No 354 and can fairly be said to have been built by Osaka Shipbuilding Co as the company which planned, organised and directed the building.

There is a line of cases which held that a minor deviation from the express terms laid down by the contract constituted a breach of condition under s 13. These decisions were said by Lord Wilberforce in *Reardon Smith Line v Hansen-Tangen* to be in need of reconsideration.

In *Arcos v Ronaasen* (1933), sellers agreed to supply a quantity of wooden staves half an inch thick. When they arrived in London, about 85% of them were found to be between half an inch and nine-sixteenths of an inch thick and 9% were found to be between nine-sixteenths of an inch and five-eighths of an inch thick. The staves were required for making cement barrels and the slight differences in thickness did not impair their use for that purpose. Nevertheless, it was held that the width of the staves was part of their description and, since it is an implied condition that goods shall correspond with the description, the buyer was entitled to repudiate the contract because the condition had been breached.

Similarly in *Re Moore and Co and Landauer and Co* (1921), sellers agreed to sell a quantity of tinned fruit to be packed in cases each containing 30 tins. When the fruit was delivered it was found that although there was the correct quantity of tins, only about half the cases contained 30 tins, the rest contained 24. The arbitrator found that 24 tins to the case was as commercially valuable as 30 to the case. Nevertheless the Court of Appeal held that the buyers were entitled to repudiate the contract since the goods did not comply with the description applied to them.

The importance of minor deviations being treated as breaches of condition under s 13 of the Sale of Goods Act has been reduced by the new s 15A. This provides that the court may treat the breach as a breach of warranty where the damage is so slight that it would be unreasonable for the buyer to reject the goods.

IMPLIED TERMS AS TO QUALITY

The Sale of Goods Act 1979 implies terms as to quality, in the following sections:

(a) s 14(2). This is the basic, and most important, implied term as to quality;

(b) s 14(4). This allows an implied condition or warranty about quality (or fitness for purpose) to be annexed to a contract of sale by trade usage;

(c) s 15(2)(a). This implies a condition that, in a sale by sample, the bulk will correspond with the sample in quality; and

(d) s 15(2)(c). This implies a condition that in a sale by sample, the goods will be free from any latent defect, rendering them unsatisfactory.

Section 14(2) implies a condition that goods supplied in a contract shall be of *satisfactory* quality. This condition applies only to sales in the course of a business, so that a private buyer has no remedy under s 14 if, for example, the camera he buys through the 'For Sale' columns of his local newspaper turns out to be incapable of taking photographs. He may, of course, have a remedy for breach of the term implied by s 13 or for breach of an express term, or for misrepresentation if statements made about the camera by the seller turn out to be untrue.

Meaning of satisfactory quality

Under s 14(2A), goods are of satisfactory quality if they meet the standard that a reasonable person would regard as satisfactory, taking account of any description of the goods, the price (if relevant) and all the other relevant circumstances.

Under s 14(2B), the quality of goods includes their state and condition and the following factors are, in appropriate cases, aspects of the quality of goods:

(a) the fitness for all the purposes for which goods of the kind in question are commonly supplied;

(b) appearance and finish;

(c) freedom from minor defects;

(d) safety; and

(e) durability.

The condition does not apply in respect of any matter making the quality of goods unsatisfactory:

(a) which is drawn specifically to the buyer's attention before the contract is made;

(b) where the buyer examines the goods before the contract is made, which that examination ought to reveal (but note that the law does not place a duty on the buyer to examine the goods before purchase); or

(c) in the case of a contract for sale by sample, would have been apparent on a reasonable examination of the sample.

Definitions of other important terms, that is, business, buyer, contract of sale, goods, quality, seller and warranty are contained in s 61(l).

The requirement of s 14(2) was originally that the goods should be of 'merchantable' quality. 'Merchantable' quality was, until the Supply of Goods (Implied Terms) Act 1973, defined by case law. The Act introduced a statutory definition of merchantable quality but, because of continued criticism, has been changed, to add more detail, by the Sale and Supply of Goods Act 1994, 'merchantable quality' becoming 'satisfactory quality' in the process.

Test of satisfactory quality

It is too early to say whether the new test of satisfactory quality is merely a semantic change with the list of criteria simply made more explicit, or whether the substance of the test has altered. It is perhaps, therefore, best to proceed on the basis that the old case law as to meaning of 'merchantable quality' will apply, except in cases where it is clearly inconsistent with the new definition.

A widely quoted test of merchantable quality is the one put forward by Dixon J in *Grant v Australian Knitting Mills*:

> The condition that goods are of merchantable quality requires that they should be in such actual state that a buyer, fully acquainted with the facts and therefore knowing what hidden defects exist ... would buy them without abatement of the price obtainable for such goods if in reasonably sound order and condition.

This effectively required that the goods should be worth the money. However, the House of Lords were unhappy with the idea of putting too much emphasis on the price paid by the buyer. In *Brown v Craiks* (below), the House disapproved of Dixon J's 'without abatement of price' formula and said that the difference between the contract price and the price at which the goods could be resold would have to be *substantial* before the goods became unmerchantable, using the price paid as evidence of unmerchantability. This means that the buyer cannot claim that the goods are unsatisfactory simply because he has made a bad bargain and paid a high price for the goods, nor if, as in *Brown v Craiks* itself, he made assumptions about the goods which turned out to be incorrect. (It was assumed that the cloth which was purchased would be suitable for dressmaking: in fact it was suitable only for industrial uses.)

However, in *Rogers v Parish* (1987), the fact that a motor vehicle was at the expensive end of the market was taken into account in deciding that the vehicle was not of merchantable quality.

Minor or repairable defects

The question sometimes arose as to whether a minor defect in goods, particularly one which is cosmetic rather than functional, rendered them unmerchantable. An analogous question arose where the defects are functional but repairable and the seller is willing to repair them. Doubtless, similar problems will arise under the requirement that the goods should be of satisfactory quality: the new definition of satisfactory quality includes 'freedom from minor defects' as a factor which the courts may take into account in determining whether goods are of satisfactory quality or not.

In practice, what happens where the buyer complains of minor defects or repairable defects is that the seller usually offers to cure them, either by repairing the goods or by replacing them. A problem may occur in one of three broad circumstances. First, there are the cases where the buyer allows the seller to cure a succession of minor defects but eventually loses patience and seeks to reject the goods on the grounds that they are not of satisfactory quality. Secondly, there are the cases where the seller refuses to remedy a minor defect. Thirdly, there are the cases where the buyer simply chooses to reject the goods and refuses to accept a repair or replacement and is relying on the breach of satisfactory quality condition to allow him to escape from the bargain.

In all three cases, if the courts hold that minor or repairable defects do not render the goods to be of unsatisfactory quality, the buyer is left without a remedy. Many people would think that it is just to deny the buyer a remedy in the third type of case. The difficulty with doing this is that the buyers in the first two types of cases, which are arguably much more deserving of the law's assistance, are also deprived of a remedy.

It was in order to try to discourage rejection of the goods on grounds of unsatisfactory quality, in circumstances where the breach is trivial, which caused the legislature to add s 15A to the Sale of Goods Act 1979. As we have already noted, this provides that the implied conditions may be treated as implied warranties (thus giving the right to claim damages, but not the right to reject) in cases where the breach is slight and the sale is not one to which a consumer is the buyer. Thus it would seem that a business buyer may be denied the right to reject for minor defects but that the consumer buyer may reject for slight defects.

The courts, conscious of the difficulties encountered by the buyer in cases of persistent defects or refusal by the seller to remedy a defect, have, in the past, been willing to hold that even minor and readily repaired defects in new goods, nonetheless render them 'unmerchantable'. In *Jackson v Rotax* (1910), a consignment of 609 motor horns (that is, the old-fashioned type consisting of a rubber bulb fixed to a brass trumpet) were sold by the plaintiff to the defendant. On delivery, over 350 of the horns were found to be dented and scratched. The horns cost £450. They could have been repaired for £35.

Nevertheless it was held that they were not of merchantable quality. Two decisions of Commonwealth courts have found that goods were not merchantable when the defects were slight. In *Winsley v Woodfield* (1929), a trivial defect in a woodworking machine rendered it inoperable. It was held that the machine was not of merchantable quality. In *IBM v Shcherban* (1925), it was held that a $300 computing scale which had a defective dial glass which did not affect the effective working of the scale and, moreover, would have cost only a few cents to replace, was not of merchantable quality.

In *Cehave NV v Bremer Handelsgesellschaft dbH: the Hansa Nord* (1976), the goods were citrus pulp pellets intended for cattle food, which had a defect which rendered them re-saleable for about one-third of the contract price. They could, nevertheless, be used for the purpose for which they were intended in more or less the same manner in which they were intended to be used. *Held* by the Court of Appeal: the goods did not have to be perfect in order to be of merchantable quality. It was sufficient if they remained saleable for the purpose for which they would normally be bought, albeit with some reduction in price. (Note that the reduction in price in this case was partly due to a fall in the market at the time of the resale.) The court also said that the proper remedy in such a case is for the seller to give the buyer some abatement in price. This seems to be tacitly recognising a 'right to cure', so that in circumstances where goods fail to meet the appropriate quality, the seller must be given an opportunity to cure the defect and fail, before he will be in breach of the condition to supply goods of satisfactory quality. Furthermore, it seems that offering an abatement in price rather than substitute goods may be regarded as a cure.

As we have seen, this is by no means a universal view and a swing back towards the older approach whereby the right to reject faulty goods as being unmerchantable was given without question, providing the goods had not been 'accepted', can be noted in *Rogers v Parish* (1987). In this case, it was argued, following cases which suggested that defects in cars were to be expected, that if it was driveable it was merchantable and that if it was repairable it was merchantable. In this case, the car in question was a new Range Rover which cost over £15,000. It had defects to the gearbox, engine and oil seals. These were repaired under the car's warranty at no cost to the buyer. The car was driveable and had, in fact, been driven for about 5,000 miles. The buyer rejected the car as being unmerchantable. It was held that the car was not merchantable. Sir Edward Everleigh said:

> Whether or not a vehicle is of merchantable quality is not determined by asking merely if it will go. One asks whether, in the condition in which it was on delivery, it was fit for use as a motor vehicle of its kind ... The fact that the plaintiff was entitled to have remedial work done under the warranty does not make it fit for its purpose at the time of delivery.

Goods must be fit for all normal purposes

Before the new definition in s 14(2B)(a) altered the situation, it was clear that goods were 'merchantable' if they were fit for *any* normal purpose for which such goods were sold, without the price being substantially reduced. Thus, if the goods were commercially saleable under the description applied to them, without any substantial abatement of price, they were merchantable.

It was irrelevant that the goods could not be used for *all* normal purposes to which such goods might be put. The reason for this was that if the buyer has a particular purpose in mind for the goods, he may inform the seller of this. If the buyer does so, showing that he relies on the seller's judgment to provide goods of the appropriate quality, then if the goods are not fit for the particular purpose which the buyer has made known to the seller, the seller will be in breach of the condition implied under s 14(3) of the Act.

Now, however, the new s 14(2B)(a) makes it clear that the goods must be fit for *all* of their normal purposes, rather than for simply any one of their normal purposes. For example, suppose S sells B a car roof rack. B loads it up with heavy-duty fencing from the DIY centre and it buckles in consequence. Evidence shows that some car roof racks would be capable of bearing the weight of the fencing. Can B argue that the roof rack is not of satisfactory quality? Using the definition laid down in the Supply of Goods (Implied Terms Act) 1973, it was held that providing goods were suitable for one of the purposes for which such goods were normally used, the goods were of merchantable quality and therefore the buyer had no remedy under s 14(2). This was not such an injustice as it may sound, because if the buyer made known the particular purpose for which the goods were required and they proved to be unsuitable for that purpose, the seller would be in breach of the condition relating to the fitness of the goods under s 14(3) of the Act. However, it would seem that in our example above, using the new definition, B may well succeed in his argument that the roof rack is not of satisfactory quality.

It would seem that in order to avoid the difficulties encountered in such cases as *Brown v Craiks* (1970) and *Aswan Engineering Establishment v Lupdine* (1987), it will be advisable for the seller to enquire the purpose of the goods rather than expect the buyer to make his own purpose known. Otherwise the seller may well find himself in breach of the new s 14(2B)(a). In *Brown v Craiks*, the buyer bought cloth of a detailed specification which he intended to use for dressmaking. The cloth supplied could be used only for industrial purposes. The House of Lords found that cloth of that specification had commonly been used for dressmaking purposes but that it had sometimes been used for industrial purposes. The buyer had not made his purpose known and therefore could not claim breach of s 14(3), (or s 14(1) as it was then). The House of Lords held that the goods were of merchantable quality because they could be could be sold under that description without any substantial abatement of price, and goods sold under that description could be used for one of the purposes for which such goods could normally be used. In the *Aswan* case, pails were sold under the description, 'Heavy duty pails suitable for export'. They were filled and then shipped to Kuwait in containers. On arrival at Kuwait the containers were left on the quayside where the heat inside them reached 70°C. The pails collapsed under the heat. Expert evidence showed that they could withstand normally high temperatures. They had been used for export to other parts of the world without difficulty. The goods were therefore merchantable.

In both cases, the buyer was denied a remedy under s 14(2) when he bought goods which were intended for a particular purpose but he did not make that purpose known to the seller. This was because in both cases the goods were fit for one of the purposes for which such goods were normally used. In the absence of special knowledge, which would have brought into play s 14(3), the seller was not liable, but, as suggested above, may well be liable now under the revised definition.

Second-hand goods

In the case of second-hand goods it is clearly not reasonable to expect perfection. It is, therefore, quite reasonable for the courts to hold that even faults of a functional nature, providing they are not too extensive, may not render the goods unsatisfactory. In *Bartlett v Sidney Marcus* (1965), the buyer bought a second-hand Jaguar car. The seller was made aware that the car needed minor repairs to the clutch. The buyer undertook to make the repair, only to find that the car engine would need to be dismantled in order to effect it. The court examined two tests of merchantability. In *Cammel Laird v Manganese Bronze* (1934), the test of unmerchantablity was whether the goods were of no use for any purpose for which such goods would normally be used. The second test, suggested in *Bristol Tramways v Fiat* (1910), asks the question: 'Is the article of such a quality and in such a condition that a reasonable man acting reasonably would, after full examination, accept it ... in performance of his offer to buy the article?' The court decided that the car was merchantable notwithstanding that the repairs were more extensive than envisaged.

In *Thain v Anniesland Trade Centre* (1997), the first case to be decided since the 1994 changes in the law, the claimant paid just under £3,000 for a second-hand Renault which was 5 years old and had done 80,000 miles. The price was reasonable for a car of its age and condition. After about two weeks the gear box developed a noise and it was found that the car needed a new gear box. The claimant claimed that the car was not fit for its purpose and not sufficiently durable. *Held*: at the time of supply, there was no indication of a fault in the gear box. However, because of the car's age, there was a risk that the gear box might fail at any time. That did not mean that the car lacked durability because a reasonable person would not expect durability in relation to the gear box of a car of that age. The court also took into account that the claimant could, if she had wished, have purchased an extended warranty.

Note: many people buy second-hand cars from dealers rather than buying them privately because, although they usually pay significantly more to a dealer than they would to a private seller, they get the benefit of the s 14 implied terms. They believe that the benefit of these implied terms gives them a protection in the event of the car developing faults within a reasonable time of purchase, which they would not get if they bought privately. Courts have often been prepared to hold that a fault which 'develops' within a short time of purchase must have been there at the time of purchase and that, therefore, the car was not of satisfactory quality. However, if the *Thain* decision is correct, it would appear that the claimant cannot count on much help from the Sale of Goods Act. He needs, instead, to add to his expense by entering into an additional contract for an extended warranty. This surely cannot be correct!

On the other hand, in *Lee v York Coach and Marine* (1977), it was held that an unroadworthy car was unmerchantable, even though it would require only a relatively small amount of money to make the car roadworthy.

In *Shine v General Guarantee Corp* (1988), a second-hand Fiat X19 was bought by the plaintiff. After he bought it, he discovered that it had previously been submerged in water for 24 hours or so and had been written off by an insurance company. The county court judge held that because the car was capable of functioning as such, it was of merchantable quality. However, the Court of Appeal acknowledged that a car is often more than simply a mode of transport and posed the fundamental question: 'What was the plaintiff entitled to think he was buying?' The answer, the court said, was that he thought he was buying an enthusiast's car at the sort of price that cars of that age and condition could be expected to fetch, a car described as 'a nice car, good runner, no problems'. He would, furthermore, expect it to have the benefit of the manufacturer's rust warranty but, because it had been written off, the rust warranty was invalid. The court further said that the car was one which 'no member of the public, knowing the facts, would touch with a barge pole unless they could get it at a substantially reduced price to reflect the risk they were taking ... A car is not just a means of transport: it is a form also of investment (though a deteriorating one) and every purchaser of a car must have in mind the eventual saleability of the car as well as, in this particular case, his pride in it as a specialist car for the enthusiast'. In the circumstances the court held that the car was not of merchantable quality.

'Sale' goods, shop-soiled goods, 'seconds'

It is clear that such goods must be of satisfactory quality. In *Kendall v Lillico* (1968), Lord Pearce said, 'It would be wrong to say that "seconds" are necessarily merchantable'. In such a case the court must look at the factors mentioned in s 14(2A) and (2B).

What is meant by 'in the course of a business'?

For s 14 to apply, the sale must be in the course of a business. This is intended to exclude private sales. Before 1973, s 14(2) applied only to goods which the seller normally sold, which was held not to include lines in which the seller had not previously traded. In adopting the formula suggested by the Law Commission, it appears that the legislature has broadened the circumstances in which a trader will be liable for the unsatisfactory quality of goods he sells. This is confirmed by *Stevenson v Rogers* (1999). In this case, R was a fisherman who sold a fishing boat, called the *Jelle*, to S for £600,000. He had previously sold a previous boat which he had owned. S claimed that the *Jelle* was not of merchantable quality but, in defending a claim under s 14(2) R claimed that the sale was not 'in the course of a business'. Previous cases relating to the Trade Descriptions Act were cited, which indicated that the sale of an item which was peripheral to the owner's business (for example, in *Davies v Sumner*, the sale by a courier of his motor vehicle) was not a sale in the course of a business. However, it was held by the Court of Appeal that the Trade Descriptions cases did not apply here, since the Sale of Goods legislation had a different purpose and a different history. Under the 1893 Act, s 14(3) had required the seller to be a dealer in the goods in question before he could be liable. This sub-section was renumbered s 14(2) by the Supply of Goods (Implied Terms) Act 1973 and the requirement was changed so that a seller no longer had to 'deal' in the goods, but merely to sell them 'in the course of a business'. Since the change in the law intended to impose liability on any person who sold in the business, there was no requirement for regular dealing in the goods, nor, indeed, for any previous dealing at all.

This case has the odd result that the defendant in *Davies v Sumner* was 'not guilty' of applying a false trade description to the car he sold, because in order to be guilty the sale had to be in the course of a business. However, if he had been sued by the purchaser because the car was not of satisfactory quality (or 'merchantable quality' as it was then) or fit for its purpose, the sale would have been in the course of a business. Similarly, in *R & B Customs Brokers v UDT* (1988), it was held that a Colt Shogun vehicle bought by a company partly for business use and partly for private use by one of its directors was not purchased in the course of a business. In reaching this decision, the court applied the test in *Davies v Sumner* as to whether there was any regularity of dealing in cars. As the answer was 'no', the vehicle was not purchased 'in the course of a business'; in consequence, it was a consumer sale. However, when R&B Brokers came to sell the vehicle, the sale would be in the course of a business, carrying potential liability under s 14(2) and (3) of the Sale of Goods Act.

Note, however, the exception contained in s 14(5). If a mercantile agent is selling on behalf of a client who is not selling in the course of a business, then the satisfactory quality condition will not apply, providing the buyer knew that the seller was not selling in the course of a business or, that reasonable steps were taken to bring the fact to the buyer's attention. It is presumably with s 14(5) in mind that motor traders sometimes describe a car as 'customer's property' in their adverts: they intend to indicate to a buyer that they are simply acting as agent for the seller and that, therefore, the implied condition as to satisfactory quality will not apply.

Why 'goods supplied under the contract' rather than 'goods sold under the contract'?

This wording was introduced in 1973 to reflect the existing case law. In *Geddling v Marsh* (1920), it applied where lemonade was sold in a defective bottle, even though the bottle itself was not sold under the contract but was returnable to the seller. Thus, the goods supplied under the contract were not of merchantable quality. In *Wilson v Rickett, Cockerell & Co* (1954), a detonator was inadvertently included in a consignment of coal. It was held that the coal was not of merchantable quality since the requirement of merchantability covered goods *supplied* under the contract not just the goods that were *sold*.

How long must the goods remain satisfactory?

It remains to be seen how the new definition relating to satisfactory quality, under which durability is one of the factors to be taken into account, affects the outcome of cases. Under the previous law as to merchantability, there was some acknowledgment that goods needed to be reasonably durable in that, although the time of delivery is accepted as being the time when merchantability (and presumably now satisfactory quality) was to be judged, the courts were willing to hold that if goods developed defects much sooner that they should have done, it followed that they were not of merchantable quality at the time they were delivered.

In the case of perishable goods, it is clear that they must be of satisfactory quality at the time they are appropriated to the contract and that they must remain merchantable for a reasonable time thereafter: see *Ollet v Jordan* (1918), *per* Atkin J, p 47: 'Where transit is envisaged by the contract, the goods must also be merchantable at the end of a normal journey', but there is no requirement that they be able to survive an abnormal journey (see *Mash and Murrell v Emmanuel* (1962), where a cargo of potatoes was left unventilated in transit during five days. The risk was on the buyer). Note that it is difficult to reconcile the above with the provisions of s 33, which provides that unless otherwise agreed, the buyer must take the risk of deterioration in the goods necessarily incident to the course of transit even where the seller has agreed to deliver the goods at his own risk.

Is the rule about the length of time goods are expected to remain satisfactory different for non-perishable goods? Winn J, in *Cordova Land Co v Victor Bros* (1966), said that there is a real distinction between perishable and non-perishable goods, though he was talking in the context of goods being transported. In *Crowther v Shannon Motor Co* (1975), it was said that fitness for purpose is judged at the time of delivery and, it is suggested, there is no reason to suppose that the rule as to the condition as to satisfactory quality is any different. However, it is clear from the cases (*Crowther* being an example; see also *Symmons v Cook* (1981) and *Spencer v Claud Rye* (1972)), that the courts are prepared to accept that a defect appearing fairly soon after delivery is evidence that the goods were not satisfactory at the time they were delivered.

A further point relating to the time at which goods must be satisfactory is that if the parties contemplate some process before use, satisfactory quality is judged after that process has taken place. In *Heil v Hedges* (1951), the plaintiff bought some pork chops. She only half-cooked them and became ill after eating them. Her illness was caused by the presence of a parasitic worm in the chops, which would have been killed if the chops had been properly cooked. *Held*: the sellers were not liable. Note, however, that it is generally no defence to an action under s 14(2) to show that the goods could have been made merchantable by a simple process, if the process was not one which was necessarily envisaged by the parties. In *Grant v Australian Knitting Mills* (1936), woollen underpants retained a residue of chemical following the manufacturing process and the plaintiff buyer suffered dermatitis as a result of wearing them. If the plaintiff had washed the underpants before use, the excessive sulphite which remained in them would have been washed out. *Held*: despite this, the goods were not merchantable at the time of sale and delivery.

Exceptions in s 14(2)(a) and (b)

In order to be able to rely on s 14(2)(a), it would appear that defects must be drawn specifically to the buyer's attention; it would not be sufficient to refer to possible defects in general terms such as 'shop-soiled' or 'seconds'. (Note, however, that such description may be taken into account when determining whether the goods are of satisfactory quality.)

In relation to s 14(2)(b), it seems clear that it is the examination which the buyer actually conducted which will be taken into account when deciding whether defects should have been revealed on examination. (Note that the wording of the Act was different when *Thornett & Fehr v Beers and Son* (1919) was decided, so that the case should not be regarded as authoritative in interpreting the current wording.) If, therefore, the buyer fails to examine the goods, or, for example, he examines the trousers of a suit, but not the jacket (in which there happens to be an easily discoverable defect), the seller will not be able to rely on s 14(2)(b).

THE IMPLIED TERM OF FITNESS FOR PURPOSE

Section 14(3) implies a condition that goods are fit for any particular purpose for which the goods are being bought, providing the buyer, expressly or by implication, makes known to the seller the particular purpose and it is not unreasonable in the circumstances for the buyer to rely on the skill and judgment of the seller. (Section 14(3) also protects the buyer where he is paying by instalments and the seller bought the goods from a credit broker to whom the buyer made his purpose known.)

Note that, as with s 14(2), s 14(3) applies only if the seller is selling in the course of a business.

Where the goods have only one particular purpose, the purpose for which the goods are required is made known to the seller by implication. In *Priest v Last* (1903), it was held that the purpose of a hot-water bottle was made known by implication and in *Grant v Australian Knitting Mills* (1936), the purpose of a pair of underpants was made known by implication.

Where goods are suitable for more than one purpose, the particular purpose for which the buyer requires them must be made known. In *Bristol Tramways v Fiat* (1910), buses were required for heavy passenger traffic in a hilly area. The buses which were supplied were suitable for touring. *Held*: the buses were not fit for the buyer's particular purpose, which had been made known to the seller. In *Kendall v Lillico* (1969), Brazilian ground-nut meal was supplied by K to G. K knew that G's purpose was to re-sell in smaller quantities to be compounded into food for cattle and poultry. It was held that the meal had to be fit for both cattle and poultry. The meal contained a latent toxin which killed the birds to which it had been fed. On behalf of K, it was argued that G's purpose was too wide to be a 'particular purpose'. However, the House of Lords held that 'particular purpose' was not necessarily a narrow purpose.

In *Manchester Liners v Rea* (1922), the buyer wrote, 'Please supply 500 tons South Wales coal for SS Manchester Importer at Partington on Friday'. The coal supplied was unsuitable for that particular ship because of the type of furnace it had and the ship, having set sail, had to turn back. *Held*: the fact that the order was accepted implied an obligation to supply coal suitable for the SS Manchester Importer. The fact that the coal supplied would have been suitable for most other vessels was not sufficient.

If there are special circumstances connected with the use of the goods, these must be made known. In *Griffiths v Peter Conway* (1939), a woman with particularly sensitive skin purchased a Harris Tweed coat without disclosing her sensitivity. She contracted dermatitis as a result of wearing the coat. The coat was suitable for wearing by a person with a normal skin. *Held*: there was no breach of s 14(1) (now 14(3)), as the buyer did not make known to the seller the special circumstances.

In *Slater v Finning* (1996), S owned a motor fishing vessel called *Aquarius II*. It was fitted with a Caterpillar engine. F's engineer (F being suppliers and fitters of Caterpillar engines and components) advised that a new crankshaft was needed and that while that was being done, it would be convenient to replace the camshaft. The new camshaft was a redesigned model which Caterpillar said would lower the stress on the cams, would lower the rate of wear and tear and extend the service life of the camshaft. In fact, the new camshaft gave nothing but trouble and, after two further replacements, S gave up and had a completely new engine fitted. S claimed that F were in breach of s 14(3) of the Sale of Goods Act 1979, in that the camshaft supplied for the old engine was not fit for its purpose. The evidence showed that the camshaft was normally suitable (the old engine had since been fitted to a different boat and the camshaft had functioned without trouble), but that the *Aquarius II* has an unusual tendency to produce excessive torsional resonance in the camshafts with the result that the camshafts became worn and unserviceable much earlier than would normally have been the case. This tendency was not known to either party. S argued that they had made known to F that the camshaft was being bought for the specific purpose of installation in *Aquarius II*, and that F, therefore, took the risk that *Aquarius II* might have some unknown and unusual characteristic such as would cause the camshafts to be subjected to excessive wear.

S relied on *Cammel Laird & Co v Manganese Bronze* (1934), in which the House of Lords held Manganese Bronze liable for a defective propeller which they had designed for a ship. In that case, said the court, the propeller in question was not a standard part to be fitted to a standard propulsion unit. It was specifically manufactured for a specific ship. More to the point was *Griffiths v Peter Conway* (1939), where the court held that where a buyer purchases goods from a seller, who deals in goods of that description, there is no breach of the implied condition of fitness where the failure of the goods to meet the intended purpose arises from an abnormal feature or idiosyncrasy not made known to the seller.

Whether the goods are reasonably fit for their purpose is a question of fact.

In the case of second-hand goods, the courts may be more willing to hold that relatively minor defects do not render the goods unfit for their purpose. In *Bartlett v Sidney Marcus* (1965), a second-hand Jaguar car which the seller said might need repair to the clutch costing £25, in fact needed repair costing £45. It was held that the car was fit for its purpose as it was reasonably fit for use as a car. In *Crowther v Shannon Motor Co* (1975), a second-hand Jaguar described as 'hardly run in' was in fact 'clapped out'. It was held that the car was not reasonably fit for its purpose.

Before 1973, the buyer had to show reliance on the seller's skill and judgment. The 1973 provision, now consolidated in the SGA 1979, presumes reliance by the buyer, unless the circumstances show that he did not rely or that it was not reasonable for him to rely on the skill and judgment of the seller, although even pre-1973, the courts tended to require little evidence to find that the buyer relied on the judgment of the seller.

Where a consumer purchases goods from a dealer, there will be little scope for arguing that the buyer did not rely on the seller's skill and judgment. However, even where the buyer and the seller were in the same line of business and equally expert, it has been held that the buyer relied on the seller's skill and judgment, because the goods were from a new source of supply and the seller recommended them: *Kendall v Lillico* (1969).

It is clear that partial reliance on the seller is sufficient to bring s 14(3) into operation. In *Ashington Piggeries v Christopher Hill* (1972), buyers used their own judgment as to the suitability of a specially mixed compound, containing herring-meal, for feeding to mink, but relied on the seller's skill and judgment to ensure that the compound was suitable for animals generally. In *Cammel Laird v Manganese Bronze* (1934), the sellers made propellers to buyer's specification, but certain matters were left to the discretion of the seller. The propellers were defective and these defects came entirely within the matters left to the defendants' skill and judgment. *Held*: the buyer partially relied on the seller's skill and judgment and this was sufficient to raise the requirement that the propellers should be reasonably fit for their purpose.

Finally, it is clear that both s 14(2) and s 14(3) impose a strict liability on the seller. It is no use the seller trying to argue that the lack of merchantability or fitness for purpose was not his fault, or, for example, that the defect could only have been discovered by protracted tests. In *Frost v Aylesbury Dairy Co* (1905), milk sold by the defendant to the plaintiff contained typhoid germs. These were only discoverable by prolonged investigation, by which time the milk would have been unusable. F's wife drank the contaminated milk and died. *Held*: asking for milk was sufficient to make its purpose known to the seller. The seller was, therefore, liable even though the defect was not discoverable at the time of sale.

IMPLIED CONDITIONS IN A SALE BY SAMPLE

Section 15(2) implies three conditions into a sale by sample. These are:

(a) that the bulk shall correspond with the sample in quality;

(b) that the buyer shall have a reasonable opportunity of comparing the bulk with the sample; and

(c) that the goods shall be free from any defect rendering them unsatisfactory which would not be apparent on reasonable examination of the sample.

In *Champanhac v Waller* (1948), C agreed to buy some government surplus balloons from W. C tested a sample of the material from which the balloons were made and found it to be satisfactory. W stated in writing that the balloons were 'as sample taken away' and 'we sell them to you with all faults and imperfections'. On delivery, the balloons were found to have perished. The seller sued for the price, arguing that the exemption clause meant that he was not responsible for defects in the goods. It was held that 'we sell them to you with all faults and imperfections' meant that the goods did not need to comply with s 15(2)(c), that is, the buyer couldn't complain about the latent defect which rendered the balloons unmerchantable, but it did not permit the seller to supply goods in respect of which the bulk failed to correspond with the sample.

In *Godley v Perry* (1960), the issue was whether defects in the goods were discoverable upon reasonable examination. In this case, a small boy bought a defective catapult, which, when he used it, caused him to lose an eye. He sued the retailer, arguing that the goods were not reasonably fit for their purpose. The retailer joined the wholesaler and the wholesaler joined the importer to the action, each in order to claim an indemnity from their own supplier. The third and fourth party claims were based on the allegation that the catapult was supplied by sample, and there was, therefore, an implied condition that the catapult would be free from any defect rendering it unmerchantable, which would not be apparent on reasonable examination of the sample. The fourth party sought to defend the claim by arguing that the defect in the sample was discoverable using one of a number of simple tests. It was held that the Act required a 'reasonable' examination, not a 'practical' examination, and testing the catapult in the normal manner of use was all that was reasonably required.

TERMS IMPLIED INTO A CONTRACT FOR SERVICES

Implied term as to care and skill

Under s 13 of the Supply of Goods and Service Act 1982, where, in a contract for the supply of a service, the supplier is acting in the course of a business, there is an implied term that the supplier will carry out the contract with reasonable care and skill. There is usually an overlap here with the tort of negligence. For example, the valuer who carelessly values property so that his client, a building society, lends more money than the property is worth and consequently loses money when the property is sold following the borrower's default; the dry cleaner who carelessly stains the dress he is employed to clean; the removal firm who carelessly damage furniture which they are employed to move, will all be liable under s 13.

Implied term as to time

Under s 14 of the Supply of Goods and Services Act 1982, where, in a contract for the supply of a service, the supplier is acting in the course of a business, and the time for the service to be carried out is not fixed by the contract, or left to be determined in a manner agreed in the contract, or determined by a course of dealing between the parties, there is an implied term that the supplier will carry out the service within a reasonable time. What is a reasonable time is a question of fact.

Implied term as to price

Under s 15 of the Supply of Goods and Services Act 1982, where the consideration for the service is not fixed by the contract, is not left to be determined in a manner agreed by the contract, or determined by a course of dealing between the parties, there is an implied term that the party contracting with the supplier will pay a reasonable price. What is reasonable is a question of fact.

Implied term as to fitness for purpose and satisfactory quality

It has been held in a case involving the supply of a service that, although the service does not amount to a sale, supply, or hire of goods, the outcome of the service must be fit for its required purpose and must be of satisfactory quality. (Though it is suggested that an alternative way of looking at the case would be to say that the supplier of the service failed to use due care and skill in supplying the service.)

In *St Albans City and District Council v International Computer Ltd* (1996), the plaintiff entered into a contract with the defendants whereby the defendants would produce a computer program which would meet all legislative requirements for the collection of the community charge. The legislative requirements were still being introduced while the program was being developed. The program overstated the relevant population by 2,966. This meant that the plaintiffs set the community charge at a lower rate than it would have done if it had been given the correct figure, resulting in a loss of £484,000. In addition, the council's rate of contribution to the county council, based on the incorrect population figure, was £685,000 more that it should have been. The plaintiffs recouped the shortfall of £484,000 in the community charge by setting a higher charge the following year. Nevertheless, they claimed both the £484,000 and £685,000 from the defendants as damages from breach of contract. The defendants contended that the error which caused the plaintiffs' loss occurred during December 1989, when a return of relevant population had (by statute) to be made to the Secretary of State. The defendants' liability under the contract was to supply a system which would not be fully operative until February 1990 and that, in the absence of negligence, the defendants were not liable.

Held: there was an express contractual term that the software supplied by the defendants would comply with legislative requirements. Once it became known that, by legislative requirement, the plaintiffs would have to supply the Secretary of State with details of relevant population by December 1989, it became an express contractual obligation for the defendants to supply the plaintiffs with software which would enable them to comply; even if there were no express term covering the contract, there is an implied term to the effect that the program would be fit for its purpose and of merchantable (now, satisfactory) quality. Having said that a disk which was supplied containing a program would be subject to the terms implied by the Sale of Goods Act 1979 if it were sold, or the Supply of Goods and Services Act 1982 if it were hired, Sir Iain Glidewell pointed out that neither would apply in this case, since the plaintiffs acquired the program *through its installation by an employee of the defendants*. However, although the *statutorily* implied terms as to fitness for purpose and quality could not be implied, corresponding terms could be implied by the *common law*.

EC DIRECTIVE ON CERTAIN ASPECTS OF THE SALE OF CONSUMER GOODS AND ASSOCIATED GUARANTEES: DIRECTIVE 1999/44/EC

The European Union is becoming increasingly active in seeking to harmonise basic laws of its Member States. A potentially far-reaching Directive, to be incorporated into the law of Member States by 1 January 2002, relates to consumer rights against the seller of goods and makes manufacturers' guarantees legally enforceable.

Will the Directive lead to any changes in the existing law?

In essence, the Directive introduces *consumer* rights which are broadly in accordance with what is given by ss 13 and 14 and the essence of s 15 of the Sale of Goods Act 1979. The primary remedies which the Directive gives are the repair or the replacement of the non-conforming goods. This is what often happens in practice, at the moment, in relation to consumer sales. However, in legal terms, the remedies of repair or replacement are inferior to those given by the Sale of Goods Act. The Act, as we have seen, gives a right to repudiate the contract and receive one's money back if repudiation takes place before the goods are accepted. If the goods have been accepted, then the remedy is damages.

The question therefore arises as to whether, since domestic law gives rights which are apparently better than those in the Directive, the Government needs to take any action in relation to the Directive. If, to be on the safe side, or if, on consideration, it is decided that the Directive might give the consumer certain rights which are superior to those already available, the Government decides to incorporate the Directive into English law, the question then arises as to how this shall be done. There are at least two possibilities: the Directive may be enacted as it stands, as was done with the Unfair Terms in Consumer Contracts Regulations 1994, or it may be given effect by primary legislation, as the Consumer Protection Act 1987 gave effect to the Product Liability Directive. If the latter approach were taken, it might be that the legislature would take the opportunity of revising our sales law in its entirety and make a clear distinction between consumer sales law and commercial sales law. However, since significant revisions to our sales law have been undertaken relatively recently, it would seem unlikely that the existing framework will be scrapped and a fresh start made, at least within the foreseeable future.

Scope of the Directive

The Directive only applies to sales to a consumer by a seller who 'sells consumer goods in the course of his trade, business or profession'. You will recall that, for the purposes of s 14 of the Sale of Goods Act, the sale has to be 'in the course of *a* business'. Originally it was thought, drawing an analogy with cases decided under the Trade Descriptions Act (TDA), that this meant that the sale had to be in the course of the core activity of the business. Thus, for the purposes of the TDA, it had been held, in *Davies v Sumner* (1984), that the sale of a car by a courier was not a sale in the course of a business. However, in *Stevenson v Rogers* (1999), in which the Court of Appeal held that a fisherman selling a fishing boat was selling in the course of a business, it was held that the same authorities did not apply to the Sale of Goods Act provision, which had a different history and a different purpose. Christian Twigg-Flessner and Robert Bradgate, writing in the Web Journal of Current Legal Issues (2000, issue 2), question whether the slight difference in wording between the Directive and the Sale of Goods Act means that, for the purposes of the Directive, the courts will adopt a different interpretive approach. They use the hypothetical example of a solicitor selling off a surplus computer, and point out that *his* trade, business or profession is the provision of legal services not the sale of computers. It seems unlikely that the courts will interpret the two provisions (that is, the Sale of Goods Act and the Directive) differently, since the purpose of both is broadly similar.

'Consumer' is defined more restrictively than it was in *R & B Customs Brokers v UDT* (1988), where it was held that a limited company, buying a car for the use of a director of the company, was dealing as a consumer. It means 'any *natural* person ... acting for purposes which are not related to his trade, business or profession'. Thus, companies, being artificial legal persons, are not included. The definition of 'seller' includes 'any *natural or legal person* who sells consumer goods in the course of his trade, business or profession'.

The Directive applies to the sale of 'consumer goods' but it is framed in such a way as to exclude piped supply of gas and water and sales of electricity. Goods sold by authority of law are also excluded.

Conformity with contract

Article 2(1) states simply that the seller must deliver to the consumer, goods which are in conformity with the contract of sale. Article 2(2) then proceeds to state that consumer goods are presumed to be in conformity with the contract if they:

(a) comply with the description given by the seller and possess the qualities of the goods which the seller has held out to the consumer as a sample or a model;

This is reminiscent of s 13 of the Sale of Goods Act. The question will inevitably arise as to what the word 'description' means. We have seen that in *Ashington Piggeries v Christopher Hill* (1972), the House of Lords ruled that only words needed to *identify* the goods were part of the description for the purposes of s 13. This was a significant restriction of the law, which had previously taken a very liberal view of what amounted to a 'description' (see above, p 363). It seems that the House of Lords ruling was intended to restrict the ability of the buyer to reject goods for non-material misdescriptions and to reduce the overlap between s 13 and the implied terms as to quality, contained in s 14. It may be, however, since this Directive seeks to establish 'a high level of consumer protection', that the *purposive* rule of interpretation, which should be pursued in interpreting an EC Directive, will lead to a return to the more liberal meaning of 'description' which was adopted prior to the *Ashington Piggeries* case.

Note that a buyer from a private seller (as in *Beale v Taylor* (1967)) will still have to rely on the Sale of Goods Act 1979 for his/her remedy, since the Directive applies only to consumer sales.

(b) are fit for any particular purpose for which the consumer requires them and which he made known to the seller at the time of conclusion of the contract and which the seller has accepted;

This is similar to s 14(3) of the Sale of Goods Act. We have seen that the original intention of the Sale of Goods Act appears to have been that, if goods were required for a *particular* purpose, which had been made known to the seller, then even if the goods were perfect, the buyer should nevertheless have an action if it turned out that the goods could not be used for that purpose.

For historical reasons, the implied term came to be extended so that if a person ordered 'milk', the court was prepared to hold that he had made his purpose known by implication. If the milk was unfit to drink, the implied term as to 'fitness for purpose' was broken: *Frost v Aylesbury Dairy Co* (1905).

(c) are fit for the purposes for which goods of the same type are normally used; and

(d) show the quality and performance which are normal in goods of the same type and which the consumer can reasonably expect, given the nature of the goods and taking into account any public statements on the specific characteristics of the goods made about them by the seller, the producer or his representative, particularly in advertising or on labelling.

Taken together, (c) and (d) equate, more or less, to s 14(2) of the Sale of Goods Act.

Public statements

It is significant that 'public statements' made not just by the seller, but also by the producer or his representative, may be taken into account. Under current English law, an aggrieved buyer could be faced with a defence that, providing the goods were fit for all their normal purposes, an inaccurate statement by the producer (rather than the seller) has the status of a misrepresentation, not a term of the contract, and as such is actionable against the producer rather than the retailer, as a negligent misrepresentation at common law (see, for example, *Hedley Byrne v Heller* (1964)). Alternatively, the court might be willing to treat a statement made by the producer as also being made by the seller, but even so, under current English law, the statement might be treated as a mere representation, with remedies either at common law, or, more likely, under the Misrepresentation Act 1967; or it might be treated as an express term of the contract. If the latter were the case, it might be held to be a warranty rather than a condition, with the result that the buyer would not be entitled to repudiate the contract. As the law stands, a buyer in a consumer sale may, under s 14(2), repudiate the contract for breach of condition and be entitled to a return of the purchase price in return for the goods, even though they have been used. Only when the buyer has 'accepted' the goods does he/she lose the right to repudiate the contract and must be content with damages as recompense for any loss.

In practice, it may be that this discussion is academic since, in a competitive retail environment, it is probable that the seller would, in such a situation, allow the buyer to exchange the misdescribed goods for goods which had characteristics which did comply with the description of the goods in the original sale. In practice, too, the disgruntled buyer would probably agree to pay extra, if necessary, in order to obtain the missing characteristics, but it may be that under the Directive, he would be entitled to a replacement free of charge. This might be the case under domestic law, though domestic law would frame the action as an action for damages (rather than replacement) and it may well be an action for breach of an express term rather than under s 13.

Article 4 does, however, provide a defence for the seller if he:

(i) shows that he was not and could not reasonably have been aware of the statement in question; or,

(ii) shows that at the time of the conclusion of the contract the statements had been corrected; or,

(iii) shows that the decision to buy the consumer goods could not have been influenced by the statement.

The first of these provisions provides an interesting contrast. The seller is strictly liable (that is, liable without fault) for defects in the quality of the goods, even though he/she had no hand in their manufacture and sold them to the consumer still in their box exactly as they left the producer's factory. However, the seller is liable for *statements* made by the producer only if (to turn the negative of the Directive into a positive) he was aware of the statement or could reasonably have been aware of it.

The second and third provisions are very similar to the common law relating to misrepresentation. Also included, presumably, is the situation where, at the time of the contract, the *buyer* was completely unaware of the statement. In that case, the court would probably hold that he could not have been influenced by the statement.

How would this work in practice?

Article 2(5) provides that any lack of conformity resulting from incorrect installation of the consumer goods shall be deemed to be the equivalent to lack of conformity, if:

(i) installation forms part of the contract of sale of goods; and,

(ii) the goods were installed by the seller or under his responsibility.

In such circumstances, the current English law gives the consumer a remedy under s 13 of the Supply of Goods and Services Act 1982, which provides that the service (that is, installation) must be carried out with due skill and care. However, this obligation can be excluded by the seller (subject to the Unfair Contract Terms Act and the Unfair Terms in Consumer Contracts Regulations, the former requiring that the exclusion shall satisfy the requirement of 'reasonableness' and the latter requiring 'good faith' on the part of the seller, though, in practice, these are likely to be substantially similar requirements). The terms implied in ss 13, 14 and 15 cannot be excluded in a consumer sale, so it may be of importance to establish whether the fault lies in the goods (where an exclusion clause is void) or in their installation (where an exclusion clause is permitted providing it is reasonable).

Article 2(5) goes on to provide that there shall be lack of conformity if the product, intended to be installed by the consumer, is installed by the consumer and the incorrect installation is due to a shortcoming in the installation instructions.

Article 2(3) of the Directive provides that there is no liability on the seller if the buyer is aware of, or could not reasonably be unaware of, the lack of conformity in the goods. This is similar, but by no means identical, to the provisions of s 14(2)(c).

Remedies

This is, arguably, the area in which the Directive may cause the most problems. Of course, it may be that the UK government will argue that, domestic law being more favourable, the Directive does not need to be implemented. However, that may be too simplistic a view, since it is arguable that, in certain respects, the Directive is more favourable and it may be that domestic law will need to be changed to take account of this.

Article 3(1) states that the seller shall be liable for any lack of conformity which exists at the time the goods were delivered.

Replacement or repair

The Article states that the consumer shall be entitled to have the goods brought into conformity, free of charge, by repair or by replacement, unless this is impossible or disproportionate. Article 3(4) provides that 'free of charge' mean the costs necessary to bring the goods into conformity, including the cost of postage, labour and materials (presumably where it is impracticable to use the post or it is cheaper to return the goods personally, the reasonable cost of using a car or other vehicle would be taken into account).

Thus, the Article reflects the commercial reality more than the Sale of Goods Act, which, if you recall, allows the buyer to repudiate the contract for breach of condition and gain rescission of the contract if he/she acts before the goods have been 'accepted'. Otherwise, there is a right to damages for breach of warranty. What happens in practice is that normally, providing the defect in the goods arises within a relatively short time of purchase, the buyer is offered, and accepts, replacement goods. (Cars tend to be an exception: once the car has been registered in the customer's name, the seller will try, at all costs, to avoid giving any remedy except a repair.) If the goods become defective after a period of time, repair is usually the remedy offered.

The significance of the 'replacement or repair' provision is that a supplier will usually prefer to replace goods rather than give money back and, in so doing, lose a sale; in relation to repair, the seller often has the resources to repair goods, or send them back to the manufacturer, and this will usually be cheaper than allowing the consumer to find his/her own repairer and then claim as damages the amount of the repairer's bill. A further reason for allowing the retailer to undertake the repair is that the manufacturer's guarantee is invalidated if repairs are undertaken by an 'unauthorised' repairer, although, if the unauthorised repairer were competent, it may be doubtful whether a court of law would uphold what is, in effect, an exemption from liability.

If replacement or repair would be disproportionate, the buyer is entitled to an appropriate reduction in the price or have the contract rescinded.

This entitlement also arises:

(a) if the seller has not completed the remedy within a reasonable time; or

(b) if the seller has not completed the remedy without significant inconvenience to the consumer.

CHAPTER 19

SALE OF GOODS: PASSING OF PROPERTY

When property in goods passes, the effect is that the buyer becomes the owner of the goods in place of the seller. If the buyer has taken delivery of, and paid for, the goods, it will be difficult to avoid the inference that he has also acquired property in the goods. However, although s 28 of the Sale of Goods Act 1979 states that, unless otherwise agreed, delivery of the goods and payment of the price are concurrent conditions, in practice payment of the price is often divorced from the delivery of the goods, particularly in commercial contracts in which it is usual for the seller to give a period of credit to the buyer. This being the case, there are two points regarding the passing of property in goods, which it is important to realise at the outset:

(a) *Property* in goods can pass to the buyer even though *possession* of the goods remains with the seller, and conversely, possession of the goods can be given to the buyer without the property in the goods also passing.

(b) Payment of the *price* of the goods by the buyer does not necessarily mean that the property in the goods passes to *him*.

WHY IT IS IMPORTANT TO KNOW WHEN THE PROPERTY IN THE GOODS PASSES

The main object of the contract of sale is to pass property in goods from the seller to the buyer. It is important to know at what stage in the transaction the property passes for two main reasons:

(a) Under s 20 of the Sale of Goods Act 1979, the person who has property in the goods also bears the risk of loss, damage, destruction or deterioration of the goods, unless the parties have agreed otherwise.

This rule applies even if the buyer has not taken delivery of the goods from the seller. For example, suppose B buys goods from S on terms that S is to keep possession of the goods pending their resale by B. Before B has resold the goods, they are destroyed by fire on S's premises. B would be liable to pay the price of the goods (assuming he had not done so already). Of course, if the loss or damage had been caused by negligence on the part of S, B could counter-claim against S and the two claims would (probably) cancel each other out. However, in case of accidental loss or damage B would have to bear the loss himself, and in the case where the loss or damage was caused by the wrongful act of a third party, B would have to claim against the third party. In practice, such *risks* are usually covered by insurance, so that any legal action may be simply to determine which of two insurance companies, B's or S's, will have to pay for the loss or damage to the goods.

(b) If the seller becomes *bankrupt* or if, in the case of a *company* being the seller, a liquidator is appointed to wind up the company and the company is insolvent, the buyer can only claim the goods (even though he has paid the price of the goods) if the property in the goods has passed to him.

In practice, the application of this rule has caused distress to consumers who have paid for goods in advance, only to find that before the goods have been delivered, the seller has gone bankrupt or gone into liquidation. In such a case, the disappointed buyer will usually lose the whole, or at least the greater part, of his advance payment.

THE RULES GOVERNING THE PASSING OF PROPERTY

The rules determining when the property passes in a sale depend on whether the goods in question are *unascertained, ascertained* or *specific.*

Unascertained goods

The term 'unascertained goods' is not defined in the Sale of Goods Act. However, the term is the antithesis of specific goods: it must mean goods not identified and agreed upon at the time of the contract.

Examples of unascertained goods

B phones the wine merchant and asks for a dozen bottles of champagne to be delivered to him. The contract is for *unascertained goods.*

B calls at the electrical shop and contracts to buy a Hoover washing machine (not knowing which of the machines will be delivered to him from stock). He is agreeing to buy *unascertained goods.*

B is shown a stock of 20,000 shirts in a warehouse. He agrees to buy 10,000 of them. The contract is for *unascertained* goods.

B contracts to buy 10,000 pairs of shoes which have not yet been made. The contract is for *unascertained goods.*

The rule in respect of unascertained goods

Section 16 of the Sale of Goods Act 1979 states: '... where there is a contract for the sale of *unascertained goods,* no property in the goods is transferred to the buyer unless and until the goods are *ascertained.*' This tells us only that the buyer cannot claim to own unascertained goods. it does not say that property necessarily passes once the goods have become ascertained. in order to discover when the property passes it becomes necessary to look at the provisions of s 17 and, if that does not help, at the provisions of s 18, r 5. Section 16 must now be read subject to the modifications introduced by the new ss 20A and 20B, dealt with below.

Ascertained goods

'Ascertained' is not defined in the Sale of Goods Act 1979. However, 'ascertained' probably means 'identified in accordance with the agreement *after the time* the contract is made', *per* Atkin LJ in *Re Wait* (1927) (see below).

Specific goods

'Specific goods' are defined in s 61 of the Sale of Goods Act 1979 as being 'goods identified and agreed on *at the time* a contract of sale is made'. Thus, an agreement with a garage to buy the red Ford Sierra displayed on their forecourt will be a sale of specific goods. An order submitted on your behalf to the Ford factory for a new, red Ford Sierra will not.

THE RULE RELATING TO SPECIFIC OR ASCERTAINED GOODS

Under s 17(1) of the Sale of Goods Act 1979, the property in *specific* or *ascertained* goods passes at such time as the parties intend it to pass. Subsection (2) goes on to say that for the purpose of ascertaining the intention of the parties, regard shall be had to the *terms* of the contract, the *conduct* of the parties and the *circumstances* of the case.

Section 18 goes on to give five rules for ascertaining the intention of the parties, which are to apply *unless a different intention appears*. The first four rules apply to contracts for the sale of specific goods. The last one applies to *unascertained* goods and *future goods sold by description* (which must, of necessity, be unascertained goods).

Rule 1

Rule 1 states: where there is an *unconditional* contract for the sale of *specific* goods in a *deliverable* state, the property in the goods passes to the buyer *when the contract is made*, and it is *immaterial* whether the time of *payment* or the time of *delivery*, or both, be *postponed*. Under s 61(5), 'deliverable state' means such a state that the buyer would be obliged to take delivery of them.

In *Tarling v Baxter* (1827), a contract for the sale of a haystack was made on 6 January, the price was to be paid on 4 February, but the hay was not to be removed until 1 May. On 20 January, the stack was destroyed by fire. The property and, therefore, the risk, passed when the contract was made and the buyer had to pay the price of the stack.

In *Dennant v Skinner and Collom* (1948), X, a rogue, bid for a car at an auction and it was knocked down to him. He was allowed to take the car away, having given the auctioneer a false name and address and having signed a form to the effect that property in the car would not pass until the cheque was cleared. X then sold the car to Y, who resold it to the defendants. The cheque which X had given the plaintiffs was dishonoured and in consequence the plaintiffs sought to recover the car from the defendants. *Held*: s 18, r 1 had already operated to pass the property in the car to X, before he signed the form by which the plaintiffs claimed to retain title. The defendants therefore had a good title to the car.

A case in which a different intention appeared was *Re Anchor Line (Henderson Bros) Ltd* (1937). In this case, specific goods were purchased on deferred payment terms. The contract provided that the goods were to be at the buyer's risk. It was held by the Court of Appeal that property had not passed, under s 18, r 1, at the time the contract was made, since the clause allocating risk would have been unnecessary if that had been the parties' intention.

In *Ward v Bignall* (1967), B contracted to buy a Ford Zodiac and a Vanguard Estate from W for a total of £850. B subsequently refused to make payment and take delivery. W exercised his right of resale under s 48(3) of the Act and resold the Vanguard but not the Ford. W then claimed the balance of the price from B, to which they were entitled only if (a) the property in the cars had passed, and (b) the resale had not had the effect of rescinding the contract. Diplock LJ said:

> ... in the opinion of the seller's solicitors, the property had already passed to the buyer. That opinion was no doubt based on s 18, r 1 of the Sale of Goods Act 1893. The governing rule, however, is s 17, and in modern times very little is needed to give rise to the inference that property in specific goods is to pass only on delivery or payment. I think the court should have inferred that in this case.

Thus, W was entitled to damages only.

Diplock LJ gives no clues as to what the 'very little' might be which gives rise to the inference and with respect, this dictum, though widely and uncritically quoted, gives rise to a number of problems.

Rule 2

Rule 2 states: where there is a contract for the sale of specific goods and the seller is bound to do something to the goods for the purpose of putting them into a deliverable state, the property does not pass until such thing is done, and the buyer has notice that it has been done.

In *Underwood Ltd v Burgh Castle Brick and Cement Syndicate* (1922), the seller sold a 30-ton condensing engine 'free on rail London'. (This means that the seller would pay for transport to a London railway station and be responsible for the goods until they had been safely loaded on to a train nominated by the buyers.) The engine was dismantled by the sellers, but as it was being loaded on to a lorry, part of the machine was accidentally broken. The question arose as to whether the property in the goods (and, therefore, the risk of accidental damage) had passed to the purchasers. *Held* by the Court of Appeal: the property in the goods had not passed because at the time the contract was made, the engine was not in a deliverable state. Therefore s 18, r 1 could not apply. Section 18, r 2 *did* apply. Property had not passed and the risk was still on the sellers. The court said that, alternatively, if the parties had expressed an intention within the meaning of s 17, their intention was that property should not pass until the engine was safely on rail.

Rule 3

Rule 3 states: where there is a contract for the sale of specific goods in a deliverable state, but the *seller* is bound to weigh, measure, test or do some other act or thing with reference to the goods for the purpose of ascertaining the price, the property does not pass until such act or thing is done and the buyer has notice that it has been done.

Rule 4

Rule 4 states: when goods are delivered to the buyer on approval or on sale or return or other similar terms, the property therein passes to the buyer:

(a) when he signifies his approval or acceptance to the seller or does any other act adopting the transaction;

(b) if he does not signify his approval or acceptance to the seller but retains the goods without giving notice of rejection, then, if a time has been fixed for the return of the goods, on the expiration of that time, and if no time has been fixed, on the expiration of a reasonable time. What is a reasonable time is a question of fact.

It can thus be seen that one of *three* events will give rise to a sale under a sale or return contract:

(i) the buyer signifies his approval or acceptance to the seller;

(ii) the buyer does any other act adopting the transaction.

In *Kirkham v Attenborough* (1897), A delivered goods to B on a sale or return basis. B pawned the goods. It was held that this was an act adopting the transaction and therefore property has passed to B. A could not, therefore, recover the goods from the pawnbroker (though, of course, he would have an action against B for the price of the goods, for what it was worth).

In *Genn v Winkel* (1912), A delivered diamonds to B on a sale or return basis. B delivered them to C on similar terms and C to D, again on similar terms. While in D's possession the diamonds were lost. Because B was unable to return the diamonds he had adopted the transaction and was liable if he was not able to return them at the time fixed for their return or, if no time had been fixed, on the expiration of a reasonable time.

(iii) if the buyer retains the goods beyond the time fixed for their return, or if no time has been fixed, beyond a reasonable time.

In *Poole v Smith's Car Sales* (1962), it was agreed that a Vauxhall car belonging to the plaintiff, which was in the possession of the defendant, could be sold by the defendant providing the plaintiff received £325 for it. (Both the plaintiff and the defendant were car dealers.) The car remained unsold for three months and the plaintiff demanded its return. When returned it was damaged, and the plaintiff refused to accept it. He sued for the price. It was held by the Court of Appeal that since the parties had treated the agreement as one of sale or return, it must be treated as such, and since the defendant had retained the car beyond a reasonable time, the property in it had passed to them and they were therefore liable for the price.

The wise seller will ensure that the contract under which he sends goods on sale or return provides for the risk to be allocated to the person to whom they are sent. Otherwise the seller, being the owner until one of the three conditions mentioned in r 4 are met, will bear the risk of any accidental loss, damage, deterioration or destruction while they are in the possession of the potential purchaser. He will also ensure that the property in the goods does not pass until the goods have been paid for, and thus avoid the problem which was encountered by the seller in *Kirkham v Attenborough* (above). The effect of such a provision is to displace the application of s 18, r 4 and replace it with s 17 (the intention of the parties).

In *Weiner v Gill* (1906), the seller A, protected himself by a provision in the contract that property was not to pass until the goods were paid for. He sent goods to B on a cash sale or return basis. C told B that he could find a customer for them and B gave the goods to C on that basis. C pawned the goods. It was held that A could recover the goods from the pawnbroker.

Where there is no contractual provision to the contrary, it will be sufficient to give notice of return without specifying the exact goods. It is not necessary that they should be available for immediate return providing they can be returned within a reasonable time.

In *Atari (UK) Ltd v Electronics Boutique Stores (UK) Ltd* (1998), A supplied E, who was a retailer wishing to test the market for electronic games manufactured by A, with a quantity of games on a sale or return basis. The games were to be returned by 31 January 1996. The price was to be paid in advance of this date, but the Court of Appeal attached no significance to this provision in relation to when and if property of the games passed to E. On 19 January 1996, E told A that the goods had not sold well and that remaining stock was to be recalled to central stock whence it would be returned to A. A argued that the notice of return was insufficient on three grounds: (a) it required further action before the goods could be returned – return from the retail outlets to central stock; (b) the exact goods to be returned were not specified; and (c) E were not in a position to return the goods at the time the notice was sent. The parties agreed that an actual return of the goods was not necessary in order to bring s 18, r 4 into play – a valid notice would be sufficient.

Held, unanimously by the Court of Appeal: the notice of return was sufficient. It was not necessary to specify the specific goods to be returned. E had indicated that they wished to return the goods and that the goods to be returned were those which were unsold. Further, it was not necessary that the goods were available for immediate return provided they could be returned within a reasonable time from the time of the notice. It would be possible to specify, by contract, that the exact goods to be returned should be specified and that they should be available for immediate return but that was not done in the present case.

UNASCERTAINED GOODS

Rule 5

Rule 5 provides:

(a) where there is a contract for the sale of unascertained or future goods by description, and goods of that description are unconditionally appropriated to the contract, either by the seller with the assent of the buyer, or by the buyer with the assent of the seller, the property in the goods then passes to the buyer; and the assent may be express or implied, and may be given either before or after the appropriation is made;

(b) where, in pursuance of the contract, the seller delivers the goods to the buyer or to a carrier or other bailee or custodier (whether named by the buyer or not) for the purpose of transmission to the buyer, and does not reserve the right of disposal, he is to be taken to have unconditionally appropriated the goods to the contract.

There are, therefore, two circumstances in which, in the absence of contrary intention, property passes in unascertained goods:

(a) Where there is an unconditional appropriation of the goods to the contract

This means that the goods have been irrevocably earmarked for the performance so that the delivery of any other goods would not suffice for the performance of the contract. A simple setting aside of the goods is not sufficient to amount to an unconditional appropriation, *per* the judgment of Pearson J in *Carlos Federspiel v Twigg* (1957).

In *Wardar's v W Norwood & Sons* (1968), S owned a stock of frozen kidneys, which were held to S's order by a warehouseman W, to B. He sold 600 cartons of them to B, and gave B an order addressed to W for W to deliver the goods to B. When B's carrier arrived at the warehouse, 600 cartons had already been set aside for him. The carrier gave the delivery order to W, who ordered that loading should commence. The kidneys were in good condition at that time, but during loading they deteriorated because: (a) the porters had a very long tea break; and (b) the carrier failed to turn on the refrigeration unit in his vehicle. The question arose as to who owned the goods and had therefore to bear the loss of the deterioration of the goods. *Held* by the Court of Appeal: where unascertained goods are in the possession of a third party, property and risk passes when the third party, having selected an appropriate part of the goods, acknowledges that he holds them on the buyer's behalf. In the present case, the property and risk passed when W received the delivery order and acted on it by ordering the loading to commence. As the goods had deteriorated after that time, the risk was on the buyer and he had to pay the price.

Where the contracted goods are mixed with other goods of the same description

(b) Where the seller delivers the goods to a carrier for transmission to the buyer

Where the contracted goods are mixed with other goods of the same description, there will be *no appropriation* until the contract goods are separated from the other goods and are *irrevocably appropriated* to the contract. Thus, if Ann agrees to buy 100 tons of coal from Ben Ltd's stock of 150 tons, the basic rule is that no property can pass to Ann until her 100 tons are unconditionally appropriated to her contract.

The difficulty with this rule is that it is not uncommon for purchasers of commodities to pay the price in advance. If this has been the case, and Ben Ltd were to go into liquidation (that is, become subject to a process which would lead to the company being wound-up) because of insolvency, before Ann's goods had been appropriated to the contract, Ann would have no property in the coal. The liquidator (that is, the person responsible for collecting in all the assets of the company with a view to paying off as much of the company debt as possible) would, therefore, be entitled to take possession of the coal and sell it for the benefit of the creditors. Ann would be able to claim the repayment of her purchase price. However, as we shall see in Chapter 31, p 704, a company's creditors are ranked in order of priority. Ann would be classified as an ordinary creditor of the company and, as such, would be way down the list of priority. It is seldom that there are any assets remaining to pay the ordinary creditors. Therefore, in all likelihood, she would receive nothing.

The case of *Re Wait* (1927) illustrates the rule. W contracted to buy 1,000 tons of wheat which was on board a ship heading for England from the USA. He contracted to sell 500 tons of this wheat to H, who paid the price in advance of delivery. W went bankrupt. Some of the wheat had been off-loaded so that 530 tons remained, all of it W's property. Nothing had been done to separate H's 500 tons from the remaining 30 tons. It was held that property in the wheat had not passed to H. H's only remedy was to prove in W's bankruptcy for the sum of £5,933 5s which had been paid for the wheat, which, as we have already seen, is usually an unsatisfactory remedy.

The law developed two main exceptions to the rule that goods must be unconditionally appropriated before property can pass. These are:

(a) ascertainment by exhaustion; and,

(b) tenancy in common.

A further important exception was created by ss 20A and 20B of the Sale of Goods Act 1979 and is dealt with below, p 402.

(a) Ascertainment by exhaustion

There may be an 'ascertainment by exhaustion', that is, if there are no other goods which would satisfy the *contract description*, other than the quantity bought by the buyer. This principle needs to be approached with caution. If the seller has the exact stock of goods bought by the buyer, the goods will not be treated as ascertained *unless those goods and only those goods* can be properly tendered in satisfaction of the contract.

For example, if Sheila agrees to sell Bruce 20 bottles of Kangaroo wine out of the stock of 100 in her cellar, it would seem that if she sells and delivers the other 80 so that only 20 remain, the goods become ascertained by exhaustion when only 20 remain. If, however, Sheila simply agrees to sell Bruce 20 bottles of Kangaroo wine, it is immaterial that the exact amount of wine remains in Sheila's cellar. Because she is not contractually bound to deliver those 20 bottles but could, without breach of contract, satisfy the contract by securing bottles from elsewhere, the goods do not become ascertained by exhaustion. Two cases will illustrate these principles.

In *Wait & James v Midland Bank* (1926), W & J owned a stock of wheat which had arrived in the UK on the *SS Thistleross* and was lying in a warehouse at Avonmouth. They had contracted to sell this wheat in various quantities to various buyers. One of the buyers, Redlers, had entered into three contracts to buy 250, 250, and 750 quarters. Redlers had taken delivery of 400 of the quarters due to them and had pledged the other 850 quarters as security to the Midland Bank. Redlers had not paid for the wheat and hadn't the means to repay the Bank. The question arose as to whether the wheat was unascertained goods and therefore still owned by W & J, or whether the wheat had become ascertained and was therefore owned by Redlers. If the goods were still owned by W & J, they could exercise their rights as unpaid sellers and resell the goods. If the goods were owned by Redlers, the Bank could realise their security by taking possession of the wheat. It was *held* that the wheat was ascertained by exhaustion. The only wheat which could satisfy the contract description was wheat which had been shipped *per* the *SS Thistleross* and was lying in a warehouse in Avonmouth.

The rule which emerged from this case has now been given statutory effect, having been incorporated into the Sale of Goods Act 1979 as s 18, r 5, para 3.

The situation was slightly different in *Karlshamns Oljefabriker v Eastport Navigation Corp* (1982). The buyers had not only one, but *five* contracts to buy part of the same bulk, a cargo of copra. The copra belonging to the other buyers was offloaded so that only the buyer's goods remained. The defendant shipowners, who were being sued for negligently damaging the goods, argued that they were not liable to the claimants because the goods did not belong to the claimants at the time of the damage. They argued that property in the goods had not passed by exhaustion because there were five contracts, and it was not possible to say that property had passed by exhaustion for each contract. *Held*: the copra belonging to K had been ascertained by exhaustion. Looking at the strict wording of s 16, the goods sold under each of the contracts had to be ascertained separately. However, the purpose of the rule is so that each separate buyer is able to identify the goods which he owns. Where, as in this case, all the goods comprising the bulk are owned by the same buyer, there is no need to impose such a solution.

The rule which emerged from this case has now been given statutory effect by being incorporated into the Sale of Goods Act as s 18, r 5, para 4.

A case in which it was argued unsuccessfully that the goods were ascertained by exhaustion is *Re London Wine Co* (1986). It was also argued in this case that a trust had been created by the seller in favour of the buyer of the goods. This claim, too, was unsuccessful.

London Wine were sellers of wine, which was stored in various warehouses. On purchase, the customers had received a 'Certificate of Title' from the company, in respect of the wine that they had bought. This described the customer as the 'sole and beneficial owner' of the purchased wine. Sales publicity asserted that the company had a lien over the wine (a lien is a right by a non-owner of goods to retain possession of them until a certain condition, in this case, the payment of the price, is fulfilled). The buyer paid storage and insurance costs in respect of the wine until either he chose to take delivery of the wine, or he sold the wine on to a third party. The company, in its circulars, referred to the wine as 'your wine'.

The circumstances of three different types of customer were considered by the court:

(a) where a customer had bought the company's entire stock of a particular wine;

(b) where two or more customers had bought the entire stock of a particular wine;

(c) where a customer had purchased a proportion of the stock of a particular wine, and the company had acknowledged that it held the appropriate quantity of that wine to the order of the customer. In some such cases, the customer had pledged the wine as security for a loan and the pledgee (that is, the lender) had been given the same assurance regarding ownership as had been given to the buyer.

In the first case, there was a strong argument to the effect that the wine had been ascertained by exhaustion. In the second case, there was a similar argument, differing from the first case in that it was argued that, because there was more than one buyer, the buyers were tenants in common (that is, they divided the wine between them in proportion to their purchases). The court did not agree with this analysis, saying that the company may have chosen to buy other wine in order to perform its contract with the buyer – the company was not compelled to use the particular wine left in their warehouses, even though it was the exact amount, in order to perform the contracts. However, it is clear that the result would have been different if the buyers had bought wine stored in a specified warehouse. The case would then have been identical in principle to *Wait & James v Midland Bank* (above), where only wheat shipped *per SS Thistleross* and lying in the warehouse in Avonmouth could have been used in performance of the contract.

In the third case, no attempt was made to argue that property in the goods had passed: it was accepted that the goods had not been irrevocably earmarked to the contract and that they could not have been ascertained by exhaustion. However, it was argued in all three cases that by referring to 'your wines', to the purchaser being the 'sole beneficial owner', to the company having a lien over the goods, a *trust* had been created in favour of the purchasers. Thus, it was argued that although the company were the legal owners of the wine, they simply held it on trust for the purchasers. However, this argument failed, since the subject matter of a trust has to be certain. In this case, it was not certain which bottles of wine were to be the subject of the trust.

(b) A tenancy in common may be created

In this situation, the goods of the buyer are appropriated to the contract but they are mixed with goods of the other buyers. It could, therefore, still be held that, as there is uncertainty about which goods belong to which buyers, there still has been no appropriation of the goods to the contract. However, in *Re Stapylton Fletcher* (1994), the court took a different view. The case was similar in its facts to *Re London Wine*. The vital difference in this case was that, in respect of some purchases, the customers' wine, although not allocated to particular customers, was separated from the normal trading stock. Although it was not always individually labelled, the seller's records were kept in proper order and recorded the transfer of ownership from the seller to the buyer, and the vendor did not act as if the goods were still their own, that is, they did not 'raid' the stock if they were short of wine for another customer. It was held that the separation and its surrounding circumstances amounted to an ascertainment of the goods for the purposes of s 16. Property therefore passed to the buyers by common intention of the seller and the buyer: the buyers became tenants in common of the wine. (The word 'tenant' is used in its original legal meaning of 'holder'.)

Sections 20A and 20B of the Sale of Goods Act 1979

The general rule that no property can pass in a case where the buyer has bought and paid for a share of a bulk of goods was thought by some to be unfair. In consequence, the Law Commission was asked to examine the issue. The Law Commission in its Report, *The Sale of Goods Forming Part of a Bulk*, No 215, 1993, recommended that where there is a contract for the sale of a specified quantity of unascertained goods, there should be a new rule which would enable property in an undivided share in the bulk to pass before ascertainment of goods relating to specific contracts. The new rule would apply only where all or part of the goods had been paid for and would apply only to the proportion of the goods which had been paid for.

These recommendations have now been put into effect by adding new ss 20A and 20B to the Sale of Goods Act. Their effect is to give statutory recognition to the concept of *common ownership of goods comprised in a bulk*. In addition, as we have seen, s 18 has been amended in order to give statutory recognition to the concept of *ascertainment by exhaustion*.

The essential effect of the provisions in ss 20A and B is to allow the property in an unascertained share of a bulk of goods to pass before the goods are ascertained. Each part-owner of the bulk becomes an owner in common with the other part-owners of the bulk.

The rules will apply only where:

(a) the goods, or some of them, form part of a bulk which is identified either in the contract or by some subsequent agreement between the parties.

Thus, the bulk must be identified, for example, 'wine in our Northampton warehouse', or 'wheat aboard SS *Thistleross*';

(b) the buyer has paid the price for some or all of the goods which are the subject of the contract and which form part of the bulk.

As soon as these two conditions are met (or at such later time as the parties may agree), the buyer becomes an owner in common of the bulk.

Example

John has bought from Kevin 100 tons of wheat from a bulk of 500 tons aboard the SS *Linda*. Kevin has retained the other 400 tons for himself. John has paid the full price for the wheat in advance. Before the wheat is delivered, Kevin goes bankrupt. Under the pre-existing law, exemplified by *Re Wait*, John would not have been entitled to the goods because they have not been unconditionally appropriated to the contract. John would, therefore, have got nothing for his money and, although he would have been entitled to claim the return of his money from Kevin (plus damages for breach of contact, if appropriate), such an entitlement against a bankrupt is usually useless. However, under the reformed law, contained in ss 20A and 20B, John is an owner in common of the bulk with Kevin and is entitled to 100 tons from the bulk of 500 tons.

Example

Mukesh has bought 100 tons of coal from Nancy, of which 50 tons are out of 300 tons which are aboard SS *Oliver*, 50 tons from an unspecified source, to be shipped later. Mukesh has paid for the whole 100 tons in advance. Nancy has gone bankrupt. Mukesh will be an owner in common of the coal which is aboard the SS *Oliver* and, therefore, will be entitled to the 50 tons which he has paid for. However, because he cannot identify the bulk out of which the remaining 50 tons will come, he can only claim his money back in respect of the remaining 50 tons.

Sub-section (4) of s 20A provides that if the aggregate of the undivided shares in the bulk would, at any time, exceed the whole of the bulk at that time, the undivided share in the bulk of each buyer shall be reduced proportionately so that the aggregate of the undivided shares is equal to the whole bulk.

Example

Paula has bought and paid for 100 tons of copper from Quentin out of 600 tons which are aboard the SS *Rover*. Owing to a miscalculation, Quentin has actually sold 1200 tons. 100 tons have been sold to Sam, 500 to Tina and 500 to Uriah. All have paid for their goods in advance. They will be co-owners of the 600 tons which are actually aboard the ship, in proportion to the quantity they have bought: that is, Tina and Uriah will each be entitled to 250 tons, and Paula and Sam will be each entitled to 50 tons. Again, their only claim in respect of the balance of their goods will be for the return of the appropriate proportion of their purchase price (and damages).

Sub-section (5) provides:

> Where the buyer has paid the price for only some of the goods due to him out of a bulk, any delivery to the buyer out of the bulk shall ... be ascribed ... to the goods in respect of which payment has been made.

Example

Ahmed buys 100 tons of potatoes from Cathy Ltd. The potatoes are part of a bulk of 800 tons aboard the *SS Beryl*. Ahmed has paid for 50 tons. Before the potatoes are delivered to Ahmed, Cathy Ltd goes into liquidation. Fifty tons are delivered to Ahmed. He cannot then claim that the 50 tons which have been delivered to him are the 50 tons which he has not paid for, and that he is therefore entitled to delivery of the remaining 50 tons from the liquidator, under the terms of S 20A, on the grounds that the remaining 50 tons are the potatoes he has paid for.

Sub-section (6) states:

> ... payment of part of the price for any goods, shall be treated as payment for a corresponding part of the goods.

Example

Suppose in the example above, Ahmed had paid only half the purchase price. In that case Ahmed will be entitled to 50 tons from the bulk. The pre-existing rules will apply to the passing of property and risk in relation to the other 50 tons.

Section 20B contains a set of provisions aimed at preventing litigation between one common owner and another, for example, where one of the owners in common receives a shortfall in relation to the goods to which he is entitled. He will, of course, be able to sue the seller in such circumstances.

Example

Gina and Harish have each bought and paid for 100 tons of cocoa aboard the *SS Java*. Owing to an error, only 100 tons have been loaded. We have seen that under s 20A(3), the shares of the buyers are reduced proportionately so that each owns 50 tons of the cocoa on board. However, suppose that Gina's cocoa is to be delivered to London and Harish's to Hull. When the *SS Java* reaches London, Gina offloads all of the 100 tons for which she has paid. It would appear that, under the provisions of s 20B, Harish would be prevented from claiming from Gina the 50 tons of which he had become the owner in common.

We have seen that s 18, r 5 has had additional paras 3 and 4 added in order to give statutory effect to the doctrine of ascertainment by exhaustion. Note that property in goods which are ascertained by exhaustion under s 18, r 5(3) will pass *irrespective of whether the price, or any part of it has been pre-paid*. This is different to the provisions of s 20A which require that the price, or part of, it has been pre-paid and, in essence, only allows property to pass in the goods which have been paid for.

Example

Suppose Drew has bought from Fatima 100 tons of barley out of a bulk of 500 tons aboard the *SS Everton* to be delivered at the port of Liverpool. After deliveries have been made at London, there are only 100 tons left aboard the vessel. The property in the 100 tons will pass to Drew. *This will be the case even though he has not paid the price of the goods or any part of the price.* This would also be the case if less than 100 tons remained. In that case, Drew would have an action for breach of contract for non-delivery of the balance.

(c) Where the seller delivers the goods to the buyer or to a carrier for transmission to the buyer

Example

Sarah sells 50 tons of coal to Richard. Sarah loads 50 tons of coal onto a lorry owned by Transport Ltd for transmission to Richard. The goods are deemed to be ascertained by s 18, r 5(2) and property will pass to Richard once the coal is loaded onto the lorry.

(d) Where more than the goods contracted for are handed to a carrier

In such a case, the property in the goods does not pass under r 5(2), but passes under r 5(1) at the time the exact amount of goods are appropriated to the contract. In *Healy v Howlett & Sons* (1917), S, an Irish fish exporter, sold 20 boxes of fish to B. S put 190 boxes of fish for various buyers including B, on the railway and instructed the railway officials to set aside 20 boxes for B's contract. At the same time, he sent B an invoice stating that the goods were at his 'sole risk'. The train was delayed and before the 20 boxes had been appropriated to the contract, the fish had deteriorated and was no longer merchantable. *Held*: the property in the boxes did not pass to B until they were appropriated. As the fish was not merchantable at the time the property passed, B was not bound to accept it. Further, the invoice stating that the goods were at B's sole risk was ineffective to allocate risk, as it was not part of the contract. In such a case, it would appear that the new s 20 would not apply to pass property, since there was not a sale from an identified bulk and there was no payment in advance.

Goods must be in a deliverable state

Property does not pass under r 5(1) unless the goods are in a deliverable state, though, for the operation of s 20A and B, an unascertained share of a bulk does not need to be in a deliverable state. In *Phillip Head v Showfronts* (1970), B ordered a carpet from S, which S was to lay on B's premises. S delivered the carpet, but it had to be sent away to be stitched. When it was redelivered it was in bales. It was then stolen from B's premises. *Held*: property had not passed to B, because the carpet, being in bales, was not in a deliverable state.

Buyer may assent by conduct to the appropriation of goods by the seller

The buyer may, by his conduct, be deemed to have assented to the appropriation of the goods by the seller. See *Pignatoro v Gilroy* (1919), in which S sold 140 bags of rice to B. A delivery note was sent in respect of 115 bags. S asked B to collect the other bags from S's premises without delay. B did nothing for one month, during which the 15 bags were stolen. The court held that as, on the evidence, there were only 15 bags at S's premises, B had assented to the appropriation of those bags to the contract by not objecting when asked to take delivery. The property and risk had therefore passed to B. Furthermore, it seems clear that the court would, if necessary, have held that the appropriation of 15 bags out of a greater quantity would have been done with the implied assent of B and property would therefore have passed.

Where the seller delivers the goods to a carrier, etc, for the purpose of transmission to the buyer: in *Wait v Baker* (1848), it was said 'the moment the goods which have been selected in pursuance of the contract are delivered to the carrier, the carrier becomes the agent of the vendee (buyer) ... there is no doubt that property passes by such delivery to the carrier'.

In *Federspiel v Charles Twigg* (1957), F, a Costa Rican company, purchased 85 bicycles from T, an English company, on fob terms. (Fob means 'free on board' and means that the seller will undertake the carriage of the goods to a designated ship and will place them on board the ship, but the buyer is responsible for paying the onward shipping costs of the goods and insurance in transit, etc.) F paid the purchase price in advance. The bicycles had been packed into cases marked with F's name and were registered for consignment. Shipping space had been booked. The bicycles then became charged to a receiver for T. (A receiver is a person appointed by creditors of a company in order to manage the assets of the company for the benefit of the creditors. The receiver becomes the legal owner of the assets.) The question arose at to whether F's property in the goods had passed to F before the goods became charged to the receiver. *Held*: the intention of the parties, as was almost invariably the case in fob contracts, was that property in the goods should pass when they were shipped (that is, placed on board ship) and not before.

Reservation of right of disposal

Under s 18, r 5(2), delivery to a carrier, etc, for transmission to the buyer passes property only if the seller does not reserve the right of disposal. 'Reserve the right of disposal' means that the seller imposes conditions upon the buyer, and until these conditions are met, the goods do not become the property of the buyer. Section 19 deals with the question of the passing of property where a right of disposal is reserved by the seller. It provides that property in the goods does not pass until the conditions imposed by the seller have been met.

RISK OF LOSS, DAMAGE, DETERIORATION OR DESTRUCTION

Section 20(1) states: 'Unless otherwise agreed, the goods remain at the *seller's risk* until the property in them is transferred to the buyer, but when the property in them is transferred to the buyer the goods are at the *buyer's risk whether delivery has been made or not.*'

In *Horn v Minister of Food* (1948), S sold potatoes to B, delivery instructions to be given by the buyer in six months, property to pass and payment to be completed on delivery. The potatoes rotted, although the seller took reasonable care. *Held*: B had to bear the risk and had to pay for the potatoes. Property and risk had been separated by the agreement. Section 20(2) provides: 'But where delivery has been *delayed* through the fault of either buyer or seller, the goods are at the risk of the party in fault as regards any loss which might not have occurred but for such fault.'

The application of s 20(2) seems to be the true explanation of the decision in *Sterns Ltd v Vickers Ltd* (1923), in which S sold to B 120,000 gallons of spirit out of a quantity of 200,000 gallons which were stored in a tank at the premises of a third party. A delivery warrant was sent to the buyer, but he failed to act on it for some months, during which time the spirit deteriorated. *Held*: although no property had passed because no appropriation had taken place, the goods were at the risk of the buyer, who was therefore liable to pay the price.

In *Demby Hamilton v Barden* (1949), S sold B 30 tons of apple juice. B agreed to give delivery instructions but failed to do so. The juice went bad. It was held that the deterioration of the juice was due to the buyer's delay in taking delivery and that, consequently, the risk passed to the buyer. This analysis would also have been appropriate to apply in the case of *Pignatoro v Gilroy* (above) if the stock of rice had exceeded the contract amount.

Section 20(3) provides: 'Nothing in this section affects the duties or liabilities of either seller or buyer as a bailee or custodier of the goods of the other party.' Thus, if B buys goods from S on terms that S will store the goods, but that the property and risk are to pass at the time of the contract, S will be liable if the goods deteriorate, etc, through his fault, but not otherwise. So that if, in the *Horn* case (above), the potatoes had deteriorated because S had stored them in a hot and humid atmosphere, S would have been liable. But as he bore no fault for their deterioration, the normal rule as to risk applied.

IMPOSSIBILITY

The question may arise as to who bears the risk where the goods are destroyed so that a contract of sale becomes impossible to perform. We saw in Chapter 9 that a contract may be impossible to perform for a number of reasons, which may arise: (a) before the contract is made; (b) between the offer and acceptance; and (c) after the contract is made. The question arises as to who bears the risk in such cases. Normally a person who contracts to deliver goods but fails to do so is liable for breach of contract. Liability is strict, so that it is immaterial that the seller is not at fault in his failure to deliver.

Initial impossibility

The contract may be impossible to perform from the outset, where two parties believe the subject matter of the contract to be in existence but, in reality, it has already been destroyed when the contract was made. This situation is often called 'common mistake'. Section 6 of the Sale of Goods Act provides that where there is a contract for the sale of specific goods, and the goods, without the knowledge of the seller, have perished at the time the contract is made, the contract is void. In *Barrow, Lane and Ballard v Phillip Phillips and Co* (1929), the claimants bought a cargo of 700 bags of Chinese groundnuts. They resold them to the defendants without moving them from the warehouse in which they were stored. Unknown to the seller, some unauthorised person had appropriated 109 of the bags so that there were only 591 bags left. It was held that the sellers were not in breach of contract because of their failure to deliver the goods. It was clear to the court that if the whole 700 bags had been destroyed before property had passed to the buyer, the contract would have been void. The same result followed, even though only part of the goods had ceased to exist.

Supervening impossibility

Section 7 of the Sale of Goods Act provides where there is an agreement to sell specific goods and subsequently the goods, without any fault on the part of the seller or the buyer, perish before the risk passes to the buyer, the agreement is avoided, (that is, void).

Therefore, if it is physically impossible to carry out the contract because the goods have perished, the seller will not be liable for failure to deliver the goods and the buyer will not be liable to pay the price.

The important point here, is that property must not have already passed. If it has, the buyer bears the risk.

The rules in ss 6 and 7 provide for the situation only where the goods have 'perished'. However, if the impossibility was due to some other cause, for example, a contract becoming impossible because it was forbidden by statute after the contract was made, or where the contract was not for specific goods but still became impossible to perform, the same rule would apply. In *Howell v Coupland* (1876), S contracted to sell a crop of 200 tons of potatoes to be grown on land belonging to the defendant. Sixty-eight acres were planted which was, in a normal year, more than enough to produce 200 tons of potatoes. However, through no fault of the defendant, the crop failed. The question arose as to whether the defendant was liable for failure to deliver the goods. *Held*: the contract was for the delivery of 200 tons out of a specific crop. If the potatoes had been fully grown and afterwards had been destroyed by disease, the defendant would have been excused performance. The fact that the crop never came into existence made no difference. In *Sainsbury v Street* (1972), there was a contract to sell 275 tons of barley grown on a particular piece of land. The crop partially failed, leaving only 140 tons. The seller claimed that the contract was frustrated and sold the goods to a different buyer at a higher price. It was held that the contract was not frustrated. The correct interpretation of the contract was that the seller intended to sell to the buyer whatever barley was in fact produced, subject to the upper limit of 275 tons.

Intervening impossibility

The statute does not provide for the situation where the goods perish between the offer and the acceptance, that is, where an offer has been made to buy goods, the goods are then destroyed, but the offeree, not knowing of this, accepts the offer. That was the situation in *Financings v Stimson Ltd* (1962), in which it was held that the acceptance was invalid. The 'buyer' was therefore not liable for breach of contract in refusing to pay for the goods which had been destroyed.

CHAPTER 20

TRANSFER OF TITLE BY A NON-OWNER

Sometimes, a seller obtains possession of goods which he does not own and which he has no right to sell, but which, nevertheless, he sells to a third party. In very many such cases, the third party who buys the goods is innocent, in the sense that he buys them in good faith, unaware of the fact that the seller did not have the right to sell the goods. The non-owner, on the other hand, is almost always a wrongdoer. Often, he has committed theft in order to obtain possession of the goods. Sometimes, he has obtained possession of the goods lawfully, with the consent of the owner, but then commits theft by wrongfully selling the goods. Occasionally, he may not have offended against the criminal law at all but, in selling the goods, is guilty of a breaching a contract which he has made with the true owner. (These examples do not claim to be exhaustive but, nevertheless, the vast majority of sales by non-owners will come within them.) In all of these cases, the law must decide who owns the goods: is it the original owner or is it the third party who has bought them from the wrongdoer?

THE PRACTICAL PROBLEM

The practical problem to which the law must give a legal answer is that, in a case where a non-owner sells goods, one of two innocent parties is generally the loser: the original owner or the innocent third party. If the innocent third party who buys the goods from the non-owner is permitted to become the owner of the goods, the original owner (in the absence of insurance) will be the loser. If, on the other hand, the innocent third party buyer is compelled to return the goods (or their value) to their original owner, the innocent buyer will be the loser. It is true that, in either case, the party who is left out of pocket would have an action against the non-owner. However, such actions are usually worthless because, first, the wrongdoer quite often remains untraced, and secondly, even in a case where the identity and whereabouts of the wrongdoer are known, he will normally have no funds available to be taken in satisfaction of any judgment against him.

THE *NEMO DAT* RULE

The original answer which the common law gave to the problem of the competing rights of the original owner and the innocent buyer was to protect the rights of the *original owner*. This was reflected by the Latin maxim *'nemo dat quod non habet'*, which means 'no one can give what he hasn't got'. Applied to the situation we are discussing, it means that no one can give a better title than he himself possesses. If the seller has no title, he cannot pass a title to anyone who buys from him.

There seems to be no compelling reason why *nemo dat* should not have remained the *only* rule. If the law had adopted this position, we would have had a rule which would protect the rights of the owner in all situations.

If, on the other hand, it should be thought that the innocent buyer is more deserving of protection than the original owner, there is, equally, no compelling reason why the law should not have gone in the opposite direction. It could have created a rule which recognised the innocent third party as being more deserving than the original owner. Thus, we could have ended up with a general rule to the effect that where a non-owner sells to a third party who buys the goods in good faith and, without any notice of the non-owner's defect in title, the innocent buyer should have title to (that is, ownership of) the goods.

If the law had adopted either of these two courses, we would have ended up with a *workable rule* which would be *reasonably certain in its application*.

As it is, the law has come down in favour of neither one side nor the other. Instead, it retains the basic rule of *nemo dat* but has then created a number of exceptions in favour of the innocent third party. If these exceptions observed a *general principle*, or even a coherent set of general principles, they might have produced a law which is logical and consistent. However, the answer to our fundamental question of 'who is the owner of the goods' nowadays often relies on the application of a series of *highly technical* and *largely unrelated rules* which have been developed *piecemeal* and which are based *on no discernible general principle*. The situation has not been helped by the fact that most proposals for reform (and, indeed, the reforms which have actually taken place) have not themselves been based on principle, but have simply amounted to tinkering with this fundamentally flawed set of somewhat arbitrary rules.

EXCEPTIONS TO THE *NEMO DAT* RULE

Section 21(1) of the Sale of Goods Act affirms the *nemo dat* rule. It provides:

> Subject to this Act, where goods are sold by a person who is not their owner and who does not sell them under the authority or with the consent of the owner, the buyer acquires no better title to the goods than the seller had unless the owner of the goods is by his conduct precluded from denying the seller's authority to sell.

As we can see, there is an exception apparent in the wording of the section itself, *where the owner of the goods is by his conduct precluded from denying the seller's authority to sell*. In addition, the words *'subject to this Act'* cover a number of exceptions which are created by the Act. Furthermore, exceptions created by the Factors Acts, the common law, statute and sales by court order are specifically preserved by s 21(2) of the Sale of Goods Act. Finally, a further exception is created by s 27 of the Hire Purchase Act 1964.

The exceptions seem to have been born either:

(a) out of *commercial expediency*, that is, a desire *to protect certain commercial transactions*, even at the expense of the original owner; or

(b) from a sense of *justice*, that is, that the original owner is *better able to stand the loss* than the innocent third party.

Unfortunately, neither of these two factors creates a *general principle*, so we will come across some situations in which commercial transactions are *not* protected, and a significant number of situations in which ideas of *justice* play little part.

Distinction between possession of goods *with* the consent of the owner and possession of goods *without* the consent of the owner

A further step in our search for a general principle could be to distinguish between the situation where the non-owner comes into possession *without the consent of the owner* and the situation where he comes into possession *with the consent of the owner*. Sometimes the non-owner has stolen the goods by dishonestly taking them *without the consent of the owner*, for example, where a thief breaks into a car and steals the CD player. We can state with some confidence a rule that where the non-owner comes into possession *without the consent of the owner*, the *nemo dat* rule will almost invariably apply: the non-owner will *not* be able to pass a good title to the innocent buyer except in extremely rare circumstances. This is so even though the owner may have been *careless* in looking after his goods. There exists a large number of hypothetical examples given by judges, such as a householder going out and leaving his doors unlocked, which underline this principle. In such a case, if the carelessness resulted in the theft of household articles, and they were then sold by the thief to an innocent third party, the *nemo dat* rule would nevertheless apply. The owner would be entitled to the return of the goods (though if the goods were insured and the insurance company has paid out on the policy of insurance, the goods will then belong to the insurance company).

Sometimes, on the other hand, the wrongdoer has come into possession *with the consent of the owner* but has sold the goods in disregard of the owner's right of ownership: an example of this is a person who is given possession of a television under a contract of hire, but then sells the television, despite having no right to do so.

A general rule could be based on the idea that if a non-owner comes into possession *without* the consent of the owner, then the owner's rights should prevail. If, on the other hand, the non-owner comes into possession *with* the consent of the owner, then the innocent third party could be given title to the goods. The basis for this would be that the owner, having put the non-owner in a position to be able to sell the goods as if he were the owner, should be the person who bears the risk of wrongdoing by the non-owner. Unfortunately, although this appears to be the rationale of certain of the exceptions, it does not constitute a general rule.

However, we can say that, generally speaking, the exceptions to the *nemo dat* rule depend upon the circumstances in which the non-owner who sells the goods came into possession of them, and that in the most important exceptions, he will have come into possession of them *with* the consent of the owner. The only way to determine which circumstances are exceptions and which are not is to learn the list of exceptions. If a circumstance does not come within the exceptions, the *nemo dat* rule applies.

The list of exceptions to the *nemo dat* rule

The main exceptions, from various sources, are:

(a) estoppel (conduct of the owner);

(b) sale under a common law or statutory power;

(c) sale under a voidable title;

(d) sale by a mercantile agent;

(e) sale by a seller in possession;

(f) sale by a buyer in possession;

(g) sale under Part III of the Hire Purchase Act 1964.

ESTOPPEL (CONDUCT OF THE OWNER)

It may be that the owner of the goods acts in such a way as to lead an innocent third party to believe that the non-owner has a right to sell the goods. In such a case, the owner is 'estopped', that is, prevented from denying the truth of what he has led the innocent purchaser to believe. This is expressed in s 21(1) where, after laying down the basic *nemo dat* rule, the section goes on to express an exception, in the form of estoppel, in the following words: 'Unless the owner of the goods is *by his conduct precluded from denying the seller's authority to sell.*'

It would have been possible for the courts to have given this provision a very wide interpretation. It could have been interpreted to cover every situation in which the owner puts a non-owner into possession of his goods and thus enables the non-owner to sell the owner's goods, wrongfully, to an innocent third party. However, the provision has been interpreted more restrictively. There are two reasons for this. In the first place, the provision in the Act was intended to codify the pre-existing law, which was of narrower scope. Secondly, if this exception were to be given such a wide interpretation, there would be no need for the exceptions contained in ss 23, 24 and 25 because they (and many more situations, to which it is not disputed that the *nemo dat* rule still applies) would be covered by this section 21 provision.

Estoppel by representation

The law before the Act was based on estoppel. Hence, the modern cases still talk in terms of estoppel, rather than using the wording of the Act. Estoppel is a rule of evidence by which, if a person misleads another, he is then estopped (that is, prevented) from denying the truth of his misleading statement.

The ingredients of estoppel occur when:

(1) Adam makes a clear representation to Bharat (note that although the basis of estoppel is that the representation is misleading, Adam is not necessarily aware at the time he makes the representation that his statement is misleading – he may well believe that what he is saying is true);

(2) Adam is aware that Bharat intends to act upon the representation; and

(3) Bharat does act on the representation to his detriment.

The effect of this series of events is that Adam cannot then deny the truth of what he has previously said.

The practical effect of this is that:

(a) if the owner of the goods informs an innocent third party that the non-owner is the owner or that the non-owner has the owner's authority to sell, as the owner's agent; and,

(b) the owner of the goods is aware that the innocent third party intends to rely on this information to buy the goods; and

(c) the innocent third party proceeds with the purchase; but

(d) if it then turns out that true owner was, for example, mistaken (see below, *Henderson v Williams*) in what he said and that, in fact, the non-owner did not have the right to sell, the rule of estoppel prevents the true owner from denying the truth of what he has previously represented to be the truth.

A major difference between a true estoppel and this rule relating to conduct contained in s 21 is that estoppel is only binding between the party who made the statement and the party to whom the statement was made. However, in relation to s 21 of the Sale of Goods Act, the so called estoppel also protects a person who buys from the innocent third party.

What is a representation (or conduct)?

We have seen that interpreting this proviso to s 21, the courts have required a *representation* to be made by the owner to the innocent third party. One problem which arises from the courts talking in terms of 'estoppel' rather than 'conduct' is that it is often said that estoppel may be by representation or by conduct, thus giving rise to the impression that 'representation' is different to 'conduct', that is, that a 'representation' is something that is *spoken* or *written* and that conduct simply refers to something which is implied by *action*. An example of the latter meaning of the word *conduct* is found in the old case of the person who dressed himself in an undergraduate gown in order to get a discount only available to undergraduates from a shop in Oxford. He did not say or write anything to the effect that he was an undergraduate – he just *acted* as if he were. However, it is clear that, in the context of s 21, the word 'representation' has been treated by the courts as meaning the same thing as the word *'conduct'* which is to be found in the Act. Thus, whether we use the word 'conduct' or 'representation' to describe what the owner does, it includes *writing, speaking* or, simply, *action*.

To whom must the representation be addressed?

It could be argued that if O (the owner) puts R (a rogue) in a position where R is able to sell O's goods to ITP (an innocent third party) wrongfully, that ITP should be able to take advantage of this exception and be able to claim that O's conduct precludes him from denying R's authority to sell (that is, ITP claims that O is 'estopped'). If that were the law, this exception would be very wide indeed. It would mean that a company that hires out goods (for example, televisions, DIY tools, etc) would, if the hirer wrongfully sold them, be unable to reclaim them from the innocent buyer; it would mean that a fraudulent employee who was put into possession of goods by his employer and then sold them as if they were his own, would be able to pass a good title. However, influenced by how the law was developing before the Act was passed, it has been held that there must be some sort of positive representation or conduct by the owner which must be aimed at the third party and which has the effect of misleading the third party.

Thus, in *Farquharson v King* (1902), F were timber merchants. They stored their imported timber with a dock warehousing company. When timber was sold, a transfer order would be sent from F to the warehousing company authorising them to release the timber to the buyer. A fraudulent employee of F, called Capon, who was authorised to issue transfer orders, issued orders to transfer timber to himself, though the name of the 'buyer' on the transfer order was an assumed name. He then sold the timber to K, an innocent third party. K claimed that F were precluded by their conduct from denying C's authority to sell. It was held that, although F had, in a sense, *enabled* Capon to transfer the timber to K, K had not in any way been *misled* by any act of F on which they had placed reliance.

An example of estoppel by representation is to be found in *Henderson v Williams* (1895). In this case, G owned some sugar which was stored in W's warehouse. G sold the sugar to F, under the mistaken impression (induced by F's fraud) that F was acting as an agent for R, who was one of G's regular customers. F paid for the sugar by cheque. F then negotiated the sale of the sugar to H. H asked W to confirm that he held the sugar to the order of F. W confirmed this, since he had an instruction from G to that effect. F's cheque bounced before the sugar had been delivered by W to H. G therefore told W not to deliver the sugar to H since G's contract of sale to F was void and therefore G still owned the sugar. H claimed the sugar. *Held*: G (through W) had represented that F was the owner of the sugar. H had acted on that representation to his detriment. Therefore, even though the correct legal position was that G owned the sugar, G was estopped from denying F's ownership. Thus, H was entitled to the sugar.

A slightly more complicated example of estoppel is contained in *Eastern Distributors v Goldring* (1957). Murphy wanted to borrow money on the security of a Bedford van which he owned, in order to be able to pay a deposit on a Chrysler motor car owned by a car dealer called Coker. He therefore colluded in a scheme with Coker, whereby Coker pretended to be the owner of the Bedford. The van would be sold by Coker to Eastern Distributors, a finance company. They would let it back to Murphy by way of a hire-purchase agreement. Coker would credit Murphy with the proceeds of the sale of the van received by Coker from Eastern Distributors. Murphy therefore signed the appropriate forms offering to take his own van on hire-purchase from Eastern Distributors, who, of course, knew nothing of the scheme. They treated it as a genuine hire-purchase application. (The reason for this somewhat convoluted fiction was that if Murphy had approached Eastern Distributors direct, he would almost certainly have been turned down, because what he would have been proposing would have been a mortgage of his van. A mortgage, although achieving the same effect in this case as the fictitious hire-purchase agreement, is a different legal transaction. It is attended by legal complications which make most finance companies unwilling to enter into such a transaction in circumstances such as Murphy's.) The scheme went wrong when the proposed deal for Murphy to take the Chrysler fell through. However, Eastern Distributors had bought the Bedford from Coker, and accepted Murphy's offer to take it on hire-purchase terms. Coker then told Murphy that the whole deal had been called off. Murphy assumed that he was still the owner of the Bedford and later sold it to Goldring. When Murphy failed to pay the hire-purchase instalments, Eastern

Distributors sought possession of the Bedford and, finding it in possession of Goldring, brought an action against him for the van. The question arose as to whether Murphy, as the true owner of the van, had passed a good title to Goldring. The alternative contention was that, by signing forms which were part of a collusive plan to mislead Eastern Distributors into believing that Coker was the owner of the van, Murphy was estopped from denying Coker's right to sell. *Held*: Murphy was estopped from denying that Coker had a good title to the Bedford. Coker had transferred the title to Eastern Distributors who were, therefore, entitled to the van (an alternative ground for the decision was that Coker was Murphy's agent and thus able to transfer a good title to Eastern Distributors).

Estoppel by negligence

If the owner has made no representation, an alternative claim open to the innocent third party is to argue that the owner is estopped by negligence from asserting his ownership. If there is a representation, it is quite clear that even a wholly innocent representation, made without negligence, will be sufficient to found the estoppel: see, for example, *Henderson v Williams* (above).

There have been, however, two important modern cases in which the court expressly found that there had been no representation by the owner, but which then went on to discuss whether there was an estoppel created by the owner's negligence.

The first of these is *Mercantile Credit v Hamblin* (1965). The facts were very similar to *Eastern Distributors v Goldring*. In this case, Mrs Hamblin wished to raise money using her Jaguar car as security. She could have done this by dealing directly with a finance company. However, as we have already seen, this would amount to a mortgage which is registrable under the Bills of Sale Acts and finance companies are generally reluctant to make such agreements with private individuals. Instead, she decided to deal through an apparently respectable car dealer called Phelan with whom she was friendly. She signed three blank forms. The first was a proposal offering to take her Jaguar on hire-purchase from Mercantile Credit; the second was a receipt acknowledging that the car had been delivered to her and that the car was insured; the third was a banker's order for payment of the instalments to Mercantile Credit. Phelan said that he would enquire how much he could get for the car and report back over the telephone to Hamblin before proceeding. Phelan gave Hamblin a blank cheque which he said she could fill in after he had told her the appropriate amount – that would save her having to make the trip to his premises to collect her money. Things went wrong when Phelan filled in the hire-purchase proposal forms which had been signed by Hamblin. He sent them to Mercantile Credit along with a further form in which Phelan claimed to be the owner of the Jaguar and offered to sell it to the finance company. The finance company would then let it on hire-purchase to Hamblin. Phelan obtained £800 for the Jaguar from the finance company and absconded with the money, leaving Hamblin to pay the hire-purchase on the car. Hamblin refused to do so. Mercantile Credit argued that Hamblin was estopped by her conduct in signing the blank forms from asserting her ownership. Hamblin's defence raised the following questions:

(a) Could she successfully plead *non est factum*? If she could, the case against her would go no further.

You will recall from Chapter 8 (*L'Estrange v Graucob* (1934), p 178) that there is a general rule in English law that if a person signs a document, he is bound by it, even though he has failed to read the document and even though, if he has read it, he has not understood it. However, in certain very narrow circumstances, the signatory can deny that he is bound by his signature – he an plead *non est factum* (meaning 'it is not my deed'). This Hamblin did. However, it was held that *the defence failed* because the document she signed was of the same character as the one she thought she was signing. There was no evidence that Phelan had misrepresented the documents to her. (Nowadays, although the rules relating to *non est factum* have changed somewhat, it is submitted that the outcome on this plea would be the same.)

(b) Had she made a representation to Mercantile Credit to the effect that the car was Phelan's to sell? If so, she would be estopped from asserting her ownership.

It was held that she had not made a representation to Mercantile Credit that Phelan was the owner of the car. You will recall that in *Henderson v Williams,* the owner of a consignment of sugar was held to be estopped by a representation which was made to the innocent third party, not by the owner himself but on his behalf, by his warehouseman. The vital difference between that case and Hamblin's was that, in the view of the Court of Appeal, Hamblin had *given no authority* to Phelan to transmit the signed papers to Mercantile Credit. Hamblin had agreed with Phelan that he would not do so until she had agreed the details of the proposed deal with Phelan. This she had never done. She was, therefore, not estopped by representation.

(c) Had she been negligent and was therefore estopped by her negligence?

It was held that in order to be estopped by negligence, it has to be shown:

- that the defendant owed the claimant a duty of care;
- that the defendant breached the duty of care; and
- that the claimant suffered damage as a result of the breach.

The court found that although Hamblin owed Mercantile Credit a duty of care, she had not, in the circumstances, breached that duty, since Phelan was well known to her and was an apparently prosperous motor dealer with three outlets in Nottingham. In addition, Pearson LJ was prepared to hold that, even if she had breached her duty of care, so that two out of the three elements of negligence would have been present, the proximate cause of the

Mercantile Credit's damage was the fraud of Phelan, not the negligence of Hamblin.

The outcome was that Mercantile Credit's pleas of estoppel failed and Mrs Hamblin retained title to her car. It could be argued that she was rather fortunate. Certainly the finding that she had not been negligent hinged largely upon the fact that Phelan was well known to her – she signed the blank documents over dinner at his home. The claimant tried to introduce evidence which showed that she had successfully concluded a similar deal with Phelan and a different finance company previously. The claimant's purpose was to argue that the current deal was fraudulent. The court refused to permit this, saying that even if it were true it would make no difference. (However, Mrs Hamblin could perhaps have used it to her advantage to re-inforce the fact that her reliance on Phelan in the current case was not negligent!)

A further case, decided by the House of Lords, in which the relationship between estoppel by representation and estoppel by negligence is much more clearly defined, is *Moorgate Mercantile Co v Twitchings* (1977). Moorgate let a car on hire-purchase to McL. Because of the continual risk that a person who obtains possession of a vehicle in pursuance of a hire-purchase agreement will wrongfully sell the vehicle, the finance companies and car dealers set up a self-help organisation called 'Hire Purchase Information' (HPI). When a finance company lets a car on hire-purchase, it registers the transaction with HPI. The idea is that if a member is offered a vehicle for sale, he is able, by making an enquiry to HPI, to determine (among other things) whether the car is the subject of a hire-purchase agreement. Moorgate would normally have registered the hire-purchase agreement between themselves and McL with HPI. However, the agreement wasn't registered with HPI. Although it wasn't clear why, the only reasonable explanation was that Moorgate had never sent the appropriate forms to HPI. In breach of his hire-purchase agreement with Moorgate, McL sold the vehicle to Twitchings. Before he bought it, Twitchings took the precaution of checking with HPI whether the vehicle was the subject of a hire-purchase agreement and was told that no agreement had been registered. Moorgate claimed damages for the tort of conversion. Twitchings argued that Moorgate were estopped from asserting their ownership. Their Lordships considered estoppel by representation: since it was HPI who had made the representation to Twitchings, Twitchings would have to show: (a) that HPI had made a clear representation that the car was not the subject of a hire-purchase agreement; and (b) that HPI had done so as an agent of Moorgate. On these points it was held that: (a) HPI had not made a representation that the car was not the subject of a hire-purchase agreement, simply that no agreement was recorded; and, in any case, (b) HPI could not be regarded as the agent of Moorgate.

Sale under a common law or statutory power

Section 21(2)(b) provides that nothing in the Act affects the validity of any contract of sale under any special common law or statutory power of sale, or under the order of a court of competent jurisdiction. There are many such situations. At common law, goods may be sold by a person to whom they have been pledged, though if the agreement is a regulated agreement within the scope of the Consumer Credit Act, there are statutory restrictions on the exercise of the power if the goods pawned are worth more than £15. An agent of necessity also has a power of sale.

Statute gives a power of sale in various circumstances, for example, to an unpaid seller of goods under s 48 of the Sale of Goods Act 1979; to an innkeeper under s 1 of the Innkeepers Act 1878; to a sheriff who has seized goods under s 15 of the Bankruptcy and Deeds of Arrangement Act 1913; a bailee of goods which remain uncollected despite reasonable efforts to obtain the instructions of the owner may sell them under the provisions of s 12 of the Tort (Interference with Goods) Act 1977, and so forth.

A court may order goods to be sold. It has power to do this to enforce a charge against the goods, for example, or under the Rules of the Supreme Court for any just or sufficient reason. One example might be where the seller has consigned goods to the buyer but, on their arrival at the appropriate port, the buyer refuses to accept them as he alleges that they are not in accordance with the contract. If the goods are perishable, rather than allow the goods to perish, the court may order them to be sold and the proceeds held for the benefit of the party to whom the goods are eventually adjudged to belong. In *Larner v Fawcett* (1950), a racehorse owner had failed to pay the bill for the training of his horse. The owner failed to collect the horse and pay his bill, because the bill almost corresponded to the value of the horse. In the face of objections from the horse's owner, the trainer succeeded in obtaining a court order to sell the horse.

Sale under a voidable title

Section 23 of the Act provides that when the seller of goods has a voidable title to them, but his title has not been avoided at the time of the sale, the buyer acquires a good title to them, provided he buys them in good faith and without notice of the seller's defect in title.

There are a number of cases in which a contract may be voidable: a contract induced by misrepresentation, duress, undue influence, mental incapacity and drunkenness are examples. The most common of these is a contract induced by fraudulent misrepresentation. The classic example is where a rogue agrees to buy a car from its owner and pays by cheque. The rogue sells the car to an innocent third party. The cheque is dishonoured and the owner claims his car back from the innocent third party. We have seen (see Chapter 12) that where the owner mistakes the identity of the rogue, in circumstances where the rogue's purported identity is of fundamental importance to the contract (which will very rarely be the case), the contract is void. It is treated as if it had never been made and the original owner can therefore recover his goods. In the normal run of events, the identity of the party with whom the owner thinks he is contracting is not of fundamental importance, in which case the contract is voidable. 'Voidable' means that the contract is valid until it is repudiated by the owner, at which time it becomes void. However, if, before the contract has been repudiated, the party with the voidable title sells the goods to an innocent third party, that party obtains a good title to the goods.

A typical scenario is as follows: on 1 June, S sells a car to R for £5,000. R pays by cheque. On 2 June, R sells the car to B for £3,000 who buys it in good faith without any notice of any irregularity. On 5 June, R's cheque is dishonoured. On the same day, S informs the police and asks them to recover his car. In this order of events, because the car is sold by R to B *before* R repudiates the contract by informing the police, B obtains a good title to the car under s 23. If the order of events was slightly different and S repudiated the contract before R sold the car to B, B would not get a good title under s 23. (He might, however, obtain a good title by virtue of a sale by a buyer in possession under s 25.)

We have said that a voidable contract is valid until repudiated. It has been held, controversially, that informing the police and asking them to recover one's property is a sufficient act of repudiation. Purists argue that the repudiation of the contract should be made known to the other contracting party before it can become valid. However, pragmatists point out that this will often be impossible since the other party is a rogue and has usually absconded and so cannot be contacted for the purpose of communicating the repudiation.

In *Car and Universal Finance v Caldwell* (1965), C sold his car to a firm called Dunn's Transport on 12 January. He was paid by a cheque signed by W Foster and F Norris on behalf of the firm. He presented it to the bank for payment the following day and it was dishonoured. He immediately told the police and asked them to recover his car. On 15 January, a firm of car dealers called Motobella bought the car from Norris with notice that he had not come by it honestly. On the same day Motobella sold it to G & C Finance who bought it in good faith. Tied in with the sale was a fictitious HP proposal, put forward by Motobella, that the car would be taken on HP by a fictitious person called Knowles. On 20 January, the police found the car in the possession of Motobella. On 29 January, C's solicitor wrote to Motobella informing them that C claimed the car. On 3 August, G & C sold the car to Car and Universal who took it in good faith.

It was held by the Court of Appeal (unanimously) that C retained title to the car (that is, he still owned it) because he had avoided the contract with

Dunn's Transport at the time he asked the police to recover the car. As this was on 13 January, two days before Motobella sold it to G & C Finance, G & C Finance had acquired no rights in the car.

Note: The Law Reform Committee (Cmnd 2958) recommended that the seller should not be able to avoid a sale which was rendered voidable by the buyer's misrepresentation, until he had informed the buyer of his decision. This proposal has not, to date, been given statutory effect.

Sale by a mercantile agent

It is clear from s 21(1) of the Sale of Goods Act 1979 that a person selling under the authority of, or with the consent of, the owner can pass the owner's title as if the sale were made by the owner directly. This represents the common law relating to sales made by agents.

A difficulty arises where the agent does something he was not authorised to do. In the case of the agent being a private person, a transaction outside the actual authority given to him by the owner will have no effect. However, in order to give some measure of protection to those dealing in good faith with professional agents, a succession of Factors Acts, culminating in the 1889 Factors Act, created exceptions to the common law rule. Section 2 of the 1889 Act provides:

> Where a mercantile agent is, with the consent of the owner, in possession of goods or documents of title to goods, any sale, pledge or other disposition of the goods made by him when acting in the ordinary course of business of a mercantile agent, shall, subject to the provisions of this Act, be as valid as if he were expressly authorised by the owner of the goods to make the same, provided that the person taking under the disposition acts in good faith, and has not at the time of the disposition notice that the person making the disposition has not authority to make the same.

Meaning of the term 'mercantile agent'

Section 1 of the Factors Act defines the term 'mercantile agent' as follows: 'The expression "mercantile agent" shall mean a mercantile agent having in the customary course of his business as such agent, authority either to sell goods, or to consign goods for the purpose of sale, or to buy goods, or to raise money on the security of goods.'

Example: suppose X asks his friend Y to sell a piano for him as a personal favour, the price to be not less than £800. Y takes the piano, shows it to Z, and sells it to him for £500. The transaction between Y and Z is void and Z does not get a good title. However, suppose that Y had been a piano dealer. In such a case Y would be a mercantile agent and s 2 of the Factors Act would operate to give Z a good title to the piano.

In most cases, the mercantile agent is a dealer in the goods in question. However, it is clear that an isolated instance of employment as an agent will still render the agent a mercantile agent within the meaning of s 2.

In *Lowther v Harris* (1927), in which P was in business as an art dealer, L wanted to sell some furniture and a tapestry and he asked P to sell it for him on commission. The goods were stored at a house rented by L. P was permitted to live in part of the house. Customers dealt with P only and knew nothing of L but P had no authority to sell without L's permission. P fraudulently told L that he had sold the tapestry for £525 to W and obtained L's permission to remove the tapestry for sale to W. Having obtained possession of the tapestry, P sold it to H for £250. H received a receipt on P's headed paper. *Held:* P was a mercantile agent even though he did not generally work as an agent and the present transaction was an isolated one. Further, P was not in possession by virtue of living in the house, but came into possession when he was allowed to take the tapestry away. The sale being in the ordinary course of business of a mercantile agent, H obtained a good title under s 2 of the Factors Act. A further example is *Hayman v Flewker* (1863), where pictures were entrusted to an insurance agent to sell on commission.

The mercantile agent must be in possession as an agent

The mercantile agent must be in possession of the goods in his capacity of mercantile agent. Therefore, the Factors Act cannot apply:

(a) if he obtains possession before he becomes a mercantile agent: *Heap v Motorist's Advisory Agency* (1923);

(b) if he is in possession for the purpose of repairing the goods rather than selling them: *Staffs Motor Guarantee v British Wagon* (1934);

(c) if he is in possession of the goods on a 'sale or return' basis: *Weiner v Gill* (1906). Contrast *Weiner v Harris* (1910) where the alleged sale or return contract clearly envisaged a sale to a third party. It was held that 'sale or return' normally meant 'sale to the recipient of the goods' or return to their original owner. Where, as in this case, the words clearly meant 'sale to a third party or return to their original owner', the correct analysis of the transaction was that the recipient was a mercantile agent within the meaning of s 2 of the Factors Act and as such could pass a good title to the goods to a third party.

However, goods are in the possession of the mercantile agent in his capacity of mercantile agent, if his possession is in some way connected with his business of mercantile agent, even if he has no authority to dispose of the goods. In *Pearson v Rose and Young* (1951), a mercantile agent was in possession of the plaintiff's car for the purpose of receiving offers for it. He decided to sell the car and misappropriate the proceeds. He therefore contrived a trick whereby he induced the plaintiff to allow him to hold the registration document of the car and then distracted the plaintiff by getting him to leave hastily on a pretext. Having obtained possession of the registration document in this way, he sold the car to the defendant. The plaintiff sued for the return of his car. The defendant claimed a good title under s 2 of the Factors Act. It was held that a mercantile agent does not sell a car in the ordinary course of business without the registration document. Although the agent was in possession of the car with the consent of the plaintiff, he was not in possession of the registration document with the consent of the plaintiff: possession of the document had been obtained by a trick. Therefore, the sale had the same effect as if it had been made without the document and was not in the ordinary course of business of a mercantile agent. The defendant did not, therefore, obtain a good title under s 2.

The agent must be in possession of the goods with the consent of the owner

The consent of the owner is presumed in the absence of evidence to the contrary: s 2(4) of the Factors Act 1889. If the agent obtains possession by false pretences, this does not nullify the owner's consent. Note that obtaining possession by a trick, as in the *Pearson* case (above), is regarded as being without the consent of the owner.

In *Folkes v King* (1923), the agent obtained possession of a car for the purpose of obtaining offers and on the express condition that he would not dispose of the car for under £575 without the owner's permission. In fact, the agent intended from the very beginning to sell the car for what he could get for it and to misappropriate the proceeds. *Held*: he had obtained the car with the consent of the owner and s 2 of the Factors Act gave the *bona fide* purchaser a good title.

However, in *Heap v Motorist's Advisory Agency* (above), where N obtained possession of H's car on the pretence that he had a friend called H (who was in fact non-existent) who would probably buy the car, it was held that H did not truly consent to N having possession of the car as a mercantile agent. He was not given possession for the purpose of finding a purchaser. He was given possession of the car to show to a particular person, who, it turned out, was non-existent. That being so, N could not be in possession as a mercantile agent since there was no-one to whom he could sell the car.

Ordinary course of business of a mercantile agent

Whether the mercantile agent is acting in the ordinary course of business as a mercantile agent is a question of fact in each case. Simply because the act of the agent is an unusual one does not necessarily take it out of the ordinary course of business: *Oppenheimer v Attenborough* (1908), in which S obtained diamonds from O on the pretext that he intended to try to sell them to one of two named diamond merchants. He did not attempt to sell them to either, but instead pawned them with A. O sued A for the return of the diamonds. The question arose as to whether S pawned the goods in the ordinary course of his business as a mercantile agent. O argued that it was not customary for a mercantile agent in the diamond trade to have authority to pledge the goods of which he had been given possession in order to sell. *Held*: S was acting in the ordinary course of his business as a mercantile agent. An express veto on pledging would not have taken the transaction outside the course of business of a mercantile agent and so, therefore, neither could an alleged trade custom.

Situations where the sale has been held to be not in the normal course of business include: where a pledge was made at an abnormal rate of interest; where a mercantile agent asked a friend to pledge an article rather than undertaking the transaction himself; where the entire stock-in-trade of a business was sold; where the seller sold goods as an agent but the buyer knew that the whole of the profits were to go to the agent, not to the principal; where a second-hand car was sold without the registration document. It may also be outside the course of the business of a mercantile agent where the sale or pledge by the agent takes place outside normal business hours, at a place other than a normal place of business, or where the transaction is in any other way abnormal.

Note that the sale of a new car without registration documents has been held to be in the ordinary course of business as a mercantile agent, where a convincing explanation was given for the absence of the documents: *Astley Industrial Trust v Miller* (1968).

Section 2(2) of the Act provides that where consent to the agent being in possession has been withdrawn, any sale or other disposition which would have been valid if the consent had continued, shall be valid providing the person undertaking the disposition had no notice that it had been determined. In *Moody v Pall Mall Deposit Co* (1917), a dealer in Paris sent some pictures to an agent in London, some for sale, others to be exhibited only. The agent's authority was revoked, after which he pledged both lots of pictures with B. B took them with no notice of the revocation. *Held*: B got a good title to the pictures. Section 2(3) makes a similar provision in relation to documents of title.

Sale by a seller in possession

Sometimes the seller may remain in possession of goods although property in the goods has passed to the buyer. For example, suppose that S, having sold goods to B in circumstances where property has passed to B, remains in possession of goods and then wrongfully re-sells them to T. It would appear, applying the *nemo dat* rule, that T obtains no title. In such circumstances, both s 24 of the Sale of Goods Act 1979 and s 8 of the Factors Act 1889 operate to give a good title to the innocent third party.

Both measures were enacted in almost identical terms. Section 8 is slightly wider. This provides:

Where a person having sold goods continues or is in possession of the goods, or documents of title to the goods, the delivery or transfer by that person or by a mercantile agent acting for him, of the goods or documents of title under any sale, pledge, or other disposition thereof or under any agreement for sale pledge or other disposition thereof, to any person receiving the same in good faith and without notice of the previous sale, shall have the same effect as if the person making the delivery or transfer were expressly authorised by the owner of the goods to make the same.

There has been some dispute as to whether the seller must remain in possession lawfully or whether it is sufficient that he remains in physical possession. The matter was fully discussed in *Worcester Works Finance Ltd v Cooden Engineering* (1972). In June, C (the defendants) sold a car to a dealer called Griffith who said he wanted it for sale to a customer. G paid for the car by cheque, which was dishonoured. G made arrangements with M (who was probably an accomplice), that G would sell the car to the plaintiffs (W) who would let the car on a HP agreement to M. W paid G for the car. M never took delivery of the car, the details of his deposit were false and he never paid any instalment under the agreement. In August, C were allowed by G to repossess the car, which C thought, as they had not been paid, they were entitled to do. G paid the HP payments for a time in order to keep W quiet. Then C, having used the car as a hire-car for some time, let it out on HP. C registered their interest with HPI, and in consequence W got to know that C claimed to be the owner of the car. Thereupon W claimed that the car was theirs. C relied on s 25(1) of the Sale of Goods Act 1893 (which is now s 24 of the Sale of Goods Act 1979), arguing: (a) that G was a seller in possession; (b) that they had taken it under 'other disposition'. *Held*: G was a seller in possession, despite the fact that he was not entitled to possession.

Sale by a buyer in possession

Sometimes, following a sale or an agreement to sell, the buyer is given possession of the goods, but has no title, or has a defective title. In such a case, the virtually identical provisions of s 9 of the Factors Act 1889 or s 25(1) of the Sale of Goods Act 1979 may apply with the effect that a person who buys from the buyer in possession, obtains a good title, even though the buyer in possession had a defective title.

Section 9 provides:

Where a person having bought or agreed to buy goods obtains, with the consent of the seller, possession of the goods or the documents of title to the goods, the delivery or transfer by that person, or by a mercantile agent acting for him, of the goods or documents of title, under any sale, pledge, or other disposition thereof or under any agreement for sale, pledge or other disposition thereof, to any person receiving the same in good faith and without notice of any lien or other right of the original seller in respect of the goods, has the same effect as if the person making the delivery or transfer were a mercantile agent in possession of the goods or documents of title with the consent of the owner.

An important thing to note at the outset is that to pass a good title under these sections, the person in possession must be a person who has bought or agreed to buy the goods. A person in possession for any other purpose cannot pass a good title under s 9 of the Factors Act or s 25(1) of the Sale of Goods Act.

The majority of cases in which s 9 (or s 25) comes to be considered are in one of the following categories:

(a) Where the seller has given the buyer 'trade credit'.

Example: a trade seller, O, has sold goods to trade buyer, B, under normal trade credit terms (typical terms are that the invoice is sent at the end of the month when the sale took place, payment to be made within seven days of invoice). Being unsure of B's creditworthiness, O includes a 'reservation of title' clause in the sale. Despite this, B re-sells the goods to a third party T, who takes in good faith. O attempts to recover the goods from T. T will obtain a good title under s 9 (see, for example, *Re Bond Worth* (1979)).

A good illustration is contained in *Four Point Garage v Carter* (1985). In this case, C agreed to purchase a Ford Escort XR 3i from Freeway, delivery to be made on 10 October. The agreement was made on 2 October, on which date C was also given the proposed registration number of the vehicle. Freeway then contacted Four Point to arrange to purchase the vehicle from them. On 8 October, C posted two cheques, representing the purchase price, to Freeway, and the delivery date of 10 October was confirmed. On 9 October, Four Point invoiced Freeway for the car. Freeway asked Four Point to deliver the car to C direct, which they did. On 10 October, C signed a delivery note and took possession of the vehicle. C thought that the delivery had been made by Freeway. Four Point believed that Freeway's business was the leasing and hiring of cars rather than their sale.

On 13 October, Four Point received notice that Freeway were going into liquidation as the company was insolvent. Four Point would not, therefore, be getting paid for the car. The best they could hope for would be a dividend (that is, so much per pound of the debt), payable to unsecured creditors. However, Four Point's contract with Freeway included a reservation of title clause (also known as a *Romalpa* clause), reserving title until the vehicle had been paid for by Freeway. Four Point therefore sought to reclaim the car from C. Because of the reservation of title clause, Freeway had never become the owner of the car and therefore, on the face of it, were unable to pass on a good title. Freeway were, however, 'a person who has bought or agreed to buy goods', and the question arose whether s 25 allowed them to pass on a good title to C. The difficulty was that s 25 refers to the buyer (that is, Freeway) being 'in possession' of the goods and making 'delivery' to the third party (that is, C). As we have seen, Freeway never actually took possession of the goods and it was Four Point who made delivery to C. In ruling that s 25 did apply to give a good title to C, the court said that Four Point made 'constructive delivery' to Freeway (and therefore put Freeway into constructive possession) and that Freeway made constructive delivery to C (via Four Point). Alternatively, Four Point acted as Freeway's agent in making delivery to C. The court gave as an alternative reason for its decision that Four Point impliedly authorised Freeway to sell the car.

(b) Where a person has bought goods on instalment credit.

The original case was *Lee v Butler* (1893). In this case, Mrs Lloyd was in possession of furniture under an agreement which called itself an agreement for hire and purchase. She agreed to hire the furniture until she had paid all the instalments, at which time it became hers. She agreed that during the continuance of the agreement she would not move the furniture from her home address with out the consent of the owners, WE Hardy. If she did, it would be lawful for WEH to repossess the goods. The agreement further provided that property in the goods did not pass until they had been paid for. Mrs L sold the goods to Butler. WEH assigned their rights to Lee who sued Butler for the return of the goods and damages for their detention. *Held*: s 9 of the Factors Act gave B a good title as Mrs L was a person who had agreed to buy the goods.

Two years later, the contrasting case of *Helby v Matthews* (1895), was heard by the House of Lords. In this case, H owned a piano which he hired to B under a hire-purchase agreement. In contravention of the agreement B pawned it. H sought to recover it. The terms of the agreement were similar to those in *Lee v Butler*. H had to pay a deposit and 36 instalments and when he had completed payment the goods were his. There was, however, one significant difference between the two agreements. In Helby's agreement, B could, if he wished, return the piano to H and if he did so he was under no further obligation, the hiring came to an end. However, in Mrs Lloyd's agreement, in *Lee v Butler* (1893), there was no such option. Mrs Lloyd had, under the terms of the contract, to complete the payments and thus become the owner of the furniture. The House of Lords held that this difference was vital because B, being able to return the piano without completing the purchase, was not a person who had bought or agreed to buy. Therefore, s 9 of the Factors Act did not apply.

Notes

(1) The decision in *Lee v Butler* has been overruled by statute as far as consumer credit agreements within the meaning of the Consumer Credit Act 1974 are concerned, so that s 9 and s 25(1) do not apply. However, the decision will still apply to agreements which are not caught by the Consumer Credit Act.

Consumer credit sales where the debtor has 'agreed to buy' but the seller has reserved title are called 'conditional sales'. Section 25(2) of the Sale of Goods

Act 1979, which came into effect in May 1985 (replacing a similar provision in s 54 of the Hire Purchase Act 1965), provides:

> For the purposes of sub-section (i) above, (the sub-section provides that a person who has bought or agreed to buy goods may transmit a good title to an innocent third party),
>
> (a)   the buyer under a conditional sale agreement is to be taken not to be a person who has bought or agreed to buy goods ... For a transaction to be a consumer credit agreement within the meaning of the Consumer Credit Act 1974, it must (a) have as its debtor an individual (or group of individuals such as a partnership), so the agreements where, for example, the debtor is a limited liability company do not qualify; and (b) involve the provision of credit not exceeding £15,000: see s 8 of the Consumer Credit Act 1974.

(2)   In *Helby v Matthews* (above), the House of Lords said that it was a matter of construction of the agreement whether the hirer was a person who had agreed to buy or whether he was simply a hirer until he had fulfilled the condition upon which he became a purchaser. Nowadays, although statute has overruled *Lee v Butler* where the agreement is a consumer credit agreement within the meaning of the 1974 Act, the case is still good law in relation to any agreement which is not a consumer credit agreement. Therefore, in order to make it clear that the possessor of the goods is merely a hirer, finance companies usually put an 'option to purchase' clause in HP agreements, whereby the hirer does not become the owner until he has exercised an option to purchase on the conclusion of the hire agreement. The option is usually exercisable at a nominal price, often £1.

(c)   Where a seller, having passed only a voidable title to the buyer because of the buyer's misrepresentation, manages to avoid the buyer's title before the buyer sells the goods to an innocent third party. In such a case, s 9 of the Factors Act or s 25(1) of the Sale of Goods Act may still operate to give the third party a good title.

In *Newtons of Wembley v Williams* (1965), which is a good example of a sale within para (c) above, the Court of Appeal placed a restriction on the operation of s 9 and s 25(1) which, if it is good law, severely cuts down the protection which the sections were thought to give to a purchaser in good faith and without notice.

In *Newtons of Wembley v Williams*, Newtons sold a Sunbeam Rapier car to Andrew on 15 June 1962. Andrew paid by cheque and was allowed to take the car and the registration document. The same day, A's name was put in the registration book. On 18 June, A's cheque was dishonoured. (As A had 16 bank accounts, mostly heavily overdrawn and as he had only £1.80 in the account on which N's cheque was drawn, the court had no hesitation in holding that A had obtained the car by false pretences and that therefore A had acquired only a voidable title.) N sent a 'stop notice' to Hire-Purchase

Information on 18 June, and told the police on 18 or 19 June. The court therefore held that N had disaffirmed the contract within a day or two of 18 June. In July 1962, A sold the car to Biss (who was buying the car with the intention of re-selling the car to a motor-dealer called Wynne) at an established street market for used cars in Warren Street, London. Biss then sold the car to one of Wynne's companies, Williams, at a loss. N claimed that as he had avoided the contract with A before A sold to Biss, A no longer had any title to pass to Biss and therefore Biss had no title which he could pass to W. *Held*: s 9 of the Factors Act and s 25(2) of the Sale of Goods Act 1893 (now s 25(1) of the Sale of Goods Act 1979) nevertheless operated to give Biss, and therefore Williams, a good title. However, the Court of Appeal, confirming the High Court judgment, went on to hold (remarkably, because this restriction had never previously been applied) that the two sections applied only where, assuming the buyer (Andrew) to have been a mercantile agent (which he wasn't), the disposition by him had been in the ordinary course of business of a mercantile agent. In other words, the disposition by the buyer in possession has to be in circumstances in which a mercantile agent would sell the goods. At the High Court hearing, the judge had said:

> The facts that A had no business premises, that the sale was in the street, and that the sale was for cash, might suggest that the transaction was not on its face an ordinary commercial one. But the evidence clearly pointed to the fact that in Warren Street and its neighbourhood there is a well-established street market for cash dealing in used cars.

Before this case, it had never been doubted that the effect of the, admittedly convoluted, wording was that the third party got a good title. However, when one reads the provisions of s 9 and s 25(1), in particular the words: '... has the same effect as if the person making the delivery or transfer were a mercantile agent in possession of goods with the consent of the owner.' If asked what effect such transfer or delivery has, one could answer either, 'It has the same effect as if it were authorised by the owner': that is, it passes a good title (see s 2(1) of the Factors Act 1889), which had always been the interpretation before the *Newton's* case, or, 'Providing the sale by the agent is made in the ordinary course of business of a mercantile agent, it has the same effect as if it were authorised by the owner'. It is the latter interpretation which the Court of Appeal chose.

In *National Employers' Mutual General Insurance Association Ltd v Jones* (1990), the House of Lords had to decide whether, if the buyer in possession was a buyer from a thief, s 25 operated to give a good title.

In this case, H owned a Ford Fiesta motor car. It was stolen, sold several times and was eventually sold to Jones. H's insurers (who had paid H her insured loss in respect of the car and thus stood in her shoes as the owner), claimed the car from J. J argued that he was a buyer in possession within the meaning of s 25. This appeared to be possible on the wording of the section, since it talks of a person who has bought or agreed to buy the goods being in possession of the goods with the consent of *the seller*. J certainly appeared to be a person who had agreed to buy the goods and was in possession with the consent of the seller. However, the only exception to the *nemo dat* rule which has ever had the acknowledged policy of giving a good title to the innocent purchaser of stolen goods, was the 'market overt' rule, which was abolished by the Sale of Goods (Amendment) Act 1994. The House of Lords held that it was not the intention of s 25(1) to give a good title in the present circumstances. The Court of Appeal had solved the problem pragmatically by finding that the 'seller' referred to in the sub-section really meant 'owner'. The House of Lords came to a similar conclusion, but by a more circuitous route. They said that the sub-section must be read as meaning that the delivery or transfer made by the intermediate transferor (initially the thief in this case), shall have the same effect as if he were a mercantile agent in possession of the goods with the consent of the owner who had entrusted them to him. Therefore, unless the initial transfer is by the owner of the goods, s 25 cannot operate to give a good title to any subsequent buyer.

Sale under Part III of the Hire Purchase Act 1964

Before the 1964 Act was passed there had been much concern at the number of buyers of motor vehicles who turned out to have no title because the 'seller' was only a hirer under an HP agreement. Section 27 of the 1964 Act therefore provided:

(a) that where a motor vehicle had been hired under an HP agreement or agreed to be sold under a conditional sale agreement and before property had passed to the hirer or buyer (that is, the debtor) he sold the vehicle, a third party who bought in good faith and without notice, providing he was a private purchaser, acquired the creditor's (that is, the finance company's) title;

(b) further, where the first disposition of the debtor is to a trade purchaser, who re-sells to a private purchaser, the private purchaser acquires the creditor's title;

(c) where the first private purchaser became the hirer under an HP agreement with a trade or finance purchaser and then bought the goods by paying off the original creditor, he gets a good title providing the HP agreement was entered into in good faith and without notice. It is immaterial that, by the time he became the purchaser, he had notice of the earlier agreement. Note that s 27 can be used only to the private purchaser's advantage, not to that of the creditor.

Note, however, that s 27 protects only the innocent private purchaser. In each of the examples above, the debtor would be liable both in tort and, almost certainly, in breach of contract to the creditor. In examples (b) and (c), the trade purchaser would be liable to the original owner for the tort of conversion (that is, wrongfully dealing with them as if he were the owner), in relation to the owner's goods. However, if a private purchaser obtains a good title under s 27, any *subsequent* trade purchaser will also obtain a good title.

In *Barber v NWS Bank plc* (1995), B entered into a conditional sale agreement with NWS to purchase a Honda Accord. Nineteen months into the agreement B discovered that the car was the subject of a previous hire-purchase agreement, with the effect that, at the time B entered into the agreement with NWS, NWS had no title to the car. B claimed to rescind the contract on the ground that a term in the contract between NWS and B, to the effect that at the date of the agreement NWS was the owner of the car, was a condition of the contract. NWS argued that it was a warranty or an innominate term and since s 27 of the Hire Purchase Act 1964 operated to give a good title to a private purchaser (as B was), damage would be nominal. It was held by the Court of Appeal that the contractual provision was a condition. It could not be an innominate term since it was not susceptible to breach in a number of ways but could be breached in one way only. B was therefore entitled to rescind the contract, since sub-s (6) of s 27 of the Hire Purchase Act expressly provided that nothing in the section was to exonerate a finance company or trade purchaser from any liability it would have been under, but for the provisions of the section. In other words, the section could have been used to B's advantage had circumstances required it, but it could not be used to advantage NWS. (Note that the seller was not in breach of s 12 of the Sale of Goods Act because by the time the sale actually took place, the seller had a right to sell as required by s 12.)

POSSIBILITIES FOR REFORM

As we have remarked, the exceptions to the *nemo dat* rule have not been based upon a general principle but have, instead, been created piecemeal by the dictates of commercial convenience or notions of justice in a particular circumstance. The result is a muddle of *inconsistency* and *contradiction*.

It might perhaps be helpful, now that we have looked at what has actually happened in English law, to look at what a general rule, to cover all cases, might lay down. There are at least five possible general rules:

(a) it would be possible to affirm the general rule of *nemo dat quod non habet* and apply it in all cases. This would have the advantage of certainty;

(b) it would be possible to move in the opposite direction and virtually to negate the *nemo dat* rule by introducing a very broad general rule to the effect that wherever a third party purchases goods in good faith from a non-owner, the third party obtains a good title.

Such a rule would mean that the owner of stolen goods would lose his property to an innocent buyer. English law, with its regard for sanctity of ownership, would be unlikely ever to favour such a rule. Indeed, most developed jurisdictions protect the property rights of an owner whose property has been stolen, though in France, if stolen goods are sold to an innocent purchaser at a fair, market, public auction or from a merchant who deals in such goods, the innocent purchaser is allowed to retain them until paid their price by the original owner. There was formerly a rule in English law that, where goods were sold by a non-owner in a 'market overt' (this meant an established market or a shop within the City of London), the innocent purchaser obtained a good title to the goods. While this rule was still in existence, there was a body of opinion in favour of extending the rule to cover sales from all retail outlets. Because many owners insure their goods against theft, such a rule would not create such hardship among owners as might be thought. Insurance has the effect of distributing the loss throughout society as a whole rather than allowing it to fall entirely upon one unfortunate person. However, in the event, the legislature took the opposite view and altered the law in favour of the original owner. In the light of a rising crime rate in relation to stolen property and amid concerns that Parliament should not be seen to be 'encouraging' criminal activity, the 'market overt' rule was abolished by the Sale of Goods (Amendment) Act 1994;

(c) a less sweeping alternative would be to have a general rule that wherever the owner has voluntarily parted with possession of his goods, for example, as a result of a hire contract, a buyer buying in good faith would acquire ownership. The idea behind such a rule is that the innocent buyer should not be disadvantaged by the fact that the owner, by his conduct, has enabled the non-owner to represent himself as being the owner. Therefore the owner must bear the consequences of his actions.

This is the general rule in Germany. It also appears to be the basis of a number of exceptions to the *nemo dat* rule in English law, but there is no *general* rule to this effect: in certain circumstances, where an owner has parted voluntarily with his goods, an innocent buyer obtains a good title, but in other circumstances he does not. An example of where the innocent buyer would get a good title is where the owner sells through an agent and the agent sells outside the term of the mandate given him by the owner. However, if an owner hires goods to a person who wrongfully sells them to an innocent third party, it is the owner who retains title to the goods;

(d) a further possibility would be to have a rule that wherever the owner has been negligent in protecting his ownership, an innocent buyer should obtain a good title.

An example of this might be where the owner has had his car stolen after having left it unlocked with the keys in the ignition and the engine running. However, although negligence can be the foundation of one of the exceptions in English law (estoppel by negligence: see below), the negligence of the owner will generally not be a factor in determining whether or not the owner retains title to his goods;

(e) apportionment of the loss between the innocent parties is a further possible solution.

Perhaps the most potent argument against this solution is that it would introduce a significant element of uncertainty into the law. The possibility of apportionment was considered in the 1966 Law Reform Committee's Report on the Transfer of Title to Chattels. The Committee did not favour such a solution. Its reasons are summarised in Chapter 12, p 286.

RETENTION OF TITLE

You will recall that the *property in goods can pass* to a buyer (that is, the buyer becomes the owner), even *though he has not paid the price of the goods*. We can say, reasonably safely, that the property in the goods will normally pass, at the latest, when the goods are delivered to the buyer. Once property has passed, the seller no longer has any rights relating to the goods – his only right is *to receive the payment of the price*.

This right is all very well, providing the buyer is able to pay the price. But what if the buyer has become insolvent? In that case, the seller is faced with the position that there is no money available to pay for the goods, yet, because the property in the goods has passed from the seller to the buyer, the goods now belong to the insolvent buyer and they may be sold for the benefit of the buyer's creditors.

One solution would be for the seller simply to refuse to sell on credit. However, the seller who asks for cash on delivery is likely to be at a substantial competitive disadvantage in relation to competitors who allow their customers the normal trade credit. Another solution is for the seller to make a thorough credit check on the buyer before selling on credit, and also ask for bank and trade references. This should always be done. However, the problem with credit checks is that circumstances change so rapidly in business and, in any case, credit information is necessarily historical, so that even the best of credit checks may fail to reveal that the buyer is on the verge of insolvency.

In order to try to combat the risks involved in supplying goods on trade credit, the seller of goods may insert a clause into the contract of sale by which he *reserves title* to goods until he has been *paid* for the goods. Such clauses, which have become increasingly common, are often called 'Romalpa' clauses, after the name of the case in which the effect of such a clause came to be considered by the courts.

Section 19 of the Sale of Goods Act provides that where the seller reserves the right of disposal until certain conditions are fulfilled, the property in the goods does not pass to the buyer until the conditions imposed by the seller are fulfilled. Thus, if the seller reserves the property in the goods (that is, the right of disposal) until the price is paid (that is, a condition is fulfilled), the property does not pass until the price has been paid. You will recall that, as a general rule, all contractual terms must be settled at the time of the contract. However, s 19 allows the reservation of the right of disposal to be made either by the terms of the contract or (and this can only apply in the case of unascertained goods) at the time of the appropriation.

The effect of a basic retention of title clause is to create a conditional sale (the condition being that property does not pass until the price is paid). The intention of the clause is to allow the seller to recover the goods from the buyer in the event of the buyer's insolvency. However, the position is complicated by the fact that in many cases, the buyer under the conditional sale agreement does not intend to retain the goods for his own use. He may intend to do one of the following:

(a) the buyer may buy them intending to sell them on to a third party. If he does this, the sub-buyer will usually get a good title to them under s 25 of the Sale of Goods Act (sale by a buyer in possession) and no provision to the contrary in a contract between the original seller and buyer can displace this rule. However, the original seller sometimes attempts to tackle this problem by inserting a clause in the contract to the effect that he will be entitled, not to the goods, but to the *proceeds of the sale* to the third party;

(b) the buyer may intend to mix the goods which are the subject of the retention of title clause, with other goods in order to manufacture new goods. In this case, the seller sometimes attempts to protect himself in this situation by providing that he shall become the *owner of the newly manufactured goods* until the buyer pays the money owed to the seller; or

(c) in some clauses, the seller may aim to combine the claims outlined in (a) and (b) above by claiming the proceeds of sale of the finished product into which the seller's goods have been incorporated and which have then been sold by the buyer to a third party.

There appears to be little doubt that a simple retention of title clause, which creates a conditional sale, will normally be effective. However, problems have arisen from the seller's point of view, where the seller has attempted to impose a more elaborate clause, of the type exemplified in examples (a), (b) and (c) above. In such cases, the validity of the clauses have been challenged by administrative receivers or liquidators, whose job is to try to preserve the assets of the insolvent company for the benefit of its creditors.

What encourages the receiver or liquidator to challenge the retention of title clause is that the circumstances of some cases are such that it is arguable that the retention of title clause goes further than a simple retention of title, and instead creates a security interest in the goods. The practical effect is often similar, but the legal distinction is crucial because, unless a security charge is registered (either with the Registrar of Companies, in the case of a company giving the security or at the High Court in the case of an individual), the charge is void.

The difference between a valid retention of title clause and a clause which creates a security charge is broadly as follows. A retention of title clause creates a conditional sale. In effect, the seller is saying to the buyer, 'If you agree to buy my goods, I will allow you to have possession of them, but the goods do not become yours until you have paid for them'. However, the position with a security charge is different. Here, the buyer is regarded as creating an encumbrance on his own rights in relation to the goods. The situation will be explained more thoroughly in the following paragraphs.

Creation and registration of charges

In order to understand the nature of the difficulties facing the more elaborate *Romalpa* clauses, it is necessary to make an excursion into the realms of insolvency and security law. This has been simplified as much as possible – more detail in relation to company insolvency may be found in Chapter 31.

The *main argument* pursued by receivers and liquidators is that the reservation of title clause creates a *charge* over the goods. A *charge* is a security interest in goods. A good example is where goods are *mortgaged*. Generally, for a charge over goods to be valid, the charge must be *registered in a public register*. This is so that a prospective purchaser of the goods may search the register and thus discover that the goods are subject to the charge. What creates the problem with *Romalpa* clauses is that there are a number of situations in which a non-owner is allowed to possess goods in circumstances where, to a third party, he may appear to be the owner, but without a legal requirement for the true owner to register his interest in the goods. Examples are conditional sales, hence the difficulties with *Romalpa* clause and hire-purchase (though, as we have seen, there is an unofficial registration scheme run for motor vehicles by HPI).

If the charge is *not registered* then it is *void*: the *right to receive payment* of the price (and to reasonable interest on the unpaid price) *remains,* but there are *no rights over the goods* themselves. Since the whole point of a retention of title clause and its variants is to be able to claim goods (or money which represents the goods), if the clause is held to be void because it is an unregistered charge, the seller is no better off than if he had not imposed the clause in the first place.

If the charge is created over the property of a *registered company*, s 395 of the Companies Act 1985 provides that the charge must be registered with the Registrar of Companies, *within 21 days of its creation*. Details of the charge are then filed with the remainder of the documents relating to the company and may be discovered by any member of the public who conducts a search relating to the company.

If goods are charged by an *individual*, rather than a company, the charge must be registered at the Central Office of the High Court, *within seven days of its creation*, under the provisions of the Bills of Sale Act (1878) Amendment Act 1882. A bill of sale transfers the ownership of the goods to the lender as security for a loan, subject to the borrower's right to have ownership of the goods returned to him when he pays off the loan. Meanwhile, the goods remain in the possession of the borrower. The theory is that if the borrower is tempted to offer the same goods as security for a further loan from a different lender, the proposed new lender can conduct a search of the register and discover the existence of the previous transaction. In practice, because of a number of technical problems associated with bills of sale, they are relatively rarely used nowadays.

It would, of course, be possible for a seller to register a retention of title clause, but even if this were done, it would often not help a great deal. This is because, where a company becomes insolvent, it has usually borrowed money from a bank. The bank will usually register a charge over *the whole of the company's assets* (called a 'floating charge', it is capable of including the goods which the seller is claiming as his) as security for the loan. Thus, we could have both the bank and the seller claiming that the goods belong to them. However, where there are competing charges, they do not rank proportionately according to the amount of the respective debts, but rank in order of *creation*. Thus, if the bank has created its charge *before* the seller, the bank will have priority. Since, under the rules of insolvency, there will usually be other creditors with priority over the seller, it is unlikely that, when creditors with prior claims have been paid, there will be anything left for the seller, even though he has registered his charge. If the seller has created a registered charge *before* the bank, then either the bank will refuse to make the proposed loan to the buyer or, alternatively, the bank will insist that the charge registered by the seller is vacated (that is, cancelled) before it will make the loan. Indeed, the bank may include in its loan to the buyer the necessary funds to pay off the amount owed to the seller, in order that the seller's charge may be vacated. Thus, any future charge registered by the seller will rank after the bank's charge, that is, the bank will have gained priority.

THE EFFECTIVENESS OF RETENTION OF TITLE CLAUSES

We are now in a position to look at the various types of retention clause and to assess their effectiveness:

(a) A relatively simple clause in which the seller reserves title to the goods until the goods have been paid for.

Because the normal rule is that the goods are at the *owner's risk* (see s 20 of the Sale of Goods Act), it is advisable from the seller's point of view for the retention clause to provide that the goods shall be at the risk of the buyer, and it is also advisable to provide that the buyer shall insure the goods against risk of loss, accidental damage, etc. In addition, the seller is usually given the right to enter the premises of the buyer in order to repossess the goods, if they are not paid for in accordance with the contract. A further provision obliges the buyer to store the seller's goods separately from his own goods, so that they can be identified should the seller need to exercise his right of repossession.

This is the type of clause which is most likely to be effective in achieving the seller's objective. In *Aluminium Industrie Vaassen BV v Romalpa Aluminium Ltd* (1976), the plaintiffs retained title to aluminium foil which they had agreed to sell and had delivered to the defendants. Romalpa became insolvent and a receiver was appointed. Romalpa had in their possession at the time £50,000 worth of aluminium foil. It was held that this still belonged to AIV. Other aspects of the *Romalpa* case have since been heavily criticised, but this particular principle has been supported in a number of cases.

However, in *Chaigley Farms v Crawford, Kaye and Grayshire* (1996), a farmer delivered livestock to an abbatoir for slaughter, under a retention of title clause. It was held that the animals lost their identity once they had been slaughtered and turned into carcasses.

A more sophisticated variant of the clause came to grief in *Re Bond Worth* (1980). Bond Worth bought carpet fibre from sellers under a retention of title clause which retained 'equitable and beneficial ownership until full payment has been received'. It also provided that if the goods were sold before they had been paid for, the seller's right transferred to the proceeds of the sale. In addition, if the goods were to be converted into other products, the sellers were to have 'equitable and beneficial' ownership of the new goods. It was held that the legal title to the goods passed to Bond Worth under s 18, r 1 when the fibre was delivered to them. The 'equitable and beneficial' ownership referred to in the contract created a floating charge, which was void, since it had not been registered in accordance with the provisions of the Companies Act 1948 (the Act which preceded the 1985 Act). The crucial point is that the contract made Bond Worth the legal owner of the fibre and, in conferring rights in relation to the fibre on the seller, Bond Worth were creating a charge over their own goods. If, as in *Romalpa*, the seller had retained the legal title, the retention of title clause would have been valid, at least in respect of the unsold fibre, though the claims to the proceeds of sale and the new goods would probably have failed.

(b) An 'all monies' clause which goes a step further than a simple retention of title clause in that the seller purports to reserve title until *all money* owing to them by the buyer has been paid.

For example, Ashok sells goods to Ben Ltd under a contract by which Ashok retains title until all monies owed by Ben to Ashok have been paid.

This was the situation in *Clough Mill v Geoffrey Martin* (1985). Clough Mill supplied yarn to the buyer under a contract which provided:

> ... the ownership of the material shall remain with the seller, which reserves the right to dispose of the material until payment in full for all the material has been received by it in accordance with the terms of this contract or until such time as the buyer sells the material to its customers ...

The buyers got into financial difficulties and a receiver was appointed. The receiver refused Clough Mill's request to allow them to enter the buyer's factory and to repossess 375 kilos of yarn which were still unused and which had not been paid for. He argued that the retention of title clause was, in effect, a *charge* over the buyer's assets and, as such, should have been registered under s 395 of the Companies Act 1985. As no registration had taken place the *charge was void*, argued the receiver. *Held*: as the buyer never obtained any title to the yarn, there was no question of the buyer creating a charge over the yarn. The seller was, therefore, entitled to the 375 kilos of unused yarn. The judges realised the possibility that the seller might be getting more than he was entitled to if the buyer had paid part of the price of the yarn, but the seller retained title to the whole of the yarn. Robert Goff LJ said that, during the subsistence of the contract, the rights of the seller were to repossess and resell only as much yarn as was necessary for the buyer to pay off his debt to the seller. If he sold more, he must account to the buyer for the surplus: that is, the seller was not allowed to make a profit out of the situation. If, however, the seller treated the buyer's non-payment as a repudiation of the contract and the seller accepted such repudiation, he could repossess the yarn and sell it at a profit. His only obligation to the buyer was to repay the amount the buyer had already paid. The buyer was entitled to that on the ground of total failure of consideration.

(c) A clause which claims ownership of new goods manufactured using the seller's goods.

A further clause in *Clough Mill v Geoffrey Martin* (1985) provided that if the buyer incorporated the seller's yarn in other goods before the yarn had been paid for, the seller should become the owner of the new goods. It was held that this clause *did* create a charge, because the manufacture of new goods involved not only the seller's goods, but the buyer would bear the cost of manufacture and might incorporate some of his own goods in the finished article. A further practical point was the possibility that a different seller might have provided goods towards the manufacture of the new article and those goods might also be subject to a similar retention of title clause. To hold that the retention of title clause was valid in relation to the newly manufactured article would mean that more than one person could validly claim to be the owner of the article! (Note, however, that it is legally possible for more than one person to have a charge over the same goods - and all such charges would be valid, providing they were registered).

A similar claim failed in *Borden (UK) Ltd v Scottish Timber Products Ltd* (1981). However, in this case, the retention of title clause related to resin which the sellers knew that the buyers intended to mix with wood chippings in order to manufacture chipboard. Borden claimed title to the finished product on the ground that they still owned the resin which had been used in the manufacture of the chipboard. The court held that the resin had ceased to exist as resin when it was subjected to an irreversible process by being mixed with hardener and incorporated into the chipboard. The ownership of the resin must, therefore, also have ceased to exist. Further, the seller could not *retain* title to the chipboard for the simple reason that they had *never possessed* any title to the chipboard.

(d) A clause claiming the proceeds of sale.

The question here is whether the seller can *trace* the proceeds of any sale of the seller's goods into the buyer's bank account. (Strictly speaking, tracing does not relate solely to funds held in a bank account, but in practice this is almost invariably the case.)

In the *Romalpa* case (above), the retention of title clause was extremely elaborate. It not only purported to retain title in goods supplied which were still in the possession of the defendants, it also asserted title to any goods which the foil had been used to manufacture. In addition to taking possession of £50,000 worth of tin foil still in the possession of the defendants, the receiver also received £35,000 cash, representing the proceeds of a sub-sale by the defendants. We have already seen that the plaintiffs were allowed to repossess their aluminium foil. The further question arose as to whether the £35,000 also belonged to the plaintiffs. The court held that as property in the foil had never passed to the defendants, the proceeds of the sale of the foil by the defendants must belong to the plaintiffs.

However, this aspect of the *Romalpa* case has been heavily criticised and subsequent cases have managed to distinguish it. One problem is that in order to trace proceeds of sale, there must be a fiduciary relationship between the buyer and the seller, which creates a duty to account for the proceeds. An example would be where the buyer, when re-selling, sells as agent of the original seller. However, in such a case, the fiduciary nature of the relationship would require the buyer to account to the original seller, not only for the price, but for any profit made on the sale. The Court of Appeal in *Romalpa* skated over this difficulty. However, in *Re Andrabell* (1984), the court refused to hold that a fiduciary relationship had been created. The relationship between the original owner and the buyer was simply one of creditor and debtor.

Comment

A continuing problem in English law is that there is a variety of transactions which have a very similar effect to a charge (that is, they allow a non-owner of goods to have possession of goods in circumstances where he may appear to be the owner), but which, because they do not fall within the legal definition of a charge, do not have to be registered. That there is no universal system of registering the interests in goods is a problem which a number of judges and authors of various reports have commented upon quite strongly (see, for example, the dissenting judgement of Wilberforce LJ in *Mercantile Credit v Hamblin* (1965) and Professor A Diamond, *A Review of Security Interests in Property*, 1989, Department of Trade and Industry). Until there is such a system, the problems with retention of title clauses appear set to continue.

CHAPTER 21

DUTIES OF THE BUYER AND SELLER

DUTY TO DELIVER THE GOODS

Section 27 of the Sale of Goods Act provides that it is the duty of the seller to deliver the goods and of the buyer to accept and pay for them, in accordance with the terms of the contract. The word 'deliver' is not used in the layperson's meaning of the word whereby the goods are taken or sent by the seller to the premises of the buyer. Indeed, in the absence of contrary intention expressed in the contract, the place of delivery is the seller's premises (see below).

Section 61(1) defines 'delivery' as a voluntary transfer of possession. The legal possession does not necessarily mean physical possession. Although the concept of legal possession has given rise to much academic debate, for our purposes 'possession' may be regarded as an intention to possess coupled with the right to possess. Thus when you leave home to go shopping, although you do not take your personal possessions with you, you still possess them in law. A complication which needs to be borne in mind is that one party may have physical possession of goods, for example a warehouseman (that is, a person whose business it is to provide storage facilities for other people's goods), while another, the owner, has legal possession. The legal possession will normally override the physical possession so that if the owner instructs the warehouseman to give physical possession of the goods to the owner's nominee (for example, the owner's employee or a person to whom the owner has resold the goods), the warehouseman must comply.

Actual, symbolic and constructive delivery

In consequence, delivery may be actual, constructive or symbolic.

Actual delivery involves transferring the possession of the goods to the buyer.

Symbolic delivery is where something which enables the buyer to take physical delivery of the goods is delivered to the buyer. The keys of a car would be an example.

Constructive delivery means that the buyer obtains legal possession of the goods without taking physical possession. For example, the seller may have sold the buyer a stock of wine which the seller keeps in his cellars, set aside and clearly labelled as the property of the buyer. In such a case, the buyer will have constructive possession. It is not uncommon in such cases for the seller to issue the buyer with a warrant acknowledging that the seller holds the goods to the order of the buyer.

Goods in possession of a third party

Where the goods sold are in the possession of a third party, s 29 provides that there is no delivery to the buyer unless and until the third person acknowledges to the buyer that he holds the goods on the buyer's behalf. The procedure by which a seller transfers constructive possession to the buyer is called an *attornment*. In practice this takes place as follows: first, the seller instructs the third party (for example, the warehouseman) to hold the goods on behalf of the buyer and, secondly, and this is the vital factor for the purposes of s 29, the third party acknowledges that he now holds the goods on the buyer's behalf.

Sometimes two documents are used to achieve this, sometimes one. S may send a delivery order to the third party instructing the third party to deliver the goods to B. The third party may simply endorse this with an acknowledgment that he will do this. Alternatively, on receipt of the delivery order the third party may make out a warrant in B's favour.

Transfer of documents of title may constitute a constructive delivery. At common law a bill of lading is a document of title. This is a detailed receipt given by the captain of a ship to a person consigning goods to his ship. For example, S in London sells goods to B in New York. The seller consigns the goods to a vessel at Tilbury bound for New York. The captain of the vessel signs a bill of lading stating that the goods are on board his vessel. The seller posts the bill of lading to the buyer in New York. When the goods arrive at New York, the buyer is able to present the bill of lading to the shipping company as evidence that he is the owner of the goods.

Section 1(4) of the Factors Act, in a definition adopted by s 61 of the Sale of Goods Act, defines 'documents of title' to include any bill of lading, dock warrant, warehouse keeper's certificate and warrant or order for the delivery of goods and any other document used in the ordinary course of business as proof of the possession or control of goods. It also includes documents which authorise, either by endorsement or delivery, the possessor of the document to transfer or receive goods thereby represented. In practice, a document of title is either a warrant or an order. A *warrant* is a document typically issued by a warehouseman acknowledging that he holds the goods described in the warrant on behalf of the person named in the warrant. A bill of lading is an example of a warrant. An *order* is a document signed by the person entitled to possession of the goods (which may be the owner or may, for example, be a third party to whom the owner has pledged the goods as security for a loan), addressed to the party who has physical possession of the goods, such as a warehouseman. The order instructs the warehouseman to deliver the goods to the person named in the order or to his nominee. In a case where S, rather than a third party, remains in physical possession of goods which B has bought, the warrant will simply be addressed by S to B.

Delivery to a carrier

If the contract authorises or requires the seller to send the goods to the buyer, s 32 provides that delivery of the goods to the carrier for transmission to the buyer is deemed to be a delivery of the goods to the buyer. This, as we have seen, means that property and therefore risk of loss or damage will pass to the buyer. The prudent buyer will therefore insure against such risks. The seller must make a contract with the carrier on behalf of the buyer on reasonable terms. If the seller does not do this and the goods are lost or damaged in transit, the buyer may decline to treat delivery to the carrier as delivery to himself. This means that the goods will be at the seller's risk. Or he may hold the seller responsible for the loss or damage and sue the seller for damages.

Time of delivery

The basic rule relating to the time of delivery is that if a time has been fixed for delivery, the time of delivery is 'of the essence' of the contract. This means that if the delivery is later or earlier than agreed, the buyer may refuse to accept delivery and may seek damages for non-delivery. In *Bowes v Shand* (1877), rice was to be shipped during the months of March and/or April 1874. The majority was put on board ship during February. The buyers refused to take delivery. *Held*: the rice was not shipped in accordance with the contract and the buyer was therefore entitled to refuse delivery. (It seems that the buyer's reason for refusing to take rice shipped in February was that they had not had time to put arrangements in place to finance the purchase.)

In *Compagnie Commerciale Sucres et Denrees v Czarnikow, The Naxos* (1990), a contract provided for the delivery of sugar from the buyer to the seller to 'one or more vessels presenting ready to load' during May–June 1986 and that the buyer was to give the seller not less than 14 days' notice of the vessel's expected readiness to load. On 15 May, the buyer notified the seller that they would have a vessel ready to load between 29 and 31 May. The vessel was ready for loading on 29 May but, despite repeated requests by the buyers and a warning on 27 May that if the sugar was not ready to load in accordance with the time stipulation, the buyers would repudiate the contract, the sugar was not forthcoming. On 3 June, the buyers informed the sellers that they repudiated the contract and had purchased the required sugar elsewhere. The buyers sued for the difference between the contract price of the sugar and the additional cost of the replacement sugar and also for the cost of keeping their vessel idle while awaiting the contract cargo. *Held*: this being a mercantile contract, time was of the essence if that was the intention of the parties. Time was essential to the buyers in this case, since punctual performance was required to enable them to carry out their obligations to their own customers who had agreed to buy the cargo.

Stipulations as to time of delivery may be, and often are, waived by the buyer. Let us suppose that the date agreed for the delivery of goods by A to B is 1 November. A is unable to meet this date and therefore B agrees that delivery by 1 December will suffice. B is not then permitted to go back on the waiver he has granted and to resume his strict legal rights by suing A for breach of contract when the goods don't arrive on 1 November.

As we have seen, sometimes a waiver is granted without a new time limit being substituted for the old one. In such a case the goods must be delivered within a reasonable time and, furthermore, the buyer may resume his right to a definite delivery date by giving reasonable notice. See *Charles Rickards v Oppenheim* (1950), the full facts of which are given in Chapter 5, p 121.

Demand for delivery or a tender of delivery may be treated as ineffectual unless it is made at a reasonable hour. This is provided for in s 29(5) of the Sale of Goods Act.

DELIVERY EXPENSES

Unless the contract states to the contrary, the place of delivery will be the seller's place of business or the seller's residence. This is the effect of s 29(1) and (2) and means that the costs of the delivery must be borne by the buyer in such cases. However, many sale contracts do make express provision relating either to the place of delivery or the costs of delivery or both. In international sales, 'Incoterms' published by the International Chamber of Commerce are often adopted. This is a reasonably comprehensive list of terms indicating where delivery will take place. Common examples are 'ex-works', which means that the buyer is responsible for the costs of transporting the goods from the seller's place of business, though in practice it is often the seller who makes the transport arrangements; 'free carrier' is a term used to encompass fob (free on board), for (free on rail) and fot (free on truck) contracts. What these mean is that the seller is responsible for the goods until they are placed on board ship, rail or truck at a named place. A sale by S in Birmingham to B in Hamburg, which is expressed to be 'fob Felixstowe' means that S will pay to transport the goods from Birmingham to the port of Felixstowe and for the goods to be put on a vessel nominated by B. The cost of the shipment and incidental expenses such as insurance are, from the time the goods are put on board ship, the responsibility of B.

Alternatively the contract may be fas (free alongside), which differs from fob in that the seller does not pay the costs of placing the goods aboard the ship.

If the seller is to pay the full costs of delivery, the contract is expressed to be cif (cost insurance and freight), in which case the seller is responsible for delivering the goods to their named destination. However, if the contract is for the sale of specific goods which to the knowledge of the parties when the contract is made are in some other place, then that place is the place of delivery. Since delivery costs are high in the modern commercial world, it is clearly of great importance for the seller of goods to make it clear where delivery will take place and to structure his prices accordingly. Section 29(6) provides that, unless otherwise agreed, the expenses of, and incidental to, putting the goods into a deliverable state must be borne by the seller. Where the goods are to be delivered to a distant place, s 33 provides that the buyer must take the risk of the deterioration of the goods which is a necessary consequence of their transit.

DELIVERY AND PAYMENT

Delivery and payment are concurrent conditions of the contract, unless otherwise agreed. The seller must be ready and willing to give possession of the goods to the buyer in exchange for the price and the buyer must be ready and willing to pay the price in exchange for possession of the goods. This is provided by s 28. In practice, in commercial sales, the seller usually gives the buyer a period of credit. Twenty-eight days from the date of the invoice is not unusual, but credit periods differ widely. Large companies placing large orders on a regular basis quite often use their bargaining power to obtain extended periods of credit.

Note that it is readiness and willingness to perform one's contractual obligations which is the requirement of s 28. If the seller is willing to pay but the buyer is not willing to deliver, the seller does not have to have paid in order to be able so sue the buyer for breach of contract: he merely has to be willing to pay. Conversely, if the buyer indicates he is not willing to pay, the buyer may sue for breach of contract without having tendered the delivery of the goods.

Delivery of the wrong quantity

Where the seller delivers less goods than were contracted for, the buyer may reject them. If he accepts them, however, he must pay for them at the contract rate. This is provided by s 30(1). In *Behrend v Produce Brokers' Co* (1920), sellers contracted to deliver 176 tons of one type of Egyptian cotton seed and 400 tons of another type to the buyer in London. When the ship arrived in London, the buyer paid the price. However, only 15 tons of the first type of seed had been unloaded and 22 tons of the second type before the ship departed to make deliveries in Hull. The ship promised to return, but on its return the buyers refused to accept delivery of the balance of the cotton. They claimed repayment of the balance of the purchase price. *Held*: the buyer had the right to delivery on the arrival of the ship. Delivery need not necessarily be immediate or continuous, since where there are other goods on board the ship, the buyer must take his turn. The buyer must submit to delays which are a necessary consequence of the ship being unloaded. However, in the absence of any agreement to the contrary, the buyer is entitled to the delivery of the whole of his goods before the vessel leaves port in order to deliver elsewhere. The buyers were therefore able to refuse delivery of the balance of the goods on the return of the ship and were entitled to recover the price attributable to the undelivered portions of the goods.

Where the seller delivers a quantity of goods larger than the quantity contracted for, the buyer may accept the goods included in the contract and reject the rest, or he may reject the whole consignment. This is the effect of s 30(2). Although s 30(2) does not, apparently, give the buyer the option of accepting the whole consignment in a case where the seller delivers more goods than were contracted for, s 30(3) provides that if the buyer accepts the whole of the goods when more were delivered than were contracted for, the buyer must pay for them at the contract rate.

The Sale and Supply of Goods Act 1994 has added a new s 30(2A) and (2B) which restrict the right of rejection. Section 30(2A) provides that a buyer who does not deal as a consumer (in other words, a business purchaser) may not reject a quantity of goods which is either less or larger than the quantity which he contracted for, if the shortfall or the excess is so slight that it would be unreasonable to reject the goods. Section 30(2B) places the burden of proof on the seller to show that the shortfall or excess fell within sub-s (2A).

Instalment deliveries

The buyer is not bound to accept delivery of the goods by instalments unless this is agreed by the contract: s 31(1). Where the contract does provide for delivery by instalments, the question arises as to what are the rights of the buyer if the seller makes defective deliveries, or the rights of the seller if the buyer refuses to take delivery of, or pay for, one or more instalments. For example, suppose that B buys from S 100 tons of coal to be delivered at the rate of 10 tons per month over 10 months beginning in January. January's delivery proceeds as per contract, but then S tenders only five tons in February. It seems clear that B can reject the short delivery. Can he, however, regard the short delivery as a repudiation of the contract by S and refuse to continue with the contract?

The answer depends on whether the court regards the defective delivery as evidence that the seller intended to repudiate the whole contract or whether the breach can be severed (that is, cut apart from) the remainder of the contract. In the latter case, B must continue with the contract and is entitled only to damages for the breach in question: see s 31(2). The term 'defective delivery' may apply to any delivery which is not in accordance with the contract, for example late delivery, delivery of the wrong quantity of goods, delivery of goods which do not correspond to the contract description or to the quality required by the contract, etc.

In *Maple Flock Co Ltd v Universal Furniture Products* (1934), M contracted to sell U 100 tons of flock to be delivered at the rate of three loads per week as required. After delivery of 18 loads U wrote to M stating that they would accept no further deliveries. The ground for doing this was that the 16th load had been analysed and had been found to contain a chlorine content of over eight times the government standard. *Held*: the buyers were not entitled to refuse to accept further deliveries under the contract. Whether U were entitled to refuse to continue with the contract on the basis of one defective load depended on the application of two tests. The first test is the ratio, quantitatively, which the breach bears to the contract as a whole. The second test is the degree of probability or improbability that the breach will be repeated. Applying the first test, the court clearly did not regard a defective one-and-a-half tons out of a contract for 100 tons to be a very high ratio. On the second test, the court pointed out that there had been 20 satisfactory deliveries both before and after the delivery objected to and that there was no indication that there was anything wrong with any of the other deliveries. The court was of the opinion that the breach was an isolated instance and unlikely to be repeated.

In *Regent OHG Aisenstadt und Barig v Francesco of Jermyn St* (1981), R agreed to manufacture 62 suits and 48 jackets for F. Delivery was by instalments as and when required by F. F wanted to cancel the order but R would not allow that because the suits were already in production. (Remember that once a contract is made it can be cancelled only by mutual agreement. If one party unilaterally cancels, he will be in breach of contract.) One delivery was one suit short. F therefore tried to take advantage of this to cancel the remainder of the contract relying on the provisions of s 30(1) in relation to delivery of the wrong quantity. However, it was held that in instalment sales, s 31(2) overrides s 30(1) and the breach was not serious enough to go to justify F's repudiation.

RIGHTS OF THE UNPAID SELLER

Where a seller has not been paid for goods, he may bring an action for the price in two circumstances:

(a) If the property *has* passed to the buyer, the seller may bring an action for the price of the goods under s 49(1).

Don't forget that in many commercial sales, the seller allows the buyer a period of credit so that the buyer obtains possession of the goods before he has to pay for them. However, unless the seller inserts an effective clause in the contract of sale, reserving property in the goods until the price is paid, the property will usually pass to the buyer on delivery of the goods at the latest. Therefore, the action in such cases will be for the price of the goods.

(b) If the contract has set a certain date for the payment of the price.

In this case, the seller may bring an action for the price even though the property has not passed and the goods have not been appropriated to the contract: s 49(2). If the contract does not provide for the price to be paid on a certain day and if property in the goods has not passed to the buyer, the buyer may bring an action for damages. The principles on which such an action is based are set out in Chapter 16.

Rights of the unpaid seller against the goods

The unpaid seller has three possible rights of action against the goods which have been sold: s 39. These are:

(a) a lien on the goods;

(b) a right of stoppage in transit;

(c) a right of rescission and re-sale.

UNPAID SELLER'S LIEN

A lien is a right to retain goods which are already in the possession of the party exercising the lien, as security for payment. Thus, a repairer of goods is entitled to retain possession until he is paid for the repairs; an innkeeper has a lien over a customer's luggage until the customer pays his bill. Similarly an unpaid seller of goods has a lien over the goods. An unpaid seller is defined in s 38 as a seller of goods:

(a) when the whole of the price has not been paid or tendered;

   Thus, an unpaid seller can exercise the rights of an unpaid seller against the whole of the goods if only part of the price remains unpaid. However, if the price has been tendered by the buyer and refused, the seller does not qualify as an unpaid seller.

(b) when a bill of exchange or other negotiable instrument has been received as conditional payment and the condition on which it was received has not been fulfilled by reason of the dishonour of the instrument or otherwise.

A negotiable instrument accepted in payment of goods is a conditional payment: that is, it does not extinguish the duty to make payment until it is honoured. However, once having accepted the negotiable instrument in payment, the seller is not an unpaid seller until the instrument is dishonoured, or until, under the provisions of s 41, the buyer becomes insolvent.

Circumstances in which the lien arises

The unpaid seller's lien arises in a case where property has passed to the buyer, in the following cases:

(a) where the goods have been sold without any stipulation as to credit;

(b) where the goods have been sold on credit but the term of credit has expired;

(c) where the buyer becomes insolvent. (The buyer becomes insolvent if he has ceased to pay his debts in the ordinary course of business or if he is unable to pay his debts as they become due: s 61(4).)

Under s 42, the seller may exercise his lien against part of the goods for the whole of the price if he has already delivered part of the goods.

The unpaid seller's lien is lost in the following circumstances:

(a) when he delivers the goods to a carrier or other bailee for the purpose of transmission to the buyer without reserving the right of disposal of the goods (though the seller will still retain his right of stoppage in transit): s 43(1)(a);

(b) when the buyer or his agent lawfully obtains possession of the goods: s 43(1)(b);

(c) by waiver of the lien or right of retention: s 43(1)(c);

(d) where there is a sale or other disposition of the goods by the buyer, which is assented to by the seller: s 47(1);

(e) where a document of title has been lawfully transferred to any person as buyer or owner of the goods and that person takes it in good faith and for value, then if the transfer was by way of sale or pledge the unpaid seller's lien is defeated: s 47(2).

Where the property in the goods has not passed to the buyer, the unpaid seller has a right to withhold delivery pending payment. This is given by s 39(2).

RIGHT OF STOPPAGE IN TRANSIT

Under s 44, the unpaid seller has the right to stop the goods in transit, resume possession of the goods and retain possession until the price is paid. This right arises if the buyer becomes insolvent. The right is exercised either by taking actual possession of the goods or by the unpaid seller giving notice of his claim to the carrier in whose possession the goods are: s 46. A difficulty faced by the seller in such circumstances is that under s 46(4), he must bear the expenses of the goods being re-delivered to him. In an export sale these can be considerable.

In *Booth Steamship Co v Cargo Fleet Iron Co* (1916), the defendants, who were unpaid sellers of goods, had received notice that their purchasers in Brazil had become insolvent. They therefore served notice on the carriers, the plaintiffs, stopping the goods in transit. The plaintiffs notified the defendants that the goods could not be landed until duty on them had been paid, whereupon the defendants repudiated any liability for the payment of the freight, landing charges or duty. At the time of the trial, the landing charges and the duty had not been paid. The plaintiffs sued for the cost of the freight. The defendants refused to pay on the ground that the voyage had not been completed. (The goods were due to be carried by ship for most of their journey and to proceed by barge for the rest of the way: the part of the journey undertaken by ship had been completed but not the rest of the journey by barge.) It was held that the carriers were entitled to their freight charge to be paid by the unpaid seller. The reason why the journey had not been fully completed was that the unpaid seller had wrongfully repudiated his obligations in respect of the goods.

Section 45 provides that goods are in transit from the time they are delivered to a carrier for the purpose of transmission to the buyer until the buyer or his agent takes delivery of them from the carrier. If the goods are delivered to a ship chartered by the buyer, it depends on the circumstances whether the ship's master is acting as a carrier of the goods (in which case the right of stoppage will continue throughout the voyage) or whether the master is acting as agent for the buyer (in which case delivery to the ship will bring the right of stoppage to an end). If the goods are rejected by the buyer and the carrier remains in possession of them, the goods remain in transit and the buyer can still, therefore, exercise his right of stoppage. This is so even if the seller has refused to take them back. Thus, if goods have arrived at their destination, where B has refused to accept delivery, following which S has refused to take the goods back (perhaps intending to sue for the price), S can nevertheless, on receiving notification of B's insolvency, exercise his right of stoppage in transit.

The transit is at an end if:

(a) the buyer or his agent obtains delivery of the goods before their arrival at the appointed destination: s 45(2);

(b) where the carrier wrongfully refuses to deliver the goods to the buyer: s 45(6);

(c) if, after the arrival of the goods at the appointed destination, the carrier acknowledges to the buyer or his agent that he holds the goods on his behalf and continues in possession of them as bailee for the buyer or his agent. It is immaterial that a further destination for the goods may have been indicated by the buyer: s 45(3).

Where part delivery of the goods has been made, the remainder may be stopped in transit: s 45(7).

EFFECT OF SUB-SALE BY THE BUYER

It may happen that the buyer has agreed to sell the goods to a third party before he has paid for them and before they have been delivered to him. This happens quite frequently in mercantile transactions. The question arises as to whether such a sub-sale defeats the unpaid seller's right of lien or retention or stoppage in transit. The basic rule is that such a re-sale does not defeat the unpaid seller's rights, unless the seller has agreed to it. However, if the seller has transferred a document of title to the buyer which enables the buyer to re-sell the goods, his unpaid seller's rights of lien or retention or stoppage in transit are defeated. If the buyer has used the documents of title to pledge the goods as security or effect a similar disposition, then the unpaid seller's rights must be exercised subject to the rights of the holder of the pledge (in other words, the unpaid seller must redeem the pledge). This is the effect of s 47(2).

In *Leask v Scott Bros* (1877), S sold a cargo of nuts to B for which B had not paid. S sent B the bill of lading. B then gave the bill of lading to T as security for a loan. B became insolvent. S attempted to stop the nuts in transit. The nuts were claimed by T in satisfaction of the loan he had made. *Held*: B's right of stoppage in transit had been defeated and T was entitled to the nuts.

THE RIGHT OF RE-SALE

The contract of sale is not rescinded by the seller exercising his right of lien or retention or stoppage in transit: s 48(1). This means that the seller who retains possession of the goods under his lien, etc, is still entitled to the price of the goods. If the seller who has exercised his right of lien does re-sell the goods, the buyer receives a good title to them as against the original buyer: s 48(2). However, if the unpaid seller had no right to sell the goods, he may be liable to the original buyer in damages. Section 48(3) and (4) go on to say that the unpaid seller has a right to re-sell the goods in the following circumstances:

(a) where the goods are of a perishable nature; or

(b) where the unpaid seller gives the buyer notice of his intention to re-sell and the buyer does not, within a reasonable time, pay or tender the price; or

(c) where the seller has expressly reserved the right of re-sale should the buyer default.

REMEDIES FOR BREACH

The remedies for breach of contract are dealt with according to whether they are the seller's remedies or the buyer's.

Seller's remedies

These are:

(a) an action for the price;

(b) an action for damages for non-acceptance.

Action for the price

The seller may bring an action for the price in a case where the property in the goods has passed to the buyer and he wrongfully neglects or refuses to pay the price.

Action for damages

The principles of such an action have been dealt with in Chapter 16. This includes an account of the Late Payment of Commercial Debts (Interest) Act 1998.

Buyer's remedies

These fall into two categories: an action for damages for non-delivery or an action for specific performance. These have both been dealt with in Chapter 16.

THE RIGHT TO REJECT THE GOODS

The question often arises: in what circumstances is the buyer entitled to reject the goods because of a breach of contract by the seller? The basic rule is that the buyer is entitled to reject the goods if the seller has breached a condition of the contract. Thus, the buyer in *Re Moore and Landauer* (1921) was entitled to reject a consignment of fruit because the goods breached the condition implied into the contract by s 13: that is, that the goods would correspond with their description. You will recall that although the correct quantity of fruit in the appropriate cans had been supplied, the goods were not all packed in cases of 30 cans, as per contract: some of them were packed in cases of 24.

However, this right to reject can be lost in a number of ways:

(a) the buyer may waive the condition. In other words, in the *Moore and Landauer* case, the buyer may simply have chosen to overlook the fact that the goods were not packaged in cases in accordance with the contract, particularly as the goods were, in every other way, fitted to the contract;

(b) the buyer may elect to treat the breach of condition as a breach of warranty. In such a case, the buyer does not reject the goods but claims damages for breach of contract; or

(c) in certain circumstances, the law *compels* the buyer to treat a breach of condition as a breach of warranty.

Section 11(4) provides that where a contract of sale is not severable and the buyer has *accepted* the goods, or part of them, a breach of condition can only be treated as a breach of warranty and not as a ground for treating the contract as repudiated unless there is an express or implied term in the contract to that effect.

Section 35 deals with the question of acceptance. It provides that the buyer is deemed to have accepted the goods:

(a) when he intimates to the seller that he has accepted them; or

(b) when goods have been delivered to him and he does any act in relation to them which is inconsistent with the ownership of the seller.

The buyer is also deemed to have accepted the goods when, after the lapse of a reasonable time, he retains the goods without intimating to the seller that he has rejected them. This causes problems in practice. In *Bernstein v Pamson Motors* (1987), B bought a Nissan from P for £8,000. After he had driven it for three weeks, covering about 140 miles in the process, it broke down. The buyer rejected the car and sought repayment of his purchase price. *Held*: although the car was in breach of the condition of merchantable quality under s 14(2) at the time it was delivered to the plaintiff, a period of three weeks and 140 miles was a sufficient time in which to examine and test the car. B had, therefore, accepted the goods within the meaning of s 35 and was therefore compelled, under s 11(4), to a treat P's breach of condition as a breach of warranty. He was therefore entitled to damages for the breach of warranty, but not entitled to repudiate the contract and reclaim the price paid. (Note, however, that when B announced his intention to appeal, the full purchase price was repaid to him, perhaps indicating that the defendant didn't have a great deal of faith that the High Court decision would be upheld by the Court of Appeal.)

However, in *Farnworth Facilities v Attryde* (1970), it was held that where the defendant had taken a motor-cycle on hire-purchase and had repeatedly complained about defects which were not properly put right, he had not accepted the vehicle, although he had had it for four months and had driven it for 4,000 miles. Where goods are delivered to the buyer and he has not previously examined the goods, he is not deemed to have accepted them until he has had a reasonable opportunity of examining them, to ascertain whether they are in conformity with the contract and, in the case of a sale by sample, an opportunity of comparing the bulk with the sample.

GOODS BOUGHT FOR RE-SALE

Where the goods are bought by a purchaser for re-sale, the reasonable period of time within which he must reject the goods, will normally extend to the time that it takes the purchaser to resell the goods and a further period of time which allows the sub-buyer to inspect and try out the goods. This is intended to get over the difficulty that if goods are retained by the buyer, who intends to resell them, he would normally (under s 35(4)) lose the right to rejection 'when, after the lapse of a reasonable time, he retains the goods without intimating to the seller that he has rejected them'. Thus, the sub-buyer would have the right to reject the goods, providing he acted within a reasonable time, but the original buyer would be entitled only to damages for breach of warranty under the provisions of s 11(4) (see above).

The law has now been clarified to the benefit of the original purchaser. In *Truk v Tokmakidis* (2000), the claimant sold a lift to the defendant, and fitted it to the defendant's truck in June. Payment was to be in December. The truck was intended for re-sale. In December, a prospective purchaser discovered that the lift had been fitted defectively. The defendant queried this with the claimant and refused to pay for the lift after having given the claimant the opportunity to cure the defect. On receiving a report from the lift manufacturers in March, confirming that the lift had been fitted wrongly, the defendants unequivocally rejected the goods. The claimant sued for the price, arguing that the defendant had lost the right of rejection, since he had had the lift for nine months. The court held that when the goods are required for re-sale, the meaning of a 'reasonable time' is extended to give the sub-buyer the opportunity to inspect and test the goods. Of course, in this case, no sub-buyer had bought the goods, but the court held that the buyer had a reasonable time from discovery of the breach in which to reject the goods. The reasonable time may be extended by dealings between the parties, as in this case, where the buyer was negotiating for the matter to be put right, at the same time waiting for an expert report to confirm the breach.

Rejection where the damage is trivial

The Sale and Supply of Goods Act 1994 inserts a new s 15A into the Sale of Goods Act and provides, in effect, that a breach of an implied term which results in damage so slight that it would be unreasonable for the buyer to reject the goods, may be treated as a breach of warranty (that is, the innocent party loses his right to rescind the contract), rather than a breach of condition. In other words, in the case of a breach in which the damage is trivial, the court may apply the doctrine of substantial performance. This provision applies only to sales which are not consumer sales. In consumer sales the right to reject for breach of condition, however slight, remains.

Acceptance of part of the goods

A new s 35A, which allows a buyer to accept part of the goods, was inserted by the Sale and Supply of Goods Act 1994. This provides that, where the buyer has the right to reject the goods by reason of a breach that affects some or all of them, he does not, by accepting some of the goods (providing that where there are some goods not affected by the breach, he accepts all of them), lose his right to reject the rest.

CHAPTER 22

THE AGENT AND THE AGENT'S AUTHORITY

Every day in the commercial world, a substantial number of transactions are undertaken by someone acting on behalf of someone else. A person who acts in this way is called an agent and it is the activities of such persons which are the subject of this chapter.

In law, the term 'agent' is given a reasonably precise meaning: it normally means a person who is employed to *alter the principal's legal relationship* with others. The agent (A) is employed by a principal (P) in order to effect a contract, on the principal's behalf, with a third party (T). The relationship is a *fiduciary* relationship, which broadly means that the agent owes a duty to act in his *principal's interest* rather than his own.

The situation where an agent makes a contract on behalf of a principal is said to be an exception to the doctrine of privity of contract. However, it is more accurate to regard the principal as having made the contract himself: he simply acts through an agent. Once the contract is made, the agent generally has no rights in relation to the contract itself. He bows out of the situation, leaving only two parties, the principal and the third party. If a dispute arises, the principal is able to sue the third party or third party sues the principal (not the agent). There are however, exceptions to this principle. For example, there is a special type of agent called a *del credere* agent, where, in return for an extra commission, the agent promises to indemnify the principal if the third party is unable to pay. Another exception is where the fact that the agent is acting as an agent, rather than on his own behalf, is not disclosed to the third party.

In most definitions of agency, the idea that the agent is able to create a legal relationship between his principal (that is, the person on whose behalf he is acting) and a third party is fundamental to the definition. For example, Fridman, *Law of Agency*, 7th edn, 1996, defines agency as follows:

> Agency is the relationship that exists between two persons when one, called the *agent* is considered in law to represent the other, called the *principal* in such a way as to be able to affect the principal's legal position in respect of strangers to the relationship by the making of contracts of the disposition of property.

Example

Alf goes in to his local Superhols travel agent and books a holiday in Spain to be organised by Flybynight Tours. Although Alf has no direct contact with Flybynight, he is nevertheless making a contract with them, through the agency of Superhols. If Alf has a claim in respect of defects in the holiday, it will generally be against Flybynight not against Superhols. In agency terms, Flybynight is the principal, Superhols is the agent and Alf is the third party.

Typical agents include solicitors, accountants, stockbrokers, insurance brokers, commodity brokers, auctioneers, company directors, business partners, etc, each of which may enter into a legal relationship with a third party on behalf of a principal. In addition, of course, many employees are given the authority to enter into legal obligations on behalf of their employers and thus will be their employer's agent. In the commercial world, 'factor' is the name given to an agent who takes possession of goods and sells them on behalf of his principal. (Though, nowadays, a person who deals in spare parts for motor vehicles and who acts on his own behalf, not as an agent, is often called a factor, though legally he is not.) A broker who deals in goods is, on the other hand, an agent who simply acts as an intermediary without taking possession of the goods.

A more difficult example is an estate agent. Estate agents are usually asked to *introduce* a third party willing to make a contract with the principal, but has *no authority* to enter into the contract on the principal's behalf. He nevertheless has power to bind his principal by, for example, issuing a description of the property. *Bowstead and Reynolds on Agency*, 16th edn, 1996, calls this type of agency 'incomplete agency'. It is, of course, possible for an estate agent to be given instructions to enter into a contract of sale on behalf of his principal, though this is rare.

Some 'agents' are not really agents at all but act on their own behalf. For example, a motor dealer may refer to himself as a 'Ford Main Agent'. However, the legal analysis of the situation is that the dealer buys cars from Ford and then sells them to his customers on his own behalf, not as agent for Ford. Thus, if the car is defective (leaving aside the effect of the manufacturer's 'guarantee'), the buyer's legal action is against the dealer, not against Ford, as it would be if the dealer were merely acting as Ford's agent.

CONSENSUAL NATURE OF THE RELATIONSHIP

It is often said that agency is a consensual relationship, that is, it arises through the consent of the principal that the agent will act on his behalf and the consent of the agent that he will act on behalf of the principal. However, this is not always the case. As we shall see, a principal may in certain circumstances be bound by the act of his agent, even though the agent has exceeded the authority given to him by the principal. Thus, although the agency is formed by consent, the actual transaction does not have the consent of the principal. There are other cases, such as the agent of necessity, where the principal does not consent at all to the relationship of principal and agent. The relationship in a commercial agency is almost always, but is not necessarily, contractual.

AUTHORITY OF THE AGENT

Crucial to the principal and agent relationship is the *authority* which the principal gives to the agent. An agent who acts outside his authority may be liable in damages to his principal and to the third party. In addition, the rights and liabilities of principal, agent and third party are dependent upon the agent's authority.

On the face of it, the principal should be bound only by the acts which he actually, either expressly or impliedly, authorises the agent to do. However, as we shall see, it is by no means as straightforward as that. The principal is also bound by the agent's acts if the principal has led the third party to believe that the agent has authority: in other words, the principal has given the agent the appearance of having authority. In addition, the principal may be deemed by law to give the agent authority in certain circumstances. Finally, the principal may ratify an act which the agent has done without authority.

We therefore need to consider the agent's authority from four different points of view:

(a) actual authority, either express or implied;

(b) apparent authority (sometimes called ostensible authority or authority by estoppel);

(c) authority by operation of law; and

(d) authority by ratification.

Actual authority and apparent authority have a number of concepts in common. It is therefore essential, when studying both actual and apparent authority, to keep in mind the *possible overlap*. Authority by operation of law and authority by ratification are, on the other hand, reasonably self-contained.

Before we begin to look at the different types of authority, let us look at the possible problems which may arise, using as our example a limited company.

Everything which is done on behalf of a limited company must be done by an agent, because the company itself is an artificial person which cannot perform an action itself but can only act through agents.

Example

Sam is the Managing Director of Company Limited. He contracts to buy a new £100,000 computer system from Information Systems, without consulting the board of directors. Is the contract binding on Company Limited?

A first reaction might be that since responsibility for the overall management of a company is in the hands of the directors, the Company is liable only for what the board of directors has expressly authorised. However, a moment's thought will show that this cannot be correct – the board of directors, unless the company is very small, cannot possibly sanction every single thing which is done by agents on the company's behalf. Thus, the constitution of a company invariably allows the board of directors to delegate their duties in respect of the day to day running of the company to a person usually called the managing director.

The managing director usually has very sweeping powers of management and usually delegates some of his authority to employees below him in the hierarchy.

He may, for example, appoint a marketing manager. If the marketing manager appoints an advertising agency on behalf of the company, without consulting the managing director, is the company bound by the appointment?

If, say, the company owns a shop, it may be that that the managing director will appoint a shop manager. A shop manager may take it upon himself to appoint a shop assistant. Is the company bound by the appointment:

(a) if the managing director has expressly authorised the appointment; or

(b) if all shop managers usually make such appointments; or,

(c) if the personnel director, having been told what the shop manager has done, retrospectively approves it?

The shop assistant has been told that he must, in no circumstances, make any promises to the customer in relation to the quality or performance of the goods he is selling. In all such cases he must refer the customer to the manager. Despite this, the shop assistant gives the customer an express warranty (that is, promise) relating to the weight which a vehicle jack will support, without consulting the shop manager. The vehicle jack collapses because it will not bear the weight which the assistant said it would. Is the company bound by the warranty?

You might like to try answer these questions for yourself after reading the remainder of this chapter.

Where does the agent's authority come from?

In analysing the authority of any agent, we are invariably asking the question, 'Has the agent the authority to enter into this *specific* transaction?' The answer will often depend upon the extent of the agent's general authority, that is, what is the overall task that the agent is employed to do?

Unless this enquiry is approached in a logical manner, there is the great danger that, because of the wide range of possible authority, the student will become confused.

It is probably best to approach the problem by applying the rules to decide, first of all, what is the agent's general authority and, having decided that, to re-apply the rules, asking this time whether, as a result of the agent's general authority, he has the usual, customary or incidental authority, actual or apparent, to enter into the particular transaction which is in question. If that enquiry does not give you the answer, then the rules may be re-applied in order to see whether, despite not having any authority derived from the agent's general authority, he has an actual or apparent authority which simply extends to this particular transaction or particular transactions of this type. Such authority is usually expressly given and cases where the matter is litigated will be relatively rare.

Types of authority

We will now examine in more detail the legal attributes of the various types of authority which we have referred to above.

Actual authority

If the principal gives the agent *actual authority* to act, or if the principal *ratifies* an act which the agent has initially done on his behalf, but without his authority, this has the following effects:

(a) the relationship of principal and agent is created;

(b) the principal and the third party are contractually bound to each other by the acts of the agent;

(c) the principal cannot sue the agent for breach of contract on the grounds that the agent has no authority (assuming, as is usually the case, that the agency has been created by contract); and

(d) the third party cannot sue the agent for breach of warranty of authority.

Most cases in which the question of the agent's actual authority is in question arise either:

(a) because the principal's instructions were ambiguous and the principal then seeks to deny that he gave authority; or

(b) because it appears that the principal may have given the agent an implied authority to act, which the principal is seeking to deny.

Actual authority may be *express* or *implied* or may be created by *ratification*.

Express actual authority

This consists of actual authority either to act in a particular capacity or to undertake a specific act. It may be that the principal has expressly authorised the agent to undertake a particular task. For example, the board of a company may have expressly authorised a particular person to act as managing director. If so, that person would have express actual authority to act in that role. There are few cases relating to express actual authority, since that is usually non-controversial.

A principal's instructions may be ambiguous. Any ambiguity must be construed in favour of the agent, providing it seems that he is genuinely attempting to carry out his principal's instructions. This applies whether we are attempting to ascertain the general authority of the agent or his specific authority.

In *Ireland v Livingstone* (1872), the principal instructed the agent to ship 500 tons of sugar, give or take 50 tons. The agent managed to procure 400 tons and shipped it to the principal, no doubt intending to ship the remaining quantity when it became available. The principal, however, contended that he had intended that the sugar should arrive all in one shipment. (In fact, he appears to have been using this as an excuse to try to escape from the contract, since the price of sugar had fallen.) He refused to accept the sugar and wrote to the agent to say that no further shipment should be made. *Held*: the principal could not use an ambiguity, caused by his own fault, to escape the consequences of the agency contract.

Implied actual authority

A general authority may be created by implied actual authority. The was the case in *Hely-Hutchinson v Brayhead* (below), where the fact that Richards was acting as managing director of Brayhead with the knowledge and acquiescence of the board of directors meant that, although he had not been expressly appointed as managing director, he nevertheless had implied actual authority to act as such.

A person who has a general authority has an implied authority to undertake the specific acts listed below. Such authority is regarded as having impliedly been given to the agent by the principal. Therefore it is an implied actual authority:

(a) any specific acts which are necessarily *incidental* to carrying out his general authority;

Thus, it was held in *Rosenbaum v Belson* (1900) that if an estate agent is instructed to sell a property, he has the incidental authority to sign an agreement of sale. However, in *Hamer v Sharp* (1874), where, as is more usual, the agent was instructed to 'find a purchaser', it was held that the agent had no authority to make an agreement to sell.

(b) any act which is it *usual* for a person with the agent's general authority to be given specific authority to undertake;

The enquiry into usual authority may involve *expert witnesses* going to court to give evidence as to what is usual.

In *Hely-Hutchinson v Brayhead Ltd* (1968), the agent derived his authority from two implied sources. The agent in question was called Richards. He had been expressly appointed as the chairman of Brayhead Ltd. He in fact also acted as the managing director, in which the other directors acquiesced, although he had not been expressly appointed as such. Brayhead Ltd held shares in Perdio, of which the plaintiff, Hely-Hutchinson, was the managing director. Perdio was in financial difficulty. Richards made a promise on behalf of Brayhead that the company would indemnify Hely-Hutchinson against any losses which he might make if he were to lend money to Perdio or if he were to guarantee any loans made to Perdio, in order to try to keep the company afloat. However, despite Hely-Hutchinson's efforts, Perdio went into liquidation. Hely-Hutchinson sued on the indemnity which had been promised to him by Brayhead through its agent, Richards. It was argued that Richards was not the agent of Brayhead, since he had not been expressly appointed as managing director. It was held that by allowing Richards to act as managing director, the board of directors of Brayhead had represented to Hely-Hutchinson that Richards was the managing director. Richards, therefore, had apparent authority to act as managing director. The court went further and found that the board had given Richards the implied actual authority to do so. (The significance of this finding is that Richards would not be liable to Brayhead for breach of contract, nor would he be liable to Hely-Hutchinson for breach of warranty of authority, since his acts would be treated as having been done with the authority of the board.) Once the authority to act as managing director had been established, whether it was implied actual authority or apparent authority, Richards then had the usual authority which is exercised by a managing director.

Analysis

In analysing this case, we begin by asking what Richards's general authority was. We examine his express actual authority, implied actual authority and apparent authority. His express actual authority was to act as chairman. This does not give him the usual or customary or incidental) authority to act on behalf of the company in guaranteeing the loans. It is not usual for the chairman to act in such a way. Nor could it be said that the company gave him a special authority, either actual or apparent, to guarantee loans as chairman of the company. We are on safer ground if we take the court's approach and say that Richards had the *implied actual authority* of the board to act as managing director. (This is his general authority.) If we then proceed to determine his authority to enter into the specific act in question, we can say that although there was no express authority to enter into the contract with Hely-Hutchinson, there was a type of implied authority. The implied authority covers anything that it is usual for a managing director to do. Therefore there was an *implied actual usual authority* to enter into the contract with Hely-Hutchinson.

(c) any act which by custom is undertaken by a person with the agent's general authority.

Unless his principal instructs otherwise, an agent has implied actual authority to act in conformity with a custom or usage of a particular locality or trade, in relation to the transactions which he has been employed to carry out. In order to amount to a usage which the court will recognise it has been held that it has to be: (i) *certain*; (ii) *notorious*, that is, so well known in the particular market that those who contract do so recognise the usage as an implied term; and (iii) *reasonable*.

In *Dingle v Hare* (1859), it was held that when manure was sold, it was customary to give a warranty, hence an agent who sold manure was held to have an implied actual authority to give a warranty.

On the other hand, in *Robinson v Mollett* (1875), an alleged custom was held to be unreasonable and was therefore not implied into the agent's authority. In this case, it was claimed that there existed a custom in the London tallow market to the effect that an agent who was employed by several principals to purchase tallow was permitted to buy in bulk, in his own name, sufficient to satisfy all his principals' orders. He could then allocate whatever was required to each order. This was held to be unreasonable, since the agent's duty is to buy at the lowest price possible, whereas when, as in this case, the agent is acting as a seller, he sells at the highest possible price. This could only be permitted with the consent of the principal.

Apparent authority

If the agent has the apparent authority to act in a particular capacity, such as managing director, then, as with actual authority, the agent will have the *implied* authority to do specific acts, which are:

(a) incidental;

(b) usual; or

(c) customary,

in exercising the general authority of managing director.

In addition, the agent will have the authority to do acts which, though they are not incidental, usual or customary to the authority of a person possessing the agent's general authority, have apparently been either actual or apparent. This type of implied authority arises independently of the agent's general authority

For example, a shop assistant may go to the bank and collect cash for the shop's petty cash account. The shop assistant is robbed of the cash on his way back to the shop. The shop's management may try to argue that the assistant had no authority to collect the cash and that, therefore, the loss is attributable to the bank, not to the shop. We would probably conclude that although the shop assistant's general authority gives him no implied usual authority to do the act in question, he has a special authority, derived from the fact that the shop manager gave him express actual authority to collect the cash.

Limitation of authority

Apparent authority to do a specific act often arises where the principal has put a limitation on the agent's authority but has not disclosed this to the third party. Suppose the board of directors has passed a resolution which limits the managing director's authority to act in specific circumstances: he is not permitted to enter into a contract which commits more than £500,000 of company funds without express authority from the board. In this case, unless the company informs anyone who deals with the managing director about this limitation, the company will still be bound by the managing director's action if he enters into a contract to borrow £1 million. We can analyse this situation by saying:

(a) that the managing director has the express authority to act as managing director;

(b) but, because of the limitation on his specific authority, his authority to enter into the specific contract is not express or implied but is apparent authority (there are other ways in which this situation may be analysed but this is relatively straightforward and will work in practice);

(c) this apparent authority extends to all actions which it is *usual* for a managing director to be authorised to undertake. Therefore, if it is usual for a managing director to be authorised to take a £1 million loan, the company will be bound by the managing director's contract even though the board has expressly forbidden it.

Basis of apparent authority

It seems to be accepted that apparent authority is based on the doctrine of estoppel: that is, if a person makes a representation to another person, intending that person to act on it, and the representation is acted upon, then the person making the representation cannot subsequently deny the truth of it.

An important point relating to apparent authority is that the representation as to the agent's authority to act must come from the *principal* or from someone who has been given *actual authority* by the principal to make the representation. This is the case where we are discussing whether the agent has a general authority or a specific authority. The effect of this is that where the principal simply puts an agent in a position where he is able to hold himself out as having a particular authority, even if this holding out is confirmed by a superior, who similarly has no authority, the principal will not be bound.

This was made clear by the House of Lords in *British Bank v Sun Life*. In *British Bank v Sun Life Assurance* (1983), the plaintiff bank advanced a short-term loan to Nellpine, a property development company. In doing this, it relied on an undertaking by a manager of Sun Life that the money was to be repaid by Sun Life. An undertaking to that effect, drafted by British Bank's solicitors, was signed by Dehnel, who was a unit manager (that is, the manager of about eight people). The management structure of Sun Life started with the unit manager at the bottom, then branch manager, then regional manager. None of these had actual authority to sign the undertaking which British Bank sought. Only certain officers at the administrative headquarters had that power. British Bank were uneasy about the fact that their draft required two signatures and it was returned with only one: that of Dehnel. They therefore wrote a letter addressed to the General Manager of Sun Life at their City branch, requesting confirmation of Dehnel's authority. A letter of confirmation was sent, signed by Clarke, the branch manager of the City branch. British Bank, relying on this, loaned the money. Two further undertakings were signed by Dehnel, bringing the total amount loaned to £120,000. When Sun Life refused to honour the repayment agreement signed by their unit manager, British bank sued, alleging: (a) that Dehnel had actual implied authority; or (b) that he had ostensible (apparent) authority. *Held* by the House of Lords: on the first point, Dehnel did not have actual implied authority to sign the undertaking, nor did Clarke have actual implied authority to represent that Dehnel had actual authority. On the second point, it was held that Clarke did not have apparent (ostensible) authority to answer the bank's letter in the way that he did. Rather, it was a case of Clarke holding himself out, without the knowledge or authority of Sun Life, as having such authority.

A similar problem arose in *Armagas v Mundogas* (1986), a case decided in the House of Lords. In this case, the somewhat simplified facts were that the defendants wished to sell a ship. They were willing to charter (that is, hire) it back from any purchaser for 12 months. The plaintiffs were willing to buy the ship, but insisted upon a 36 month charter at $350,000 per month. An important factor in what happened was that the directors of Armagas and Mundogas never met face to face to discuss the deal but allowed the arrangements to be made by J, a ship broker, and M, the vice president (transportation) and chartering manager for Mundogas. J stood to gain a great deal, including a share of the ship, if the deal went through. To overcome the difficulties, J persuaded M (by offering him a share in the ship) to join him in a fraudulent scheme. Armagas would be told that Mundogas had agreed to a 36 month charter. They were presented with a 36 month charter signed by M, on behalf of Mundogas. They knew that M had no general authority to enter into such a transaction but were told that M had specific authority for this particular contract. The directors of Mundogas knew nothing about this. They were told that the charter was for 12 months and, accordingly, they signed a 12 month charter. J tried unsuccessfully, by fraudulently stating that it was required for Mundogas's records, to get Armagas to sign the 12 month charter. It was then hoped that Mundogas would renew the charter after 12 months and then again after 24 months so that the fraud would remain undiscovered: Armagas would have got their 36 months' charter and Mundogas would never have been committed for more than 12 months at a time. Meanwhile, J and M would have made a nice profit from the deal. Unfortunately, the bottom dropped out of the charter market and Mundogas returned the ship to Armagas after 12 months, at what they thought was the end of the charter period. Armagas, relying on the charter signed by M, sought damages for breach of contract. *Held*: that Mundogas was not bound by the terms of the 36 month charter because:

(a) M had no actual authority to enter into such contracts generally;

(b) M could not, *in the absence of any representation* by Mundogas, be reasonably believed by Armagas to have authority to enter into this specific contract (that is, M had neither actual nor apparent authority); and

(c) that an employer whose employee causes loss, because of his fraud, to an innocent third party is liable only when the employee is doing an act which he is authorised to do or is within the class of acts which an employee in his position is usually authorised to do. In this case, the loss had been brought about by misguided reliance on the employee himself in the course of performing an unauthorised act.

General authority created by apparent authority

A general authority can be created by apparent authority. In *Freeman and Lockyer v Buckhurst Park Properties* (1964), Kapoor, with the knowledge and acquiescence of the other directors, acted as managing director of the defendant company, although he had never been appointed as such. He entered, on the company's behalf, into a contract with a firm of architects to apply for planning permission and undertake other duties in relation to the development of land owned by the company. The issue arose as to whether he had the authority to do so. It was held that Kapoor had apparent authority to act as the managing director and once given that authority, he had all the usual authority of a managing director, which included making a contract with architects. In order to create an apparent authority in the circumstances, Diplock LJ stated that the following must be shown:

(a) that a representation that the agent had authority to enter on behalf of the company into a contract of the kind sought to be enforced was made to the contractor;

(b) that such representation was made by a person or persons who had 'actual authority' to manage the business of the company either generally or in respect of those matters to which the contract relates;

(c) that he (the contractor) was induced by such representation to enter into the contract, that is, that he in fact relied upon it; and

(d) that under its memorandum or articles of association the company was not deprived of the capacity either to enter into a contract of the kind sought to be enforced or to delegate authority to enter into a contract of that kind, to the agent. This fourth requirement *is no longer relevant* (unless the contractor (that is, the third party) is aware of the lack of authority). There used to be a rule to the effect that if a company entered into a contract which was *ultra vires* (that is, 'beyond its powers' – as set out in the company's constitution which is examinable by any member of the public at Companies House), it could not be enforced against the company. However, this rule has now substantially gone. This is the effect of ss 35A and B of the Companies Act 1985. These provide:

s 35A(1)   In favour of a person dealing with the company in good faith, the power of the board of directors to bind the company, or authorise others to do so, shall be deemed to be free of any limitation under the company's constitution.

s 35B   A party to a transaction with a company is not bound to enquire as to whether it is permitted by the company's memorandum or as to any limitation on the powers of the board of directors to bind the company or authorise others to do so.

In *Barrett v Deere* (1828), T owed money to P, a merchant. T called at the merchant's counting house and paid the debt to A, who appeared to be in charge of the house and responsible for conducting its business. In fact, he had no authority. *Held*: P should not allow a stranger to appear to be conducting his business. The payment to A by T therefore discharged T's debt to P.

Barrett's case must be read with caution. It has been held repeatedly in more modern cases that simply putting the so called agent in a position where he can hold himself out as the agent is not sufficient to amount to a representation by the principal that the so called agent has the principal's authority.

See, also, *Hely-Hutchinson v Brayhead* (above), in which it was held that Richards, in addition to having an implied actual authority to act as managing director, also had an apparent authority.

The agent with general authority has an apparent implied usual, customary or incidental authority

If the agent has a general authority, whether express, implied or apparent, he will have the apparent authority to do any specific acts which are usual, customary or incidental in the carrying out of his general authority. Problems which give rise to an apparent authority in this context arise usually where the agent has had a limitation put on his authority by his principal, but the limitation has not been made known to the third party. Thus, it appears to the third party that the agent has the usual authority of someone in his position.

Example

Egyptian International Foreign Trade Co v.Soplex Wholesale Supplies ('The Raffaella') (1985)

Booth was an employee of Repson (a trading bank). Booth's position was described as 'documentary credit manager'. One of the bank's customers, Soplex, had entered into a contract with the Egyptian International Foreign Trade Co (EIFTC) to supply them with a quantity of cement (aboard *The Raffaella*), for which EIFTC had paid Soplex in advance. EIFTC became concerned when the cement repeatedly failed to arrive as promised and in order to try to allay their concern, Soplex asked their trading bank, Repson, to guarantee payment of 570,000 dollars to EIFTC if Soplex defaulted on the contract. Booth provided a guarantee, and EIFTC claimed against Repson under the terms of the guarantee. Repson's defence was that Booth had no authority, as the bank's agent, to sign the guarantee, without obtaining a second signature. The court held that Repson had made a representation which led EIFTC to believe that Booth was able to authorise the guarantee on his own signature alone. The factors which led to this conclusion included:

(a) evidence showed that although there were employees in the banking business, in Booth's position, who did not have the authority to authorise guarantees without a second signature, there were also those who did have such authority;

(b) that Booth saw the representatives of EIFTC at the premises of Repson, where he had his own substantial office from which he could supervise the staff under him;

(c) Booth reported directly to the board of directors at Repson;

(d) Booth had the letter of guarantee stamped with Repson's company stamp;

(e) Booth appeared to have Repson's full authority to deal with Soplex's affairs on the bank's behalf.

It was therefore held that Booth had *apparent usual* authority to sign the guarantee and that the bank was liable to pay.

A less obvious example is *First Energy (UK) Ltd v Hungarian International Bank Ltd* (1993). In this case, the plaintiffs applied for a loan through the

Manchester regional office of the bank. The plaintiffs were aware that the Mr Jamieson, the manager, did not have authority to approve the loan and that it would have to be referred to head office. (Most branch managers of banks have a lending limit, beyond which they must refer the matter to higher authority. The limit tends to depend upon (a) the size of the branch and (b) the seniority of the manager.) However, First Energy received a letter, signed by Jamieson, making an offer of finance. They accepted the offer, on the reasonable assumption that head office had sanctioned it. The bank denied that this was the case, pointing out that it was a rule of the bank that such offers had to bear two signatures. *Held*: although it was clear that Jamieson had neither the actual authority nor apparent authority to make the offer of the loan, his express actual authority to act as regional manager gave him the apparent authority usual to such a position. It was usual for a branch manager to have the authority to communicate the decision of his superiors in such matters and it was not reasonable to expect First Energy to make enquiries as to whether Jamieson had the authority to communicate the offer.

We have looked at four very similar cases in relation to apparent authority: *Mundogas, First Energy, British Bank* and *The Raffaella*. How do we reconcile them? In each case there was no actual authority, express or implied, to undertake the act in question. In the absence of actual authority, nevertheless in each case the employee, by virtue of being appointed to a particular position, would have the apparent authority to act in a way usually given to employees in that position.

In the *Raffaella*, the evidence showed that the agent's general authority as documentary credit manager gave him the apparent usual authority to act as he did. In *First Energy*, although it was not within the authority of the general manager to grant the loan in question (and the third party was aware of that) it was held to be within a regional manager's usual authority to communicate the decision of head office regarding loans. Therefore, there was a implied representation on behalf of the Hungarian Bank that Jamieson had authority to do so: he had apparent usual authority. However, in *Mundogas* and *British Bank* there was no such authority usually given to employees in that particular employee's position. So, there was no actual authority in either case. The only further possibility is that the 'agent' had been given an apparent authority to do that particular act. In this case, a positive representation on the part of the employer is required. In *Mundogas*, although M claimed to have an authority to enter into the three year charter, there was no evidence that Mundogas had misled Armagas in any way into believing that M had any such authority. In *British Bank*, there was the letter written, without authority, by the branch manager. With *Mundogas*, we can say that: (a) the third party knew that there was no actual authority; (b) M was not acting within the usual authority given to employees in his position; (c) therefore it needed a representation from Mundogas to give M apparent authority. This was never forthcoming.

If, in *British Bank*, the only suggestion of authority had come from Dehnel it would clearly have not been sufficient to create an apparent authority. However, because a branch manager had represented Dehnel as having an express authority, it was arguable that Dehnel had at least apparent authority. However, it was held that any apparent authority must have as its source someone with actual authority. That was not the case here. With *First Energy*: (a) the third party knew that there was no actual authority to agree to the loan; b) however, employees with Jamieson's seniority would have the actual implied usual authority to communicate a decision made by Head Office. Therefore, Jamieson had apparent authority to communicate that decision.

There will also be an apparent authority where:

(a) the agency has terminated but the principal fails to inform third parties;

In *Summers v Salomon* (1857), Salomon employed his nephew to manage his jewellery shop. Salomon paid for jewellery ordered by his nephew from Summers. The nephew left the shop, terminating the agency. However, he obtained goods from Summers, using Salomon's name, and absconded with them. *Held*: the nephew was the agent of Salomon until such time as Salomon notified Summers that the agency was terminated.

A partnership will be liable for the acts of a former partner who is dealing with a person who knew him to be a partner and who is unaware that he is no longer a partner. It is, therefore, essential to give notice to all persons with whom the retiring partner is known to have dealt immediately on that partner's retirement from the partnership. Otherwise he will have apparent authority to bind the partnership.

(b) the principal limits the agent's actual implied authority without informing third party of the limitation.

(c) where the principal's subsequent conduct prevents him from denying that a contract was made on his behalf. In *Spiro v Lintern* (1973), a wife was asked by her husband to find an estate agent to sell the husband's house. The wife entered into a contract without her husband's authority to sell the house. Nevertheless, the husband permitted the 'purchaser' to carry out repair work on the house and generally behaved as if the contract made by the wife was authorised by him. *Held*: the husband was estopped from denying his wife's authority to act (note: if the husband had not been an undisclosed principal, he could have been liable under the doctrine of ratification).

Example

The managing director of a company, validly appointed, has his borrowing power restricted to £50,000 by resolution of the board of directors. The managing director borrows £100,000 on behalf of the company. As we shall see, it is possible for the company to ratify the contract. This might be important to the managing director because a ratification gives him actual authority retrospectively, which means that the managing director cannot be brought to account for breaching his contract with the company. However, as far as the lender (that is, the third party) is concerned, he can enforce the contract against the company on the basis of apparent (usual) authority.

The exceptional case of Watteau v Fenwick

There is one category of authority which does not appear to fit the general framework. This was created in the case of *Watteau v Fenwick* (1893). In this case, Humble was the manager of a public house and his name appeared over the door as licensee. He was told not to buy cigars on credit. Disregarding this instruction, he bought cigars on credit from the plaintiff. The plaintiff did not, however, realise that Humble was an agent. The question arose as to whether the owner was liable on the contract. *Held*: once it was established that Fenwick (the owner) was the real principal, the ordinary doctrine of principal and agent applied and the owner was liable for all acts which are usually confided to agents of that character. In other words, because it was usual for a public house manager to have the authority to buy cigars on credit, the principal was liable.

This case has been subject to some forthright criticism, not least from Canadian jurisdictions, where some courts have refused to follow it. If we analyse the case in the terms of the principles we have learned, we get the following: Humble had general authority to manage the public house; this was express actual authority. Once we have established that, we enquire as to whether he had implied authority to buy the cigars. Normally he would have had implied actual usual authority to undertake that transaction, but the express limitation on his authority meant that he had no actual authority. We then move on to the question of apparent authority. Had Fenwick represented to Watteau that Humble had the authority to act as Fenwick's agent in the specific matter of buying the cigars? Wills J, giving the judgment of the court, said: '... once it is established that the defendant is the real principal, the ordinary doctrine of principal and agent applies – that the principal is liable for all the acts of the agent which are within the authority usually confided to an agent of that character, not withstanding limitations ... put upon that authority.' Thus, once we have established that Humble had actual authority to act as the public house manager, we then proceed to enquire as to whether he had the authority in relation to purchasing the cigars. To the third party, he had an apparent authority and such authority would be that which is usual for a person in Humble's position. This is probably the best analysis of the situation. The difficulty with this analysis is that the agency was undisclosed: Watteau thought that he was contracting with the owner of the pub, not with the manager. Thus, it is argued that as the third party knew nothing of the principal and, in fact, thought he was dealing with the principal, he cannot have been misled by a representation made by the principal as to the agent's authority. If such facts were repeated today, it is possible that the decision in *Watteau v Fenwick* would not be followed. However, that does not mean that the pub owner would be allowed to keep the cigars without payment. There are one or two possibilities: the owner would be ordered to restore the cigars or their value under the law against permitting unjust enrichment; or it may be held that the real owner, by allowing Humble to appear to be the owner of the pub, is estopped by his conduct from denying Humble's authority to act as owner.

RATIFICATION

A person may purport to act as an agent, but without any prior authority, or he may exceed whatever authority he has. In either case, the intended principal may validate the agent's actions retrospectively by ratifying them. Authority by ratification is, in certain respects, the equivalent of actual authority. Thus, the principal and third party come into a contractual relationship with each other as a result of the ratified agency. However, if the principal has suffered damage because of the agent's action, he may be able to sue the agent for breach of duty. Similarly, if the third party has suffered damage by the agent's original breach of warranty of his authority, the third party will have an action for damages.

The main rules as to ratification are as follows.

(a) The agent must contract as an agent and not as a principal

We will see that it is possible, subject to special rules of liability, for an agent to contract on behalf of an undisclosed principal, that is, the agent appears to be making the contract on his own behalf and it is only after the contract has been made that the existence of the real principal is made known. However, it is the rule that an undisclosed principal cannot ratify a contract made on his behalf. In *Keighley, Maxted and Co v Durant* (1901), KM instructed R to buy wheat at a certain price for the joint account of KM and R. R could not obtain the wheat at the authorised price, but purchased from D at a higher price. KM purported to ratify the purchase but later changed their minds. D sued KM for the price of the wheat. *Held*, by the House of Lords: KM's ratification was ineffective, on the grounds that liability should not be created by, or based upon, undisclosed intentions. Note, however, that where the agent is acting within his actual authority the law allows the undisclosed principal to sue and be sued on a contract which was made on his behalf. The court in the *Keighly Maxted* case recognised this as an anomaly but said, in effect, that the anomaly was based on reality (that is, .

the agent has actual authority) and that there was no commercial need to create a further anomaly where there was no authority.

(b) The principal must be in existence at the time the agent made the contract

This rule is mainly of importance to promoters of companies. For example, suppose Micawber is promoting a company, Copperfield Ltd, in order to purchase and operate the tanker *SS Goodison*. Micawber agrees, as agent for Copperfield Ltd, to buy the tanker from Dora, before the company has been incorporated. The company cannot ratify the contract after incorporation, since it was not in existence when the contract was made.

At common law, such a contract was a nullity. However, the position has now been altered as a result of s 36C of the Companies Act 1985. This provides that in the case of a contract which purports to be made by or on behalf of a company which has not yet been formed, then subject to any agreement to the contrary, the contract is to be treated as having been made with the person purporting to act for the company or as agent for it and he is personally liable on the contract accordingly.

Thus, in the above example, unless the contract makes it clear that Micawber is not to be held personally liable, he will have personal liability. In most cases, this would not matter since, providing Micawber is the moving spirit behind Copperfield Ltd, the company may simply agree to buy the vessel from Micawber, or Micawber can assign the benefit of the contract to Copperfield Ltd. However, should something go wrong relating to the formation of the company, or should the company's management be placed in the hands of someone other than Micawber, the personal liability could be onerous.

The question might arise whether the Contracts (Rights of Third Parties) Act 1999 would give the company the right to sue on the contract. The Act provides for third parties (that is, third parties in the sense of being third parties to the contract, not the third parties in an agency situation), to be able to sue on a contract made for their benefit, whether or not the third party was in existence when the contract was made. Of course, if the agency were valid, the company would not be a 'third party' within the meaning of the Act, because the contract would be treated as having been made by the company and thus they would be party to it. But since the agency is not valid, there seems to be no reason why the would-be principal cannot be treated as a 'third party' for the purposes of the Act. Thus, although Micawber would be liable to Dora on the contract, it may be that Copperfield Ltd could sue on it.

(c) The principal must be capable of being ascertained

Although, as we have seen, an undisclosed principal cannot ratify a contract purportedly made on his behalf, an unnamed principal can do so, providing the principal is capable of being ascertained at the time of the contract. In *Watson v Swann* (1862), Willes J said: '... the person for whom the agent professes to act must be a person capable of being ascertained at the time. It is not necessary that he should be named; but there must be such a description of him as shall amount to a reasonable designation of the person intended to be bound by the contract.' In this case, A had made a contract of insurance for himself. Later P instructed A to effect an insurance on behalf of P. A was unable to do so, but listed P's goods on his own policy. P ratified what A had done. However, it was held that P could not sue on the policy. He could not ratify it since at the time A made the contract, P was not known at A and could not, therefore, have been ascertained.

This rule is viewed by a number of commentators as being too restrictive and, in the case of marine insurance, it is possible for P to ratify contracts which have been made 'for the benefit of all those to whom they may appertain'.

(d) The principal must be legally competent

The principal must be competent to have made the contract himself, both at the time the contract was made on his behalf and at the time he ratifies it.

We have seen that most contracts made by a minor are not enforceable against him (though they may become enforceable when he comes of age). Thus he cannot, while a minor, ratify such contracts. There are two exceptions to this rule. The first is that a minor may make a contract for necessaries (though he only has to pay a reasonable price – not necessarily the contract price – and then only if the necessaries have been delivered to him). The second is that a minor may make a contract of service (that is, employment) or similar contract aimed at providing the minor with a living, providing the contract is beneficial to the minor. In either of these two cases, it would seem that a minor can ratify a contract made on his behalf by an agent. Other classes of person who may be incompetent include intoxicated persons, persons with a mental disability, and enemy aliens.

In *Dibbins v Dibbins* (1896), the solicitor of an insane person purported to exercise an option on his behalf. The option was open for three months. The agent had no authority, since the principal was insane. An application was made to the court to permit ratification of the agreement made by the solicitor. The court made the appropriate order but by then it was too late – the three months had expired.

(e) A void act cannot be ratified

It has been held that a void act cannot be ratified. However, it would seem that both a voidable act and an illegal act may be ratified where appropriate. A difficulty for any future court approaching the problem will be to distinguish between void, on the one hand, and voidable or illegal on the other.

In *Brook v Hook* (1871), the question arose as to whether a 'principal' could ratify his signature, which his brother-in-law had forged on a promissory note. The principal did this in order to avoid his brother-in-law being prosecuted. When the 'principal' was sued on the note, the court drew a distinction between a voidable act, which can be ratified, and an act which is void and which cannot be ratified. The court held that the act of the 'agent' was void and could, therefore, not be ratified.

However, in the contrasting case of *Danish Mercantile v Beaumont* (1951), it was held that the principal could ratify in a case where a solicitor had issued proceedings without authority. This case is regarded as holding that a voidable act can be ratified.

In *Whitehead v Taylor* (1839), it was held that a principal may ratify an act by an agent which was initially unlawful, in order to make it lawful. In this case, an 'agent' took possession of a tenant's goods in circumstances in which, had the landlord's authority been given, it would have been lawful, but without authority it was unlawful. *Held*: the landlord was permitted to ratify his agent's act so as to render it lawful.

Time limit for ratification

Ratification must take place within the time agreed by the parties for ratification. If no time limit is agreed, the ratification must take place within a reasonable time. In *Metropolitan Asylum Board Managers v Kingham* (1890), it was held that ratification 10 days after the contract was made was too late. It was also suggested in this case that ratification must take effect, in any event, not later than the contract was to be carried out. However, this was questioned in *Bedford Insurance Co v Instituto de Resseguros do Brasil* (1984), so that the matter may be regarded as not having been decided.

The ratification must be done at a time when the ratifying principal could lawfully have made the contract himself. We have seen in *Dibbins v Dibbins* (above) that a purported ratification of an option which was open for three months was ineffective after the three months had passed. In *Bird v Brown* (1850), an agent, acting without his principal's authority, sent notice to stop goods in transit. (You may remember that recovery of possession by stopping the goods in transit is one of the rights of the unpaid seller of goods.) However, by the time the notice had reached the ship's master, the buyer's assignee in bankruptcy had already made a formal demand for the goods. The notice sent by the agent was ratified. It was held that the ratification came too late. The assignees in bankruptcy, consequent upon their formal demand, had a right to possession and the transit could not be extended artificially in order to allow ratification.

In *Presentaciones Musicales v Secunda* (1994), it was held that a legal action which had been begun without authority within the appropriate limitation period (you will remember that all types of legal action, except serious crimes, have a limitation period, by statute, within which a legal action must be started or the right to action will expire – it is said to be 'statute-barred'), was ratified by the principal after the expiry of the limitation period. It was argued that *Dibbins v Dibbins* was authority for the proposition that the action could not be ratified after it had become statute-barred. *Held*: the difference between this case and that of *Dibbins* was that the ratification in this case did not have the effect of extending the limitation period. Therefore, the ratification was effective.

REVOCATION OF THE AGREEMENT TO CONTRACT

We have seen that, as a general rule of the law of contract, an offer may be revoked at any time before it has been accepted. But, again subject to exceptions, a contract, once concluded, is binding and can only be cancelled by mutual agreement.

A question which has arisen on a number of occasions in connection with ratification is whether the third party, having made an agreement with the agent to contract with the principal, may revoke his offer before the principal has ratified the contract.

It seems that the answer to this question is that if the third party is unaware that the contract must be ratified, that is, if it appears that he has concluded a binding contract with the agent, the contract cannot then be revoked.

This seems to be the consequence of *Bolton and Partners v Lambert* (1889). In this case, Scratchly, acting on behalf on Bolton, accepted an offer by Lambert to take a lease of certain of Bolton's properties. Because Scratchly was acting without authority, the agreement had to be ratified by Bolton. Before Bolton had ratified, Lambert purported to withdraw from the contract. Bolton sued for specific performance of the agreement. *Held*: Bolton were entitled to succeed. While it is true that an *offer* may be revoked at any time before it has been accepted, a *binding contract* had come into being when Scratchly accepted Lambert's offer. Bolton's ratification related back to that time.

This appears to give the principal the best of both worlds. He can ratify the contract if he wishes, or refuse to ratify it if not. However, the third party must wait and see. However, the rule in *Bolton v Lambert*, seen by many as being unfair, has been modified to a large extent by exceptions.

The principal exception is that if the third party knows that the contract he has made with the agent is subject to ratification, the position is as if the third party had made an offer to contract, in which case the offer may be withdrawn at any time before it has been accepted. This is the effect of *Watson v Davies* (1931), where an offer was made to sell property to a deputation of a board of a charity. They had no authority to contract without the authority of the full board. They accepted the offer, but it was clearly subject to ratification. The defendant revoked the offer to sell before the 'contract' was ratified by the full board. The board later ratified the contract and relied on *Bolton v Lambert* in arguing that the defendant was in breach of contract. *Held*: because it was clear that the deputation did not have the authority to bind the full board, the defendant could revoke the 'contract' at any time before the full board ratified it.

It appears that the third party will not be liable for any breach of contact between the making of the contract with the third party and the ratification by the principal: *Kidderminster Corp v Hardwick* (1873), though since it was held in *Bolton v Lambert* that ratification relates back to when the contract was made, it is not easy to understand the principle on which this ruling was made.

Act of ratification

The principal may ratify the agent's action either expressly or impliedly. Express ratification, like express authority, poses little difficulty.

Whether ratification has taken place impliedly must depend upon the particular circumstances. In *Waithman v Wakefield* (1807), a husband refused to pay for non-necessary goods purchased by his wife, but refused to return the goods. *Held*: this refusal amounted to ratification.

There are a number of uncertainties about implied ratification: in particular, whether mere inactivity can amount to ratification. It would seem that if the principal is aware of the material facts and takes no steps to disown the position of principal, he may be bound.

UNDISCLOSED AGENCY

It is possible for an agent to act on behalf of a principal without disclosing the fact to a third party. In this case, it is essential that the agent acts within his authority since, as we have seen, it was held in *Keighly Maxted and Co v Durant* (1901) that the act of an undisclosed principal cannot be ratified.

The outward appearance of the contract is that it has been made by the agent on his own behalf: the third party knows nothing of the principal. Despite this, it is possible for the principal to intervene in the contract which was made on his behalf. This is a situation unique to English law and must be regarded as anomalous. Its development is all the more surprising in the light of English law's fairly strict adherence to the doctrine of privity of contract until relatively recently. Whereas, in a normal agency situation, the agent drops out of the picture and the contract is treated as being made between the principal and the third party, an undisclosed agency is a true exception to the doctrine of privity. The rationale behind the doctrine is simply one of commercial convenience: it happens frequently in practice that a principal is undisclosed at the time of the contract.

An undisclosed principal is not permitted to intervene in a contract made between his agent and a third party in the following circumstances.

(a) Where there is an express or implied term in the contract to that effect

The leading case is *Humble v Hunter* (1848). The agent described himself in the charterparty as the 'owner' of the vessel '*Ann*', indicating that he had contracted as principal. The undisclosed principal sought to intervene by introducing evidence to the effect that the agent was not the owner. The court refused to allow him to do this as the description of the agent as the 'owner' was unambiguous.

(b) Where there is a strong personal element in the contract and the third party would not have contracted with the undisclosed principal

In *Said v Butt* (1920), Butt was the managing director of a theatre, with whom Said had had a dispute. Said was anxious to acquire tickets for the first night of a play at the theatre and, on personal application, had been refused. He therefore got a friend to buy a ticket for him. On arrival at the theatre, he was turned away. He sued for breach of contract, claiming to intervene as undisclosed principal. The action failed. The theatre would not have sold the ticket to the agent if it had known he was acting on behalf of Said.

However, in *Dyster v Randall* (1926), the plaintiff wished to buy land belonging to the defendant. Knowing that the defendant would not, under any circumstances, sell the land to him, he instructed an agent to enter into a contract, on his behalf, to buy the land without disclosing the agency. The defendant discovered the true situation and refused to complete the sale. The plaintiff sued for specific performance of the contract. *Held*: the identity of the principal was not important in relation to the contract. Therefore the undisclosed principal could intervene and enforce the contract.

One further point: if the agent has been asked whether he is contracting on behalf of another and he lies about the matter, neither the principal nor the agent will be allowed to enforce the contract. This is the effect of *Archer v Stone* (1898).

AGENCY BY OPERATION OF LAW

As we saw earlier, agency is generally referred to as a consensual relationship, in that it arises from the consent or the apparent consent of the principal. However, there are certain circumstances where agency may arise by operation of law.

The two main circumstances in which agency by operation of law arises are (a) agency of necessity and (b) agency by cohabitation.

Agency of necessity

In an emergency, it is sometimes necessary for a person to contract with a third party, on behalf of another, without authority, in order to preserve the other's property or protect his interests. If the 'agent' does this, an agency of necessity will be created and the principal will be liable to the third party.

A good example is *Great Northern Railway v Swaffield* (1874), in which a horse was transported by the plaintiffs' railway on behalf of the defendants. When the horse arrived at its destination, there was no one to take possession of it. The plaintiffs therefore paid for it to be kept at a livery stable until it could be collected. It was held that the plaintiffs were able to recover the cost from the defendant. An agency of necessity had been created.

The master of a vessel being forced to take emergency steps to preserve a cargo, or to preserve the vessel itself, is a good example of a circumstance in which an agency of necessity has arisen regularly in the past, although with modern means of communication, it is unlikely to occur quite so often in the future.

However, a relatively modern case is *China Pacific SA v Food Corp of India The Winson* (1982). The defendant chartered a ship to carry a cargo of wheat. The ship became stranded. The captain authorised a salvage operation. In order to lighten the ship, the salvors unloaded some of the wheat and put it in storage. The salvors were now suing the cargo owners for the cost of storing the wheat, as agents of necessity. It was held by the House of Lords that an agency of necessity had been created and the salvors were entitled to reimbursement.

For an agency of necessity to be created, the following factors must be present:

(a) the principal must not have given express instructions to the contrary;

(b) it must be impossible for the agent to get instructions from the principal;
In *Sims v Midland Railway Co* (1913), a claim of agency of necessity failed on the ground that the railway company could have secured the instructions of the principal. In this case, a cargo of tomatoes being shipped by the railway company was delayed during a dock strike. The company sold them. The original owner sued for conversion (that is, the wrongful sale of the goods). The company defended their action by pleading agency of necessity. *Held*: there was no necessity, since the railway company could have contacted the owners and secured their instructions. In *Surrey Breakdown v Knight* (1999), a breakdown service

dragged a car from a pond without the authority of the owner. They claimed the cost plus the cost of subsequent storage charges from the owner as agents of necessity. It was held that there was no immediate urgency: they could have waited until they were able to communicate with the owner and ascertain his wishes;

(c) there must be an emergency which makes the agent's action necessary for the benefit of the principal;

(d) the agent's act must be reasonable, prudent and *bona fide* in the interests of the principal. These requirements were laid down in *Prager v Blatspiel, Stamp and Heacock* (1924). In the event, the judge held that there was no necessity in this case. This was because the agent, who sold furs belonging to the principal without authority, could have retained the furs (since they were not perishable) until such time as he could have communicated with the principal.

Agency by reason of cohabitation

There is a presumption that a *female cohabitee* has the authority of the male cohabitee, to pledge his credit for *necessaries*. This presumption may be regarded as anachronistic, dating as it does from the time when the woman was regarded as the manager of the household and the man as the breadwinner. However, although the presumption may be rebutted, it still exists. There appears to be no reason why, in modern times, the presumption could not be applied in circumstances where the male manages the household while the woman is the breadwinner, or indeed, between cohabiting same-sex couples where one adopts a household management role while the other adopts the breadwinning role. Although the legal theory behind this type of agency could be the subject of a fascinating debate (Professor Treitel, for example, thinks that the agency arises from implied authority), it is not important enough in commercial practice to merit further debate here.

CHAPTER 23

THE DUTIES OF THE AGENT
AND THE PRINCIPAL

DUTIES OF AN AGENT TO HIS PRINCIPAL

As we noted at the outset, the vast majority of commercial agencies arise through contract, so that the agent has a contractual duty to his principal and vice versa. However, because the relationship of principal and agent is one which it is often easy for the agent to abuse, equity has imposed a number of *fiduciary* duties (that is, duties of which the basic requirement is loyalty) upon the agent. Thus, in domestic law the duties of an agent come from two sources: (a) duties under the contract of agency; and (b) duties imposed by equity.

The Commercial Agents (Council Directive) Regulations 1993

Regulations passed in pursuance of an EU Directive lay down duties for a 'commercial agent' which are more or less on a par with those which were established by English law. However, 'commercial agent' as defined applies only to 'a self-employed intermediary who has continuing authority to negotiate the sale or purchase of goods on behalf of another person ('the principal') or to negotiate and conclude the sale or purchase of goods on behalf of and in the name of the principal.

Agents not covered by the Regulations

As we have seen from the above definition, agents who are not involved in buying and selling goods will not be covered by the Regulations, for example, solicitors, insurance brokers, travel agents, etc. In addition, the Regulations *expressly exclude* officers of a company, (for example, directors and company secretary) or an association, partners and any person who acts as an insolvency practitioner (the Directive names receiver, receiver and manager, liquidator or trustee in bankruptcy). The Regulations also do not apply unless the agency is a continuing one so that, for example, the employment of an auctioneer for a one-off transaction would not be covered. In addition, the Regulations are not applicable to unpaid agents, agents who operate on the commodity exchanges or in the commodity market, or agents whose activities as commercial agents are to be considered 'secondary'.

In *Parkes v Esso Petroleum* (1999), the issue arose of a licensee of a petrol station whose main activity was to sell fuel oils mainly by self-service on behalf of Esso. The licence described the claimant as an agent. He received a commission on sales. He argued that he was a commercial agent within the meaning of the Regulations. It was held that because the majority of the sales in the petrol station were self-service, the claimant did not negotiate those sales. Thus, the claimant's activities in relation to negotiated sales (refer back to the definition of 'commercial agent' above) were secondary. He was, therefore, not a commercial agent within the meaning of the Regulations.

Duties of an agent under the Regulations

Regulation 3 of the Commercial Agents (Council Directive) Regulations 1993 provides:

(1) In performing his activities a commercial agent must look after the interests of his principal and act dutifully and in good faith.

(2) In particular a commercial agent must–

(a) make proper efforts to negotiate and, where appropriate, conclude the transactions he is instructed to take care of;

(b) communicate to his principal all the necessary information available to him;

(c) comply with reasonable instructions given by his principal.

It can be seen that the Regulations cover agents employed to effect introductions as well as agents employed to complete sales.

Regulation 5 contains a prohibition on derogation from reg 3 (and 4, which deals with the duties of a principal to his agent). This means that the duties cannot be excluded by contractual agreement.

We will see that the controversial provisions of the Regulations relate not to the duties of the agent or principal, but to the fact that they introduce a statutory right to compensation in the event that the agency is discontinued, somewhat akin to the right of an employee to claim unfair dismissal. This concept of compensation is entirely new to English law, so that we may look forward to increasing litigation in which agents who may be on the borderline of the Regulations, seek to bring themselves within the scope of the Regulations in order to claim compensation. There has been no effort to rationalise the law relating to agency in order to incorporate the regulation and so there is a significant overlap between the Regulations and the common law. It may well be that because the duties of an agent under the Regulations are so similar to those developed by English law, the case law developed in English law will continue to be relevant for the purpose of interpretation of the regulations. We will, therefore, proceed on that assumption. In any case, we need to know the duties of an agent under domestic law because a significant number of agents (that is, all those who supply services rather than sell goods) will continue to be subject only to domestic law.

Contractual duties

Duty to perform his instructions

The agent has a duty to carry out the task which he has contracted to undertake. Thus, in *Turpin v Bilton* (1843), the agent contracted to effect a contract of insurance with relation to the principal's ship. The agent failed to do this. The uninsured ship was subsequently lost. The principal sued the agent in respect of his loses. *Held*: the agent was liable to the principal for breach of contract.

However, if the contract which the agent is asked to make is illegal (in the sense that it is void or unenforceable – not in the sense that it breaches the criminal law), the agent will not be liable if he fails to make the contract. In *Cohen v Kittell* (1889), the principal instructed the agent, who was a horse-racing commission agent, to place a number of bets for him. The agent failed to do so and the principal sued him in respect of the winnings which the principal had failed to receive as a result. *Held*: the agent was not liable since the contract he was asked to make was a wagering contract and, as such, was illegal.

Duty to carry out the agency with due care and skill

Section 13 of the Supply of Goods and Services Act 1982 implies a term into all contracts under which a service is provided, that the service will be carried out with due care and skill. The common law implies such a duty in the case of an agent. This is a duty which arises contractually but it also arises independently from the tort of negligence. Thus, the claimant has the choice of whether to sue in contract or in tort. This might be more than academic, since the rules relating to remoteness of damage are different in contract and in tort, so that there may be some situations in which a contract action is more advantageous and some in which negligence is more advantageous.

The duty requires that the agent show the standard of skill and care of a reasonably competent practitioner in the trade or business in which the agent is employed.

It used to be thought that the standard of care to be expected from a gratuitous agent was lower than that of a contractual agent. However, it would seem, since the case of *Chaudhry v Prabhakar* (1988), in which Chaudhry was given negligent advice by Prabhakar, acting as a friend, in relation to the purchase of a car, the standard to be expected from a contractual agent and that from a gratuitous agent is the same.

Duty to perform personally

The agent has a duty to perform his task personally. This is often expressed by the latin maxim *delegatus non potest delegare*, which means 'a delegate cannot delegate'. The reason for the rule is because the principal is entitled to expect personally from the agent: (a) the use by the agent of his own skill; and (b) the personal relationship which requires the agent to act in good faith.

Two issues arise from delegation:

(a) *Has the agent the right to delegate his duties?*

If it is held that the agent has no authority, either express or implied, to delegate his duties, he will be liable to his principal for any damage caused to the principal by reason of the unauthorised delegation. Moreover, he will not be entitled to remuneration.

Example

McCann v Pow (1975)

In this case, the plaintiffs were employed to find a purchaser for the defendant's property. He sent the details to another estate agent, Douglas, who found a purchaser. The plaintiff sued for the agreed commission. *Held*: the plaintiff had no authority, express or implied, to delegate his task. He was not, therefore, entitled to his commission. Note: one argument on behalf of the plaintiff was that the act of selling the property was purely ministerial (see below), requiring no particular skill or care – the argument was not accepted by the court.

(b) *If the agent is found to have the right to delegate, is the principal in a direct contractual relationship with the sub-agent? Or, alternatively, does the principal's agent remain responsible for any defaults of the sub-agent?*

To answer this question, let us first look at the circumstances in which it might be held that the agent has authority to delegate to a sub agent. These are:

(i) where there is *express authority to delegate*. For an example see *De Bussche v Alt* (1878) (below);

(ii) where authority to delegate is the conclusion to be drawn from the *conduct of the parties*. In *De Bussche v Alt* (1878), although the authority to delegate was express, the court held that the express authority to delegate to a sub-agent who had an office only in Japan, meant that it was within the contemplation of the parties that a sub-agent might have been appointed in ports where the sub-agent had no offices. Thus, had any such delegation been made, it would have been done with implied authority;

(iii) where, in the course of the employment, *unforeseen emergencies* arise which impose upon the agent the necessity to employ a substitute;

(iv) where it is done in accordance with a *usage of the trade*: for example, where a country solicitor appoints a town solicitor as a sub-agent;

(v) where it is *reasonable* bearing in mind the nature of the particular business which is the subject of the agency;

(vi) where the act delegated is *a purely ministerial act* which does not require his particular skill or the principal's confidence in the agent. For example, in *Allam v European Poster Services* (1968), agents were authorised to issue notices to quit. They delegated this duty to a firm of solicitors. The issue of whether this was a permissible delegation arose. It was held that the act of the solicitor was purely ministerial and that, therefore, the delegation was permissible.

However, simply because the delegation is within the authority of the agent, this *does not necessarily mean that the sub-agent takes the principal's place as agent*. This will only be the case if it is held that there is privity of contract between the principal and the sub-agent. It has been held that there will be no privity of contract unless there is 'precise proof' that privity of contract was intended to be created. In *Calico Printers' Association v Barclays Bank* (1931), the plaintiffs had appointed Barclays Bank as their agent in relation to a sale of cotton in Beirut. However, as Barclays had no office in Beirut, they appointed the Anglo-Palestine Bank as sub-agents. The arrangement was the normal one in international trade, whereby the shipping documents evidencing that the goods had been shipped were sent to the local agents. The agents were instructed to present the documents to the buyer in return for payment. If the buyer refused to accept the documents, the sub-agent was instructed to warehouse the goods and insure them. The sub-agents failed to present the shipping documents for payment and failed to insure the goods. The goods were destroyed by fire. The plaintiffs sued Barclays and the Anglo-Palestine Bank for the loss caused by the breach of duty. It was held: (a) that the plaintiffs could not recover against the Anglo-Palestinian Bank because there was no privity of contract between the plaintiffs and the Bank; and (b) they could not recover against Barclays because there was an effective exemption clause in the contract between the plaintiffs and Barclays which exempted Barclays from liability.

Note: because it was held that there was no privity of contract between Calico Printers and the Anglo-Palestinian Bank, it meant that the duties of an agent to his principal were still owed by Barclays. Normally Calico Printers would have succeeded against Barclays, who would then have had a similar action against Anglo-Palestinian. Thus the buck would have stopped where the fault lay. If this case were repeated today, the issue would arise as to whether Barclays' exemption from liability was reasonable under ss 2 or 3 of the Unfair Contract Terms Act. One of the factors which is expressly taken into account in deciding that issue, is the incidence of insurance. So, if Calico Printers had the goods insured (or if it was reasonable to expect them to have the goods insured), the result of the case might well be the same. Otherwise, if Calico Printers were uninsured and were, as a result of the exemption clause, going to have to stand the loss themselves, the exemption clause may well be held to be unreasonable.

A contrasting case in which it was held that there was privity of contract between the principal and the sub-agent was *De Bussche v Alt* (1878). In this case, the principal owned a vessel called the *Columbine*. He authorised an agent to sell it on his behalf. The agent was unable to sell it at the price stated and asked the principal's permission, which the principal gave, to appoint a sub-agent. The sub-agent sold the ship to himself and then resold it at a profit. It was held that the delegation was valid because it was authorised by the principal. It was also held that the principal and the sub-agent were in a direct contractual relationship (that is, privity of contract existed between them). Because of this, the principal was able to recover the profit made by the sub-agent: the sub-agent was in breach of duty in selling the ship to himself and re-selling at a profit. If there had been no privity of contract, the owner would have had to sue his agent, who in turn would have had to sue the sub-agent.

We will try to summarise the effect of these cases. If there is no privity of contract, the agent remains liable to the principal for the default of the sub-agent. Therefore, for example, if a sub-agent is paid a sum of money due to the principal but fails to pay it over to him, the principal's remedy is to sue his agent, not the sub-agent. However, this does not mean that the sub-agent gets away with his breach of duty. He is himself the agent of the agent and as such, the sub-agent will be in breach of his duty to the agent.

If there is privity of contract, the agent's duty is restricted to the duty to select the sub-agent with due care and skill. There his duty ends and in relation to breaches of duty by the sub-agent to the principal or the principal to the sub-agent, each may sue the other.

The agent's fiduciary duties

Duty to account

The agent has a duty to account for all the principal's money which may be in his possession. This applies whether the money has come from the principal or from a third party. He must keep the principal's money or property separate from his own. He must keep accurate accounts of his transactions on behalf of the principal and must produce them on request.

Duty to avoid conflict of interest

The agent must avoid putting himself in a situation where his own interest conflicts with that of his principal. If, after having been employed to sell the principal's property, he buys it himself he will be in breach of duty. The reason for this is that as agent he owes a duty to obtain the best price possible for his principal. It is immaterial that he pays the principal's asking price (as happened in *De Bussche v Alt* (above). It is immaterial that he deals fairly with the principal – simply putting himself in a position where his duty to his principal may conflict with his own self-interest is sufficient to amount to a breach of duty. For example, in *McPherson v Watt* (1877), an agent who was employed to sell a property and who wanted the property for himself, agreed to buy it in his brother's name. When this was discovered the principal refused to complete the sale. The agent sued for specific performance but failed on the ground that his conflict of interest amounted to a breach of duty.

Similarly, if the agent is instructed to buy property for the principal but sells the principal the agent's own property, the agent will be in breach of duty. The agent owes the principal a duty to purchase the property for the lowest price possible, whereas his own personal interest means that he may be seeking to sell for the highest price possible. In *Armstrong v Jackson* (1917), Jackson, a stockbroker, was instructed to buy 600 shares in a company on behalf of Armstrong. Jackson pretended to acquire the shares on the stockmarket but in fact sold the principal 600 of his own shares in the company. Some years later the principal discovered the truth and sued to have the contract set aside. *Held*: a conflict of interest had arisen and consequently Armstrong was entitled to have the contract set aside. Although delay is normally a bar to claiming rescission of a contract, in the case of breach of this duty, time does not begin to run against the principal until the breach of duty is discovered.

The agent will not have breached his duty if he makes full disclosure of all the facts to the principal and obtains the principal's consent.

In addition, if the conflict of interest involves the agent in selling the principal his own property, or the agent buys the principal's property, he must show that the price was fair and that he did not abuse his position in any way.

The question may arise as to what is the agent's duty if he acts for two different principals whose interests conflict? This happened in *Kelly v Cooper* (1993). Kelly instructed Cooper's estate agents to sell his property. Brant, who owned the adjacent property, also instructed Coopers to sell it. Cooper took Perot to view both properties. Perot made an offer for Brant's property, which Brant accepted. Perot then made an offer for Kelly's property, which Kelly accepted, in ignorance of Perot's offer to buy Brant's house. When Kelly discovered the full facts, he brought an action against Coopers alleging breach of duty in failing to disclose to him Perot's offer for Brant's property. He argued that if he had known that Perot wanted both properties, he could have used the knowledge to negotiate a better price for his own property. He also argued that Coopers were in breach of their duty by putting themselves in a position where their duties to two principals could conflict. The court held that there was no conflict of interest. The matter was to be resolved by looking at the contract of agency. The plaintiff was aware that Coopers would be acting for vendors of comparable properties, and that in doing so would receive confidential information from those other vendors. In order for there to be a breach of duty, the agency contract between the plaintiff and the defendant would have to include: (a) a term requiring the defendants to disclose such confidential information to the plaintiff; and (b) a term precluding the defendant from acting for rival vendors; and (c) a term precluding the vendors from seeking to earn commission by acting for a rival vendor. The court was of the opinion that no such terms were included.

Duty not to make a secret profit

An agent is must not use his position to make a secret profit. A secret profit consists of an advantage, over and above the agent's remuneration, which the agent has gained from using his principal's property, or his position of authority, or information and knowledge which he has gained on the principal's behalf while acting as agent.

In principle, if the agent has made a secret profit: (a) he will be made to give up the profit to his principal; and (b) he will lose his entitlement to remuneration. However, the latter rule is not enforced where it appears that the agent did not act dishonestly, that is, where he did not realise that what he was doing was in breach of duty.

In *Boardman v Phipps* (1967), two people, who had not been appointed as agents but who were, nevertheless, acting as agents for trustees, were appointed to negotiate with a company in which the trust had shares. As a result of information received while acting as agents, they recommended that the trust should buy a controlling interest, since there was a large profit to be made. The trustees turned down the suggestion. The two agents therefore bought the shares for themselves. They made a large profit for themselves and also made a profit for the trust. It was held that they were in breach of duty to the trust. They could only have made the profit because of the information they received as agents: such information would not have been available to them as members of the public. They were, therefore, compelled to hand over their profits to the trust, although they were allowed 'a generous remuneration' from the trustees for producing the profit.

In *Hippisley v Knee Bros* (1905), Hippisley employed Knee Bros to sell goods by auction. This involved Knee Bros in placing advertisements, for which they charged Hippisley the gross amount. However, they had been allowed a customary discount from the gross amount. They argued that they should be allowed to keep the discount since, if Hippisley had placed the adverts themselves, they would not have been granted a discount. *Held*: this was a secret profit and the discount received must be accounted for. However, since the agents had not acted dishonestly, they were entitled to their remuneration under the agency contract.

Duty not to take a bribe

A bribe, in layman's language, is a dishonest inducement to take a particular course of action. It is associated in the public mind with corruption. In relation to the agent's duty not to take a bribe, the word 'bribe' is used with a much broader meaning. There is not necessarily any dishonesty.

A bribe was defined in *Anangel Atlas Compania v Ishikawajima-Harima Heavy Industries* (1990), at p 171, as 'a commission or other inducement which is given by a third party to an agent as such and which is secret from his principal'.

In *Boston Deep Sea Fishing and Ice Co v Ansell* (1888), Ansell was the managing director of the plaintiff. He ordered the construction of two new fishing boats for the company. Unknown to the plaintiff, the shipbuilders paid Ansell a commission on the orders. In addition, Ansell accepted payments from two other companies (in both of which he held shares), with which he placed orders on behalf of the plaintiff. When the company found out, Ansell was dismissed and the company brought an action to recover the amount of the bribes, in which they were successful.

The remedies available to the principal where his agent fails to act in good faith are as follows:

(a) the agent may be dismissed without notice;

(b) the principal may recover any remuneration paid to the agent in respect of the transaction;

(c) where the agent has been given a bribe or made a secret profit, the principal may recover the amount of the bribe or profit. Where the agent has been fraudulent, the principal may sue the agent for damages for the tort of deceit. However, this is an alternative to suing for the amount of the profit or the bribe;

(d) where the agent has been given a bribe by the third party, the principal may rescind the contract made with the third party.

THE RIGHTS OF THE AGENT

The agent's right to payment

The agent may be entitled to payment from one of three sources: by way of remuneration; by way of lien; and by way of indemnity.

Remuneration

There is no restriction upon the source from which the remuneration may be derived. It is commonly made by way of salary, fee, commission, or share of profits. The agent has a right to remuneration only if remuneration has been agreed. However, where it is clear from the circumstances that the agent expected to receive remuneration and the principal expected to pay it, the court will usually imply a term giving a right to remuneration where none has been expressly stated.

Section 15 of the Supply of Goods and Services Act 1982 provides that where, under a contract for the supply of a service, the consideration for the contract is:

(a) not determined by the contract; or

(b) left to be determined in a manner agreed by the contract; or

(c) determined by the course of dealing between the parties,

there is an implied term that the party contracting with the supplier will pay a reasonable price. What is a reasonable price is a question of fact.

In such a case, the court will decide what remuneration is reasonable in the circumstances. They will give a *quantum meruit,* that is, 'as much as it is worth'. (An alternative way of looking at this problem is under the law relating to restitution. Where the circumstances indicate that at the outset both parties expected the agent to be remunerated, an amount of remuneration may be awarded, to avoid the principal unjustly enriching himself at the expense of the agent.)

In *Way v Latilla* (1937), W (the agent) agreed with L (the principal) to send L information regarding gold mines and concessions in West Africa. His contract did not provide for any remuneration, although W had understood that he would be remunerated by a share in any concessions obtained. W sued for remuneration. The trial judge awarded him a one third share of the value of the concession. This amounted to £30,000. However, the trial judge also stated that if he had made an award based upon a *quantum meruit* the amount of the award would have been £5,000. On appeal to the House of Lords, it was held that the trial judge was not entitled to write the contract for the parties by determining that L was entitled to a particular percentage of the concession. W was, therefore, not entitled to a share in the concession but was entitled to a *quantum meruit* which the House of Lords, accepting the trial judge's valuation, valued at £5,000.

If the remuneration is by the terms of the contract, left to be fixed at the discretion of the principal, the agent will only be entitled to such remuneration as the principal decides. In *Re Richmond Gate Property Ltd* (1965), the plaintiff was appointed joint managing director of the company. His remuneration was to be, under the Articles of the company, 'such remuneration ... as the directors may determine'. The company was wound up after the plaintiff had acted as managing director for four months. He received no remuneration. He sued for £400, either as a result of contract or by way of *quantum meruit. Held*: he was entitled to nothing. The articles gave the board of directors a discretion whether or not to award remuneration and, as the directors had made no award, the plaintiff had no entitlement.

If there is a custom of the agent's trade or profession which relates to the amount of commission payable, such amount must be reasonable.

The agent must be the effective cause of the operative event

If the terms of the contract are that the agent is entitled to remuneration on his being responsible for the happening of a particular event, for example, introducing a purchaser, effecting a sale, etc, he will be entitled to his remuneration only if he is the effective cause of the operative event.

In *Coles v Enoch* (1939), the plaintiff was told that he could seek a tenant for an empty shop owned by the defendant. If he succeeded he would be paid a commission. The plaintiff phoned A, whom he thought might be interested. A third party, W, overheard the call and, on being informed of the general location of the shop by A, searched and found it. It had a notice in the window that it was to let. W leased the shop from Enoch. Coles claimed commission on the lease on the basis that he had been the effective cause of the introduction of W. *Held*: Coles was not the effective cause of the lease: W had found the shop for himself (although the court stated that this was a borderline case).

For a case which came on the other side of the borderline, see *Nahum v Royal Holloway and Bedford New College* (1999), where the claimant was asked to find buyers for certain paintings on commission. The paintings included a Gainsborough and a Constable. He found a buyer for the Gainsborough, for which he was paid the agreed commission. A considerable time afterwards, the same buyer bought the Constable. The claimant claimed the agreed commission. *Held*: the claimant was the effective cause of the sale. He had brought about the introduction of the buyer to the seller and so was entitled to the agreed commission.

Note that there are provisions relating to the entitlement of commercial agents to commission under the 1993 Regulations set out below. They provide for commission to be paid to an agent where a transaction comes about 'as a result of his action'. It has been suggested by a number of authors that this requirement is not as rigorous as the common law's 'effective cause' and that, to be entitled to commission under the Regulations, it may be sufficient if the agent plays some sort of part, though not necessarily a major part, in securing the customer.

The right to earn commission

As a general rule, there is no implied promise by the principal that he will not act in such a way as to deprive the agent of the opportunity to earn his commission. In *Luxor (Eastbourne) Ltd v Cooper* (1941), L employed C, an estate agent, to find a purchaser for a chain of four cinemas. C was to be paid £10,000 on completion of the sale. C found a suitable purchaser, 'subject to contract'. However, before a binding contract of sale was concluded, the seller decided to withdraw the properties from the market. C was, therefore, not entitled to his contractual commission, since the event upon which the commission was payable, that is, 'on completion' of the sale, had not happened. C therefore sued for the agreed remuneration on the basis that there was an implied term in the contract of agency to the effect that L would not deprive C of the opportunity to earn the agreed commission. *Held*: the court would not imply such a term. It was not necessary in order to give the contract business efficacy (that is, to make the contract workable – you may recall that this is one of the tests which the court apply in deciding whether a term should be implied). The agreed commission (which in those days was the equivalent of the Lord Chancellor's annual salary) was a very high reward for 8 or 9 days' work. Therefore, C must be deemed to have taken the risk that the owner might decide not to sell.

Estate agents nowadays seek to get round this ruling by contracting that their commission will become payable upon them introducing a person 'ready, willing and able' to complete the purchase. Thus, if the agent introduces such a person and then the owner withdraws his property from the market, the agent will nevertheless have brought about the event upon which commission was payable and will, therefore, be entitled to the commission.

The Commercial Agents (Council Directive) Regulations 1993

Regulation 6 provides that a commercial agent shall be entitled to remuneration according to the customary practice of the place where he carries on his activities and, if there is no such customary practice, to reasonable remuneration. Do not forget that this Regulation applies only to those who buy or sell goods but that those who supply a service are entitled to reasonable remuneration under s 15 of the Supply of Goods and Service Act 1982.

Regulations 7 to 12 deal only with the situation where an agent is remunerated either wholly or in part by commission.

Regulation 7(1) provides that the agent shall be entitled to commission on commercial transactions concluded during the agency period:

(i) where the transaction has been concluded as a result of his action; or

(ii) where the transaction has been concluded with a third party whom the agent has previously acquired as a customer for transactions of the same kind.

Regulation 7(2) provides that a commercial agent shall also be entitled to commission on transactions concluded within a specific geographical area or by one of a specific group of customers, where the agent has been given exclusive rights of agency in respect to that geographical area or that group of customers.

Regulation 8 gives a right to commission after the agency is terminated, where the transaction was due to the efforts of the agent during his agency and is entered into within a reasonable time after the agency terminates, or where, in relation to the circumstance laid down in reg 7, the order of the third party reached either the principal or the commercial agent before the agency terminated.

Regulation 9 provides that where commission is due to a previous agent under regs 7 and 8, it shall not also be payable to a new agent unless it is equitable in the circumstances to share the commission between the new agent and the previous agent.

Regulation 10(1) provides that the commission becomes due as soon as either: (a) the principal has executed the transaction; or (b) the principal should have executed the transaction; or (c) the third party has executed the transaction. Paragraph 2 provides that commission shall become due at the latest when the third party has executed his part of the transaction or would have done so if the principal had executed his part of the contract. Paragraph 3 provides for the commission to be paid not later than the last day of the month following the quarter in which it became due.

Regulation 11(1) provides that the right to commission can only be extinguished if it is established that the contract between the principal and the third party will not be executed and that the principal is not to blame for this. Regulation 11(2) provides a right for the principal to reclaim the commission on such a transaction if it has already been paid.

The Regulations provide that any exemption clause in relation to regs 10(2) or (3) or reg 11(1) which is to the detriment of the agent, shall be void.

Any exemption clause which, in relation to paras 2 and 3, operates to the detriment of the agent, is void.

Indemnity

An agent is entitled to be indemnified in relation to expenses necessarily incurred in carrying out the duties of his agency. This principle applies also to agents who are acting without entitlement to remuneration.

The entitlement to an indemnity only arises in relation to acts authorised by the principal, but this will include unauthorised acts which the principal has ratified.

The principal may instruct the agent to act in a way which, unknown to the agent, constitutes a tort, or a breach of contract, for example, where a principal, who appears to be the owner of goods, instructs an auctioneer to auction goods which, unknown to the agent, do not belong to the principal. In such a case, the auctioneer may be liable for the tort of conversion but would be entitled to an indemnity from his principal in relation to costs and damages. If the agent is aware that there is some doubt about his principal's ownership of goods he is asked to deal with, the agent is well advised to refuse to deal with them unless the principal gives him an express promise of an indemnity.

Lien

A lien is a right to retain property belonging to another, by way of security, until a debt is paid. There are two kinds of lien: a general lien and a particular lien. A general lien is the right to retain any and all property of the debtor which happens to be in the possession of the party who holds the lien. A particular lien is the entitlement to hold only property relating to the transaction, or a related transaction, from which the debt arises.

Most agents are entitled only to a particular lien, but the law has been prepared to recognise a right to a general lien in favour of stockbrokers, bankers and solicitors.

The agent's right will depend upon him having carried out the task he was instructed to perform, or, in the case of a continuing agency, it will depend upon him continuing to act as instructed, within the actual authority given by the principal. If the agent binds the principal with an apparent authority, he will generally be entitled to no remuneration unless the principal ratifies the agent's actions. In this case, as we have seen, the ratification has the effect of giving actual authority to the agent's actions.

TERMINATION OF AGENCY

The agency may be terminated:

(a) by consent of both parties; or

(b) by the unilateral act of one of the parties; or

(c) by the operation of law.

Consent of both parties

The contract of agency may be terminated by express agreement. If this is the case, the consideration given by each party is that he forgoes his own right under the contract. Where the agency is for a fixed period of time or is to perform a specific task, the agency will come to an end at the expiry of the period of time or when the agreed task has been completed.

Unilateral termination

If one party terminates the agency before the expiry of the fixed term or before the purpose for which the agency was created is completed, that party will be guilty of a breach of contract. It will amount to a repudiatory breach and entitle the other party to refuse further performance.

Revocation of authority

However, despite the fact that he may be in breach of contract, there is a general rule that either party may unilaterally terminate the agency at any time. Thus, a principal may revoke the agent's authority, or the agent may renounce the agency, at any time, even though the revocation takes place within the time period of the agency or before the task for which the agency was created is completed. However, if this is done the party terminating the agency may be in breach of contract and liable to pay damages.

Example

Lynn appoints Mary as her agent to sell a quantity of antiques. After six months, Lynn decides she would prefer to sell them herself rather than employ an agent. She therefore terminates the agency. Mary would not be able to insist that she should continue to act as agent. She would no longer have the right to possess the antiques and would have to return them to Lynn. However, she would have an action against Lynn for breach of the contract of agency.

Irrevocable agencies

There are however, circumstances in which the agency is not revocable. These are:

(a) where one of the purposes of the agency is to protect an interest of the agent;

In *Gaussen v Morton* (1830), a principal owed a significant sum of money to F. In order to discharge this debt, he conferred a power of attorney (that is, an authority to act as agent, created by deed) on F to sell certain property and for F to recoup his loan out of the proceeds of sale. The principal then purported to revoke the authority. *Held*: he was unable to do so, since F had an interest in the agency.

(b) where the agent has completed the task which he was authorised to do;

In such a case, the principal cannot deprive the agent of his rights (for example, to remuneration or to an indemnity) by purporting to revoke the agent's authority.

(c) where statute prevents the revocation.

Revocation of authority and breach of contract

Where either party purports to terminate the agency while it is current, it will be a matter of interpretation of the agency agreement whether or not the party terminating is in breach of contract.

In *Rhodes v Forwood* (1876), Paton and Forwood, the owners of the Risca colliery in South Wales, appointed Rhodes of Liverpool as an agent to sell coal from that colliery for a period of seven years, or for so long as the agent carried on business in Liverpool. However, it was the colliery owner, not the agent, who went out of business after the agreement had been running for three and a half years. The question arose whether, by reason of ceasing in business and therefore revoking the agency, the colliery owner was in breach of an implied term in the contract. It was held by the House of Lords that since there was no express agreement that the colliery owner would send any coal to Liverpool, or any particular quantity, or continue to send coal to Liverpool for any particular length of time, there was no express agreement entitling Rhodes to sue for breach of contract. On the other hand, there was an express agreement which allowed Rhodes to terminate the agreement if Paton and Forwood didn't sell a minimum amount of coal in any particular year, or Paton and Forwood could terminate if Rhodes didn't supply a particular amount. The plaintiff argued that there was an implied term to the effect that those were the only situations in which the agreement could be terminated within the seven years, without the payment of damages. However, the court held that the way the contract was drafted, the agent was taking the risk that the contract might be terminated within the seven years. The only remedy given to the agent was that if a stipulated amount of coal was not provided to him to sell, he could terminate the agreement. In hindsight, that was not satisfactory from the agent's point of view, but the court was not prepared to reform the agreement on that account.

In the contrasting case of *Turner v Goldsmith* (1891–94), Goldsmith employed Turner as a commercial traveller for a period of five years. He sold shirts manufactured at Goldsmith's factory. He was paid on commission. Goldsmith's factory burnt down. Goldsmith therefore gave up business. Turner sued for damages for the unexpired term of the agency agreement. In this case, it was held that there was an express contract to employ the plaintiff for five years. There was nothing in the contract to say that Turner would sell only shirts manufactured at Goldsmith's factory. Therefore, the contract was not frustrated as Goldsmith could have acquired shirts elsewhere in order to carry on his business.

If the contract provides expressly or impliedly for a certain period of notice to be given in order to terminate it, then the party terminating must give the appropriate notice. If there is no express or implied provision relating to notice, it may be that the agency may be ended without notice. In *Motion v Michaud* (1892), an agent was appointed to sell the agent's brandies in England on a commission basis. It was held that the agency could be terminated without notice.

However, even where there is no stipulation in the contract as to a period of notice to be given, it may be that there are special circumstances which entitle the agent to a reasonable period of notice. What will be reasonable will depend upon the circumstances of the case.

In *Martin-Baker Aircraft Co v Canadian Flight Equipment Ltd* (1955), the principal granted an agency to sell the principal's equipment throughout North America. The agent acted in many ways like an employee, in that he worked exclusively for the principal, agreed not to sell competing products and expended much time and effort in building up the principal's North American business. There was no provision for notice on termination. *Held*: the agreement was analogous to a contract of service. Therefore, reasonable notice was required. A reasonable period in the circumstances was 12 months.

Operation of law

The law operates to terminate the agents' authority in the following cases:

(a) death of the principal or the agent;

    The death of the principal or the agent will terminate the agency.

    In *Campanari v Woodburn* (1854), an agent was employed to sell a picture. He would receive a commission of £100 if he was successful. The principal died before the agent sold the property. The agent then sold the property and the deceased's widow, without knowledge of the original agreement between her late husband and the agent, confirmed the sale. *Held*: the agent's authority had been revoked by operation of law on the death of the principal. The widow had not entered into a contract on similar terms. Thus, although the confirmation of the sale by the deceased's widow might render her liable to pay a reasonable sum in commission, it did not entitle the agent to the £100 commission which he had agreed with the deceased.

(b) insanity;

    It seems that the insanity of the principal or the agent will terminate the agency. However, although it will operate to revoke the agent's actual authority to act, there may remain in existence an apparent authority for the agent to bind the principal.

    In *Drew v Nunn* (1879), a man gave his wife authority to act as his agent. He then became insane. After he became insane, his wife ordered boots and shoes. When he recovered his sanity, the supplier sued the husband, arguing that in ordering the boots and shoes his wife was acting as his agent. It was held that the insanity of the principal put an end to the actual authority of the agent. The further question arose as to whether, if a third party continued dealing with the agent, after the insanity and without notice of the insanity, the agent had an apparent authority to bind the principal. It was held that, since the third party had not been notified by the principal of the withdrawal of the agent's authority, the agent had apparent authority to bind the principal. The third party, therefore, recovered the price of the boots and shoes.

Alternatively, it seems that in such a case the third party may make the agent liable for breach of warranty of authority. In *Yonge v Toynbee* (1910), a firm of solicitors continued to act for a principal who, unknown to them, had become insane. It was held that the solicitors were liable to the third party for breach of warranty of authority.

(c) frustration;

A contract of agency may be frustrated under the normal rules relating to frustration if the agency contract becomes impossible to carry out because it becomes illegal, or physically impossible or, because of supervening events, performance would be radically different from what the parties envisaged. This pre-supposes that neither party was responsible for bringing about the supervening event.

(d) bankruptcy or liquidation.

The appointment of a provisional liquidator of a company will terminate the authority of the board of directors to act as agents in the management of the company. It follows that the authority of any agent appointed by the directors also comes to an end.

The bankruptcy of the principal or agent will terminate the agency.

Termination under the Commercial Agents (Council Directive) Regulations 1993

The Regulations set out detailed provision in relation to agents to whom the Regulations apply (see above, p 485).

These are reminiscent, to some extent, of the provisions relating to unfair dismissal of a person employed under a contract of employment (service). Agents have never been thought to require such protection under UK law, though in *Martin-Baker Aircraft Co v Canadian Flight Equipment Ltd* (1955), where the court thought that contract of agency had features in common with a contract of service, the court was prepared to imply a term into the contract requiring a reasonable period of notice.

Regulation 15 provides that, where an agency contract is for an indefinite period, either party may terminate it by notice. Regulation 15(2) provides minimum periods of notice. The parties may not agree to shorter periods. The contract may provide for longer periods than the minimum, providing that the period of notice to be given by the principal to the agent is not shorter than that to be given by the agent to the principal. The minimum periods are: one month during the first year of the contract; two months during the second year; three months during the third or subsequent years.

Regulation 16 provides that the Regulations do not affect the situation where the contract is immediately terminated by operation of law where exceptional circumstances arise, or where one party fails to carry out all or part of his obligation under the contract.

Indemnity or compensation

Regulation 17 provides that after termination of the contract the agent is entitled to be compensated or indemnified. The idea is that the agent, having spent time and energy helping to build up his employer's business, has established a stake in that business. If his agency is then terminated, he is entitled to compensation for loss of his 'property'. This is similar to the 'property in the job' theory which some commentators think underpins the employee's right to compensation for unfair dismissal or redundancy.

Compensation is based upon a concept of French law and indemnity upon a concept of German law. Neither of them equates to the concept of damages or indemnity in English law. The Directive appears to have envisaged that domestic law should choose one or the other. The UK Regulations merely provide that the agent is entitled to compensation unless the contract provides for an indemnity.

Indemnity

Regulation 17(3) provides that the indemnity is payable where the agent:

(a) has brought the principal new customers or has significantly increased the volume of business from existing customers and the principal continues to derive substantial benefits from the business with such customers; and

(b) the payment of this indemnity is equitable having regard to all the circumstances and, in particular, the commission lost by the agent on the business transacted with such customers.

Thus there are two principles here: first, the benefit the agent has given to the principal; and, secondly, the commission which has been lost by the agent.

However, reg 17(4) provides that an indemnity shall not exceed one year's average remuneration. Regulation 17(5) provides that the grant of an indemnity shall not prevent the agent from seeking damages

Compensation

Regulation 17(6) provides that the commercial agent shall be entitled to compensation for the damage he suffers as a result of termination of his relations with the principal.

Regulation 17(7) provides that such damage shall be deemed to occur particularly when the termination takes place in either or both of the following circumstances, namely circumstances which:

(a) deprive the commercial agent of the commission which proper performance of the agency contract would have procured for him whilst providing his principal with substantial benefits linked to the activities of the commercial agent; or

(b) have not enabled the commercial agent to amortise (that is, recover) the costs and expenses that he had incurred in the performance of the agency contract on the advice of his principal.

At first glance, since there is no limit on the amount of compensation (as there is with indemnity) and since there is no express provision that damages can be claimed in addition to compensation (there is such a provision in relation to indemnity), it would seem that compensation may have been intended to cover full compensation for the loss of the agency. The principal can avoid this by providing in the contract that the agent is entitled to an indemnity only (though, in such a case, the agent's right to claim damages in addition is preserved). All this appears to be rather ill thought-out but, nevertheless, workable.

However, in *King v Tunnock* (2000), reference was made to French law on which the idea of compensation is based. The French idea is that compensation equates to the amount for which the agency is re-sold by the principal, or the amount of money which it would take to build up the agency. Conventionally, compensation is the amount of two years' gross commission. Such an amount was awarded in this case.

The question then remains as to whether, in addition to compensation, the agent is entitled to claim damages where appropriate. It would appear that the answer is 'yes', but the whole relationship between indemnity, compensation and damages awaits a definitive judgment by the courts.

CHAPTER 24

CONSUMER CREDIT

Credit is the lifeblood of business. Most supplies of goods and services between businesses take place on credit, typically 30 days. In addition, some businesses 'factor' their debts: that is, they have their trade debts collected by specialists, called factors, in which there is often an element of credit in that the factor will advance to the customer a proportion of 'approved' debts before the factor has collected them. Businesses regularly borrow money, often from banks and often 'charging' the assets of the business as security. Because the credit elements of business are dealt with to some extent elsewhere, for example, the power of a company to create a charge over its business is dealt with in Chapter 31, p 656, it is proposed to deal in this chapter solely with a particular type of credit: consumer credit.

Granting of credit to consumers is an important aspect of many businesses. It is governed principally by the Consumer Credit Act 1974, though there are other provisions which are relevant, such as the terms relating to quality, etc, of goods supplied under a hire-purchase agreement (Supply of Goods (Implied Terms) Act 1973), credit sale or conditional sale (both Sale of Goods Act 1979) or supply of goods not coming within the definition of a sale or hire of goods or supply of services (Supply of Goods and Services Act 1982).

The Consumer Credit Act 1974 was passed following the Report of the Crowther Committee in 1971. The Act seeks to achieve three main aims:

(a) to supervise those involved in granting credit by means of a licensing system;

(b) to place controls on the advertising and canvassing of credit; and

(c) to regulate individual credit agreements and to provide the debtor with certain rights.

TYPES OF CREDIT

A 'credit agreement' is the description applied to an agreement where a person, 'the borrower', is given a credit facility by another, 'the lender', which takes the form either (a) of a loan of money, or (b) of allowing the borrower to defer payment for goods or services supplied to him. An analogous type of agreement, where a consumer hires goods, paying a periodic rental for the privilege, is called a 'hire agreement'.

Credit agreements can be classified into the following main types.

Bank overdraft

This is the cheapest form of borrowing. As far as the consumer is concerned, it is essentially short term borrowing, intended to tide the borrower over a temporary financial embarrassment (though a corporate giant may well run a permanent overdraft). Very often, the overdraft is not for a specific amount of money, but the borrower is given a maximum level of cash he may draw against the overdraft.

The overdraft is repayable on demand, though it is usual to agree with the bank the period for which the overdraft is required. It has the advantage that interest accrues from day to day only on the balance outstanding, which means that, unlike a bank loan, the flat rate of interest quoted is the true rate of interest. Before the Consumer Credit Act 1974, overdrafts granted by banks were subject to no statutory control.

Bank loan

This tends to be more expensive than an overdraft, but cheaper than some other forms of consumer borrowing. The difference between a bank loan and a bank overdraft is that a loan is granted for a specific period (say, two years), usually at a set rate of interest (that is, it doesn't vary when bank base rates vary). Furthermore, the interest is calculated on the whole sum over the relevant period, despite the fact that the borrower begins to pay back the loan shortly after he has borrowed it. For example, suppose A borrowed £2,000 over two years at 10% from the bank. Interest of £400 would be added to the loan, making the sum repayable £2,400. This would be repaid at £200 per month. Because A begins paying back the loan a month after he borrowed it, it is inaccurate to say that the interest rate is 10%, because after the first repayment is made, the balance outstanding is no longer £2,000. The true interest rate is, in fact, about 19.5%. Because the quoting of flat rates of interest is often misleading, regulations made under the Consumer Credit Act 1974 provide a formula for working out the true rate of interest (APR, meaning Annual Percentage Rate). Under the Consumer Credit (Advertisements) Regulations 1989, as amended, the APR must be quoted in all advertisements other than those classified as 'simple'. Before the Consumer Credit Act 1974, loans made by banks were subject to no statutory control.

Loans of money made other than by a bank

Such loans are usually based on the same principle as a bank loan. However, before the Consumer Credit Act 1974 came into force, they were regulated by the Moneylenders Acts 1900 and 1927. The moneylender had to be licensed, which involved an annual application to the magistrates' court for a certificate, which had to be granted before the local authority could issue a licence. Advertising was severely restricted and the loan itself was subject to formalities and regulation. Banks were exempt from the requirements of the Moneylenders Acts and before 1967, it was not too difficult for a moneylender to avoid the requirements of the Acts by calling himself a bank. The Companies Act 1967 empowered the Board of Trade to issue a certificate that a person could be properly treated as a bank for the purposes of the Moneylenders Acts, which curbed this practice.

Credit tokens

A credit token is a card, voucher, etc, on the production of which the debtor is able to secure credit. The best known type of credit token is a credit card. This is the name given to a card, on production of which the consumer can obtain goods on credit, at selected outlets. It is often possible to draw cash using the card, from a bank which subscribes to the scheme. The consumer is sent a statement of indebtedness, usually at monthly intervals, and must pay within a specified time thereafter. With some cards, for example, American Express and Diners' Club, the amount on the statement is payable in full. With others, For example, Visa and Access, the cardholder may choose to pay off only part of the debt, leaving a balance to be paid off later. This type of credit is called 'running account credit', since the cardholder is given a financial limit beyond which he may not spend.

Some credit cards are 'in house' cards, which means that they can only be used to purchase goods or services from one particular store or group of stores. They work largely on the same principle as Visa and Access and are usually operated by a finance company on behalf of the store.

Club checks work on a similar principle, except the total amount of credit available to the checkholder is fixed at the outset and is not topped up once the checkholder has drawn against the credit. The finance company gives the customer a check to a specific value (say, £50). The customer may then take the check to outlets which subscribe to the scheme and offer it in payment for goods or services. If he spends £10 at one shop, the check is endorsed accordingly and the remaining value to be spent becomes £40. With both credit cards and club checks, in addition to receiving interest from the card or check holder, the finance company also receives a discount on the goods from the supplier. Before the Consumer Credit Act, such transactions were unregulated by statute. Section 14 of the Act now makes provision for their regulation.

Hire-purchase

A hire-purchase agreement is an agreement, other than a conditional sale agreement, under which:

(a) goods are bailed in return for periodical payments by the person to whom they are bailed; and

(b) the property in the goods will pass to that person if the terms of the agreement are complied with and one or more of the following occurs:

(1) the exercise of an option to purchase by that person;

(2) the doing of any other specified act by any party to the agreement;

(3) the happening of some other specified event (see s 189 of the Consumer Credit Act 1974).

Hire-purchase was initially a device to overcome the operation of the Factors Act, where goods were being sold on instalment credit. The difficulty created by the Factors Act was that if there was an agreement to sell at the outset of the transaction, the person buying on instalments could, in breach of the agreement, sell the goods to an innocent third party who would, under s 9 of the Factors Act 1889, obtain a good title. This was so even if the seller retained title to the goods. Of course, the finance company could sue the original buyer, but the security which retention of title of the goods was supposed to provide would be gone, and without it the buyer may well not be worth suing.

An attempt to get round the Factors Act which came before the House of Lords in 1893 in *Lee v Butler* (1893) (for the facts, see Chapter 20) was unsuccessful. The basic idea was on the right lines in that, instead of agreeing to buy the goods at the outset, the buyer agreed to hire them until she had paid all the instalments, at which time the goods (title to which, meanwhile, remained with the seller) would become hers. The idea was that if the purchaser was only a 'hirer' until the goods were paid for, she was not a person who was in possession of the goods 'having agreed to buy them', and thus the Factors Act did not apply. Unfortunately for the seller, the House of Lords held that the hirer was a person who had agreed to buy the goods, since there was no provision in the agreement which enabled her to hand the goods back without completing the purchase. As the agreement must inevitably end in the purchase of the goods, the hirer was a person who had agreed to buy and therefore she could pass a good title to an innocent third party under s 9 of the Factors Act 1889. This type of agreement, where the buyer had agreed to buy but the seller retained title until he was paid, became called a conditional sale agreement (see below).

Providers of finance reacted quickly and in the next case to come before the House of Lords, *Helby v Matthews* (1895) (for the facts, see Chapter 20), a right to discontinue the hire and to hand the goods back was incorporated into the contract. This did the trick. The House of Lords held that the contract was one of hire until the final instalment was paid because at any time before that happened, the hirer could terminate the hire and hand back the goods. He was not forced to buy them. This meant that the hirer was not a person who had agreed to buy and therefore s 9 of the Factors Act did not apply, with the result that, where the goods were sold by the hirer to an innocent third party, the third party did not get a good title to the goods. Before the Consumer Credit Act came into force, hire-purchase agreements were regulated by the Hire Purchase Acts 1964 and 1965.

Conditional sales

A conditional sale agreement is an agreement for the sale of goods or land under which the purchase price or part of it is payable by instalments, and the property in the goods or land is to remain in the seller (notwithstanding that the buyer is to be in possession of the goods or land) until such conditions as to the payment of instalments or otherwise as may be specified in the agreement are fulfilled (s 189 of the Consumer Credit Act 1974).

At common law, there is an important difference between conditional sales and contracts of hire-purchase in that the buyer under a conditional sale agreement can pass a good title to an innocent third party if, in contravention of his contract with the owner of the goods, he sells them before he has paid for them. In contrast, the hirer under a hire-purchase agreement cannot pass a good title (see *Helby v Matthews* (above)). However, s 9 of the Factors Act 1889 has been amended by the Consumer Credit Act 1974, so that in relation to a consumer credit agreement within the meaning of the Consumer Credit Act (this is one where the total credit granted is not more than £15,000 and where the debtor is not a body corporate), a buyer under a conditional sale agreement is deemed not to be a person who has bought or agreed to buy goods. Note that in circumstances where the credit agreement is not a consumer credit agreement, the Factors Act 1889 will apply to a conditional sale agreement. Before the Consumer Credit Act 1974, conditional sales were controlled by the Hire Purchase Acts 1964 and 1965.

Credit sale

A credit sale agreement means an agreement for the sale of goods, under which the purchase price or part of it is payable by instalments, but which is not a conditional sale agreement (s 189 of the Consumer Credit Act 1974). The fundamental distinction between a credit sale and a conditional sale is that with a credit sale there is no reservation of title to the goods by the seller and thus the instalment buyer obtains property in the goods, either when provided by the contract or under the rules in ss 16–18 of the Sale of Goods Act 1979 (this will usually be when delivery of the goods takes place, at the latest). Once property in the goods has passed to the buyer, the seller has no further legal interest in the goods. If the buyer fails to pay, the seller's remedy is an action for money: there is no question of him being able to retake the goods. The buyer may, therefore, sell the goods (though he may be obliged under the agreement to pay the outstanding amount in full if he does sell) and pass a good title to the goods to a third party in the normal way. Before the Consumer Credit Act 1974, credit sales were regulated by the Hire Purchase Acts 1964 and 1965.

Pawnbroking

A pawnbroker is a person who lends cash against the security of goods. The transaction differs from hire-purchase and mortgage in that the pawnbroker takes possession of the pledged goods. Before the Consumer Credit Act 1974, pawnbroking was regulated by the Pawnbrokers Acts 1872 and 1960. Under the Acts, a pawnbroker had to be licensed in the same way as a moneylender, in that application was made to magistrates who granted authorisation (or not, as the case may be) to the local authority to issue a licence. The business authorised by the licence related to loans of £50 or less. Loans above that amount were probably regulated by the Moneylenders Acts, but this was not certain. Pawns of £2 or less were automatically forfeit on the expiry of the period of the loan. Over that amount they had to be auctioned, though on a loan above £5 the parties could make a special contract, in which case the Pawnbrokers' Acts did not apply.

Pawnbroking is now regulated by ss 114–21 of the Consumer Credit Act 1974. Under the Act, a pawn may be redeemed at any time within six months after it was taken or such longer period as the parties may agree. In the case of pawns on the security of which not more than £15 has been advanced, the property in the unredeemed pledge passes to the pawnbroker at the end of the redemption period. In other cases, the pawnbroker must follow the prescribed procedure, involving, among other things, giving the borrower notice of his intention to sell.

Mortgages of goods

A legal mortgage of goods is where the mortgagor (the owner) transfers the title to the goods to the mortgagee (the lender), subject to the right of the mortgagor to redeem (pay off) the mortgage and resume the ownership of his goods. The mortgagor remains in possession of the goods throughout. In order to reduce the opportunity for fraud (for example, the borrower claiming to have an unfettered title to the goods), a chattel mortgage, made by an individual, where the amount borrowed is not less than £30, must be evidenced by a security bill of sale. The Bills of Sale Acts 1878 and 1882 regulate bills of sale. Under the Acts, the bill of sale must be in statutory form and attested by one or more witnesses. An affidavit of due execution must be sworn by the attesting witness and filed when the bill is registered. Registration is effected in the Royal Courts of Justice. Failure to register the bill within seven days renders the bill void as regards the goods comprised in it (that is, the debt remains but the goods cannot be used as security for it). The Bills of Sale Acts have survived the Consumer Credit Act 1974 and still regulate chattel mortgages made by individuals.

Note that a mortgage of chattels which is made by a registered company does not need to be registered as a bill of sale. However, if it had been made by an individual it would have to have been registered as a bill of sale; it must be registered with the Companies Registry within 21 days of the charge being created. This means that anyone who does a 'search' on the company (that is, looks at its filed records) will become aware of the charge.

Hire of goods

These are all legally similar, but for practical purposes can be divided into three groups:

(a) leases. This usually denotes an agreement of three to five years. Expensive office equipment is often leased;

(b) contract hire. This is the term applied to the hire of goods, particularly cars, for a period which is longer than a week or so, and extends up to three years;

(c) rental. This is the term applied to the hire to the consumer of consumer goods for a short or indefinite period.

It should be emphasised that the above terms are used in order to make a practical distinction between the three situations. They have no legal significance. Contracts of hire were unregulated before the Consumer Credit Act 1974. Consumer hire agreements, as defined by the Act, are now regulated by the Act.

NEED FOR *COMPREHENSIVE* LEGISLATION

It can be seen that the regulation of providers of credit was, before the Consumer Credit Act, largely arbitrary, often relying on legal distinctions between the transaction or the lender, where, in practice, the effect to be achieved by the transaction was indistinguishable. Thus, a loan of money from a moneylender or a pawnbroker or by way of a credit sale, was regulated by law. On the other hand, a loan of money from a bank was unregulated. Similarly, a hire-purchase contract or a conditional sale were regulated by law, whereas the acquisition of goods by way of credit card or club check or by a contract of hire, were unregulated. Moreover, where the law regulated transactions, it regulated them in different ways. There was no uniformity of approach.

In the light of this unsatisfactory situation, a Committee was set up in September 1968, under the chairmanship of Lord Crowther, to enquire into the law and to make recommendations. Their Report, *The Crowther Report*, was presented to Parliament in March 1971. Its recommendations were far-reaching. Two new Acts of Parliament were recommended by the Committee: a Lending and Security Act containing provisions relating to credit transactions generally, and a Consumer Sale and Loan Act containing any special provisions necessary to regulate, in any of their aspects, those transactions which fall within the definition of a consumer credit transaction. In the event, a compromise was reached in the shape of the Consumer Credit Act 1974, which was enacted in order to replace the existing fragmentary law with a comprehensive code for consumer credit. The Act was intended to sweep away arbitrary distinctions between transactions which, though legally treated as different, were practically the same.

THE SCOPE OF THE CONSUMER CREDIT ACT

For the Act to fully regulate a particular transaction, the amount of credit granted (or the total amount payable under the contract of hire) must not be more than £25,000 and the debtor or hirer must not be a body corporate. Where the amount of credit given under the transaction exceeds £25,000, or where the debtor is a body corporate, the common law will apply to the transaction, though there are one or two matters in respect of which the Consumer Credit Act will apply (for example, the power of the court to re-open extortionate credit bargains).

The Act has been brought into effect piecemeal over the years since 1974. This was necessary since the Act itself, generally speaking, provides a broad framework, so that for many of the provisions to be operative, detailed regulations need to be made. Thus the regulations needed to be prepared before, and brought into effect at the same time as, the relevant sections of the Act were made operative. The Act was finally brought fully into effect in May 1985.

Although the 1974 Act is the principal means by which consumer credit and consumer hire agreements are regulated, both the common law and other statutes may also be relevant. The common law will be relevant as follows:

(a) certain formalities are required by the 1974 Act for the formation of a consumer credit agreement. For example, the agreement must, among other things, be in writing and signed by both the debtor and the creditor or hirer, whereas in ordinary contracts for the sale of goods or supply of services, no formality is needed, not even writing. Similarly, the 1974 Act places certain constraints on the remedies available to the creditor in the event of a breach of contract by the debtor. However, within the limits imposed by the Act, the common law rules as to offer, acceptance, consideration, intention to create legal relations, misrepresentation, damages, etc, will apply;

(b) the Sale of Goods Act 1979 will apply to all sales of goods, including sales on credit and conditional sales. Thus the implied terms contained in ss 12–15 will apply, as will the rules relating to passing of property and transfer of title, etc;

(c) the Supply of Goods and Services Act implies terms similar to those contained in ss 12–15 of the Sale of Goods Act 1979 in relation to (1) contracts which are not within the definition of a sale of goods but under which, nevertheless, property in goods is transferred (ss 2–5), and (2) contracts for the hire of goods (ss 7–10). The Act also contains implied terms in relation to the supply of services, which will apply where the services are supplied on credit (ss 13–15);

(d) the Supply of Goods (Implied Terms) Act 1973 (as amended) implies terms similar to those found in ss 12–15 of the SGA 1979 into all hire-purchase agreements;

(e) the Unfair Contract Terms Act controls the use of exemption clauses and notices and is relevant to consumer credit and consumer hire agreements;

(f) s 27 of the Hire Purchase Act 1964 relating to transfer of title in the case of motor vehicles will apply;

(g) the Fair Trading Act 1973, for example, in relation to harmful consumer trade practices, codes of practice, etc, may apply;

(h) the Bills of Sale Acts 1878–82 still regulate mortgages and other security interests which are granted in relation to personal property.

DEFINITION OF A CONSUMER CREDIT AGREEMENT

Section 8 provides:

(a) a personal credit agreement is an agreement between an individual (the debtor) and any other person (the creditor) by which the creditor provides the debtor with credit of any amount;

(b) a consumer credit agreement is a personal credit agreement by which the creditor provides the debtor with credit not exceeding £15,000; and

(c) a consumer credit agreement is a regulated agreement within the meaning of the Act if it is not an agreement (an exempt agreement) specified in or under s 16.

Section 189 defines an individual as including a partnership or other unincorporated body of persons not consisting entirely of bodies corporate. The combined effect of all this is that a consumer credit agreement is an agreement with anyone except a body corporate to give credit not exceeding £15,000, unless the agreement is exempt under s 16.

It is rather odd that a commercial enterprise in the form of a partnership comes within the definition of an individual and is, therefore, a 'consumer'. Thus the Act will regulate an agreement to take credit made by Sharp & Co, a partnership with a multi-million pound turnover, providing credit given does not exceed £25,000, but it will not regulate an agreement to take credit by Smith Ltd, a one-man company with a turnover of £30,000.

For the purpose of s 8, 'credit' means the total credit price for the goods or services, less the aggregate of the deposit (if any) and the total charge for credit. For example: Drew buys a BMW motor car. He agrees to pay a total of £32,500 for goods under a hire-purchase agreement. He pays a deposit of £3,000 and a total charge for credit by way of interest of £4,500 is to be paid. The credit given is £32,500, less the sum of £3,000 and £4,500. This equals £25,000. The agreement is a regulated consumer credit agreement.

One problem with this definition is that, although it works with some certainty where the credit provided is a fixed sum, it may be difficult to ascertain whether or not the agreement is within the specified limit in a case where the credit is given on a running account, such as with an overdraft or Visa. A further problem is that a sharp operator may grant a high credit limit on a running account (say £30,000), but specify that no more than, say, £1,000 may be drawn in one year, or specify that the interest shall be sharply increased if, for example, the credit taken exceeds £2,000. The object in both cases is to take the agreement outside the scope of the Consumer Credit Act, but at the same time to make it difficult or onerous for the debtor to borrow beyond a permissible level.

To meet these difficulties, s 10(3) makes provision regarding running account credit as follows: 'For the purposes of s 8(2) (that is, the sub-section which specifies the £25,000 limit in relation to regulated agreements), running-account credit shall be taken not to exceed the amount specified in that sub-section if:

(a) the credit limit does not exceed the specified amount (that is, £25,000); or

(b) whether or not there is a credit limit, and if there is, notwithstanding that it exceeds £25,000:

   (1) the debtor is not enabled to draw at any one time an amount which … exceeds £25,000; or

   (2) the agreement provides that, if the debit balance rises above a given amount (not exceeding £25,000), the rate of the total charge for credit

increases or any other condition favouring the creditor or his associate comes into operation; or

(3) at the time the agreement is made it is probable ... that the debit balance will not at any time rise above the specified amount.'

RESTRICTED-USE AND UNRESTRICTED-USE CREDIT

A consumer credit agreement may be a restricted-use agreement or an unrestricted-use agreement. Section 11 defines both categories. It provides:

(1) A restricted-use credit agreement is a regulated consumer credit agreement:

    (a) to finance a transaction between the debtor and the creditor, whether forming part of that agreement or not; or

    (b) to finance a transaction between the debtor and a person (the 'supplier') other than the creditor; or

    (b) to refinance any existing indebtedness of the debtor's whether to the creditor or another person.

(2) An unrestricted-use credit agreement is a regulated consumer credit agreement not falling within sub-s (1).

(3) An agreement does not fall within sub-s (1) if the credit is, in fact, provided in such a way as to leave the debtor free to use it as he chooses, even though certain uses would contravene that or any other agreement.

Briefly it amounts to this: an agreement is a restricted-use agreement where the debtor is not able to get his hands on the money. Where he is able to get his hands on the money if he wishes, even though he is bound by contract to use the money in a particular way, the agreement is an unrestricted-use agreement.

DEBTOR-CREDITOR-SUPPLIER AGREEMENTS AND DEBTOR-CREDITOR AGREEMENTS

The debtor may use his credit to obtain goods and services:

(a) from the creditor himself;

(b) from a supplier who has a pre-existing arrangement with the creditor, whereby he will introduce customers requiring credit;

(c) from a supplier who has no connection with the creditor.

The Act refers to (a) and (b) as debtor-creditor-supplier agreements: (c) is a debtor-creditor agreement. The distinction between debtor-creditor-supplier agreements, on the one hand, and debtor-creditor agreements on the other is important because:

(a) it may be necessary in order to identify an 'exempt agreement' (for details of these, see below). For example, a debtor-creditor-supplier agreement for fixed-sum credit, under which the total number of payments to be made by the debtor in respect of the credit does not exceed four, is exempt. However, a similar debtor-creditor agreement is not. The critical factor in determining whether a debtor-creditor agreement is exempt is the interest rate charged;

(b) door-to-door canvassing of debtor-creditor agreements is prohibited, but not the door-to-door canvassing of debtor-creditor-supplier agreements;

(c) the creditor is liable for the breaches of contract and the misrepresentations of the supplier in debtor-creditor-supplier agreements, but not in debtor-creditor agreements (ss 56 and 75);

(d) where a debtor-creditor-supplier agreement is a cancellable one, the creditor and the supplier are jointly and severally liable to repay any sum repayable to the debtor (s 70).

Definition of debtor-creditor-supplier and debtor-creditor agreements

The definitions in s 11 of restricted-use and unrestricted-use agreements are employed in ss 12 and 13 to define debtor-creditor-supplier and debtor-creditor agreements. Section 12 provides that a debtor-creditor-supplier agreement is a regulated consumer credit agreement being:

(a) a restricted-use credit agreement which falls within s 11(1)(a); or

(b) a restricted-use credit agreement which falls within s 11(1)(b) and is made by the creditor under pre-existing arrangements, or in contemplation of future arrangements, between himself and the supplier; or

(c) an unrestricted-use credit agreement which is made by the creditor under pre-existing arrangements between himself and a person ('the supplier') other than the debtor in the knowledge that the credit is to be used to finance a transaction between the debtor and the supplier.

Examples

(a) Supplier enters into a hire-purchase agreement with debtor. This is a two-party debtor-creditor-supplier agreement, since the credit given is restricted use.

(b) Supplier agrees with finance company whereby finance company will consider applications for finance from supplier's customers. Debtor makes an application which is granted. This is a debtor-creditor-supplier agreement, even though the credit granted may be unrestricted use, since it is made under pre-existing arrangements between the creditor and the supplier.

Section 13 provides that a debtor-creditor agreement is:

(a) a restricted-use credit agreement which falls within s 11(1)(b) but is not made by the creditor under pre-existing arrangements, or in contemplation of future arrangements, between himself and the supplier; or

(b) a restricted-use credit agreement which falls within s 11(1)(c); or

(c) an unrestricted-use credit agreement which is not made by the creditor under pre-existing arrangements between himself and a person (the 'supplier') other than the debtor in the knowledge that the transaction is to be used to finance a transaction between the debtor and the supplier.

Examples

(a) Bank makes personal loan to customer. Customer uses it to buy a car from supplier. This is a debtor-creditor agreement, since there are no pre-existing arrangements between the bank and the supplier.

(b) Supplier agrees to sell a car to buyer. Buyer requires finance. Supplier offers to ring round on buyer's behalf to see if he can get an offer of finance. Eventually finance is arranged with finance company. As there are no pre-existing arrangements between supplier and finance company, the agreement is a debtor-creditor agreement.

EXEMPT AGREEMENTS

Section 8 provides that a consumer credit agreement is a regulated agreement within the meaning of the Act, unless it is an 'exempt agreement' under s 16 and the orders made under it. The Consumer Credit (Exempt Agreements) Order 1989, gives five categories of exempt agreement. These are:

(a) Certain credit agreements secured on land entered into by specified bodies.

(b) Where the credit is essentially short term. Thus, Art 3 of the 1989 Order provides for exemption in a number of circumstances where the credit is short term. Among them are:

(1) a debtor-creditor-supplier agreement for fixed sum credit under which the total number of payments in respect of the credit does not exceed four. The payments must be required to be made within a period not exceeding 12 months beginning with the date of the agreement. This would exempt most trade credit granted to sole traders and partnerships;

(2) a debtor-creditor-supplier agreement for running-account credit under which:

(i) provides for periodic payments by the debtor (for example, every week, month, etc); and

(ii) the debtor is bound to discharge the total credit for that period by a single payment (examples: milk bill, paper bill, American Express card, Diners' Club card).

Neither of the above two exceptions applies to (a) hire-purchase or conditional sale agreements, or (b) an agreement secured by pledge (that is, a pawn) or (c) an agreement to finance land purchase.

(3) a debtor-creditor-supplier agreement to finance the purchase of land where the total payments to be made by the debtor in respect of the credit and in respect of the total charge for credit does not exceed four;

(4) a debtor-creditor-supplier agreement for fixed-sum credit to finance a premium under a contract of insurance relating to land or to do anything on the land, subject to the conditions contained in the 1989 Order.

(c) Where the total charge for credit is a relatively low one. This is covered by Article 4 of the 1989 Order, which gives exemption to loans where the total charge for credit (to be calculated in accordance with the Consumer Credit (Total Charge for Credit Agreements and Advertisements) (Amendment) Regulations 1999) does not exceed the higher of:

(1) 1% plus the highest of any base rate published by a number of specified banks; and

(2) 13%.

The relevant base rate is the base rate in operation 28 days before the date on which the agreement is made. Note that:

(i) any later fluctuation in base rate will not affect the exemption. Thus if A makes a loan to B, interest to be 1% above the Barclays Bank base rate currently in force, it will remain exempt if, for example, a month after the loan is made the base rate increases from 9% to 10%;

(ii) the exemption does not apply if the amount payable by the debtor in respect of the credit can vary according to a formula or index;

(iii) an exception to the 'no-indexing' rule is where an employer grants a loan to an employee and the agreement provides that a higher rate of interest shall become payable on the termination of the employment.

(d) Where the purpose of the credit is to finance foreign trade. This may be either import or export trade. The exemption only applies where the credit is provided to the debtor in the course of a business carried on by the debtor.

(e) Debit and cash card credit token agreements by virtue of s 89 of the Banking Act 1987. The reason for this is that the customer's account is debited with a single sum within a few days of the credit being granted.

A 1999 Amendment Order exempts a debtor/creditor agreement where the creditor is a credit union and the total charges for credit does not exceed 12.7%.

SMALL AGREEMENTS

A small agreement is a regulated agreement where the credit given does not exceed £50. Neither a hire-purchase agreement nor a conditional sale agreement may qualify as a small agreement. The significance of a small agreement is that the provisions of Part V of the Act, except s 56, do not apply to small debtor-creditor-supplier agreements for restricted-use credit.

NON-COMMERCIAL AGREEMENTS AND ISOLATED TRANSACTIONS

A non-commercial agreement means a consumer credit agreement or a consumer hire agreement not made by the creditor or owner in the course of a business carried on by him (s 189(1)). Under s 40, a non-commercial agreement made by an unlicensed trader may be enforced by him without an order from the Director General of Fair Trading.

Section 189(2) provides that a person is not to be treated as carrying on a particular type of business merely because occasionally he enters into transactions belonging to a business of that type. Thus, a person who occasionally collects debts will not need a licence under the Act.

LINKED TRANSACTIONS

Section 19 contains detailed definitions of what amounts to a linked transaction. If a transaction is treated as a linked transaction it has the following effects: if it is made before the principal agreement it has no effect until the principal agreement is entered into; if the prospective debtor withdraws from a prospective regulated agreement or if he exercises his right to cancel the agreement, any linked transaction is cancelled.

A linked transaction is one that is ancillary to the main credit transaction. An example might be a maintenance agreement in respect of a computer which is being bought on credit. However, since most linked transactions are contracts of insurance or contracts guaranteeing the debt, and such contracts have been excluded from the effect of s 19, it would seem that the practical effect of s 19 will be comparatively slight.

Consumer hire agreements

The Act also regulates consumer hire agreements. A consumer hire agreement is defined by s 15 as follows:

(1) A consumer hire agreement is an agreement made by a person with an individual (the 'hirer') for the bailment of goods to the hirer, being an agreement which:

(a) is not a hire-purchase agreement; and

(b) is capable of subsisting for more than three months; and

(c) does not require the hirer to make payments exceeding £15,000.

(2) A consumer hire agreement is a regulated agreement if it is not an exempt agreement.

TOTAL CHARGE FOR CREDIT AND ANNUAL PERCENTAGE RATE

It is important that the consumer is aware of the charge which is being made for the credit. Thus, the Consumer Credit (Total Charge for Credit) Regulations 1980, as amended by the Consumer Credit (Total Charge for Credit, Agreements and Advertisements) (Amendment) Regulations 1999 (SI 1999/3177) provides a formula whereby this can be calculated. The 1980 Regulations gave three formulae. The 1999 Regulations have replaced them with a single formula.

As we pointed out earlier in the chapter, the quotation of a flat rate of interest is usually deceptive. The true rate is often around *double*, or more. In addition, a trader quoting a rate of interest may fail to include sums which are realistically part of the credit charge but which are not 'interest'. The Regulations therefore give a system of working out the Annual Percentage Rate of interest (the APR quoted in advertisements). It is an offence to mislead by quoting the APR incorrectly.

Regulation 4, as amended, requires the following to be included in the total charge for credit: (a) the total interest on the credit; (b) other charges at any time payable under the agreement; (c) a premium under a contract of insurance which is a condition of making the agreement and is for the sole purpose of ensuring complete or partial repayment of the credit ... in the event of death, invalidity, illness or unemployment. Regulation 5 gives a long list of items to be excluded. These are generally items of expenditure which are not compulsory under the agreement, for example, a premium to insure a motor vehicle.

Once the total charge for credit has been ascertained, the Regulations provide a formula for working out the APR. Fortunately for the non-mathematicians, the Office of Fair Trading provides sets of calculation tables which do the job for you.

CREDIT TOKENS

As we have seen, 'credit tokens' is the expression used to describe instruments of credit such as credit cards, store charge cards, etc. Section 14 of the Consumer Credit Act 1974 defines a credit token as follows:

(1) A credit token is a card, check, voucher, coupon, stamp, form, booklet or other document or thing given to an individual by a person carrying on a consumer credit business who undertakes:

    (a) that on production of it (whether or not some other action is required) he or she will supply cash, goods and services (or any part of them) on credit; or

    (b) that where on production of it to a third party (whether or not any other action is required) the third party supplies cash, goods and services (or any of them) he or she will pay the third party (whether or not deducting any discount or commission) in return for payment by the individual.

'Tokens' include book tokens, meal vouchers, gift tokens, cheques, gift stamps, and cash, debit, charge and credit cards. However, certain tokens such as book tokens may well be exempt as they will be below the £50 small agreement limit.

Types of payment card

Credit cards

Credit cards allow the holder to obtain cash, goods or services on credit from particular outlets on production of the card. The holder receives a periodic account (usually monthly) from the creditor. This requires him to pay off a specified amount of the balance (usually 5%) but allows him to remain the debtor of the issuer as far as the balance is concerned. This is an example of debtor-creditor-supplier running-account credit.

The major examples of such cards are Visa and Mastercard. The credit agreements are regulated agreements within the meaning of the Act. Paying for a transaction with Mastercard or Visa will mean that where the creditor is not the supplier of the goods or services supplied on credit, the creditor will nevertheless be jointly and severally liable under s 56 in respect of representations made to the debtor in antecedent negotiations and under s 75 in respect of any breach of contract by the supplier. Thus, if you pay by Access for a motor car which turns out not to be of satisfactory quality, you would have a remedy against Access, providing the amount of the cash price exceeded £100 but was not more than £30,000. This is known as 'connected lender liability'.

Cash card

A cash card enables the holder to obtain cash from an automated teller machine (ATM). The withdrawal is debited immediately from the holder's account. This is therefore not a provision of credit. A difficulty arises in that if the card is used in the machine of another bank, the withdrawal may not be debited immediately. Therefore, there would be a provision of credit which would be within the definition of a regulated agreement. In order to cover this potential anomaly, s 89 of the Banking Act 1987 makes the transaction exempt.

Many cards are multi-function, that is, they enable the holder to withdraw cash from his bank account and they enable him to obtain cash, goods or services on credit. If a card is used as a credit card then the agreement will be a regulated agreement within the meaning of the Act.

Debit cards

Debit cards enable bank customers to allow a third party (usually a retailer) to receive payment from their respective current accounts immediately at the point of sale. No provision of credit is involved in this transaction. Nevertheless the transaction comes within s 14. However, it is exempt from regulation under the Act by virtue of s 89 of the Banking Act 1987.

Cheque guarantee cards

These are not credit tokens within the meaning of s 14. Such cards simply offer a guarantee that providing the payee of a cheque complies with the conditions, the main one being that the payee must write the guarantee card number on the back of the cheque, the bank will guarantee payment of the cheque up to a specified limit, providing the cheque is given in respect of one particular transaction. Guarantee cards are not regulated by the Consumer Credit Act.

Charge cards

These allow the holder to obtain cash, goods or services against the production of the card. They are not linked to the debiting of a bank account and therefore are credit tokens within the meaning of s 14. Where they differ from credit cards is that the issuer of the card expects the balance to be paid in full following the issue of a periodic statement to the holder. American Express cards provide an example of charge cards. Charge cards are exempt from regulation by virtue of the Consumer Credit (Exempt Agreements) Order 1989 because of the obligation to discharge the balance in one payment. It should be noted that although users of Visa and Mastercard credit cards are able to take advantage of connected lender liability under ss 56 and 75 of the Act, the fact that charge cards are exempt means that those who pay by such cards are not able to take advantage of connected lender liability.

It can be seen that although a number of payment cards are credit tokens, within the meaning of s 14, and create debtor-creditor-supplier agreements, only credit cards are regulated agreements since the remainder are exempt.

UNAUTHORISED USE OF CREDIT CARD TOKENS BY THIRD PARTIES

Generally speaking, because the bank or other creditor has no mandate to debit a customer's account unless the customer has authorised the debit either by signature, personal identification number or other means of identification, the bank, not the customer, must bear the loss if the credit token is used without authority by a third party, for example, a thief.

Section 83 states that the debtor under a regulated consumer credit agreement shall not be liable to the creditor for any loss arising from the use of the credit facility by another person not acting as the debtor's agent. However, s 84 allows the card holder to be made liable to the extent of £50 arising from the use of a credit token by other persons during which the credit token ceases to be in the possession of an authorised person.

Liability for unauthorised misuse ends once the card holder has given oral or written notice that it is lost or stolen or liable to misuse for any other reason, providing the credit token agreement contains particulars of the name, address and telephone number of a person to whom notice must be given. The credit agreement may require oral notice to be confirmed in writing within seven days.

CONNECTED LENDER LIABILITY

Because both creditor and supplier benefit from a consumer credit contract, s 75 provides for the creditor to be jointly and severally liable with the supplier in the case of the latter's breach of contract or misrepresentation. It is, therefore, not a bad idea to pay for important items such as holidays with your credit card, even if you intend paying off the full amount when your statement arrives. If the holiday fails to materialise or is defective, you will then be able to claim against the supplier of the credit: very useful if the tour operator who has contracted to supply your holiday has become insolvent!

The creditor's liability arises in the case of debtor-creditor-supplier agreements which are either for restricted-use credit made under pre-existing arrangements, or for unrestricted-use credit made under pre-existing arrangements between a person (the supplier) other than the debtor, in the knowledge that the credit is to be used to finance a transaction between the debtor and the supplier. The lender is not liable under s 75 if the cash value of the contract was less than £100 or more than £30,000: Consumer Credit (Increased Monetary Limits) Order 1983.

Section 56 contains a provision to the effect that in negotiations conducted by a credit-broker for restricted-use credit or negotiations conducted by a supplier either for restricted-use credit or unrestricted-use credit where a pre-existing arrangement exists between the supplier or the creditor, the negotiator is deemed to be conducting the negotiations as agent for the creditor as well as in his actual capacity. This seems to mean that any misrepresentation in antecedent negotiations will be the liability of the creditor as well as the negotiator. Note that, unlike s 75, there are no financial limits placed on s 56.

Where a borrower takes out a personal loan (say, from his bank) even though it is for a particular purpose, unless there is a pre-existing arrangement between the bank and the supplier (which is unlikely), neither s 56 nor s 75 will apply.

EXTORTIONATE CREDIT BARGAINS

Sections 137–39 of the Act gives the court power to re-open and make appropriate orders in relation to a credit agreement which requires the debtor to make payments which the court finds are 'grossly exorbitant' or which otherwise grossly contravene ordinary principles of fair dealing. In deciding whether the rate is grossly exorbitant, the court must have regard to:

(a) prevailing interests rates;

(b) factors applicable to the debtor which include: his age, experience, business capacity and state of health, and the degree and nature of the financial pressure he was under when making the credit bargain;

(c) factors applicable to the creditor which include: the degree of risk accepted by him, having regard to the value of any security provided; his relationship to the debtor; and whether or not a colourable cash price was quoted for any goods or services included in the credit bargain. (A 'colourable cash price' describes the situation where a dealer falsely inflates the cash price of a product. This is sometimes done in order to make it appear that a debtor has paid a deposit when, in fact, he was unable to. For example, a dealer has a car for sale for £6,000. The company providing the finance requires the buyer to pay a 25% deposit, that is, £1,500. If the dealer 'colours' the price to £8,000 and tells the finance company that a £2,000 deposit has been paid, the effect is that the debtor obtains the car on 100% finance and the dealer receives the £6,000 required.)

(d) any other relevant considerations.

In *Barcabe v Edwards* (1983), an agreement was re-opened where the flat rate of interest was 100%, giving an annual percentage rate of over 300%. The court had evidence that elsewhere the flat rate was 18-20%. Thus, the interest rate was grossly exorbitant in relation to prevailing rates of interest. The court reduced the interest to 40%.

In *Castle Phillips Co v Wilkinson* (1992), a secured loan of £21,000 had an interest rate of 48%. The security was worth more than the loan. Prevailing building society interest rates were around 15%. Therefore, the court decided, taking these factors into account, to reduce the rate to 20%.

In *Falco Finance v Gough* (1999), it was held that a credit bargain was extortionate in that it was grossly exorbitant or otherwise contravened the ordinary principles of fair dealing because: (a) there was a misrepresentation on the part of the creditor in relation to the debtor's position if he wanted to redeem the loan early; and (b) the concessionary rate of interest at which the loan was taken out was lost if the debtor defaulted. It led to a higher rate being payable for the rest of the mortgage. The full rate would be payable, which added £125 per month to the debtor's payments, even though the default had cost the creditor nothing. The court found that it was so easy to default on the terms of the mortgage that it was virtually impossible to maintain the right to the concessionary rate. It was also held that the terms in question were unfair terms within the meaning of the Unfair Terms in Consumer Contracts Regulations 1994.

In the Office of Fair Trading Annual Report 1999, it was reported that the provisions relating to extortionate credit bargains are not working. It referred back to its recommendations in its 1991 Reports, which have not yet been implemented. The recommendations were:

(a) the court's power to re-open an agreement should be on the basis of an unjust credit transaction rather than an exorbitant credit bargain;

(b) a finding that the transaction involved 'excessive' – rather than grossly exorbitant – payments should be a factor in determining whether the transaction was unjust;

(c) a further factor should be whether the transaction involved business activity which was deceitful or oppressive or otherwise unfair or improper (whether unlawful or not);

(d) the court should be empowered to re-open a credit transaction of its own motion – without the need for application by the debtor – in both defended and undefended cases;

(e) the court should be required to notify the Director General of each case where it found a credit transaction to be unjust;

(f) in cases of public interest, the Director General or local Trading Standards Officers should be empowered to apply to the court; and

(g) tougher penalties should be introduced for unlicensed provision of credit.

UNFAIR TERMS IN CONSUMER CONTRACTS REGULATIONS 1999

Unjust bargains can, to a certain extent, be dealt with under the Unfair Terms in Consumer Contracts Act 1999. However, it would seem that a 'core provision', such as the basic interest rate, cannot be challenged under the Regulations (the reason why it could be challenged in the *Falco* case, above, is that the agreement provided for a substantially higher rate to be applied in circumstances which were not fair to the debtor. If the agreement had contained a basic rate which applied throughout the mortgage, it could only have been challenged using ss 137–39).

In *Director General of Fair Trading v First National Bank plc* (2000), the contractual term in question provided that if judgment were given against a borrower, the borrower had to pay interest on the judgment debt. This was an unusual provision, and the DG argued that it created an 'unfair surprise' for the borrower who, when he thought he had paid off the judgment, was presented with a bill for interest. *Held*: the term breached the requirement of good faith and created an unfair imbalance in the rights and obligations of the parties, to the detriment of the customer. (Note: a fuller account of this case is given in Chapter 8, p 202.)

Applications made under the Act are likely to relate to money lent at very high rates of interest, although that is not the only consideration. The court had a similar power under the Moneylenders Acts, which referred to the transaction being 'harsh and unconscionable'. However, in *Davies v Direct Loans* (1986), it was held in the High Court that Moneylenders Acts cases on harsh and unconscionable agreements are not authoritative under the Consumer Credit Act, which refers to extortionate agreements. In this case, a couple were lent money by way of mortgage for house purchase at a rate of 21.6% which, on behalf of the plaintiffs, was said to be 3.6% more than the going rate. However, even if this was correct, the difference between 18% and 21.6% was not so great as to render the agreement extortionate.

Application may be made to the court in respect of any consumer credit bargain: the limit of £25,000 does not apply.

APPLICATION FOR A CONSUMER CREDIT LICENCE

There are two types of licence: a standard licence, which is granted to an individual, and a group licence, which is granted to a group of individuals, for example, solicitors, chartered accountants, etc, though named members of the group may be excluded from the licence. Application for a licence is made to the Director General of Fair Trading (DG). The applicant must state what type of consumer credit business he intends to engage in and the licence, if granted, will specify this. One licence may cover more than one category of business. The categories are:

(a) Consumer credit. This is the provision of credit to the consumer.

(b) Consumer hire. This is the hiring of goods to the consumer.

(c) Credit brokerage. This is the introduction of the consumer to the person who provides the credit or hires the goods.

(d) Debt adjusting and debt counselling. Debt adjusting is negotiating with the creditor on the debtor's behalf for the discharge of a debt, taking over the debt on the debtor's behalf in return for payment or any similar activity. Debt counselling is the giving of advice to debtors or hirers about the liquidation of debts under consumer credit or consumer hire agreements.

(e) Debt collecting. This is taking steps to procure the payment of debts.

(f) Credit reference agency. This is collecting information regarding the financial standing of individuals and furnishing it to others.

Since licensing was introduced in 1976, up to the end of 2000, 477,794 applications for licences have been granted. By far the greatest number have been in respect of credit brokerage. If the licensee wishes to canvas off trade premises, his licence must be endorsed with permission to do so.

Refusal, suspension, variation or revocation of licences

Although s 25(1) provides that the DG must satisfy himself that the applicant is a fit person to engage in activities covered by the licence and that the name the applicant proposes to use is not misleading or otherwise undesirable, in practice a licence is granted unless the DG has notice of matters which make the applicant unfit. In 2000, only 35 applications out of 16,986 were refused.

Because most applications are granted and because of the substantial resources needed to operate a positive licensing system, when estate agents were made the subject of regulation by the Estate Agents Act 1979, a negative licensing system was used. This means that the estate agent can carry on business until such time as the DG issues a prohibition order.

Under s 27(1), if the DG proposes to refuse a licence, or to grant it on different terms from those applied for, he must first send a notice to the applicant inviting him to make representations. Under s 30(1), a licence can be varied on the request of the licence holder, (for example, the holder might have changed his trading name, or he might wish his licence to be endorsed with permission to canvass off trade premises). The DG has power to vary (s 31), suspend or revoke (s 32) a licence. Thirty-two licences were dealt with in this way in the year ending December 2000.

Where the DG refuses to issue, renew or vary a licence in accordance with the terms of an application, or where he compulsorily varies, suspends or revokes a licence, the applicant or licensee, as the case may be, may appeal to the Secretary of State. There is further appeal on point of law to the High Court (s 41). Under s 189(2) of the Act, a person who only occasionally enters into a transaction regulated by the Consumer Credit Act is not to be treated as carrying on a business and, therefore, will not need a licence.

Enforcement of agreements made by unlicensed traders (s 40), or of agreements for the services of an unlicensed trader (s 148), or of agreements where the introduction was made by an unlicensed credit broker (s 149)

In all three cases, the agreement can be enforced only where the DG makes an order allowing the agreement to be enforced. The DG may grant an application in the terms in which it is made (which will usually be for payment of all outstanding monies due under the agreement), or he may grant it on different terms. Usually, there are a number of agreements in respect of which an order is applied for. In such a case, the applicant must give details of each one separately. If the DG thinks fit to make an order for enforcement, he may:

(a) limit the order to specified agreements, or agreements of a specified description, or made at a specified time; or

(b) make the order conditional on the doing of specified acts by the applicant.

In determining whether or not to make an order in respect of an unlicensed trader, the DG shall have regard to:

(a) how far customers were prejudiced by the trader's conduct;

(b) whether or not the DG would have been likely to have granted a licence covering the period in the application;

(c) the degree of culpability for failure to obtain a licence (see ss 40 and 148).

In determining whether or not to make an order in respect of an unlicensed broker, on the application of a trader, the DG shall consider, in addition to any other relevant factors:

(a) how far, if at all, debtors or hirers were prejudiced by the credit broker's conduct; and

(b) the degree of culpability of the applicant (that is, the trader who granted the credit and to whom, therefore, the debtor or hirer owes the money) in facilitating the carrying on by the credit broker of his business when unlicensed.

ADVERTISEMENTS, QUOTATIONS AND CANVASSING FOR BUSINESS

The potential social dangers of unrestricted credit advertising have long been recognised. The first attempt by the law to restrict such advertising was the Betting and Loans (Infants) Act 1892, which made it an offence to write to minors offering loans. The Moneylenders Act 1927 prohibited the use by moneylenders of unsolicited circulars, agents or canvassers. In addition, the content of newspaper advertisements was strictly controlled. In 1957 came the Advertisements (Hire Purchase) Act, which first regulated advertisements in relation to hire-purchase and credit sales. All these controls have now been replaced with the provisions of the Consumer Credit Act ss 43–54 and ss 151–53, supplemented by the Consumer Credit (Advertisements) Regulations 1989. Quotations are dealt with by the Consumer Credit (Quotations) Regulations 1989.

Advertisements

Section 189 (which is the definition section of the Act) provides that: 'advertisement' includes every form of advertising, whether in a publication, by television or radio, by display of notices, signs, labels, showcards or goods, by distribution of samples, circulars, catalogues, price lists or other material, by exhibition of pictures, models or films, or in any other way, and references to the publishing of advertisements shall be construed accordingly.

It can be seen that the draftsman of the Act has gone to great lengths to ensure that his definition is comprehensive. The same s 189 also contains a definition of 'advertiser'. This is not restricted to the person who places the advert but 'means any person indicated by the advertisement as willing to enter into transactions to which the advertisement relates'.

Two basic criminal offences are created by the Act:

(a) Section 46(1) provides: 'If an advertisement ... conveys information which in a material respect is false or misleading the advertiser commits an offence.'

In *Mersoja v Pitt* (1989), a car dealer offered '0%' finance. However, in order to offer this deal, he offered less money on a trade-in deal than if the purchaser were paying cash or arranging his own finance. It was held that an offence had been committed, since the advertisement was misleading.

(b) Section 45 provides:

> If an advertisement ... indicates that the advertiser is willing to provide goods on credit under a restricted-use credit agreement ... but ... that person is not holding himself out as prepared to sell ... for cash, the advertiser commits an offence.

The advertising regulations

The other controls on advertising are contained in the Consumer Credit (Advertising) Regulations 1989, made under s 44 of the Act. Advertisements may be simple, intermediate or full. The regulations provide for maximum information which is to be given in simple and intermediate advertisements and minimum information which must be given in full advertisements. There is a long list of matters to be covered in the latter, including details of the Annual Percentage Rate (APR) and, if security to be given comprises a mortgage on the debtor's home, a warning must be given to the effect that the borrower's home is at risk if the payments are not kept up. The validity of this has been challenged in the courts by First National Bank, who argued that s 44 of the Consumer Credit Act did not give the power to make such a regulation. The validity of the Regulation was, however, upheld: *R v Secretary of State for Trade and Industry ex p First National Bank plc*.

Section 50 of the 1974 Act provides that any person who, with a view to financial gain, sends to a minor any document inviting him to borrow money, obtain goods on credit or hire, obtain services on credit, or apply for information or advice on borrowing money or otherwise obtaining credit, or hiring goods, commits an offence. A defence is available where the person sending the document had no reasonable cause to suspect that the addressee was a minor.

Regulation 8 provides that where the advert contains the APR, it must be of greater prominence than any other charge mentioned and must be at least as prominent as statements relating to periods of time, advance payments, and the amount, number and frequency of any other payments. It may, however, be less prominent than the cash price.

Quotations

Section 52(1) of the 1974 Act provides that regulations may be made: (a) as to the form and content of quotations; and (b) requiring quotations to be given in specified circumstances. The Consumer Credit (Quotations) Regulations 1989 deal with the form and content and require that a trader or credit-broker must provide a written quotation on request, except where he does not intend to deal with the prospective customer.

A quotation must contain substantially the same information as a full credit advertisement. Where the quotation relates to fixed-sum credit to be provided under a debtor-creditor agreement, it must state the amount of credit the trader is willing to provide. Where the quotation relates to running account credit, it must state the credit limit or how this is determined.

Canvassing

This is orally soliciting an individual to enter a credit agreement. This is permitted if it occurs on the trade premises but is generally not permitted off trade premises.

Canvassing regulated agreements

Canvassing off trade premises involves:

(a) making oral representations during a visit by the canvasser for that purpose; and

(b) making a visit to somewhere other than the business premises of the canvasser, creditor, supplier or consumer; and

(c) not making the visit in response to an earlier request by the consumer.

Since the visit must be for the purposes of canvassing then casual conversations are exempt. Canvassing debtor-creditor agreements off trade premises is a criminal offence. Canvassing other agreements off trade premises is permitted only under licence. An exception is in the case of overdrafts on current accounts where the canvasser is the creditor or an employee of the creditor.

Canvassing ancillary credit activities

It is a criminal offence to canvass the services of a credit broker, debt adjuster or debt counsellor off trade premises: s 154. It is also a criminal offence to issue a credit token to a person who has not requested one in writing: s 51.

FORMALITIES OF REGULATED AGREEMENTS

The debtor may withdraw from a credit agreement at any time until the agreement has been fully executed.

The agreement

It would appear that the common law rules relating to offer, acceptance, consideration and so forth apply to the Act, except where they are overridden. For example, there is no general requirement that a contract must be in writing, but the Act provides that an agreement is not properly executed unless the agreement is in writing in the prescribed form, the document embodies all the terms of the agreement except the implied terms, and the document is legible when presented or sent to the debtor for signature. In addition, an agreement is not properly executed if: (a) a copy of the unexecuted agreement, where appropriate; (b) a copy of the executed agreement, where appropriate; or (c) notice of cancellation rights, where appropriate, are not given to the debtor. If the agreement is not properly executed, it can be enforced only by order of the court. The agreement becomes fully executed when signed for and on behalf of both parties.

Copies

If the debtor signs an agreement presented to him for signature, he must be given a copy there and then. If he is sent a copy for signature, he must be sent a duplicate. If the agreement was not executed by the signature of the debtor (that is, if, when he signed it, the creditor had not yet done so), he must be sent a copy within seven days. A copy of a cancellable agreement must be sent by post.

Cancellable agreements

Under s 67, a cancellable agreement is one where there have been oral representations made to the debtor or hirer by an individual acting as, or on behalf of, the negotiator, unless:

(a) the agreement is secured on land or is a restricted-use agreement to finance the purchase of land or is an agreement for a bridging loan in connection with a purchase of land; or

(b) the unexecuted agreement is signed by the debtor or hirer at premises at which any of the following carry on business: the creditor or owner; any party to a linked transaction; the negotiator in the antecedent negotiations.

The broad effect of this is that an agreement signed by the debtor away from the trade premises of the creditor or supplier may be cancelled unless it is secured on land. The reason for these provisions is that high pressure doorstep sales people have taken advantage of a person, alone and vulnerable, in order to get them to sign agreements which, on reflection, they have regretted. Under s 64, the debtor must be given written notice of the right to cancel, and under s 68 has a 'cooling off' period of five clear days (14 days in certain circumstances) from the date of receipt of the notice, within which to cancel. Section 69 provides that the cancellation must be in writing and is effective as soon as it is posted.

It would seem that 'representation' has a wider meaning than it bears in the general law of contract. In *Moorgate Services v Humayon Kabir* (1995), the defendant appealed against judgment given against him for the payment of £14,673.85 in relation to a regulated credit agreement. The agreement had been signed at the defendant's home and oral statements had been made to the defendant at the time of signing. Section 189 provides that 'representation' includes any condition or warranty and any other statement or undertaking, whether oral or in writing. *Held*: the statement must be a statement of fact or opinion or an undertaking as to the future (that is, much wider than 'representation' for the purposes of misrepresentation in contract). It must be capable of inducing the prospective borrower to enter into the contract. However, it is not necessary to show that the representation did in fact induce the borrower to sign the agreement. Nor is it necessary to show that it was intended to have that effect. Since the representation was made, the agreement was cancellable within the meaning of s 67. Where a cancellable agreement is improperly executed, it can only be enforced by order of the court. However, s 127(4)(b) provides that if s 64(1) is not complied with (that is, notification to the debtor that the agreement is a cancellable one to which cooling-off rights apply), the court may not make an enforcement order. Therefore the agreement could not be enforced against the debtor.

Section 70 provides that on cancellation of the agreement:

(a) any sum paid by the debtor or hirer or his relative shall become repayable;

(b) any sum which is or would or might become payable ceases to become payable; and

(c) in the case of a debtor-creditor-supplier agreement any sum paid on the debtor's behalf by the creditor to the supplier shall become repayable to the creditor.

Goods in the possession of the debtor may be recovered within 21 days, during which time the debtor is obliged to take reasonable care of them. The debtor has a lien on the goods in relation to money repayable to him. The effect of cancellation upon a debtor-creditor agreement is that the debtor must repay the loan.

Note that the Consumer Protection (Cancellation of Contracts Concluded Away from Business Premises) Regulations 1987 give a 7 day cooling-off period to a customer who enters into a contract to buy goods or services during an *unsolicited* visit by the trader to the customer's home, place of work, or someone else's home. For more detail, see Chapter 3, p 88. These Regulations give a longer basic cooling-off period (7 days rather than 5), but can only be used where the visit is unsolicited. The cooling-off period given by the Consumer Credit Act applies even though the customer requested the trader to visit.

Unenforceable agreements

It may be useful at this stage to list the circumstances in which a consumer credit agreement may be unenforceable. There are two situations: (a) agreements which may only be enforced by order of the court; and (b) agreement which may only be enforced by order of the Director General of Fair Trading.

Enforcement by order of the court

The following are the situations in which the creditor must apply to the court for an enforcement order:

(a) Where an agreement is not properly executed. In order to be properly executed, the agreement must be in the prescribed form; it must contain all the terms of the agreement; all the terms must be legible; it must be signed by both the debtor and creditor; the rules as to the supply of copies to the debtor must have been complied with; in the case of a cancellable agreement, the debtor must have been given notice of his cancellation rights and how they might be exercised.

A number of companies have offered a new kind of service which has become called 'repair hire' and which has already provoked a flood of litigation centred on the question of when an agreement is unenforceable. The scheme is as follows. A's car is damaged by the fault of B. A will need to hire a car for the period while his own car is being repaired. Normally, A will pay the hire charge out of his own pocket. He can recoup the charge from B's insurance company when his claim is eventually settled. The 'repair hire' service takes care of this and more. A enters into an agreement with the repair hire company, whereby the repair hire company hires a car to A while his own is off the road. In addition, the repair hire company undertakes to pursue A's claim against B. However, A is not liable to pay the repair hire company's hire charge until his claim against B has been settled, so A need pay nothing out of his own pocket. So where is the profit for the repair hire company? The answer is that their hire charges are substantially in excess of the normal car hire charges. The problem, of course, arises when B's insurance company are presented with A's inflated bill for hire charges. They, not unnaturally, have sought a way to avoid paying, and the answer they have found is in the provisions of the Consumer Credit Act.

The leading case, heard by the House of Lords, is *Dimond v Lovell* (2000). In this case, the claimant's car had been damaged by the negligence of the defendant. While the claimant's car was being repaired, a replacement vehicle was hired to her by First Automotive. Normally, the defendant's insurers will pay the cost of a hire vehicle. However, liability to pay in this case was disputed because the hire agreement had some unusual features. In the first place, the hire charge was much higher than the normal hire rate. Secondly, the hire-charge made by First Automotive included the handling of the claimant's claim against the defendant. Thirdly, the charge was not payable at the end of the hire (at the latest) as is usually the case. The charge was not payable until First Automotive had pursued the claimant's claim to a successful conclusion. The defendant, therefore, argued that the agreement between the claimant and First Automotive was unenforceable, since it was an improperly executed consumer credit agreement, and, furthermore, since the impropriety consisted of there not being an agreement containing the prescribed terms, the court did not have power to order that the agreement should be enforced. That being so, since First Automotive could not legally compel the claimant to pay the hire charge, there was no liability for which the claimant could claim compensation from the defendant. *Held*: (a) giving the word 'credit' its normal meaning of 'allowing payment to be deferred', this was a credit agreement. Moreover, the agreement between Dimond and First Automotive described the agreement as a 'credit facility'; (b) the question then arose as to whether the agreement was an 'exempt' agreement, to which the formalities of s 61, etc, would not apply (see p 517, above). It would be an exempt agreement if the number of payments made by the debtor did not exceed four and those payments were required within 12 months beginning with the date of the agreement. The number of payments did not exceed four *but* the agreement did not contain a clause requiring the hire charge to be paid within 12 months. Therefore, the agreement was not an exempt agreement. It was a regulated agreement which had been improperly executed. As the improper execution related to failure to give prescribed details, the court could not, under the terms of s 127(3), order that the contract should be enforced; (c) furthermore, the hire charge was not really a hire charge, since it also covered payment for services in relation to pursuing the claim. Even if, therefore, the court had had the power to order the agreement to be enforced, the additional services provided by First Automotive did not qualify for compensation. Thus, the amount of the claimant's claim would have been restricted to what she would have been willing to pay an ordinary car-hire company for the hire of a replacement car. Finally, the House of Lords dismissed the argument that Dimond should be ordered to make restitution to First Automotive for the benefit she had received at their expense. Such an order would undermine the policy of the Consumer Credit Act.

This type of business, whereby a credit hire company takes over the conduct of a claim in cases where it is clear that the claimant was not at fault in causing the accident from which he suffered, seems to have grown considerably. However, it is clear from *Dimond v Lovell* (above) that these companies need to adjust their terms of business if they are not to fall foul of the Consumer Credit Act. In *Ketley v Gilbert* (2001), a similar agreement was brought into question. In this case, the car hire company had provided that its charges were payable by the claimant 'on the expiry of 12 months starting with the date of this agreement'. The idea was clear – to create the agreement in such a form that it became an exempt agreement. However, the Regulations provide that an agreement will be exempt if it required the payments to be made 'within a period not exceeding 12 months beginning with the date of the agreement'. The court held that the wording of the agreement failed to make it exempt. The Regulations require payment to be made 'within 12 months' not 'on the expiry of 12 months'. The agreement was, therefore, regulated and unenforceable since it was improperly executed.

A group of cases involving similar issues were heard together at the Oxford County Court. In *Seddon v Tekin, Dowsett v Clifford, Beesley v PPP Columbus Healthcare* (2000), the credit hire company ensured that the agreements were exempt agreements by providing that the credit must be repaid within the 12 month statutory limit. The difficulty with doing this is that it defeats the object of the repair hire agreement as far as the accident victim is concerned. He still has to pay the charges out of his own pocket, until such time as the defendant's insurance company settles his case. However, in order to avoid this, the agreements in these cases introduced a new twist. For a small insurance premium (£10), the accident victim could insure against the risk that the defendant motorist's insurance company had not settled the claim by the time the repair hire agreement expired. If this were the case, instead of the claimant having to pay, the insurance company would pay. Then the claimant would claim back the hire charges on behalf of the insurance company. Each of the claimants was claiming the hire charges. *Held*: (a) that the agreements were not a sham and a pretence, as contended by the defendants. It was perfectly right and proper to make an exempt agreement as provided for in the 1989 Order; (b) that in the case of *Seddon*, as the insurance premium had not been paid, there was no valid insurance. Therefore, when the insurance company paid the victim's hire charges, it was under no legal obligation to do so. (If there had been a valid insurance, the company would have been legally liable to pay the credit hire charges on S's behalf. S would have been obliged, under his contract with the insurance company, to claim the hire charges from the defendant (Tekin) and the insurance company would then have had the right to claim them back from S.) Because the insurance company had no legal obligation to pay S's hire charges, they could not legally insist that S should claim them back from T. Therefore, S had lost nothing; (c) otherwise the credit repair agreements were exempt agreements not regulated by the CCA and were enforceable. However, following *Dimond v Lovell*, the car hire tariff must be reduced since it covers services other than car hire. It was therefore reduced by 30%. Permission to appeal to the Court of Appeal has been given.

Comment: the fact that the claimant is only able to recover normal hire charges from the defendant appears to put the viability of the credit hire business in jeopardy. The answer to the problem might be to use the insurance scheme which was used in the Oxford group of cases and to increase the premiums. The question then will be whether the scheme will lose its attractiveness as far as accident victims are concerned. In the event, the credit hire companies have got round the regulated agreement problem quite easily. Ironically, the real problem is the ruling of the House of Lords in *Dimond v Lovell* that only normal hire charges are recoverable. I say 'ironically' because it was the credit hire company which was behind the appeal to the House of Lords. If they had simply accepted the Court of Appeal judgment that the agreement was an unenforceable credit agreement and adjusted their operations for the future to sidestep the judgment, they could have continued charging the inflated hire charges, though, of course, it probably wouldn't have been too long before another defendant challenged them.

(b) Where a security instrument is not properly executed (s 105 of the Consumer Credit Act). In this case, the security given by the debtor will not be enforceable.

(c) Where a copy of a default notice which is served on a debtor or hirer, is not served upon a surety. For example, B borrows £5,000 from X under a regulated agreement. Because B has no acceptable credit history, B's father A acts as surety for the loan (that is, he agrees to pay the loan back in the event of B's default). B defaults and X serves a default notice on B but not on A. X's failure to serve a notice on A means that X can only enforce the surety agreement against A if the court makes an order to that effect.

(d) Where a debtor or surety gives a negotiable instrument, other than a bank note or a cheque, in discharge of any sum payable under a regulated agreement, then the agreement under which the sum is payable is unenforceable or the security given by the surety is enforceable only by order of the court. Thus if, for example, a promissory note or a bill of exchange is given by the debtor or surety, the whole agreement made by the debtor or surety is unenforceable.

Section 127 of the Consumer Credit Act provides that the court shall only dismiss the application to enforce the agreement if it considers it just and equitable to do so. It also empowers the court to reduce any sum payable by the debtor, hirer or surety to compensate for any prejudice suffered (that is, any loss sustained) by the contravention in question.

Section 127 goes on to provide that, in certain circumstances, the court *may not* make an order to enforce the agreement. These are:

(a) where a document in prescribed form, containing all the prescribed terms of the agreement, was not signed by the debtor or hirer, unless the debtor or hirer did sign an agreement, not in prescribed form, which contained all the prescribed terms of the agreement (s 127(3));

(b) where, in relation to a cancellable agreement, the rules relating to copies to the debtor were not complied with (s 127(4)(a));

(c) where, in relation to a cancellable agreement, the creditor failed to give the debtor notice of his cancellation rights and how to exercise them s 127(4)(b).

These provisions which disable the court from making an enforcement order may, it seems, fall foul of the European Convention on Human Rights, which is incorporated into UK law by the Human Rights Act 1998.

In *Wilson v First County Trust* (2001), FCT agreed to lend W £5,000. FCT charged a document fee of £250 in respect of the loan, which W was unwilling or unable to pay immediately. This sum was therefore added to the amount of the loan. The agreement stated that the amount of the loan was £5,250. W brought an action arguing, among other things, that the loan agreement was unenforceable because the agreement did not state the prescribed terms correctly, in that it stated the wrong figure as the amount of the loan. *Held*: the agreement mis-stated the amount of credit and therefore contravened reg 61 of the Consumer Credit (Agreements) Regulations 1983, under which one of the prescribed terms for an agreement is the total amount of the credit. Therefore, the agreement was unenforceable. Furthermore, under the terms of s 127(3), this was a situation in which it was not open to the court to decide whether it was just and equitable for the agreement to be enforced. However, this being the case, the court was of the opinion that the provisions in s 127(3) (and, also, presumably s 127(4)), which prohibit the court from making an enforcement order in the circumstances laid down in the sub-sections, may be incompatible with Article 6 and Protocol 1, Article 1 of the European Convention on Human Rights. Article 6 gives the right to a just and fair trial. Protocol 1, Article 1 guarantees peaceful enjoyment of possessions. First County Trust had been denied a trial of the case on its merits – thus Article 6 may have been infringed. The effect of this was to deprive First County of its property, that is, the amount of the loan. The court does not have the power to strike down the legislation in such a case. It makes a 'declaration of incompatibility' which then puts the onus on the government to change the law. The appeal was, therefore, adjourned pending argument of the matter before the court (should the Crown decide to oppose the proposal to make the declaration).

Comment: the provisions against enforceability may be regarded as imposing a penalty for non-compliance with the formalities of the Act. This conflicts with the purpose of the civil law, which is primarily to compensate for loss. Non-compliance could have been made a criminal offence instead of enacting these penal provisions. The argument against doing this is that the credit companies would have been able to flout the law and get away with a relatively small fine. The counter-argument is that, if a credit company persistently flouted the law, the Director General could remove its consumer credit licence, thus putting it out of business altogether. Therefore, on balance, the view of the Court of Appeal in the *Wilson* case, that the sanction was disproportionate to the contravention, is arguably correct on a practical level, as well as on human rights considerations.

Enforcement by order of the Director General of Fair Trading

There are three circumstances where a regulated agreement can be enforced only where the Director General makes an order to the effect that they may be enforced. These are:

(a) where the agreement is made by an unlicensed trader;

(b) where there is an agreement for the services of an unlicensed trader; and

(c) where the introduction leading to the agreement was made by an unlicensed credit broker.

Details of the requirements for enforcement in these cases are set out on p 528.

TERMINATION OF THE AGREEMENT

An agreement may be terminated by the creditor or by the debtor. The debtor is given a statutory right to terminate. The creditor's right is given either by the contract in circumstances where the debtor has not defaulted, or on the failure by the debtor to observe the terms of the contract in such a way that his breach goes to the root of the contract and is therefore treated as repudiating the contract.

Early settlement by the debtor

Section 94 of the Act confers on the debtor the right to settle the debt early on payment of all sums outstanding under the agreement. This right cannot be excluded and a statement of the debtor's rights in this respect must be included in the agreement. Section 95 provides for the debtor to receive a rebate for early settlement. Where the debtor settles early any linked transaction, other than one which itself gives credit, is also discharged, except for any sum which has already become payable (s 96).

Duty to give information

The creditor is, under s 97, obliged to give the debtor a statement of his indebtedness. This right cannot be excluded. A failure to comply with the request means the creditor cannot enforce the agreement while the default continues. If the default continues for one month, the creditor commits an offence.

Termination by the debtor

Although, under normal contractual rules, once an agreement is made it must be carried out otherwise the party in default is in breach, the Consumer Credit Act provides a number of exceptions to the rule. One is in relation to cancellable agreements. Another allows the debtor to terminate an agreement at any time before the final payment is made. Sections 99 and 100 provide that in a regulated hire-purchase or conditional sale agreement the debtor is entitled to terminate the agreement. The debtor must return the goods to the creditor. The debtor may be ordered to bring the amount of his payments up to one half of the purchase price, although the court can order him to pay a lesser sum if it thinks that a lesser sum would adequately compensate the creditor for any loss sustained in consequence of the termination.

Termination by the creditor

Default notice

The creditor cannot take certain steps to enforce the agreement against the debtor, in the event of the debtor's default, unless he has issued a 'default notice'. Section 88 specifies the contents and effect of the notice. It must be in a prescribed form (that is, the law lays down the form: it is not open to the creditor to create his own form) and must specify:

(a) the nature of the alleged breach;

(b) if the breach is capable of remedy, what action is required to remedy it and the date before which that action is to be taken; and

(c) if the breach is not capable of remedy, the sum (if any) required to be paid as compensation for the breach, and the date before which it is to be repaid.

The date specified by which the debtor must remedy the breach must be not less than 7 days after the date of service of the notice or, if no date is specified, no action may be taken until 7 days have elapsed. If steps are taken to remedy the breach within the time limit imposed, the breach is to be treated as if it never occurred.

A default notice must be issued if the creditor wishes:

(a) to terminate the agreement; or

(b) to demand earlier repayment of any sum; or

(c) to recover possession of any goods or land; or

(d) to treat any right conferred on the debtor or hirer by the agreement as terminated, restricted or deferred; or

(e) to enforce any security.

A default notice must comply accurately and precisely with the terms of the Act, otherwise it will be invalid. In *Woodchester Lease Management Services v Swain and Co* (1999), a default notice, aimed at terminating an agreement, specified the amount of the payment required to remedy the breach as £879.90, when in fact it was only £634.30. The defendant argued that the notice was substantially correct and should be treated as valid, subject to correction. They argued that the defendant had at least 7 days in which to check the agreement and seek advice. The Court of Appeal did not accept these arguments and held that the notice must be correct in that it must specify exactly the sum which was owed (though the court accepted that a mistake in very minor details might be overlooked). The aim of the Act was to protect debtors. Most debtors were at a disadvantage dealing with financial organisations whose contracts were likely to be in standard form and relatively complex. The defaulting debtor needed to know precisely what to do to put things right.

Sometimes the contract may contain terms which allow the creditor to terminate the contract and demand early repayment or the return of goods, etc, even if the debtor is not in breach, for example, if a debtor becomes bankrupt or makes a composition with his creditors. In such a case, s 98 provides that the creditor shall give the debtor 7 days' notice of the termination. Further, if a creditor wishes to enforce a term of a contract which gives the right to earlier payment of any sum due, or repossession of goods or land or treat any right of the debtor as having been terminated or restricted or deferred, he must, under s 76, give the debtor 7 days' notice of his intention to do so by issuing a notice which is very similar in terms and effect to a default notice.

PROTECTED GOODS

If the debtor is in breach of a hire-purchase or conditional sale agreement and he or she has paid at least one third of the total price for the goods, then the goods are 'protected goods' which may not be repossessed by the creditor without a court order: s 90. If the creditor recovers 'protected goods' from the debtor without a court order the regulated agreement is terminated and the debtor is released from all liability under the agreement and may recover all sums paid: s 91. Furthermore, the creditor cannot 'cure' a wrongful repossession by redelivering the goods to the debtor. This is so even if the repossession was made in error. No court order is required if goods are repossessed with the consent of the debtor. However, case law strongly suggests that such 'consent' does not really amount to consent unless the debtor takes the action voluntarily having been fully informed as to his rights in the matter.

If the protected goods have been abandoned by the debtor, the creditor may recover them without a court order: *Bentinck v Cromwell Engineering* (1971), in which the debtor was involved in a collision in which a car he had taken on hire-purchase was seriously damaged. He left it at a garage for repair and disappeared, having given a false telephone number to the finance company which owned the car. Nine months later, the finance company traced the car to the garage where it had been left and repossessed it. The Court of Appeal held, applying provisions which were similar to those in place under the Consumer Credit Act, that the car had been abandoned by the debtor and that, therefore, the creditor had not recovered possession from the debtor. However, this will not always be the case. Unless it is clear that the debtor intended to abandon the property, the court may hold that a bailee who is in possession of protected goods for the purpose of repairing them, is in possession as agent of the debtor. Any repossession from the garage will, therefore, be a repossession from the debtor.

TIME ORDERS

The court may, under s 129, make a time order which does one of the following:

(a) provides for payment to be made under a regulated agreement at such times as the court, having regard to the means of the debtor, considers reasonable;

(b) provides for the debtor to remedy any breach within such period as the court may specify.

The court may do this in the following circumstances:

(a) on application for an enforcement order. Most such applications are where the creditor applies to enforce an improperly executed agreement, although there are a number of other circumstances in which an agreement can be enforced only by order of the court; or

(b) on an application made by the debtor after a default notice has been served on him (or a notice having similar effect under s 76 or 98 where the debtor is not in default); or

(c) in an action brought by the creditor to enforce any regulated agreement or any security or recover possession of any goods or land to which a regulated agreement relates.

In *Southern District Finance v Barnes* (1995), B borrowed £12,000 against the security of their house, repayable at £260 per month over 10 years. They fell into arrears of £1,300. When SDF sought to possess the house in order to sell it and use the proceeds to recoup their loan, B applied for a time order. SDF argued:

(a) that the use of the words 'any sum owed' in s 129 meant that a time order could be made only in respect of the debt outstanding; it could not relate to future payments not yet due; and

(b) that s 136 (which provides that the court may include in any order made by it, any provision it considers just for amending any agreement) did not permit the court to vary the rate of interest payable in relation to a time order.

Held by the Court of Appeal:

(a) although in ordinary circumstances, a time order may only be made in relation to existing arrears, the position is different where land is used as security. In such a case, when the creditor brings a possession action, he demands payment of the whole sum outstanding. This effectively calls in the whole loan, which consequently becomes 'any sum owed' within s 129. Accordingly, a court may make a time order which reschedules repayment of the whole loan;

(b) s 136 empowers a court to vary an agreement 'in consequence of a term of the order'. This gives a court the power to vary the interest charge in relation to the payments rescheduled under the time order. (It was argued that such a power would render s 137, relating to extortionate agreements, superfluous. However, it would not, since s 136 applies only to regulated agreements whereas s 137 applies to all credit agreements. Also, s 137 applies whether or not the debtor is in arrears.)

B's application for a time order, which rescheduled the payments and reduced the rate of interest, was granted, and the order for possession suspended so long as the rescheduled payments were made.

Termination of a consumer hire agreement by the hirer

Section 101 gives the hirer, under a regulated consumer hire agreement, the right to terminate the agreement after 18 months, on giving notice. Where payments are at equal intervals, the length of the notice is of an interval between payments or three months, whichever is the less. Where they are at differing intervals, notice is the length of the shortest interval or three months, whichever is the less. In all other cases, the period is three months. There are exceptions to this right of the hirer to terminate, chiefly in relation to hire for business purposes.

CHAPTER 25

LIABILITY FOR UNSAFE PRODUCTS

Liability for unsafe products is both civil and criminal. It is contained in the Consumer Protection Act 1987. Part I deals with civil liability and Part II with criminal liability.

CIVIL LIABILITY: LEGAL BACKGROUND

We have seen that if a purchaser of goods suffers damage as a result of the goods proving defective, the seller, providing that he sold the goods in the course of a business, is liable to the buyer under s 14 of the Sale of Goods Act or analogous legislation. The buyer alleges that the goods were not of satisfactory quality or that they were not fit for their purpose. In such a case, liability is *strict*. This means that it is imposed irrespective of fault on the part of the supplier. Thus, if your new television explodes, burning your hand, when you switch it on for the first time, it is no use your high street retailer arguing that he did not manufacture the television which came straight out of the manufacturer's box into your lounge and that, therefore, he is not liable for the damage. He is liable to you for breach of contract. The injustice in this is often more apparent than real, since the retailer will have an action against his supplier for breach of s 14, and so forth back along the chain of supply until the buck stops with the manufacturer. The only time that this might not happen is if one person in the chain of supply cannot effectively be sued for some reason, for example, because he is insolvent or because he is protected from liability by an effective exemption clause.

Strict liability may mean, however, that the retailer is liable for an occurrence which could not have been avoided, however much care had been taken by all parties in the chain of supply. In *Frost v Aylesbury Dairy Co* (1905), the plaintiff bought milk from the defendant. The milk contained typhoid germs, which could not be detected except by prolonged tests, by which time the milk would have become unusable. The defendant argued that they had taken all reasonable care in their production of the milk and that there was nothing they could practicably have done in relation to the typhoid germs. It was held that the defendant was liable because liability for breach of contract is strict, that is, liability arose irrespective of whether the defendant was at fault or not.

WHERE DAMAGE IS SUFFERED BY A NON-PURCHASER

A problem arises in a case where it is not the purchaser who is injured, but a third party. For example, Alice purchases the defective television but it is her mother, Barbara, who switches it on and is injured in consequence. In such a case, there is no privity of contract between Barbara and the retailer. This means that Barbara must sue not the retailer but the manufacturer. The action is for the tort of negligence. The action was established by the case of *Donoghue v Stevenson* (1932). In this case, D's friend bought some ice cream and ginger beer from M. Both D and her friend consumed the ice cream and beer. D was pouring herself a second helping of beer when the decomposed remains of a snail emerged from the bottle. D alleged that she suffered gastro-enteritis in consequence. As she was unable to sue M for breach of contract because her friend had bought the beer, D sued the manufacturers of the ginger beer, S, for negligence. The case went to the House of Lords on the issue of whether, even if D were to prove the facts, S would be liable. S's argument, which was thought to represent the law at the time, was that since S had a potential contractual liability to M in respect of the ginger beer, he could not have a concurrent liability to D in relation to the same goods: he did not owe D a duty of care. In a landmark judgment, which marks the beginning of the development of the modern law of negligence, the House of Lords held (but only by a three to two majority!) that S did indeed owe a duty of care to S, so that, if she proved her case, she would be entitled to damages. Reports state that the case was subsequently settled out of court for £100.

The judgment paved the way for future claims against manufacturers, repairers, etc, who did their work carelessly and, as a result, injured persons with whom they had no contractual relationship. However, because in a negligence action it is necessary to prove that the defendant was at fault, it is possible that a contractual action and a negligence action will give different results *on the same facts*.

In *Daniels v White* (1938), D bought some beer and a bottle of lemonade from T. He took it home and mixed the two drinks into a shandy. He drank some and his wife drank some. The lemonade was contaminated with carbolic acid and both D and his wife suffered illness as a result. D had a straightforward action for breach of contract against the public house: the lemonade did not comply with the quality requirements of s 14. However, his wife, not being a party to the contract, had to sue the manufacturer for negligence. The manufacturer brought evidence to show that they had an up-to-date bottle-cleaning procedure which should have ensured that no impurities remained in the bottles at the time the lemonade was poured in. On that evidence, the court held that the manufacturer had taken all reasonable care and that he was not liable to D's wife for negligence.

Res ipsa loquitur

Proof of negligence may be made easier if the court allows the plaintiff to use the evidential rule *res ipsa loquitur*, which raises a rebuttable presumption of negligence against the *defendant*. Its effect is that the defendant must then rebut the presumption by showing that he was not negligent, or he becomes liable. In order that *res ipsa loquitur* may apply, three conditions must be met:

(a) the cause of the occurrence must be unknown;

(b) the events leading up to the occurrence must have been wholly in the control of the defendant; and

(c) the accident must be such as would not have happened without negligence; in other words, the fact that the defendant has been negligent must be the only reasonable explanation of the occurrence. Thus, if a manufacturer is sued and he brings evidence to show that the occurrence could equally well be explained by the fact that the retailer has been negligent, the plaintiff will have to prove his case in the normal way.

A case in which *res ipsa loquitur* was successfully invoked was the case of *Grant v Australian Knitting Mills* (1936). In this case, G bought a pair of long woollen underpants which had been manufactured by Australian Knitting Mills. He suffered illness because the wool used in the manufacture of the pants contained a quantity of sulphite. The manufacturer operated a system which would normally mean that the sulphite was washed out of the pants at the manufacturing stage and there was no evidence to show how the sulphite had remained in the wool. G alleged breach of contract against the retailers and negligence against Australian Knitting Mills. In support of his allegation of negligence, he was allowed to use *res ipsa loquitur*, the effect of which was to reverse the burden of proof so that, instead of G having to prove that the defendants were negligent, the defendants had to prove that they were not. They failed to do this, despite showing that they had manufactured 4,737,600 pairs of underpants without complaint. (Negligence was an alternative head of claim: G also succeeded in his claim for breach of contract under the South Australian equivalent of s 14 of the English Sale of Goods Act.)

Who to sue?

One situation which the potential plaintiff may find difficult is where he did not purchase the goods and cannot therefore sue the retailer and, in addition, where it is for some reason impracticable to sue the manufacturer. In that case, the injured party is left with the sole option of suing someone in the chain of supply, other than the manufacturer, for negligence. Such an action depends upon proving that either:

(a) there is a defect in the goods which is discoverable on reasonable examination and it was reasonable to expect that the defendant would have examined the goods; or

(b) that the goods were purchased from a supplier not known to the seller and because of this the seller ought to have made independent checks on the quality of the goods.

The first of these criteria arises relatively rarely nowadays, since most goods are pre-packed by the manufacturer in a way that makes an intermediate examination impracticable, if not impossible. However, the duty might arise in relation to a motor-vehicle, for example, where the retail seller has a duty to carry out a pre-delivery inspection on behalf of the manufacturer.

A case based on the second of the above criteria, which demonstrates the duty to make appropriate checks when buying from an unknown supplier, is *Fisher v Harrods* (1966). In this case, the defendants, a well known London department store, sold some jewellery cleaning fluid called Couronne. It was sold to a third party, who bought it for use by the plaintiff. There was thus no privity of contract between the plaintiff and the store. The fluid contained alcohol and ammonium oleate. It was supplied in a plastic bottle with a screw top and a plastic bung. The bung should have been removed before the bottle was squeezed, but it seems that the plaintiff (and a number of other ladies who bought the fluid) didn't realise this (they thought that the bung must have a tiny hole in it through which the fluid could escape from the bottle), and squeezed the bottle with the bung in place. The bung shot out and, in the plaintiff's case, some fluid splashed into the plaintiff's eye, causing damage. The plaintiff chose to sue the retailer for negligence (she had no privity of contract with the retailer, otherwise her claim would have been more straightforward), rather than the manufacturer against whom, in all probability, she would have had a more straightforward case. She made this decision because the manufacturer was a person with no assets, against whom a judgment would have been of doubtful value. Harrods' buyer had agreed to stock the fluid following a visit from the manufacturer of the fluid. The buyer said in evidence that it was not Harrods' practice to make any enquiries as to the status of a manufacturer, even when approached by an unknown salesman selling a new product produced by an unknown manufacturer. In this case, Harrods' buyer made no enquiries about the previous experience of the manufacturer, or whether he had any qualifications. Nor did he have the jewellery cleaner tested by a chemist, though the defendants have an analytical department. As it turned out, the manufacturer was a man without qualifications for, or experience in, the manufacture of a cleaning product and without qualifications for making a proper choice of ingredients. An experienced industrial chemist stated that he would not expect a product of this kind to be put on the market without some warning. It was held that Harrods were liable for negligence, following an earlier case of *Watson v Buckley, Osborne, Garrett & Co* (1940), in which a distributor of a hair-dye produced by an unknown foreign manufacturer was held to be liable for the damage it caused because they failed to make proper enquiries and tests. In the present case, the judge was of the opinion that Couronne should not have been put on the market, even with a pierced plug, without instructions as to how to get the fluid out of the bottle and also with a warning that the product should be kept away from the eyes.

The thalidomide case

However, it is very difficult to establish negligence against a supplier who was not involved in the manufacture of the goods. The classic, tragic, example is to be found in the thalidomide case. In this case, the first of the criteria for suing a supplier who is neither the retailer or the manufacturer, set out above, was not applicable; and the second appeared not to be, because the supplier was a reputable supplier, so there appeared to be no reason to carry out intermediate tests. The case for the children was that this was a special case: because of the fact that the drug was specially recommended for pregnant women and because, therefore, the drug had a greater potential for doing harm than normal, the manufacturers had a duty to carry out their own, independent tests. This argument was never tested in court, but the level at which the initial cases were settled out of court indicates that the balance of opinion was against the argument being successful.

The case is not reported as such, because it was settled out of court: the only two reported cases were not concerned with the issue of liability. However, the facts are well documented. Distillers imported and marketed a drug manufactured in West Germany by a reputable chemical company. The drug was a relaxant for pregnant women. It was described as being safe with no side effects. The drug appears to have worked satisfactorily as a relaxant. However, it produced horrendous injuries in the women's offspring. There was little doubt that the German company had been negligent from the outset in making insufficient tests on the drug. Later, it seems that the company was involved in a deliberate cover-up in that, once the malformations suffered by the newly-born children started being attributed to thalidomide, the drug's manufacturers continued to market the drug while, at the same time, making strenuous attempts to suppress the evidence against it. In Britain there were more than 300 reported cases of malformation due to thalidomide. Suing the German manufacturer was the obvious course of action, but it was not practicable in those days, for a variety of reasons. This left the children to sue Distillers for negligence. The Distillers defence was two-pronged. First, they said they were not negligent: they argued that they had no duty to carry out their own testing on a drug bought from a reputable manufacturer. Secondly, the damaged children were not legal persons at the time the damage was done to them, therefore they could not sue in respect of it. The second defence failed in Australia and would have been likely to have failed in Britain. (The Congenital Disabilities (Civil Liability) Act 1976 has now clarified the matter: it gives the child a right to sue.)

On the other hand, the first defence was more likely than not to succeed. This is reflected by the fact that damages were discounted by 60% in the first two cases settled out of court, the discount reflecting the chance of complete failure if the cases had actually been heard in court. This means that the children's legal advisers accepted that the children had only a 40% chance of winning, should the matter be decided in court. Significantly, the settlement had to be approved by the court since it involved children who were minors. The settlement was approved, indicating that the court took a similar view of matters to that of those who negotiated the settlement. Eventually, mainly because of a campaign run by *The Sunday Times*, Distillers were cajoled into setting up a decently funded trust fund, to which HM Government made unique tax concessions. So, in the end, justice was just about done, but it was done by the strength of public opinion: the law had shown itself to be impotent in the face of the crisis.

What about s 14 of the Sale of Goods Act and the notion of strict liability? Surely the goods were not of merchantable quality (as the law then required) nor were they fit for their purpose. Why was the action brought against Distillers and not against the retailer who supplied the drug? The short answer is that even if there were a contract for the sale of the thalidomide to the consumer, the contract was between the children's mothers and the retail chemist.

However, even if the injury had been caused not to the children but to their mothers, there would have been no contractual liability since it has been held that when a chemist supplies a drug to a patient under NHS prescription, there is no contract between the chemist and the patient. This, says the law, is because a contract is *consensual* (that is, entered into by consent of the parties) and this is not the case when a chemist fills a prescription because the chemist has a *statutory duty* to fill the prescription: see *Pfizer v Ministry of Health* (1965). With respect, that view was hardly tenable in 1965 (the agency of necessity being one obvious example of compulsory liability overriding the notion of consent). At the present day, when the law inserts non-excludable implied terms into consumer contracts and puts other restraints on the freedom of contract, the view is substantially discredited. In any case, whether *Pfizer* is legally logical or not, to fund the supply of medical goods by enforced deductions from workers' remuneration, without giving them the option of contracting for their needs privately, and then to attenuate the normal legal liability of the providers of the goods by denying that the supply of the goods is contractual, strikes one as being an attitude of very dubious morality.

CHOOSING THE CORRECT DEFENDANT

Sometimes, while it is clear that someone must have been negligent, it is not clear who has been negligent. The obvious course of action in such cases is to join all the persons who may have been negligent as defendants in the proceedings. This was done in *Walton and Walton v British Leyland, Dutton Forshaw and Blue House Garage* (1978), where the manufacturers, retail suppliers and the garage which serviced the car were all joined as defendants where the purchaser's wife was injured in consequence of a defect in the car. In this case, a car called the Austin Allegro suffered from a problem which could cause the wheels to come off. This was quickly discovered. There were over 100 early cases, 50 of them in seven weeks. British Leyland, the car's manufacturer, though they could not cure the problem itself, could prevent the wheels coming off by fitting oversize washers. This was done on cars manufactured after the defect became known. However, the cars manufactured before the oversize washers began to be fitted remained in a dangerous state. Leyland issued a 'warning' to franchised dealers only. It contained an instruction as to how to put the problem right (that is, by fitting oversize washers), but did not indicate the precise reason for this (that is, the wheels were liable to come off if it was not done). The plaintiff had his car serviced by a competent but non-franchised garage, which knew nothing about the wheel problem. The wheel of his car came off, causing injury to Mr W and severe injury to his wife. It was held that Leyland were negligent in failing to recall the cars manufactured before the problem became known. However, neither the retail suppliers nor the garage that had last serviced the car were in any way liable.

On the other hand, in *Evans v Triplex*, (1936), E was driving his one year old car when the windscreen disintegrated without warning. Some of the glass fell on each of the passengers. E's son suffered cuts and his wife suffered shock. The windscreen was made by the defendants, Triplex, of specially toughened glass. E chose to sue the manufacturers of the glass for negligence, though the better course would appear to have been for Mrs E to sue the manufacturer and for Mr E to sue the retailer who sold the car, for breach of contract. Porter J held that negligence on the part of the manufacturer had not been proved. Evidence showed that the glass would shatter if it was cut on the outside or if it had been strained when it was being screwed into its frame. The judge concluded that the disintegration was due to an error in fitting rather than in manufacture.

Reasons why even a purchaser may choose to sue the manufacturer for negligence rather than the retailer for breach of the contractual terms implied by s 14 of the Sale of Goods Act 1979 are as follows:

(a) the seller may be insolvent or his capacity to pay substantial damages may be in doubt;

It may be that the seller has insufficient resources to meet the claims against him. The seller may join, as a third party to the action, the person who sold the seller the goods, since the seller is entitled to the benefit of the terms implied by the Sale of Goods Act as against his supplier. This process of joining one's immediate supplier can continue all the way up the vertical chain of supply until the manufacturer or importer is reached. Thus, the manufacturer will indemnify the distributor, the distributor will indemnify the wholesaler and the wholesaler will indemnify the seller and, providing the seller's insolvency relates only to his inability to meet his customer's claim for damages, the seller will be able to pay his customer. Thus, even though the seller is unable to pay out of his own resources, the customer may succeed in obtaining his damages.

The case we examined above was where the seller was insolvent in the sense that, although he could pay his normal trade debts, he was unable to shoulder the unexpected burden of paying damages to his injured customer. However, if the seller is insolvent to the extent that he is also unable to meet his trade creditors, the injured customer is again in difficulties as regards his damages. This is because it has been held that the indemnity which is paid by the supplier to the seller in respect of the faulty goods, is a contribution to the seller's general assets. This means that the indemnity is available to pay off the seller's other creditors as well as the injured customer. Thus, the injured customer is unlikely to receive more than a proportion of his claim, at best, by way of dividend in the seller's insolvency.

(b) it may be impracticable to sue the seller;

It may be that the seller is protected by an effective exemption clause, although since the Unfair Contract Terms Act this is not very likely, since attempts to exclude s 14 from a contract are void if the contract is made with a consumer and must satisfy the test of reasonableness if the contract is between businesses. A further possibility is that the supplier is a limited company which has been liquidated and has, therefore, ceased to exist. Suppose, for example, that C (a consumer) has been injured by faulty goods bought from R (an insolvent retailer) who bought them from W (a wholesaler, a limited company which has been liquidated, that is, it has ceased to exist in law), who bought them from D (a distributor), who bought them from M (the manufacturer). In such a case, C will sue R, but R cannot join W to the action, since W no longer exists as a legal entity. Nor can he leapfrog over W and join D instead, since he has no privity of contract with D. Thus, C will be left without a remedy, since R is unable to pay the damages awarded against him.

On the other hand, the seller may be effectively out of reach. Suppose that, in the above example, R bought the goods directly from a foreign supplier. Unless the supplier has assets in this country, there may be a problem in enforcing the judgment if the supplier is domiciled outside the European Union. It may be possible, in some cases, to sue the supplier in his own country but this, in itself, raises daunting problems. (For a discussion on the reciprocal enforcement of judgments between EEC countries, see the section on the Consumer Protection Act 1987, below.)

Insurance

The prudent retailer will be insured against his liability to pay damages to a customer who is injured by faulty goods. In such a case, it will be immaterial that the retailer is unable to pursue his action against his supplier. Furthermore, under the Third Parties (Rights Against Insurers) Act 1930, the rights under the insurance policy are transferred to the customer, whose claim is then met directly by the insurance company. It seems odd that the same rule does not apply to money paid by way of indemnity to the retailer by the party who sold the goods to the retailer.

PRODUCT LIABILITY

We have seen that whereas the purchaser of faulty goods had an action for breach of contract against the seller, the non-purchaser who suffered damage as a result of faulty goods had to bring a negligence action, generally against the manufacturer, which involved proving that the manufacturer had been negligent. An example of a negligence case which was based on liability for unsafe goods is to be found in *Vacwell Engineering v BDH Chemicals* (1969). The defendants manufactured a chemical called 'boron tribromidel', which they marketed for industrial use. The chemical was packed in glass ampoules, each of which bore a label giving the warning, 'harmful vapour'. The plaintiffs used the chemical in their business, following discussions with the defendants. Before use, the labels had to be washed off the ampoules. This was done in batches, a number of ampoules being placed in two adjacent sinks containing water and detergent. A visiting Russian chemist was engaged in this task when there was a violent explosion, resulting in his death and extensive damage to the plaintiffs' property. The probable cause of the explosion was that one of the ampoules had been dropped into a sink where it became mixed with the water. The consequent chemical reaction had broken the glass of the other ampoules, releasing sufficient of the chemical to cause the explosion. The fact that the chemical was liable to explode on contact with water was not known to the defendants, nor was it mentioned in the standard work on the hazards of modern chemicals, nor in three other works which the defendants had consulted. It was, however, mentioned in a work by the French chemist, Gautier, published in 1878. Rees J held that the defendants were liable in contract for breach of the implied condition of fitness for purpose. Furthermore, the defendants were liable in the tort of negligence for two reasons: first, they failed to provide and maintain a system for carrying out an adequate research into scientific literature to ascertain known hazards, and secondly, they failed to carry out adequate research into the scientific literature available to them to discover the industrial hazards of a new or little known chemical. The judge added that if the defendants had complied with that duty, he had no doubt that the explosion noted by Gautier would have come to light and a suitable warning given. This would have prevented the plaintiffs from handling the chemical in the way in which they did.

Despite the success of some plaintiffs in establishing negligence, a negligence action was thought to be too uncertain as regards its outcome to be a reliable method of compensating those who were harmed by defective products. What many thought was needed was a system of *strict liability* for defective products, whereby the injured party could sue the producer of the product without the need to prove that the producer had been negligent. In other words, the non-purchaser would be able to sue the producer in the same manner as an injured purchaser is able to sue the party he contracted with (who, as you will remember, can sue others in the chain of supply until the manufacturer is reached). Such liability is generally called 'product liability'. The United States pioneered the idea of the strict liability of the manufacturer towards the non-purchaser injured by a defect in the manufacturer's goods.

The American experience

The USA has sought to meet the problems arising from damage caused by defective goods by imposing *strict liability* on manufacturers and, in some states, on any person in the distributive chain. This development started by extending the rights given by the implied terms as to quality of goods in the contract of sale, to users of the goods other than the owner, and the doctrine of privity of contract was suitably modified to allow this. For example, in *Henningsen v Bloomfield Motors* (1960), a Chrysler car was purchased from an authorised Chrysler dealer. The purchaser bought it as a gift for his wife. When the wife was driving the car, a steering fault caused it to go out of control. Both the wife and the husband claimed against Bloomfield and Chrysler. Their claims were based on an allegation that the car was not of merchantable quality. Chrysler defended the claim by asserting that there was no privity of contract between them and the plaintiffs. The judge held in favour of the plaintiffs. He dealt with Mr Henningsen's claim by stating that:

> ... the ordinary layman, on responding to the importuning of colourful advertising, has neither the opportunity nor the capacity to inspect or determine the fitness of an automobile for use; he must rely on the manufacturer who has control of its constructions and to some degree the dealer who, to the limited extent called for by the manufacturer's instructions, inspects and services it before delivery. In such a marketing milieu, his remedies and those of persons who properly claim through him should not depend 'upon the intricacies of the law of sales'. The obligation of the manufacturer should not be based alone on privity of contract. It should rest, as was once said, upon 'the demands of social justice'.

The judge proceeded to hold that the manufacturer gives an implied warranty that his product is reasonably suitable for use and that this warranty accompanies the product into the hands of the ultimate purchaser. In relation to Mrs Henningsen, the judge extended the implied warranty to cover members of the purchaser's family and any person using the car with his consent.

There are, however, conceptual difficulties in applying the principle of an implied warranty to someone who is not a user of the defective product, for example, a bystander injured when the defective car runs into him. For this reason, product liability in US law is now governed by the law of tort, so that questions of privity of contract, even the extended privity created in the *Henningsen* case, have now become obsolete. In *Greenman v Yuba Power Products* (1962), the Supreme Court of California held that:

> A manufacturer is strictly liable in tort when an article he places on the market, knowing that it is to be used without inspection for defects, proves to have a defect which causes injury to a human being.

The American Restatement of the Law of Torts, published by the American Law Institute, has been followed by the courts of some States. This makes the plaintiff's claim slightly more difficult to establish by requiring that, in addition to the product being defective, it must be 'unreasonably dangerous'. The Restatement imposes liability on any person who is a seller: this would include anyone in the distributive chain. The Restatement allows claims for both personal injury and damage to property but does not allow claims for pure economic loss (for example, a claim for loss of profits which arises because the plaintiff's factory is put out of action: but don't forget that most businesses will insure against such eventualities).

The United States Model Uniform Product Liability Act

In 1979, the United States Department of Commerce produced a Model Uniform Product Liability Act. It did this to try to secure uniformity in product liability so that insurance rates would stabilise, and also because it was concerned about bankruptcies engendered by the product liability laws of some states. However, although parts of the Act have been adopted by over half of the states, few have adopted the Act as a whole.

The Act provides that a product manufacturer is liable for harm caused by a defective product. This eliminates other persons in the distributive chain (apart from the retailer who is liable in contract), who, however, are liable in California and other States which have chosen to adopt the Californian approach. It provides four circumstances in which a product may be defective:

(a) if it was unreasonably unsafe in construction;

(b) if it was unreasonably unsafe in design;

(c) if it was unreasonably unsafe because adequate warnings or instructions were not provided; or

(d) if it was unreasonably unsafe because it did not conform to the product.

The cost of product liability in the US has led to the imposition of high insurance premiums and has led to some companies withdrawing from the US market.

In *Grimshaw v Ford Motor Co* (1981), Ford manufactured a car called the Pinto, in which the fuel tank was too near the rear of the car so that, if there was a collision with the rear of the car, there was a severe risk from explosion or fire. Ford discovered this but nevertheless proceeded with the manufacture. Substantial damages were awarded against them in a number of claims. These included a sum for *punitive* damages to prevent them profiting from their tort: they had calculated that the cost of paying damages would be less than the cost of redesigning and re-tooling for the manufacture of the car. The total cost of claims faced by Ford was some four billion dollars.

The Consumer Protection Act 1987

Virtually concurrent with the developments in the United States, strict liability for defective products was developed in France, Germany and Holland in the 1960s. In England, a Law Commission Report, 'Liability for Defective Products' (Report No 82, Cmnd 6831, 1977), recommended a system of strict liability in respect of defective products. The Pearson Commission (1978 Cmnd 7054) also recommended strict liability along very similar lines in favour of persons who suffered death or bodily injury caused by a defective product.

The EEC was also active in this area. After producing a draft directive, which was followed by amendments (for example, one amendment excluded primary agricultural products from the scope of the directive), it came up with a final version in 1985 in the form of the EEC Directive on Product Liability (85/374/EEC). The final version was not so robust as the draft in that, in particular, it allows a 'state of the art' defence, which was specifically excluded in the draft. The Directive was given effect in the UK by the Consumer Protection Act, which became law early in 1987. It provides in s 1 that it is intended to give effect to the Directive and shall be construed accordingly. This would appear to mean that if the Act is unclear about any matter, the Directive may be referred to. This, in any case, would be the position if the wording of the Act is construed purposively in accordance with such cases as *Litster v Forth Dry Dock and Engineering Co* (1989) (see Chapter 1).

Who is liable?

Section 2(2) provides that the following shall be liable for damage caused wholly or partly by a defect in the product:

(a) the producer of the product. A producer includes:

    (1) the person who manufactured it;

    (2) in the case of a product which has not been manufactured but has been won or abstracted (in the case, for example, of coal dug out of the ground), the person who won or abstracted it;

    (3) in the case of a product which has not been manufactured, won or abstracted, but the essential characteristics of which are attributable to an industrial or other process having been carried out (for example, in relation to industrial produce), the person who carried out that process.

(b) any person who, by putting his name on the product or using a trade mark or other distinguishing mark in relation to the product, has held himself out to be the producer of the product; and

(c) any person who has imported the product into a Member State from a place outside the Member States (that is, of the EEC) in order, in the course of any business of his, to supply it to another.

In addition, any person who *supplied the product* is liable if the person who suffered the damage requests the supplier to identify one or more of the persons listed in (a), (b) or (c), within a reasonable time of the damage occurring, and the supplier fails to supply the information within a reasonable time.

The question might arise whether a supermarket such as Sainsbury's, which has its own brand put on to many of the goods it sells, would be liable by virtue of s 2(2)(c). The answer might well depend on the way in which the goods are labelled. Suppose a tin of rice pudding is labelled 'Manufactured for Sainsbury's': it might well be held that Sainsbury's are not holding themselves out as the producer. If, however, the tin is simply labelled 'Sainsbury's', it is arguable that they are holding themselves out as producer, though it is common knowledge that 'own brands' are almost invariably manufactured by specialist producers.

It may be that the injured party is unable to identify the producer of the product if, for example, there is no manufacturer's name on the product or if the manufacturer is based outside the European Union and there is no indication on the goods as to who imported them into the UK. It is to meet such difficulties that a supplier who has received a request from a person suffering damage to name a person who is a producer, brander or importer and fails to do so within a reasonable time, is liable as if he were the producer.

WHICH COURTS HAVE JURISDICTION?

Liability attaches only to the importer into the EEC, not the importer into Member States. Thus, if a German imports from outside the EEC and sells to a

British importer, it is the German importer who is liable. Articles 5 and 6 of the 1968 Convention on Jurisdiction and the enforcement of Judgments in Civil and Commercial Matters (The Judgments Convention) and a 1971 Protocol, to which Britain acceded by a Convention of Accession in 1978, make special provision for such a circumstance. The Conventions and Protocol, which are part of European Law (since they were entered into in pursuance of Article 220 of the Treaty of Rome), were given effect in the UK by the Civil Jurisdiction and Judgments Act 1982.

Under Article 5(3) of the 1968 Convention, a person domiciled in a contracting state may, in another contracting state be sued ... (3) in matters relating to tort ... 'in the courts for the place where the harmful event occurred'. Article 6 provides, *inter alia*, that where there are a number of defendants, a person may be sued in the courts for the place where any one of them is domiciled. This provision is intended to avoid multiple actions where a number of parties are liable though, since it would seem that under Art 5, the plaintiff can sue them all on his own 'home' ground, he might be well advised to do this.

The question might arise as to where 'the harmful event' occurred. If goods are manufactured in one country and cause damage in another, it might be thought that the harm occurred where the damage was caused. However, in *Bier v Mines de Potasse* (1978), the defendant was a French company which daily discharged 11,000 tons of chloride into the Rhine. B was a nurseryman in Holland who used water from the Rhine for irrigation. It was so polluted by the chloride that he had to use an expensive purification system. B brought an action for damages. The question arose as to where the harm occurred. B brought an action in the Dutch courts which declined jurisdiction. (He particularly wished to avoid bringing his action in France, since the problem had arisen partly because of the refusal of the French government to take effective steps to avoid the pollution: he was afraid that this would affect the attitude of the French courts.) B appealed to the European Court, which held that either the Dutch or the French courts had jurisdiction. Thus, the principle is that harm is treated as having occurred either where the defendant acted or where the damage was caused, and this principle will hold good for product liability actions.

GAME AND AGRICULTURAL PRODUCE

Originally, the Act excluded from its scope any liability for game or agricultural process which had not undergone an industrial process. However, in the wake of the BSE crisis, the Directive was amended in 1999 (Directive 99/34/EC) to remove this exemption. The exception in respect of game and agricultural produce was, in consequence, removed by the Consumer Protection Act (Product Liability)(Modification) Order 2000.

DAMAGE

The Act requires, not unreasonably, that the product caused the damage. This is the rock on which many claims in respect of allegedly defective pharmaceutical drugs founder. A manufacturer may argue, when his drug is alleged to have caused headaches and sickness, that many illnesses have headaches and sickness as side effects and that there is no proof that the headaches and sickness suffered by the claimant have been caused by the manufacturer's drug rather than being the normal side effects of the illness itself. This may well bring into play the rules of causation in negligence. For example, was the cause of the claimant's illness the manufacturer's defective drug? Or was it that it had been prescribed by the doctor in inappropriate circumstances? Or was it that the chemist had failed to print appropriate instructions as to the proper use of the product?

A further question arises as to the foreseeability of the damage. The general rule in relation to the tort of negligence is that if the plaintiff's injury arose in an unforeseeable way, even though it was a direct result of the defendant's carelessness, the defendant is not liable: see, for example, *Doughty v Turner Manufacturing* (1964), in which the plaintiff was injured when an asbestos lid was carelessly dropped into a vat of molten metal, causing an explosion. The possibility of such an explosion had not been known until it happened, and only a controlled experiment after it had happened revealed the cause: a chemical reaction between the asbestos in the lid and the metal in the vat, when the metal reached a certain temperature. It was held that the defendants were not liable. The damage had been unforeseeable and was, therefore, too remote a consequence of the defendant's action. However, it is probable that the test of remoteness of damage would be modified to accord with the principle laid down in relation to strict liability under the Factories Act in *Millard v Serck Tubes* (1969). In this case, the defendant had failed to fence a machine, though required to do so in accordance with the Factories Act. The Act imposed strict liability in respect of failure to comply. The plaintiff was injured, but in an unforeseeable manner. It was held that it was irrelevant that the plaintiff's injury was caused in an unforeseeable way: it was sufficient that if the machine had been fenced, the injury would not have occurred. It would appear likely, therefore, that if a defective product causes injury in an unforeseeable manner, the defendant may nevertheless be liable.

WHAT IS A 'DEFECT' IN GOODS?

Section 3 provides that there is a defect in a product if the safety of the product is not such as persons are generally entitled to expect. (Goods which simply wear out quickly or do not work properly are not, simply because of that fact, defective within the meaning of the Act.) In determining what persons are entitled to expect, all the circumstances must be taken into account, particularly the following:

(a) the manner in which and the purposes for which the product has been marketed, its get-up, the use of any mark in relation to the product (for example, the British Standards kitemark) and any instructions for, or warnings with respect to, doing or refraining from doing anything with or in relation to the product;

The issue of whether a warning should have been included, or whether the warning actually included was adequate, has been at issue in a number of cases.

In *Iman Abouzaid v Mothercare* (2000), the claimant was injured in 1990 when he was 12 years old. He was helping his mother to attach a product called 'Cosytoes' to his younger brother's pushchair. The product was held to the pushchair by elastic straps, on one of which was a metal buckle. The claimant was attempting to join one elastic strap to the other, which contained the buckle, when the strap slipped from his grasp. This caused the buckle to hit him in the eye, resulting in permanent damage. An expert report said that in 1990, no manufacturer could have been expected to foresee that the straps might cause a hazard, but by the date of the trial, it could be said that the product had a safety defect. The trial judge held that if a safety defect existed in 2000, it also existed in 1990, and awarded damages accordingly. On appeal, the Court of Appeal said that it wasn't clear whether the judge was finding Mothercare liable for negligence, or under the Consumer Protection Act. However, the court confirmed liability, holding that it arose under the Consumer Protection Act. The defendant's reliance on the idea that what was defective now would not have been defective in 1990 was misplaced. Elasticated products have been around for some time now and there was no suggestion of any technical advances which might reasonably have affected the expectations of the public. The product was supplied with a design that permitted the risk to arise. The manufacturer should therefore have issued a warning that the user should position himself so as to avoid the risk. The defendant pleaded the 'state of the art' defence, relying on the absence of reported accidents. However, the court held that the defect was present in the goods at the time, whether or not there had been any previous accidents. In any case, the court was doubtful whether a record of accidents fell within the category of scientific knowledge.

It was further held that there was no negligence at common law – a good illustration of the fact that the Consumer Protection Act imposes strict liability. In relation to the negligence claim, the absence of previous accidents was relevant, as was the claim that, in any case, accidents to the face were unlikely. Elastic tape was a commonly used fabric and experience had not shown that its use in children's products was likely to cause injury.

In *Worsley v Tambrands* (1999), the claimant claimed damages for toxic shock syndrome (TSS) which she alleged was caused by using one of the defendant's products, Tampax Regular. TSS is a very rare but potentially fatal disease which is caused by bacteria and has been associated with tampon use. The main issues to be decided were whether the defendant's product was defective within the meaning of ss 2 and 3 of the Act, taking into account, in particular, the nature of the warnings provided by the defendant, or alternatively whether the warning was so deficient that it amounted to a breach of the defendant's duty of care and therefore made the defendant liable for the tort of negligence. On Tuesday, when the claimant realised she might be suffering from the condition, she looked at the box which gave a warning in general terms and referred the user to a leaflet inside the box. The leaflet gave a detailed list of symptoms and advice as to what to do if the user manifested any of the symptoms. (She had read previous versions of the leaflet and recalled some of the content but not all of it.) However, her husband had thrown the current leaflet away. If Mrs Worsley had read the most recent leaflet, she would have seen that it advised her to remove the tampon (which she did, but only for a short time), visit her doctor and tell him she had been using a tampon. She did not visit her doctor until Thursday, and did not tell him that she was using a tampon. He diagnosed food poisoning. She later collapsed and was taken to hospital where she was found to have TSS. She argued that the warning given in the leaflet was not sufficiently emphatic and, therefore, did not have the impact that it should. She pointed out that the UK version was multi-lingual and therefore in relatively smaller type. It was not as clear as a similar warning in the United States version. In addition, the United States version contained advice on alternating tampons with towels or not using tampons at all. The (female) judge accepted that the United States version was superior, but that was not the issue. The issue was whether the UK version fell below the statutory or common law requirement and whether, if it did, a different design would have caused the claimant to act differently. The judge found:

(a) there was a clearly legible warning on the box, directing the user to the leaflet;

(b) the leaflet was legible, literate, and unambiguous and contained all the information necessary to recognise the warning signs and the action required if any warning signs were present; and

(c) the defendants cannot cater for lost leaflets or for users who, having discovered the loss, as the defendant did on the Tuesday, choose not to replace them.

There was therefore no case for the defendants to answer.

In *Relph v Yamaha* (1996), a claim of negligence and a claim under the Consumer Protection Act in relation to an accident sustained by the plaintiff while riding a three-wheeled all-terrain vehicle (ATV) failed. The court accepted expert testimony that such vehicles are stable if used properly. The plaintiff was warned that the ATV was dangerous if used by novices. The plaintiff read the warnings and instructions. Some he ignored: he was a novice; he did not wear a helmet; he gave rides to passengers. His reading of the manual and label should have alerted him to the danger.

(b) what might be expected to be done with, or in relation to, the product;

In *Richardson v LRC Products* (2000), a condom split during intercourse. The claimant became pregnant. The evidence showed that the teat of the condom had parted from the body of the condom at about shoulder level. The claimant alleged that the fracture was attributable to: (a) a weakening of the latex due to ozone damage; or (b) some other cause which, although it could not be precisely identified, was attributable to a manufacturing defect. R admitted in evidence that she had heard of the morning-after pill but had taken no steps to enquire as to whether it could be used in her case to avoid conception. *Held*: (a) it was more likely that the ozone damage had occurred while the condom was being stored to be used as evidence at the trial; (b) that there was no evidence that the failure of the condom was due to a manufacturing defect; and (c) R had failed to attempt to mitigate her damage which she might have done by using the morning-after pill.

(c) the time when the product was supplied by the producer to another.

Section 3(2) also provides that safety includes risks to property as well as risks to persons, so that damage to property as well as death and bodily injury are covered. However, sub-s (2) goes on to provide, in effect, that any reliance by the injured party on a false or misleading promise or statement which is incorporated into the product does not, in itself, make the product defective. There are four possible sources of defects in goods. These are: manufacturing defects; design defects; failure to give warning of a possible danger connected with the use of the goods; failure to comply with an express warranty. Of possible defects in products, manufacturing defects are possibly the easiest to identify. Goods are normally manufactured to a particular specification and it is probable that goods which do not meet the specification, or whose components fall short of the specification, will be held to be defective. Failure to comply with an express warranty should also be relatively easy to identify.

Design defects, on the other hand, might result in tests being applied which are not dissimilar to the negligence tests, for example, the social utility of the product balanced against the cost of eliminating the design defect. Similarly, the question of whether a warning should have been issued might turn on whether it was reasonably foreseeable that a warning would be needed in the circumstances. However, the preamble to the Directive states that: '... liability without fault on the part of the producer is the sole means of solving the problem, peculiar to our age, of increasing technicality, of a fair apportionment of the risks inherent in modern technological production.' This might be taken to indicate that the negligence concept of foreseeability is not to be applied.

DEFENCES

Section 4 gives the following defences:

(a) that the defect is attributable to compliance with any requirement imposed by or under any enactment or with any Community obligation;

Regulations have been made, which must be complied with, in relation to many kinds of goods ranging from perambulators and pushchairs to aerosol dispensers. They have been made under the Consumer Protection Acts 1961 and 1971 and the Consumer Safety Act 1978 (both of which have been repealed and replaced by the 1987 Act) and, in respect of EEC requirements, by Orders made under the European Communities Act 1972. Thus, if a producer must manufacture goods to a particular specification in order to comply with any of these Regulations, he has a defence *providing* the defect was attributable to compliance with the Regulation.

(b) that the person proceeded against did not supply the product to another;

An obvious example here would be if goods are stolen from Y, the manufacturer, and then sold to X, who purchases in good faith and is injured by a defect in the goods. Since Y did not supply the goods within the meaning of the Act, he is not liable;

(c) that the defendant did not supply the product in the course of a business and was not a producer, brander or importer unless otherwise than with a view to profit;

This intends to exempt the non-business producer, etc, such as the father who makes a toy for his child for Christmas. Note, however, that a producer who supplies a promotional free gift will be supplying in the course of a business;

(d) that the defect did not exist in the product at the relevant time;

'Relevant' time is defined in s 2. The effect of s 4(1)(d) and s 4(2) is that a producer, etc, has to show that the defect was not present when it was last supplied by him. However, where the person who is being sued is one who has failed to identify who supplied the product to him and also failed to identify the producer, he has to show that the defect was not present when the goods were last supplied by the producer.

(e) that the state of scientific or technical knowledge at the relevant time was not such that a producer of products of the same description as the product in question might be expected to have discovered the defect if it had existed in his products while they were under his control (this is the so called 'state of the art' or 'development risks' defence);

In *EC Commission v UK* (1997), the European Commission brought infringement proceedings against the UK, arguing that the wording of the Consumer Protection Act did not reflect that of the Directive in relation to this defence. It was held, however, that there was no evidence that the UK legislation would not achieve the effect intended by the Directive, given the obligation of the UK courts to interpret domestic legislation to reflect EU legislation.

Given that the pressure for the introduction of product liability in Britain stemmed from the thalidomide tragedy, it is perhaps odd that the UK government chose to include this defence (which is permitted by the Directive but not obligatory), which seems to give a large measure of protection to producers of new drugs. Note that it does not absolve drug suppliers, as such, from liability. What it does is to give drug producers (and others engaged in developing 'high risk' products) a special, but limited, defence.

The Law Commission, the Pearson Commission and the EEC have all turned down the idea that a special exemption should be made for drugs, though there are a number of arguments in favour, for example, that drugs combat pain and disease by interfering with the natural processes of the body and that if drugs were completely safe they would not work; drugs are available only on prescription, and the suitability of a particular drug for a particular patient is monitored by persons and bodies other than the producer of the drug, including the medical practitioner who makes out the prescription; the imposition of strict liability might inhibit research into new products – and retard the availability to the public of new medicinal remedies. (See *Liability for Defective Products*, Law Commission No 82, Cmnd 7054, 1977, para 56.)

It is probably not sufficient for a drug producer to assert that the particular side effect of the drug was not known at the time of the supply. He would have to go further and show that he could not have been expected to discover the side effect.

(f) that the product was comprised in another product and the defect was wholly attributable to the design of the other product or to compliance by the producer of the product with instructions given by the producer of the other product.

Suppose that a manufacturer of brake systems, Y, manufactures a system for X a car manufacturer, to X's specifications, for X to incorporate in his cars. The design is faulty, with the result that Z, a passenger in one of X's cars, is injured as a result of brake failure. Y would be able to use the defence that the defect was wholly attributable to compliance by him with instructions given by X. Similarly, if the brake failure was due entirely to a fault in the design of the car, the brake manufacturer could use this defence. Note, however, that if Y simply supplied a faulty system which X incorporated in his cars, both Y and X would be liable to anyone injured as a result of the defect. Both would be 'producers'.

Damage which gives rise to liability

Section 5 contains various limiting provisions relating to the type and amount of damage for which damages are recoverable under the Act. Section 5(1) provides that 'damage' means death or personal injury or any loss of or damage to property. It may be that this is more narrow than the type of damage recoverable for negligence. For example, suppose that Z suffered damage to himself and his car because of defective brakes manufactured by Y. It may be that consequential loss, for example, the hiring of an alternative car while Z's car is being repaired, though recoverable in negligence, would be excluded under the Act. Section 5(2) provides that the producer, etc, shall not be liable for the loss of, or any damage to, the product itself or for the loss of, or any damage to, a product which has been supplied with the defective product. (Note that in such a case, the purchaser of the product will have his remedies under the Sale of Goods Act.)

Sub-section (3) limits claims for damage to property to property ordinarily intended for private use or consumption and intended by the claimant for his own private use, occupation or consumption. The effect of this is to exclude commercial property. Thus damage to, for example, a factory or a lorry used in business, will be excluded. However, the factory owner or the lorry owner will still have the possibility of an action in negligence. Sub-section (4) puts a lower limit on the *damage* suffered *to property* at a minimum of £275. This is permitted by Article 9 of the Directive. It is intended to avoid the system becoming overburdened with small claims. The £275 is not an excess. If someone suffers £300 worth of damage to property, he will recover the entire amount. However, there is no upper limit in the Act on the amount of damages which may be awarded in relation to total damage caused by products with the same defects, though this is permitted by the Directive, Articles 15 and 16.

Limitation of claims

Under s 11A of the Limitation Act 1980, claims must be brought within three years from the date of the damage or injury, or within three years of the date when the claimant knew, or could reasonably have known, of the claim. No action may be brought against a producer more than 10 years from the date on which the product was first put into circulation.

CONTRIBUTORY NEGLIGENCE

Contributory negligence is a defence to an action in negligence or breach of statutory duty, in which the defendant alleges either that the plaintiff contributed to the *cause* of the harm which befell him, or that the defendant contributed to the resulting damage. An example of the first type of contributory negligence would be where a person ran out into the road from behind a parked car and was knocked down by a bus. The second type of contributory negligence is where the victim does not contribute at all towards the accident but fails to take steps which would reduce the damage he suffers in consequence. Failure to wear a seat belt while travelling as a passenger in a car would be an example of the second type of contributory negligence. In either case, the court assesses the full amount of damages which would be awarded to the claimant if he had not been contributorily negligent and then reduces it by a percentage to allow for the contributory negligence. Contributory negligence in the second type of case, where the victim is in no way responsible for the occurrence which injured him, is seldom very high.

Section 6(3) of the Consumer Protection Act permits the defence of contributory negligence as provided for in the Law Reform (Contributory Negligence) Act 1945 and s 5 of the Fatal Accidents Act 1976. However, in a negligence action the court is comparing the claimant's negligence with that of the defendant. In a product liability action the defendant is liable irrespective of fault, so that to engage in a comparison of fault will not be appropriate. In cases involving strict liability under the Factories Acts and similar legislation imposing strict liability, it has been held that the contribution of the claimant must not be judged too harshly. For example, in *Quintas v National Smelting Co* (1961), Sellars LJ said: 'It has often been held that there is a high responsibility on a defendant who fails to comply with his statutory duty. A workman is not to be judged too severely.' Similarly, in *Stavely Iron and Chemical Co v Jones* (1956), Lord Tucker said: 'In Factory Act cases the purpose of imposing the absolute obligation is to protect the workman against those very acts of inattention which are sometimes relied upon as constituting contributory negligence so that too strict a standard would defeat the object of the statute.' It would therefore seem reasonable to conclude that under the Act, contributory negligence will be assessed with greater lenience towards the plaintiff than is the situation in negligence cases.

Exemption of liability

Section 7 provides that liability to a person who has suffered damage or to a relative or dependant of that person cannot be limited or excluded by any contract term or by notice or by any other provision. Note that this does not prevent adjustment of liability between defendants: liability under the Act is joint and several as between the producer, the 'own-brander', the importer into the EEC and, where appropriate, the supplier. They can adjust liability between themselves (subject to the provisions of the Unfair Contract Terms Act 1977) but cannot limit or exclude liability as between themselves and the consumer. In *Thompson v T Lohan* (1987), the second defendants hired an excavator, with a driver, from the first defendants. Clause 8 of the contract provided that, in relation to the operation of the plant, the driver was to be regarded as a servant or agent of the second defendants who alone was to be responsible for all claims arising in connection with the operation of the plant by the drivers. The plaintiff's husband, who was also an employee of the first defendants, was killed as a result of the driver's negligence in operating the excavator when working for the second defendants at a quarry. The plaintiff, as her husband's personal representative, obtained damages and costs against the first defendants, her husband's employers. In third party proceedings, the first defendants argued that they were entitled to an indemnity from the second defendants. The second defendants resisted the claim, arguing that clause 8 was void under s 2(1) of the Unfair Contract Terms Act 1977, because it sought to limit or exclude liability for death or personal injury contrary to the provisions of the sub-section. *Held*: clause 8 was effective as between the parties to the contract. On its true construction, s 2 was concerned with protecting the victim of negligence and those who claimed under him, and not with the arrangements between the wrongdoer and other persons as to the sharing or bearing of the burden of compensating the victim. Since such arrangements did not exclude or restrict the wrongdoer's liability, clause 8 did not fall within the prohibition of s 2(1).

However, in a case where the plaintiffs were the hirers of the plant and they suffered damage to their property caused by the negligence of the driver they had hired with the plant, the defendants were not allowed to use clause 8 to exempt them from liability. In this case, damage was to property and it was held by the Court of Appeal that the exemption from liability, which under s 2(2) of UCTA 1977 has to be reasonable, was unreasonable and therefore ineffective to absolve the defendants from liability: *Phillips Products v Hyland* (1987).

CRIMINAL LIABILITY FOR UNSAFE PRODUCTS

Part 2 of the Consumer Protection Act places *criminal* liability on the *supplier* of goods in respect of unsafe goods. (To remind you, Part 1 places *civil* liability on the *producer, own-brander*, or *importer*, though the supplier will still be liable for breach of contract to the person he or she supplies.) The advantage of the criminal law provisions is that they enable the enforcement authorities to take action to remove unsafe goods from circulation before anyone is harmed by them. A civil action, on the other hand, can only be brought after a person has suffered injury from the goods.

Section 10 of the Act provides that a person who supplies, offers or agrees to supply, or exposes or possesses for supply, any consumer goods which fail to comply with the general safety requirement shall be guilty of an offence. The section goes on to state that consumer goods fail to comply with the general safety requirement if they are not reasonably safe, having regard to all the circumstances. The circumstances include: the manner in which, and the purposes for which, the goods are being marketed; the use of any mark in relation to the goods; any instructions or warnings which are given with respect to the keeping, use or consumption of the goods; any standards of safety published by any person for goods of that description; the existence of any means by which it would have been reasonable (taking into account the cost, likelihood and extent of any improvement) for the goods to have been made safer. Consumer goods are defined as goods ordinarily intended for private use and consumption, but there are a number of exceptions (for example, tobacco products), to which the general safety requirement does not apply. If goods comply with safety standards imposed by or under regulations, they will be treated as complying with the general safety requirement as regards matters which the regulations cover. Similarly, goods are not regarded as failing to meet the general safety requirement in respect of anything which is done in order to comply with European Union obligations. The current regulations are the General Product Safety Regulations (SI 1994/1828).

In addition to the general safety requirement, a number of regulations are in force which have been made both under the Consumer Protection Act and preceding legislation. These cover a wide range of matters from an ignitability test for furniture (Furniture and Furnishings (Fire) (Safety) Regulations 1988); prohibition of the supply of manufactured goods which, though not food, might be mistaken for food (Food Imitation (Safety) Regulations 1989); flammability performance for children's nightwear and labelling of certain garments in relation to their flammability (Nightwear (Safety) Regulations 1985). Other regulations apply to carry-cots, ceramic ware, toys, cosmetic products, tobacco products, pencils and graphite instruments, oil heaters, tyres, fireworks, plugs and sockets, etc. A person who suffers injury as a result of a breach of the safety requirements contained in regulations may bring a civil action against the person responsible, for breach of statutory duty. There are a number of defences available under the Act. There is no liability where the accused could show that they reasonably believed the goods would be used outside the UK. A retailer has a defence if they reasonably believed that the goods complied with the general safety requirement. A defence is also available where the goods are second-hand.

Enforcement provisions

An enforcement authority (that is, the local Trading Standards Office), may serve a suspension notice on the supplier concerned. This may last for a period of up to six months and prevents the supplier from supplying the goods during that time. This is intended to give time for the safety of the goods to be investigated and, where appropriate, for the Secretary of State to issue a prohibition notice relating to the goods. This prohibits the supplier from supplying the goods. The Secretary of State may serve a *notice to warn*. This requires the supplier, at their own expense, to publish in a specified manner, a warning about the unsafe goods. This power has never, up to the time of writing, been used. This is probably because a supplier of goods which are a safety hazard will voluntarily recall the goods for replacement, in order to avoid the adverse publicity which would ensue if he were forced to publish a warning about them.

An enforcement authority has powers to make test purchases, to search premises and seize goods for testing, etc, require the production of and take copies of, records relating to the business concerned. Customs officers may seize imported goods and detain them for not more than two working days in order to facilitate the investigations of the enforcement authority. Failure to comply with a suspension notice, prohibition notice or notice to warn, or any other offence under the Act, may be punished by a period of imprisonment of up to six months and or a fine of up to £5,000.

Other Acts dealing with the safety of goods

The Food Safety Act 1990 established three principal offences in relation to the supply of food. These are:

(a) to render food injurious to health by the addition or abstraction of articles or constituents;

(b) to sell, offer, expose or advertise for sale, food which does not comply with the food safety requirement. This means either that the food is unfit for human consumption or that it has been rendered injurious to health (but not necessarily by the seller); and

(c) to sell food which is not of the nature, quality or substance demanded by the purchaser.

The Medicines Act 1968 contains similar offences to those contained in the Food Safety Act. The Road Traffic Act 1988 makes provisions about the safety of motor vehicles, trailers and crash helmets. There are also Acts which place control over explosives, fireworks and farm and garden chemicals, among other things.

CHAPTER 26

CRIMINAL LIABILITY FOR STATEMENTS

We have seen that if a seller misdescribes goods he may be liable in one of several ways. He may be liable under s 13 of the Sale of Goods Act; he may be liable for breach of an express term; he may be liable for misrepresentation. Each of these three may entitle the innocent party to recover damages and/or to rescind the contract as against the guilty party.

There is, however, a potential criminal liability in respect of making false statements. Criminal liability for statements derives largely from two sources. The Trade Descriptions Act 1968 contains penalties for statements which misdescribe goods or services. The Consumer Protection Act 1987 penalises misleading statements about the price at which goods or services are to be provided. Although the customer to whom the goods or services are misdescribed will usually have a civil action for breach of contract, there is usually no civil action available to the person who is misled by a mis-statement of price.

THE TRADE DESCRIPTIONS ACT 1968

The Trade Descriptions Act provides for criminal penalties in two circumstances where the consumer may be misled by a trader. These are: (a) misdescription of goods; and (b) false statements about services. The Act has been most effective in relation to the misdescription of goods. It seems to have had very little impact in relation to services, the reason being that mis-statements regarding services do not, unlike mis-statements relating to goods, attract strict liability.

False or misleading descriptions of goods

Section 1(1) of the Trade Descriptions Act provides: any person who, in the course of a trade or business (a) applies a false trade description to any goods; or (b) supplies or offers to supply any goods to which a false trade description is applied, shall, subject to the provisions of this Act, be guilty of an offence.

The meaning of the key words and phrases in s 1

It will be useful to look at the meaning of the key words and phrases used in s 1.

Trade description

Section 2(1) provides: A trade description is an indication, direct or indirect, and by whatever means given, of any of the following matters with respect to any goods or parts of goods, that is to say:

(a) quantity, size or gauge (including length, width, height, area, volume, capacity, weight and number);

(b) method of manufacture, production, processing or reconditioning;

(c) composition;

(d) fitness for purpose, strength, performance, behaviour or accuracy;

In *Sherratt v Geralds, the American Jewellers Ltd* (1970), it was held that a watch described as a 'diver's watch' and 'waterproof' was misdescribed when it filled with water after being immersed in a bowl of water for an hour.

(e) any physical characteristics not included in the preceding paragraphs;

Descriptions of second-hand cars have frequently been false within the provisions of this paragraph. In *Hawkins v Smith* (1978), a dealer placed the following advertisement for a car: 'Showroom condition throughout is the only way to describe this 1968 Austin 1100 estate.' The car was sold and three weeks afterwards, the purchaser took it to a garage which discovered certain defects. The garage advised the purchaser to contact her local trading-standards office, which she did. Their consulting engineer reported the following defects: corrosion of front nearside box section of the suspension; corrosion of brake pipe; damage to rear sub-frame mountings; excessive wear on front suspension ball pin assemblies; corrosion of front offside wing; badly fitted and misaligned tailgate. The dealer contended that the words 'showroom condition' were a mere trade puff. *Held*: the words amounted to a false trade description.

In other cases, 'excellent condition throughout' and 'really exceptional condition throughout' have been held to be false trade descriptions.

(f) testing by any person and the results thereof;

(g) approval by any person or conformity with a type approved by any person;

(h) place or date of manufacture, production, processing or reconditioning;

In *Routledge v Ansa Motors* (1980), a van which was manufactured in 1972, converted into a caravanette and first registered on 1 August 1975 was described in a sales invoice as 'one used 1975 Ford Escort Fiesta'. The defendant was charged with applying a false trade description to the vehicle. The justices accepted a submission by the defence that there was no case to answer. On appeal it was held that the justices should have considered whether it was likely that the average customer on reading these words would believe that the date of manufacture was 1975. If that were so, the justices should consider whether the date given was false to a material degree.

However, in *R v Ford Motor Co* (1974), Ford were charged with supplying a vehicle, a Ford Cortina, to which a false trade description had been applied in that it had been sold as a new vehicle when it had been crashed in the factory compound. Evidence showed that it was as good as new, but the jury in the Crown Court convicted, the judge having indicated to them that if we say that something is as good as new, we are saying it is not new. However, the Court of Appeal quashed the conviction. Bridge J said that two questions should be asked: first, what is the extent and nature of the damage; and secondly, what is the quality of the repairs which have been effected? He then went on: 'If the damage which a new car after leaving the factory has sustained is, although perhaps extensive, either superficial in character or limited to certain defined parts of the vehicle which can simply be replaced with new parts, then provided that such damage is in practical terms perfectly repaired so that it can in truth be said after repairs have been effected that the vehicle is as good as new, in our judgment it would not be a false trade description to describe such a vehicle as new.'

(i) person by whom manufactured, produced, processed or reconditioned;

It has been held that a conspiracy to manufacture bogus Chanel No 5 was an offence under the TDA 1968: *R v Pain*; *R v Jory*; *R v Hawkins* (1985).

(j) other history including previous ownership or use.

'Clocking' cars comes under this heading. 'Clocking' describes the practice, allegedly common in the motor trade, of turning back the odometer of a car so that it reads a lesser mileage figure than the car has actually done. In 1978 the Director General of Fair Trading stated that in the course of making 1,614 routine checks, over 50% of the vehicles checked were found to have been 'clocked', at an estimated cost to the consumer of £53 million per annum. The DG said that in order to try to counter this practice, he would withhold, suspend or revoke a dealer's consumer credit licence, or he would use his power under Part 3 of the Fair Trading Act 1973, to demand assurances from the trader that he or she would cease the practice. 'Clocking' is an offence which is regarded seriously by the courts. For example, in *R v Hewitt* (1991), a motor trader was jailed for two months for 'clocking' offences, which he carried out routinely.

In November 1980, the Office of Fair Trading made a report to the Secretary of State for Trade and the Ministry of Transport, recommending legislation:

(a) for the compulsory provision of dealers of a pre-sales report about the condition of used cars under 10 years old;

(b) for the introduction of tamper-proof odometers;

(c) for the provision of a standard notice to be used by all dealers unable to verify a mileage reading;

(d) for the provision of an expanded vehicle registration document giving details of previous owners.

No legislation has yet been introduced, though a new motor trade code of practice has been introduced making it compulsory for members of the Motor Traders Association to verify odometer readings or to warn customers that this has not been done.

In *Holloway v Cross* (1981), Holloway, a motor trader, bought a 1973 Triumph with an odometer reading of 700 miles. The true mileage was over 70,000 miles. A prospective purchaser asked Holloway what the true mileage was. He said he didn't know but would make enquiries. The prospective purchaser came back with a view to buying the car and Holloway asked him what his estimate of the car's mileage would be. The purchaser didn't know. Holloway then asked whether he thought that the figure of 45,000 (which was, in fact, an average figure for a vehicle of that age) sounded correct. The purchaser accepted this and the invoice was completed by the appellant to read, 'Recorded mileage indicator reading is 715, estimated 45,000'. The purchaser wouldn't have bought the car if he had known its true mileage. Holloway was prosecuted under s 1 of the Trade Descriptions Act. On the evidence, the magistrates concluded that the description 'estimated 45,000' was not a trade description as such within s 2 of the Trade Descriptions Act, but that it was a trade description within the extended meaning given to the phrase by s 3(3). (Note that if the seller had given a firm indication that the mileage was 45,000, the case would clearly have come within s 2(1)(j).) On appeal to the Divisional Court, Donaldson LJ felt that the finding that there was no trade description within s 2 was 'somewhat debatable'. However, both he and Hodgson J agreed that the words used were a trade description within the extended meaning given to the words by s 3(3).

Section 2(3) provides that in this section, 'quantity' includes length, width, height, area, volume, capacity, weight and number. In 1976, the DG published a *Review of the Trade Descriptions Act 1968*, Cmnd 6628. It drew attention to possible gaps in the definition of 'trade description'. In particular, the DG noted doubts as to whether 'indications of the identity of a supplier or distributor and the standing, commercial importance or capabilities of a manufacturer of goods or indications of the contents of books, films, recordings, etc, including their authorship' came within s 2(1).

The Review dealt with, among other things, the problems of 'bait-advertising' and 'switch-selling'. Bait-advertising is advertising goods which the trader either has not got in stock, or has no intention of selling, at a very low price in order to induce persons to visit the trader's premises. The hope is that the potential customer, once there, will buy something else at the normal price. 'Switch-selling' is where a trader interests a potential customer in certain goods (usually at a bargain price) and, having hooked the customer, tells them that for one reason or another (for example, that the goods are not in stock), the sale cannot take place. The trader then proceeds to try to sell alternative, more expensive, goods to the customer.

It was proposed that false indications as to the availability of goods should be made an offence. This was welcomed by the National Consumer Council. However, traders thought that the offence could have serious repercussions on the activities of honest traders who miscalculated demand, and that it could cause cash-flow problems in forcing them to acquire stock before seeking to advertise it, and to hold stock until the advert was published, which in the case of publications with a substantial 'lead-time' (that is, where there is a substantial gap between the date the advertising copy has to be with the publisher, and the date on which it is published) could run into months. For these reasons, the DG concluded that the abuse was too small to justify amending legislation to deal with it.

False trade description

Section 3 defines the term 'false trade description'. Section 3(1) provides: 'A false trade description is a trade description which is false to a material degree.' Section 3(2) provides: 'A trade description which, though not false, is misleading ... shall be deemed to be a false trade description.' Thus, in *R v Southwestern Justices and Hallcrest ex p London Borough of Wandsworth*, a car was accurately described as 'one owner' but the one owner had leased it out to five different registered keepers. It was held that the words 'one owner', though strictly true, were misleading and therefore amounted to a false trade description within the meaning of s 3(2).

Section 3(3) provides: 'Anything which, though not a trade description, is likely to be taken for an indication of any of those matters (that is, the matters listed in s 2), and ... would be false to a material degree, shall be deemed to be a false trade description.' Thus, in *Holloway v Cross* (1981) (above), the Divisional Court was not sure whether the words 'estimated mileage 45,000' amounted to a false trade description within the meaning of s 2(1)(j), but as the words were likely to be taken as an indication of 'other history', the description was a false trade description within the meaning of s 3(3).

Any person

This includes a corporation: Sched 1 to the Interpretation Act 1978. In the case of a corporation, the corporation cannot itself perform the act complained of, since it must always act through agents. However, the act of an employee is not necessarily the act of the company. In order to amount to an act of the company the act must be performed by a person in a senior management position. Thus, in *Tesco v Nattrass*, it was held that the act of a Tesco store manager was not the act of the company.

In order that the prosecution may reach the real culprit in a case where a company is prosecuted, s 20 provides that where an offence which has been committed by a body corporate (for example a limited liability company) is proved to have been committed with the consent or connivance of, or to be attributable to any neglect on the part of, any director, manager, secretary, or other similar officer of the body corporate, or any person who was purporting to act in any such capacity, he as well as the body corporate shall be guilty of an offence.

'Any person' includes a buyer as well as a seller. So that, in *Fletcher v Budgen* (1974), where a dealer bought a car for scrap, having made disparaging remarks about it and then resold it at a substantial profit, it was held that he had committed an offence under the Act. The words 'any person' can also include a person who has no contractual relationship with the complainant. In *Fletcher v Sledmore* (1973), S was a panel-beater who bought, repaired and sold old cars. A car dealer and his prospective customer visited him to look at a car and he falsely told them that it had a good little engine. S sold the car to the dealer who resold it to his customer. Despite the fact that S had no contractual relationship with the customer, he was convicted of an offence under s 1(1)(a).

Applies

Section 1 states that an offence is committed where a person 'applies' a false trade description to goods, or supplies or offers to supply goods to which a false trade description is applied. Section 4 amplifies the meaning of the word 'applies'. It states:

(1) A person applies a trade description to goods if he:

    (a) affixes or annexes it to or in any manner marks on it or incorporates it with:

        (i) the goods themselves; or

        (ii) anything in, on or with which the goods are supplied; or

    (b) places the goods in, on or with anything which the trade description has been affixed or annexed to, marked on or incorporated with, or places any such thing with the goods; or

    (c) uses the trade description in any manner likely to be taken as referring to the goods.

In *Roberts v Severn Petroleum and Trading Co* (1981), a petrol company supplied petrol which was not Esso, to a garage which displayed an Esso sign outside.

The garage owners knew that the petrol supplied was not Esso but members of the public di not necessarily know. It was held that the petrol company was guilty of applying a false trade description to the petrol it supplied.

In *R v AF Pears* (1982), a cosmetics company supplied moisturising cream in a double-skinned jar which looked as if it held substantially more than it did. They were convicted of applying a false trade description despite the fact that the amount of the contents was indicated accurately on the jar.

In the course of a trade or business

The Act is aimed principally at dishonest tradespeople. Thus a private seller or buyer cannot be guilty of an offence under s 1. However, a private individual can be guilty of an offence under s 23.

In *Olzeirsson v Kitching* (1985), the defendant, a private individual, sold a car to a trader knowing that the odometer reading was false. The trader resold it. The defendant was convicted of an offence under s 23, which provides: 'Where the commission of an offence under this Act is due to the act or default of *some other person*, that other person shall be guilty of the offence, and a person may be charged with and convicted of the offence by virtue of this section, whether or not proceedings are taken against the first-mentioned person.' The trader, the 'first-mentioned person', was guilty of an offence under s 1. The defendant was 'some other person' within the meaning of s 23. The court resisted an argument that s 23, like s 1, should apply only to a trader. The statute is clearly worded and there is no reference in s 23 to any requirement that 'some other person' must be a trader.

It seems that to amount to a description made in the course of a trade or business, the description must relate to a transaction which is an integral part of the defendant's business. In *Davies v Sumner* (1984), the appellant, a self-employed courier engaged exclusively by Harlech Television, sold a car with a false odometer reading of 18,100 miles. The car had, in fact, done 118,100 miles (in one year between June 1980 and July 1981). The justices convicted. However, it was held by the House of Lords that the conviction must be quashed. The appropriate question was 'Was the sale of the car an integral part of the appellant's business?' not 'Was the *use* of the car an integral part of the appellant's business?'. Since the sale of the car was not an integral part of the appellant's business, he was not acting in the course of a business within the meaning of s 1. (But note that the courier would have been guilty of an offence under s 23 if the dealer had resold the vehicle without correction or disclaimer of the false mileage.)

In cases where a transaction, though not the main business of the defendant, is an integral part of the defendant's business, the courts have held that the transaction is in the course of a business. In *Havering Borough Council v Stevenson* (1970), a car-hire firm with a fleet of 24 cars had a normal practice of selling off its hire cars after they had been used for two years. The firm never bought cars for the purpose of reselling them at a greater price. They had a Ford Corsair which had a recorded mileage of 34,000 miles. They sold it to Mr Carter. In fact, the vehicle had covered more than 50,000 miles. The firm was charged under s 1(1)(b) of the Trade Descriptions Act 1968. The justices dismissed the case on the ground that the trade description was not made 'in the course of a trade or business' as required by s 1. The prosecutor appealed. In allowing the appeal the Lord Chief Justice, Lord Parker, said: 'Once it is found that a car-hire business *as part of its normal practice* buys and disposes of cars, it seems to me almost inevitable that the sale of a car ... was an integral part of the business carried on as a car hire firm.'

Supplies or offers to supply

Difficulties have been experienced in the past in relation to criminal offences where the offence has consisted of 'offering to sell or supply'. In such cases, the law of contract has been applied to decide whether or not an offer has been made. Under the law of contract, there is no offer to sell unless the person making the offer unequivocally indicates an intention to be contractually bound should their offer be accepted by the other party.

In *Pharmaceutical Society v Boots* (1953), it was held that a display of goods on the shelves of a supermarket was not an offer. In *Fisher v Bell* (1961), it was held that a display of goods in a shop window with price tags attached is not an offer to sell them. In *Partridge v Crittenden* (1968), it was held that an advert, 'Bramblefinch cocks and hens, 25s each', was not an offer. To avoid these difficulties, s 6 enacts: 'A person exposing goods for supply or having goods in his possession for supply shall be deemed to offer to supply them.'

Where goods are ordered to a specification and the goods supplied do not meet the specification, an offence is committed.

In *Walker v Simon Dudley Ltd* (1997), Shropshire Fire and Rescue Service sent the defendants a specification for a fire engine which the defendants agreed to supply. Prior to delivery, several modifications were agreed. The engine supplied did not meet the original specification, nor had the modifications been undertaken. *Held*: where the trade description is false at the time of the supply, the supplier commits an offence.

False descriptions of services

Section 14(1) of the Trade Descriptions Act 1968 provides that it shall be an offence for any person in the course of any trade or business: (a) to make a statement which he knows to be false; or (b) recklessly to make a statement which is false; as to any of the following matters relating to services, accommodation or facilities:

(i) the provision of them in the course of any trade or business;

(ii) the nature of them;

(iii) the time at which or the manner in which or the persons by whom they are provided;

(iv) the examination, approval or evaluation of them by any person;

(v) the location or amenities of any accommodation provided.

In each case the provision of the services, etc, as well as the statement made in relation to them, has to be in the course of a business.

Sub-section (2) provides:

(a) anything (whether or not a statement as to any of the matters specified in the preceding sub-section) likely to be taken for such a statement as to any of those matters as would be false shall be deemed to be a false statement as to that matter;

(b) a statement made regardless of whether it is true or false shall be deemed to be made recklessly, whether or not the person making it had reasons for believing that it might be true.

The difficulties with s 14

Section 14 has proved disappointingly inadequate as a means of bringing unscrupulous traders to account, for two reasons:

(a) a mental element is required before an offence is committed, whereas the offences established by s 1 of the Act are offences of *strict liability*; and

(b) in construing the offence created by s 14, the courts have followed the law of misrepresentation in holding that, in order to be actionable as an offence, a statement must be one of existing fact (that is, it must relate to something present or past), *it cannot relate to a statement of future intention*.

We will deal with these difficulties in turn:

The mental element

For an offence to be committed, the accused must either:

(a) know that their statement was false; or

(b) have made the statement recklessly.

Knowledge that the statement was false

It is sufficient for the purposes of s 14 if the defendant, though not knowing that his statement was false at the time it was made, was aware that his statement was untrue at the time it was read by the complainant.

In *Wings Ltd v Ellis* (1985), the defendant's brochure had advertised that a hotel in Sri Lanka was equipped with air-conditioning. Before the complainant, Mr Wade, read the brochure and booked a holiday on the strength of it, the defendants became aware that the statement about the air-conditioning was untrue and that the hotel was equipped only with overhead fans. They therefore instructed their employee salesagent to tell travel agents orally that the information was false and that it should be corrected when dealing with customers. Mr Wade was not informed by the travel agent or by Wings, and only discovered the untruth of the statement when he arrived in Sri Lanka. Wings Ltd were convicted by the magistrates of an offence under s 14(1). The House of Lords held that the offence had been committed because by the time Mr Wade read the brochure, the defendants knew that their statement was false: once the defendants knew their statement was false, they nevertheless continued to make it.

Recklessness

It has been held that the requirement of recklessness does not necessarily import dishonesty, as it does in other areas of the law: it is sufficient if the accused has exhibited 'the degree of irresponsibility implied in the phrase "careless whether it be true or false"', used in s 14(2)(b).

This was laid down in *MFI Warehouses v Nattrass* (1973). MFI sold folding doors on term which included a period of approval without pre-payment and a carriage charge of 25p each door. MFI later started to sell sliding gear with these doors so that they could be used as a sliding partition. They placed an advert in the *Practical Householder* which said, 'Folding door gear (carriage free)'. The advert also referred to the door being sent on approval. When a customer ordered some sliding gear only, he was charged 25p carriage and the goods were not sent on approval: pre-payment was required. In its defence, the company argued that it had not been reckless as required by s 14, in that it hadn't envisaged selling the sliding gear separately from the doors. It had intended to make a carriage charge of 25p in respect of the doors, which would also cover the sliding gear; hence the gear was carriage free. It was held by the divisional court that the conclusion reached by the purchaser to the effect that he could buy the gear separately and that it would be carriage free and on approval was a reasonable one. On the question of whether MFI had been reckless, it was held that 'recklessly' in the context of the Trade Descriptions Act did not import dishonesty. For recklessness to be present, it was sufficient that MFI had exhibited the degree of carelessness implied by s 14(2)(b).

The statement of future intention

The law of trade descriptions has followed the law of deceit and the old criminal law of false pretences in holding that a statement of future intention, which turns out to be unfounded, will not, save in special circumstances, amount to a false statement for the purposes of the Trade Descriptions Act. To be actionable, a statement has to relate to an existing or a past state of facts.

This point is illustrated by *R v Sunair Holidays* (1973), in which the appellants published a brochure offering accommodation at a number of holiday resorts. One of the hotels at which accommodation was offered was the Hotel Cadi at Calella on Spain's Costa Brava. Mr Bateman booked a holiday. He was dissatisfied with it and reported the company to the trading standards authority. As a result of his complaint, they began criminal proceedings against the company. The indictment alleged six false statements:

(1) that the hotel had a swimming pool;

(2) that there were pushchairs for hire;

(3) that the hotel had its own night club;

(4) that cots were available;

(5) that there was dancing every night in the hotel's discothèque (the hotel, in fact, had no discothèque);

(6) that the hotel provided good food with English dishes available as well as special meals for children.

Each of these statements was untrue. There were plans for a swimming pool and a discothèque. The swimming pool had been built but there were cracks in it and it could not be filled with water. The larger room for the discothèque and night club had not been finished. The food consisted of steak, chops or chicken, always served with chips, but cooked in the Spanish style. The children could have their meals one hour earlier than the adults but there were no special dishes provided for them. Pushchairs were not available at the hotel itself though they were available from a shop in a neighbouring street.

What the judge said

On count 4, the judge had ruled that Sunair had no case to answer. In relation to the other counts, the judge told the jury that they had to decide what Sunair were saying in their brochure. Were they saying that the facilities existed on 7 January when Mr Bateman booked, or on 7 March, which was said to be the earliest possible booking date, or on 27 May when Mr Bateman arrived at the hotel? Once they had decided on the operative date they should then decide whether it was true on that date and if it were not, and they found that the statement had been made recklessly, then they could convict.

What the Court of Appeal said

Sunair's appeal would be allowed because the judge had misdirected the jury, in that he had failed to direct them as to the possibility of Sunair's statements being statements of future intention rather than statements of existing fact. He should have directed the jury to acquit on counts 2 and 6, since both sides agreed that they related to the future. As regards count 1 (and presumably 3 and 5), he should have directed the jury as to the possibility of Sunair's statements being promises as to what would be in the future (as Sunair contended they were), rather than representations of existing fact.

Thus, because of the judge's inadequate direction to the jury, the appeal was allowed. However, it is difficult to see how, if the judge had directed the jury properly, they could have found that the representation as to the swimming pool was anything but a representation of existing fact. It is perhaps significant that the Court of Appeal did not feel it appropriate to use its powers under the Criminal Appeal Act 1968 to affirm the conviction on the ground that no miscarriage of justice had actually occurred (that is, the result would have been the same even if the judge had given correct directions to the jury). Nevertheless, tour operators who wish to protect themselves from allegations of false trade descriptions will say something to the effect, 'A swimming pool is now in the course of construction and is expected to be open in summer 1970'. Such phrasing could have been used by Sunair and it has the advantage that it is clearly outside the scope of s 14.

Beckett v Cohen (1973), provides a clear example of a statement of future intention: the only way in which a conviction could have been achieved in this case would have been if the prosecution had been able to show that there was no such intention when the statement was made. In this case, a builder promised that he would complete a garage within 10 days and that it would be similar to an existing garage. He took longer than 10 days and the garage he built was in some respects dissimilar to the existing garage. He was charged under s 14. The justices upheld the builder's submission that s 14 caught only representations as to what was currently being done or what had been done. The prosecutor appealed. *Held* by the divisional court of QBD: the appeal would be dismissed. Section 14 dealt only with statements of fact, past or present, not with promises about the future.

On the other hand, in *British Airways Board v Taylor* (1976), the House of Lords ruled that justices had been entitled to find that a statement that seats had been reserved on an aircraft was a statement of existing fact, rather than one of future intention. The case concerned the practice of overbooking, which is prevalent among airlines and tour operators. In the event, British Airways were acquitted on a technicality.

Cases where the maker of a statement of future intention never had any such intention

A distinction must be made between a genuine statement of future intention where, when the statement was made, there was every intention of carrying it out, and the situation where there was never any intention of carrying it out. In the latter case, the statement of future intention will be a false statement at the time it was made.

In *Bambury v Hounslow Borough Council* (1971), a customer saw a car at the premises of a company of which Bambury was a director. It had the word 'guaranteed' on it. Bambury told the customer that the word meant that if anything went wrong with the car within the next three months, the company would put it right. The customer bought the car and received an invoice which contained a clause which excluded the company's liability for faults. (The clause would have been ineffective since, although such exclusions of liability were permitted at that time, the exclusion clause came too late to be part of the contract.) The car developed several faults, including one in the clutch. The company repaired some of the faults but said there was nothing wrong with the clutch. This was put right by another garage. Bambury was charged under s 14 and convicted by the justices on the ground that when he made the statement about the guarantee, he made it knowing that it would not be honoured or recklessly without caring whether it would or would not be honoured. On appeal, the conviction was confirmed.

PROPOSALS FOR REFORM

In the *Review of the Trade Descriptions Act 1968: A Report by the Director General of Fair Trading* (Cmnd 6628, October 1975), the following proposals were made (see para 106):

(1) that the offences under s 14 should be made absolute (that is, strict liability should be imposed) subject only to the defences in s 24;

(2) that a new offence consisting of supplying services, to which a false description has been applied should be created. A defence to this offence would be available if, before the services were provided, the provider took reasonable steps to inform the intending recipient that the description was false but that he will be providing services which differ in certain respects;

(3) that ss 4 and 5 should apply, with the necessary changes, to the new offence;

(4) it should continue to be an offence to make false statements about the past or present supply of services;

(5) it should continue to be an offence to make false statements in respect of future supply of any services, accommodation or facilities but only in the following circumstances:

    (a) where the falsity of the statement can be demonstrated at the time it is made, irrespective of whether the services are provided; or

    (b) where the statement involves holding out or undertaking that services will be supplied and the person making the statement can be shown to have no intention of supplying them, or no reasonable expectation that they can be supplied by him or any other person, either at all, or in the form that has been described.

These recommendations have not, as yet, been given legislative effect.

Defences

Section 24 provides a range of defences to a prosecution under the Act. A further defence is provided by s 25, in circumstances where an advertisement is the means by which an offence is committed.

Section 24

Section 24(1) provides a defence where the commission of the offence was due to:

(a) a mistake; or

(b) reliance on information supplied by another; or

(c) the act or default of another; or

(d) an accident; or

(e) some other cause beyond the accused's control,

providing that the accused took all reasonable precautions and exercised all due diligence to avoid the commission of such an offence by himself or any person under his control.

Sub-section (2) goes on to say that where the defence relies on 'the act or default of another' or 'reliance on information supplied by another' the person charged shall not, without the leave of the court, be entitled to rely on the defence unless, seven clear days before the hearing, he has served a notice on the prosecutor giving such information identifying, or assisting in the identification of, the other person as was in his possession.

We will look now at some difficulties which have been encountered by the defence.

Another person

In *Tesco v Nattrass* (1971), Tesco displayed a poster at one of their stores advertising money off the usual price of a washing-powder. The shelf-stocker found that there were no more of the specially priced packs in stock. There were, however, some marked at the normal price so she put them out. She should have told the store manager but failed to do so. It was the manager's duty to ensure that the special offers were correctly on sale, but on his daily return to the company, he said that all special offers were OK. If he had known about the soap-powder, he would either have withdrawn the advertising poster or would have reduced the price of the normal packs. In their defence to a prosecution for mispricing the goods (the law as to which was at that time contained in the Trade Descriptions Act), Tesco put forward the defence that the offence was due to the act or default of another person. The store manager was duly named as the other person. On appeal to the House of Lords, it was held that the defence succeeded. The 'other person' could be someone in the employment of the alleged offender, providing that the other person was not part of the directing mind and will of the company. The directing mind and will of the company consists of the board of directors, the managing director and perhaps other superior officers who carry out the functions of management and speak and act as the company, plus persons to whom they delegate their functions. Of course, the 'other person', once named, could be prosecuted. However, it is not the policy of Trading Standards Officers to prosecute relatively minor employees.

One solution would be to impose vicarious liability on the company (that is, make the company liable for the default of its employee). However, in the 1976 Report (referred to above), it was concluded that the imposition of strict liability would not be justified. Lord Reid, one of the judges in the *Tesco* case, clearly thought that to impose liability on Tesco when the company had done all it could would be unjustifiable. However, the Law Commission, in its Working Paper No 44, *Criminal Liability of Corporations* (1972), was strongly of the opinion that vicarious liability should be imposed in relation to regulatory offences such as those contained in the Trade Descriptions Act.

What amounts to 'reasonable precautions' and 'all due diligence'?

Where the accused satisfies the requirements of para (a) of s 24(1) by showing, for example, that the offence was due to the act of a minor employee or that his supplier gave him faulty information about the goods, he must then show that he took 'reasonable precautions' and exercised 'all due diligence' as required by para (b). It would seem that this requirement is not easily satisfied. In the *Tesco* case (above), the court was clearly satisfied that the company had given proper instructions and training to its manager and that the manager's default could not, therefore, be laid at the door of the company. However, in *Garrett v Boot Chemists Ltd* (1980), Boots were charged with having on sale pencils which breached the Pencils and Graphic Instruments (Safety) Regulations 1974, to which a similar defence applies. They had informed their supplier about the regulations but the court held that this was not sufficient: they should have taken random samples, even though the court recognised that random sampling might not have disclosed the problem.

Disclaimers

The practice of using disclaimers in an attempt to avoid the provisions of the Act is widespread. It is particularly widespread in relation to odometer readings on used cars. To be effective the disclaimer 'must be as bold, precise and compelling as the trade description itself and must be effectively brought to the notice of any person to whom the goods may be supplied'. A leading case as to the form that disclaimers must take is *Norman v Bennett* (1974), in which Lord Widgery CJ said that in order to be effective the disclaimer 'must be as bold, precise and compelling as the trade description itself and must be effectively brought to the notice of any person to whom the goods may be supplied'.

In *K Lill Holdings v White* (1979), the practice of 'zeroing' the odometer, coupled with the use of a disclaimer, was approved by the divisional court of QBD since the purchaser would not be misled into thinking that the used car had covered no miles at all. However, this gives difficulties when the car passes into less scrupulous hands and the car is resold without the new low reading being disclaimed. It also seems to offend against the general principle laid down by the divisional court in *Newman v Hackney Borough Council* (below), to the effect that if you give the false description you cannot then disclaim the truth of it.

In *Corfield v Starr* (1981), the defendant took an odometer from one car and put it in another. He then put a notice on the dashboard which read: 'With deep regret due to the Customer's Protection Act we can no longer verify that the mileage shown on this vehicle is correct.' The divisional court of QBD directed the justices to convict on the grounds that the defendant should have made it clear that no reliance could be placed on the mileage reading or that the reading was meaningless. However, the court did not rule out the possibility that the mileage on a deliberately 'clocked' car could be disclaimed.

In *Newman v Hackney Borough Council* (1982), the odometer of a Triumph car was deliberately turned back from 46,328 miles to about 21,000 miles and then a disclaimer sticker was stuck over it. The divisional court of QBD approved the judgment of the circuit judge sitting in the Crown Court, to the effect that where the charge is one of supplying falsely described goods under s 1(1)(b) a disclaimer can validly be used, whereas when the charge is one of applying a false trade description to goods under s 1(1)(a), a disclaimer cannot be valid. The court realised that this might lead to difficulties where a trader had to alter the odometer for a legitimate reason but preferred to leave such a case to be dealt with as it arose.

In his *Review of the Trade Descriptions Act 1968* (Cmnd 6628, 1976), the DG, having reviewed the use of disclaimers, concluded that no legislation was required at the time. However, he thought that it might be advantageous to confer a power on the Secretary of State to regulate disclaimers by statutory order.

Misleading price indications

Part 3 of the Consumer Protection Act 1987 makes it a criminal offence to give a misleading price indication to a consumer, in the course of a business. There is also an offence relating to a price indication which, though correct when given, later becomes misleading. The misleading indication may relate to the price payable for goods, services, accommodation or facilities. The misleading indication must relate to the aggregate price payable.

The price indication is misleading if it indicates:

(a) that the price is less than it is. An example of this would be where goods are marked £2 on a supermarket shelf and £2.50 is demanded at the check-out;

(b) that the applicability of the prices does not depend on facts or circumstances on which its applicability does, in fact, depend. An example of this would be where, in order to obtain goods at the stated price, you would need to purchase more than one item and this fact was not made clear in the offer;

(c) that the price covers matters in respect of which an additional charge is, in fact, made. An example would be where an additional charge is made for post and packing which was not indicated in the offer;

(d) that a person who has in fact no such expectation:

   (i) expects the price to be increased or reduced (whether or not at a particular time or by a particular amount). An example would be where an offer is made at a lower price, with an indication that the post-sale price is to be higher. If there is no intention to increase the price post-sale, an offence will have been committed;

   (ii) expects the price, or the price as increased or reduced, to be maintained (whether or not for a particular period). An example would be where an offer was expressed to end on a particular date, when there was no intention of ending it on that date;

(e) that the facts or circumstances by reference to which the consumers might reasonably be expected to judge the validity of any relevant comparison made or implied by the (price) indication, are not what in fact they are. An example would be a comparison between a flat-pack price and a ready-assembled price when the goods are not, in fact, available ready-assembled.

A code of practice has been issued under the Act. This does not in itself create offences but may be used in support of the contention that the person who has contravened the code has committed an offence.

Defences

There are a number of defences to the offence. Four are limited in scope. The fifth is the 'due diligence' defence, found in other legislation. This provides that it shall be a defence for a person to show that he took all reasonable steps and exercised all due diligence to avoid committing an offence.

CHAPTER 27

NEGLIGENCE (1)

LAW OF TORT

Nature of a tort

A tort is a civil wrong, like a breach of contract or a breach of trust. It differs from those two because, instead of being a breach of a duty which has been undertaken by agreement, the duty which is breached in tort is a duty which is imposed by the law, irrespective of agreement. There is, nevertheless, an overlap between contract and tort, particularly where a party has contracted to supply a service. The law of contract implies a term into the contract that it will be undertaken with due care and skill. However, such a duty will arise independently of the contract by virtue of the tort of negligence. The effect of this is that there is a concurrent duty in tort and contract in such cases. The claimant may choose whether to sue for breach of contract or for the tort of negligence (usually he will hedge his bets by including both). In practice, unless the employee's loss is purely economic (a concept we will look at later), the tort action offers advantages over the contract action (for example, the operation of the rules relating to the remoteness of damage will normally be more advantageous in tort), so that it is the tort action which we will consider here.

The law of tort covers a wide number of differing situations. It has a wide application among the whole of society. It covers private activities as well as business activities. Thus, if your property emits smells or noise, for example, which affect your neighbour's enjoyment of his property (for example, he can't get to sleep at night), this may amount to the tort of nuisance. If you copy sheet music composed by another person or copy someone else's patented invention, this may be breach of copyright or infringement of patent. If you induce someone to buy shares in a company by dishonest statements as to the current level of profits, you commit the tort of deceit. If you claim that your competitor's fast food restaurant sells horseburgers rather than beefburgers, this may amount to the tort of libel or slander. However, in this book we don't have space for all the torts you may encounter in business. Therefore, we will deal only with negligence, which is by far the most important tort of general application, and with two torts which are closely associated with negligence, breach of statutory duty and occupiers' liability.

Breach of duty and its consequences

The torts we are considering in this text each have general principles of general application. Thus, some of the examples we will use do not relate to business. However, wherever possible, examples have been chosen which relate to business (including public services), so that the student may recognise the implications of the principle in a business context.

Many of our illustrative cases involve an employee suing an employer. Where there is a contract of employment, there is an implied term in each employee's contract of employment that the employer will provide a safe working environment. This is a concept which includes a matrix of factors. However, in relation to contractual duties which are carried out negligently, in breach of statutory duty, or in breach of the Occupiers' Liability Act, and which result in physical damage to the employee or his/her property, there is usually a concurrent liability in the law of tort. (Though, in such a case, the victim doesn't get double the damages!)

Importance of the three torts

The three torts with which we are dealing, negligence, breach of statutory duty and occupiers' liability, are of great importance in the workplace. They establish principles governing liability in the following circumstances relating to business (and in many other circumstances besides these):

(a) employers' and employees' civil liability for health and safety issues;

(b) employers' and employees' civil liability for the safety of members of the public;

(c) liability of professionals such as solicitors, accountants and estate agents for professional negligence;

(d) liability of public services such as the police, the fire brigade, the ambulance service, the Crown Prosecution Service, local authority social services, etc, to members of the public or to the 'clients' with whom they deal.

Importance of insurance in tort claims

At the outset, it is important to take note of the relevance of insurance to negligence claims. Most negligence claims come from one of two sources:

(a) road traffic accidents (which often involve employees, particularly lorry drivers, who are driving in the course of their employment); and

(b) accidents in the workplace.

However, increasing numbers are coming from:

(c) medical negligence;

(d) professional negligence (for example, a solicitor or accountant who gives negligent advice to his/her client); and

(e) from the negligence of public authorities towards claimants who were relying upon the authority to take care in their dealings with the claimant. Examples include: prisons or police ensuring the safety of persons in their custody; police ensuring the safety of the spectators at a football match; or social services responsibility for ensuring that persons in their care are not physically abused.

In almost all of these cases, the real defendant is an insurance company unless, as is the case with certain large organisations (such as the National Health Service), the organisation is permitted to act as its own insurer. An important point to remember is that an insurance company is not compelled to pay out under a liability insurance unless the insured party would be legally liable to pay. Sometimes students assume that if an insured person causes an injury or illness to another person, then the insured person's insurance company will automatically pay damages. This is not the case. The insurance company is only bound to pay if it is established that the insured party would be liable to pay, most usually because of negligence, breach of statutory duty or occupiers' liability. If the insured is not liable, then neither is his insurance company (though it must be added that an insurance company will often settle a case where liability has not been fully established, simply in order to avoid the expense of protracted legal proceedings which, in the end, they might lose).

Example

Paula is employed by Richard. She is injured at work by a fork-lift truck driven by Quentin. Paula claims that Quentin is wholly to blame. Quentin says that Paula ran out from behind a row of storage racks, right into the path of the truck (that is, he is claiming that she was contributorily negligent – a defence which, if established, will have the effect of reducing the amount of damages to which Paula is entitled). Paula is making a claim of negligence. The claim may be that Quentin was driving the truck negligently. On the other hand, it may be that Richard has been negligent by not ensuring that Quentin had the appropriate training or that the layout of the warehouse was such that it was inherently dangerous for anyone to walk through it. Or it may be both. In such a case, Paula may join Quentin and Richard as defendants. However, in reality, neither of those two are the real defendants in the case. The real defendant is Mega Insurance, with whom Richard has an insurance covering him against tort liability to pay damages in the case of injury or illness of an employee. Such insurance is compulsory under the Employers' Liability (Compulsory Insurance) Act 1969. The insurance must be for payment of up to £2 million in respect of each occurrence. As we shall see, the fact that Quentin, a fairly low-paid employee, is unable to meet the financial burden of damages will not matter in practice. This is because Richard is vicariously liable for Quentin's negligence. Therefore, in practice, Paula may not bother to include Quentin as a defendant, or if she does so initially, it may be that she will not pursue the case against Quentin, once it becomes clear that the insurance company will shoulder any liability.

What happens in practice is that Mega Insurance takes over the conduct of Richard's (and therefore, indirectly, Quentin's) defence. What will happen is that Mega will make an offer to settle Paula's claim. It may be that the process will become protracted, as offers are refused and counter-offers are made. It would not be unusual for Mega to offer Paula as little as they think they can get away with in relation to damages and also to protract the correspondence so that, eventually, Paula will become so frustrated by the whole process that she will be willing to settle her claim for whatever the insurance company's offer happens to amount to at the moment when Paula reaches the end of her tether. In fairness, we should balance this somewhat cynical view by pointing out that insurance companies are not philanthropic organisations. They would argue that they owe a duty to their shareholders to bargain with claimants in order to keep claims within reasonable bounds. They would also point to the increasing incidence of fraudulent claims – with claimants not only exaggerating the injuries they have suffered but also exaggerating the financial costs they have incurred as a result of those injuries.

From Paula's point of view, there may be two inducements to settle. First she needs to keep an eye on her mounting legal costs, though she may enter into a conditional fee arrangement with her solicitor (see below) and cover them by an insurance. Secondly, the insurance company may make a payment into court (known in lawyers' shorthand as a 'payment in'). This is a procedure which favours the skilful defendant. Mega assesses the amount of damages which Paula may receive if she is successful. The insurers will come up with a maximum amount and a minimum amount. They then pay into the court office a settlement sum which is usually towards the minimum amount which Paula may expect to receive. The significance of this is that if Paula proceeds with the case and, after judgment, it transpires that the award of damages is equal to or less than the amount of the payment in, the costs of the case from the time of the payment in fall upon the claimant rather than, as would normally be the case, upon the defendant.

Should Paula refuse to compromise her claim, with the result that the case reaches court, the case will be entered as *Paula v Richard*. However, any costs and damages ordered to be paid by Richard as a result of the case will be paid by Mega Insurance, under the terms of Richard's insurance policy.

If Quentin had injured a member of the public, rather than a fellow employee, by his negligence, Richard will still be vicariously liable. However, the relevant insurance will be a public liability insurance. This is not compulsory, though it is strongly arguable that it should be. Most businesses carry public liability insurance. If Richard is insured, the outcome is similar to that in Paula's case, above. If not, Richard will be responsible for any damages and costs awarded against him.

Solicitors must insure against liability for professional negligence. As might be expected, insurance premiums have risen significantly in the light of the sharp increase in claims over the past two decades. Hospital doctors no longer have to insure. Claims for medical negligence are settled by the health authority which employs them.

Who can be sued?

There are two matters to be considered. The first relates to the circumstances in which one person can be vicariously liable for the tort of another. Since we are dealing mainly with injuries arising in the course of employment, we will restrict ourselves to considering the vicarious liability of an employer for the torts of his employees. The second relates to the situation where more than one person is liable for a tort.

Vicarious liability

An employer is vicariously liable for the torts of his employees if they are committed in the course of the employee's employment. There is no fundamental logic underlying this principle. It is simply a matter of practical justice. The employer puts his employee in a position where the employee may commit a tort. Therefore, the employer is liable to the injured party. This is the case even though the employer was not present when the tort was committed and even though the employer may have expressly forbidden the employee to do the act which caused the damage.

The fact that the employer is vicariously liable does not negative the liability of the employee. The employer and employee are, in law, joint tortfeasors (a 'tortfeasor' is a person who has committed a tort). Because the employer will usually be insured, the claimant will normally proceed against the employer in order to get the benefit of the insurance. However, there is nothing in law to stop the claimant suing the employee and enforcing the judgment against him. (Similarly, if the employer is sued, the employer can seek an indemnity from the employee – see below.)

Some cases involve the employer in a purely vicarious liability in that the employer was in no way to blame for the events in respect of which he is being made liable. In other cases, the allegation may be that the employer is vicariously liable for his employee's negligence and is also liable because he, the employer, was negligent in his own right.

As we have seen, in nearly all cases, the real defendant in the case is not the employer but the employer's insurance company.

In order for the employer to be made liable, two conditions must be satisfied:

(a) *The employer is liable only for the torts of his employees, employed under a contract of service*

The employer is generally not liable for the torts of independent contractors. The distinction is between a person who is employed under a contract of service (an employee) and one who is employed under a contract for services (an independent contractor).

Example

Sally owns a large factory. She employs Terry as a maintenance man, deducting PAYE tax and Class 1 National Insurance Contributions from Terry's wages and paying employers' National Insurance Contributions herself, in respect of Terry. It is reasonably clear that Terry is employed under a contract of service and, as such, is an employee for whom Sally will be vicariously liable.

On the other hand, suppose that, whenever Sally required maintenance work to be done, she called in Unwin's Property Services. They send someone to carry out the specified work and then send Sally a bill, including VAT. Unwin's Property Services will be employed under a contract for services and, as such, will be an independent contractor (or self-employed person), for whom Sally will not be vicariously liable.

Borderline cases

It can be difficult in borderline cases to determine whether the person in question is an employee or an independent contractor. Because of the rise in the cost of employing people, and because of the cost of employment protection provisions (employees are entitled to compensation for unfair dismissal, redundancy pay, maternity pay, etc, – independent contractors are not) there has been some activity by employers, over the past 30 years or so, aimed at dressing up a contract of service (employer liable) so that it appears to be a contract for services (employer not liable).

The attraction to the employee to agree to this is that, at least in the short term, he makes a financial gain because the tax and national insurance systems tend to extract less money from people employed under a contract for services (that is, self-employed people). It is when he gets injured or seeks compensation for dismissal that he begins to see the other side of the picture and to claim that he is, in legal reality, an employee.

Of course, the courts could answer any such claims by saying that if a person has agreed to become employed under a contract for services, then that is an end to the matter. However, the courts have not done this, perhaps because, in certain cases, there is a real question mark over whether the employee has genuinely agreed to become employed under a contract for services, or whether he has agreed as an alternative to losing his job. Another reason may be a wish to prevent employer and compliant employees effectively reducing government revenue from tax and national insurance.

The courts decide the issue by applying one or more of a number of tests. Only in cases where the scales are equally balanced between the two will the court take into account the parties' wishes. The main factors which the courts use to determine the issue include the following.

Control: to what extent has the employer the right to control not only what is done but also the way in which it is done. The more control exerted by the employer the more likely the court is to hold that the employee is employed under a contract of service.

The incidence of risk and potential for gain: to what extent is the employee risking his own money in the enterprise? Does the employee or the employer own the tools, machinery, etc, necessary to do the job? The heavier the investment in tools, etc, by the employee, the more likely it is that he is self-employed rather than employed. To what extent can the employee make a greater income by more efficient organisation of his work? The greater the potential for gain through efficiency, the more likely it is that the employee is self-employed (that is, employed under a contact for services).

Mutuality of obligation: this question usually arises with respect to casual workers. The question is whether the employer is bound to offer the work to the employee if work is available and, if the work is offered, whether the worker is obliged to accept the work. If there is an obligation by the employer to offer and a corresponding obligation by the employee to accept, the worker is likely to be employed under a contract of service (it is said that there is a 'mutuality of obligation').

The commercial reality of the situation: this simply consists of asking whether the employee is, realistically, in business on his own account. Thus, if a supermarket tried to 'dress-up' the contracts of its check-out assistants and designate them as being employed under a 'contract for services' (or self-employed), it might purport to hire out a check-out position to the employee and pay the employee a commission on the amount of cash passing through the check-out, after deducting the hire charge. In such circumstances, the court would be likely to hold that the employee was engaged in the business of the supermarket, not in a business of his own.

Payment of tax and national insurance: the fact that the employee pays his own tax and national insurance, which self-employed people do, rather than having it deducted at source by the employer, as employed persons do, is not conclusive one way or the other. However, in a borderline case, it may be that because the employee has been accepted by the Inland Revenue and Social Security authorities as being self-employed, the court is prepared to acquiesce in their decision.

It would be pointless citing a list of cases to illustrate the distinction because, for one case which says that there is a mutuality of obligation and therefore the employee is employed under a contract of service, there is an identical case which holds that there is no mutuality of obligation and therefore the employee is self-employed. Similar remarks apply in relation to the other tests. The best we can say is that each case is decided on its own particular facts, taking into account the factors we have identified above.

We will, nevertheless, look at one or two illustrative examples. The THF case has been chosen because the tribunal analysed the various important factors with extreme thoroughness. Nevertheless, it is strongly arguable that they came to the wrong conclusion. What do you think?

In *O'Kelly v Trust House Forte* (1983), O'Kelly had worked as a 'regular casual' at THF's banqueting department at Grosvenor House Hotel. He claimed unfair dismissal and the tribunal had to decide, as a preliminary point, whether or not he was an employee. The tribunal delivered a very careful judgment in which they listed all the factors which they saw as being consistent with a contract of employment; all the factors which they viewed as pointing to a contract for services; and all the factors which they regarded as being inconclusive one way or the other.

The factors in favour of O'Kelly being an employee were as follows:

(a) he performed his services in return for remuneration for the work actually performed. He did not invest his own capital and did not stand to gain or lose from the commercial success of the functions organised by the banqueting department;

(b) he performed his work under the control of THF;

(c) when he attended at functions, he was part of the employer's organisation and for the purpose of ensuring the smooth running of the business, he and the other casuals were represented in the staff consultation process;

(d) when he was working, he was carrying on the business of THF;

(e) clothing and equipment were provided by THF;

(f) O'Kelly was paid weekly in arrears and had PAYE tax and social security contributions deducted;

(g) the casuals' work was organised on a rota basis and they required permission to take time off from rostered duties;

(h) there was a disciplinary and grievance procedure;

(i) there was holiday pay or an incentive bonus calculated by reference to past service.

The following factors were found to be not inconsistent with a contract of employment (that is, the factors were regarded as being neutral):

(j) the applicants were paid for work they actually performed and did not receive a regular wage or retainer. However, the method of calculating the remuneration is not an essential part of the employment relationship;

(k) casual workers were not remunerated on the same basis as permanent employees, did not receive sick pay, were not included in THF's staff pension scheme, and did not receive fringe benefits accorded to established employees. There was, however, no objection to employers adopting different terms and conditions for different categories of employee (note that if the casuals were treated as part-time employees, which despite the finding of the tribunal it is arguable that they were, the Part-Time Workers (Prevention of Less Favourable Treatment) Regulations 2000 would apply);

(l) there were no regular or assured working hours. It is not a requirement of employment that there should be normal working hours;

(m) casual workers were not provided with written particulars of employment. If it is established that casual workers are employees there is a statutory obligation to furnish written particulars.

The following factors were found to be inconsistent with the relationship being one of employer/employee:

(n) the engagement was terminable without notice on either side;

(o) the applicants had the right to decide whether or not to accept the work, although whether or not it would be in their interest to exercise the right is another matter (that is, they might not be offered work in the future);

(p) THF had no obligation to provide any work;

(q) during the subsistence of the relationship it was the parties' view that casual workers were engaged under successive contracts for services;

(r) it is the recognised custom and practice of the industry that casual workers are engaged under contracts for services.

Despite the fact that this process of analysis seemed to favour the conclusion that the contract was one of service, the tribunal reached the conclusion that one overriding factor must lead to the conclusion that the workers were in business on their own account. The overriding factor was the lack of mutuality of obligation, that is, if the work was available, THF were not bound to offer the work to O'Kelly and, conversely, if the work were offered, O'Kelly had no obligation to accept it. There are, however, similar cases where the courts have given less emphasis to the mutuality of obligation factor and have been prepared to hold that the employees were employed under a contract of service. It is submitted that this should also have been the decision in this case.

Note: sometimes the employee is allowed to have his cake (that is, the lower tax and national insurance payments which go with being self-employed) and eat it too. There are certain cases in which the employee was designated 'self-employed' but was injured at work. If he could show that he was employed under a contract of service rather than a contract for services, the employer would be in breach of duty towards him. If, however, he was self-employed, the employer owed him no duty and therefore, if the employee did not carry accident insurance, he went uncompensated, except by the state social security system, which does not offer particularly generous levels of benefit.

In *Ferguson v Dawson and Partners* (1976), F worked for the defendant on terms which involved 'no cards' and working the 'lump' (that is, wages were paid in a lump sum without deduction of PAYE tax or national insurance contributions). F gave a false name which he signed when receiving his wages. He was working on a flat roof when he fell and suffered serious injuries. He was awarded damages of £30,387.88 against the defendants for breach of statutory duty, because contrary to the Construction (Working Places) Regulations 1966, there was no guard rail on the roof. However, the company was liable only if F was employed under a contract of service rather than being an independent contractor. The company therefore appealed on the grounds that F was not an employee. *Held*: while the agreement of the parties as to the nature of the contract between them was a relevant factor, it was not conclusive. On the facts of the case, the trial judge had correctly found that, according to the established tests, in reality the relationship of employer/employee existed. Note: the issue of illegality will be relevant where the parties have colluded to defraud the Inland Revenue (see Chapter 14, p 302). However, as this issue was not raised by either party at the original trial, the Court of Appeal felt that it would be unjust to hold that the contract was affected by illegality, since F had not been given the opportunity of being cross-examined (and thus giving an explanation) on the issue.

Similarly, in *Lane v Shire Roofing* (1995), lane had carried on business as a self-employed roofing contractor for some considerable time. He agreed to do a job for the defendant for a lump sum, with the defendant supplying the materials. He took his own ladder to the site and fell off it while doing the job. It was held that Lane was employed under a contract of service and that the defendant was liable.

Employees on loan to a sub-employer

The general rule here is that the main employer remains the employer, particularly where the employee is hired out to operate plant or machinery which has been hired by the main employer to the sub-employer. However, in the case of plant-hire companies, for example, it is usual for the contract between the main employer and the sub-employer to contain a standard term that the sub-employer shall be liable for meeting any claims arising out of the operation of the plant. Thus, although the main employer remains, in law, the employer, the issue of liability is decided by the contract between the main employer and the sub-employer.

Independent contractors

The employer will not be liable for the torts of independent contractors, (for example, a company called in to do repairs to the employer's factory), unless:

(a) the employer has authorised or ratified the tort;

(b) the employer has selected an incompetent contractor or gives a competent contractor incomplete or incorrect instructions;

(c) where the work done by the contractor is to satisfy the employer's statutory duty – responsibility for complying with statutory duty generally cannot be delegated and if the contractor performs his task inadequately, the employer nevertheless remains liable;

(d) the work being done by the independent contractor is on or near the highway;

(e) where a hospital patient is being treated by an independent practitioner selected by the hospital rather than by the patient.

Note that where the independent contractor is in breach of contract to the employer, although the employer will be primarily liable to pay damages, he will be able to recoup them if, as will often be the case, the independent contractor is in breach of his contract with the employer or if the independent contractor is liable to the employer for negligence.

(b) The employee must commit the tort in the course of his/her employment

As a general rule, providing the employee is doing what he/she has been paid to do, the employer will be liable for a tort committed by the employee. This is so even though the employee is doing something he has been forbidden to do.

Limpus v London General Omnibus Co (1862)

Drivers employed by the bus company to drive horse drawn buses were specifically forbidden to race with other drivers. Nevertheless, a driver employed by the company injured the plaintiff while racing with the driver of a rival company. The London General Omnibus Company denied they were vicariously liable since they had instructed their driver not to race. *Held*: the Company was liable since the driver was doing what he was paid to do, albeit wrongfully.

In *Century Insurance v Northern Ireland Transport Board* (1942), a tanker driver decided to have a cigarette while delivering petrol to a petrol station. He threw down a lighted match. The resulting explosion destroyed the station. *Held*: the driver's employer was vicariously liable. The fact that he was doing something for his own convenience did not take him outside the course of his employment.

However, if the employee is undertaking an activity which he is not paid to do, the employer will not be vicariously liable.

Beard v London General Omnibus Co (1900)

A bus conductor decided, in the absence of the driver, to turn the bus round when it reached its terminus. In doing so he ran over a pedestrian. It was held that his employer was not vicariously liable since the driver was doing something which was outside the scope of his employment

In a more modern example, it has been held that a cleaner, employed by cleaning contractors, was not in the course of employment when he used a customer's telephone to make unauthorised international telephone calls. He was employed to clean telephones, not to use them.

A deviation *while in the course of the employer's business* will be treated as being in the course of employment. For example, a bus driver who, while carrying a bus load of boys, took an unauthorised route in order to follow a bus load of girls, was held to be in the course of his employment. However, a driver who, *after completing his deliveries*, went on a detour to visit his brother-in-law was held to be not in the course of his employment.

Joint tortfeasors

Where more than one person is liable in respect of the same tort they are called 'joint tortfeasors'. Where two or more persons cause the same damage, even though they act separately, they are liable jointly. This means that the injured party may sue any one or more of them. In such a case, the court will apportion the blame between the defendants. However, the claimant may enforce the full amount of the judgment against any one of them, leaving that party to claim back the appropriate contribution from his fellow defendants.

An employer who is vicariously liable for his employee will be entitled either:

(a) to an *indemnity* (that is, the employee must reimburse the employer for what he has paid out in respect of the employee's tort) because of the employee's breach of contract; or

(b) a *contribution* because the employer and employee are treated as joint-tortfeasors. In the latter case, the contribution will be 100% unless the employer is in some way at fault.

(a) Breach of contract by the employee

The employee has a duty to exercise due care and skill in performing his contract of employment. If he fails to do his, he is in breach of his contract of employment and will be liable to pay damages to his employer.

Lister v Romford Ice and Cold Storage Co (1957)

L Jnr was employed by R as a lorry driver. His father was also employed by the Company and acted as L Jnr's 'mate'. One day, L performed a backing manoeuvre during which he knocked down and injured his father. L Snr claimed damages from the company as being vicariously liable for the negligent driving of his son. The company, in turn, claimed an indemnity from the son on the grounds (a) that he was in breach of an implied term in his contract of employment that he would carry out his duties with due skill and care, and (b) that he owed them a 100% contribution as a joint tortfeasor.

Damages of £2,400 were awarded to the father, reduced by one third on the ground of the father's contributory negligence.

Held by the House of Lords: Lister Jnr had been in breach of an implied term in the contract of employment to the effect that he would carry out his duties with due care and skill. Lister Jnr had, therefore, to indemnify his employer both as to the damages paid to his father and as to the costs of defending the case. Two of the Lords also held that L Jnr owed his employer a 100% contribution as a joint tortfeasor.

(b) Contribution

Even where there is no breach of contract, the employee will have to pay a contribution on the ground that he/she is a joint tortfeasor. In a case where there is no fault on the part of the employer, the employee's contribution will be assessed at 100%.

Harvey v RG O'Dell (1958)

A storekeeper who sometimes used his motor-cycle and sidecar combination on his employer's business was held not liable for breach of contract when he injured a fellow workman whilst driving the combination negligently. This was because he was employed as a storeman, not as a motor-cycle and sidecar driver. However, in the case of joint tortfeasors, the court has the power to apportion the blame between them. Since the employer was himself in no way to blame, his liability deriving entirely vicariously because he was the employer of the driver of the combination, the driver's contribution was assessed at 100% (which will normally always be the case where the employer's liability is purely vicarious). This means that although the victim is entitled to claim 100% of his damages from whichever can afford to pay, the party who does pay can claim the appropriate contribution from the other. In this case, the driver was ordered to pay a 100% contribution, so that, although the employer paid the full amount of the damages initially, he was entitled to claim a full indemnity from the estate of the motor-cycle driver.

In practice, this can give rise to a complex chain of events: Len is a lorry driver employed by Ellen. Len negligently injures Tessa. Tessa sues Len and Ellen (who is vicariously liable for Len's tort and is thus a joint tortfeasor). Ellen and Len are found liable. Ellen is insured against such liability and therefore Insurers (Ellen's insurance company) pays the damages to Tessa. However, in such a case, the insurance company has a right of subrogation, which means that the insurance company can put itself in the shoes of the insured and therefore may pursue whatever claims the insured may have against the person who actually caused the loss which was insured. Insurers therefore insists that Ellen should claim against Len for breach of contract (subject to Insurers promising to indemnify Ellen in respect of her costs). In practice, all the related issues are usually decided at one hearing in order to minimise costs. Len is found liable and must indemnify Ellen, who in turn must indemnify Insurers, in respect of the damages paid to Tessa.

As a result of the *Lister* and the *Harvey* cases, MPs began to raise doubts as to whether this potentially financially crippling liability was socially acceptable. In the face of threats of a parliamentary enquiry, which might have resulted in legislation adverse to the insurance companies, the companies announced their intention not to pursue claims for indemnities from persons who injured fellow employees, unless the injury was caused by outrageous conduct or the legal action is a collusion between the injured employee and the employee who has caused the injury. In practice, this concession appears to have been extended to cases where third parties are injured also.

THE TORT OF NEGLIGENCE

As its name suggests, the tort of negligence exists to compensate one party for harm caused to him/her by the negligent conduct of another party. We commonly call these situations 'accidents' or 'mistakes' but where, as is almost always the case, one party is at fault, there is a potential liability for negligence.

Furthermore, it does not matter if the injured party is himself partly to blame. Until the Law Reform (Contributory Negligence Act) 1945, if the claimant bore more than an insignificant share of the blame for an accident, the law refused his claim in its entirety. Thus, if the claimant were severely injured in an accident for which he was adjudged to be 20% to blame, the law would give him no recompense. However, since the 1945 Act, the court may assess the damage which the claimant has suffered and then reduce the amount of his damages by the proportion for which the claimant was to blame. This is the case even where the claimant is substantially to blame (for example, contributory negligence has been assessed as high as 80%).

The compensation culture

The tort of negligence has developed at a tremendous rate in recent years and is likely to continue to do so. The 'compensation culture', developed in the 1980s and 90s has led to aggressive advertising of the services of solicitors and 'accident specialists'. If a person has been injured in any way through the fault of another person ('person' here includes corporate bodies, such as companies, who can be liable where someone who is acting on their behalf does so negligently), the specialist will pursue a claim on their behalf, usually using a conditional fee arrangement (see below). Fundamental to the agreement is that the potential claimant enter into an insurance against the risk that they might lose and might, therefore, need to pay costs. A number of solicitors are members of an organisation which offers such insurance at a very modest premium. However, a criticism which has been levelled against independent companies which pursue personal injury claims on behalf of clients is that they make significant profits from charging large insurance premiums, which are then deducted from the damages which are secured on behalf of the successful claimant.

For many years, claims were somewhat restricted by two main factors:

(a) If the claimant were to lose the case, he was forced to pay the legal costs not only of himself, but also of the winning party. This was a powerful disincentive unless the claimant had a reasonably water-tight case. Legal costs, even in a case which is compromised (or abandoned) before it reaches court, can be substantial. If the case is lost after a court hearing, the costs can be enormous. However, negligence claims have now been made easier by the 'no win, no pay' situation introduced by the conditional fee. In this case, a claimant pays a one-off insurance fee and, if the client loses, the other party's costs are paid by the insurance company, not by the losing client as would normally be the case. If the client wins, the solicitor gets his costs plus, where agreed, an additional fixed percentage (which can be as much as 100%) of his costs. This will be partially offset by the fact that any disbursements and basic costs will be recovered from the other side. This is not like the US system of contingency fees, where the lawyer gets a percentage of the damages awarded. The US system is thought to encourage unethical conduct (for example, ambulance chasing) and to inflate the amount of awards because the court is aware that a substantial slice will go to the claimant's lawyer.

(b) Until the case of *Anns v Merton Borough Council* (1978), the courts tended to be cautious in relation to allowing a negligence claim, unless it was similar in type to a claim which had been allowed previously. The case of *Anns* suggested a more liberal approach. However, this approach has been much criticised both by judges and academics, to the extent where, nowadays, it can be regarded as having been discredited. Thus, although, no doubt, the range of situations in which a duty is owed will continue to expand, they are likely to do so 'incrementally', that is, the new circumstance will bear a very close relationship to a circumstance in which a duty has previously been held to exist.

Scope of negligence

The tort of negligence is defined in *Winfield and Jolowicz on Tort* as follows:

> Negligence as a tort is the breach of a legal duty to take care which results in damage, undesired by the defendant, to the claimant.

We should note that the word 'negligence' is used in a special way. It means a complex of factors which must be proved before the claimant is able to succeed. So, the person who is found liable for negligence will always have been careless, but carelessness does not necessarily amount to negligence. For example, in *Barnett v Kensington and Chelsea Hospital Management Committee* (1968), B drank some tea which had been contaminated with arsenic and complained of vomiting for three hours. He went to a hospital casualty department. No-one examined him but the doctor on duty sent a message telling him to go to his GP. Five hours later he died. His widow sued for negligence. it was found as a fact that the poison in his system had reached such an advanced state that whatever had been done for him at the hospital, he would have died anyway. *Held*: although the duty doctor had been careless and had breached his duty of care, this *did not amount* to the tort of negligence since the carelessness was not the cause of B's death.

Balancing risks

The tort of negligence compels those who take *unjustifiable risks* in the conduct of their activities, to pay damages to anyone who suffers injury as a result. The law does not expect people not to take any risks. For example, the annual horrendous toll which road accidents take in relation to human life, limb and property could be significantly reduced if society were to return to the horse and cart as a means of transport. However, such a move would have a disastrously damaging effect on the quality of many areas of human activity. So, the law does not prohibit activities which involve risk, but it does say that the risks which are taken must be reasonable in the circumstances. For example, in *Watt v Hertfordshire County Council* (1954), a fire brigade transported a jack on an unsuitable vehicle because a suitable one was not available. The reason it did this was in order to save the life of a person trapped in a motor vehicle. The jack was not properly secured and, as a result, fell upon the plaintiff's ankle and injured it. It was held that the purpose to be achieve justified the risk and that, therefore, the brigade was not negligent.

One problem which is recurring in relation to negligence relates to the question of allocation of resources, particularly in the public sector where the allocation of resources is politically sensitive. At government level, it is politically unpopular to increase taxes in order to provide additional funding. The alternative, if additional funding is required, is to cut the level of expenditure elsewhere. However, it is often difficult to cut expenditure without engendering political protest. This inevitably has an effect at local level. For example, suppose a health authority is found liable because a patient dies owing to the fact that his illness was not diagnosed quickly enough in the casualty department. The hospital reacts by employing more casualty staff. However, it must save money elsewhere and therefore cuts down on security staff. The hospital is then found liable for an injury caused by a violent patient to a nurse, which could have been prevented with a better level of security.

It is perhaps, therefore, not surprising that there has been a significant rise in negligence actions against public bodies over the last decade or so. Many of these do not involve blameworthy conduct in the sense that the defendant has been completely inadvertent to the risk which has eventually materialised and caused damage. More commonly, it has been a case of a hard-pressed service vainly trying to juggle resources in order to achieve its objectives and, in doing so, taking risks which occasionally turn out to be an unfortunate miscalculation.

Ironically, the Audit Commission has calculated that the increase in funding which was allocated to the health service for the year 2000 will be entirely swallowed up in settling claims for medical negligence.

What must be proved?

To succeed in a claim for negligence, the claimant must prove three things. These are:

(a) that he comes within the category of people in respect of whom the defendant had a duty to take care when he was doing (or not doing) what he did (or did not) do. This is often shortened to 'duty of care';

(b) that the defendant breached the duty to take care;

(c) that the defendant's breach caused the damage that the claimant is claiming.

Once it is found that the defendant is liable for negligence, there is the further issue as to how much compensation (that is, damages) should be awarded to the claimant in consequence.

We will deal with these matters in turn.

(a) The existence of a duty of care

The concept of duty of care is *a control mechanism* imposed in law in order to contain the number of possible actions against a negligent party within reasonable bounds. If a court holds that a defendant owes the claimant no duty of care, the action is struck-out and proceeds no further. Establishing the existence of a duty of care is clearly an important hurdle to get over. However, since the decision of the European Court of Human Rights in the *Osman* case (see below), the courts have become noticeably less willing to hold that a duty of care does not exist, particularly when the main reason why not is simply a matter of policy. However, it is important to note that simply because a case is allowed to proceed it does not necessarily mean that the claimant will be successful. He still has to proved that the duty of care was breached and that damage resulted from the breach.

This control mechanism of duty of care has been criticised by certain academic writers, who contend that if a person has suffered damage which can be attributed to the negligent action of another, then the other should be liable. It is arguable that the law is now progressing in this direction. Opponents of this view usually invoke the *floodgates argument*; that is, if we adopt this view where will it end? For example, if an outbreak of foot and mouth disease is traced to one particular farm and is attributed to the negligence of the farmer, is the farmer to be liable to everyone up and down the country who may suffer loss or injury because of the spread of the disease? This may include not just other farmers whose livestock has to be destroyed, but transport firms who lose money because they are not able to make their usual deliveries until the disease is cleared up; meat exporters; auctioneers who cannot hold their usual livestock markets, etc.

The courts approach such extensions of liability with extreme caution and, in essence, the requirement of a duty of care allows only a foreseeable claimant, who is reasonably 'proximate' to the defendant, to sue. It denies claimants who are not reasonably foreseeable and are not 'proximate' a remedy. The law does this on the ground that the defendant did not owe the claimant a duty of care.

The 'neighbour' test

The principle behind the idea of the duty of care, which has been modified over the years, is famously set-out by Lord Atkin in the case of *Donoghue v Stevenson* (1932), p 580 (see Chapter 25, p 546 for the facts of the case) as follows:

> The rule that you are to love your neighbour becomes in law, you must not injure your neighbour; and the lawyer's question, Who is my neighbour? receives a restricted reply. You must take reasonable care to avoid acts or omissions which you can reasonably foresee would be likely to injure your neighbour. Who, then, in law, is my neighbour? The answer seems to be – persons who are so closely and directly affected by my act that I ought to have them in contemplation as being so affected when I am directing my mind to the acts or omissions which are called into question.

Thus, it has to be foreseeable that the act (or omission) will injure someone, and that he must be someone closely and directly affected by the act or omission.

The 'neighbour test' has been widely criticised by academics as concentrating too much on foreseeability, but the idea that the person injured has to be 'someone closely and directly affected' clearly imports the idea that there must be some proximity between the claimant and the defendant's action or failure to act.

Established 'duty of care' situations

In many cases, it will be undeniable that the defendant owes the claimant a duty of care. This is because the claimant and the defendant have a particular relationship (or proximity) to each other, which is established as giving rise to a duty of care.

Thus, an employer owes a duty of care to his employee; a manufacturer or repairer of goods owes a duty of care to those who use the goods (whether a duty is owed to a non-user injured by a defect in negligently manufactured or repaired goods is a matter determined by general principle); road users owe a duty of care to other road users, within a reasonable physical proximity; a doctor owes a duty of care to his patient; a teacher owes a duty of care to his child-pupil, etc.

Controversial cases

Where the circumstance which is said to give rise to the duty does not lie within one of the established categories, it must be specially considered.

There has long been controversy concerning whether, and if so, to what extent, a duty of care is owed in two particular types of case: (a) those where the claimant has suffered psychiatric injury; and (b) those where the claimant has suffered 'pure' economic loss: that is, the defendant has caused no damage to the claimant or his property but has caused him a purely financial loss (an example might be where the defendant has carelessly turned his car over, blocking the road, with the consequence that the claimant is unable to get to work on time and thus loses pay).

We need also to examine a third category of case: where the claimant is attempting to persuade the court that a duty should be created in his favour, where no duty has previously been recognised. Thus we will examine the concept of duty of care under three headings:

(a) new duty situations;

(b) pure economic loss; and

(c) psychiatric damage (or 'nervous shock').

New duty situations

There now exists a three-fold test of whether or not the defendant owes the claimant a duty of care in any particular circumstance:

(1) was it foreseeable that the defendant would injure the claimant by the action in question?

(2) was there a sufficient proximity between the defendant and the claimant?

(3) is it fair, just and reasonable that the court should impose a duty?

This test emerges from *Caparo v Dickman* (1990), the facts of which can be found in Chapter 10 which we have previously examined when looking at liability for misrepresentation.

Foreseeability and proximity

The question as to whether it was foreseeable that the defendant's act would injure the claimant is often bound up with the idea of proximity. Proximity is an idea which has hitherto defied definition but it clearly includes, where appropriate, the ideas of a proximity which arises:

(1) from a special relationship;

(2) from a geographical proximity; and

(3) from a proximity relating to time.

Special relationship

Thus, in *Hill v Chief Constable of West Yorkshire* (1988), the mother of a victim of the murderer known as 'the Yorkshire Ripper' claimed damages against the police on behalf of her murdered daughter, Jacqueline. Mrs Hill alleged that the police had been negligent in not detecting the murderer before the time when he had killed Jacqueline (she was the last of his 13 known victims). It was held that there is no general duty of care owed by the police to individual members of the public. In the absence of a special relationship or proximity between Jacqueline and the police, no duty of care arose.

In the contrasting case of *Swinney v Chief Constable of Northumbria Police (No 2)* (1999), a woman gave the police information regarding a possible criminal. The police failed to keep the information secure. It was stolen and made known to the suspect. It was held that the police owed the woman a duty of care. She had a special relationship with the police which gave rise to proximity.

Geographical proximity

In *Dorset Yacht Co v Home Office* (1970), the issue of proximity was a main issue. In this case, seven young offenders who were normally kept in a secure custodial unit, five of whom had previously escaped, were on a training exercise in Poole Harbour. There were three officers in charge but the accommodation in which the party was lodged was not secure. One night when, contrary to instructions, the three officers were in bed, the boys escaped and did damage to the plaintiff's yacht in Poole Harbour. The question arose as to whether the Home Office (which is responsible for the operation of custodial units) owed the yacht owner a duty of care. Despite arguments that it was against public policy to allow the yacht owner to sue, the House of Lords held that the Home Office owed a duty of care based on the foreseeability of damage should they negligently allow a prisoner to escape. Although there is a general risk of damage from criminal attack, for which no-one but the criminal is generally liable, in this case, there was a relationship (that is, a proximity) between the Home Office and the person damaged. The duty of care was owed only to persons whom the negligent officers could reasonably foresee had property in the vicinity of the escape which the escapees were likely to steal or damage in the course of eluding immediate pursuit and recapture. Thus, once the criminals were clear of the immediate vicinity, the negligent officers would no longer owe a duty of care in respect of the boys' criminal activities (even though, of course, it was foreseeable that the boys might commit further crimes).

By contrast, in *King v Phillips* (1953), a taxi-driver carelessly backed his taxi-cab into a small boy on a tricycle, slightly injuring the boy and the tricycle. His mother was 70 or 80 yards away and, as a consequence of hearing her son scream and seeing the immediate aftermath of the accident, she suffered nervous shock. *Held*: the taxi-driver did not owe a duty of care. It was not reasonable to expect a taxi-driver to foresee that if he was careless when backing his taxi he would cause damage to a woman in a house some 70 to 80 yards away up a side street.

Proximity in relation to time

Sometimes the injury is caused some time after the alleged act of negligence. This problem arises principally in connection with psychiatric cases, where an accident occurs and then, some time later, the claimant suffers psychiatric damage when encountering the aftermath of the negligent act. Providing the damage comes in the immediate aftermath of the event, the claimant may succeed: *McLoughlin v O'Brian* (1983), where a mother hurried to the hospital after being told of a road accident in which her daughter had died. The rest of the family who had been involved in the crash were at the hospital. One daughter had died. Her son was badly injured and screaming. Her other daughter and her husband were covered in oil and the daughter was bleeding from a cut. The mother suffered psychiatric injury as a result of this. *Held*: although she had not seen or heard the accident, she had encountered the immediate aftermath and the negligent party owed her a duty of care. On the other hand, in *Tranmore v Scudder* (1998), it was held that when a father arrived at the scene of an accident two hours after his son's death no duty of care was owed.

Public policy

Sometimes the court fails to impose a duty because it thinks that it is contrary to public policy that the defendant shall be held liable: it is not fair, just and reasonable. The role of policy in relation to establishing a duty of care is a controversial one. Until *Arthur JS Hall & Co v Simons* (2000), barristers and solicitors were given immunity in relation to their conduct of cases in court, as a matter of public policy. This was on several grounds, the main one being that to decide whether or not they had been negligent, it would be necessary, in effect, to retry the case. That immunity has now gone for both civil and criminal cases, though there was only a 4:3 majority in the House of Lords in favour of its removal in relation to criminal cases.

In addition, it used to be thought that the police had a general immunity from negligence action on the ground that they had to make decisions as to priorities when using resources, and if they were open to negligence actions this might lead to a diversion of manpower. We have seen, above, however, there is no absolute rule that the police do not owe a duty of care in carrying out their functions. If the police have a special relationship with a particular victim, this can give rise to a finding that duty of care exists.

However, in the *Hill* case, while there was a finding that there was insufficient proximity, a second reason for the decision was that it was against public policy to hold that the police owed a duty of care. Since the ruling of the European Court of Human Rights in *Osman v UK* (1999), future cases are, however, likely to be based on the proximity question rather than the policy question. The facts of the case were that a school teacher suffering from a serious psychiatric condition, which made it likely that he would commit offences against property or person, was infatuated with a pupil. The police failed to take action. The teacher killed the pupil's father and injured the pupil. In an action against the police for negligence, the Court of Appeal, following *Hill*, held that although there was proximity between the claimant and the police, the police were entitled to immunity as a matter of public policy. The court therefore refused to hear the case on its merits. Osman brought proceedings under the European Convention on Human Rights, which has now been incorporated into English law by the Human Rights Act 1998. Article 6 provides that everyone has a right to a fair trial. By holding that the police had immunity as a matter of policy, the Court of Appeal denied Osman that right.

Pure economic loss

For many years, the law did not recognise a duty of care when the loss complained of was pure economic loss. The law of contract exists to compensate pure economic loss. This is partly the reason why, for many years, the law of negligence did not do so: claims for economic loss tend to be brought in circumstances where the claimant has suffered loss because the defendant has breached a contract to which, however, the claimant is not a party. Not being able to sue for breach of contract, the claimant sues for negligence instead.

Example

A company contracts with an auditor to audit its accounts. The auditor does the job negligently. The company suffers no loss and therefore brings no action for breach of contract. However, an investor, relying on the accounts, invests money in the company and loses the money. He cannot sue the auditor for breach of contract, since he has no contract with the auditor. However, the question arises as to whether he can sue the auditor for negligence.

Originally, the law made a distinction between *economic loss arising from injury to the claimant or damage to the claimant's property*, on the one hand, and *pure economic loss* on the other. It was said that there was no duty of care in negligence to avoid causing pure economic loss. One reason, as we have seen, was that it was not policy to allow a defendant to be sued in negligence when he was liable in contract to a third party. That was the original reason why it was held that a manufacturer did not owe a duty of care to a consumer. However, that reasoning fell by the wayside in *Donoghue v Stevenson* in respect of negligence which causes *physical damage*. However, it was retained until the 1960s in relation to negligence which causes pure economic loss.

The other reason was the 'floodgates' argument. This is really two arguments in one. First, that it will give rise to a large number of individual claims; secondly, each act of 'negligence' could involve the defendant in what may turn out to be thousands of claims.

As we have seen, in the landmark case of *Hedley Byrne v Heller* (1964), it was held that there may be a duty of care, where a special relationship exists, in relation to negligent mis-statements which cause pure economic loss. Thus, for example, an auditor may be liable for negligence if he has a special relationship with the persons who relied on his negligent audit: *Morgan Crucible v Hill Samuel* (1991) (see the discussion in Chapter 10, p 240 *et seq*).

For a time, the decision in *Junior Books v Veitchi* (1983) appeared to be a radical turning point, and it seemed that there would emerge a general duty not to cause economic loss. However, it has since been affirmed that the Junior Books case should be restricted to its own particular facts and that a special relationship, or assumption of responsibility, akin to a contractual relationship, must exist before a defendant can be liable for economic loss. Thus, an auditor is not liable to everyone who may rely on his negligent audit: see *Caparo v Dickman* (1990).

Such a special relationship was held to exist, by reason of an *assumption of responsibility*, in *Spring v Guardian Assurance* (1994). Spring had been dismissed from his employment with the Guardian Assurance. They gave him a reference which, wrongly, stated that he had sold clients inappropriate insurance. This caused him economic loss, since it prevented him getting another job. Although the reference was, on the face of it, defamatory, the defence of qualified privilege is available to the defendant in relation to communications such as an employer's reference. This means that, even if the reference is incorrect, the claimant will only succeed if he can prove that the defendant was actuated by malice. Therefore, the claimant sued for negligence. It was argued that it was contrary to public policy to allow such a claim because, by allowing the claimant to circumvent the law of libel, it would undermine the law. It was also argued that because the reference was for the benefit of the prospective employer, there was no proximity between the employer and the employee which would give rise to a duty of care in negligence. *Held*: there were no reasons of policy to prevent the employee suing in negligence. Further, the reference was for the benefit of the employee as much as for the prospective employer. There was, therefore, an assumption of responsibility by the employer to the employee which gave rise to a duty of care.

The idea of *assumption of responsibility* was applied in relation to negligence in education in a number of related factual situations in *Phelps v Hillingdon LBC* (2000). The House of Lords dealt with four cases together, each raising similar issues. The issues were whether teachers, educational psychologists and local education authorities owe a duty of care to school children to ensure that their special needs are properly diagnosed and that, in consequence, they are provided with the most suitable education and educational support. There was a further issue in relation to whether failure to diagnose a pupil's condition with the result that the pupil's level of achievement suffered or the pupil suffered psychologically, could constitute damage meriting compensation. It was held that teachers, educational psychologists and local authorities all owe a duty of care to pupils to ensure that their needs are properly diagnosed. In each case, there is an *assumption of responsibility*. In addition, a local authority can be vicariously liable for the negligence of teachers and educational psychologists. Furthermore, failure to achieve potential or suffering psychological damage as a result of the failure to diagnose can be compensated as damage.

There have been claims for economic loss involving the amount of money needed to bring up an unwanted child after a failed vasectomy. In *McFarlane v Tayside Health Board* (1999), the House of Lords held that it would not be fair, just and reasonable (that is, it would be contrary to policy) to impose a duty on the doctor in the circumstances. In *Greenfield v Irwin* (2001), a nurse administered a contraceptive injection without examining the claimant for pregnancy. If this had been done (as it should have been), it would have been found that the claimant was already pregnant. The claimant would then have terminated the pregnancy. Despite the claimant's attempt to distinguish the case from *McFarlane*, it was held that the defendant owed no duty of care to prevent economic loss through an unwanted pregnancy. However, in *Rand v Dorset Health Authority* (2000), doctors negligently failed to inform prospective parents the result of a scan, which showed that the child was likely to be born with Downs Syndrome. If the parents had been given the correct information, the mother would have had an abortion. The parents claimed, among other things, for the cost of maintaining the child. *Held*: the claim would be restricted to the additional cost caused by the child's disability.

Since the decision of the ECHR in the *Osman* case, it would seem that any attempt to deny a claimant a hearing on the merits of his case on the ground that no duty of care exists, is likely to be based on a finding that there is insufficient proximity or that there has been no assumption of responsibility, rather than that it is against public policy. Thus, it may be that if a case like *Willmore v South Eastern Electricity Board* (1957) (see Chapter 6, p 135) were to be based on negligence rather than on breach of contract, the claim may well succeed nowadays. In this case, a chicken farmer, relying on assurances from the electricity board as to the suitability of their installations, lost a quantity of chicks when the electricity supply failed. He failed in his action for breach of contract on the rather dubious ground that his relationship with the electricity company was not contractual. However, it would seem difficult to sustain the argument that he has insufficient proximity to enable him to sue in negligence.

The distinction between negligence which causes physical damage and negligence which causes pure economic loss is well illustrated by the Court of Appeal case of *Spartan Steel v Martin* (1973). In that case, the defendant was excavating with a mechanical shovel when he carelessly damaged a cable and interrupted the supply of electricity to the claimant's factory 400 yards away. To avoid damage to the furnace, the claimants had to damage its contents (on which they would have made a profit of £400) to the extent of £368 and, in addition, had to abandon plans for a further four 'melts' on which they would have made £1,767 profit. The claimants recovered the losses in respect of the melt that was in the furnace at the time the electricity supply was halted, because this was economic loss consequent upon physical damage, but failed in the claim for the loss of profit on the subsequent melts which had not taken place because that loss was independent of the physical damage.

Psychiatric damage

An area of liability which has given rise to problems over the years is where the defendant has caused psychiatric damage rather than physical damage to the claimant. At first, possibly because it was thought that psychiatric damage was difficult to fake and certainly because mental damage has never been regarded by the law as seriously as physical damage, it was held that such damage was *too remote.* (This latter concept prevents the claimant from claiming in respect of unforeseeable damage; see Chapter 28, p 627.)

Later, the argument centred upon whether the defendant owed the claimant a duty of care to avoid causing him psychiatric damage. It was held that a claim was permitted if the psychiatric damage was caused by fear, caused by the negligent act of the defendant, by the primary victim, for her own safety. In *Dully v White* (1901), the defendant drove a horse and cart towards the plaintiff, causing her to fear for her life. She was pregnant and alleged that her child was born defective because of the shock. It was held that the defendant did owe a duty to avoid causing the plaintiff psychiatric damage, but only where the shock resulted from fear for the plaintiff's personal safety. In *Hambrook v Stokes* (1925), the duty was extended to avoid causing shock where the shock arose for the safety of one's family.

The recognition of post-traumatic stress disorder, and other forms of psychiatric illness caused by shock, has led to an upsurge in claims in recent years. Most cases involve shock caused by witnessing injury caused to the primary, or being involved in the immediate aftermath, for example, seeing dead bodies in the road after a road accident. Occasionally, a person who suffers physical injury himself, and is therefore the primary victim, also suffers psychiatric damage in consequence.

The older cases, on what used to be called 'nervous shock', are of limited value nowadays. We will therefore restrict our studies to relatively recent cases. The starting point must be the tragic case of the Hillsborough football disaster, in *Alcock v Chief Constable of South Yorkshire* (1991). The *Alcock* and subsequent cases distinguished between *primary* victims and *secondary* victims. A primary victim is one who participates in the events, in that he is in fear for his own safety or he puts his own safety at risk by acting as a rescuer. In such a case, the person causing the event will owe a duty to avoid causing psychiatric injury equally with a duty to avoid causing physical injury. This is so even though the physical injury does not, in the event, materialise. A secondary victim is one whose own safety is not at risk and he must, therefore, prove the factors set out in (a) and (b) below.

In the *Alcock* case, police negligence in controlling the crowd at an FA Cup semi-final at Hillsborough football ground in Sheffield, was responsible for 95 deaths. Ten relatives of victims who died in the disaster brought claims against the police alleging that they had suffered psychiatric damage as a result of these events. The question arose as to whether the police owed the relatives a duty of care to avoid causing them psychiatric damage.

It was held that none of the plaintiffs succeeded. The effect of the *Alcock* case and later cases is that, in order to succeed as a *secondary victim*, the claimant must:

(a) *have a relationship of the 'closest ties of love and affection'* with the person for whose safety the claimant is in fear. Such a relationship may be presumed in the case of a parent or fiancé, but in the case of a brother or a brother-in-law it must be proved to the court. It is possible for it to exist in an even remoter relative (or, presumably, in a friend or workmate, etc) but for it to be foreseeable that the claimant would suffer psychiatric injury as a result of the events which injure the primary victim, the relationship will require 'most cautious scrutiny'; and

(b) *be within sight or hearing of the event or its immediate aftermath*. In the *Alcock* case, the two claimants who witnessed the events in the stadium had not proved the ties of love and affection. Those who had the ties of love and affection had only witnessed the events on TV, and then not in close-up. If the pictures had broken the broadcasting code and had been in close-up, then the Chief Constable would still not have been liable. The close-up, because it was not reasonably foreseeable, would count as an intervening act (see below, p 631). In such a case, it would be the television company that was liable. In *Tranmore v Scudder* (1998), it was held that a father who arrived at the scene where a building had collapsed, killing his son, two hours after the accident, was owed no duty of care in relation to the psychiatric damage which he suffered. Two hours was too long to be classed as 'the immediate aftermath'.

Primary victims

The claimant is *a primary victim* in the sense that the claimant has participated in the events and has been in physical danger. In this case, it does not have to be foreseeable that the reaction to the danger will cause psychiatric injury. In *Page v Smith* (1994), the plaintiff was involved in a minor road accident. He had a pre-existing mental illness from which he was recovering at the time of the accident. The accident caused him a serious set-back and, as a result, it was unlikely that he would ever work again. *Held*: he was a primary victim. As such, it was not necessary for the negligent party to foresee that psychiatric injury would be caused. Once it was foreseeable that the negligence would cause some injury, the negligent party was responsible for all injury arising from the event (this is a version of the 'egg-shell skull rule' (see below) and is sometimes called the 'egg-shell personality rule').

A *rescuer* is also a primary victim. If a person suffers injury, either physical or psychiatric, in attempting to rescue the victims of someone else's negligence, then a duty of care is owed to them. However, the rescuer must be a primary victim in that he perceives himself to be in danger. It was held, in *Frost v Chief Constable of South Yorkshire Police* (1999), that police officers who had witnessed the events and tried to assist the injured parties and who suffered post traumatic stress were not eligible to claim: no duty of care was owed to them.

In *McFarlane v EE Caledonia Ltd* (1994), the plaintiff suffered psychiatric injury witnessing the fire on the Piper Alpha oil rig. He was a worker on the rig, but on the night of the disaster was off-duty on a support vessel nearby. He never got closer than 100 metres to the rig's platform. It was held that the claim failed. A mere bystander, in the absence of proximity in the sense of nearness of time and place and close ties of affection to the primary victim, is owed no duty of care.

The courts are being invited to extend the category of claimants who may claim psychiatric damage. In *W v Essex County Council* (2000), two parents claimed that they had suffered psychiatric damage when, despite the fact that they had expressly asked that no child abuser should be given them to foster, the Council placed in their care a child known to be a child abuser. He sexually abused the claimants' own daughters. The Council applied for the action by the parents to be struck out on the ground that the Council did not owe them a duty of care in respect of the psychiatric damage. However, the House of Lords held that the parents had a case which they were entitled to have heard in court. Because the parents had a feeling of responsibility at having brought the abuser into their home, they were arguably primary victims, and the fact that they did not witness the abuse but were told about it some days later did not prevent them from being secondary victims by experiencing the 'immediate aftermath'. However, the parental case in this respect is not easy to argue: hitherto it has been held that the immediate aftermath must be witnessed. Will the courts establish a less rigid requirement in the case where an event causes psychiatric damage when it is reported some days later?

Type of illness

The victim must suffer a *genuine psychiatric illness caused by shock*. It is not enough that the victim suffers normal human emotions of, for example, fear, grief or depression. Although some of the older cases do not seem to have applied this requirement strictly, it is now a clear requirement

In *McLoughlin v O'Brian* (1982), a borderline case, where a mother whose family had suffered a horrendous road accident did not see or hear it but encountered the aftermath when she saw the family in hospital, Lord Bridge said:

The common law gives no damages for the emotional distress which any normal person experiences when someone he loves is killed or injured. Anxiety and depression are normal human emotions. Yet an anxiety neurosis or a reactive depression may be recognisable psychiatric illnesses, with or without psychosomatic symptoms. So, the first hurdle which a claimant claiming damages of the kind in question must surmount is to establish that he is suffering, not merely from grief, distress or any other normal emotion, but a positive psychiatric illness.

Does the 'egg-shell skull rule' apply to nervous shock?

There is a rule at common law that you must take your victim as you find him. For example, if the defendant has negligently splashed with a spot of hot liquid a person who has a pre-disposition to cancer, then the defendant is not permitted to argue that he is liable only for the damage which was foreseeable as a result of a tiny splash: if the victim dies, the defendant will be liable in negligence for his death: *Smith v Leech Brain* (1962).

As we have seen, the egg-shell rule applies to primary victims who suffer psychiatric damage.

However, in relation to secondary victims, the court must find that a person of ordinary phlegm and fortitude would suffer psychiatric damage by what he saw: *McFarlane v EE Caledonia Ltd* (1994), above.

The Law Commission, in its Report, *Liability for Psychiatric Illness*, 1998, Law Com 249, has recommended a number of changes in the law relating to psychiatric injury. It proposes a statutory duty of care where the plaintiff has a close tie of love and affection to an accident victim. It would abolish the restriction as to time, so that the rule that the claimant must see or hear the event or its immediate aftermath would be abolished. It would also abolish the requirements that the illness be caused by shock and that the illness should not be cause by fear for the safety of the defendant himself.

Employer's liability

We have seen that there may be some dispute as to whether a duty of care is owed in the case of new duties, economic loss and psychiatric damage. However, there is no question that an employer owes his employee a duty to take care, and, moreover, this has been broken down into four specific duties. These are:

(a) the duty to provide a competent workforce;

Hudson v Ridge Manufacturing Co (1957)

C, an employee of the defendants, had, for four years, made a nuisance of himself to fellow employees. These included the plaintiff, who was crippled, whom C was constantly tripping up. C had been reprimanded by his superior, but to no effect. Eventually, C injured the plaintiff who claimed damages from their employer. *Held*: the employers were liable since this dangerous behaviour had been known to them for some time and they had failed to prevent it.

In a contrasting case, *Smith v Crossley Bros* (1951), two apprentices put a compressed air pipe up the plaintiff's rectum. He sued his employer but failed, since this was an isolated act and his employer had no reason to believe that the apprentices would behave in that way.

(b) to provide adequate plant and equipment;

Where an employer fails to provide equipment which a reasonable employer would regard as necessary, the employer is liable if the employee is injured because the equipment is unavailable.

Lovell v Blundells and Crompton (1944)

L was a boilermaker who was employed by the defendants to overhaul the boiler of a ship. To do this he required staging to a height of four feet. He was not provided with it, nor was he told where to get it. He therefore made a staging from a plank and a wooden wedge. The staging collapsed and L was injured. *Held*: his employers were in breach of their duty to provide proper equipment

At common law, the employer was not liable for latent defects (that is, defects which were not discoverable on reasonable examination) in plant and machinery unless he had acquired it from an unreputable source. In respect of latent defects in equipment supplied by a source, the employee had to sue the manufacturer, which might present one of a number of difficulties. The common law position has now been overruled by statute. Under the provisions of the Employer's Liability (Defective Equipment) Act 1969, an employer is liable to an employee who is injured during the course of his employment, in consequence of a defect in equipment provided by the employer, even though the defect is due to the fault of a third party.

(c) to provide a safe place of work;

This duty overlaps with the duty of an occupier under the Occupiers' Liability Act 1957 and also with a number of specific duties relating to the safety of the workplace, laid down in a number of Regulations.

(d) to provide a safe system of working.

This duty is a very broad one and requires the employer to put in place safe working procedures. The duty is imposed by the common law and may also be the subject of specific Regulations. In *Bullerwell v Darlington Insulation Co* (1999), the claimant alleged that his employer had failed to provide a safe system of work under the common law and under reg 6(2) of the Construction (Working Places) Regulations 1996. Scaffolding had been placed round a tall cylinder, leaving triangular-shaped gaps of some 12 inches by 9 inches. The claimant, who was an experienced thermal insulation engineer, was injured when his foot slipped through one of the gaps. He argued that if the gap had been in a factory floor or a pavement, there would have been a breach of duty and that, therefore, the court should hold that a breach of duty had taken place in this case. *Held*: the gap in the scaffolding had been large enough to see and small enough to avoid. The court was assessing the safety of the system of work applicable to placing scaffolding round a cylinder, not a hole in pavement or a factory floor. The system of work was safe in the circumstances.

CHAPTER 28

NEGLIGENCE (2)

BREACH OF DUTY OF CARE

Once the claimant has established that the defendant owed him a duty of care, he has a second hurdle to get over. He must show that the defendant has actually breached the duty. Whether a duty of care has been breached involves consideration of two questions: (a) what standard must be reached?; and (b) has the defendant, in fact, fallen short of the required standard?

(a) What standard of care is expected from the party alleged to have been negligent?

The standard of care expected is objective. It expects the defendant to have done what a reasonable person would have done (or not done) in the circumstances. Where a person is undertaking a task which requires a particular skill, such as driving, running a garage, performing a medical operation, etc, that person is expected to exhibit the skill of a reasonable practitioner of the skill.

Where the defendant is practising a particular skill

In a case where a person purports to have a particular skill, the standard to be expected is that of a *reasonably competent*, (not perfect) practitioner of that skill.

The Lady Gwendolen (1965)

Brewers operated a ship for carrying stout from Dublin to Liverpool. The captain collided with another ship when he sailed full steam ahead up the Mersey in a thick fog, relying only on radar. The owners argued that they should be judged by the standard of reasonable brewers in the management of their ships. The argument was rejected by the court. They were expected to behave as reasonable ship-owners if they engaged in maritime operations.

An important point to emphasis is that the standard is objective not subjective. This means that the court imposes the standard of care which the defendant should have reached, even though, perhaps through lack of experience, the defendant might have been incapable of reaching that standard. Thus, in *Nettleship v Weston* (1971), it was held that a learner driver must be judged by the standard of a reasonably competent experienced driver.

However, it was held in *Phillips v Whitely* (1938) that a jeweller who pierces ears must show the competence of a reasonably experienced jeweller who undertakes such tasks. He does not have to show the competence of a surgeon. In this case, a customer developed a blood disorder after having her ear pierced by a jeweller. However, it was held that the hygiene methods which he used to disinfect his instruments were reasonable in the circumstances.

A more controversial decision is *Wells v Cooper* (1958), in which a door handle came off in the plaintiff's hand, causing him to fall and injure himself. The handle had been put in place by the householder – an amateur handyman. It was held that the householder did not need to exhibit the skill of a professional carpenter, merely that of an amateur handyman. With respect, this decision appears to be unsound. In the *Weston* case, we have seen that the standard required was objective, even though the driver was driving a car carrying a warning that she was a learner. In the *Phillips* case, the plaintiff knew that the defendant was a jeweller, so that it was reasonable to impose the standard of care that the plaintiff must have expected to receive. However, in the *Wells* case, in the absence of any warning sign, the injured party would not have expected the door to have been mended by an amateur handyman and would have had no warning to take extra care.

(b) Has the defendant fallen short of the standard of care required? In other words, 'Has the defendant been guilty of taking an unjustifiable risk?'

In answering this question of whether the risk is justifiable, the court tends to impose one (or sometimes both) of two broad tests.

The first test, often called the 'Salmond' test after the distinguished legal author who expounded it in his text-book, looks at the following complex involving four questions:

(1) What is the degree of probability that damage will be done by the conduct in question? The greater the probability that the conduct complained of will cause harm, the more likely it is that the conduct will be negligent

Haley v London Electricity Board (1965)

The defendants excavated a pavement, leaving a hole in it. They sought to guard against anyone falling into the hole by placing a hammer diagonally across the pavement in front of the hole. The plaintiff was a blind person who failed to detect the hole and fell into it. The fall rendered him deaf. The Electricity Board argued that they had not been negligent, since the likelihood of a blind person encountering the hole was not great. However, after hearing evidence about the number of blind persons in the locality, the court decided that there was sufficient probability of a blind person being injured, and that the Board ought to have taken further steps to guard against the eventuality.

Contrast *Bolton v Stone* (1951), where a woman who was standing by her front gate was hit by a cricket ball which had travelled 100 yards and cleared a 17 foot high fence which surrounded the cricket ground, in the process. The court thought that this was a borderline case, but held that there was no breach of the duty of care since the ball had been hit out of the ground only six times in the past 30 years. Thus the risk was not disproportionately great.

(2) What are the consequences of the injury that is risked in terms of seriousness?

It may be that, although damage is not very probable, nevertheless the injury that is risked is so serious that the risk is not justifiable.

Paris v Stepney Borough Council (1951)

P was a one-eyed mechanic working for the council. He was engaged in removing rusty bolts from a vehicle, a job which involved a relatively small risk of injury from splintering metal. The risk materialised. A splinter of metal entered the plaintiff's good eye, rendering him blind. He argued that his employer should have provided him with goggles. His employer argued that the relatively slight risk did not justify the expense. *Held*: it was true that the risk of injury did not justify the expense of provision of goggles to a normally sighted person. However, the seriousness of the injury that was risked in the case of Paris meant that the council should have provided him with goggles.

(3) What is the social utility that the conduct in question is trying to achieve?

It seems that an abnormal risk may be justified if the social objective which the defendant is trying to achieve is thought to justify the risk. In *Watt v Hertfordshire County Council* (1954), a fire brigade transported a jack on an unsuitable vehicle because a suitable one was not available and could not be obtained without a significant delay. The reason the brigade did not wait for a suitable vehicle was that time was of the essence in order to save the life of a person trapped in a motor vehicle. The jack could not be properly secured on the vehicle that was actually used and, as a result, fell upon the plaintiff's ankle and injured it. It was held that the purpose to be achieved justified the risk and that, therefore, the brigade was not negligent.

We have seen that the fact that a fire brigade was trying to save life was held to justify a risk which would otherwise have been unjustifiable. However, this principle is of relatively narrow scope. Drivers of ambulances, fire-engines and police vehicles are permitted to exceed the speed limit, but this does not affect their civil liability. For example, in *Ward v LCC* (1938), a fire engine jumped a red light in attending a fire and was held to have been negligent, and in *Gaynor v Allen* (1959), a police motor-cyclist travelling at 60 mph on a road with a 40 mph speed limit, was held to be negligent.

(4) What would be the cost (in time, effort, monetary terms, etc) of avoiding the harm?

The cost must be balanced against the risk of injury. One of the factors which led to the Electricity Board being liable in the *Haley* case, above, was that it would have cost relatively little to erect a guard round the hole which would have been sufficient to prevent Mr. Haley from falling into the hole.

Latimer v AEC (1953)

Heavy rain flooded the employer's factory and in doing so washed waste oil up from the channels in the floor where it normally ran on to the floor itself. The employer spread sawdust on the oil as a precaution until the floor could be properly cleaned. However, there was not enough sawdust to cover the whole floor. The plaintiff slipped on a part of the floor not covered with sawdust and injured himself. He argued that his employer's precautions were not sufficient. They should have closed the factory until the oil had been cleaned from the floor. *Held*: the risk of injury was relatively slight compared to the loss to the employer if the factory had been closed. In the circumstances, the employer's response to the situation was reasonable. Note that there have been criticisms of this decision because of the court's failure to consider the feasibility of alternatives, such as closing down the area of the factory for which there was no sawdust available.

Conformity with accepted practice

A further test which may be applied to decide whether the defendant's conduct is negligent, is whether the defendant acted in accordance with accepted practice, in the light of knowledge existing at the time. If he did, then the conduct is less likely to have been negligent.

Roe v Ministry of Health (1954)

Roe entered hospital for a minor operation. This involved being given a local anaesthetic called nupercaine. The nupercaine was contained in glass ampoules which were stored in a jar containing a disinfectant chemical called phenol. The major problem with this was that if the nupercaine became contaminated with the phenol, it formed a compound which corroded human nerve tissue. It was accepted practice, therefore, to examine the ampoules of nupercaine for cracks, to ensure that no phenol could have seeped into the nupercaine, before the anaesthetic was used. On this occasion, the anaesthetist examined the ampoule by holding it up and examining it for cracks before using the anaesthetic. However, there were hairline cracks in the nupercaine ampoules invisible to the naked eye. The phenol had become mixed with the nupercaine and, in consequence, Roe was paralysed for life from the waist down. He sued for negligence. *Held*: the anaesthetist had followed accepted practice. As the possibility of hairline cracks in the ampoules was not known at the time, he was not negligent. (Once the risk was known, it became the practice to dye the phenol deep blue so that if it entered the ampoule of nupercaine it was highly visible. An anaesthetist failing to follow this practice would probably be held to be negligent.)

The 'accepted practice' test may be used in conjunction with the 'Salmond' test set out above, so that the court may examine the cost of complying with accepted practice and set it against the risk incurred in not doing so.

Where there is a difference of opinion as to what the practice should be, adherence to a widely held *minority opinion* will not justify a finding of negligence, providing it is reasonable and responsible (that is, based on logic). This has been discussed extensively in medical negligence cases where the practitioner has chosen a particular form of treatment which, with hindsight, has been seen to be unsuccessful. The leading case is now *Bolitho v City and Hackney Health Authority* (1997). Patrick, a small child, was admitted to hospital with breathing difficulties. He was not attended properly by Dr Horn, who was in charge of his case. As a result of his inability to breathe, he suffered a cardiac arrest which led to brain damage. In consequence of this, he died some time later. It was suggested that intubation (that is, inserting a tube to provide an airway) would have prevented his problems. The question was, what would Dr Horn have done if she had attended Patrick? In particular, if she had not intubated him, would she have been negligent? The defence witnesses claimed that intubation would not have been appropriate, while the plaintiff's witnesses thought that it would. It was held that, although Dr Horn had been in breach of her duty to Patrick, the breach of duty had not caused the damage. Strictly speaking, this is a case on causation (see below), but its significance is that the House of Lords held that the court was not required to accept expert views unless they were reasonable and responsible, and this meant that they must be based on logic. The same rule will apply when considering whether a defendant has breached his duty of care.

Failure to observe accepted practice is more likely to result in a finding of negligence.

Stokes v GKN

Mrs Stokes's husband died of scrotal cancer as a result of leaning over oily machines in the course of his employment as a toolsetter. She alleged that GKN, his employers, had been negligent in that they did not warn against the possibility of contracting the disease and took no steps to conduct medical examinations with a view to detecting it. The evidence indicated that the GKN company doctor did not do this because of the administrative and economic cost.

Held: where a substantial body of medical opinion advocates a particular practice, a minority practice is not necessarily negligent if there is evidence that it is widely accepted. However, in this case an individual was acting on his own personal opinion. In such a case, the practice must be judged on what is reasonable. The practice was not reasonable and was therefore negligent. GKN were vicariously liable for the negligence of their company doctor.

In a small number of cases the courts have ruled that accepted practice is, nevertheless, negligent.

General Cleaning Contractors v Christmas (1953)

A window cleaner stood on the sill holding on to the open window when the sash, which was loose and moved easily, moved down and dislodged the plaintiff's fingers. This caused him to fall and hurt himself. Evidence was showed that it was widely accepted practice to clean windows standing on the sill while holding on to the open window.

Held: the employer was negligent in not providing wedges to prevent the window from closing.

The courts have also ruled that failing to follow accepted practice is not necessarily negligent.

Brown v Rolls Royce (1960)

Brown contracted dermatitis on his hands as a result of being in constant contact with oil in the course of his employment. He alleged that his employers, Rolls Royce, had been negligent in failing to supply him with a barrier cream. Rolls Royce had relied on medical advice in not supplying the cream, but it was common practice for other employers to supply their employees with a barrier cream.

Held: although departure from accepted practice is evidence from which negligence may be inferred, the court does not have to infer it. In this case the evidence as to whether the employer had been negligent or not was finely balanced and, therefore, the court had to rule in favour of the defendants.

Foreseeable damage

It is not sufficient to show that the defendant breached a duty of care that he owed to the claimant. He also has to prove that he suffered foreseeable damage as a result of the breach.

There are three issues to be examined. These are: (a) causation; (b) remoteness of damage; and (c) new acts intervening.

(a) Did the defendant's action cause the damage?

It is often difficult, especially in industrial cases involving disease, for the claimant worker to prove conclusively that the defendant employer's negligence was responsible for his damage. What the claimant has to prove is that the defendant's breach of duty materially increased the risk of the claimant's injuries. (The burden of proof in a civil case is 'on balance of probabilities', which means 'more likely than not'.)

McGhee v NCB (1973)

The plaintiff was sent for several days, by his employers, to clean out brick kilns. The defendants failed to provide him with washing facilities. He then cycled home covered in sweat and dirt. He contracted dermatitis. He was unable to prove conclusively that the journey home unwashed caused the dermatitis, but it was accepted that lack of washing facilities materially increased the risk and, therefore, his employer was liable.

We have seen that in the *Bolitho* case (above), there was a breach of duty of care where a doctor failed to attend properly to a sick child, who suffered cardiac arrest leading to brain damage in consequence. However, had she attended him properly, it was held to be unlikely that she would have been able to save him. Therefore, the breach of duty was not responsible for the damage.

Similarly, in *Barnett v Kensington and Chelsea Hospital Management Committee* (1968), B drank some tea which had been contaminated with arsenic and complained of vomiting for three hours. He went to a hospital casualty department. No-one examined him but the doctor on duty sent a message telling him to go to his GP. Five hours later he died. His widow sued for negligence. It was found as a fact that the poison in his system had reached such an advanced state that, whatever had been done for him at the hospital, he would have died anyway. *Held*: although the duty doctor had been careless and had breached his duty of care, this did not amount to the tort of negligence since the carelessness was not the cause of B's death.

(b) *Was the damage caused by the defendant of the type that was* foreseeable *in the circumstances? If not the defendant* will not be liable – *the law regards the damage as being too* remote *a consequence of the careless act*

The most far-reaching and unexpected damage can ensue from a careless act. Originally, the law of negligence compensated the claimant for all *direct damage* resulting from the defendant's act, no matter how unforeseeable it might be. In *Re Polemis* (1921), a stevedore (a dock worker) negligently dropped a plank into the hold of a ship. It struck against the wooden bulwark (wall), created a spark (in true boy scout fashion) and ignited some vapour which had remained in the hold from a previous cargo. The ship was destroyed by fire. *Held*: the defendant stevedoring firm was liable, even though it was not foreseeable that their employee's negligent act would lead to the destruction of the ship.

There was some dissatisfaction with the rule in *Re Polemis*: it was thought that the defendant in negligence should be liable only for damage which was foreseeable. (Though the foreseeable damage could have been as bad as that which actually happened. For example, the plank might have fallen on a person working below and caused serious personal injury, or even death!)

The Privy Council effectively changed the law in *The Wagon Mound* so that the test of remoteness is now one of foreseeability. In *Overseas Tankship v Morts Docks Engineering (No 1)* (1961) (usually called '*The Wagon Mound*' after the name of the ship involved), a ship discharged oil in Sydney Harbour. Welders working on a wharf were afraid that a spark or molten metal from the welding operation would fall on the oil and cause it to ignite. They therefore stopped welding while expert advice was taken. Expert advice was that the intensity of heat given by a spark was not sufficient to ignite the oil. They therefore continued welding. Unfortunately, more than two days after the original discharge, some molten metal from the welding operations landed on some cotton waste and ignited it. This was sufficient to set fire to the oil and the resultant conflagration did considerable damage to the wharf and congealed in the slipways so that they could not be used. It was held that the shipowners were liable only for the foreseeable damage cause by their negligence. It is foreseeable that an oil spillage will cause damage by fouling the slipways, but not by causing a fire.

The application of the foreseeability rule can be seen in the following example:

Doughty v Turner Manufacturing Co (1964)

The plaintiff was employed by the defendant. An asbestos cover was carelessly knocked into a cauldron of molten metal by a fellow employee. The asbestos underwent a chemical change which resulted in an explosion, injuring the plaintiff. The possibility of this happening had not previously been known. *Held*: although injury from splashing was reasonably foreseeable, injury from an explosion was not. Therefore, the defendants were not liable

If the type of damage is foreseeable, although the damage is caused in an *unusual* way, the damage will *not be too remote*.

Hughes v Lord Advocate (1963)

In this case, employees of the Post Office were working in a manhole. They had left it covered over by a tent with red lamps as a warning. Some boys began to play at the site and one of them dropped a lamp into the hole. An explosion occurred and a fire resulted. One of the boys was thrown into the manhole and severely burnt. It was argued on behalf of the defendants that although a fire was foreseeable, an explosion was not. *Held*: although the precise way in which the damage would occur was not foreseeable, it was nevertheless foreseeable that damage by burning would take place, which is exactly what happened.

If damage of *a type which is foreseeable* occurs, it does not matter that it is *more extreme in extent* than was foreseeable, the defendant will be liable.

Bradford v Robinson Rentals (1967)

B's employer sent him on a 600 mile round trip in the middle of a severe winter in a van which lacked a heater. This meant that the windscreen iced up and that the plaintiff had to open the windscreen (it had a mechanism which allowed it to be raised) to see where he was going. The radiator was also defective and needed refilling with water at regular intervals. The plaintiff suffered from frostbite in consequence of these events. Frostbite is extremely rare in Britain and it was therefore argued on behalf of B's employer that the damage was not reasonably foreseeable and was therefore too remote. *Held*: frostbite was merely an acute form of cold. It was foreseeable that B would suffer from the cold. Therefore, the defendant was liable for all the consequences of the cold: it was immaterial that the precise nature of the injury was not foreseeable.

A similar rule states that *you must take your victim as you find him*. This means that if the victim is unduly susceptible so that he suffers greater injuries than could be foreseen, the defendant will nevertheless be liable. This is sometimes called the 'egg-shell skull' or 'thin skull' rule.

Smith v Leech Brain (1962)

Smith was employed by the defendants. His job involved removing galvanised articles from a tank of molten metal. He was splashed on the lip by a drop of molten metal. His lip was burned and he developed cancer. The evidence showed that he had a predisposition to cancer. He died of cancer as a result. The defendants argued that it was not reasonably foreseeable that a small drop of molten metal would cause cancer. *Held*: it was reasonably foreseeable that the plaintiff would suffer the type of injury that he did, namely injury by burning. It was immaterial that the consequences were more extreme in form than could have been foreseen: the defendants were liable.

Relationship between 'duty of care' and 'remoteness of damage'

In examining the scope of the concept of duty of care, we come across an immediate difficulty in that the concept of remoteness of damage, which we will consider when we come to deal with damage, does a similar job. They both act as control mechanisms – one tries to limit the number of potential claimants, the other tries to limit the type of damage for which the law will give compensation.

However, the two concepts operate from different approaches. With the duty of care, the law tries to keep the number of potential claimants within reasonable bounds, from a policy point of view, by holding that unless the claimant is foreseeable and has proximity to the defendant, the claimant has no case. With remoteness of damage, it is acknowledged that the defendant owes the claimant a duty of care, but refuses to allow the claimant to claim for damage which was an unforeseeable consequence of the defendant's negligent act.

Example

Cleo is driving to an airfield near London in order to catch a chartered aeroplane to North Wales. There she is due to have an on-site conference to discuss the suitability of the site for use as a theme park. Her proposed financial backer is Pierre, who has flown from Paris specially for the conference. Unfortunately, though Cleo is in no way at fault, her car is in collision with a car which was being driven negligently by Dave and, in consequence, Cleo has to spend a week in hospital. As a result, she misses four weeks' work, suffers damage to her legs which will cause her pain for the rest of her life and also suffers damage to her property, principally her car. In addition, she has to pay the charter cost of the plane which she didn't use. Pierre's expenses were also wasted.

The question arises as to how far Dave's liability extends for the loss and damage caused by his negligence.

It would be possible to make him liable for the entire loss and damage, but the law tends to be cautious in its approach to negligence claims and requires that claims must be confined within manageable parameters. It would, therefore, probably deny Pierre any recompense at all, on the grounds that Dave did not owe him a duty of care. The law would rationalise this by saying that it is not reasonably foreseeable that Pierre would suffer loss as a result of an accident to Cleo and that Pierre was not sufficiently proximate to Dave. In other words, Pierre is not one of the category of persons whom Dave should have in mind as being at risk as a result of Dave's careless driving. However, it cannot be denied that it is reasonably foreseeable that if you drive your motor car carelessly you will cause damage to another road user. Therefore, Dave owed a duty of care to Cleo. However, this does not necessarily mean that Cleo will be able to claim the full extent of her loss. She will get recompense for her reasonably foreseeable damage, such as her loss of earnings, the damage to her leg, and the damage to her car. However, it is likely that the court will regard the loss of her aeroplane charter fee as an unforeseeable consequence of Dave's negligence and this damage will therefore be too remote.

(c) *Sometimes the damage suffered by the claimant is caused or aggravated by an occurrence which takes place after the defendant's original act of carelessness. In such a case it is possible that the defendant will be liable for such damage. Whether he is or not depends upon whether the later damage is causally connected with the defendant's earlier act. The later act is called a* novus actus interveniens *(meaning 'a new act intervening')*

The effect of an intervening act depends upon whether it is an intervening act of a third party or an intervening act of the claimant himself.

Intervening acts of third parties

As a broad rule, the person who was originally careless will be liable providing the later act which caused or aggravated the damage was foreseeable.

The leading case is *Scott v Shepherd* (1773), in which the defendant threw a lighted firework on to a market stall. It was thrown from stall to stall until it exploded, injuring the plaintiff. It was held that as the intervening acts were foreseeable, the defendant was liable.

Stansbie v Trowman (1948)

A decorator was working in a house. He went to fetch more wallpaper and carelessly left the empty house unlocked. A thief entered while he was out and stole from the premises. It was held that the decorator was liable for the value of the property stolen. It was foreseeable that if a house was left empty and unlocked, thieves might enter and take property.

On the other hand, where the later act is not foreseeable, the defendant will not be liable.

Hogan v Bentinck Collieries (1949)

Hogan's thumb was injured in an accident at the colliery where he worked, caused by his employer's negligence. He was then given negligent medical advice that an amputation was necessary when it wasn't. Following this advice he had his thumb amputated. It was held that the colliery was not liable for the loss of the thumb. It was not foreseeable that negligent advice would be given. (Of course, the surgeon who had given the negligent advice, together with his employer, unless he was self-employed, would have been liable. The colliery would have been liable for the pain and suffering endured between the accident and the amputation, but this is unlikely to have been enough to be worth suing for.)

Intervening acts of the claimant

If the intervening act is the act of the claimant himself, the later act has not only to be *foreseeable*, it is the further requirement that it must also be *reasonable*.

If the intervening act of the claimant was reasonable, the defendant will be liable.

Sayers v Harlow UDC (1958)

Sayers was locked in a public lavatory through the defendant's carelessness. This in itself did not cause her injury. Her injury was caused by her own later action of trying to climb out of the toilet over the partition wall between her compartment and the next one. She tried to climb up by putting her foot on a toilet roll holder. It revolved under her weight and she slipped and injured herself. The question arose as to whether the defendants were liable for her injury. It was held that they were. The act of the plaintiff in trying to escape from the toilet was both foreseeable and reasonable (her damages were, however, reduced by 25% on the ground of her contributory negligence).

If the later act of the plaintiff was unreasonable, the defendant will not be liable.

McKew v Holland and Hannen and Cubitts (1969)

McKew's leg was injured by the defendant's negligence. It occasionally gave way. He suffered a broken ankle when his leg gave way and he fell down a flight of steep stairs. The stairs had no hand-rail and he was descending holding his daughter's hand. It was held that the defendants were not liable for this later injury since the defendant's conduct was unreasonable

Breach of statutory duty

Where a statute gives rise to a duty, breach of the duty usually carries penalties imposed by the *criminal law*. The question may then arise as to whether a person who suffers damage as a result of the breach may bring a *civil action* for damage, relying on the breach.

A principal advantage of doing this is that many statutory duties are strict or absolute. This means that possible defences are limited (as in the case of strict liability) or non-existent (as is the case with absolute liability). The important point is that if a strict or absolute duty is breached the victim is not required to prove that the defendant was at fault, as he would have to do if he brought a claim based on negligence.

Summers v Frost (1955)

Frost's thumb was injured when it came into contact with a grinding wheel belonging to his employer. The employer had failed to fence the machine as required by s 14 of the Factories Act 1961. The reason for the employer's failure was that fencing the machine would have rendered it inoperable. Nevertheless, it was held that the employer was in breach of statutory duty since the duty was absolute. The fact that it was not reasonably practicable to fence the machine was no defence.

On the other hand, certain statutory duties are not strict or absolute. They only require compliance 'so far as is reasonably practicable'. Failure to do what is reasonably practicable is akin to negligence. Even so, an action for breach of statutory duty has advantages over a negligence action.

Advantages of breach of statutory duty action over an action for negligence

Breach of statutory duty offers two main advantages over an action for negligence:

(a) in a negligence action, the burden of proving that the employer has not taken the precautions that a reasonable person would have done in the circumstances, is placed upon the claimant employee. However, in an action for breach of statutory duty, if the employer has a duty to do something 'so far as is reasonably practicable', the normal burden of proof is reversed and it is up to the employer to prove that he has done all that is reasonably practicable; and

(b) the duties which the statute lays down are reasonably precise. Let us say, for example, that an employer fails to cover or fence a tank, as required by the Workplace (Health, Safety and Welfare) Regulations 1992. In consequence an employee falls into the tank, which contains a hot liquid, and is injured. The employee would not have to prove that failure to fence or cover amounted to negligence. It is sufficient to show that there was a statutory duty to fence and that the employer had not complied with it. It would then be up to the employer to show that he had complied as far as is practicable.

Does breach of the statutory duty give a right to bring a civil action?

Not all statutory duties give rise to a civil action if they are breached. For example, the Health and Safety at Work Act 1974, the Safety of Sports Grounds Act 1975 and the Guard Dogs Act 1975 all expressly state that a breach of their provisions may not be used as the basis for a civil action. However, a breach of any of them might amount to negligence or liability under the Occupiers' Liability Act. For example, in *Barrett v London Borough of Enfield* (1999), it was held that a claim for negligence, in that the claimant had not been properly cared for by a local authority under the Children Act 1989, should not be struck out: there was no civil liability for breach of statutory duty under the Act, but failure to carry out the statutory duty might be evidence of negligence.

In the case of health and safety, the Health and Safety at Work Act 1974 provides that the breach of Regulations made under the Act *may give rise to a civil action* unless the Regulations expressly state otherwise. Thus we have the situation that the Act itself does not give a civil action but breach of the Regulations will give an action.

Where a statute is silent as to whether it gives a civil action for breach of statutory duty, it is up to the court to decide whether Parliament intended to give a civil action. The principles on which the court decides the issue are not themselves consistent, nor have they been applied consistently. It is, in consequence, often difficult to determine how a court will decide the issue.

Defences to a breach of statutory duty action

Even where liability for breach of statutory duty exists and is strict, the employer may have one of a number of defences.

(a) That the damage caused was not the type of damage which the statute was passed to prevent

This requirement dates from a nineteenth century case, *Gorris v Scott* (1874), in which sheep were being carried, unrestrained, on the deck of a ship. This was contrary to statutory provisions which required them to be carried in pens. The sheep were washed overboard and lost. The owner failed in his action for breach of statutory duty, since the purpose of the statute was to prevent the spread of disease among the animals, not to prevent them being washed overboard.

The following case shows how the principle was applied in a health and safety situation.

Close v Steel Company of Wales (1961)

Close was injured when a drill with which he was working shattered and fragments hit him. This would not have happened had the drill been fenced in accordance with the provisions of the Factories Act. However, the plaintiff failed in his action for breach of statutory duty since the House of Lords held that the purpose of the fencing provisions was to prevent the machine operator's body from coming into contact with the machine rather than prevent injury from material being thrown out of the machine.

Subsequent cases have, fortunately for injured workers, tended to be more sympathetic towards the worker in their interpretation of the purposes of statutory provisions aimed at promoting health and safety. For example, in *Wearing v Pirelli Ltd* (1977), an unfenced part of a machine knocked the employee's hand against the materials on which he was working. It was held that the employer was liable.

(b) That the employer's breach did not cause the employee's injury

The employer may defend a case by arguing that, although he was in breach of statutory duty, his breach was not the cause of the employee's injury.

Cummings v Sir William Arrol (1962)

Cummings was a steel erector. His employer failed to provide a safety belt, in breach of his statutory duty. Cummings fell and was injured. If he had been wearing a safety belt, his injuries would not have occurred. Nevertheless, the House of Lords, accepting evidence that even if safety belts had been provided, Cummings would not have worn one, held that the employer's failure to provide a safety belt was not the cause of Cummings's injuries.

Defences which apply to both negligence and breach of statutory duty

Contributory negligence

Until the Law Reform (Contributory Negligence) Act 1945, if the claimant himself was partly responsible for his injuries, he was unable to claim. Despite modifications to the rule, it still operated to cause injustice in a number of cases. Therefore the idea of contributory negligence, whereby the court apportions the blame for the claimant's damage between the claimant and the defendant, was introduced by the 1945 Act. The apportionment is effected on the basis of what the court thinks is just and equitable.

The effect of the defence is that, although the defendant is found liable, it reduces the amount of damages which he has to pay. The court apportions the blame for the damage between the claimant and the defendant on a percentage basis and awards the employee the appropriate proportion of his damage.

This does not mean that if the claimant and the defendant are found equally to blame, the one liability cancels out the other. What it means is that if the claimant's damages are set at £10,000 and the claimant is found to be 50% at fault, he will receive £5,000.

In apportioning the damages, the court considers two factors:

(a) To what extent was the defendant blameworthy in causing the occurrence?

In *Jones v Livox Quarries* (1952), an employee was crushed when riding on the back of a traxcavator contrary to instructions. A dumper truck driven by a fellow employee negligently crashed into the back of the traxcavator. The injured employee was held to be contributorily negligent.

If there is more than one defendant, and contributory negligence is claimed, the court must undertake two processes. First, it must ask what proportion of the blame for the accident should be attributed to the claimant's acts. Then it must apportion the blame among the defendants as joint-tortfeasors. This must be done on two stages rather than one, otherwise a distorted result might be produced. In *Fitzgerald v Lane* (1989), it was originally held that the plaintiff and each of the two defendants were equally to blame for the occurrence. Therefore, contributory negligence was one third. However, the fallacy in this approach lies in the fact that the more parties who are equally to blame, the less the contributory negligence of the plaintiff (for example, if 10 parties were equally to blame, the plaintiff's contributory negligence would be only 10%). The House of Lords therefore held that the correct approach is to ask what proportion of blame does the plaintiff bear for the occurrence? The House decided in this case that it was 50%. The court should then proceed to allocate the blame between the joint-tortfeasors.

(b) To what extent was the defendant blameworthy in causing the damage acts rather than the claimant's acts causing the actual damage?

Sometimes a person may be blameless in causing the occurrence which injures him but may, nevertheless, be guilty of contributory negligence because his actions contributed towards the damage he suffered. A good example is where a passenger in a car fails to wear a seat-belt. In such a case, the claimant might be quite blameless in relation to the cause of the occurrence, but if his injuries are made worse because he failed to wear a seat belt, he will be guilty of contributory negligence.

Froom v Butcher (1976)

In this case, the plaintiff's car was struck by the defendant's car travelling on the wrong side of the road. He was not wearing a seat-belt. In consequence his injuries were worse than they would have been. The court laid down the following guidelines in relation to wearing seat-belts (which apply equally to the failure to wear a crash-helmet while riding a motor-bike):

(i) if wearing a seat belt would have made no difference to the injuries suffered, there will be no deduction for contributory negligence from the plaintiff's damages;

(ii) if wearing a seat-belt would have reduced the injuries suffered, there will be a 15% reduction for contributory negligence; and

(iii) if wearing a seat-belt would have meant that the plaintiff would have suffered no damage, there will be a 25% reduction on account of contributory negligence.

The question has also arisen on a number of occasions where the claimant has accepted a lift with a driver he knows to be drunk. In *Owens v Brimmel* (1977), where the plaintiff and the defendant had been on a pub crawl together before driving home, the plaintiff's damages were reduced by 20%. However, the proportion might be more if the court judges the claimant to be more blameworthy. In *Donelan v Donelan* (1993), the plaintiff and defendant had been drinking together. The plaintiff persuaded the defendant, an inexperienced driver, to drive his large and powerful car. The plaintiff was injured owing to the defendant's negligence. However, as the plaintiff was the dominant party in the venture, his damages were reduced by 75%.

Since the concept of contributory negligence pre-supposes fault on both sides, it is not possible to award 100% contributory negligence. However, findings of contributory negligence as high as 80% have been made. For example, in *Stapley v Gypsum Mines* (1953), where the plaintiff's husband was killed by a mine roof which collapsed, he was found to be 80% contributorily negligent because he had been told that the roof was unsafe and disobeyed orders to bring it down.

Consent (volenti non fit injuria)

Sometimes the claimant may be held to have consented to his injury or to run the risk of injury. This is expressed in the Latin maxim *volenti non fit injuria*, which means 'no injury is done to one who consents'. It seems to have originated from the situation where a free citizen of Rome, in order to raise money, would sell himself as a slave. Having received the money, he would then attempt to assert that it was unlawful to treat him as a slave since he was really a free man. The answer the law gave was that no legal injury was done to one who consented.

There are two forms of consent:

(a) Where the potential claimant knows that what would otherwise be a legal wrong is going to be done to him and he nevertheless consents to it

A good example is a surgical operation. To operate on someone without their consent amounts to the tort of battery. Some people are not happy with the risks of an operation; others, especially members of certain religious groups, simply do not believe in the use of surgery. Hence, wherever possible, a patient is asked to sign a 'consent form' when undergoing surgery. Even then, there may be liability where the doctor has not properly explained the effects of the surgery or other medical treatment. Whether there is liability in such circumstances depends upon whether the doctor who was doing the explaining adhered to accepted principles: *Sidaway v Governors of Bethlem Royal and Maudsley Hospitals* (1985). As may be expected, there is now a significant body of case law building up on the subject, but it is beyond the scope of this text to go into detail.

Where the consent of the patient is not possible, the consent of the next of kin is sought, though in cases of life-saving emergency it is possible that the surgeon would be able to plead the defence of *necessity*. Consent can be implied so that, for example, holding out an arm to receive an injection would probably amount to implied consent.

(b) Where the claimant consents to run the risk of injury

This type of consent has been heavily criticised because it deprives the claimant of any compensation at all for his injuries. Consent (or *volenti*) is a *complete defence* to an action for negligence or breach of statutory duty. It presupposes that the claimant is entirely responsible for his own injuries. However, nowadays, where the alleged consent takes the form of consent to run the risk of injury, the courts are reluctant to apply this defence. Where appropriate, they are much more likely to hold that the 'consent' amounts to *contributory negligence* and to reduce the claimant's damages accordingly.

The defence is restricted by the Unfair Contract Terms Act 1977 which provides, in effect, that liability for *death or personal injury* which arises from negligence in a business context (including breach of statutory duty and liability under the Occupiers' Liability Act) cannot be excluded by agreement or by notice. In addition, s 149 of the Road Traffic Act 1988, provides that liability cannot be excluded by agreement or notice in relation to risks in respect of which insurance is compulsory (that is, death, personal injury and damage to property). The Transport Act 1962 and the Public Passenger Vehicles Act 1981 make similar provisions relating to public transport by rail and road respectively.

Example

Jack drives Jill home after they have been out drinking together. Jill knows that Jack is too drunk to drive. Jack crashes the car, injuring Jill. Jack argues that Jill has consented to run the risk of injury, knowing that he was drunk. Section 149 of the Road Traffic Act 1988 provides that the defence of consent cannot be employed in circumstances where the driver must be covered by compulsory motor insurance (as would be the case here). Therefore, although the partial defence of contributory negligence might succeed, Jill would not be held to have consented.

However, in a case not covered by statute, it was held that there was an implied consent to run the risk of injury. In *Morris v Murray* (1990), a passenger in a private plane was severely injured when the plane crashed. The pilot and the claimant had been drinking heavily together before the flight and it was found that, as a result, the pilot was not fit to fly the aircraft. It was held that as the claimant was a willing participant in the drunken enterprise, he must be deemed to have consented to run the risk of injury.

In employment cases, it has been held that the defence of consent cannot apply where the employer is in breach of statutory duty. However, it may apply where the employee is in breach of the employee's own statutory duty. In *ICI v Shatwell* (1964), two qualified employees were working with explosives. They failed to take proper precautions and an explosion occurred which injured them. One of them claimed that the employer was vicariously liable for the other's breach of statutory duty. It was held that the employee was in breach of his own statutory duty and must therefore be deemed to have consented to the risk of injury. His claim therefore failed.

By and large, the courts have been reluctant to find that a claimant has consented unless there is very strong evidence to that effect. Knowledge of the potential danger is not sufficient. In a number of cases where an employer sent the employee to do a task which both the employer and employee knew was dangerous, it has been held that the employee's advance knowledge of the risk did not mean that he consented to run the risk of injury. For example, in *Smith v Baker* (1891), a workman was sent to work in a quarry where stones were being slung above his head by a crane. He realised that there was a risk of the crane dropping a stone upon him but it was held that he did not consent to run the risk of injury from falling stones.

Rescue cases

If a person is injured while rescuing another from a dangerous situation created by the negligence of a third person, the person who created the danger cannot argue that the rescuer consented to run the risk of being hurt while making the rescue. This principle applies even where the rescuer is employed in a profession where he would be expected to undertake a rescue as part of his employment duties.

In *Haynes v Harwood* (1935), it was held that a policeman was injured when he tried to stop a runaway horse and cart, which was a danger to passers-by. It was argued that he consented to run the risk. However, it as held that when a person acts through compulsion of a moral or social duty to go to the rescue of someone in danger, his claim for damages cannot be defeated by the defence of consent (*volenti*).

For a person to be classed as a rescuer, there must be a dangerous situation requiring the rescuer to take a risk to remove the danger. Thus, in *Cutler v United Dairies* (1933), a runaway horse had run into a field. The plaintiff tried to calm it and was injured. It was held that the plaintiff could not claim to be a rescuer since there was no immediate danger requiring a rescue.

OCCUPIERS' LIABILITY ACTS 1957 AND 1984

If a person is injured as a result of premises being unsafe or an unsafe activity being carried out on the premises, he or she may have one of three legal actions. We have already considered the actions of breach of statutory duty and the tort of negligence. The third possibility is under the Occupiers' Liability Act 1957. This provides that occupiers of premises owe a duty to visitors to take such care as is reasonable in order to see that the visitor will be reasonably safe in using the premises. The later Act, passed in 1984, deals mainly with the thorny question of trespassers.

Relationship between negligence and occupiers' liability

In theory, the Occupiers' Liability Act creates a duty in relation to the state of the premises. Thus, the occupier is liable for any injury arising from the defective state of the premises. Negligence creates a duty to take care in relation to activities carried out on the premises. However, in practice the courts do not always make this distinction. Perhaps, in any case, the distinction in many cases will be academic, since it seems that the duty laid down by the Act and the duty laid down by the tort of negligence are so similar in effect as to produce similar outcomes.

Definition of 'premises'

The Act defines 'premises' in such a way as to include 'any fixed or moveable structure including any vessel, vehicle or aircraft'. Thus 'premises' includes not only land and buildings upon the land but also appliances or objects on the land of which the visitor has been invited or allowed to make use, for example, grandstands, theatre stages, diving-boards, ladders, etc.

Who is an occupier?

The duty is owed by an occupier of premises. This is not necessarily the owner. Thus, if property is rented, the duty will normally be owed by the tenant. This, however, depends on the circumstances of the case. If two or more persons have control over premises, they may all be occupiers. In *Wheat v Lacon* (1966), the owner of a public house allowed the manager to take in paying guests on the upper floor. An accident occurred whereby a guest was injured when slipping on an unlighted staircase leading to the upper floor. The question arose as to whether the pub owners were also occupiers. *Held*: if more than one person had effective control over the premises, each may be an 'occupier' and each owes a duty of care to a lawful visitor.

In the case of a block of rented flats, for example, it may be that while the tenants were occupiers of their particular flats, the owner remained the occupier of common parts such as staircases, lifts, etc.

Lawful visitors

The duty of care imposed by the Act applies only to lawful visitors. This means that they must have entered the premises at the invitation, express or implied, of the occupier, or must have a right of entry on to the premises (for example, a policeman entering under the authority of a search warrant). However, people entering by virtue of the fact that the premises constitute a public or private right of way, will not be owed a duty as visitors. Similarly, persons entering under the Countryside and Rights of Way Act 2000 and the National Parks and Access to Countryside Act 1949, are not to be treated as visitors.

Implied permission to enter premises will normally be held to exist except where it is clear that the occupier would have forbidden entry had he or she been asked in advance. So that, for example, a person who delivers post, newspapers or consignments of goods addressed to the occupant of the premises, even canvassers or beggars, will enter under an implied permission, unless their entry is expressly forbidden, for example, by a notice posted up at the gate of the premises.

Implied permission may also be gained if the occupier of the premises has habitually allowed persons who have no lawful business on the premises to enter them nevertheless. There has been some judicial disagreement as to whether such persons are 'visitors' to whom a duty of care is owed within the meaning of the Act and the law is therefore not clear on this point.

Trespassers

A common problem for enterprises is to what extent the enterprise is liable for injury to persons who have no lawful business on the premises. Such persons are called trespassers, whether they are burglars or simply children who stray while they are playing.

At common law, the only duty owed to a trespasser was not to injure the trespasser intentionally or recklessly (beyond using reasonable force to evict him from the premises). This duty has now been modified by the Occupiers' Liability Act 1984, which also covers other non-visitors such as those who enter under Countryside and Rights of Way Act 2000 and the National Parks and Access to the Countryside Act 1949, so that where the *occupier is aware of a danger or has reasonable grounds to believe it exists*, the occupier owes the trespasser (and other non-visitors) a duty *'to take such care as is reasonable* in all the circumstances of the case to see that he (that is, the non-visitor) does not suffer injury on the premises by reason of danger concerned'.

In relation to countryside access, the 2000 Act amends the 1984 Act by providing that no duty is owed to persons in respect of risks created by natural hazards such as rivers, or the crossing of walls, etc, unless the risk is intentionally or recklessly created by the landowner.

Trespassers can be divided into two categories: they may be persons who enter premises by invitation or right of entry but, once there, abuse their permission to be there by making wrongful use of the permission. In the words of one judge, 'When you invite a person into your house to use the stairs, you do not invite him to slide down the bannisters'. Thus, for example, the football fan who has paid for entry to the match is a visitor to whom the common duty of care is owed while he or she stays on the terraces. However, the fan becomes a trespasser, to whom only the limited duty of care established by the 1984 Act is owed, when he or she invades the pitch.

Alternatively, trespassers may be persons who enter premises without invitation or right of entry and whose presence is either unknown or, if known, is objected to in a practical manner.

However, in the case of children, trespass may be negatived (that is, the child may be found to be a visitor) if it is held that the occupier of the premises set a 'trap' or 'allurement' for the child. (The word 'trap' seems simply to be a variation of 'allurement'.) For example in *Glasgow Corp v Taylor* (1922), while walking in a public park, a child aged seven was attracted by a bush bearing bright berries. The child picked and ate some of the berries. They were poisonous and the child died as a result. On the face of it, the child was a trespasser in that permitting it to use the public park did not permit it to pick and eat the berries. However, it was held that the berries were an allurement and that, therefore, the child was not a trespasser. The corporation thus owed the child a duty of care.

The child in the *Taylor* case was not accompanied by an adult, but the court held that, nevertheless, the corporation was liable. However, in *Phipps v Rochester Corp* (1955), where a child aged five (that is, two years younger than the child in the *Taylor* case), using an open space owned by the local authority, fell into an open trench and broke his leg. He was accompanied by his sister, aged seven. Nevertheless, the court held that the corporation were entitled to assume that small children would be accompanied by their parents.

Defences

The defences to an action under the Occupiers' Liability Act 1957 include contributory negligence and consent, both of which have been dealt with earlier (see p 634). Consent is also a defence under s 1(6) of the 1984 Act which deals with liability to trespassers. In *Ratcliffe v McConnell* (1998), a student entered a college swimming pool as a trespasser, after having drunk four pints of beer. The pool was enclosed by a high wall and the entrance was through gates which were kept locked when the pool was closed. The deep end and the shallow end were clearly marked. The student dived in the shallow end and suffered very severe injury when his head hit the bottom of the pool. It was held that the student had consented to run the risk of injury.

DAMAGES

The assessment of damages in personal injury cases is a complex matter. What follows is simply an overview of how the court approaches the matter. Current levels of award for particular types of damage can be found in the monthly editions of Current Law. It is essential that any business, such as liability insurance, keeps up-to-date with the levels of award, since although most cases are settled out of court, any settlement will normally reflect current judicial practice.

The method of assessment of damages in any injury case depends upon whether the injured person survived the injuries or whether she died as a result. As a general rule, the claimant in a disputed claim must issue a High Court writ or County Court summons within three years of the injury being incurred. How long the case may drag on after that is anyone's guess!

The award of damages is intended to represent 'full compensation'. It is generally made as a lump sum, but the Damages Act 1996, allows the court to make an order for 'structured payment'. In such a case, the award is calculated as a lump sum but the insurance company (the real defendant in most cases) purchases an annuity for the claimant, which bears interest and is paid out over each year of the claimant's life. One advantage to this is that the interest, which is added to the award, is not subject to income tax as it would be if the claimant himself were paid a lump sum which he then invested. However, it seems that structured settlements are not often used where the lump sum award is less than half a million pounds. Alternatives to structured settlements, where the claimant may receive damages otherwise than in a lump sum, are: (a) split trials where an interim award of damages is made, pending the final award; and (b) provisional damages.

The successful claimant who is awarded a lump sum is expected to invest the money so as to provide an income over his lifetime. Until the case of *Page v Sheerness Steel* (1996), the award was made on the assumption that the plaintiff would invest it in stock-market securities. However, in the *Page* case, the House of Lords ruled that awards should be calculated on the basis that they would be invested in safe, index-linked government securities. This will inevitably produce an increase in the amounts awarded to successful claimants.

There is a professional body of people called actuaries (facetiously defined as 'a person who found accountancy too exciting'!) who specialise in the assessment of the likelihood of future events. Insurance companies use them in setting insurance premiums. It has been suggested that they should be used by the courts in the assessment of damages. However, hitherto, there has not been a widespread use of actuarial evidence.

The rule that 'you must take your victim as you find him' applies to the payment of damages. If the defendant negligently causes the death of a high earner with a host of dependants, it is no use arguing that he thought he was causing the death of a lone homeless person with no family. Damages for injuring or causing the death of a high earner can literally run into millions of pounds!

LIVING CLAIMANTS

Loss of earnings to the date of the trial

A living claimant is entitled to loss of earnings up to the date of the trial. The figure arrived at is net of tax and social security contributions.

It is often said that calculating the claimant's damages for loss of earnings up to the date of the trial is a relatively straightforward process. However, as the trial often takes place several years after the claimant's injury, it is necessary to take into account the possibility of a salary rise and possible promotion or, on the other hand, possible redundancy. Evidence will be heard to determine the likelihood of any of these events. So that, for example, should the claimant's company have made widespread redundancies in its enterprise between the date of the injury and the date of trial, the court will have to assess the likelihood that the claimant would have been among the redundancies.

There are two types of deduction made from the net figure. First is the amount of social security benefits received by the claimant over a maximum period of five years (this does not apply if the damages are assessed at less than £2,500). The amount of the benefits is then paid over by the defendant to the Department of Social Security. Second is the amount of any wages paid by the employer, after the injury, under the employee's contract of employment. Occupational sick pay will be the prime example of this.

Expenses

Expenses incurred in respect of the injury may be claimed. These may include travelling to and from hospital, including travel by wife and children; private medical expenses; private nursing care; cost of prescriptions; damage to clothing, etc.

Loss of future earnings

The claimant may claim for loss of future earnings. In practice, the calculation made by the court is rather rough and ready, involving a large degree of prophesy. The court tends not to make use of the professional services of actuaries who are experts in making this kind of calculation. One text calls the process 'educated guesswork' and certainly guesswork plays a prominent part in the process.

Broadly, the calculation involves arriving at a sum which is sufficient, if prudently invested, to maintain the claimant's lifestyle during his working life. A calculation is made as to the injured party's net earnings. Account may be taken of the possibility of future promotion or future redundancy. The lawyers call the figure arrived at by this process the 'multiplicand'.

The multiplicand is multiplied by a multiplier which represents the number of years the claimant will be off work as a result of his injury. In practice, the maximum multiplier for loss of future earnings is 18. There are two reasons for this. The first is because the money is received in a lump sum, often years before the actual earnings would have been received. The second is what the courts call 'the vicissitudes of life', for example, the claimant may have become ill at sometime in the future and have been forced to give up work irrespective of the current accident.

A special adjustment is made to the calculation where it is likely that the claimant will die as a result of her injuries before the end of her normal working life. In such a case, the cost of her own maintenance for the years during which she will not be alive, is deducted from the award.

Nursing care and medical expenses

The claimant may be entitled to damages to pay for future nursing care and medical expenses. This is also calculated on a multiplicand and multiplier basis, although the multiplier in this case is not restricted to 18 as it is in loss of earnings calculations.

Other expenses

If the claimant is severely disabled and needs specially adapted accommodation and transport, the defendant will be liable to pay an appropriate amount in compensation.

Pain and suffering

The claimant may claim for pain and suffering. This takes into account the pain caused by the injury and by subsequent operations needed to treat the injury. It takes into account embarrassment or humiliation caused by disfiguring injuries. It also takes into account the claimant's awareness that her lifespan is likely to be shortened as a result of the injuries.

Loss of amenity

A claim may be made for loss of amenity. This compensates for loss of faculty such as loss of hearing, loss of sight, loss of a limb, etc. It also compensates for loss of ability to do the things which the claimant previously enjoyed doing. For example, a keen footballer may claim for loss of enjoyment if, as a result of the defendant's negligence, his leg were amputated.

Awards for loss of amenity and pain and suffering tend to be lumped together. The amount awarded tends to be at the rate prescribed by a tariff.

DAMAGES ON DEATH

There are three possible sources of claim where a person dies as a result of the defendant's negligence.

Claim on behalf of the deceased

The deceased's personal representative may bring an action on the deceased's behalf. This is made under the Law Reform (Miscellaneous Provisions) Act 1934. Claims in such a case are restricted to expenses caused by the deceased's death (for example, funeral expenses) and items of loss which arise after the injury but before the death (unless, of course, death is instantaneous). Examples of the latter would be the same sort of loss which is claimable by a living claimant, for example, loss of earnings between the accident and the date of death.

Claim by the deceased's dependants

The deceased's dependants may bring an action under the Fatal Accidents Act 1976. The range of dependants entitled to bring such an action is wide. Damages are calculated in one of two ways. The first way is to calculate the net amount the deceased would have earned during the period of dependency. The calculation is done in the same way as that for living claimants. A deduction is then made for the amount the deceased would have spent on himself. What remains is divided among dependants proportionately to their dependence on the deceased.

Alternatively, the court may calculate the amount which the deceased would have spent on each dependent and make that the basis of the award.

In claims involving the dependency of a widow and children, it is customary to award a large part of the total sum to the widow on the assumption that she will maintain the children while they are dependent.

Claim for bereavement

This was introduced by the Administration of Justice Act 1982. The spouse of the deceased or the parents of an unmarried minor (the mother in the case of a minor whose parents are not married), may bring a claim for bereavement. The action is not available to a cohabitee, nor, it was decided in *Doleman v Deakin*, is it available in a case where the injuries which cause the death are inflicted while the minor is 17, but death does not actually occur until the victim has become 18.

The action is somewhat arbitrary in effect. So that, for example, the loving parents of a 20 year old will not (unless they are dependants) be entitled to a bereavement award in respect of his/her death. On the other hand, the parents of a 17 year old who are estranged from him will, nevertheless, be entitled to the bereavement award. The amount awarded is fixed by statute. Currently it is £7,500. Where there is more than one claimant it is apportioned between them.

Lump sum awards

It used to be the case that damages were always awarded in a lump sum. This was a 'once and for all' payment. The court tried to predict whether the claimant's medical condition would worsen and make appropriate allowance.

Nowadays, there is provision for courts to make a provisional award which is made on the basis of the claimant's present state of health but which can later be increased if the claimant suffers some serious deterioration or develops a disease as a result of his injuries. This power is rarely used and the lump sum predominates.

There is also the possibility of a 'structured settlement', under the Damages Act 1996, where the court orders that damages will be paid periodically rather than by way of a lump sum.

It is also possible for the court to have a split trial. This means that the issue of liability can be settled at one trial, leaving the issue of damages to be settled at a later trial. Meanwhile, the claimant is given an interim award pending the final award.

The lump sum has the further disadvantage that the courts do not take inflation into account, so that the value of the award may be reduced in the longer term.

CHAPTER 29

CORPORATIONS

This chapter deals with the concept of corporate personality; the distinction between companies and partnerships; the formalities for forming a company, which includes an account of the contractual capacity of the company; and the distinction between public and private companies.

A 'limited liability company' is one of three main types of business entity. It is useful to consider all three before going on to look at the particular characteristics of a limited company. They are as follows.

(a) Sole trader

There is relatively little regulation of a sole trader, and there is no general requirement of registration. A sole trader has unlimited liability for any debts that his business incurs.

When he becomes insolvent, he may be made bankrupt, which means, among other things, that he cannot be a company director. If he trades in any name other than his own, he must comply with the Business Names Act 1985. If his turnover exceeds the current VAT threshold, he must register for VAT. He must keep sufficient accounts to enable the Inland Revenue to determine his profits, but there is no requirement that his accounts should be audited or even, indeed, prepared by a professional accountant.

(b) Partnership

The legal definition of a partnership is a relationship of 'two or more persons carrying on business in common with a view to profit'. partnerships are known as 'firms'. They are not companies, even though many professional firms have the word 'company' in their title. (Commonly, the title consists of the name of the principal partner or partners followed by '& Co'.)

The relationship is governed by the Partnership Act 1890. This generally provides for rules which operate in the absence of contrary agreement between the partners.

The legal controls over a partnership are not extensive – there is no need for registration. There is no need for the parties to have a partnership agreement but this is advisable. Accounts need only be sufficient to satisfy the Inland Revenue. They need not be audited or prepared by a professional accountant. Registration for VAT is on similar terms to a sole trader. The rules relating to business names also apply to a partnership which is not trading in the names of all the partners.

Each partner is an agent of the firm and has the power to enter into a legally binding agreement on its behalf. This is so even if, by their partnership agreement, the partners have placed restrictions on a partner's power (unless the restrictions have been made known to the party with whom the partner is contracting). As a general rule, partners have unlimited liability for the debts of their firm. Liability of partners is, in effect, joint and several (that is, separate).

It is possible to have a partnership where one or more partners has limited liability.

At present, the Limited Partnerships Act 1907 governs this situation. There must be at least one 'general partner' with unlimited liability. Because of the greater advantages of the limited liability company, very few of these partnerships have been formed: there were only just over 5,000 registered on 31 March 1997. With a normal partnership there is no need for registration. A limited partnership must be registered with the registrar of companies, though the cost of this is only a nominal £2. If a limited partnership is not registered, the liability of the limited partners becomes unlimited. A limited partner does not have the power to bind his firm. With the introduction of the limited liability partnership under the Limited Liability Partnerships Act 2000, care must be taken not to confuse such a partnership with the limited partnership under the Limited Partnerships Act 1907. The possibility of forming such a partnership still remains.

Limited liability partnerships

From 6 April 2001, it will be possible to register a new legal entity, a limited partnership. This is the effect of the provisions of the Limited Liability Partnerships Act 2000 and Regulations to be made under the Act. It is expected that many large professional partnerships will take advantage of the legislation and register as limited liability partnerships.

It will be a corporate body with a legal personality separate from that of its members and, as such, will have much more in common with a limited liability company than it will with a partnership. One small difference is that the new entity can only be formed for the carrying on of a business, whereas a limited liability company can be formed for non-business purposes.

Each member will be an agent of the partnership. As such, if an individual member is liable to any person for any wrongful act or omission in the course of partnership business, the limited liability partnership will be liable to the same extent as the member. A partnership will have 'designated members', presumably to fulfil the role which directors take in the management of a company.

The rules relating to the registration of the limited liability partnership are similar to those relating to limited liability companies and it seems to be intended that the rules of company law, where appropriate, shall be applied to the new entity. The registration will be undertaken by the Registrar of Companies. An 'incorporation document' (the equivalent of a memorandum of association) must be submitted, in a form approved by the Registrar, which must state:

(a) the name of the limited liability partnership (which must end in llp or LLP or its Welsh equivalent);

(b) the country in which the registered office is to be situated (England and Wales, Wales or Scotland);

(c) the address of the registered office;

(d) the names and addresses of each of the persons who are to be members of the limited liability partnership on incorporation; and

(e) either specify which of those persons are to be designated members, or state that every person who, from time to time, is a member of the limited liability partnership is a designated member (as, presumably, will be the case with smaller partnerships).

(c) Corporations

A corporation is a legally created artificial person. Its principal characteristic is that it can continue in perpetuity; it doesn't die, like a natural person. Its existence can only come to an end in a manner prescribed by law.

Corporations are artificial legal persons. As such, they can act only through agents. They can, however, through these agents, be guilty of a crime (though they cannot be sent to prison as a punishment!) and can be liable for torts.

TYPES OF CORPORATION

There are two types of corporation: sole and aggregate.

A corporation sole is where one person has two legal personalities: the corporate one is artificial, the human one is natural. The Crown is an example of a corporation sole. The advantage of a corporation sole is that property owned by the present incumbent in its corporate personality continues to be owned by the corporation after the death of the current holder. For example, property owned by the Queen as a corporation sole will continue to be owned by the Crown after her death. However, property owned by her in her personal capacity will devolve according to the laws of succession.

A corporation aggregate is a corporation, for example, a public limited company, which consists of two or more persons.

Types of aggregate corporation

A corporation aggregate may be created in one of three ways:

(a) by Royal Charter;

(b) by Act of Parliament; and

(c) by registration under the Companies Act 1985.

A chartered corporation is one which is established by Royal Charter. The BBC is an example. It is possible for a chartered corporation to exist by prescription: that is, it has existed as a corporation for so long that the law presumes that it originally had a charter which has now been lost.

A statutory corporation is one which is established directly by statute. It is not the same as a company formed under the Companies Act 1985. Such companies are formed by promoters acting under the provisions of the Act which enable them to form the company.

Corporations registered under the Companies Act 1985 are by far the most common, and of these, companies limited by shares are the most common.

Companies and partnerships contrasted

If a person is thinking of beginning a business enterprise with others, he may consider entering into a partnership or may consider forming a registered company, of which the most popular type is a company with liability limited by shares: a limited liability company. The limited liability company is a corporation: the partnership is an unincorporated association. The main differences between the two are as follows.

Registered company is a separate legal person

A registered company is a legal person, separate from the persons who have subscribed for shares in the company even if these persons own substantially the whole of the shares.

A leading case which illustrates this is *Salomon v Salomon* (1897). S carried on business as a boot and shoe manufacturer. He sold this business to a company called Salomon and Co Ltd. The minimum number of shareholders required by the existing legislation was seven. Therefore, Salomon, his wife, four sons and a daughter each subscribed for one share each. The company paid Mr Salomon for his business by giving him 20,000 £1 shares in the company (so that S ended up with 20,001 shares), £10,000 in debentures and £9,000 in cash. The debentures were secured by a floating charge on the company's assets. A short time later the company became insolvent. A total of £7,000 was available to pay creditors. S claimed this amount by virtue of his debenture. The unsecured creditors resisted the claim on the ground that S was the same as Salomon Ltd and he could not owe money to himself. *Held* by the House of Lords: S and S Ltd were, in law, different people. It was possible for S to make a secured loan to S Ltd and S was therefore entitled to be paid ahead of the unsecured creditors.

A Privy Council case to similar effect is *Lee v Lee's Air Farming* (1960), in which Mrs Lee's husband had been governing director of Lee's Air Farming. He was also the controlling shareholder since he held 2,999 of the 3,000 shares which had been issued. The company carried on the business of crop spraying from aeroplanes and Mr Lee had been employed by the company as its chief pilot 'at a salary to be arranged by the governing director'. Mr Lee was piloting a plane on behalf of the company when he was killed. The question arose whether he had entered into a contract of service with the company. Lord Morris of Borth-y-Gest said:

> It is well-established that the mere fact that someone is a director of the company is no impediment to his entering into a contract to serve the company … Control would remain with the company whoever might be the agent of the company to exercise it. The fact that so long as the deceased continued to be the governing director, with amplitude of powers, it would be for him to act as the agent of the company to give the orders, does not alter the fact that the company and the deceased were two separate and distinct legal persons. If the deceased had a contract of service with the company then the company had a right of control.

It was held that Lee was an employee of the company.

A partnership, on the other hand, is regulated principally by the Partnership Act 1890, which defines a partnership as 'the relationship which subsists between persons carrying on business with a view to profit'. It is simply the sum total of its members, although the rules of the Supreme Court allow a partnership to sue and be sued in the partnership name. However, if the partnership is the plaintiff, the defendant can require it to disclose the names and addresses of all its members.

No limit on the number of members a company may have

The number of partners in a partnership is limited to 20 but this may be exceeded in the case of solicitors, accountants and stockbrokers and any other profession named in regulations. Regulations have listed a number of professions where the limit might be exceeded. Although there is a minimum number of persons permitted in a company, there is no maximum.

Limited liability

If, as is usual, a company is formed with limited liability, the liability of its individual members is limited to the amount which the member has agreed to subscribe. Thus if a member has agreed to take 100 shares of £1 each, that represents the extent of his liability. If he has actually paid for his shares, he has no further liability should the company go into liquidation. Note that persons who are asked to lend money to private companies often ask the controlling shareholder(s) to guarantee repayment of the loan (the legal form by which this is done is called an indemnity). This means that, in effect, the benefit of limited liability is lost in respect of the loan. It is also not uncommon for landlords to ask for such guarantees when renting premises to the company. It is, however, unusual for ordinary trade creditors to ask for such guarantees so that if the directors of a small company can avoid giving guarantees to creditors such as banks, they can trade with little or no risk to their own private assets should the company become insolvent.

In a partnership, on the other hand, liability is, in effect, joint and several. This means that each member of the partnership is fully liable to the extent of his private assets, for the debts of the partnership. For example A, who has private assets of £100,000, is in partnership with B, who has no private assets. The partnership is dissolved with debts of £100,000. A will be liable to the partnership's creditors to the extent of his private assets of £100,000. This is so even if the insolvency has been caused by factors which are mainly B's responsibility, for example, unpaid tax on B's share of partnership profits, or where B has entered into ill-considered contracts for goods or services which the partnership does not need.

In such a case, where A satisfied the partnership debts, A would be entitled to an appropriate contribution from B. However, where B lacks assets, the practical effect will be that A funds the shortfall in the partnership assets.

There is the possibility of creating a limited partnership under the Limited Partnerships Act 1907. These are registered with the Registrar of Companies. They must have at least one general partner with unlimited liability and one partner with limited liability. The maximum number of partners is limited as with a general partnership. A limited partner contributes a stated amount to the partnership assets and his liability to contribute towards the firms debts is limited to that amount. He may take no part in the management of the partnership (if he does he loses his limited liability for the period during which he participates in management) and is not an agent of the firm. Limited partnerships are not common owing to the general superiority of the private limited liability company.

Management of the company

The company's affairs are managed by its directors who are the agents of the company for that purpose. A director is usually a member of the company, though there is no legal requirement to this effect. Some directors, particularly of large multinational companies, may possess simply a token shareholding. The individual member has no power to act as agent on behalf of the company (unless specifically appointed for the purpose) or to manage its affairs.

Each partner is an agent for the firm. This has the effect that if one partner makes unauthorised contracts on behalf of the partnership, which are within his apparent authority to make, the partnership as a whole is liable on those contracts.

Continuous existence

A company, being a legal person, exists independently of its natural members. Thus the death or bankruptcy of a member does not affect the existence of a company. In the case of a partnership, however, the death or bankruptcy (unless there is an agreement to the contrary) of a partner will cause the partnership to be dissolved. In practice, the partnership is usually reconstituted by the remaining members but the need to find the money for the deceased partner's share can cause difficulty. In the case of the death of a company member, their shares devolve according to the laws of succession. There is no compulsion upon the remaining members to purchase the shares of the deceased member.

Contracts with members

A company, being a distinct legal person, can contract with its members: see *Lee v Lee's Air Farming* (above). A partnership, on the other hand, cannot contract with its members. In *Green v Hertzog* (1954), a partner brought an action against his partners for the repayment of a loan which he had made to the partnership. The action was dismissed because a partner lending money to a partnership is lending part of the money to himself. The proper proceeding for recovering the money was by bringing an action under the rule for distribution of assets on final settlement of accounts, as laid down in s 44 of the 1890 Act.

Shares are freely transferable

Shares in a company can be transferred or mortgaged without reference to other members of the company, though in the case of a small private company there is often a requirement in the articles of the company requiring the directors to approve any transfer of shares. This allows the directors to prevent a transfer of shares to someone who may not have the company's best interests at heart or someone with whom they feel unable to work. In the case of a partnership, no new partner can be introduced without the consent of all the others, unless the partnership agreement provides to that effect.

Borrowing powers

A company can borrow money more easily because it is able to create a *floating charge* over the property of the company. A floating charge is a procedure by which the company's assets, for the time being, are offered as security to the lender of money. The floating charge is created by a document called a debenture which provides for the lender/debenture holder to appoint a receiver to look after the lender's interest in certain circumstances, usually if the borrower falls down on its obligations in relation to repayment of the loan. Sometimes the receiver simply collects the assets of the company together and sells them for the benefit of the lender; at other times the receiver is able to sell the company as a going concern and pay off the lender with the proceeds.

The best type of security is a fixed charge (that is, a mortgage) of real property. Both a partnership and a company can create this type of charge. However, though property other than real property can be mortgaged, for example a car or a computer or a piece of machinery, there are difficulties with such mortgages. First, if the borrower wishes to sell the mortgaged property in order to replace it, the existing mortgage on the property has to be discharged and a fresh mortgage on the new property entered into. If there is a regular turnover in the mortgaged property this would create practical difficulties.

Secondly, a mortgage of chattels (that is, goods) is subject to registration under the Bills of Sale Act 1878. The formalities for doing this are so strewn with pitfalls for the lender that financiers prefer to avoid taking security by way of chattel mortgages: alternative forms of secured finance such as hire-purchase are preferred. Thus the floating charge which can be entered into by a company, effectively mortgaging all its assets for the time being, including debts owed to the company, gives the company a solid advantage in raising finance.

TYPES OF REGISTERED COMPANY

There are three main types of registered company:

(a) unlimited;

(b) limited by guarantee;

(c) limited by shares.

Unlimited companies

This type of company is not very popular. One reason for its use was that until relatively recently all limited liability companies had to file full accounts at Companies House, where they were open to inspection by anyone who chose to inspect them, including the company's competitors. Unlimited companies were exempt from that requirement. Nowadays, however, the information which small private limited companies are required to file is minimal and unlikely to give much information away to competitors, particularly in view of the time lag between the accounting period and the time when the accounts have to be filed. Thus a private limited company will usually be the better option for those requiring the benefit of incorporation. In contrast to a partnership, the main advantage of an unlimited liability company over a partnership, nowadays, is that the company has perpetual succession (that is, continuous existence).

An unlimited company must be formed as a private company, though until 1980 it could be formed as a private or a public company.

Companies limited by guarantee

Where a company is limited by guarantee, each member guarantees a particular amount of money which he will pay in the event of a liquidation of the company. In such a case, each member is liable up to the amount of his guarantee, which will be the amount stated in the memorandum of association.

Until the Companies Act 1980 changed the law, a company limited by guarantee could be registered with or without a share capital. Now such a company can be formed only without a share capital. However, companies which were formed prior to the Act and which have a share capital, remain in existence. In such a case, in the case of a liquidation, a subscriber will be liable to pay up any amount outstanding in relation to the shares which have been allotted to him.

Companies limited by guarantee are usually formed for charitable or educational purposes or for professional or trade associations, where the resources of the company come from donations or subscriptions. Under s 30, a company limited by guarantee may omit the word 'limited' from its name if certain criteria are met.

Companies limited by shares

A share in a company indicates two things:

(a) the shareholder's liability to the company; and

(b) the extent of the shareholder's interest in the company.

In relation to liability, it means that where a company is limited by shares, the liability of members in the event of a liquidation of the company is limited to any amount outstanding on the shares allotted to the member.

EUROPEAN ECONOMIC INTEREST GROUPINGS

The idea of European Economic Interest Groupings (EEIGs) was introduced in order to allow businesses to develop by cross-border co-operation between businesses which are perhaps too small to enter into the expense of mergers, take-overs, etc. EEIGs are regulated by the European Economic Interest Grouping Regulations (SI 1989/638).

The members of a group do not need to be companies but may be sole traders, partnerships, or, from April 2001, limited liability partnerships. The group will have unlimited liability and members will be jointly liable on any contracts it makes.

A group may be set up in any Member State of the European Union. It is a corporate body and, as such, it has its own legal personality. It is registered with the Registrar of Companies and the fees payable are the same as those which are payable on the registration of a company. It must have a 'formation contract' which is the equivalent of a company's memorandum. The filing requirements, though in some respects similar to those of a company, are much less onerous. In particular, it does not have to have audited accounts and does not need to file an annual return.

Each member must have at least one vote in the decision-making process, but the formation contract can give more than one vote to a certain member or members, providing no one member holds a majority of the votes. The members must appoint at least one manager. An EEIG registered in the UK may appoint a company as its manager providing a natural person is registered as the company's representative.

The members decide on the powers of the managers. The group may restrict the power of its managers by requiring a double signature. However, it will only bind third parties if its existence is advertised in the London Gazette.

The group must use European Economic Interest Grouping or EEIG in its name. It is not permitted to use 'limited', 'unlimited' or 'public limited company' as part of its name. Apart from this, similar restrictions apply to naming the EEIG as apply to naming companies registered under the Companies Act 1985.

SHAREHOLDERS AND DEBENTURE HOLDERS

A registered company limited by shares is financed by shares and debentures. It may also be financed by loan capital, which in turn may be secured and the security evidenced by a document called a debenture.

Advantages and disadvantages of share capital rather than loan capital.

Advantages

(a) If a company is in difficult financial circumstances, it need pay no return (known as a 'dividend') on the capital that it is using. On the other hand, interest on a loan has to be paid when it is contractually due (although the lender will often reschedule the debt if it is clear that pursuing his money too assiduously may turn a temporary difficulty into a terminal one).

(b) The capital itself does not have to be repaid.

Disadvantages

(a) If the issue is done through a stock market, the costs of making the issue (for example, stockbrokers, solicitors, prospectuses, merchant bank, etc) tend to be expensive.

(b) Investors may expect a greater return from a 'new' company, to reflect the perceived additional risk they are taking.

(c) The more shares that are issued, the greater the risk of loss of control of the company.

(d) Paying dividends on share capital is not as tax efficient (under the current tax regime) as paying interest on loan capital.

Types of share

Shareholders subscribe for shares because:

(1) they may receive a return on their investment in the form of a dividend (though small private companies often do not declare dividends); and

(2) the value of their shares increases as the value of the company increases; and

(3) they have an opportunity to be involved in the management of the company by a vote in the general meeting.

The two main types of share are' preference' and 'ordinary'. There is, in addition, a class of shares called 'deferred' shares. There are no standard rights attaching to any of these classes of share: the rights in relation to a particular class of shares are those which are set out in the articles of the company. The usual differences between classes of share relate to different voting rights and different dividend rights. There may, therefore, be a wide range of shares within a company, each carrying different rights.

Preference shares

Preference shares carry some preference over ordinary shares in the company. In practical terms, they are a sort of hybrid of share capital and loan capital. They are usually the first to be paid a dividend, which may mean that if the company makes insufficient profits, the preference shareholders get a dividend but the ordinary shareholders do not. However, the preferential dividend is usually at a fixed rate, which means that, although the preferential shares are a safer investment, if the company shows good profits the ordinary shareholders will reap the greater dividend, since the dividend paid to ordinary shareholders is usually related to the profitability of the company. Preference shareholders are also usually entitled to preferential repayment of capital if the company is wound up.

There are a number of different types of preference share. These are:

Cumulative: if the company fails to pay a dividend on its preference shares in any year, the dividend is carried forward. Dividends accumulated in this way must be paid before the ordinary shareholders receive any dividend.

Convertible: these carry an option to convert into ordinary shares at a future date. However, they may carry a lower dividend rate because of the potential capital gain which may be realised when they are converted.

Participating: in addition to the fixed interest dividend, the shares may carry a right to participate in the profits of the company. Thus participating preference shareholders get the best of both worlds.

Redeemable: these shares are redeemable at a future date.

Ordinary shares: ordinary shareholders are entitled to be paid a dividend on their shares only after the preference shareholders have been paid. (If the company is a small one, where all the shareholders are employed by the company, it may well be that the income of the shareholders is given by way of salary or other remuneration rather than by dividend.) In a company where the preference shares have priority in respect of repayment of capital where the company is wound up, the ordinary shareholder will have his capital returned only after the preference shareholder has been repaid.

Deferred shares: deferred shares are not common nowadays. The holders of deferred shares are entitled to a dividend only when a specified minimum dividend has been paid to the ordinary shareholders. They often rank behind the ordinary shareholders in respect of a return of capital in a winding-up. Deferred shareholders often have special voting rights which entitle them to a disproportionately large voice in general meetings of the company.

Non-voting shares: sometimes non-voting shares are issued. These are usually called 'A' shares. They often have the same rights as ordinary shares except in relation to voting. Companies might use these when they wish to raise additional capital without diluting the voting rights of the existing members (family-owned companies often use them in order to raise capital, while keeping control of the company within the family).

Golden shares: a golden share is a share with a special power. The special power is usually the ability to veto a takeover of the company. The government retained a golden share in certain former nationalised companies which it sold under its privatisation policy.

Debentures

A debenture is a document which creates or acknowledges a debt due from a company. Debenture holders receive interest on their loan rather than a dividend. This generally carries greater security than a share, since the interest on it may be paid out of the company's capital whereas a dividend to a shareholder may only be paid out of profits. Debentures are often secured by either a fixed charge or a floating charge. Debenture holders are not members of the company and, unless the terms of the debenture expressly permit, are not entitled to attend and vote at company meetings.

What the member owns

The member owns an unspecified part of the company's undertaking. The member's rights are given by way of shares in the company. For example, if a company has issued 100 ordinary shares at £1 each and Alice has subscribed for 20 of them, this means that she owns one-fifth of the company's undertaking, but there are no particular company assets which she can claim to own.

Authorised or nominal share capital

Each company has an *authorised* or *nominal* share capital. Conventionally this almost always used to be £100, since stamp duty used to be levied on the amount of a company's authorised capital. However, the law has now changed so that stamp duty is levied only on the company's *issued* share capital. This means that it is immaterial at what level the nominal capital is set: it is no more costly to have £1 million nominal capital than it is to have £100. When registering a company, therefore, it is advisable to register it with the level of nominal capital that the company might need in the foreseeable future. If this is not done, s 121 of the Companies Act permits a company to increase its share capital. However, this may only be done if the company's articles of association give it the power to do so. If they do not give such a power, the articles must be altered by special resolution in order to give the power.

The company may *issue* or *allot* shares up to a maximum of its authorised capital. If the price of the shares is paid in full by the time they are issued, they are said to be 'fully paid-up'. If the price of the shares is only partly paid, leaving part of the price to be paid at a later date (this may be a specific date or may, for example, be at an unspecified date when the company needs to call up the additional capital), they are said to be 'partly paid'. The capital which is outstanding on such shares is called 'unpaid' or 'uncalled' capital.

The shares in a company might be issued at *par*. This means that for each £1 share the company will receive £1 in cash or in kind. The shares might be issued at a *premium*. This means that the company will receive more than the nominal value of each share either in cash or in kind. For example, if Alice sold her business, worth £20,000, to Alice Ltd in return for 100 shares of £1, the shares would have been issued at a premium since they would have been sold by the company for £200 each. If shares are quoted on the stock exchange and the current price is below par value, for example, where each £1 share is selling for 50p, they are said to be standing at a discount. It is not possible to *issue* shares at a discount, since the possibilities for fraud are too great.

FLOATING A COMPANY ON THE LONDON STOCK EXCHANGE

As we will see, a private company is not allowed to offer its shares to the public. Its potential for raising money through a share issue is therefore restricted to a private subscriber or subscribers. An alternative is to convert the private limited company into a public limited company and to seek to raise money through the stock market. In addition, public limited companies exist which are not members of a stock market or which are only members of a privately run market. It may be that they will seek to upgrade their status by securing a quotation on the London Stock Exchange (LSE), or the less onerous (in terms of controls and expense) Alternative Investment Market (AIM). The stock market is also used to raise additional finance from companies whose shares are already quoted in the market.

A listing on the LSE is achieved by reference to the Listing Rules. These are regulated by three EU Directives. The Directives are currently implemented in domestic law by Part IV of the Financial Services Act 1986, but are shortly to be replaced by Part VI of the Financial Markets and Services Act 2000. The Directives require a Listing Authority to be authorised. In the UK, this is the Financial Services Authority (formerly the LSE was the Listing Authority). The Directives allow the Listing Rules to be more stringent than those laid down by the Directives and, in some respects, the rules of the UK Listing Authority are, in fact, more stringent.

The LSE lags behind the two largest American exchanges in terms of turnover, but has been the most successful in attracting the shares of foreign companies – over 50% of the trade on the LSE is in foreign shares. In the case of some countries, there is as large (or nearly as large) a trade in the shares of their companies on the London Exchange as there is on their own Exchanges, for example, France, Belgium, the Netherlands and Spain.

Listed companies must sign a Listing Agreement which commits the directors to high standards of conduct of their company's affairs and high levels of reporting to their shareholders. There is a choice between the Official List (OL) and the AIM. The regulations and the costs for the AIM are lower than those on the OL. For companies which wish their shares to be traded but are unable or unwilling (for example, because of the cost involved) to achieve a listing on the OL or AIM, there is a market called OFEX which is run by a stockbroker, JP Jenkins. Weetabix and Arsenal Football Club are traded on OFEX. Where a company is offering shares to the public in the European Union, otherwise than by a listing on a stock exchange, the person making the offer must comply with Directive 89/298/EEC, which has been implemented by the Public Offers of Securities Regulations 1995. A principal requirement is that the company offering the shares should publish a prospectus and that the prospectus should be available to members of the public free of charge. The Financial Services and Markets Act 2000 contains provisions relating to what will become called 'non-listing' prospectuses. When those come into force, presumably, the 1995 Regulations will be revoked.

The cost of obtaining and maintaining a listing on the Official List is substantial, much more so than a listing on AIM. The lead time is often one to two years. To obtain a listing, at least 25% of the company's share capital must be available to the public. The Exchange also requires that a company has a profitable trading record stretching back for three years, although this requirement may be relaxed in certain types of case. So, for example, Eurotunnel, which was undertaking a major capital project but without any trading record, was given a listing.

The company must obtain a sponsor (this will be a merchant bank or a stockbroker who is officially approved to act as such) who will co-ordinate the whole of the complex process. Provisions relating to sponsors are contained in ss 88 and 89 of the Financial Services and Markets Act 2000. The sponsor will initially ascertain the suitability of the company to be floated on the stock exchange and will draw up a timetable for the issue and advise on the manner in which the shares will be issued. The sponsor will also ensure that the company complies with the Listing Rules and also oversee the preparation of a detailed prospectus. This will contain financial detail, details of the proposed directors, valuations of the company's assets, details regarding major contracts, detail regarding the companies operations in relation to geographical locality, etc.

Methods of issue

There are three main methods, which are as follows:

Offer for sale: in this case, the company fixes the price at which it is prepared to sell its shares and offers them to the public, usually via a newspaper advertisement. Strictly speaking, it is the potential subscriber who makes the offer since, in a popular issue, the shares may be over-subscribed, in which case the subscriber will only receive a proportion of the shares he applied for. (Sometimes, in order to encourage wider participation, those who subscribe for only a small number of shares (say 200) will get the full amount of their application, with only larger applications suffering a reduction.)

Offer for sale by tender: this method has become increasingly popular in recent years. In this case, investors are invited to subscribe for shares and state the price they are willing to pay (there is usually a minimum price stipulated). The company then sells the shares at the highest price which enables them to sell the issue.

Example

Let us say 5 million shares are on offer. Subscribers bid £2 for 1 million, £2.50 for 2 million, £3 for 2 million and £3.50 for 3 million. The 'strike' price, that is, the price at which the shares will be sold, is £3, that is, the highest price at which they can sell the whole 5 million. Those who bid below £3 will receive no allocation. Those who bid £3.50 will receive their allocation at £3.

Placing: this is increasingly popular since it tends to be cheaper than an offer for sale. Publicity costs and underwriting costs, among others, are not incurred. Most new issues nowadays are effected by 'placing'. The shares are 'placed', usually with institutions like insurance companies or pension funds. The Stock Exchange requires the placing to involve a range of investors. However, there is no longer any control over the maximum amount (formerly less than £15 million) for which the placing method may be used.

Underwriting

It is possible that, in an offer for sale or offer for sale by tender, the new shares will not all be sold. The issue is said to be 'under-subscribed'. To ensure that the company does not face undue problems caused by the under-subscription, a new issue is usually underwritten. This means that, for a fee, a financial institution (usually the sponsor of the issue), will agree to take up any shares which are left unsold. The fee charged is usually 2% of the proceeds of the issue. They usually spend some of this fee in employing sub-underwriters, in order to spread the risk.

Rights issues

A rights issue is a method of raising new capital from existing shareholders. If the company is doing well, rights issues tend to be popular. If not, shareholders may decline to take up their rights. However, to guard against this risk, rights issues are usually underwritten. The rights issue is usually priced lower than the market value of the shares, as an incentive for shareholders to take them up. However, if shareholders do not wish to take up the issue, they can sell their rights through the market.

Example

A supermarket has issued 50 million shares. The market price is £2.30 each. The company is therefore valued at £115 million. It wishes to raise an extra £10 million by a rights issue. It therefore creates an extra 5 million shares which are offered to existing shareholders, *pro rata* to their existing holding, at £2 each. The rights issue is said to be a 'one for ten' issue because shareholders are offered one additional share for each ten shares they already own. Theoretically, this dilutes the value of each share. The company now has 55 million shares and its value is £125 million (that is, £115 million plus the extra £10 million realised by the rights issue). The value of each share is, therefore, £125 million divided by 55 million: approximately £2.27. The reason this is theoretical is because the market sets the price of the shares and, with a thriving company, the share price may remain the same or even increase after the issue. On the other hand, if the rights issue is seen by the market as a desperate move, it may be that the share price will fall.

Scrip issues

Sometimes a company may wish to revalue its shares in the market without raising fresh capital. This may be because it is a perception that investors are less likely to buy high-priced shares. Thus, for example, suppose a company has 5 million shares trading at £20 each, valuing the company at £100 million. It is desired to bring the share price down to around £5. It may make a scrip issue of three shares for each one already owned. Thus the company will now have 20 million shares trading at £5 each to achieve its market capitalisation of £100 million.

MANAGEMENT OF THE COMPANY

The company is managed by:

(a) the shareholders in general meeting who have various responsibilities allocated to them by the Companies Act. Examples are: to alter the Memorandum and Articles; to alter share capital; to authorise the issue of share; to remove and appoint directors and the auditor;

(b) the board of directors which deals with the day to day running of the company. As a general rule, the shareholders cannot override the exercise of power which has been given to directors by the Articles, even by unanimous vote in general meeting.

Decisions of general meetings are decisions of the company and are made by resolutions which are passed by those attending in person or by proxy. These are of three types:

Ordinary resolutions: these require a majority of the members voting in person and, where this is permitted by the articles of the company, voting by proxy, at a meeting of which notice has duly been given. The length of notice required depends on a number of factors including the type of meeting at which the resolution is proposed, but is usually 14 days.

Extraordinary resolutions: these must be passed by 75% of the members voting in person, or by proxy, at a meeting of which notice has duly been given. The length of notice required depends on a number of factors including the type of meeting at which the resolution is proposed, but is usually 14 days.

Special resolutions: these must be passed by 75% of the members voting in person, or by proxy, at a meeting of which at least 21 days' notice has been given specifying the intention to propose the resolution as a special resolution.

TYPES OF COMPANY LIMITED BY SHARES

There are two types of registered company limited by shares: public and private.

The main advantage of a public company is that the public may be asked to subscribe for shares, though unless the company is quoted on a *recognised* market, the subscriber may be in no better position to sell the shares, in practice, than the holder of shares in a private company.

The main advantages of a private company (and they are many) include:

(a) it is able to commence trading immediately on incorporation: it does not need a trading certificate;

(b) it does not need a minimum share capital or need to have a certain amount of its capital allotted and paid-up;

(c) it needs to have one member and one director: a public company must have a minimum of two members and two directors;

(d) private companies which qualify as small or medium-sized companies may file abbreviated accounts with the registrar of companies;

(e) the company secretary of a private company does not have to be qualified as such or experienced as such; and

(f) a private company is able to use the written resolution procedure under s 381 without the need to hold a formal meeting.

There are a wide number of other advantages to having a private company. Most of them require less formality to achieve a particular purpose than does a public company, especially in relation to financial matters.

PUBLIC COMPANIES

A public company must be one which is limited by shares or is limited by guarantee with a share capital (s 1 of the Companies Act 1985). It may offer its shares and debentures to the public. The company is identified as a public company by using the words 'public limited company' after its name. The phrase may be abbreviated by use of the letters 'plc'. The company's memorandum of association must state that it is a public company.

The authorised capital of the company must be not less than £50,000. Before it can commence business or exercise any borrowing powers, it must receive a trading certificate from the Registrar of Companies, under s 117 of the Companies Act. An application for the certificate must be made in prescribed form and must be signed by a director of the company or by the company secretary. The principal matters about which the registrar must be satisfied before he grants a certificate are:

(a) that the nominal value of the company's allotted share capital is not less than the authorised minimum, that is, £50,000; and

(b) that not less than one quarter of the nominal value of each allotted share in the company has been received by the company. If the shares are issued at a premium, the whole of the premium must have been paid up.

This means that if 50,000 x £1 shares have been allotted at a price of £2 each, £1.25 (that is, 25 pence in the pound in relation to the par value of the shares plus £1, which is the premium) must be fully paid up.

Shares allotted to employees under employees' share schemes do not count towards determining the nominal value of the company's allotted share capital unless such shares are paid-up as to one quarter of their nominal value plus the full amount of any premium.

A public company must have at least two members. It must have at least two directors (s 282 of the Companies Act).

PRIVATE COMPANIES

A private company is any kind of Registered Company, not being a public company. A private company may not advertise its shares or debentures for sale to the public: s 170 of the Financial Services Act 1986. Like a public company, a private company used to be required to have a minimum of two members. It had to be formed with two members and was not permitted to allow its membership to fall below two. However, many private companies (known as 'one-person companies' in acknowledgment of the practical reality of the situation) were formed with one controlling member, the other member being a nominee in order to conform to legal requirement. Thus, Gerry Builders Ltd might be formed with a share capital of £100, Gerry being allotted 99 of the shares and his accountant, solicitor, or a member of his family being allotted the other share.

Now, pursuant to the 12th EC Company Law Directive, the Companies (Single Member Private Limited Companies) Regulations 1992 (SI 1992/1699) have been passed, with effect from July 1992, to permit private companies limited by shares or by guarantee, to be formed with one member, or to allow the company's membership to fall to one member. The regulations do not apply to unlimited private companies, which must still be formed with a minimum of two members. A private company must have at least one director. The company must also have a secretary. Neither person needs to be a member of the company but, in practice, in small private companies directors are almost invariably members and company secretaries usually are. A sole director may not be the secretary. Thus, in a one-person company, it is not unusual for the controlling person to be the sole director and for the nominee shareholder to be the secretary. If there are two directors, there is nothing to prevent one of them acting as secretary. Though there are no statutory restrictions on the transfer of shares in a private company (beyond the fact that they must not be advertised for sale to members of the public), it is customary to place such restrictions in the company's articles of association. The reason for this is to be able to reject as members, persons whom the existing members or directors regard as undesirable.

All companies must prepare full accounts for presentation to their shareholders. However, there are special concessions relating to private companies which qualify as small companies or medium-sized companies, whereby they may file abbreviated accounts with the Registrar of Companies. The concessions vary according to the classification of the company: those given to small companies are extensive. Small and medium-sized companies are defined by reference to annual turnover, balance-sheet value and average weekly number of employees. A company must meet two of the three criteria set out for the classification in order to qualify. The filing concessions are intended to preserve some of the privacy of the company relating to its financial affairs, though it is arguable that limited liability confers a significant benefit for which loss of financial privacy is a small price to pay.

The purpose of the distinction between private and public companies is to allow small companies to enjoy a less rigorous control over their affairs (though it must not be assumed that all private companies are small: Littlewoods, the football pools and mail-order empire, is a private company), as there is no need to safeguard the public in relation to investment in the companies. There are much stricter controls in relation to public companies.

The main purpose of creating a public company is to raise money by public subscription. This is usually done by a flotation on the stock exchange. The requirements for a flotation on the stock exchange are rigorous and go well beyond the controls exercised over a public company by the Companies Acts.

FORMATION OF THE COMPANY

In order to form a company, prescribed documentation has to be filed with the Registrar of Companies, together with the appropriate fee. At present, this is £20, though there is a same-day service if the documents are presented at Companies House before 3 pm. The same-day service costs £100. If everything is in order, the registrar duly issues a certificate of incorporation. In the case of a private company, this enables the company to begin trading immediately. In the case of a public company, a trading certificate issued under s 117 of the Companies Act 1985 is a further necessity.

The documents to be filed with the Registrar are listed below. Under the Companies Act 1985 (Electronic Communications) Order 2000, the documents may be filed electronically, in which case the requirements for signature in the presence of a witness and the attestation of the signature by a witness, do not apply.

Memorandum of Association

This is the document which gives basic information about the company to the outside world. The memorandum must be signed by each subscriber in the presence of a witness. Table B of the 1985 Companies Act provides a model memorandum for a private company limited by shares; Table F gives a model memorandum for a public company limited by shares. The contents of the memorandum are prescribed by s 2 of the Companies Act 1985. It must contain the following.

(a) The name of the company

Section 25 provides that if a company is limited, the last word of its name must be 'limited' if it is a private company; and the last words must be 'public limited company' if it is a public company. This warns people that they are dealing with an enterprise which has limited liability in respect of its corporate debts.

There are provisions which allow the words to be abbreviated to 'Ltd' and 'plc' for private and public companies respectively and which allow for their Welsh equivalents to be used in certain circumstances. Section 30 permits the word 'limited' to be dispensed with by a private company limited by guarantee, provided the company's objects meet certain criteria and its memorandum or articles contain specified restrictions as to the way in which the company may deal with its assets.

Section 26 of the Companies Act contains restrictions on the names which the registrar will register. The most important restriction is that a name will not be registered if it is the same as a name appearing on the index of names of companies held by the Registrar. The index can be searched free of charge on the Companies House website. Further restrictions are: where the use of the name would be a criminal offence or would be offensive; where the words 'limited', 'unlimited' or 'public limited company' or their abbreviations, appear anywhere except at the end of the name.

To try to prevent the public from being misled, certain names will not be registered without approval. Others require that a 'relevant body' be given the opportunity to register its objection to the name. In addition, there are provisions relating to 'phoenix companies'.

The Secretary of State must approve the registration of a name which implies national or multi-national pre-eminence; local or central government connection, patronage or sponsorship; business pre-eminence or representative status; objects or status, such as insurance. Certain names require that a 'relevant body' be given the opportunity to make objections to the name. Thus, for example, in order to use a name including the word 'Royal' or 'Royalty', a written request must be sent to the Home Secretary asking him if he has any objections to the proposed use of the word, and, if so, to state the reason for them. The reply must be forwarded to the Registrar of Companies, who has a discretion to decline to register the name.

The Insolvency Act 1986 introduced measures aimed at preventing people from being misled by so called 'phoenix companies'. A phoenix company was an insolvent company which was purchased from the liquidator by its existing management and then continued to trade as before, but free of its creditors. Sections 216 and 217 of the Insolvency Act provide that where a company goes into insolvent liquidation, anyone who was a director or shadow director of that company at any time during the previous 12 months, who becomes a director of a company using the name or trading name of the insolvent company, within five years of the insolvency, commits an offence.

Change of name

A company may change its name voluntarily, subject to the above rules, by passing a special resolution and sending a copy to the registrar with the appropriate fee.

There are three circumstances in which a company can be compelled to change its name. There is also a circumstance at common law where a company can be prevented, by injunction, from continuing to use its registered name. In such a case, in order to carry on trading, the company will be compelled to change its name.

The three circumstances in which, under the Act, a company may be compelled to change its name are:

(a) where a company is registered under a name which is the same as, or too like, a name which appears, or should have appeared, in the index of names of companies at the time the company was registered. In such circumstances the Secretary of State may, within 12 months of the name being registered, give a written direction to change the name: s 28(2) of the Companies Act 1985;

(b) where it appears to the Secretary of State that a company has provided misleading information for the purpose of securing the registration of a particular name, or has given undertakings or assurances which have not been fulfilled. In such a case, the Secretary of State may, within five years of the name being registered, give the company a written direction to change the name: s 28(3) of the Companies Act 1985;

(c) where the registered name gives so misleading an indication of the nature of its activities as to be likely to cause harm to the public. In such a case, the Department of Trade and Industry may direct a company to change its name. There is no time limit within which such a direction must be made. The direction must be complied with within six weeks, unless the company applies to a court within three weeks to have the direction set aside. The court may set the direction aside or confirm it.

Before the Business Names Act 1985, it was possible for a company to circumvent the above rules by adopting a trade name which was not the company name. For example, a small tyre company trading only in Northampton might register itself as Smith's Tyres Ltd, but trade under the name of International Tyre Services. However, under the Business Names Act, similar rules apply to the trading names of a company as they do to its registered name.

Despite these rules, it may be that a company secures the registration of a name which is so similar to that of an existing company or trading name that the existing enterprise has justifiable fears that the new company may be mistaken for the existing enterprise. In such a case, the existing enterprise may apply to the court for an injunction preventing the new company from using its registered name. In doing so, it alleges that the new company is committing the tort of 'passing off', that is, it is passing off its business as that of the existing business. The leading case is *Ewing v Buttercup Margarine Co Ltd* (1917). In this case the plaintiff carried on business under the name Buttercup Dairy Co. He obtained an injunction to prevent the defendant trading under the registered name of the company on the grounds that the public might think the two businesses were connected.

(b) The domicile of the company

The place where the registered office of the company is situated determines its domicile. The registered office is the address to which communications to the company may be sent and writs may be served. There is also a list of important documents which, under various sections of the Companies Act, must be kept at the registered office.

(c) The objects of the company

The objects clause of the memorandum, originally of substantial significance, has become much reduced in importance over recent years. A final step was the introduction of a new s 3A, which provides that a company may be registered with the object to carry on business as a general commercial company.

Ultra vires

Originally the doctrine of *ultra vires* (meaning 'beyond one's powers') meant that if the company embarked on any business or undertaking which was not included in its objects clause, any contracts relating to such a business were not enforceable either on behalf of, or against, the company. This meant that a person dealing with the company had to take the trouble to seek out and examine the objects clause of the memorandum. If he did not, the doctrine of constructive notice deemed that he had done so and he was therefore regarded as having had notice of the limitation on the company's powers. This problem was partly overcome by including a large number of powers within the objects clause so that the ultimate effect was that the company could undertake virtually whatever business the directors decided upon.

In 1972, the European Communities Act made changes which are now in s 35 of the Companies Act 1985. It provided that, in relation to a person dealing with the company in good faith, any transaction decided on by the directors was deemed to be within the company's powers. This meant that a person dealing in good faith could enforce an *ultra vires* transaction. The company or a person of whom it could be proved that he was not dealing in good faith could not, however, enforce such a transaction. The position was changed by the Companies Act 1989, which amended the 1985 Act. Under s 35A, transactions are enforceable against the company even by persons who have actual knowledge that the transaction is not within the company's power. Thus the requirement of good faith on behalf of the company's creditor in relation to an *ultra vires* transaction has disappeared.

Section 35 provides that any member may seek an injunction from the court to restrain the directors from entering into an *ultra vires* transaction. If the directors have already entered into the transaction, no injunction is available. Similarly, no injunction can be granted if members have ratified the *ultra vires* transaction by a special, or (in the case of a single member company), a written resolution. Directors are liable to pay damages to the company in respect of any loss caused to it by an *ultra vires* transaction. However, the company may relieve the directors of this liability by passing a special (or written) resolution to that effect.

Ultra vires transactions undertaken by a director, with the company or with the company's holding company, are voidable, that is, they can be set aside at the instance of the company. *Ultra vires* contracts made with persons connected with the director are voidable, as are contracts made with associated companies, that is, a company in which the director has 20% or more of the issued share capital or controls 20% or more of the votes. Connected persons comprise the director's spouse or child or step-child (under the age of 18). Also connected are trustees of trusts whose beneficiaries include the director, the director's spouse, child or step-child, or any associated company. In addition, a partner (that is, business partner) of the director or of any of the director's connected persons is connected.

The problems with objects clauses can now be almost entirely avoided as between the company and its creditors. A new s 3A provides that a company may be registered with objects (or alter its objects) to carry on business as a general commercial company. This allows the company to carry on any trade or business whatsoever. It also allows the company to do any act incidental or conducive to such trade or business.

(d) That the liability of members is limited, though, of course, this will normally be apparent from the name of the company

(e) The amount of its authorised share capital and its division into shares of a particular value

For example, 100 shares of £1 each.

In addition, the memorandum of a public company must contain a clause stating that it is a public company. Section 14 of the Companies Act provides that the memorandum of a company binds the company and the members as though it had been signed and sealed by each member and as though it contained covenants by each member to observe its provisions.

Articles of association

Articles of association regulate the internal government of the company. They deal with such matters as the issue and transfer of shares, the calling of meetings together with the procedure to be adopted and the taking of votes at them, the appointment of directors and their powers, etc. It is not compulsory for a company limited by shares to register articles of association, though an unlimited company or a company limited by guarantee must do so. Table A to the Companies Act sets out a model form of articles for both public and private companies. Section 8 provides that Table A will automatically apply to companies limited by shares unless it is excluded or modified. The normal practice is for a company to expressly adopt Table A as its articles but to include modifications where appropriate. For example, Art 73 of Table A requires directors to retire in rotation. Though they can, of course, be reappointed following their compulsory retirement, most private companies find it convenient to exclude this Article.

Section 7 provides that articles must be printed, in numbered paragraphs and signed by the subscribers to the memorandum in the presence of at least one witness. Where the memorandum and articles conflict, the memorandum will prevail. The company may alter its articles by special resolution under the provisions of s 9 of the Companies Act, subject to the restrictions contained in the section. Section 14 of the Companies Act provides that the articles of a company (like its memorandum) bind the company and the members as though they had been signed and sealed by each member and as though they contained covenants by each member to observe their provisions. The broad effect of this is that the company is contractually bound to its members, and members are contractually bound to each other in respect of the provisions of the articles.

In addition to the Memorandum and Articles, those involved in the formation of the company must file a statement signed by the subscribers to the memorandum which:

(a) gives particulars of the first directors and company secretary; and

(b) specifies the intended situation of the company's registered office;

This is done on standard form 10.

(c) a statement of the company's capital;

(d) a statutory declaration that those engaged in the formation of the company have taken all the required steps in relation to the formation.

This is done on standard form 12, though the purpose is not apparent. If all the required steps have *not* been taken, the Registrar will simply refuse to register the company irrespective of the fact that form 12 has been submitted.

Lifting the veil

We saw earlier that a company is a legal person quite distinct from its members and that this is so even where, as in the *Salomon* case and the *Lee* case, one person effectively 'owns' the company. This is called 'the veil of incorporation'.

There are circumstances, however, where the law will 'lift the veil' of incorporation and look at the reality behind the veil. Some of these are as a result of statutory provisions, some as a result of judicial decisions.

There are two situations in which statute may lift the veil. The first is where a public company carries on business for more than six months with less than the statutory minimum of two members. In this case, any person who was a member of the company during any of that time and who knew that business was being carried on with less than two members is jointly and severally (that is, separately) liable for all of the company's debts contracted during that time.

The second is where an officer of the company, or any person acting on the company's behalf, signs and authorises the signing of a bill of exchange, promissory note, cheque, endorsement or orders for money or goods which purports to be signed on behalf of the company but in which the company's name is not mentioned. The officer (or other person) is personally liable to the holder of the bill of exchange, etc, unless the company honours the obligation (see s 349).

The veil may be lifted by a decision of the court. However, the judicial decisions as to when it is appropriate to lift the veil do not seem to follow any defined principle. The main principle originally was that the veil would be lifted if the company was a 'sham', formed or operated to avoid the enforcement of rights which had accrued against an individual or another company.

In *Gilford Motor Co v Horne* (1933), EB Horne had covenanted with his employer that on leaving the employer's employment, he would not solicit his employer's customers. He left his employer and set up a competing business. In order to avoid the restraint on soliciting his former employer's customers, he carried on the business through a company set up by his wife, JM Horne Ltd. *Held:* the plaintiff would be granted an injunction against Horne and against JM Horne Ltd, since the company was nothing but a sham set up in order to avoid Horne's obligations under his agreement with the plaintiff.

In a contrasting case, *Hilton v Plustile* (1989), H owned a flat which Miss Rose wished to rent. However, if H rented the flat to an individual, that individual would be entitled to protection (for example, protection against eviction) under the Rent Act 1977. H would therefore only let the flat to a company. Miss R acquired a company called Plustile Ltd to which H rented the flat. Miss R contended that the reality of the situation was that H had rented the flat to her. *Held* by the Court of Appeal: there was no reason to override the transaction since it was the intention of both parties to structure their transaction in such a way that the Rent Acts would be avoided.

Thus, in the *Hilton* case, the court was drawing a distinction between the situation where the device of a company is used to try to avoid existing rights to the detriment of an unwilling party and the situation where, initially at any rate, both parties are agreed upon using a company to prevent rights arising.

In certain cases, particularly where a group of companies is involved, it has been suggested that the corporate veil may be pierced 'in the interests of justice'. However, in *Adams v Cape Industries* (1990), the Court of Appeal stated that the court was not 'free to disregard the principle of *Salomon v Salomon & Co Ltd* merely because it considers that justice so requires'.

Phoenix companies

A 'phoenix' company is a company which is controlled by the persons who were previously in control of a company of the same or very similar name, which has gone into insolvent liquidation. They have usually sold the assets of the old company to the new company, often at an under-valuation.

To try to combat this, s 216 of the Insolvency Act 1986 makes it an offence for a person who has been a director of a company within 12 months before it goes into insolvent liquidation to be a director of, or to be concerned directly or indirectly in the promotion, formation, or management of another company without leave of the court, within five years after the original company went into liquidation, if the other company is known by a name which is the same as one by which the original company was known at any time within 12 months before it went into liquidation, or by a name which is so similar to such a name by which the original company was known that it suggests an association between the original and the new companies.

It is also an offence for a director of the original company, within the same five year period, to be concerned in the management of a business, other than a company, which is known by the prohibited name (s 216). In other words, the prohibition cannot be got round by using a sole tradership or partnership instead of a company.

A person who is a director of, or concerned in the management of, a successor company in contravention of these provisions, or if a person acts or is willing to act on instructions given without the leave of the court, by another person whom he knows to be acting in contravention of any of these prohibitions, that person is personally liable for the debts or other liabilities of the successor company which are incurred while he is a director of it, or is involved in its management, or while he acts or is willing to act under instructions. This personal liability is enforceable by the other party to the contract which the director negotiates on behalf of the successor company, even though the other party is aware that the contract is entered into in breach of the prohibition.

Insider dealing

Sometimes a person obtains price-sensitive information about a company which has not yet been made public. If the company is quoted on the stock-exchange, that person may make a profit by making use of his information. However, a person who wishes to do this commits a criminal offence and will probably need to act fairly quickly since the Listing Rules of the LSE require price-sensitive information (that is, information which might affect the price of the relevant securities) to be disclosed promptly to the Company Announcements Office of the LSE. Certain other information, such as any information received regarding substantial shareholdings (which might indicate that a takeover bid is being prepared) must be disclosed, whether or not it is regarded by the company as being price-sensitive.

Example

Suppose that the shares of Everpool United Football Club are quoted on the LSE. The chairman of the club has been negotiating secretly regarding the formation of a new European Super League, of which Everpool United are to be founder members. The negotiations are concluded favourably. Before the agreed time for the press release, the chairman's personal assistant buys himself a substantial number of shares in the club. When, later that day, the news of the proposed League is made public, the value of the shares rise and the personal assistant ends up with a substantial profit.

This is called 'insider dealing'. Typical examples might be where the chairman of a company who becomes aware that his company is a target for a takeover bid (which tends to push the share price up) buys a large number of shares in his company in order to make a profit; or the finance director of a company which is about to announce a large loss sells his shares in the company before the announcement is made; or a telecommunications company is about to be awarded a large government contract and a director of the company, being aware of this, buys a significant number of shares in the company, shortly before the public announcement is made.

Some people think that insider dealing is perfectly legitimate. After all, no one is harmed by the personal assistant's activities: the profit he makes could be regarded as additional remuneration. If it is treated as a crime, it is argued that it is a crime without a victim.

Nevertheless, UK law and European law does treat insider dealing as a crime. It is thought by many that a stock-market loses credibility unless it includes the concept that dealing shall be fair to all. Insider dealing is now regulated by the Criminal Justice Act 1993. There are two basic concepts: one is 'inside information'; the other is 'having information as an insider'.

Inside information

This is defined by s 56(1) of the Criminal Justice Act 1993 to mean information which:

(a) relates to particular securities or to a particular issuer of securities and not to securities generally or to issuers of securities generally. Thus, in our example of Everpool Football Club above, if the inside information were to the effect that the government intended to reduce corporation tax, this would not be inside information, since it would relate to securities generally – all shares would tend to rise;

(b) is specific or precise;

(c) has not been made public; and

(d) if it were made public would be likely to have a significant effect on the price of any securities.

However, the definition of when information has been made public does not necessarily conform to everyone's idea of being made public. Section 58(3) provides that information may be treated as having been made public even though:

(a) it can be acquired only by persons exercising diligence or expertise;

(b) it is communicated to a section of the public and not the public at large;

(c) it can be acquired only by observation;

(d) it is communicated only upon the payment of a fee;

(e) it is published only outside the UK.

Having information as an insider

A person is regarded as having information as an insider if:

(a) he has information which he knows is inside information; and

(b) he has the information which he knows comes from an inside source.

A person has information from an inside source if:

(a) he has it through:

   (i) being a director, employee or shareholder of an issuer of securities; or

   (ii) having access to the information by reason of his employment, office or profession.

(b) the direct or indirect source of the information is a person within para (a).

This is widely drafted and will potentially cover a very wide range of persons. It will not only cover the directors of the company concerned, but it will, for example, cover the company's professional advisers and its employees; the office clerk who overhears the information; a shareholder in company X who learns that company X is about to make a takeover bid for company Y and so buys shares in company Y; and, in addition, anyone who learns the information through them.

In order for an offence to be committed, the securities must be 'price-affected'. Securities are price-affected in relation to inside information if the information would, if made public, be likely to have a significant effect on the price of the securities.

A person deals in securities if he:

(a) acquires or disposes of the securities; or

(b) procures, directly or indirectly, an acquisition or disposal of the securities by any other person.

The dealing must be in a regulated market or through a professional intermediary (for example, bank, stockbroker).

There are three offences relating to insider dealing:

(a) dealing as an insider with price-affected securities;

(b) encouraging another to deal in price-affected securities; and

(c) disclosing inside information, otherwise than in the proper performance of his employment office or profession, to another person.

There are a number of defences to the crime of insider dealing:

(a) that the defendant did not expect any of the activities listed above to result in a profit (or loss) attributable to the fact that the information was price-sensitive information;

(b) that the defendant believed on reasonable grounds that the information had been disclosed widely enough to ensure that none of those taking part in the dealing would be prejudiced by not having the information;

(c) that the defendant would have acted as he did even if he had not had the information;

(d) market makers on regulated markets may deal, or encourage others to deal, on the basis of inside information, provided they act in good faith in the course of the market-making business. However, they must not disclose the information. Thus, it would appear that a stockbroker may recommend a share to his clients when he knows that profits are going to be substantially improved, but is not able to say why he is making the recommendation.

CHAPTER 30

COMPANY DIRECTORS, SECRETARY AND AUDITORS

A private company must appoint at least one director; a public company registered on or after 1 November 1929 must appoint at least two (s 282 of the Companies Act 1985). A director does not need to be a shareholder in the company, though he usually is. However, sometimes the directors of large public companies are not shareholders.

The directors are agents of the company for the purpose of managing the company. It is necessary for a company to have at least one director because a company, being an artificial person, cannot act on its own behalf. The powers of the directors in relation to the running of the company are unlimited, unless they have been limited in some way under the articles of association of the company. The articles usually give the directors the power to appoint one of their number to be the managing director. In that case, the managing director has authority to make decisions relating to the day to day running of the company except insofar as the board of directors or the articles of association have placed a limitation on his authority. Even then, if the managing director performs some action which is beyond his authority but which is usually within the authority of a managing director, the company may be bound by the managing director's action.

DE FACTO DIRECTORS AND SHADOW DIRECTORS

In addition to properly appointed directors, the following categories are treated as directors for certain purposes.

De facto directors

A director whose appointment is defective is called a *de facto* director; one who is properly appointed is called a *de jure* director. A *de facto* director will be treated as a *de jure* director for the purpose of liability.

Shadow directors

A shadow director is a person (or company) who is neither a *de facto* or a *de jure* director but one who:

(a) directed the directors to act in a particular manner;

(b) the directors did act in that manner; and

(c) the directors were accustomed to act in accordance with the directions given to them by that person.

Majority rule

The rule in *Foss v Harbottle* (1843) is the principle of majority rule. The rule states that, where there has been an alleged irregularity in the management of the company, the correct plaintiff is the company.

A number of exceptions have been developed which enable minority shareholders to sue in limited circumstances:

(a) where the wrong complained of is a fraud on the minority committed by a majority who control the company in general meeting;

(b) where the act which is complained of is an *ultra vires* or illegal act;

(c) where the act is one which has been sanctioned by a simple majority but which, under the Articles, can only be done by a special majority;

(d) where the member is taking action to enforce his personal rights, for example, the right to a declared dividend;

(e) where a contributory of the company (and a shareholder whose shares are fully paid is a contributory) petitions for the winding-up of the company on the grounds that it is just and equitable.

There are four grounds on which this can be done:

(1) where the company is a quasi-partnership (that is, the equivalent of a partnership). (A company which is managed by a few shareholders who are also directors would come under this rule.)

The leading case is *Ebrahimi v Westbourne Galleries Ltd* (1973) in which a partnership carried on by Ebrahimi and Nazar was converted into a company. Later, Nazar's son entered the company and became a director. The Nazars owned 60% of the shares and Ebrahimi 40%. The Nazars then removed Ebrahimi as a director, acting under what is now s 303 of the Companies Act 1985, which was strictly within their legal right to do. Ebrahimi petitioned for the winding-up of the company. *Held*: the petition would be granted. The company was a quasi-partnership and there was an underlying obligation of his fellow members to permit him to participate in the management of the company, 'an obligation so basic that, if broken, the conclusion must be that the association must be dissolved';

(2) where there has been an irretrievable breakdown of the business relationship;

(3) where the substratum (that is, the purpose for which the company was formed) has failed;

(4) where there has been a lack of probity on the part of the directors.

In the case of a winding-up application, the petitioner must pay the court fee plus a deposit of £500 to cover the official receiver's fees.

(f) where, under s 459 of the Companies Act 1985, the affairs of the company are being conducted in a manner which is unfairly prejudicial to the interests of its members.

Under s 210 of the Companies Act 1948, the conduct complained of had to be oppressive. This is now modified to the 'unfair prejudice' formula. This often involves the court going into the detailed history of the company and, in consequence, the costs of such actions are often high in relation to the value of the subject of the litigation. In *Re Elgindata Ltd* (1991), costs of £320,000 were incurred in litigation over shares worth £24,000.

Originally, an 'unfair prejudice action could only be brought where only some of the members were unfairly prejudiced. For example, in *Re Cumana Ltd* (1986), a rights issue was made on apparently favourable terms to all members. However, it was known that the issue could not be taken up by a minority member because of his lack of the necessary finance.

In *Re Elgindata*, it was held that, although poor management is one of the risks of investment and that, therefore, it will not in itself amount to unfairly prejudicial conduct, the managing director was using company assets for his personal benefit, which reduced the value of the shares in the company. The managing director was therefore ordered to buy the petitioners' shares.

If the court finds a complaint of unfair prejudice well-founded, the court may, under s 461:

(1) regulate the conduct of the company's affairs in future; for example, making an alteration to the company's memorandum or articles;

(2) require the company to refrain from doing or continuing an act complained of by the petitioner or to do an act which the petitioner has complained it has omitted to do;

(3) authorise civil proceedings to be brought in the name of and on behalf of the company by such persons and on such terms as the court may direct; and

(4) provide for the purchase of the shares of any members of the company by other members or by the company itself and, in the case of a purchase by the company itself, the reduction of the company's capital accordingly.

Sometimes the problem arises from the fact that the petitioner wished to sell shares in a private company and the petitioner is dissatisfied with the return.

This might happen if:

(a) the articles provide for an arbitrary method of valuation, which does not reflect the true value;

(b) there has been mismanagement of the company which reduces the value of the shares;

(c) the person who will value the shares is not independent;

(d) there is no procedure for the petitioner to make representations to the valuer and the valuer has inadequate means of valuing the shares.

If an offer is made to purchase the shares, which is arrived at by a truly independent valuation, the petition will be struck out.

Investigations of a company's affairs

Appointment of inspectors

There are certain circumstances in which the Secretary of State for Trade and Industry may or must order an investigation into the affairs of a company.

The Secretary of State (SoS) may, on the application of not less than 200 members or of members holding not less than one tenth of the shares issued, appoint one or more inspectors to investigate the affairs of the company. The application must be supported by evidence showing that the applicants have good reason for requiring the investigation. The SoS may require security of up to £5,000 for the costs of the inquiry.

The SoS must appoint an inspector/s if a court order declares that an investigation ought to be made. (s 432 of the Companies Act 1985).

The SoS may order an investigation on his own initiative if it appears:

(a) that the company's affairs are being or have been conducted with intent to defraud creditors of any person or otherwise for a fraudulent or unlawful purpose, or in a manner which is unfairly prejudicial to part of its members, or that any actual or proposed act or omission of the company is or would be so prejudicial, or that it was formed for a fraudulent or unlawful purpose;

(b) that the promoters or the person managing its affairs have been guilty of fraud, misfeasance or other misconduct towards the company or its members;

(c) that the members have not been given all the information as to the company's affairs which they might reasonably expect.

The inspector has wide powers of investigation, including taking statements on oath. However, it is not a trial, so there is no prosecution, defence, etc. The investigation is conducted in private. The reason for this is that it is not a court proceeding and, therefore, a defamatory statement is not open to challenge by cross examination (though this is sometimes true of a defamatory statement made in court).

Proceedings on the inspectors report

If it appears from the report that it is expedient in the public interest that the company be wound up, the SoS may petition the court that the company should be wound up by the court if the court thinks it just and equitable to do so (s 124A of the Insolvency Act 1986).

A minority shareholder may use the report to support his own petition that the company should be wound up on the grounds that it is just and equitable under s 122(1)(g) of the 1986 Act.

If, from the report, it appears that civil proceedings ought to be brought by the company, the SoS is empowered to bring such proceedings (s 438). The SoS must indemnify the company against costs or expenses incurred in connection with any such proceedings.

The expenses of the investigation are borne by the SoS but he can claim repayment from any of the following:

(a) any person convicted on a prosecution instituted as a result of the proceedings, or ordered to pay the cost of proceedings brought under s 438;

(b) any company in whose name proceedings are brought is liable to repay to the extent of money or property recovered by it as a result of the proceedings;

(c) where the inspector was appointed otherwise than on the motion of the SoS, and where it was not the applicant (for example, where the investigation was ordered by the court), is liable except so far as the SoS otherwise directs;

(d) where the investigation was the consequence of an application under s 431 (company members), the applicants are liable to such extent as the SoS shall direct.

Investigation into the ownership of a company

Where he considers there is good reason to do so, the SoS may appoint one or more inspectors to investigate and report on the membership of a company for the purpose of determining the true persons who are, or have been, financially interested in the success or failure of the company, or able to control or materially influence its policy (s 442).

The powers of the inspectors and the rules as to defraying costs are the same as for an investigation into a company's affairs.

If the SoS has difficulty in discovering the owners of shares, etc, he may put restrictions on them. The restrictions prevent transfers, exercise of voting rights, issue of further shares, payment of dividends, etc.

The SoS also has power to investigate share dealings and to inspect a company's books and documents.

Duties of Directors

Fiduciary duty

Directors must act for the benefit of the company as a whole. Directors are trustees of the company's property and money. If directors breach this duty and misappropriate the company's money for their own benefit, they can be made to reimburse the company.

In *Piercy v Mills* (1920), a company did not need money but, nevertheless, the directors issued additional shares in order to resist the appointment of additional directors and thus keep themselves in power. It was held that this was an abuse of the directors' fiduciary position and the share issue was therefore void.

Agents

Directors are the agents through which the company, being an artificial person, must act. The company is the principal. It is a general rule of the law of agency that an agent is not personally liable on a contract he makes on behalf of a principal.

Skill

A director is not required to have any special qualifications nor even any skill in the business of the company of which he is a director. However, if he does have special skill, he must give the company the advantage of it.

A director is not under a duty to perform any definite function in the conduct of the company's business unless he has a contract of employment specifying such duties. The director is not liable for negligence in respect of what he doesn't do, since he has no duty, but will be liable if he fails to take reasonable care in doing what he undertakes to do. Provided the directors have acted only negligently and have not been guilty of illegality, fraud or bad faith, the directors may be forgiven by a unanimous vote of the members, even though the vote has been procured owing to the control of the director who was negligent.

Company Directors' Disqualification Act 1986

A person may be disqualified by order of the court from being a director, liquidator, or administrator of any company and from being a receiver or manager of the undertaking or assets or any property of any company, or indirectly concerned in or taking part in the promotion, formation or management of any company, unless the court gives him leave to do so. The disqualification period must not exceed 15 years from the date of the court's order, except where the disqualification is imposed for persistent default in delivering returns, accounts, or other documents to the Registrar of Companies or is imposed by the magistrates' court on summary conviction for failure to deliver returns, etc. In this case, the disqualification period may not exceed five years. Acting in contravention of a disqualification order is an offence triable either way (that is, summarily by magistrates or on indictment in the Crown Court).

Disqualification by undertaking

About 2,800 disqualifications were made in 1998/99. The difficulty with the court proceedings is that that there are inevitably delays in getting the matter dealt with. Therefore, s 6 of the Insolvency Act 2000 has amended the Directors' Disqualification Act 1986 by introducing a new procedure whereby disqualification can be achieved through an administrative process. In a case where the director is willing to give an undertaking to the Secretary of State that he will not act as a director of a company, etc, for a specified period, the maximum period for an undertaking is 15 years. The disqualified person may subsequently apply to the court to vary the undertaking he has given. Of course, if a director is not willing to give an undertaking, the case may proceed to court.

Disqualification by order of the court

The grounds of disqualification by order of the court are as follows:

(a) He has been convicted of an indictable offence (whether on indictment or summarily) in connection with the promotion, formation, management or liquidation of a company or with the receivership or management of property of the company.

The offence can be one which could have been committed by a non-director, for example, insider dealing as a result of unpublished price sensitive information in relation to the shares of the company, but it must have been committed in the exercise of his functions as a director.

In *R v Austen* (1985), A's companies sold cars. A was convicted of making fraudulent hire-purchase arrangements for cars sold by his companies. He was disqualified for 10 years.

In *R v Georgiou* (1988), it was held that a director who carried on insurance business through a company without the authorisation of the Insurance Companies Act 1982 was committing an offence in connection with the management of the company. He was disqualified for five years.

(b) In the winding up of the company, if it is found in civil or criminal proceedings that he had been guilty of fraudulent trading or that while an officer or liquidator of a company, or while a receiver or manager of any of its property, he has been guilty of any fraud in relation to the company or a breach of duty towards it.

(c) He has been a director or a shadow director of a company which has, at any time, become insolvent (whether while he was a director or shadow director of it or subsequently) and his conduct as a director or shadow director of that company (either taken alone or together with his conduct as a director or shadow director of any other company or companies) makes him unfit to be concerned in the management of a company.

A company becomes insolvent for this purpose if it goes into liquidation at a time when its assets are insufficient to discharge its debts and liabilities in full, together with the expenses of the liquidation.

(d) He is or has been a director or shadow director of a company whose affairs have been investigated by inspectors appointed by the Secretary of State or about whose affairs the SoS has exercised his powers to obtain information or documents and his conduct in relation to that company, as revealed by the inspector's report or the SoS's enquiries, shows that he is unfit to be concerned in the management of a company.

(e) He has persistently defaulted as a director or secretary of any company or companies in making returns, delivering accounts or other documents or giving notifications required by the Companies Act 1985 (as amended) to the Registrar of Companies.

A person is conclusively deemed to be in persistent default if he has been convicted of a default or required by a court to make good a default on at least three occasions during the five years before an application for a disqualification order is made.

(f) The court has made an order under the Insolvency Act 1986 that he shall contribute such amount to the assets of a company in liquidation as the court directs on the ground that he has been guilty of wrongful or fraudulent trading.

Bankruptcy

It is a criminal offence for an undischarged bankrupt to act as a company director or to take part in the management of a company without the leave of the court which declared him bankrupt. However, the law does not prevent a bankrupt from being appointed a director and there are some functions, not classed as management, which the director could undertake. It is, therefore, usual for the articles of a company to provide that an undischarged bankrupt shall not be appointed.

COMPANY SECRETARY

All companies must appoint a secretary (s 283(1) of the Companies Act 1985). The secretary is an officer of the company. A sole director cannot also be the secretary of the company. The secretary does not need to be a shareholder in the company. In practice, many small private companies appoint their solicitor as company secretary. When a company is formed, a statement of who are to be the first directors and secretary (or joint secretaries) must be filed with the Registrar.

Qualifications

The secretary of a private company needs no formal qualifications. However, the secretary of a public company needs to be qualified. The main qualifications include:

(a) he can be a solicitor, barrister or advocate;

(b) he can be a member of one of a number of professional bodies, including the four main accountancy bodies and the Chartered Institute of Secretaries; or

(c) he can be a person who, by virtue of his previous experience or membership of another body, appears to the directors to be capable of discharging the functions of secretary.

The secretary's duties are not specified in the Companies Act, but the Combined Code, which applies to companies listed on the stock exchange, provides that all directors should have access to the advice and services of a company secretary, who is responsible to the board for ensuring that board procedures are followed and the applicable rules and regulation are complied with.

The secretary may be liable under the criminal law for any default in respect of which a duty is placed on the officers of the company. For example, failure to file the company's annual return or failure to file changes in the details of a company's directors and secretary.

The secretary usually takes responsibility for the following (among many other things):

(a) maintaining the company's statutory registers;

These are: the register of members; register of directors and secretaries; register of charges (that is, details of company property which has been designated as security, usually for a loan); register of directors' interests (there are detailed rules in ss 325–29 of the Companies Act about the disclosure of directors' interests in the shares or debentures of the company or other companies within the group). In relation to public companies there is a further register: register of directors' interests in shares (s 211 requires a director to notify an interest in the shares of a public company when his material interest reaches 3% of the nominal value of relevant share capital, or where the aggregate of his material and non-material interest reaches 10%. A non-material interest might occur when he buys the shares on behalf of others. A register must be kept of such interests).

(2) sending out notice of meetings to company members and the auditor;

The Annual General Meeting or a meeting to pass a special resolution requires 21 days' notice. Other meetings require 14 days.

(3) ensuring that minutes of company meetings and directors' meetings are kept and, where appropriate, ensuring that the Registrar of Companies is provided with copies of resolutions passed at meetings (for example, in relation to special and extraordinary resolutions);

(4) ensuring that statutory forms which must be filed with the Registrar are filed within the appropriate time limit;

For example, notification of changes in particulars of directors or secretaries must be filed within 14 days of the change.

(5) ensuring copies of the accounts are available to every person who is entitled to a copy.

AUDITORS

It used to be the case that all companies must appoint an auditor. However, very small companies and certain charitable companies do not need to have their accounts audited. If turnover is less than £90,000, accounts do not need to be audited nor accompanied by a report. If the turnover is between £90,000 and £350,000, the accounts do not need to be audited but an independent accountant's report must accompany accounts delivered to the Registrar of Companies. Even where companies meet these criteria, there are exceptions, for example, public companies or where a member requests, and it may be advisable, if the company may wish to borrow money, to have the accounts audited in any case.

The company's first auditor is appointed by the directors. The auditor then holds office until the end of the first meeting of the company at which its accounts are laid before the members. At the meeting, the members may reappoint the auditor or appoint a different auditor. However, a private company may pass a resolution not to have its accounts laid before it in general meeting. If this is done, the auditor must be appointed or reappointed at a meeting to be held within 28 days beginning with the day that the accounts are sent to members.

An auditor must be a member of one of certain accounting bodies: a Chartered Accountant, a Certified Accountant or a member of the Association of Authorised Public Accountants.

It is not the auditor's responsibility to file the accounts and report, but the auditor often undertakes this job for small companies. Nevertheless, if it is not done, the company must pay a penalty according to a sliding scale tariff. The penalty is different for private and public companies.

The auditor must ensure that the company has kept proper accounting records, that the accounts agree with those records, that the accounts comply with the requirements of the Companies Act 1985, that the accounts give a true and fair view of the company's affairs and that the information given in the directors' report is consistent with the accounts.

The auditor must then make a report to the company. If, in the opinion of the auditor, the director's report is not consistent with the accounts, or proper accounting records have not been kept, or proper returns have not been received from branches of the company he has not visited, then the accounts are not in agreement with the accounting records or returns, and the auditor must say that in his report. His report is then said to be *qualified*.

CHAPTER 31

COMPANY INSOLVENCY

This chapter is mainly about what happens when a company is unable to pay its debts as they become due. In such a case, the company is said to be insolvent. Insolvency is not a particularly rare occurrence: many companies become insolvent at some stage in their lives and where the insolvency is essentially short term, the company will often continue trading as normal, except that they will ask for some forbearance from their creditors or will use more dubious tactics, such as taking an unauthorised extension of their agreed credit periods, until the financial difficulty has passed.

Where the insolvency is more serious, there are various options open to the company and its creditors. These will normally involve the participation of a qualified insolvency practitioner, who will often, but not always, be a chartered accountant. The steps taken will be governed by insolvency law, the main plank of which is the Insolvency Act 1986. All references in this chapter are to sections of the Insolvency Act, unless otherwise stated in the text.

The Insolvency Act tries to resolve the conflicting ideas of, on the one hand, allowing secured creditors to realise their security and, on the other hand, protecting the company's assets and ensuring that, with some exceptions, the creditors are treated equally favourably if the company does not recover and, in consequence, has to be wound up and its assets distributed among the creditors. However, since the 1986 Act, there has been more emphasis on attempting to keep an insolvent company afloat. To that end the Act introduced a concept new to English law, the administration order, and improved the procedure for the concept of voluntary compromises or arrangements with creditors, which had been in existence for a long time but which had become largely ineffective because of procedural defects.

The following steps may be taken in relation to an insolvent company:

(a) it may be put into liquidation either by its creditors or of its own volition;

(b) secured creditors may appoint an administrative receiver, where they have a debenture which permits this; otherwise they may apply to the court for the appointment of a receiver;

(c) it may be made the subject of an administration order; or

(d) it may make a voluntary arrangement with its creditors.

Of these four alternatives, liquidation (or winding up) is the most drastic since that means that the company is dissolved, that is, it ceases to exist. The preferred outcome of each of the other three is that the company should continue to operate as a going concern so that the creditors get paid at least part of their debt and jobs are preserved. However, in the case of the appointment of an administrative receiver or the making of an administration order, although some companies are saved, the ultimate outcome is likely to be that the company goes into liquidation.

LIQUIDATION

Liquidation (or winding up) is the name given to the process whereby a company is dissolved, that is, it ceases to exist. The process of liquidation involves the realisation of the company's assets and the discharge of its liabilities, in as far as this is possible, out of the assets. If a surplus remains (which will be extremely rare), the surplus is distributed according to the rules laid down by the company's articles of association. A company that is dissolved has its name is removed from the Register of Companies.

If it appears to the Registrar of Companies that a company is defunct then he may remove the company from the register under s 652 of the Companies Act 1985. Many companies are dissolved by this method every year. If a company has not been trading, a request to the Registrar to remove it from the register is the quickest, easiest and cheapest method to dissolve it. However, where a company is operational, it must be put into liquidation and wound up before being dissolved. A company may be wound up:

(a) compulsorily; or

(b) voluntarily; by either the members or the creditors.

COMPULSORY LIQUIDATION

The process of compulsory liquidation begins with a petition being presented to the Companies Court which is part of the Chancery Division of the High Court. Alternatively, if the paid-up share capital does not exceed £120,000, the petition may be presented to a county court which has bankruptcy jurisdiction. Bankruptcy is the procedure by which the estates of insolvent individuals and partnerships are dealt with. An insolvent company is not subject to the bankruptcy procedure: it is wound up. Note that while it is possible to wind up a solvent company, it is not possible to make a solvent individual bankrupt.

The petition may be presented by:

(a) A creditor

The vast majority of petitions are presented by creditors on the ground that the company is unable to pay its debts. The creditor does not need to have brought a legal action in respect of his claim, though the claim must be for a liquidated sum, that is, a certain sum of money. Money owed on an invoice relating to a sale of goods would be an example. On the other hand, if the claim is for an unliquidated sum (that is, an uncertain amount), such as a claim for damages in respect of defective goods supplied by the company, the claimant is not a creditor of the company until he has secured judgment against the company. A prospective or contingent creditor or an assignee of a creditor may petition.

(b) A contributory

This implies that the petitioner must be someone who has an outstanding liability to contribute to the assets of the company in the event of a winding up, such as the holder of partly paid shares in a limited liability company. However, the definition of 'contributory' laid down in s 79 is wider than this and it has been held that members of a limited liability company whose shares are fully paid come within the definition of a contributory. Under s 124, a member can petition only if:

(1) the number of members of the company has fallen below two; or

(2) the shares were originally allotted to the member; or

(3) the member has held his shares for at least six months of the 18 months prior to the winding up; or

(4) the member has succeeded to the shares of a deceased shareholder.

There is then an overriding requirement that the contributory must have an interest in the winding up. If the contributory holds fully paid shares in a limited liability company which is unlikely to show a surplus on being wound up, the contributory will have no interest. If, however, he is the holder of partly paid shares, he will have an interest, since he will be liable to contribute the balance outstanding on the shares in the event of a winding up.

(c) The company itself

This is unusual since, if the members want the company to be wound up, they can pass a resolution for a members' voluntary winding up which will be quicker and cheaper.

(d) All the directors

Although the directors are agents of the company, there is some doubt as to whether they can petition for a winding up in the company's name even if the articles expressly provide that the directors may do so. However, in Re Instrumentation Electrical Services (1988), it was held that a petition may be presented by the directors in their own names, providing all of them are in agreement.

(e) The Secretary of State for Trade and Industry

The Secretary of State may petition on the ground that it is just and equitable that the company be wound up, but only after an inspection or investigation shows that it appears to be expedient in the public interest that the company be wound up. There are special provisions under the Insurance Companies Act 1982 (as amended) which provide a number of grounds (for example, that the company has not kept proper accounting records), in which the Secretary of State may petition for the winding up of an insurance company.

(f) The Bank of England

The Bank may petition for the winding up of a company which has been authorised as a deposit-taking institution under the Banking Act 1987. It may do so on the ground that it is just and equitable that the company should be wound up, that it cannot pay its debts or that it cannot meet a demand by a customer for a deposit made with it.

(g) The Attorney General

The Attorney General may petition for the winding up of any company formed for a charitable purpose on any of the grounds mentioned below.

(h) The official receiver

The official receiver may petition for a winding up by the court in respect of a company which is already in voluntary liquidation. The court will only grant an order for compulsory winding up if it is satisfied that the existing liquidation is not being conducted with proper regard for the interests of the creditors or contributories.

GROUNDS FOR WINDING UP

There are seven grounds, set out in s 122, on which a petition for a compulsory winding up may be based. These are:

(1) The company has by special resolution resolved that it should be wound up by the court (as has been pointed out above, such a resolution is extremely rare).

(2) The company was registered as a public company on or after 22 December 1980 and has failed to obtain a trading certificate within one year of incorporation.

As you will recall from Chapter 29, p 667, s 117 of the Companies Act does not permit a public company to trade or borrow money until it has obtained a trading certificate. Failure to obtain one within a year of incorporation constitutes grounds for petitioning for the winding up of the company:

(3) That the company was a public company immediately before 22 December 1980 and has failed to re-register either as a public or private company.

The Companies Act 1980 required old public companies to re-register either as public companies (subject to the new requirements relating to public companies imposed by the 1980 Act), or as private companies, if they were unable or unwilling to comply with the new requirements. In addition to failure to re-register being a ground for a winding up petition, the company and its officers are committing a criminal offence. In addition, since the company is no longer regarded as a public company, it is unable to invite the public to subscribe for shares or debentures.

(4) The company has not commenced business within one year of incorporation or has suspended its business for a year.

This is intended to remove defunct companies from the register. The court will only grant an order if the company has failed to pursue all its main objects for a year and there is no prospect of the company doing so within a reasonable time.

(5) The number of members of the company has been reduced below two.

Where the membership of a limited company falls below two, the single member may, under s 24 of the Companies Act 1985, become personally liable for its debts. This provision enables the single member to petition for winding up and therefore avoid personal liability. However, the Companies (Single Member Private Limited Companies) Regulations 1992 provide that neither s 122(1)(e) of the Insolvency Act or s 24 of the Companies Act apply to private companies limited by shares or guarantee.

(6) The company is unable to pay its debts as they fall due.

A creditor may rely upon one of the following situations to show that the company is unable to pay its debts:

(a) a creditor to whom the company owes a statutory specified sum, currently £750, serves on the company at its registered office a statutory demand for payment;

In such a case, if the company fails within three weeks either to pay the debt or offer reasonable security for it, the creditor may proceed to the issue of a petition. If, however, the company is able to deny that it owes the sum upon apparently reasonable grounds, the court will dismiss the petition and the creditor will be left to prove his claim by taking legal proceedings. In practice, a statutory demand is sometimes issued as a tactic in an attempt to persuade a debtor to pay the debt. If the demand is ignored (as it often is), the creditor may proceed to obtain a petition and serve it on the offending company. If, following the service of the petition, the company still fails to pay, it is usually best for an ordinary creditor to withdraw the petition, since, if he proceeds, he will probably find that preferential creditors and holders of fixed and/or floating charges have left nothing in the kitty for the ordinary creditors. In addition, the withdrawal of the petition will mean the return of the deposit which has to be made against the official receiver's fees.

(b) a creditor obtains judgment against a company for a debt and attempts to enforce the judgment but is unable to obtain payment, as insufficient assets can be seized to satisfy the claim;

(c) if it is proved to the satisfaction of the court that the company is unable to pay its debts as they fall due;

This requires that the company is unable to pay its existing debts out of cash or the disposition of readily realisable assets. This ground can be used even though the creditor has not made a statutory demand for the debt.

(d) the value of the company's assets is less than its liabilities, taking into account contingent and prospective liabilities.

This takes a longer term view of the company's prospects and, although it takes into account liabilities which may never arise, it also allows the court to take into account a steady realisation of the company's assets.

(7) The court considers that it is just and equitable to wind up the company.

This allows the court to consider reasons not covered by the six grounds already set out. So, for example, orders have been granted where the majority shareholders of the company were oppressing the minority; where two opposing groups controlling the company were unable to agree, so it was impossible to manage the company; where the company was formed for fraudulent purposes. By far the most common reason for a winding up is that a company is unable to pay its debts, and since we are concerned in this chapter with insolvency, this is the only ground we will examine in any detail.

COMMENCEMENT OF LIQUIDATION

A compulsory liquidation commences on the date the petition is presented. However, there is often an interval of several months between the petition being presented and the court hearing which grants the winding up order. The order therefore has a retrospective effect to the date of presentation of the petition. Under s 127, any dispositions of the company's property made after the presentation of the petition and before the making of the winding up order are void. The reason for this provision is to avoid the improper disposition of the company's assets, with the intention of defeating the legitimate claims of the company's creditors. However, the provision may have an adverse effect if the company wishes to carry on trading, either with a view to recovery or with a view to selling the company as a going concern.

A company which wishes to continue trading after the presentation of the winding up petition is left with three possible courses of action:

(a) application may be made to the court, under s 135, for the appointment of a provisional liquidator to take control of the company's assets pending the hearing of the petition;

One consequence of the application being granted is that the liquidator takes over the function of the directors, so that this course of action is really more suitable for the case where the applicant fears that the company's assets will be disposed of or dissipated before the winding-up order is granted.

(b) application may be made to the court under s 127 for a validation order to authorise the company to carry on its business;

In *Re Operator Control Cabs* (1970), the court permitted the directors to carry on the business of the company, dispose of its assets and pay its debts without it being necessary to seek the court's approval for each transaction. However, in *Re Gray's Inn Construction Co Ltd* (1980), it was held that such an order should be made only if it is probable that the company's business will be saleable as a going concern if the order is made.

(c) the officers of the company may carry on in the hope that the court will not in the event make an order of compulsory liquidation, or, if it does, that it will ratify the transactions of the company which would otherwise be void.

Effects of a compulsory liquidation order

We have already seen that one effect of an order is that any dispositions between the presentation of the petition and the making of the order are void unless the court sanctions them. Other effects of an order are as follows:

(a) The official receiver becomes the liquidator;

The official receiver must decide whether to call a meeting of creditors and contributories so that they may decide whether a liquidator should be appointed in his place and must decide whether to constitute a liquidation committee to supervise the winding up. In addition, he must investigate the cause of the company's insolvency and make such report as he deems fit.

(b) Any legal proceedings against the company are halted;

(c) The employees of the company are automatically dismissed;

Where the court makes a winding up order, the contracts of service or contracts for services of the company's directors, employees and agents are automatically terminated, though if the employees are re-engaged by the liquidator, their continuity of employment is not broken for the purposes of claiming a redundancy payment.

(d) The liquidator assumes the powers of the directors of the company;

The liquidator is an agent of the company and is also an officer of the company. He has the power to undertake virtually any transaction necessary to ensure its efficient winding up, including selling any or all the company's assets. He needs the approval of the court in two circumstances: first, to bring or defend legal proceedings (in a voluntary winding up the liquidator does not need the court's approval to do this); secondly, to carry on the company's business, with a view to selling it as a going concern or obtaining a better price for the assets.

(e) Every invoice, order for goods or business letter issued on behalf of the company, on which the company's name appears, must contain a statement that the company is being wound up.

PROCEDURE FOLLOWING THE MAKING OF AN ORDER

On the making of the order for compulsory liquidation the following events may, or in some circumstances must, occur.

Statement of company's affairs

The official receiver has a duty to investigate the cause of a company's failure and to investigate its promotion, formation, business dealings and affairs. To facilitate this, he may require certain persons connected with the management of the company to deliver a statement of its affairs. The list of persons, contained in s 131, who may be required to do this includes present and former directors and officers of the company and its present and former employees. The information contained in the statement relates to a comprehensive range of matters relating to the company and its finances. The information is given on affidavit, which is a statement given under oath.

Public examination of persons concerned with the company

The official receiver may, and if requested by half of the creditors or three-quarters of the contributories must, apply to the court for public examination (that is, the person is subjected to questioning in open court) of certain categories of person. The categories include anyone who is, or has been, an officer of the company or has been a liquidator, administrator, receiver or manager of the company or has been concerned with its promotion, formation or management.

Appointment of a liquidator and liquidation committee

The official receiver may decide to call separate first meetings of the creditors and contributories to nominate a liquidator in place of the official receiver and to decide whether to establish a liquidation committee to oversee the liquidator's conduct of the winding up. He *must* summon such meetings if requested to do so by one quarter in value of the creditors. If the official receiver decides to call first meetings, he must do so within 12 weeks of the order. If the creditors' meeting and the contributories' meeting each nominate different liquidators, the creditors' nominee is appointed. However, a creditor or contributory may apply to the court for some other person to be appointed as liquidator.

If the creditors' or contributories' meetings fail to appoint a liquidator, the official receiver may apply to the Secretary of State for the appointment of a liquidator. Section 137 gives the Secretary of State a discretion whether or not to appoint a liquidator. If no liquidator is appointed under either of these two procedures, the official receiver remains as the liquidator. This will usually be the case where the company in question has little or nothing in the way of assets so that there is likely to be no money with which to pay a professional liquidator. If no liquidation committee is appointed, its functions become vested in the Secretary of State.

Members' voluntary winding up

A members' voluntary winding up has the advantage that it has fewer formalities and is therefore generally quicker and cheaper than a winding up by the court or a creditors' voluntary winding up. However, such a winding up may take place only if the company is solvent.

The type of resolution to be passed by the general meeting of shareholders depends on the circumstances in which the winding up is sought.

(a) If the company is set up for a specific purpose and the articles of association provide for liquidation once that purpose has been achieved, only an ordinary resolution is required. This is one for which only 14 days' notice is required prior to the meeting and for which only a bare majority is required.

(b) If a company cannot continue its business because it is insolvent then it may be wound up by extraordinary resolution. This is one for which only 14 days' notice is required prior to the meeting but a 75% majority is required.

(c) If the company is to be wound up for any other reason, then it may do so by special resolution. This is one for which 21 days' notice must be given prior to the meeting and a majority of 75% is required.

The winding up commences on the passing of the resolution. A signed copy of the resolution must be delivered to the Registrar within 15 days. A liquidator is normally appointed at the same meeting and his or her appointment must be notified to the Registrar and advertised in the Gazette within 14 days.

Declaration of solvency

A voluntary winding up is only a members' voluntary winding up if the directors make and deliver to the Registrar a declaration of solvency under s 89. This is a statutory declaration that the directors have made a full inquiry into the affairs of the company and are of the opinion that it will be able to pay its debts in full within a specified period not exceeding 12 months. It is a criminal offence, punishable by imprisonment, for a director to make a declaration of solvency without reasonable grounds for believing it to be true. If the company is, in fact, unable to pay its debts, there is a presumption that the directors did not have reasonable grounds for their belief, although it is open to the directors to prove otherwise.

The declaration of solvency:

(a) is made by all the directors or, if there is more than two, by the majority;

(b) includes a statement of the company's assets and liabilities at the latest practicable date before the declaration is made;

(c) must be made within the five weeks preceding the date of the resolution to wind up; and

(d) must be filed with the Registrar within 15 days of the passing of the resolution to wind up.

A liquidator may be appointed by members in a general meeting; this may be done at the meeting at which the resolution to wind up is passed. If no liquidator is appointed, the court may appoint one. If the liquidator concludes that the company will be unable to pay its debts, they then call a meeting of the creditors and the matter proceeds as a creditors' voluntary winding up. In a members' voluntary winding up, the creditors play no part as it is assumed that they will be paid in full. After holding a final meeting, the liquidator sends a copy of the accounts to the registrar who dissolves the company three months later by removing its name from the register.

Creditors' voluntary winding up

If no declaration of solvency is made, the liquidation proceeds as a creditors' voluntary winding up even if, in the end, the company pays all its debts in full. To commence a creditors' voluntary winding up, the directors convene a general meeting of members to pass an extraordinary resolution. They also convene a meeting of creditors: s 98. The meeting of members is held first and its business is to resolve to wind up the company, appoint a liquidator, and nominate up to five representatives for a liquidation committee.

The creditors' meeting is convened for a date within 14 days of the members' meeting. The delay between the two meetings has in the past enabled the members' liquidator to dispose of the assets, thereby defeating the claims of the creditors before the creditors have a chance to appoint their own liquidator. This has been restricted by s 166 which limits the powers of the members' liquidator until his appointment is ratified by the creditors or they appoint their own.

Proceedings in liquidations

The role of the liquidator is to gather in all the assets of the company and seek to pay all its liabilities in accordance with their priority. The assets of the company will include property that is subject to a charge, that is, has been used to secure loans received by the company. These charges are usually created by a document called a debenture. (It is not necessary for a debenture to create a charge – the debenture is simply a formal acknowledgment of the company's indebtedness – however, it usually does.) Debentures are usually made under seal and the charges they create are of two kinds: fixed charge or floating charge.

Fixed charge

This is a charge over specific identifiable assets of the company, such as land or buildings. The main advantage of a fixed charge is that it enables the holder to realise his security, independently of any other creditor, in the event of the company's winding up. A fixed charge even takes precedence over the costs of the winding up. In theory, a fixed charge could also be given over such assets as stock in trade or work in progress. However, as such assets are constantly changing, it is impracticable for them to be used as security for a fixed charge since they could not be sold without the debenture holder's consent and, in addition, a fresh charge would have to be created in respect of the property which replaced them. Such property is, therefore, used to secure a floating charge instead.

Floating charge

This is a charge which 'floats' either over the whole of a company's assets (except those which are secured by a fixed charge) for the time being, whatever they may be, or over a specific range of the company's assets, for example, debts owed to the company or the company's stock in trade or work in progress. Such a charge will continue to float until an event such as a liquidation causes the charge to crystallise. When the charge crystallises, the property which is subject to the floating charge may be realised for the benefit of the holder of the charge. A floating charge is inferior to a fixed charge in that, first, the floating charge ranks only fourth in the list of classes of creditors to be paid in a liquidation and, secondly, the risk is that at the time of the liquidation there may be no assets remaining to which the charge relates.

Registration of charges

Any charge must be registered with the registrar within 21 days of its creation, otherwise it will be void against the liquidator and the holder of the charge will be treated as an unsecured creditor. (As we shall see, unsecured creditors rarely receive more than a very small proportion of their claim, if anything.)

Proof of debts

A creditor must prove his or her debt. Which debts are provable and the manner in which they are to be proved is governed by the Insolvency Rules 1986. Liability must exist at the commencement of the winding up but may be a future or uncertain liability. The liquidator may value an uncertain liability or may apply to the court for directions if valuation is difficult. The rules give a right of set-off. This allows a person who both owes money to and is owed money by, the company to set-off the amounts against one another.

Priority of claims

Schedule 6 to the Insolvency Act 1986 sets out the priority in which debts are paid as follows:

(a) secured creditors who have fixed charges;

(b) costs, charges and expenses of the winding up;

(c) preferential debts;

(d) secured creditors who have floating charges;

(e) unsecured debts;

(f) deferred debts.

Secured creditors

A secured creditor is one who holds a mortgage, a charge or a lien over the company's property. A secured creditor has one of four options. He may:

(1) rely on his security and not prove his debt;

(2) value his security and prove as an unsecured creditor in relation to any shortfall. There is a procedure whereby the liquidator may challenge the creditor's valuation since the creditor may be tempted to value the security on the low side;

(3) realise his security and prove as an unsecured creditor for the balance of his debt;

(4) surrender his security (though he is likely to do this only if it has little or no value) and prove for his debt as an unsecured creditor.

Costs, charges and expenses

Preferential creditors and unsecured creditors all rank equally in respect of the priority of their claims as between themselves (that is, no preferential creditor or unsecured creditor is entitled to payment in priority over any other preferential or unsecured creditor). However, there is an internal order of priority in respect of the costs of the winding up. There is a list of nine items in ranking order. Top of the list are the fees and expenses incurred in preserving, realising or getting in the assets, followed by the costs of the petition itself. At the bottom of the list are the costs of the liquidation committee, preceded by the remuneration of the liquidator.

Preferential debts

Certain debts are designated as preferential. This means that they are paid in preference to other creditors. Preferential creditors have been created as a matter of policy and broadly consist of money collected by the company on behalf of the public revenue and which has not been paid over to the appropriate authority and money owing to employees by way of wages. To some extent this category of creditor is controversial, since ordinary creditors often receive little or nothing in liquidations in which preferential creditors get paid. Because of this, the 1986 Act reduced the range of preferential creditors. It did not, however, give effect to the recommendations of the Cork Committee, to the effect that 10% of an insolvent company's assets should be retained for distribution among ordinary creditors.

Preferential creditors are:

(1) PAYE deducted from employees' wages for the previous 12 months;

(2) VAT referable to the six months before the liquidation;

(3) car tax, and betting and gaming duties due in respect of the preceding 12 months;

(4) arrears of unpaid wages. Unpaid wages are subject to a limit of four months' arrears or £800, whichever is the less, in each individual case.

Loans to pay wages are treated as preferential debts and as a result banks encourage customers to open wages accounts. If these are overdrawn on a liquidation, they will be treated as a preferential debt;

(5) National Insurance Contributions for the previous 12 months;

(6) accrued holiday pay in respect of an employee whose employment has been terminated on or before the liquidation. There is no limit placed on the amount of this debt;

(7) debts due under Sched 3 to the Social Security Pensions Act 1975;

(8) debts due under the European Coal and Steel Treaty.

Unsecured creditors

These are paid out of the balance of funds left after the uncharged assets have been realised and the preferential debts have been paid.

Deferred creditors

These are members of the company who have lent money to the company as members. These debts are paid after the unsecured creditors.

Voidable transactions

If a company goes into liquidation, the liquidator may be able to challenge a previous transaction and have it set aside and therefore the asset or funds will be available for the creditors if:

(a) it is at an undervalue and was made within two years before the commencement of the liquidation;

(b) it gives a creditor a preference and was made within two years before the commencement of a liquidation if with a 'connected' person or within six months if 'unconnected';

(c) it is an extortionate credit transaction made within three years of the commencement of the liquidation;

(d) it is a floating charge created within 12 months of the commencement of the liquidation when the company was unable to pay its debts.

A 'connected' person is a director or shadow director of the company or his minor children, spouse, partners or any company in which the director and his other associates control one fifth of the equity, share capital or voting powers. A shadow director is one who, though not a director, is a person on whose orders the directors are accustomed to act.

DIRECTORS' LIABILITY FOR MISCONDUCT

In the following cases, directors will be personally liable for the debts or losses suffered by the company.

Fraudulent trading

Section 213 provides that if a company is in liquidation and the court finds that its business has been carried on with intent to defraud creditors or for fraudulent purposes, the court may make such order as it thinks fit in respect of any person who knowingly carried on the business to contribute to the company's assets. Fraudulent trading is also a criminal offence under s 458 of the Companies Act 1985. The company will be guilty of fraudulent trading if, knowing that there is no reasonable prospect of new creditors being paid, it nevertheless carries on business and incurs debts.

Wrongful trading

Fraudulent trading requires proof that the person responsible *knew* that there was no reasonable prospect of the creditor being paid or was reckless as to whether the creditors would be paid: in other words, the person responsible must have been dishonest. Dishonesty is difficult to prove in this particular context: it is not sufficient to show that the person or persons responsible were over-optimistic about the company's chances of recovery. Thus, before the 1986 Act introduced the concept of wrongful trading, many persons who had carried on a business in circumstances where they *ought to have known* that there was no reasonable prospect of creditors being paid, were able to escape liability because it could not be shown that they had been dishonest. Because of this difficulty, the 1986 Act introduced the new concept of 'wrongful trading'. Unlike fraudulent trading, this is not a criminal offence and it applies only to directors or shadow directors of the company, whereas fraudulent trading applies to 'any person'.

In relation to wrongful trading, the court may order that the directors contribute to the debts of the company if it appears that:

(a) the company in liquidation cannot pay its debts; and

(b) at some previous time the directors knew, or should have concluded, that the company had no reasonable prospect of avoiding insolvent liquidation; and

(c) the directors did not take every reasonable step to minimise the potential loss to the company's creditors.

Disqualification of directors

Under the Company Directors' Disqualification Act 1986, a court may disqualify a person from being a director if they have committed offences in respect of company legislation. The maximum period of disqualification is 15 years. The Insolvency Act 2000 provides for a 'fast track' disqualification procedure, whereby the director concerned may give an undertaking to the Secretary of State that he will not serve as a company director. The maximum period of disqualification which the Secretary of State may order under the procedure is 15 years.

Members' liability for company debts

The shareholders with fully paid up shares are not liable for the debts of the company. Shareholders who have only partly paid the subscription of their shares will be liable for that part which is unpaid.

Completion of the winding up

When all the assets have been collected and distributed by the liquidator, the liquidator must call a final general meeting of the company. If the liquidator is able to give notice of the final distribution of the company's property, the meeting will generally release him from his duties. The liquidator then gives notice to the registrar of these facts. Alternatively, if the winding up is being conducted by the official receiver, he gives notice that the winding up is complete. Three months from the date of notice being given, the company will be automatically dissolved. However, on the application of an interested party, the Secretary of State may defer the date of the dissolution.

RECEIVERS AND ADMINISTRATIVE RECEIVERS

A receiver is a person appointed to collect in debts owed to a company and distribute the proceeds to those entitled to them. It is possible for the creditors of a company to apply to the court for the appointment of a receiver. Should the court appoint a receiver it will usually also appoint a manager with a view to keeping the business going and: (a) selling it as a going concern; or (b) enabling it to survive in its existing form; or (c) obtaining the best possible price for its assets if the company has to be liquidated. The same person will usually act as both receiver and manager. A receiver appointed by the court does not have to be a qualified insolvency practitioner, but usually will be.

An administrative receiver is a person appointed on behalf of the debenture holders in a company. As we have seen, a company may raise money by offering its assets as security. It may create a fixed charge over particular assets: this means that the creditor may take possession of the assets and sell them in order to recoup his loan. A company may also create a floating charge. This means that the creditor is not entitled to any particular asset but is entitled to whatever assets the company owns (often all the assets of the company but sometimes assets of a particular type such as book debts owed to the company or plant and machinery owned by it) at the time the charge 'crystallises', that is, when an event occurs which entitles the creditor to realise his security.

His appointment is made under the terms of the deed which creates the debenture. It is made following the occurrence of a specified event, for example, that the company has failed to pay the interest due on the loan made to it. There are a number of distinctions between receivers appointed by the court and administrative receivers appointed by debenture holders, but probably the most significant is that, whereas a receiver has a duty to act impartially in the interests of all the company's creditors, an administrative receiver is entitled to act in the interests of the debenture holders.

The purpose of appointing a receiver instead of putting the company into liquidation is that the debenture holder hopes to protect the assets of the company over which he has a charge, especially if the debenture holder has a floating charge, to try and ensure that they obtain payment in full. The receiver is really only interested in the assets of the company over which the creditor has a charge. However, since charges, especially bank charges, are usually drafted in such a way as to ensure that the loan to the company is secured against all the assets of the company, the receiver will, in effect, take over the running of the entire company.

Express appointment

The debenture which creates a floating charge will usually expressly give a power to appoint a receiver to the debenture holder in specified circumstances, such as default by the company in payment of interest or capital on the loan as it falls due or the company's financial position deteriorates, for example, profits fall below a certain level or the company is not managed prudently. If one of the specified circumstances occurs, then the debenture holder has a contractual right to appoint a receiver. However, before doing so the debenture holder must first demand payment in writing of the company's debt and only on default can a receiver be appointed.

Appointment by the court

If the debenture does not give an express power to appoint a receiver, then the creditor may apply to the court to appoint the official receiver. In such circumstances, the official receiver will not be an agent of the debenture holder or the company, but an officer of the court whose remuneration is fixed by the court and will be payable by the company.

Acceptance of the appointment

A receiver must be an authorised insolvency practitioner. He must be appointed in writing and the appointment only takes effect if the appointee accepts the day after receiving notice of the appointment. If he accepts, the appointment will be from the day the notice was received. It is important that the administrative receiver goes to the company's offices immediately to ensure that the assets of the company are not appropriated by others.

Functions of the receiver

The function of a receiver is to manage or to realise assets which are subject to the charge by virtue of which he is appointed with a view to paying out of those assets what is due to the debenture holders whom he represents (plus expenses, including their own remuneration). If he is able to discharge those debts, he will then vacate the office of receiver and the directors resume full control.

If the company is put into liquidation by another creditor or by the members, then the receiver will remain in office but only until such time as he has been able to obtain the discharge of the debt which was the subject of the charge by virtue of which he was appointed. However, the receiver in such circumstances will no longer be the agent of the company but only that of the debenture holder. The liquidator will be responsible for the winding up of the company. The difference between a receiver and a liquidator is that the receiver represents the debenture holders with control of the assets which secure their loans to the company. His task is only to obtain payment of the loan. The liquidator is appointed to realise *all* the assets and to pay *all* the debts of the company and distribute the surplus, if any, to the shareholders.

The directors only lose control over the assets over which there is a charge, although, in the case of a floating charge by a bank, this is likely to be all the assets. Nevertheless, the directors remain in office and retain their powers. For example, they may convene a general meeting to wind up the company or take action to protect the interests of the company, as in *Newhart Developments Ltd v Cooperative Commercial Bank Ltd* (1978), where the directors were held to be entitled to commence an action for breach of contract against the debenture holder who appointed a receiver.

Powers of an administrative receiver

A receiver who is appointed with reference to a fixed charge is only responsible for the secured asset and therefore needs no more powers than those of sale, in the same way as a mortgagee. This type of receiver is an agent of the debenture holder appointing him. However, an administrative receiver who, by virtue of the floating charge over the whole of the available assets of the company, will be responsible for the management of the company will be the agent of the company (unless appointed by the court) and, therefore, needs the power to run it.

The administrative receiver has a number of statutory powers which are conferred automatically, unless the debenture provides to the contrary, (Schedule 1, s 42) as follows:

(a) to borrow money and give security;

(b) to carry on the business of the company;

(c) to sell the company's property over which the charge extends;

(d) to transfer the business of the company or a part of it to a subsidiary (hiving down).

As agent of the company the administrative receiver:

(a) is personally liable on contracts made in the course of the receivership;

(b) is entitled to an indemnity for that liability from the company's assets;

(c) can bind the company by their acts.

Effect of the administrative receiver's appointment

On appointment of an administrative receiver:

(a) the receiver takes control of the assets of the company that are subject to the charge and the director's powers in respect of those assets are suspended during the receivership;

(b) all company stationery must state that a receiver has been appointed;

(c) if the administrative receiver is appointed by the court or as agent of the debenture holder, then the employees of the company are automatically dismissed, although the receiver may re-appoint them. If the receiver is the agent of the company he has 14 days within which he may decide whether or not to continue their employment. At the end of that period, if the receiver has not dismissed the employees he is deemed to have adopted their existing contracts of employment: s 44;

(d) all floating charges crystallise;

(e) within 28 days of appointment the company must send to the receiver a statement of affairs which will show the company's assets and liabilities and give a list of all known creditors of the company. The receiver must then, in turn, inform the creditors of his appointment: ss 46 and 47;

(f) the receiver must, within three months, send a copy of the statement and of his comments upon it to the registrar, the company and the debenture holders (and the court if he was appointed by the court). This must cover the events leading up to their appointment and details of the sums that are likely to be available for secured, preferential and unsecured creditors: s 48. The administrative receiver must also send a copy to unsecured creditors and convene a meeting where they can consider it. At this meeting, the creditors may appoint a committee to maintain contact with the receiver.

Priority of claims in receivership

The order of application of assets in the hands of the receiver are as follows:

(a) payment of expenses;

(b) receiver's expenses;

(c) costs of any court application;

(d) preferential debts if the charge is a floating one;

(e) payment of the secured debt.

Liability of the receiver

The receiver is not liable upon contracts made before his appointment, although he may repudiate contracts that are outstanding when he takes office as part of the management function. This may lead to the company being in breach of contract, but this may be preferable to performing the contracts if it would be more costly to do so. The receiver must obtain the leave of the court to repudiate a contract if it would destroy the goodwill of the company's business. However, this will not be refused if, for example, the receiver would have to borrow money to perform the contracts.

The receiver is personally liable upon contracts that are entered into after the company is put into receivership. To avoid this personal liability when the receiver intends to carry on the business of the company, it is now common for the receiver to transfer the assets of the company to a wholly owned subsidiary, of which the receiver is the managing director, which will carry on the business while the main company remains in receivership. Since the subsidiary is not in receivership, the normal rules regarding limitation of liability apply and the receiver is, therefore, not personally liable in respect of any liability incurred by the subsidiary.

It is essential that the receiver ensures that the charge under which he obtains his authority is valid, otherwise the receiver's appointment will be void and he will be personally liable for his actions. As a result, before they will accept an appointment, receivers usually require an indemnity from the debenture holder.

ADMINISTRATION ORDERS

Administration orders were introduced by the Insolvency Act 1986. They represent an alternative to putting an insolvent company into immediate liquidation and there is some evidence that debenture holders are allowing administration orders to be made rather than exercising their rights to appoint an administrative receiver. The disadvantage to the debenture holder of this course of action is that the administrator acts in the interests of the creditors generally, whereas an administrative receiver acts in the interests of the debenture holder. However, an advantage to an administration order is that it prevents an unsecured creditor from jumping the gun and petitioning for a winding up of the company.

The idea behind them is that a company in financial difficulty is given breathing space during which it may recover entirely or may be sold as a going concern or, at least, parts of the undertaking may be sold as a going concern. In any event, the order gives some possibility of saving at least part of the company with consequential benefits for the creditors, the employees and the members.

The main disadvantages in relation to the appointment of a receiver are that only a secured creditor may appoint a receiver, and a petition for the liquidation and winding up of the company may still be made by an unsecured creditor. The procedure for obtaining an administrative order from the court is intended to offer an alternative to both receivership and liquidation. An administration order and a receivership and liquidation are mutually exclusive. If an administrative receiver has already been appointed when an administration order is applied for, the administration order may not be granted unless the person who appointed the receiver consents.

The effect of the administration order is to put an insolvency practitioner in control of the company with a defined programme, and meanwhile prevent any of the creditors, secured or unsecured, from collecting their debts, thereby giving the administrator an opportunity, not available to the receiver, to perhaps save the company for the benefit of all the creditors. The company itself, through the members in general meeting, the directors or the creditors, may present a petition to the court for an administration order: s 9. To make such an order, the court must be satisfied that:

(a) the company is or likely to become unable to pay its debts; and

(b) the making of an administration order is likely to do one or more of the following:

   (1) ensure the survival of the company as a going concern; or

   (2) ensure the approval of a voluntary arrangement; or

   (3) the sanctioning of a scheme of arrangement under s 425 of the Companies Act 1985; or

   (4) a more advantageous realisation of the company's assets than would be effected by a liquidation: s 8.

The effect of the administration order is to:

(a) prevent a voluntary or compulsory liquidation order being made;

(b) prevent seizure of the company's goods in execution of a judgment debt;

(c) prevent re-possession of goods held on hire-purchase; and

(d) prevent the institution of legal proceedings against the company.

Appointment

The administrator is appointed by the court and is an insolvency practitioner. He acts as the company's agent but does not have the liability upon contracts that the administrative receiver has. All company correspondence must give the administrator's name and state that an order has been made: s 12. The administrator must give notice to the company immediately an order is made. Notice must also be given to the registrar within 14 days and to creditors within 28 days: s 21. On taking up appointment the administrator's main concern will be to implement the order and he is entitled to a statement of affairs of the company. Within three months, the administrator must produce and circulate to the creditors (members are informed where a copy may be obtained) his proposals for implementing the purpose of the order. Then, within 14 days, the administrator holds a meeting of creditors to consider and approve the proposals. The administrator then reports to the court which will allow the order to continue or, if the proposals are not approved, will discharge the order (receivership or liquidation may follow): s 24. In approving the proposals, the creditors may appoint a committee to work with the administrator: s 24. There are also statutory provisions to allow modification of the proposals: s 25. At any time that the order is in force, a creditor or member may petition the court on the grounds of unfair prejudice and the court may make such order as it thinks fit: s 27.

Powers

An administrator has the following statutory powers:

(a) to borrow money and give security;

(b) to carry on the business of the company;

(c) to sell the company's property;

(d) to transfer the business of the company to a subsidiary;

(e) to challenge past transactions of the company with a view to having them reversed by court order;

(f) to sell the assets of the company that are subject to a fixed charge with the charge holder's agreement and also the assets that are subject to a floating charge. The charge then becomes attached to the proceeds of sale: s 15;

(g) to remove and appoint directors;

(h) to call meetings of creditors and members.

Voluntary arrangements

Voluntary arrangements under which a company can, for example, agree to pay a proportion of its debts to each creditor and be released from the remainder (a 'composition') have been possible for some considerable time. Such provisions are now contained in ss 425–27 of the Companies Act 1985. However, a major defect with these provisions is that they are only operable if all the creditors agree to the arrangement: there is no provision for compelling a reluctant creditor to accept an arrangement in the general interest. A valid compromise is possible at common law but, again, there is no power to bind dissentient creditors.

Because of the defects in both the statutory and the common law procedures, the Insolvency Act 1986 introduced a procedure, contained in ss 1 to 7, whereby, under a properly constituted scheme, a reluctant creditor can be compelled to accept the arrangement. Sometimes a voluntary arrangement may be entered into in the hope of avoiding the costs of liquidating the company and, for the unsecured creditors, there is the hope of receiving part of their debt when, in a liquidation, they will quite often receive nothing after the secured creditors, the preferential creditors and the costs of the liquidation have been paid. At other times, a voluntary arrangement may be entered into as part of an administration or liquidation of the company.

Moratorium for small companies

A disadvantage of Company Voluntary Arrangements (CVA) made under the 1986 Act was that, unlike the case with administration orders, there was no moratorium on the company's debts while the arrangement was being considered. This meant that, until the CVA was formally approved, any creditor could jeopardise the prospective arrangement by bringing an action for his debt. This disadvantage still remains for all but small companies.

In the case of small companies as defined by s 247(3) of the Companies Act 1985 (that is, companies which satisfy two out of three of the following criteria: (a) a turnover of not more than £2.8 million; (b) a balance sheet total of not more than £1.4 million; (c) less than 50 employees), the Insolvency Act 2000 provides that a moratorium is available. Certain companies, largely insurance companies and those involved in the provision of financial services, such as banks, cannot qualify.

A moratorium means that, unless a petition is presented by the Secretary of State, no insolvency proceeding may be brought against the company, nor can any other proceeding be brought, such as an action on a debt or an enforcement of security, which might lead to the company's assets being diminished. Any insolvency proceedings already begun are stayed (that is, not proceeded with) during the period of the moratorium. The maximum initial period of the moratorium is 28 days. The moratorium may be brought to an end by a decision of the meetings of creditors and the company to approve the CVA. Alternatively, it may be brought to an end by: decision of the court; the withdrawal of the nominee of his consent to act; a decision of the meetings of the creditors and the company; on the expiry of 28 days, if the nominee (an insolvency practitioner nominated to orchestrate the scheme) has failed to summon either of the first meetings of the company or creditors; or if a first meeting of the company or creditors has not been held when summoned.

The company can continue trading as usual during the moratorium, but is subject to a number of restrictions, such as not obtaining credit of more than £250 without informing the creditor that a moratorium is in force, advertising the fact on letters, invoices, etc. It may only settle a debt which existed at the start of the moratorium if it is believed that the settlement will assist the company's business and it is approved by the moratorium committee or, if there is no committee, the nominee.

Nature of a voluntary arrangement

A voluntary arrangement may be either a composition with creditors in satisfaction of the full debt; or a scheme of arrangement, whereby the company may make various undertakings to its creditors about the way the business will be conducted in future. The initiative in proposing a voluntary arrangement may be taken either by the directors, if the company is not already subject to an administration order or in liquidation, or by a liquidator or administrator in office at the time. Whoever proposes the voluntary arrangement is required to employ an insolvency practitioner to put forward a suitable scheme and apply to the court for preliminary approval. The practitioner is known at this initial stage as a 'nominee'.

The nominee holds separate meetings of the members and the creditors and puts the proposals for the arrangement to them. If both meetings approve, the voluntary arrangement becomes binding on the company and all its creditors. However, any secured or preferential creditor whose rights are modified by the arrangement is not bound by the scheme unless they have expressly consented to it. Any creditor or member of the company may raise objections to the scheme by showing that it is unfairly prejudicial; or that there has been some material irregularity in relation to one of the meetings.

If the court upholds the objection, the arrangement may be revoked or suspended pending the submission of revised proposals. It the company is already subject to an administration order or is in liquidation, then the court may make an order terminating or suspending those proceedings. The voluntary arrangement, when approved, is administered by the insolvency practitioner then known as the 'supervisor'. The supervisor is controlled by the court and any interested party may apply to the court if the conduct of the supervisor is unsatisfactory. In such a case, or if the supervisor himself makes application, the court may issue directions.

INDEX